THE RISE
OF THE WEST

The
New American Nation Series

EDITED BY

HENRY STEELE COMMAGER

AND

RICHARD B. MORRIS

THE RISE
OF THE WEST
1754 ★ 1830

By FRANCIS S. PHILBRICK

ILLUSTRATED

HARPER & ROW, PUBLISHERS
NEW YORK

LIBRARY OF CONGRESS CATALOG CARD NUMBER: 65-21377

Contents

EDITORS' INTRODUCTION   xi

PREFACE   xv

1. BRITISH RULE IN THE WEST, 1763–68   1

2. BRITISH RULE: CONFUSION AND COLLAPSE,
    1768–74   34

3. THE WEST IN WAR AND IN MAKING PEACE   53

4. SETTLEMENT AND SEPARATISM IN THE CONFEDER-
    ATION ERA   80

5. A NATIONAL WEST AND NEW COLONIAL SYSTEM   104

6. PEACE WITHOUT FRUITS IN THE NORTHWEST,
    1783–94   134

7. THE SOUTHWEST AND EUROPEAN RELATIONS TO
    1798   163

8. ACQUISITION OF LOUISIANA AND THE FLORIDAS   201

9. BURR'S CONSPIRACY AND NATIONALISM   234

10. THE WEST IN RELATIONS WITH CANADA AND
    BRITAIN, 1795–1830   253

11. REMOVING INDIANS AND SELLING PUBLIC LANDS   284

12. THE GREAT MIGRATION   303

13. SETTLING DOWN: INDUSTRY AND TRADE   322

14. THE WEST AS A FRONTIER SOCIETY   344

    ABBREVIATIONS   375

    APPENDIX   379

    INDEX   389

Illustrations

These photographs, grouped in a separate section,
will be found following page 142

1. Immigrants on the way westward

2. Chicago in 1820

3. SIR WILLIAM JOHNSON

4. DANIEL BOONE

5. JOSEPH BRANT

6. GENERAL SIR GUY CARLETON

7. Dorton's Fort, near Nickelsville, Virginia

8. Ground plan of Fort Defiance

9. Fort Sackville in Vincennes, Indiana

10. Fort Harmer

11. Campus Martius, initial settlement of Marietta, Ohio

12. GEORGE ROGERS CLARK

13. The Saucier House, the first courthouse of the Old Northwest

14. WILLIAM HENRY HARRISON

15. Medical College of Ohio, Cincinnati

16. Public landing in Cincinnati

17. MAJOR GENERAL ARTHUR ST. CLAIR

18. ANTHONY WAYNE

19. The first floating mill on the Ohio

20. A flat-bottom boat used on the Ohio and the Mississippi

21. The Detroit River front in 1794

22. An American log house

23. Grease lamp

24. Printing press

25. The rifle, tomahawk, sword, etc., of General George Rogers Clark

26. Flatboat, family boat and steamboat on the Mississippi

27. Interior of *The Philanthropist*

28. Scene on steamboat

29. Natchez ballroom

30. A typical Indian village

Maps

NORTHWESTERN BOUNDARIES CONSIDERED IN THE PEACE
    NEGOTIATIONS OF 1782–1783   69

PROPOSED COLONIES IN THE SOUTHWEST   88

STATE LAND CLAIMS AND CESSIONS AFTER 1783   118

INDIAN WAR, 1789–1794   153

WEST FLORIDA: CLAIMS AND CESSIONS 1763–1819   214

THE WEST IN THE WAR OF 1812   267

Editors' Introduction

FROM THE AGE of Reconnaissance and Discovery down to our own Nuclear Space Age, the exploration of the unknown and the untamed has challenged the imagination of man. The westward movement was almost a preoccupation of American writers and historians from James Fenimore Cooper to Frederick Jackson Turner. Natty Bumppo, Cooper's hero of forest and prairie, epitomized the clash of Indian and white cultures, that dichotomy of freedom against order which became a part of the frontier mythos.

This book is the first of a series of volumes on the history of the West included in *The New American Nation Series,* a comprehensive and cooperative survey of the history of the area now embraced in the United States. Its successor volume is Ray Billington's treatment of *The Far Western Frontier, 1830–1860,* and two additional volumes will describe the extraordinary story of Western growth from the Civil War to the present day.

The author of this book, himself of a generation of the last frontier, does not sentimentalize the early West. Instead, he submits the myths which have gathered about the area to the most up-to-date and rigorous scholarly review. While he does not regard the West either as a romantic sanctuary or a springboard of democratic egalitarianism, he recognizes its unique and central role in the shaping of American nationalism. Thus, if he rejects some of the hypotheses of Frederick Jackson Turner and Clarence W. Alvord about the early West, he is also quick to point out how many uncertainties still remain. Even cartographers do not know how to draw the Proclamation Line of 1763, for example; nor are historians still decided on what that Line intended.

With Frederick Jackson Turner Professor Philbrick stands at Cumberland Gap and watches the procession of civilization marching single file—the buffalo following the trail to salt springs, the Indian, the fur trader and hunter, the cattle raiser, the pioneer farmer—and with Turner he sees that frontier pass by. However, while he stands on the same ground, he sees many things about the West quite differently from Turner. He questions the thesis that American democracy came out of the forest, gaining new strength each time it touched a new frontier, and the extent of "political squatter sovereignty." He implies that Turnerian interpretations do not oversimplify and overdraw the contrasts between the sections. He casts doubt on the depth of the antagonism between interior and coast, between creditor and debtor. In place of Turner's romantic primitivism Professor Philbrick would substitute hard and often dreary work, great isolation, and the virtually limitless resource of the early West in making free land available.

There is much else, too, which is significant and fresh in this volume. Mr. Philbrick ties together the multiple threads of conflicting land company claims, gives us a masterly treatment of the Northwest Territorial Ordinance of 1787 and the organization of the public lands during the Confederation, and provides forthright, albeit controversial, pen portraits of frontier "heroes" like William Blount, James Wilkinson, and Aaron Burr. He explains why migration came when it did and why it could not be postponed. To the author the American character took root on the Atlantic frontier, not the trans-Appalachian, and it was in the area east of the mountains that nationalism first evolved. At the same time he concedes to nationalism a more consequential role in the growth of the West than he does to sectionalism. Just as Mr. Philbrick would play down democratic impulse as especially characteristic of the Early West, so he would also lessen the pervasiveness of Western lawlessness and separatism.

In addition, this book provides a fresh examination of the great issue of the free navigation of the Mississippi, which, in the author's opinion, was overlaid with dubious arguments about economic needs and emotional issues. He explores early cases of conflict of interest, an area which still needs clarification and policing, and gives us a sensible and balanced account of the role of the West in the War of 1812.

If this treatment of the early West is as much a reconsideration of the legends which have grown up about the historic area as it is a fresh look at the historical facts, it serves all the more to point to the distortion of the concept of a land frontier as the central theme in American life. Having come to the furthest limits of the continental West, we today recognize that there are other frontiers besides land, frontiers of creativity, of science, and technology which remain to be more fully explored and developed. In that sense the frontier has not disappeared, nor has the American dream.

HENRY STEELE COMMAGER
RICHARD B. MORRIS

Preface

FOR undertaking to write this volume the author can only offer the common excuse that he has long been interested in the subject— in fact, ever since he was allowed in 1899 to teach a college course on the territorial expansion of the United States.

There is no attempt, except in rare instances, to tell the whole story of anything. The book is a *commentary* on the West's role in our history, and, to some extent, on traditional presentations of its story. Great limitations of the story being inevitable, they have been determined by the volume's objective as defined by the editors: namely, to present the West's "rise," or development. This, as interpreted by the writer, means not merely in area, population, and industry, but also as affecting—or affected by—the rest of the country.

Many lesser inquiries are included in that general inquiry. What policies and agencies accelerated or retarded it? To what extent was favor to "squatters" consistent with English law? Did the Proclamation of 1763 have any actual effect? Did the land companies sensibly affect western settlement? What was sound statesmanship? Was the British government's failure to colonize the Illinois country before 1776 obtuse, or was it sound statesmanship, or a necessity? Although a past era may be properly judged on the basis of present knowledge and ideals, it is not just that its actors should be individually so judged. This is just. Moreover, unless observed, it is impossible to distinguish the wise from the stupid, the effective from the inadequate, among all who acted within the general restrictions and imperfections of their time.

The book is necessarily a prosaic substitute for what is popularly understood as western history. "The West" is a phrase which has never had a merely geographical significance for Americans; its meaning has always been overlaid with emotional connotations. Fresh in European interest when the romantic movement in literature was in its heyday, it fascinated a remarkable group of European poets and other celebrities. Its endless forest captivated both Chateaubriand and Francis Parkman. The latter's first volume on the romance of the American forest (as he described his histories) commemorated the blood, fire, and terror of Pontiac's War. Indian wars remained the dominant background of western romanticism until fences ended the open range and the Indians abandoned war. In addition to this, various causes gave to the history of the Southwest during the first two decades of our national existence an exaggerated color of intrigue and infidelity which still persists.

The writer's minimization of romance is a sacrifice to truth—not to the writer's disdain. His boyhood was spent on the last frontier—for one summer in a sod house on an unstocked ranch, thereafter in a nearby town, which in 1958 celebrated its seventy-fifth anniversary with a pageant concluding with "the hanging of Kid Wade," that area's last rustler. The location was sufficiently near an Indian reservation to disquiet eastern friends, but with an army post nearer. Droves of horses for eastern markets grazed each spring beyond the railroad's head before shipment, and competition between the drovers and local riders in breaking broncos was an everyday free show. The writer remembers vividly the buffalo wallows in the prairie; every boy old enough to have a gun had a buffalo powder horn; buffalo laprobes and overcoats were numerous. An antelope (today a nuisance in a stock country) could occasionally be seen in the distance. Oxen, displaced by horses in travel to the West early in the 1800's, were long continued in heavy tasks. In the city of two million inhabitants in which he now lives, the writer is very likely the only one who ever rode behind oxen all day. On his first railroad ride, taken into the smoking car, he witnessed a robbery: the snatching of a roll of bills from a rancher (who had doubtless just sold a herd in Omaha). Paperback stories of life in army posts or of range life and wars are in the writer's bedroom bookcase, and they stir a hundred memories—particularly those of the old cavalry uniform of dark blue tunic and light blue trousers with broad yellow stripes. This book is dedicated *con amore* to these boyhood memories—that is to say, to romance.

However, there was only one form of romance that greatly affected western development. Indeed, it made the West. That was the love between man and woman, and for their children, which moved millions to the frontier in search of better lives—including the writer's four New England grandparents.

Various persons interested in the early West have answered questions, permitted reproduction of illustrations, or otherwise given aid in the preparation of this volume. Their kindness is most appreciatively acknowledged. To Mrs. Margaret W. Halsey, whose experience as a proofreader has saved me from errors in spelling and lessened shortcomings in phrasing, and to Mr. James F. McRee, Jr., who has done for me in the last stages of the manuscript's preparation much work which I could not do myself, I am particularly indebted.

F.S.P.

CHAPTER 1

British Rule in the West, 1763-68

A LARGE portion of the West that is the subject of this volume became British by the treaty which ended the French and Indian War. Of the long French rule in the Mississippi Valley, in 1763 no signs remained between Louisiana and Canada save some two thousand souls in scattered settlements, some fur traders, and the names (still in use today) of some threescore settlements, rivers, and other geographical features.[1] Of Britain's gain, nothing was clear beyond the acquisition of the territory.

In southern and central Illinois there were several French villages, three of them fifty to sixty years old. At Detroit there was a fortified trading post and a small settlement older than those in Illinois, at Vincennes another younger settlement. Army garrisons of French or English troops rarely exceeded a few hundred soldiers. Traders gathered seasonally about a number of forts or trading posts; some hundreds of them were in and out of both Northwest and Southwest every season. Halfbreeds were a considerable part of the permanent population of every post. Hunters and an occasional explorer made up the rest of those, other than Indians, within the vast wilderness.

The war had revealed some weaknesses in British control of the colonies and, far more plainly, colonial disunity. This localism had been manifested in matters distinctly intercolonial in incidence, which were relations with the Indians, and so primarily of the West—Indian trade, the purchase of Indian lands, the maintenance of peace. The Albany

[1] L. P. Kellogg, *MVHR* (XVIII), 20-21.

Congress of 1754 was notable for its attempt to secure a colonial union to deal with precisely these problems.[2] They had been presented to the home government by the petition of that Congress after the war department had learned the immense difficulties and expense of forest war, and the importance of finding a basis for permanent peace.

Elimination of the causes of Indian hostility required the extirpation of unfair treatment in trade, of frauds in land purchases, and of constant border encroachments. Evidence of these evils had poured into government offices during the war.[3] They were common to all the colonies, as was recognized both by the Board of Trade and the Privy Council.[4] As a result of the information and advice before it, the Board prepared in 1754, even before receiving the proposals of the Albany Congress, a general plan for what was essentially a military supervision of the colonies.[5] Soon afterward, in a report on the Albany Congress which made pacification of the Indians a primary objective, it advised the King to assume control of Indian affairs.[6] The offices of commander in chief of the forces in North America and of superintendent of Indian affairs were accordingly created. Sir William Johnson was made superintendent in a northern department, and Edmund Atkin (John Stuart soon succeeding the latter) of a southern. Sir William (a former colonel) had long been an Indian trader and lived baronially among the Mohawks—after his wife's death, with Indian mates. He thoroughly understood the Indians, particularly their instability; joined understandingly in their ritualistic formalism; was generous to those in need.

[2] *N.Y. Col. Docs.*, VI, 889–91, 853–897, 916–920; Franklin, *Writings* (Smyth ed.), III, 203–207, gives the reasons for each recommendation.

[3] In particular, C. H. McIlwain (ed.), *Peter Wraxall's Abridgment of the Indian Affairs of New York, 1678–1850* (Cambridge, 1915), pp. xcvi, xcvii–ix; *Johnson Papers*, I, 253.

[4] *N.Y. Col. Docs.*, VII, 47, 77, 221; O'Callaghan (ed.), *Doc. Hist.*, pp. 777, 780; *Wraxall's Abridgment*, p. 204; C. E. Carter (ed.), *The Correspondence of General Thomas Gage with the Secretaries of State, 1762–1775* (2 vols., New Haven, 1931–33), I, 152. The cost of Indian affairs to Pennsylvania from 1748 to 1752 was equal to that for thirty years preceding. A. T. Volwiler, *George Croghan and the Western Movement, 1748–1782* (Cleveland, 1926), p. 56.

[5] Of August 19, 1754. The government acted on advice of the Board of Trade of June 14, 1754—*N.Y. Col. Docs.*, VI, 844, 901–906, 916–920. See C. E. Carter, "The Significance of the Military Office in America, 1763–1775," *AHR*, XXVIII (1922), and "The Office of Commander in Chief: A Phase of Imperial Unity . . . ," in R. B. Morris (ed.), *The Era of the American Revolution* (New York, 1939), p. 740.

[6] Oct. 29, 1754, *N.Y. Col. Docs.*, VI, 916–920.

The policy of the home government was soon seen in America. In 1758, by a treaty made by Johnson for Pennsylvania with the eastern Delawares, that colony promised that no settlements would be made west of the Susquehanna without prior agreement.[7] The British commandant at Fort Pitt (Pittsburgh), Colonel Henry Bouquet, interpreted this as equally binding on Maryland and Virginia, whose lands also adjoined the hunting grounds of the Delawares. He therefore issued a proclamation (October, 1761) which forbade any hunting or settlement west of the Alleghenies unless licensed by provincial governors or the commander in chief, and enforced it by driving away and burning the cabins of "vagabonds" making settlements in the Monongahela country.[8] Even before this the Board of Trade had been ordered to draft instructions to the colonial governors forbidding grants or settlements that might interfere with the Indians, and ordering that proclamations be issued requiring settlers on Indian lands to remove. The basis of this policy was a declaration in these instructions that since "the peace and Security of our Colonies . . . does greatly depend upon the amity and alliance" of nearby Indians, the government was resolved "to protect their just rights and possessions." The instructions went out in 1762.[9]

As a result of these actions in America and England, the home government had assumed direct control both of Indian affairs and of the disposition of crown lands. And the purpose behind this was explicitly stated to be peace with, and justice for, the Indians.

The government's general policy was formally expressed in a royal proclamation prepared by the Board of Trade.[10]

[7] This involved a famous case of fraud, years of rankling resentment by the Indians, government action in America and London. *N.Y. Col. Docs.*, VII, 130, 329–333, 221–222; Volwiler, *Croghan*, pp. 127–128; *Johnson Papers*, III, 849–850; O'Callaghan, *Doc. Hist.*, II, 770–772, 775, 783. For the important Easton Indian Treaty of 1758 releasing to the Indians the transappalachian lands up to Pennsylvania's western boundary, see L. H. Gipson, *The Great War for Empire* (New York, 1959), VII, 278, 279.

[8] K. P. Bailey, *The Ohio Company of Virginia and the Westward Movement, 1748–1792* (Glendale, Calif., 1939), pp. 223–226; Canad. Archives, *Report* for 1889, "Note E," pp. 72–79.

[9] *N.Y. Col. Docs.*, VII, 472–480 (quotations, 473, 478). The instructions (pp. 478–479) were embodied in general instructions sent at different times to the governors, but they received little emphasis. See *Acts of the Privy Council of England, Colonial Series*, IV, 475, 479, 481, 482.

[10] That its president, Lord Shelburne, made no original contribution to its substance or form was made almost certain by V. W. Crane, in *MVHR*, VIII (1921), 368, and R. A. Humphrey, in *Eng. Hist. Rev.*, XLIX (1934), 241–242, 248, 250; and it has been confirmed after study of the original manu-

The Proclamation of 1763 created three new colonies: East Florida, West Florida, and a greatly diminished Province of Quebec.[11] This last was cut off from western Canada by a line running from the intersection of the St. Lawrence River with 45° north latitude (at Cornwall, Ontario) to Lake Nipissing. Pacification of the Indians was a primary objective. The great area west of Quebec, north of Florida, and "westward of the sources of the rivers which fall into the sea from the west and northwest" was reserved to the Indians. Land grants and settlements were forbidden within this reservation, and the Indian trade was opened to any licensed British subject under certain regulations.

The Board also emphasized the desirability of a "secure settling of the whole Coast . . . from the Mouth of the Mississippi to . . . the Hudson's Bay Settlements," by "emigrants from Europe, or from the Overflow of . . . [the] ancient Colonies." Finally, the Proclamation provided for land bounties in all the new colonies for soldiers of the war, just ended; those in Quebec were located within Virginia's indefinite northwest—part of the new reservation. This was bound to become fatefully inconsistent with the policy of Indian peace.

The Proclamation had little if any effect upon the development of the West. It has interest as an attempt to affect it, and for its failure. Whether it was the basis of government policy from 1763 to 1768 or on the contrary was flouted by the actions that followed it; whether there *was* any continuing policy, and what that was if there was any— these are beclouded and controverted questions. A few points respecting the Proclamation seem clear.

1. All cartographic representations of the boundary, as described, are merely conventional. No line has ever been drawn, because none can be drawn, that is demonstrably consistent with both the government's purpose and actual geography. The Board knew little of the latter, and various uncertainties exist respecting its purpose.[12]

---

scripts by J. M. Sosin, *Whitehall and the Wilderness* (Lincoln, Neb., 1961), pp. 27, 39, 46, 47.

[11] The papers embodying its preparation are in Shortt and Doughty, *Papers,* I, 163–168, 127–163, respectively. The Proclamation alone is in H. Commager, *Documents of American History* (5th ed., New York, 1949), p. 47; A. C. Douglas (ed.), *English Historical Documents* (Cambridge, 1955), IX, 639; *Amer. Archives,* I, 172–175; *Ill. Hist. Coll.,* X, 39–45. Important related documents are in *N.Y. Col. Docs,* VII, 15, 473, 478–479, 520–521.

[12] The desire was perhaps to stop travel up river valleys. The reservation included "all the Lands . . . not . . . within the limits of Our said Three New Governments . . . as also all the Lands . . . Westward of the Sources of the

2. The Proclamation nowhere indicated an intent to alter the western boundaries of the seaboard colonies. It is obvious that political boundaries earlier fixed by formal royal acts could not possibly have been altered by a later act which did not even refer to them or to boundaries, and did refer to settlement.[13] It was a settlement line merely. It is difficult to find any reason why the idea arose that the intent was to fix colonial bounds, but for more than a century an idea persisted—seemingly on that basis—that the Proclamation was hostile to the colonies.[14] That view has largely disappeared. However, the same failure to distinguish between a settlement line and a political boundary later generated confusion and international discord, particularly in American-Canadian relations, and it still underlies unacceptable views.[15]

There are likewise views which unjustifiably aggrandize the Proclamation—for example, as an act "for the reconstruction of the American colonial empire." It was not at all "a readjustment of the legal relations between" Britain and the colonies.[16] Again, since the Proclamation's purpose required the exclusion of all inhabitants save Indians, and provided for no government save military police, it was only in that negative sense "the fundamental law of the West in the years preceding the revolutionary war."[17]

Rivers which fall into the Sea from the West and Northwest." Obviously, therefore, its boundary could not run into and around the peninsula of East Florida. It is also obvious that no reservation land lay north of East Florida except westward of Georgia, but that a reservation boundary necessarily crossed rivers emptying through West Florida into the Gulf of Mexico—if the Gulf was part of the "sea" or "Atlantic ocean." Almost all historians have ended the Proclamation line at the south end of the Great Valley of Virginia, on the assumption that the intent was to indicate the watershed between the Mississippi River and Atlantic Ocean. This was John Stuart's view in *MVHR*, XVII, 364–365. But it is a certainty that the intent was to protect the reservation, and the description of the reservation requires a line north of West Florida.

[13] The question is one of what the Proclamation said, not of what Lord Shelburne's secretary thought (*Eng. Hist. Rev.*, XLIX, 247), or of vague later statements of Shelburne. *Ill. Hist. Coll.*, XVI, 17, 106.

[14] A vague suggestion, supposedly made by Edmund Burke (*Annual Register for 1763*, 6th ed., 1810, p. 21), has sometimes been relied on.

[15] Examples, old and recent, are in *Ill. Hist. Coll.*, XVI, 182; of Trade; P. C. Phillips, *The West in the Diplomacy of the Revolution* (Urbana, Ill., 1913), p. 60; Carter, *Gage Correspondence*, I, 222. Lord Hillsborough was not confused, *N.Y. Col. Docs.*, VIII, 94–95, 102, nor G. E. Howard, *Preliminaries of the Revolution* (New York, 1905), p. 233.

[16] F. L. Paxson, *When the West Is Gone* (New York, 1930), pp. 8, 10.

[17] C. W. Alvord, in *MVHR*, III, 37.

3. The three new colonies created by the Proclamation were all coastal, and so accessible to British ships and trade. The emphasis upon seaboard settlement, and the unavoidable deflection from the interior to the new provinces of migrants from the old, were congruent with a mercantilistic purpose. But they do not prove the accuracy of Lord Hillsborough's later statement that such was the Proclamation's basic policy—if he meant that.

4. The most important disagreements respecting the Proclamation have related to the intended duration of its provisions and their relation to future administrative acts. The provisions were in several ways necessarily tentative, but their temporary quality has been overemphasized. Pontiac's War revealed an administrative emergency, but it is no more true of politics than of surgery that what is done in an emergency is either in fact or in intent provisional. A document is always construed in the light of the circumstances with which it was to deal, or within which it was to operate. That a strong and long-term policy was called for seems perfectly clear.[18] However, over and over in the documents which record the Proclamation's formulation, the prohibition of western settlement was characterized as proposed, or desirable, or approved, "for the present." Did this indicate that conflicting views of the Board members permitted only a short-term policy? Or that, despite agreement on a long-term policy, administrative discretion dictated avoidance of explicit long-term commitments? Neither contention has ever been made. Until recent decades the prevailing view was that "for the present" meant for the foreseeable future, and unless and until basic conditions should change; but that this intent to plan for a long period was defeated by the influence of land speculation in London. The evidence in the document was equivocal, but in informing Sir William Johnson and General Gage of its measures, which they were to make effective, not only did the Board give no hint of a time restriction but it expressed the belief that the Proclamation would definitely end encroachments on Indian areas.[19] One other view makes Lord Shelburne the author of the Proclamation's provisions respecting the West, assumes them underlain by a definite policy of steady settlement,

[18] Cf. C. E. Carter, *Great Britain and the Illinois Country* (Washington, 1910), p. 140.

[19] The framers coupled the reservation provision with a reference to Senegal and Newfoundland as territories where no "permanent" residents were contemplated, but then added, "immediately at least." Shortt and Doughty, *Papers,* p. 139; *N.Y. Col. Docs.,* VII, 535; *Gage Correspondence,* II, 10.

and makes a vast land purchase made in 1768 part of Shelburne's original idea.[20] This view relieves the government of liability to charges of
uncertain purpose or unsteady resolution, and adjusts the Proclamation's purposes to the actual fact that there was no possibility of long
preventing settlement of the West. There is, however, a complete absence of satisfactory evidence to support it.

West Florida was virtually without inhabitants when organized save
for a Spanish garrison, some French around Mobile, and Americans
around Natchez. The northern boundary, originally placed on 31°
north latitude, was moved in 1767 to that of the mouth of the Yazoo
River, to include the Natchez region, which by that time had become
important.[21] This was one of the first excisions made by the government from the Indian reservation just created.

The only direct relation of the colony in its early years to the development of the West was through the influx of emigrants from the
coastal colonies—at first of wanderers, primarily from Georgia, later
of loyalists from all the colonies, for whom it was made a special haven
by the British government.[22] On the other hand, the history of the
colony epitomizes the causes of the West's creation—that is, of the
Revolution; for there was a repetition in it of all the vices and blunders
by which discontent was hardened in the old colonies. Great and precipitate land grants illustrated the pattern of land and class control.
Repression of the legislature was petty and excessive. Legislation dealt,
of necessity, primarily with local problems, mainly economic, yet nearly
a quarter of all laws were disallowed by the Crown, and in some cases

[20] C. W. Alvord, "Genesis of the Proclamation of 1763," *Mich. Hist. Coll.*,
XXXVI (1909), 42–43, 52; "The British Ministry and the Treaty of Fort
Stanwix," Wisconsin State Historical Society, *Proceedings* for 1908, LVI
(1909), 179; *The Illinois Country, 1678–1818* (Springfield, 1920), p. 255.
He admitted that the policy "had been so concealed in the proclamation . . .
that few had understood it." *Mississippi Valley*, I, 171. Indeed, this expansion
policy supposedly hidden in the Proclamation was forgotten by Shelburne himself when, in 1767, just before its first great application in the Fort Stanwix
purchase, he characterized that instrument as "founded on a contracted policy"
of limiting "the extension of [British] dominions." *Ill. Hist. Coll.*, XVI, 106.

[21] C. E. Carter, "Some Aspects of British Administration in West Florida,"
MVHR I (1914–15), 364–366, 368. Previously, in 1763, and in 1765–67,
land cessions were secured from the Creeks and Cherokees west of the Proclamation Line.

[22] C. Johnson, *British West Florida, 1763–1783* (New Haven, 1943), and
C. N. Howard, *The British Development of West Florida, 1763–1769* (Berkeley,
1947), afford abundant illustrations; the second volume deals with land policies
in detail.

this action shockingly illustrated the vice of that royal power. Two early governors were removed for embezzlement of an Indian fund. Another was a former naval officer who embarrassed General Gage in intercolonial administration by quarrels with army officers; prorogued the legislature several times for long periods, even for years; feuded with the chief justice and with minor executive officers of his colony; quarreled endlessly with the regimental commander in Pensacola (a petty stockaded settlement of bark huts along narrow roadways) over salutes, military returns, the exclusive right to entertain Indian chiefs, and a hut for occupancy by those dignitaries. He was finally removed for insubordination.

The history of the West from 1763 to the Revolution centered in attempts by the British government to decide whether the Indian reservation created there should remain as such, and, meanwhile, to enforce rules of trade and prevent land grants and settlement therein. Both attempts were complete failures. But whether or not an uncertainty of policy weakened the will to enforce these rules and prohibitions, it was not the primary cause for the administrative failure. This was relatively simple.

In the military posts, British military law replaced French. In the old French villages of Illinois the affairs of some two thousand civilians had needed, and had received, regulation by French civil law—which General Gage rightly treated as continuing. But outside these posts and villages all was a void save for the British sovereignty that had displaced French. No British statutes relating to private law and crimes ran, even in wording, to America. No provincial laws could be actualities beyond the limits of effective government—that is, control. Moreover, reservation of the area for exclusive Indian use, necessarily excluding British subjects, impliedly excluded British law for regulation of their acts and relations. There could therefore be only such conduct of intruders as the military commanders might regard as breaches of good order, to be punished by them as police officers. Attention to these facts is important as a basis for judging both the merits of government policy and the intelligence of its administrators in America.

The Board of Trade, when preparing the Proclamation of 1763, remarked that no "regular Government" was "either necessary or indeed [could] be established, where no perpetual Residence or planting [was] intended." When the King objected that criminals might, in the absence of government, seek asylum there, the Board gave reasons why it was inadvisable to extend over it the government of any seaboard colony, and particularly that of Quebec. Yet the Board inconsistently agreed that it needed some government—though simultaneously making it impossible—"with a most precise description of its Boundaries."[23]

The Board, seemingly, did not recognize the conflict. The government was never able to remove it, nor, therefore, able to solve the problems it created. By no possibility could military police by a few hundred soldiers be effective over a region of some 300,000 square miles.[24] However, that being the only possibility, the Board recommended that the commission of the commander in chief give him authority "for the Government" of the region—which was unnecessary, since his commission, ever since 1754, had covered it.[25] This was a proper exercise of military power. Colonel Henry Bouquet had so enforced his proclamation of 1761.

The paramountcy of the commander in chief over the Indian superintendents was clear in theory from 1755 to 1764.[26] Johnson's instructions in 1756 and 1761 were to obey punctually "in all matters" the orders of the commanders, and this was undoubtedly the case for Stuart also. Both were specifically so instructed in 1766. But from 1764 onward, obscurity covered this paramountcy because utterly different powers were assigned to the Indian superintendents in a plan, which never became law, prepared in 1764 by the Board of Trade for the management of Indian affairs.[27] This plan was in two parts, one dealing with the Indian trade. Since the difficulties now in question arose from the other part, we may briefly dismiss the trading plan.

That it was a failure even in the Southwest, where it had its best trial, was agreed.[28] This was owing primarily to its maladjustment to the conditions of the trade. Since the different tribes did not occupy

[23] Shortt and Doughty, *Papers*, I, 139, 148, 151–152.

[24] There was one "battalion" for "Chartres, Pitt, &c." and another for the "Great Lakes," and one in West Florida. *Gage Correspondence*, II, 589. This applies to the entire period, 1763–74.

[25] *Ibid.*, p. 152. No special commission was ever prepared. As respects Amherst's, Carter, *Illinois Country*, p. 19; presumably Gage's was the same. Compare Alvord, *Mississippi Valley*, I, 205.

[26] *Ill. Hist. Coll.*, XI, 450, 453, for the orders to the superintendents in 1756. See Carter, "The Significance of the Military Office in America, 1763–1775," *AHR*, XXVIII (1923), 475–488, and "Office of Commander in Chief," in Morris (ed.), *Era of the Revolution;* Introduction to Carter, *Gage Correspondence.*

[27] Its antecedents are in *N.Y. Col. Docs.*, VII, 535–536, 572–581, 634–636. The plan is *ibid.*, pp. 637–641, 657–666; *Ill. Hist. Coll.*, X, 273–281; Shortt and Doughty, *Papers*, pp. 614–620.

[28] *Gage Correspondence*, I, 278; II, 49.

definite territories, trade was supervised tribally.[29] However, licenses
were issued by the governors.[30] Though many licenses in the south
specified the Indian towns at which the licensees should trade (as the
plan required), different provinces had long had special relations with
particular tribes, and even uncertain boundaries were more or less disregarded. Illegalities and interprovincial jealousies were inevitable. In
addition, the southern governors resented subordination to the superintendents. Governor Johnstone of West Florida sent his own agents to
the Cherokee.[31] Governor Fauquier of Virginia ignored imperial regulations and appointed his own commissioners.[32] The Board of Trade
itself sent over to the governors quantities of goods for them to distribute.[33] The governors profited financially at the expense of administrative reforms ordered in the plan. Both in the north and south the
Indians also had ideas that defied regulation. The Creeks preferred to
continue trade with Georgia and not to shift to Pensacola, as John
Stuart desired. Johnson sought to confine trade in the Northwest to the
military posts, in accordance with the plan's provision. The traders preferred to sell, and the Indians to secure, unlimited rum in the woods.
The British traders violated the post restriction in order to meet the
competition of Canadian traders. Even the post commanders and
George Croghan, Sir William's deputy, violated it. By 1768 it was
everywhere a nullity.[34] North and south the general results were much
the same, perhaps less calamitous in the north.[35]

[29] *Ill. Hist. Coll.*, X, 281, 17.

[30] The importance of this is stressed by C. E. Carter, "British Policy towards
the American Indians in the South, 1763–1768," in *Eng. Hist. Rev.*, XXXIII
(1918), 37–56.

[31] *Ibid.*, p. 47; H. L. Shaw, *British Administration of the Southern Indians,
1763–1776* (Lancaster, 1931), pp. 38–41; *Gage Correspondence*, I, 321; *Ill.
Hist. Coll.*, XI, 459–461, 496.

[32] *Gage Correspondence*, I, 144.

[33] *Ibid.*, p. 145.

[34] Johnson letters in S. Pargellis (ed.), *Military Affairs in North America,
1748–1765: Selected Documents* (New York, 1936), pp. 458–459; *Ill. Hist.
Coll.*, X, 307, 328; XI, 509; *Gage Correspondence*, I, 96, 113–114, 123, 126,
276. On opposition of British Canadians and London merchants, *ibid.*, pp.
96, 97; opinion of Sir Guy Carleton, *N.Y. Col. Docs.*, VIII, 655; *Ill. Hist.
Coll.*, XI, 4, 5, 43–44, 76–77, 80, 105, 209, 367, 378–382, 509, 533–534
(Carleton), 543, 574; M. J. Reid, "The Quebec Fur Traders and Western
Policy, 1763–1774," *Canad. Hist. Rev.*, VII, 22, 26; *Johnson Papers*, V, 346,
399, 738, VI, 19, 199. Indian opinion was divided; *Johnson Papers*, IV, 852;
Gage Correspondence, I, 155; O'Callaghan, *Doc. Hist.*, II, 881.

[35] C. E. Carter, *Eng. Hist. Rev.*, XXXIII, 40, 47–51; J. Stuart, "Observations on the Plan," *AHR*, XX, 817, 818.

In addition to these weaknesses in the plan itself that ensured its failure, there was another which would have made any regulatory plan unworkable—the absence of effective government.[36] This brings us back to the provisions in the plan which dealt with matters other than trade. A main objective of these was to free Sir William Johnson—whose plan, substantially, it was—from control by the commander in chief.[37] Control of all public affairs of the Indians (including even the bestowal of military commissions upon them) was entrusted to the superintendent. Such was Johnson's thirst for absolute power that he desired "that all private persons, Societies, or Bodies Corporate, be prohibited from *Intermeddling,* in like manner as the *Civil and Military* [authorities]."[38] Moreover, the plan conferred upon the superintendents and their subordinates powers for maintaining peace and good order, for deciding civil cases and punishing crimes; and proposed the repeal of all provincial laws regulating "Indian affairs or commerce."[39] Thus, within both the reservation and the provinces, the superintendents or their deputies would have bestowed justice (in cases affecting the Indians) like absolute monarchs on tour among their subjects.[40] Even the provincial governors were to be pushed aside. Thereafter, only the superintendents might "buy" Indian lands, and only for the Crown or colony proprietaries.[41]

Portions of the plan could have been established by act of the King, but only in 1768 was it even laid before him, and he never made any part thereof effective.[42] Obviously, legislation was required by the third item. Obviously, too, the fourth—and the second, if construed as broadly as a tyrant would have desired—were beyond even the power

[36] Shelburne's vague condemnation of it (*Gage Correspondence,* II, 48; *Ill. Hist. Coll.,* XI, 456) presumably refers both to these and to those next discussed. Few of all the comments on the plan solicited by government (listed by Carter in *Gage Correspondence,* II, 48, n. 34, and in *AHR,* XX, 817) showed the remotest consciousness of this difficulty.

[37] *N.Y. Col. Docs.,* VII, 964–965; *Ill. Hist. Coll.,* X, 221, 256–263, 273; *Amer. Hist. Rev.,* XX, 816.

[38] Sections 10, 11, 17 of the plan, *Ill. Hist. Coll.,* X, 273 *et seq.,* and letters of Johnson to Board, *ibid.,* pp. 330, 332.

[39] *Ill. Hist. Coll.,* X, 274, 329. Only Richard Jackson (*ibid.,* XI, 423) commented on the unwisdom of this proposal.

[40] *Ibid.,* pp. 276, 332. By 1767 Johnson wanted power to render "speedy Justice without Dispute or Evasion" (no court, no lawyers, no arguments), *ibid.,* XI, 573.

[41] *Ibid.,* X, 280, secs. 41, 43.

[42] *Ibid.,* XVI, 245, or *N.Y. Col. Docs.,* VIII, 55.

of Parliament. And the Board itself could only express opinions.[43] The plan, then, was without any legal character whatever. Lord Hillsborough had earlier correctly described it as "suggested by this Board in 1764, and adopted by the Superintendents," and again in writing of laying before the King "the plan adopted by the Superintendents." Lord Shelburne once criticized Stuart for having "too hastily adopted" it.[44] The superintendents did try to put it into effect (just what parts does not appear), and Gage, whether or not he resented Johnson's ambitions, aided him as best he could.[45]

Legal action by the superintendents (within their commissions) undoubtedly contributed greatly to the chief objective of their office, the maintenance of peace. Johnson simply resented the disregard of the governors, and others, who realized that his commission powers were "very trifling, uncertain and in general . . . disputed."[46]

While the Proclamation was being drafted, the King suggested that all army officers and Indian agents be empowered (1) to seize "criminals" and other offenders, and (2) "send them to be tried in any of the old colonies (if that can be done)" or else (3) "to that Government, from which They respectively fled."[47] There could be "criminals" only where English law existed and defined the crimes. Even had there been such law, the first provision for trial was banned by one of the most ancient and basic principles of criminal law, and the second was likely to be impracticable because of lack of knowledge, time, expense, and guards. The Proclamation did direct officers to seize persons "[known to be] charged" with crime and send them to the colony

[43] A. H. Basye, *The Lords Commissioners of Trade and Plantations* . . . *1748–1782* (New Haven, 1925), p. 176, and "The Secretary of State for the Colonies," *AHR*, XXXVIII (1932), 15.

[44] *Ill. Hist. Coll.*, XI, 454, 245, 191, 187. Compare *Ill. Hist. Coll.*, X, 337. On Shelburne's in 1766, *Johnson Papers*, VIII, p. 37.

[45] Shaw, *Southern Indians*, p. 23; C. E. Carter, *Eng. Hist. Rev.*, XXXIII (1918), 45–46; R. C. Downes, *Council Fires on the Upper Ohio* . . . *until 1795* (Pittsburgh, 1940), pp. 127–128; *Ill. Hist. Coll.*, X, 400; *Gage Correspondence*, I, 123, 144, 276; Carter, "Commander in Chief," in R. B. Morris (ed.), *Era of the Revolution*, p. 192; Alvord, *Illinois Country*, p. 255; J. R. Alden, *John Stuart and the Southern Frontier* . . . *1754–1775* (Ann Arbor, 1944), pp. 140, 149; Alden, *Gage in America*, pp. 137–138.

[46] *N.Y. Col. Docs.*, VII, 872, 964. Shelburne's comments were highly creditable to his intelligence. *Ill. Hist. Coll.*, XVI, 16, XI, 539.

[47] Shortt and Doughty, *Papers*, p. 154. For later orders of this character by Lord Carleton, see *Mich. Hist. Colls.*, IX, 346, X, 424.

where the crime was allegedly committed.[48] The Mutiny Act, by an amendment of 1765, made it possible to send civilians accused of crimes committed at British "forts, garrisons or places" (where there *was* law, French civil or British military) to the nearest province, and to be there tried, "any law, usage, custom, matter, or thing whatsoever to the contrary notwithstanding."[49] And those words only justly describe the centuries-old rule which Parliament in extraordinary circumstances thus overrode.

Outside this provision everything was left to military police. There seems to be little information about how many or what offenses were noted. General Gage resorted to persuasion, travel regulations, perhaps trials, in cases whose facts do not appear, and possibly attempted to punish lawlessness in the wilderness; but in 1772 he wrote that "the Indian Country is become not only an asylum for Fugitive Debtors, but for People guilty of all Crimes."[50]

It remains to note one extraordinary aspect of these problems. The law of civilized people is territorial. Pennsylvania rightly disclaimed any power to punish acts committed beyond her borders, even by her own citizens. Members of the Board of Trade certainly knew that England and Scotland had distinct legal systems enforceable only within their respective borders. Yet they gave no thought to that fact in considering problems of the reservation. Sir William Johnson was steadily confused, and it is not unfair to say that he never understood the nature of the reservation.[51] General Gage had a chance to learn that while governor of Montreal, since the Quebec Council was perfectly clear both on law's territorial limitation and on the difference between paper law and law in fact.[52] Indeed, Gage did write in 1772 that he "never could comprehend by what Right or Claim the American Col-

[48] Shortt and Doughty, *Papers*, p. 168.
[49] Reprinted in *Ill. Hist. Coll.*, X, 484–486. Compare *Gage Correspondence*, I, 239, II, 263, 266; *Johnson Papers*, VIII, 616, 635, 641, 1005.
[50] The instances noted (all due to Carter's research) will be found in Carter, *Illinois Country*, p. 19; *Ill. Hist. Coll.*, X, 348, 485, XVI, 630; *Gage Correspondence*, I, 156, 239, 316, 350; Carter in Morris (ed.), *Era of the Revolution*, pp. 185–189.
[51] *Ill. Hist. Coll.*, XVI, 44, a short passage which requires outright rejection or substantial qualifications on six points; XI, 543, XVI, 61–62, 64; *N.Y. Col. Docs.*, VII, 964–965.
[52] See V. Coffin, *The Province of Quebec and the Early American Revolution* (Madison, 1896), p. 417.

onies should make Laws for . . . a Trade out of their Respective Limits and consequently out of their Jurisdictions." However, his letters and his actions were by no means consistent with this statement.[53] The plan of 1764 prepared by the Board of Trade strikingly attests its ignorance, and the language of some of the secretaries of state indicates an equal lack of understanding.[54]

The plan called for performance of an impossible task. The legal difficulties that made it impossible have been emphasized because an awareness not only that it was impossible but that almost all the responsible officials were unaware of that fact or its reason is essential to a just judgment of them and of their efforts.[55] They were wholly unenlightened, but the most enlightened civil service could have done little better.

From 1763 to 1774 the British government vacillated in its attitude toward administration of the West, and this vacillation was manifestly not caused by realization of the impossibility of effective government. The hindrances to stability of policy were plain. Individuals ignored the King's prohibition of settlement beyond the "line" of 1763, and far beyond it great grants of land were sought by speculators. British fur merchants and their American factors demanded primary consideration over settlers and speculators for their trade.

The progress of overmountain settlement was steady, but it was neither great nor rapid. Proposals of colonization had begun when the war with France was scarcely under way. As advocated by the Albany Congress, Governor Thomas Pownall, Franklin, and General Amherst, such settlements were planned to join the West and the seaboard with

[53] *Gage Correspondence*, I, 123, 144, 328, 350; *Ill. Hist. Coll.*, XI, 499, 509, 543; XVI, 50, 62, 64; Carter, in Morris (ed.), *Era of the Revolution*, p. 187, 185.

[54] It is said that the Board of Trade had as legal counsel "one of His Majesty's counsel-at-law," and that from 1770 to 1782 the counsel was Richard ("Omniscient") Jackson. M. P. Clark, in *AHR*, XVII, 23. There is only scant evidence of advice. In 1768 the Board still ignored the difference between law on paper and law that was enforceable, but Samuel Wharton did not. Franklin, *Writings* (Smyth ed.), V, 525; *Gage Correspondence*, I, ix, 176; *Conn. Hist. Coll.*, XIX, 29; *Ill. Hist. Coll.*, XVI, 247; *N.Y. Col. Docs.*, VIII, 655; Shortt and Doughty, *Papers*, pp. 168, 607, 614–620; W. H. Mohr, *Federal Indian Relations, 1774–1778* (Philadelphia, 1933), pp. 12–13, 16.

[55] British officials charged with colonial administration necessarily ignored its lack of legal basis. American historians have all, so far as the writer's reading reveals, merely repeated the erroneous assumptions, and judgments thereon based, of two centuries ago.

new provinces as parts of a developing empire.[56] After the peace of 1763, large amounts of military bounty lands were granted to soldiers, and colonization of the newly acquired territory was urged by various pamphleteers.[57] Some of these advocated military colonies on the frontier, but pressure soon concentrated on petitions for royal grants of the Indian reservation to land companies.[58] Most of the schemes were for colonies in the Old Northwest—necessarily so, since grants by North Carolina and Virginia had covered much of the Southwest before the late war had more than started. The first of these groups of partners was the Mississippi Company, a score or more Virginians and Marylanders, headed by Lees and Washingtons, who sought a grant between the Mississippi and the Wabash rivers. They wanted nearly four thousand square miles, free of quitrents for twelve years, in return for settling at least two hundred families on the land within that period. Even this first company reserved "shares" for prospective British partners, to secure favorable action by the government. Originally ten, these were later made five double shares, since "Gentlemen of Power, Fortune and Interest" were not to be gained by one share of 50,000 acres.[59] This and other plans were ignored, and their proposed sites were included in the reservation of 1763.[60]

By that time British government circles were awake to the profit potential of American land. The French ambassador reported to his government that "here, M. Bute excepted, all the persons in office are interested in the trade, speculations, privileges, and monopolies of . . . the American, and the East Indian merchants."[61] George Croghan, in London in 1764 on business of his own and of Sir William Johnson,

[56] Franklin, *Writings* (Smyth ed.), III, 212–220, 358–366; G. H. Alden, *New Governments West of the Alleghanies before 1780* (Madison, 1899), pp. 3–15, and Carter, *Illinois Country,* pp. 103–110. In *Gage Correspondence,* II, 53, Carter cites the material in the *Ill. Hist. Coll.,* X, XI, XVI, on plans antedating 1767. One notable pamphlet is reprinted *ibid.,* X, 134–161 (see *ibid.,* XXVII, 301 n.).

[57] In 1754 Governor Dinwiddie had promised 250,000 acres to Virginia troops. For 1763, see Shortt and Doughty, *Papers,* I, 149, 153, 166. Gage, Johnson and Stuart, Croghan, and others received large tracts in New York in 1765 under the Proclamation; Volwiler, *Croghan,* p. 244.

[58] *Gage Correspondence,* I, 149, 25, 26; *Ill. Hist. Coll.,* XI, 198–199.

[59] Carter, *Illinois Country,* pp. 165–171; *Ill. Hist. Coll.,* X, 19, 22–29; XI, 517, 570–572; C. E. Carter (ed.), "Documents Relating to the Mississippi Land Company, 1763–1768," *AHR,* XVI (1911), 311–319.

[60] *Ibid.,* p. 318; Carter, *Illinois Country,* p. 109; L. S. Mays, *Jeffrey Amherst . . . 1717–1797* (New York, 1916), p. 245.

[61] *Ill. Hist. Coll.,* XXVII, 561.

wrote to the latter upon his return that "half of England is Now Land
Mad & Every body has thire eys fixt on this Cuntry"; on going again
into the West, Croghan kept a special journal, descriptive of the land,
for speculators.[62] The result was the next great scheme for a colony in
the Illinois Country. It introduced a new idea in proposing a government colony of 100,000 square miles and asking for itself only 2,000
(free of quitrents) in return for settling at least six persons on each
square mile of its portion.[63] The latter would then thrive parasitically
upon the government colony as its host. The company was organized
by Sir William and Croghan with a few other speculators, Johnson and
Benjamin Franklin being secret partners. The latter worked hard for
the company in London, and presumably converted Lord Shelburne to
the policy of colonizing the West.

By 1765, division of opinion concerning problems of western administration and settlement was pronounced in government circles.[64] In
1766, Lord Shelburne became secretary of state, and spent a year
studying these problems. He started and ended with the professed convictions that the government's prime objectives must be a reduction of
American expenses and an improvement of Indian relations.[65] The
latter obviously required the preservation of the reservation, the rejection of interior colonization, and the continuance of trade.

The costs of the military establishment in the West involved maintenance of the forts (all save Chartres wooden stockades, constantly
disintegrating), transfer of troops, and provisionment posts.[66] The ex-

[62] Ibid., XI, 206; journal for speculators, ibid., pp. 23–38; official journal,
pp. 38–56, or N.Y. Col. Docs., VII, 779–788.

[63] General Gage declined membership. The changes in Johnson's letter suggesting to the government a vast colony deep in the Indian reservation show
great embarrassment, even though his partnership was hidden and despite his
extraordinary assuredness. He finally sent the letter to Franklin for presentation
to the government. Ill. Hist. Coll., X, 318, 342; XI, 203, 221, 248–257; Franklin, Writings (Smyth ed.), V, 47–48, Complete Works (J. Bigelow ed.), IV,
136–149.

[64] Ill. Hist. Coll., XI, 335, 234–242; Gage Correspondence, I, 323 n., 319–
324.

[65] Ibid., II, 48, 49, 66; compare Hillsborough, p. 62.

[66] Pargellis, Military Affairs; Gage Correspondence, I, 90, 184, 210; II, 321,
351, 553; Ill. Hist. Coll., XI, 474, 475, 478, 553. The forces in the Illinois
Country were provisioned from Montreal at monstrous cost and delay. Gage
Correspondence, II, 321 (compare I, 176), 552; I, 179, 239. An American
company offered a bribe to Shelburne's secretary to get a contract for supplies
from Illinois. Ill. Hist. Coll., XI, 474–475, 478. Either Gage was favoring old

penses of the Indian department combined the slight outlays for the administrative staff and the never-ending and very considerable costs of presents.[67] There were three obvious means of lessening these burdens on the British treasury without need of actually reducing them. One was to tax the fur trade, but this was seemingly never seriously considered.[68] A second, ultimately adopted, was to return to the provinces the responsibility for supervising the Indian trade. A third was the sale of western lands, outright or with reserve of quitrents. Outright sales would never have occurred to Englishmen; American speculators were to contribute the notion of land as an object of commerce. Quitrents would be of scant aid unless settlement could be made heavy and continuous, and such settlement would not only vastly increase government expenses but would inevitably bring war and vaster expenses in its wake. Gage gave Shelburne sound advice on quitrents, and he had even higher official warning.[69] Nevertheless, though forced to rely provisionally on requisitions made to the provinces, he became convinced that quitrents "would in a few years not only defray the Expence but form a Fund for other purposes."[70] The decision, therefore, was for a plan inconsistent alike with economy and with the improvement of relations with the Indians. Whether this plan was statesmanlike, notwithstanding its inconsistency with the convictions with which he had started, will be considered later.[71]

The actual problem was not that of retaining or abandoning control

Canadian friends or he was inefficient in this matter. There is also evidence that some provisioning was done locally or from Philadelphia.

[67] Amherst saw no charity in them, considered them mere bribes—*Ill. Hist. Coll.*, XI, 101. Gage often questioned or rejected them, *ibid.*, 390, 221, 98, 258, 511, 316; *Gage Correspondence*, I, 167, 239, 90 n.

[68] Croghan thought it feasible (*Ill. Hist. Coll.*, XI, 63); *Johnson Papers*, IV, 463. It seems highly probable that any tax could have been evaded; compare Coffin, *Province of Quebec*, pp. 313–314; *Ill. Hist. Colls.*, XI, 502. Besides, the trade was essentially one of British subjects. See *N.Y. Col. Docs.*, VII, 376–377 (Johnson, 1759); Franklin, *Writings* (Smyth ed.), V, 438–439; *Ill. Hist. Coll.*, XI, 429 (Richard Jackson); Gage's comments on this, *Gage Correspondence*, I, 216. The opinion of R. Coupland, *The Quebec Act: a Study in Statesmanship* (Oxford, 1925), p. 106, is counter to these authorities.

[69] B. Bond, *The Quit-Rent System in the American Colonies* (New Haven, 1919); *Gage Correspondence*, I, 162.

[70] *Ill. Hist. Coll.*, XI, 457, 540; XVI, 3; *Gage Correspondence*, II, 50; I, 131–132; *N.Y. Col. Docs.*, VII, 880.

[71] Compare W. E. Lecky, *A History of England in the Eighteenth Century* (8 vols., London, 1878–90), IV, 210–215.

of the fur trade; there *was* no control, and the question was whether to confess that. In the Southwest, local trade was perhaps not being drawn through New Orleans. But the yield of the Illinois Country was being increasingly drawn off, with that of the Missouri and upper Mississippi, into the French-Spanish trade through the southern outlet.[72] By 1769 Gage wondered whether holding the Illinois Country was worth while. As early as 1765 he wrote to the secretary of war: "Was it not that Great Britain is a gainer by the Furr Trade, and possibly the cry of the Merchants should Inconvenience arise from abandoning the Forts; there would be no difficulty in deciding at once that the Forts should be abandoned, and the Provinces left to Manage their trade . . . and defend their Frontiers . . . at their own risque and Expence."[73] And the next year he repeated that both these changes should be made, provided Britain would "firmly resist the Sollicitations and Outcrys of the . . . Furr Trade," and disregard the petitions of provincial governors if the Indians should drive stragglers back from Indian territory.[74] On the basis of a policy of imperative economy as transmitted to him by the secretaries of state, Gage's advice was intelligent and sound.

The question of the posts thus became the basic issue with respect to future relations in the West between Britain and the colonies, with respect to their usefulness to the fur trade, and in relation to the budget and the possibility of new colonies.[75]

The first was a relatively simple matter. The posts had no appreciable value for protection of the colonies after ouster of the French. Their value as a bar to French "influence" is frequently referred to, but there is no evidence of influence by traders or otherwise. Gage belittled the idea, and the secretary of war agreed with him.[76] Only aid to the colonies in Indian war was in question, and opinions expressed

---

[72] *Gage Correspondence,* I, 99, 119, 121–122, 177–178, 184, 215–216, 260, 350; II, 262; *Ill. Hist. Coll.,* XI, 117, 242, 243, 462, 497–499, 501–504, 506–508; *Doc. Hist. of N.Y.,* II, 835.

[73] December 18, 1765, *Gage Correspondence,* II, 321; I, 216, as to Illinois.

[74] *Ibid.,* II, 350.

[75] General Gage discussed all these points (as he said, "very fully and with freedom") in letters to Lords Hillsborough and Barrington. *Gage Correspondence,* I, 275–277, 278; II, 318–321, 339, 349, 350, 449, 570, 615, 622–623, 631. Compare Croghan, *Ill. Hist. Coll.,* X, 259–260.

[76] *Gage Correspondence,* I, 350. Canadian historians echo the charges of British traders; see Coupland, *Quebec Act,* p. 16; M. J. Reid in *Canad. Hist. Rev.,* VII, 32. Compare *Ill. Hist. Rev.,* X, 423, 426, 539; XVI, 20.

by Gage and Washington strongly suggest that in such wars forts had been of no value beyond serving as stockades in which civilians, together with militia or regulars, found refuge from Indian attacks.[77] However, Gage was always deferential to superiors; and though he conceded no value to the posts, he advised the government that if Britain, after abandoning supervision of trade, would still feel obliged to join in wars between the Indians and colonials—and such wars would, he thought, inevitably result from provincial management of the Indian trade—then the posts should not be abandoned.[78] The government, without referring to his condition, adopted the conclusion. If Gage was also inconsistent, it was presumably because the posts, by concentrating Indian attacks, undoubtedly facilitated the escape of some scattered settlers.

A belief that the posts could protect the Montreal traders against the French traders in Missouri was seemingly the chief reason why Sir William Johnson and others wanted even more posts.[79] But Gage rejected this belief utterly. It was evident to him that the posts were incapable of cutting off French trade with New Orleans or of weakening French competition in the wilderness around them. He treated as scarcely worthy of contradiction the ideas that the forts protected traders against frauds, gave them safety, or protected the trade.[80]

The choices available with respect to budget and colonies have already been indicated. Quite remarkably, Shelburne finally urged the establishment of colonies in the Illinois Country, the erection of two new forts to save fur trade that was going to New Orleans, and return to the provinces of responsibility for the fur trade.[81] His cynicism in discussing land purchases from the Indians would have satisfied the

[77] J. C. Fitzpatrick (ed.), *The Writings of George Washington* (39 vols., Washington, 1931–44), I, 492, 493, 494. In Pontiac's War the British garrisons could not leave the forts, as one attempt at Detroit proved. *Ill. Hist. Coll.*, X, 307; Pargellis (ed.), *Military Affairs in North America*, pp. 455, 458–459. Gage wrote in 1766 that the situation was then the same, *Gage Correspondence*, II, 351, 62, 64; I, 276.

[78] *Ibid.*, I, 350, 449.

[79] September 11, *ibid.*, I, 76, 77, 80, 209, 244, 348–382, 533–534, 574.

[80] *Ibid.*, I, 113–114 (Southwest), 123, 276, 350; *Ill. Hist. Coll.*, XI, 509, 543. The French had vainly attempted to restrict trade to their posts. L. P. Kellogg, *Minnesota History*, XII, 356.

[81] *Ill. Hist. Coll.*, XI, 376, 431, 536–541, XVI, 12–21; Franklin, *Works* (Bigelow ed.), IV, 142–145.

most acquisitive speculators.[82] In recommending renunciation of trade regulation, he unreservedly condemned the plan of 1764.[83]

Shelburne's suggestions were referred to the Board of Trade.[84] In January, 1768, Lord Hillsborough became the first secretary of state for American affairs, a newly created department, and the Board's report was made to him with exceptional promptitude. Its definite and unequivocal character contrasts sharply with many other papers, and its ideas or authorship have always been attributed to Hillsborough. It disapproved on mercantilistic principles of the far-inland colonies proposed by Shelburne, but conceded that colonies created on the back of the old colonies by gradual extension of population would not conflict with those principles, and would be desirable.[85] It recommended relinquishment of trade control to the provinces, but continued imperial control of border encroachments, land purchases, treaties, boundaries, and presents.

On the subject of posts, the one subject demanding and capable of a clear-cut decision, indecision continued. A few posts were abandoned, chiefly in the Southwest, but most of them only temporarily.[86] Endless correspondence continued; decisions were seemingly made only to prove unstable.

Hillsborough's attempts to state the government's intent reflected its obscurity. He indicated to Gage that "public security" (protection of the colonies?) was no longer to be one of the main objects of the Indian department, yet somewhat weakened this instruction by others on abandonment of posts. As respects the fur trade, the instructions to Gage and others unquestionably made its protection the ultimate basis of the government's policy. This also appears from the instructions of the secretary at war respecting the posts, in which protection "necessary to commerce" and maintenance of the "alliance between His

[82] Ill. Hist. Coll., XVI, 17, 20; advice of Richard Jackson, ibid., XI, 426, 429.

[83] Ibid., XI, 539, XVI, 13, 16.

[84] Ibid., pp. 77–81, with another argument for Shelburne's views.

[85] March 7, 1768, Ill. Hist. Coll., XVI, 183–204, particularly 197–203; or N.Y. Col. Docs., VIII, 19–31. Compare Gage Correspondence, II, 108–110. The obscurities in Hillsborough's circular letter to the provincial governors (April 15, 1768, Ill. Hist. Coll., XVI, 245–247, or N.Y. Col. Docs., VIII, 55) suggest that different writers wrote report and letter.

[86] Johnson, British West Florida, pp. 67, 68, 134; Howard, British Development of West Florida, pp. 39, 123, 124. In the Northwest there was little change.

Majesty & the Indians" were explicitly declared paramount to motives of economy, of army discipline, and of peace as objectives of the new policy.[87]

Beyond this objective of unfettered and facilitated trade, the government's later decisions and orders merely prolonged the irresolution that had filled past years. Nothing was definitive. Hillsborough wrote, seemingly with contentment, of the recommendations of the new plan; "The Completion of the boundary Line, the Passing of severe Laws to prevent Encroachments, the taking effectual Methods to punish the . . . Murders that have been commited, the Abandonment of unnecessary Forts . . . the leaving Direction of the Trade to the several Colonies, and the Intention that if they bring on an Indian War they shall bear the Expence of it . . . make the principal Part."[88]

The new settlement line was soon drawn. Only ignorance permitted belief that anything could come of the other recommendations, which obviously rested on continuing assumptions that effective political and legal jurisdiction existed within the Indian reservation. The letters of Johnson and of Gage and the reports of the Board of Trade all exhibit the total confusion earlier noted in other connections.[89] Richard Jackson had advised the Board not to repeal provincial laws regulating Indian affairs within the provinces and requiring "the authority of law" for their enforcement.[90] So far was this simple principle beyond the Board's comprehension that it was repeated as the Board's reason for discontinuing imperial regulation outside the provinces. And this fatuity was made plainer by a recommendation "that the Colonies should be *required* . . . to provide by proper Laws for the Punishment of all Persons who [should] endanger the publick peace . . . by . . . occupying Lands beyond" the new settlement line.

As nomads the Indians were interested in land solely as hunting

[87] On the assumption that trade was primarily the affair of the colonies, *Ill. Hist. Coll.*, XVI, 514; on the economy motive, *Gage Correspondence*, II, 61. For the last quoted instructions, *Ill. Hist. Coll.*, XVI, 248, 250; *Gage Correspondence*, II, 62. For other instructions—muddled, but giving paramountcy to "the Trade"—see *Ill. Hist. Coll.*, XVI, 219, 247; *Gage Correspondence*, II, 63, 108, 136, 138, 478; I, 175–179, 349.

[88] *Ibid.*, II, 67.

[89] *Johnson Papers*, VI, 147; VIII, 639; *Ill. Hist. Coll.*, XI, 509; *Gage Correspondence*, I, 209.

[90] Jackson's advice, *Ill. Hist. Coll.*, XI, 429. The Board's recommendations, *ibid.*, XVI, 189; compare *Gage Correspondence*, II, 86, 87 (n. 58), Alvord, *Illinois Country*, pp. 292–293, 320.

grounds, which they changed often and for various reasons.[91] Before white interference, great areas were sometimes full of Indian towns, sometimes virtually deserted.[92] Within the historical and inferable past, intertribal war was continual, and territorial displacement of defeated enemies was a common incident. Large numbers sometimes moved to be near a new or favored trading post.[93] But removals were more often the result of official influence or pressure. The French policy of removals "completely changed the Indian geography of the Mississippi Valley." An order of the French government in 1752 forbade continuance of "the practice inaugurated by La Salle and afterwards persistently followed . . . of moving the tribes to places near the French posts," condemning it as "costly and useless."[94]

Evidence is abundant of great migration by the seven tribes which in the period of this volume have most historical importance in the Old Northwest: the Shawnee, Delawares, Miami, Wyandot, Potawatomi, Kickapoo, and Cherokee. Consider, on one hand, the "home" states of these tribes (the states with which they respectively were historically most closely related) and the number of other states with which each had habitat relations sufficiently important to require mention in its tribal history. The historic homes of these seven tribes, respectively, were Tennessee, New Jersey, Indiana, Ohio, Michigan, Wisconsin, and again Tennessee. The states of secondary residence for the same tribes numbered twelve, seven, five, six, five, five, and seven.[95] Again, for the five states of the Old Northwest, we find that the number of tribes having important habitat relations with each (excluding all "home" tribes) is nineteen for Wisconsin, eleven for Michigan and for Ohio, ten for Illinois, and eight for Indiana. It is agreed by ethnologists that Ohio and Kentucky were virtually void of Indians when first discovered by whites, and only the Cherokee, Shawnee, and Chickasaw were later associated with them even in the secondary sense.[96] It was

[91] See the historical account of each tribe indicated in index of J. R. Swanton, *The Indian Tribes of North America* (Washington, 1952).

[92] *Ibid.*, p. 4.

[93] Volwiler, *Croghan*, pp. 36, 46; G. Foreman, *Pioneer Days of the Early Southwest* (Cleveland, 1926), p. 24.

[94] L. P. Kellogg, "The French and the Ohio Valley," *MVHR*, XVIII (1931), 6–7, 12, 13, 14; Alvord, *Illinois Country*, pp. 227, 129, 172.

[95] Swanton, *Indian Tribes*, pp. 225, 227 (Shawnee); 49, 54 (Delawares); 237, 238 (Miami); 233, 235 (Wyandot); 247, 248, 253 (Potawatomi); 253 (Kickapoo); 216, 221 (Cherokee). See also in index, under name of each state, the citations for each tribe.

[96] Kroeber, *Cultural and Natural Areas of Native North America* (Berkeley,

merely a hunting and feuding ground between northern and southern tribes.[97]

It has been authoritatively estimated that the northern side of the Ohio valley, together with Illinois and the lower peninsula of Michigan, perhaps had a total Indian population, somewhat after 1700, of about 20,000.[98] This is almost precisely three Indians (men, women, and children) to thirty-six square miles. The corresponding estimates for the Old Southwest, including almost all of Georgia and the Gulf strip of Florida, are 49,000 and eleven per township.[99]

The preceding facts were conclusive of the relations of the Indians to the land in law. As stated by one of the greatest authorities, "of uncivilized natives, international law takes no account,"[100] but recent decades have witnessed a revulsion against this attitude of "advanced" toward "retarded" races. Changing ethics, however, cannot alter the fact that, in the words of Chief Justice Marshall, both American continents were claimed, occupied, and exploited by the greatest Christian powers of Europe on the principle just stated. On mere sightings of coast or far-separated landings England and France claimed most of North America. In 1713, by the Treaty of Utrecht, all of northern America was divided between France and England without consultation of the Indians or representation of them in the negotiations and treaty. The same was true of the treaties of 1748, 1763, and 1783—notwithstanding that in all three of the wars which they closed, Indians were "allies" on one side or on both. In all other actions, also, the territory was considered, legally, as *res nullius.* This was true of the colonial charters granted by Great Britain, and colonial land was later granted out by the Crown, the colonial governors, and colonial proprietors on the assumption that they held and could dispose of the legal title to the soil. "All our institutions recognize the absolute title of the crown," which was acquired by the United States in 1783.[101] "The ultimate fee, encumbered with the right of Indian occupancy," was in the crown previous to the revolution, and in the states of the union afterward, and

---

1939), p. 184; map in Wissler, *Indians of the United States* (New York, 1940), p. 50.

  [97] *Ibid.,* pp. 229–230.

  [98] Kroeber, *Cultural and Natural Areas,* p. 140.

  [99] *Ibid.,* p. 138, and map on p. 66.

  [100] J. Westlake, *Collected Papers on Public International Law* (London, 1914), p. 138.

  [101] Chief Justice Marshall in Johnson & G's Lessee *v.* McIntosh, 21 U.S. (8 Wheaton) 543; compare 574–584.

subject to grant.[102] British legal writers have followed American decisions.[103]

Misapprehension of these matters was doubtless common in colonial times, and has been perpetuated. Correctly assuming crown title, the idea was once common that by the Proclamation of 1763 the King limited the western boundary of the colonies, instead of prohibiting settlement beyond it. Another misconception arose, after Sir William Johnson's great "purchase," for such settlement in 1768. In 1775 George Mason wrote of "the new fangled doctrine . . . of the Crown's having no Title beyond the Alleghany Mountains 'til after the purchase at Fort Stanwix."[104]

Denial to the Indians of title to land, and their consequent exclusion from international agreements, were not substantive injustices to them; such agreements did not affect their enjoyment of the land. Nor did transfer of the title from Crown to colonist affect it. Title is only a right to hold and enjoy, and there was no civil or military power, imperial or colonial, which could assure occupation and enjoyment unless the Indians consented. That consent was necessarily bought with blood or trading goods. The substantial injustice done to the Indians was the use of rum and fraud in buying the renunciation of hunting usage— that is, buying the assurance of safe settlement by the whites. Such was the Indians' ignorance that the opportunities for defrauding them were illimitable.[105] Scores of pages in Sir William Johnson's reports are filled with examples and denunciations of these practices. Despite this, and despite proper legal advice from the attorney general of New York that title was in the Crown, he took "deeds" from them as did all other land speculators—deeds which would all have been legally worthless even if the Indians had had title and even if there was no fraud in the transaction.

As time passed, ethical attitudes toward the Indians slowly improved, and they received—even within the years dealt with in this volume— increasingly large payments when displaced. Moreover, because claims were only memories of past wanderings, the same area was not infre-

---

[102] Clark *v.* Smith, 38 U.S. (13 Peters) 195.

[103] Westlake, *Chapters on the Principles of International Law,* 134–139, 156–159; A. P. Higgins, in *Cambridge History of the British Empire,* I, 544–545.

[104] S. M. Hamilton (ed.), *Letters to Washington* (5 vols., Boston, 1898–1902), V, 134; see K. M. Rowland, *Life of George Mason, 1725–1792* (2 vols., New York, 1892), I, 398–399.

[105] McIlwain, *Wraxall's Abridgment,* pp. 153, 154, 212.

quently cleared repeatedly of claims by different tribes, particularly in the Old Northwest.[106] Confusion between purchase of title and purchase of safe occupation was inevitable. Even in the Proclamation of 1763 its writer, John Pownall, secretary of the Board of Trade, made the King himself describe the land set aside for exclusive Indian use as "such part of our Dominions and Territories as, not having been ceded to or purchased by us [from the Indians] are hereby [by royal act and power!] reserved to them . . . as their Hunting Grounds." As Lord Shelburne said, "the land [was] and [had] always been acknowledged to be the King's."[107] And "the right of nations to countries discovered in the sixteenth century is to be determined by the law of nations as understood at that time, and not by . . . the opinion of three centuries later."[108] However, England did not renounce after 1600 the practice of claiming sovereignty over lands whose shores were first sighted or locally explored by her sea captains. James Cook, in the years immediately preceding and during the American Revolution, was thus extending the British empire in the Pacific.

The policy of a new settlement line did not originate in England. Sir William Johnson originated the policy, selected the line, began the negotiation of it without orders, and ultimately altered it to suit himself in disregard of orders, his ends being in part pecuniary. His attention had been fixed on this area for many years. Its establishment involved removal from the Indian reservation of a great area south of the Ohio. Since the Six Nations asserted conquest title to it, he could use his control of them to secure it—even in disregard of claims to it made by their "dependents" (and his), the Delawares and Shawnee, just north of it above the Ohio. By three Indian treaties Virginia had acquired settlement rights within a vaguely indefinite territory south of the Ohio. Two of these treaties, of 1744 and 1751, were with the Six

[106] In Indiana, for example, all claims were not extinguished until 1872 after fifty-four treaties, of which less than half proved to be free of overlapping claims. C. C. Royce in Bureau of American Ethnology, *Annual Report,* I (1881), 257–262, with maps. For similar reasons, all the land within Illinois was "bought" twice, and some portions three times, by eighteen treaties in which there were thirty overlappings, varying from one in eight treaties to eight in one treaty. *Ibid.,* pp. 254–256.

[107] Shortt and Doughty, *Papers Relating to the Constitutional History of Canada, 1759–1791* (1 vol. in 2, paged continuously, 2nd ed., Toronto, 1918), p. 16; E. G. Fitzmaurice, *Life of William, Earl of Shelburne* (2nd ed., 2 vols., London, 1912), II, 194.

[108] J. B. Moore, *Digest of International Law* (8 vols., Washington, 1906), I, 259.

Nations, and a third, of 1752, was with the Delawares, Shawnee, and Seneca.[109] What the Six Nations had once done they could, Johnson reasoned, do again; and if the Cherokee had not objected in 1752, perhaps they would not make trouble later, nor would Virginia if her interests were satisfactorily protected.

It was necessary only to prepare the way with the government in London for further proceeding. In 1764 Croghan presented in London claims by himself and other traders for losses suffered during Pontiac's War. When he failed to secure either pecuniary satisfaction for them or confirmation of his claim to a great tract of land allegedly purchased by him from the Indians in 1749, he and Johnson proceeded with another plan. The line limiting white settlement in the Proclamation of 1763 was loosely described even at its starting point in New York; whether or not it was intended to be relatively permanent, Johnson never conceded to it the slightest trace of that quality. Just eight months after the King had assured the Indians of their great reservation, Croghan—admitting past encroachments "contrary to repeated promises" to them—blandly assured the Board of Trade that the Indians would live in friendship with the whites "if they saw a Tract"— that is, a new one—"secured to them under the . . . Protection of His Majesty . . . and a Trade . . . to supply them with . . . Necessaries."[110] One line had even earlier been suggested to Johnson, and he suggested another a little later.[111] The Board informed him of its rec-

---

[109] Volwiler, *Croghan,* pp. 68, 74–76, 257, 266. They were typical in the facts that clear descriptions were impossible (and possibly undesired), with consequent disputable results. *Colonial Records of Pa.,* IV, 698–773 (Lancaster); *Va. Magazine of History and Biography,* XIII, 139–142 (Lancaster), 143–174 (Logstown); K. L. Bailey, *The Ohio Company of Virginia and the Westward Movement, 1748–1792* (Glendale, Calif., 1939), pp. 125–139.

[110] *Ill. Hist. Coll.,* X, 257, 258, 260 (or *N.Y. Col. Docs.,* VII, 605). Croghan had already found Lord Halifax and others receptive to his ideas. Two years later, after deciding to create three great colonies in the Illinois Country, Shelburne repeated this hypocrisy, writing to Johnson (*Ill. Hist. Coll.,* XI, 450): "As soon as they find that their Boundaries are not encroached upon; that they are not cheated in their Dealings, that Frauds when commit'd are punish'd, that strict Justice is done to them upon all Occasions, and that we really mean to cherish and protect them . . . we shall become . . . the only Refuge they will think of seeking in their Distress." With all these blessings, what distress could there be?

[111] Croghan's suggested line was "from the heads of the Delaware [at Hancock, New York] to the mouth of the Ohio." Johnson's are in *N.Y. Col. Docs.,* VII, 573; *Ill. Hist. Coll.,* X, 328.

ommendation to the King that he declare his "final determination" not
to permit land grants or settlements under any pretext within a territory set aside for the Indians. Sir William, to make certain that he and
the Board understood each other, replied that he approved of a boundary, but only "until the whole Six Nations should think proper of selling part" of the land already reserved—and that he was ready to settle
immediately with them a boundary to their satisfaction.[112] It promptly
appeared that this made understanding perfect.

The plan of 1764 promised a new boundary, and thereafter Sir
William repeatedly urged its establishment. One result in the spring of
1765 was Croghan's journal of a western tour, written for prospective
speculators, and the formation of the Illinois Company for the profit
of Johnson, Croghan, and others, including Franklin.

Another result was virtually simultaneous. The plan for the management of Indian affairs was one for times of peace. It gave to the superintendents of Indian affairs the power to make treaties—that is, of
course, for trade and for opening land to settlement. Nevertheless,
Johnson claimed authority to make the peace ending Pontiac's War.
The waging of imperial war was not an affair incidental to trade,
presents, and land cessions. Moreover, the supremacy of the commander in chief was declared as basic in the whole plan. Gage should
have asserted his supremacy by dictating peace in the field. But he was
pliant, and permitted Sir William to make the treaty of peace at his
home in New York in May, 1765, Gage merely drafting a few provisions for inclusion. In addition, Johnson exacted other promises from
the Indians. One of these was that whenever the King should direct
settlement of a boundary "with the Indians with their consent" (thus
discrediting the boundary proclaimed by the King in 1763), the western Indians (Delawares and Shawnee) would "abide by whatever limits [should] be agreed upon between the English and the Six Nations."
And such a boundary of white settlement was then and there discussed
with the Six Nations by Sir William, and agreed upon by them, subject
only to the King's approval. This line ran down the Ohio River to the
mouth of the Tennessee.[113] Thus, without waiting for the King to
"direct" negotiation of a settlement line, Sir William did it all in ad-

[112] *N.Y. Col. Docs.*, VII, 535, 581.
[113] *Ibid.*, VII, 738–741; report to Board of Trade, 711–718; *Ill. Hist. Coll.*,
X, 323, 333, 350, 500, 511; XI, 361.

vance. And we shall now see how he then suggested to the government negotiation of a line; urged it until ordered, though already negotiated; and finally had it approved in 1768, with last-minute alterations which, incidentally, were to his own great profit.

Another promise exacted by Johnson was that land should be given by the Indians in reparation for the pillage of traders during Pontiac's War.[114] Croghan reported from the West that same year that the Indians were "not only very willing, but anxious," to make reparation. With both him and Johnson they agreed to make it by ceding "their Country" south of the Ohio, which was no longer needed for hunting.[115] Well might Johnson rejoice over the Tennessee River terminus down the Ohio, and well might all speculators rejoice over an agreement to make reparation with land, which was exhaustless, for frontier pillaging that was never ending. But Croghan and Sir William and their associates had special reason, for the claims of the Suffering Traders of 1763 had long been in process of acquisition by a group known as the Indiana Company, composed of much the same associates of Johnson as had formed in 1766 the company to seek a colony grant in Illinois. Franklin was later repeatedly urged to give precedence in London to the Traders' claims as "of infinitely more consequence"; but though he defended these to the end, it is highly probable that his own preference was strong for a policy of colonization.[116] He made great progress with the colony and no progress with the claims.

Johnson now had the word of the Board of Trade that there should be a new settlement line. He was empowered to make all Indian treaties. He had long had an agreement with the Delawares and Shawnee for a land cession to quiet the Suffering Traders of 1763, and a tentative agreement respecting a settlement line down the Ohio to the Tennessee. As time passed, the Indians, expectant of lavish presents, became impatient for the treaty. It was, of course, Johnson himself who stimulated their desires. He was the only person by whom (in his own words respecting traders' frauds and border intrusions) "they [could]

[114] N.Y. Col. Docs., VII, 738–741, sec. 8; Johnson Papers, VI, 627; Documentary Hist. of N.Y., II, 881; Gage Correspondence, I, 59.

[115] Ill. Hist. Coll., X, 374; XI, 62, 152.

[116] Volwiler, Croghan, pp. 265–266; Ill. Hist. Coll., XI, 367, 465–466, 468, 473, 519. On efforts to secure aid from the government, ibid., pp. 62, 152, 207, 365, 378, 465, 468, 506. On the Indiana Company, M. Savelle, George Morgan, Colony Builder (New York, 1932), Chap. 5, and W. V. Byars, Bernard and Michael Gratz (Jefferson City, 1916).

have been repeatedly assured that persons shod be appointed Vested with powers" to end those wrongs.[117]

Trouble might come from the Ohio tribes north of that line or from the Cherokee. He decided that it was more likely to come from the former, but that they could be controlled by the Six Nations, to whom that task would be committed by having the Six (as long since planned) make the cession.[118] Meanwhile, in order to insure Virginia's co-opera-tion and quiet the Cherokee by restraining frontier inhabitants, treaties with the southern Indians were essential. With some prodding from the home government, Stuart undertook to locate settlement lines north of West Florida and up back of the seaboard colonies to meet John-son's line. He brought his line up to the headwaters of the Kanawha (near Wytheville) in southwestern Virginia, and down that river to its mouth.[119]

It is clear that the Board of Trade had been completely ignorant of Johnson's past acts, and was equally blind to his immediate purpose. In considering Stuart's southern line to and down the Kanawha, the Board learned and complained of Sir William's earlier and unauthor-ized negotiations and treaty with the Ohio tribes.[120] For approval of the Kanawha "terminus" south of the Ohio it found good reason in the fact that, although the Six Nations might "have pretensions" to lands south of the Ohio, it was more used by the southern tribes.[121] It

[117] *Gage Correspondence,* I, 157 (adding that the new line had been "so much wished for by others, that large tracts of rich land may be added to several of the Provinces") ; *Documentary Hist. of N.Y.,* II, 881; *Ill. Hist. Coll.,* VI, 57, 119; W. L. Stone, *Life and Times of Sir William Johnson* (2 vols., Albany, 1865), II, 303, 309.

[118] He was superintendent of the Six Nations "and of their dependents," the Shawnee and Delawares, placed in Ohio by the Five Nations, "as sort of Frontier dependents," after conquest by the Five Nations of various tribes in that region. *Johnson Papers,* VII, 640. The Six Nations were to make the cession under claim of a prehistoric conquest of the territory by the Five Nations. The claims to be quieted were those of the Cherokee, who denied such a conquest and hunted much in Kentucky, and the Delawares and Shaw-nee, of whom Kentucky was likewise the favorite hunting ground. Preliminary councils were held to placate the Cherokee. *N.Y. Col. Docs.,* VIII, 38–53; *Gage Correspondence,* I, 170.

[119] *Johnson Papers,* V, 333, 513, 536, 537, 652, 691; VII, 119. See also John R. Alden, *John Stuart and the Southern Colonial Frontier* (Ann Arbor, Mich., 1944).

[120] *Ill. Hist. Coll.,* XVI, 20, 151, 155, XI, 426, 423, 539; *Johnson Papers,* VI, 200; *Gage Correspondence,* I, 209, 214, 232, II, 85; *Documentary Hist. of N.Y.,* II, 881.

[121] *Ill. Hist. Coll.,* XVI, 189.

had no suspicion that Sir William was about to use the Six Nations, as owners, to renounce all Indian hunting rights far west of the Kanawha —leaving to Virginia the problem of more definite agreement with the Cherokee.

Shelburne was cynical in Cabinet argument. The objection, he said, that settlements at different places "might give offence to the Indians . . . [might] at any time in Case of a new Settlement be got over by . . . purchasing the Lands under the Pretext of supplying them better with such Necessaries as they may want. . . . [They] have never been averse to sell . . . when they have not suspected an Intention to defraud them."[122] In December, 1767, the government authorized final settlement of a line with a terminus at the Kanawha's mouth. There is nothing to justify an assumption that the line was to be permanent. After preliminary councils with the western tribes Johnson concluded at Fort Stanwix the cession treaty with the Six Nations. As the Delawares and Shawnee disappointed Sir William, and received no part of the presents (worth £10,500), their resentment was left to rankle until other causes combined with it in causing another war.[123]

That the line, in conception and execution, was wholly Johnson's is obvious, but several remarkable things about the treaty which adopted it call for special comment.[124] Johnson was reprimanded for disobedience in taking a cession down to the Tennessee's mouth, and the King was averse to accepting from the Six Nations the area west of the Kanawha. In the end, however, all was accepted.[125] Without orders, the boundary was also extended eastward in New York to a point between Rome and Oneida. This was well beyond any line suggested as

[122] *Ibid.*, XI, 450.

[123] Western councils, *N.Y. Colonial Docs.*, VIII, 38–53; *Gage Correspondence*, I, 170, 193; W. L. Stone, *Life and Times of Sir William Johnson* (2 vols., New York, 1865), II, 303–309. Fort Stanwix treaty, *N.Y. Col. Docs.*, VIII, 112–134 (proceedings), 135–137 (map, deed); 110, 145, 151–152, 159, 163, 165–166; *Johnson Papers*, VI, 331–334, 536, 652, VII, 49, 55–56; *Gage Correspondence*, I, 193; *Documentary History of N.Y.*, II, 938–939; R. A. Billington, "The Ft. Stanwix Treaty of 1768," *New York History*, xxv, 182–194.

[124] Alvord regarded the line of 1768 as merely carrying out Shelburne's policy of 1763. *Illinois Country*, p. 292. Shelburne did not know until 1767 that any line had been settled between Johnson and the Indians in 1765. *N.Y. Col. Docs.*, VIII, 86; Franklin, *Writings* (Smyth ed.), V, 67, 68.

[125] Criticisms of Johnson by the Board, *N.Y. Col. Docs.*, VII, 611; *Ill. Hist. Coll.*, X, 222, 325, 131–136 (map), 332, 395, XI, 224. Hillsborough thought the price too high. *N.Y. Col. Docs.*, VIII, 102; T. Bodley, *Our First Great West* (Louisville, 1938), p. 39, estimated it at $0.01 per fifty acres.

having been fixed by the Proclamation. The total result was to open land for settlement in Pennsylvania, central New York, Kentucky, West Virginia, Tennessee, and even northern Alabama.[126] There was, of course, no possibility of actual early settlement in most of this enormous area. Almost all of it was taken out of the Indian reservation. Much of it was of direct interest to speculators and in New York immediately enriched Johnson and his coterie.[127]

Within the region thus cleared of Indian use there were two tracts which Johnson and Croghan wished the Crown to recognize as having been earlier disposed of by the Indians. One tract was purportedly conveyed by the Indians to the Indiana Company. The other purportedly conveyed land from them to Croghan to compensate him for land which the Indians had vainly attempted to convey to him in 1749, because it lay within Pennsylvania.[128] The character of these instruments, the facts regarding them, and their relations to each other and to the Stanwix grant to the King have been greatly misunderstood. The King hesitated to accept the grant to him because of what Hillsborough called "improper conditions" imposed upon it, that is, by the claims for recognition of the traders' and Croghan's deeds.[129] His words were not technical. There were words of request and expectation, of slight moral suasion, at most, but none of condition.[130] Ignoring all the instruments as worthless in law, some regard was presumably due to the Indiana Company claimants as a matter of ethics if their claims had been vastly reduced—the speculators involved were of Gargantuan breed.

Such difficulties as were to arise in the north from the Fort Stanwix cession lay in the future. Those in the south accompanied and imme-

---

[126] R. L. Higgins, *Expansion in New York* (Columbus, 1931), p. 93. Volwiler (*Croghan,* p. 268) estimated the area as 2,500,000 acres; Bodley (p. 35) as more than 5,000,000.

[127] A group identical in large part with the Indiana Company, Abernethy, *Western Lands,* pp. 33–34; *Ill. Hist. Coll.,* X, 17, 21. By 1770, Johnson and Croghan each owned some 200,000 acres in central New York, though Croghan later lost his. Higgins, *Expansion in New York,* pp. 92, 13, 94, 95, 96, 140; Volwiler, *Croghan,* pp. 24–25; *Ill. Hist. Coll.,* XI, 224, 353; *Gage Correspondence,* I, 216–217.

[128] *Ill. Hist. Coll.,* XVI, 513; *Johnson Papers,* VII, 65.

[129] The words of request and expectation were in the proceedings only, *N.Y. Col. Docs.,* VIII, 127–128, 130–131; in the deed to the Crown there was merely a reference to the equity raised in favor of the Indiana Company by its payment for the land.

[130] Bodley (pp. 39, 45) states a contrary view, but other statements on p. 39 exclude the possibility of any legal condition, express or implied.

diately followed it. As Virginia believed her bounds to include the
whole Northwest, imperial plans for new colonies therein, or imperial
restriction of interior settlement, necessarily commanded the attention
of both her speculators and statesmen. She acquiesced in Johnson's
acts because she could not prevent them, and also because, as a leading
authority on her history has said, "The great majority of Virginians,
including most of the leaders . . . were indifferent in the matter of
Western lands. . . . [The matter was] a question of what a few powerful speculators wanted, and . . . an immediate opening of lands for
exploitation was their object." [131] For this reason Virginia sent to Fort
Stanwix the heads of her two great groups of speculators, Dr. Thomas
Walker and Andrew Lewis, representing the Loyal and Greenbrier
Companies respectively, and the former signed the treaty.[132] But she
was resolved to remove for her citizens the Cherokee claims that Johnson had ignored. This was done by two treaties and a happily inaccurate survey. By a Treaty of Hard Labor, negotiated by Lewis, the
settlement line was run directly overland from Criswell's Mine to the
Kanawha's mouth, thus gaining a considerable area.[133] John Stuart then
suggested another line, which Walker and Lewis secured by the Treaty
of Lochaber.[134] This moved the starting point considerably westward
from the mine along Virginia's southern boundary, and ran thence
directly to the Kanawha's mouth, adding twice as much land as had
been gained at Hard Labor.[135] The King approved this treaty, but
Johnson was told that it was not the King's "intention" that settlement
should be made westward of that line.[136] Notwithstanding that intention, however, when the Lochaber line was surveyed for Virginia, the
surveyor and the Indians adopted as part of the line to the Ohio a
river, one of three called the Louisa, that did not (as did one of the
other two) merge with the Kanawha and carry the line to the latter's
mouth. It was in fact the Kentucky, and so (for a promise of £500 that

[131] Abernethy, *Western Lands.*
[132] On Virginia's reasons for having Walker sign, see Bodley, p. 44; Abernethy, *Western Lands,* p. 38.
[133] The treaty is in *No. Carolina Col. Rec.,* VII, 815–855; also in *Va. Mag.
of Hist. and Biog.,* XIII, 20–36.
[134] Abernethy, *Western Lands,* pp. 67–72; *Gage Correspondence,* I, 222.
[135] The Treaty is in *Va. Mag. of Hist. and Biog.,* IX, 360–364. Henderson
estimated that it cleared for sale some 800,000 acres of the area in which the
Loyal Company wished to locate its grant. *MVHR,* XVII (1930), 199.
[136] *Ill. Hist. Coll.,* XVI, 540.

was never paid) a third and very great area was renounced by the Cherokee.[137]

Johnson had promised the government that a new settlement line would bring a blessed end to all colonial troubles. He assured the Board of Trade that it "would encourage the thick settlement of the Frontiers, oblige the Proprietors of large tracts to get them Inhabited, and secure the Indians from being further deceived." [138] The complete dominance of speculators in the conception and realization of the line is manifest. Necessarily, too, the line shifted their interest to the country south of the Ohio. Much of the great area which it removed from the Indian reservation remained scantily settled for many years, and part of it, in Tennessee, was even temporarily turned back to the Indians twenty-eight years later. The new line, by removing resistance to migration further westward, may possibly have stimulated migration somewhat, though the line was far less significant to emigrants than to the Virginia speculators who participated in Johnson's treaty and bought up, in addition, the Cherokee claims. In time the new line would itself be passed, as General Gage warned the government.[139]

[137] Much disagreement exists with respect to facts or motives. Abernethy, *Western Lands*, p. 75; Alvord, *Mississippi Valley*, II, 83–89; *MVHR*, III, 25; J. R. Alden, *John Stuart and the Southern Colonial Frontier* (Ann Arbor, 1944), p. 344 *et seq.*; R. G. Thwaites and Kellogg (eds.), *Documentary History of Dunmore's War* (Madison, 1905), pp. 5, 20, 26.

[138] *N.Y. Col. Docs.*, VII, 578.

[139] *Gage Correspondence*, I, 157.

CHAPTER 2

British Rule: Confusion and Collapse, 1768-74

THE new settlement line did not allay the anxieties of the Indians, and five years of steady deterioration in Indian-white relations ended in war. The British government manifested responsibility for a conscionable land policy. Parliament, concerned with colonial problems, reaffirmed the policy of an Indian reservation north of the Ohio. Speculators, however, continued to ignore legal prohibitions, and a falsified opinion of the Crown's highest legal officers was used to justify great land "purchases" from the Indians in the Northwest and Southwest. Virginia's last royal governor (John Murray, Earl of Dunmore, father of the King's son-in-law) ignored and suppressed royal orders, both general and personal; recommended approval by the home government of the illegal land purchases, of which he was a secret beneficiary; made grants and permitted surveys specifically prohibited; brought Virginia and Pennsylvania to the verge of war; and precipitated an Indian war. When the provincial governments in the South added to this disregard of imperial orders their own outright repudiation of them, the collapse of British control was complete.

The Shawnee, who had lost their Kentucky hunting ground without recompense, bitterly resented the cession of Fort Stanwix. In 1772 Johnson found it necessary to advise the Six Nations to withdraw the Seneca from south of the Ohio—though theirs was one of the Six Nations that had made the cession. The Cherokee, victims of Sir William and the Six Nations in the cession, were now at odds with the Wabash tribes and wanted an alliance with the Six Nations. Because the Shawnee continued their discontent, Sir William incited the Six

Nations to make war on them, and for political reasons the Cherokee joined in the threat. Four considerable Indian councils were held in 1770–73, but all attempts to secure attendance by tribes west of the Wabash failed.[1]

"As far as I can understand these Affairs," Gage wrote to Lord Hillsborough, "the Cession . . . is the Cause of all the Commotions that have lately happened among the Indians." And the Secretary replied: "I can only lament that a Measure of the Utility of which such great expectation was held out, and which has been adopted at so great an Expense, should have so entirely failed in its Object, as to have produced the very Evils to which it was proposed as a Remedy."[2] Hillsborough justifiably complained that the cession had been "so managed" by Johnson, but what followed added to the danger of his misjudgments. After a great purchase, prudence would have counseled slow settlement, but the cession of 1768 was followed at once by plans for immediate settlement on a great scale, and Johnson, as always, was at the center of the new plans. Hillsborough originally hoped for their success, but ultimately opposed them.[3]

Early in 1769, Samuel Wharton went to London to seek recognition for the claims of the Suffering Traders of 1763. He proved to be a lobbyist of extraordinary ability. A company headed by a London banker, Thomas Walpole, and with the members of the Indiana Company as its nucleus, was formed to buy a tract of 4,000 square miles within the Fort Stanwix purchase. For this tiny portion the Crown was to be repaid the entire cost of that purchase, and the company assumed no responsibility for colonization. However, on Lord Hillsborough's suggestion, it substituted a petition for what is now West Virginia and much of Kentucky (about eight times the amount first applied for) with no increase in price.[4] The new plan was for a proprietary colony, and the company had become the Grand Ohio Company, with various English partners. Eventually these became more than half the members, and by January, 1770, the despoiled traders of 1754 and the members

[1] *Johnson Papers*, VIII, 6–11, 219, 251, 277, 348, 406, 688, 689; *Gage Correspondence*, I, 227, 235, 236, 245–246; *N.Y. Col. Docs.*, VIII, 183, 203, 211, 222, 233, 236, 280, 314, 348, 364.
[2] *Gage Correspondence*, II, 98, 104.
[3] *Ill. Hist. Coll.*, XI, 212, 220.
[4] The losses claimed amounted to £25,916, *Pa. Mag. Hist. and Biog.*, XXXIV, 30. The ministry overruled Lord Hillsborough, *Johnson Papers*, VII, 16–17.

of the old Ohio Company were partners.[5] The enlarged purchase had been approved, but the petition of the enlarged company, when finally made, was rejected (April, 1772) by Lord Hillsborough, speaking for the Board of Trade.[6] His arguments were mercantilistic, and at least superficially inconsistent with his position in 1768, for the colony now proposed was relatively near Virginia.

This report evoked a reply that did not challenge mercantilism but held its principles to be inapplicable to the proposed colony.[7] In positive support of the Company's petition, it offered several arguments of slight weight, but one which would have been of great merit if true. It was, the writer averred, "obvious and certain truth," which he would "from undoubted testimony prove," that there were "not less than five thousand families, of at least six persons to a family," located "southward of, and adjoining to, the southern line of Pennsylvania . . . independent of some thousand families . . . over the mountains, within . . . Pennsylvania."[8] Whoever argued for the Company's petition presumably presented this pamphlet, which contains no evidence in support of assertions which were vast exaggerations.[9] Nevertheless, the Privy Council ruled against Hillsborough, expressing the opinions "That the lands in question . . . were then in an actual state of settling," and that the proposed colony would not lie "beyond all advantageous intercourse with . . . Great Britain." The Council's prime decision therefore rested on the misrepresentations of actual settlements.

Hillsborough resigned, and was succeeded by Lord Dartmouth. The plans for the grant and colony were approved by the Board of Trade and by the King in Council in August, 1772. Orders were given to

[5] C. W. Alvord, *The Mississippi Valley in British Politics* (2 vols., Cleveland, 1917), II, 119–149; *MVHR*, XVII, 22; K. L. Bailey, *The Ohio Company of Virginia and the Westward Movement, 1748–1792* (Glendale, Calif., 1939), pp. 233–249.

[6] The report, of April 15, 1768, is in Franklin, *Writings* (Smyth ed.), IV, 467–478.

[7] *Ibid.,* IV, 490, 491, 509.

[8] *Ibid.,* pp. 527, 522, 519–520.

[9] The paper was long ascribed to Franklin, but probably was by Wharton. The strongest evidence against Franklin's authorship is not the style but the substance of the paper. It is incredible that Franklin could have believed dependable the population data stated; not believing them, it is incredible that he would have cited them with approval to the government. Moreover, the argument that the Fort Stanwix deeds to Crown and Indiana Company were valid rested on the assumption of original land title in the Indians (*ibid.,* pp. 468, 479, 480, 481, 484, 487, 489, 520, 527, 529). Franklin could never have written thus for argument before Crown lawyers.

inform the Indians that the land ceded at Fort Stanwix was to be settled. Plans for a charter and government were in preparation. The grant to the proprietors was ordered (October, 1773).[10] Nothing more was done, however, and the reasons are unknown. Worsening relations between the colonies and mother country may be the explanation.

The inadequacy of revenue from crown lands, and the subterfuges by which the collection of quitrents was impeded, had long been matters of concern. A policy was initiated of remedying this situation by drastic control of land grants and the checking of disorderly settlement. Incidentally, this included an attempt to enforce the long-standing prohibition of private "purchases" of Indian lands. From 1770 to 1773 a series of orders to provincial governors forbade grants west of the Proclamation line, the issue of patents for or survey of land earlier granted, or licenses to individuals to purchase Indian lands. All these Dunmore (and others) ignored.[11]

These orders were followed by a new plan (of February 3, 1774) for the sale of unseated lands beyond the Proclamation line. It required survey into small tracts before sales; sale by auction after long advertisement, at prices based on quality, with a fixed minimum price of sixpence per acre; and a minimum annual quitrent.[12] The last requirement was unpalatable to everybody and the rest were anathema to speculators. The first struck down the long-established practice by which a great part of the back country of Virginia had been given away to political leaders and speculators of that province. Since Dartmouth (secretary for the colonies) left evidence of his understanding that the new system would conflict with the plans of the British authorities in West Florida, he presumably foresaw strong opposition in older colonies.[13]

All these orders were given, Lord Dartmouth stated, to protect the interests of the Walpole Company.[14] Dunmore suppressed the land plan

---

[10] *Gage Correspondence*, II, 148, 337; *Johnson Papers*, VIII, 639, 755, 889; *N.Y. Col. Docs.*, VIII, 31. After Donelson's survey of the Lochaber line, the government added to Vandalia (but not to the Walpole grant) the area west of the Kentucky River; it had earlier added the southwest corner of Virginia.

[11] Mass. Hist. Soc., *Coll.*, 4th Series, X, 655 (Sec. 60 of Dartmouth's instructions of February 7, 1771); *N.Y. Col. Docs.*, VIII, 257 (Order in Council of April 7, 1773); Abernethy, *Western Lands*, pp. 35, 72, 73, 84.

[12] *N.Y. Col. Docs.*, VIII, 410–413 (409); *American Archives*, II, 174.

[13] C. E. Carter, "British Administration in West Florida," *MVHR*, I, 374.

[14] Instructions of February 7, 1773, to Lord Dunmore, Mass. Hist. Soc., *Collections*, 4th Series, X (1930), 655, 723, 728.

for a year, during which he pursued purely personal ends in the West in contemptuous disregard of the royal policy, until at its end, when he belatedly attempted to enforce it, the provincial government likewise flouted it and toppled the King's "cousin" and royal administration in the first tremors of revolution.

Meanwhile, the home government proceeded in the formulation of its new plans. The first steps having been tentatively taken for a colony south of the Fort Stanwix line, a second step was taken, four months later, in a reorganization of the Northwest. By the Quebec Act (June 24, 1774, to become effective one year later) the country northwest of the Ohio River was added to the province of Quebec.[15] The purpose of the Act was to deal with difficulties that had arisen in the legal system and church establishment of that province, which was to become Lower Canada (French Canada) in 1791. There must have been some special reason for adding to the French area, with its peculiar problems, all the northwestern wilderness, notwithstanding the fact that the adoption of the Stanwix settlement line in 1768 indicated that no settlement or regular government of that wilderness was presently contemplated. There were no local interests to consider save the fur trade and the French villages in Illinois. However important or unimportant the former, the fact that the government showed it special favor needs no attention, for the government's decision was seemingly necessitated by other conditions. In 1763 there had been a reason, deemed by the government decisive, for not attaching the area to any one of the southern colonies; that reason had weakened, but in an altered and more important form it persisted. On the other hand, the government's possible reason in 1763 for not attaching the region to Quebec had long since disappeared, and both the fur traders and those who hoped to lessen abuses in the trade desired the annexation. As for the French villages, originally settled from Canada, clearly they were properly added to Quebec, notwithstanding that Virginia and Pennsylvania were nearer.[16]

Continued participation in the fur trade by the southern colonies was

[15] 14 Geo. III, c. 83 (Imp.); Shortt and Doughty, pp. 594–614; *Amer. Archives*, I, 140–216 (debates in Parliament), 217–219 (the act); Henry Steele Commager, *Documents of American History* (5th ed., New York, 1949), p. 74; V. Coffin, *The Province of Quebec and the Early American Revolution* (Madison, 1896), and R. Coupland, *The Quebec Act: a Study in Statesmanship* (Oxford, 1925).

[16] The annexation admittedly favored Quebec over other colonies in the fur trade—as in 1763, 1768, and 1782. But to have added the area in 1774 to any

assumed, and Parliament altered the regulations of Quebec's border customs in order not to handicap New York.[17] On the other hand, the Quebec Act, unlike the Proclamation of 1763, did affect the boundary claims of such colonies as Pennsylvania, Virginia, and New York.[18] There was almost no reference to this effect of the Act in the Parliamentary debate.

However, there is a view that it was the Act's intent to "enclose" the southern colonies within a barrier of French law and Roman Catholicism. There is some evidence that government policy at the time was explicitly *contrary* to this, and time has proved it to be a demographic absurdity.[19] The idea derives from the extravagant propaganda directed against the Act by Congress at the outset of the Revolution.[20] It has been conclusively demonstrated that all the main provisions were drafted without anything in the record to connect it with the "coercive acts" against Massachusetts that were concurrently in preparation.[21] There is no evidence that it was motivated by hostility to the southern colonies. The once-common view that only the Revolution saved the West from becoming a French-Catholic preserve ignored many other facts, among them the history of Upper Canada. Nor is there evidence that the Act had significant influence in causing the Revolution.

Lord Dunmore's disregard of government orders was a favor to

---

one of the southern colonies would have provoked far more dangerous political jealousies.

[17] New York's "Remonstrance" is in T. C. Hansard, *Parliamentary History of England* . . . , XVIII, 650–655. It dealt with a provision in the Quebec Revenue Act of 1774. See Shortt and Doughty, pp. 576–580; the Act just cited was promptly amended, *ibid.*, p. 580.

[18] Coffin, *Province of Quebec,* pp. 420–422, and Coupland, *Quebec Act,* pp. 60–61, 117, point out that British soldiers and ministers reflected upon the possible future usefulness of Canada in case of future serious trouble with the southern colonies. No further evidence is cited to sustain a suggestion that this was the reason for attaching the Northwest to Quebec. M. J. Reed, *CHR,* VI, 31.

[19] Shortt and Doughty, pp. 551, 554, 605. Nearly 2,000,000 Americans (including some Catholics) were doubling every twenty-five years; possibly 80,-000 French Canadians were very slowly increasing. The fact is that there was no more French law after 1774 than there had been before.

[20] In the Declaration of Independence, "abolishing [in French Canada] the free system of English laws . . . establishing therein an arbitrary [English] government, and enlarging its boundaries so as to render it a fit instrument for introducing the same absolute rule in these colonies."

[21] Coffin, *Province of Quebec,* pp. 393–396, 399–403, 419, 423, 431, 472, 530–532.

speculators. Military bounty claims had merit and official preference, and they were gilt-edged investments. In large degree they had been bought by speculators, to a notable extent by Washington.[22] He had ignored the offer to enter the Walpole Company, but had located claims within Vandalia. Other important claims were under Virginia's old grants to the Loyal and Greenbrier Companies. In October, 1773, the Virginia assembly declared these valid, and later that year they and the claims of actual squatters were given priority over bounty claims.[23] These companies looked to the Hard Labor and Lochaber lands.

Dunmore possibly acted primarily in his own interest. Before his trip to the West in 1773, he had petitioned the King for a grant of 100,000 acres "in the back part of Virginia." That summer, after the activities of surveyors along both sides of the Ohio had so disturbed the Indians that forebodings of war filled the West, he went to Pittsburgh and began acts of irresponsibility which continued for months. These acts, after interruption by return to Williamsburg, were continued in 1774. He made various grants and permitted various surveys, and thousands of acres covered by these are believed to have been taken for him, as well as for George Croghan or associates.[24]

Trouble between settlers in an area in dispute between Virginia and Pennsylvania (later recognized as the latter's) was one reason for Dunmore's trip to Fort Pitt in 1773. This area was the Monongahela region. If not in Pennsylvania, it was (1) in or very near to the site fixed for Vandalia, or (2) to Croghan's alleged great Indian grant of 1749 (which Dunmore, guardian of the interests of the King, pronounced valid), or (3) to the Indiana Company grant of 1768 that was to take the place of that of 1749. Whatever might be the fate of Vandalia, there was clearly every reason for Croghan and Dunmore to join against Pennsylvania. Dr. John Connolly, Croghan's nephew, was put in charge of Fort Pitt as the seat of a Virginia county. Arrested by Pennsylvania authorities when he asserted control over local militia, then released, he in turn caused the arrest of county officials acting for Pennsylvania. The governors of the two provinces issued proclamations. Innumerable frauds, bickerings, and lawsuits arose from conflicting land titles, and from claims of jurisdiction by rival county courts. The controversy was

[22] See *AHR*, I, 99–100.

[23] Abernethy, *Western Lands*, pp. 70–71, 12, 73.

[24] The surveys in the West were full of Virginia politics. See Abernethy, *Western Lands*, pp. 84–88, 99, 100, 101, 103; Henderson, "A Pre-Revolutionary Revolt in the Old Southwest," *MVHR*, XVII (1930), 197.

not settled until 1782.[25] The Croghan-Virginia group of speculators conceived a plan for a fourteenth state of the Confederation to take the place of Vandalia in protecting the land claims of Croghan and the Indiana Company. This state, Westsylvania, was first heard of in 1776. It was virtually deprived of any trace of vitality by a Pennsylvania statute of 1782.

Early in 1774, when an official Virginia surveyor was along the Ohio, the frontier became tense and belligerent. New settlers in the southwest tip of Virginia gathered within stockades, isolated outrages by both whites and Indians increased, and Connolly, in a panic, put out a circular declaring that a state of war existed. In June, Dunmore called out the Virginia militia. After the colonies bought the neutrality of the Delawares and Six Nations, the isolated Shawnee were successfully subdued, and they renounced their claims to hunting privileges south of the Ohio, thus finally recognizing the Fort Stanwix cession. Dunmore proclaimed peace in January.[26]

Ironically enough, it was in the Illinois Country—just dedicated a third time to the Indians and the fur merchants—that the land speculators made their last great gamble; the irony is doubled by the fact that in this flouting of the law two official guardians of the crown's interests, Dunmore and Croghan, played the most conspicuous roles. Though it had not yet been passed, they doubtless knew of the Quebec Act. Private "purchases" of land from the Indians by British colonials and officials had nowhere been wholly prevented.[27] Croghan had never ceased to buy for himself and others on a great scale; in part, at least, by virtually bribing the governor of New York to make acquisitions for him through dummy grantees. And though royal instructions prohibited grants with their main dimension riparian, Sir William Johnson held one stretching for many miles along a river.[28] In 1773 an excuse became

[25] B. Crumrine, "The Boundary Controversy between Pennsylvania and Virginia, 1745–1785," Carnegie Institute, *Annals of the Carnegie Museum,* I, 505–524; N. B. Craig, *The Olden Time* (2 vols., Pittsburgh, 1846, 1848), I, 433–519, with many letters and proclamations.

[26] R. G. Thwaites and Kellogg (eds.), *Documentary History of Dunmore's War, 1774* (Madison, Wis., 1905), Introduction and pp. 368–395 for general account; *Amer. Archives,* I, 283, 468, 479, 790, 871–876.

[27] See W. H. Mohr, *Federal Indian Relations, 1774–1788* (Philadelphia, 1933), pp. 12–15, and H. L. Shaw, *British Administration of the Southern Indians, 1763–1776* (Lancaster, 1931).

[28] *N.Y. Col. Docs.,* VIII, 373–375. On Johnson's ribbon strip, see R. L. Higgins, *Expansion in New York* (Columbus, 1931), pp. 94, 95. Sir William

available for disregarding the prohibition of private purchases.

In 1757, the attorney general of England (Charles Pratt) and the solicitor general (Charles Yorke, counsel to the East India Company) gave the British government an opinion that perfect legal title to land in India passed to a purchaser "from the Mogul or any of the Indian princes or governments."[29] Those rulers *owned* land, under law far more ancient than England's. The opinion was obviously sound, but no lawyer of competence would have applied it to the tribal chiefs of American Indians. Yet some have believed, on the authority of an Indian trader (William Trent), an associate of Croghan, that the Lord Chancellor of England, as Pratt had become, and Yorke, who was soon to succeed him in that office, together with Franklin, advised him in 1769 that the Fort Stanwix deed to the Suffering Traders was valid without royal confirmation.[30] This also requires one to believe that the crown's highest legal officers would ignore the doctrine of American crown lands.

Lord Mansfield's reputation has also been besmirched in this connection without the production of any semblance of authority.[31] Although the Camden-Yorke opinion is said to have been circulating since 1768 or 1769 among speculators, no action was taken on it until 1773. As usual to justify purchases in America, the opinion's reference to "the Mogul" was omitted. In that year Lord Mansfield bought from the Illinois Indians, for himself and other subscribers to a land agreement, two tracts in Illinois, and in 1775 another agent bought two tracts on the Wabash River for other individuals. These groups later became, respectively, the Illinois Land Company and the Wabash Land Company, and in 1779 they were merged in order to prosecute more effectively their claims before Congress. George Croghan also bought

---

bought 18,000 acres for General Gage in 1768. *Johnson Papers*, V, 187–188; VI, 120, 296; VIII, 157.

[29] A copy of this opinion made at the Indian Office by Mr. W. E. Stevens is printed in S. Livermore, *Early American Land Companies: Their Influence on Corporate Development* (New York, 1939), p. 106.

[30] A. T. Volwiler, *George Croghan and the Western Movement, 1741–1782* (Cleveland, 1926), p. 298, 299. J. M. Sosin, *Whitehall and the Wilderness* (Lincoln, Neb., 1961), pp. 229–239; "The Yorke-Camden Opinion and American Land Speculators," *Pa. Mag. of Hist. and Biog.*, LXXXV, 38–49.

[31] *Pa. Mag. Hist. and Biog.*, XXXIII, 332; A. Henderson in *MVHR*, II, 447, XVII, 204, and *The Conquest of the Old Southwest . . . 1740–1790* (New York, 1920), pp. 201, 204, 357 (n. 137).

a tract of 1,500,000 acres and another of above 6,000,000 after Murray showed him the Camden-Yorke opinion—all for $8,000.[32] In this he may have acted in part for others; at any rate, various great speculators of the eastern states later held claims in his purchases.[33]

Murray had learned from Croghan, early in 1773, of the Camden-Yorke opinion. Croghan became closely associated that summer with Lord Dunmore. In view of the latter's approval of Croghan's alleged purchase of 1749, it is easy to understand that Murray's group would have sought the aid of Dunmore in support of their claims, and in May, 1774, he did strongly recommend that at least the Murray purchase be included in some existing colony. It has also been believed that the Wabash purchase was made, or at least Dunmore received an interest in it, to secure this aid.[34]

Murray's purchases were known in London in November, 1773, and no doubt they were known earlier to Sir William Johnson. When Murray, before making his purchases, had shown the Camden-Yorke opinion to Captain Lord, commander at Kaskaskia, the latter had promptly pronounced it contrary to royal orders and forwarded word (Gage being in London) to General Haldimand, in Quebec. In consequence, the latter issued on March 10, 1774, a proclamation, obviously under orders from the Crown, which reissued in the King's name the pertinent portions of the Proclamation of 1763, prohibiting settlement in, and land grants within, the West, thus reaffirming the reservation north of the Ohio which the Quebec Act would once more affirm three months later. And it also declared that *all* land purchases from the Indians made since 1763 without royal license would be considered "void and fraudulent."[35] That action, the land plan of February, 1774, and the Quebec Act were all parts of a consistent policy. But that policy obviously resulted from the lawless actions of speculators and not from

[32] C. E. Carter, *Great Britain and the Illinois Country* (Washington, 1910), p. 160; Volwiler, *Croghan*, 296, 297. In S. Livermore, *Early American Land Companies*, pp. 106 *et seq.* and 305, some details are given that are almost inaccessible.

[33] Among them, Silas Deane, Robert Morris, Gérard (the French minister), Dr. Thomas Walker. Abernethy, *Western Lands*, pp. 189, 234.

[34] Alvord, *Illinois Country*, pp. 302–303; but compare Henderson, *Old Southwest*, p. 239. Both grants were to lists of persons, and the lists are seemingly nonexistent.

[35] *Johnson Papers*, VIII, 844, 885, 898, 1074 (Haldimand's proclamation), 1136.

any "lawless rush of settlement westward." The British position being thus taken, the land companies necessarily turned for recognition to Virginia, and later to Congress.

These acts of the speculators, made known when Gage was in London and the Quebec Act in preparation, very probably suggested the wisdom of annexing the Northwest to Quebec.

After Dunmore's return from the war with the Shawnee, he was of course censured for disregard of orders. He replied, as respected his grants in the West, that government could not prevent settlement of the back country, and advised that new settlements should be incorporated into the seaboard colonies. In the same letter, doubtless in realization of the difficulty he would face in enforcing the land plan, he reported the pre-Revolutionary movement in Virginia. "As to the power of Government," he wrote, ". . . I can assure your Lordship that it is entirely disregarded, if not wholly overturned."[36]

Against the land plan Dunmore, and likewise the governors of the Carolinas and Georgia, had immediately protested, alleging that it would be injurious if enforced. The loss of executive revenue in fees was mentioned by some and probably bewailed by all.[37] Dunmore, at least, added that the gentry of the colonies would tolerate no limitation of purchases to one thousand acres.

The real danger to crown interests lay in provincial grants; that is, by imperial agents and politics.[38]

In Virginia, it had always been Crown against Council in land policy. Dunmore had continued disregard of royal orders in making grants even west of the Kentucky River, and had ignored the Proclamation policy, "which . . . seemed," he said, "to everybody in this Country, not at all to have been considered when the grant to Walpole and others was intended."[39] And he had ignored Vandalia too as it lost vitality.

Another challenge to the Crown's policy was given in the spring of

[36] Letter of December 24, 1774, in Thwaites and Kellogg, *Dunmore's War*, pp. 368–372.

[37] *Amer. Archives*, I, 1061–63.

[38] *Colonial Records of North Carolina*, IX, 820–824, 989–994; S. L. Sioussat, "The Breakdown of the Royal Management of Lands in the Southern Provinces, 1773–1775," *Agricultural History*, III (1929), 67–98; C. H. Laub, "British Regulation of Crown Lands in the West . . . 1773–1775," Wm. and Mary College, *Quarterly Historical Magazine*, 2nd Series, X (1930), 52–55.

[39] Thwaites and Kellogg, *Dunmore's War*, p. 370.

1775 by another speculator, a member of the colonial judiciary, Richard Henderson of North Carolina. Like Dunmore, he proposed to profit by the Camden-Yorke opinion, on the strength of which he bought from the Cherokee a great tract on which to establish a new proprietary colony, Transylvania. It was to lie between the Kentucky, Ohio, Holston, and Cumberland rivers; and as this would be in large part within limits claimed by Virginia,[40] Dunmore was compelled to publish the imperial land plan (which he had suppressed), to denounce Henderson as a conspicuous violator of its provisions, and to attempt enforcement of the plan. Four days before Dunmore's proclamation was issued, Henderson consummated his plan by a treaty at Watauga.

In the spring of 1775, in Virginia, the fate of the land plan and of Transylvania depended on the popular house of the legislature, and then on the revolutionary Convention. Popular control did not necessarily ensure wise action. In one case, wisdom prevailed; in the other, speculators.

Washington had immediately protested against the land plan. Within a week the Virginia Convention pronounced it "an innovation," and a committee was appointed to consider it. By July, William Preston, surveyor for the region west of the Kanawha, to whom it was sent for public notification, turned to the Convention for orders, and in August that body forbade any surveying or sales in accordance with the plan. Thomas Jefferson, a member of the committee which was considering it, was prompted to write *A Summary View of the Rights of British America*.[41]

As for Henderson, he had the task of overcoming both Virginia patriotism and the opposition of Kentucky settlers. Many land claimants in Kentucky, Virginians and others, whose claims were adjusted to Virginia's law, had no desire to start anew under Henderson's. George Rogers Clark, claimant and speculator, was also an ardently patriotic Virginian, and led the opposition both in Kentucky meetings and in debate with Henderson before the Virginia assembly, which rejected

[40] It included a large part of Kentucky and much of middle Tennessee. See Henderson, *Old Southwest*, pp. 218, 220, 239–240, 248, 256–259, 278–279; T. P. Abernethy, *Western Lands*, p. 125.

[41] He charged that the King had raised the price of land, and declared "fictitious" the doctrine "that all lands belong originally to the King," asserting that he had therefore no right of himself to grant lands (as he had done, for example, in creating Virginia in 1609)—nor any right, therefore, to protect them for the people, as he was now trying to do. *Writings* (Ford ed.).

the Transylvania Company's plea and made Kentucky a county of Virginia. However, both North Carolina, which likewise rejected his plea, and Virginia made generous consolation grants to the Company.[42]

For fifteen years of war and peace Great Britain had now been in control of the West. Its problems had been limited to the Indians, the fur trade, and land. It had happened that these were the only common interests of the seaboard colonies that could be dealt with through common effort, if at all. The fur trade, in particular, had always created inter-provincial jealousies and irritations.[43] The recommendations of the Albany Congress showed that colonial leaders realized the necessity of dealing with all these problems collectively, and, as Britain refused to approve a colonial authority for the purpose, she had undertaken the task herself.[44] However, it has been seen that the causes of her failure were beyond control by empire or colonies, or by both combined.

What was actually done and not done seems clear enough. The fur trade enjoyed virtually complete immunity from control. Yet much was done by the government which appears to be irreconcilable with a policy of giving the trade pre-eminence—that is, in considering plans for colonization of the fur country that would have destroyed the trade. Adoption of a stable western policy was prevented by persistent hesitancy in choosing between these irreconcilable interests.

Did this hesitancy arise from any difficulty of choosing between the two policies as a matter of long-term importance? Some condemnations of the government rest on the assumption that the fur trade was deliberately preferred. More probably, hesitation in policy resulted from an equilibrium between lobbying interests. Those interested in the fur trade were a very few English merchants, a few dozen American and Canadian agents, and some hundreds of traders and packers. These were actual interests, representing a considerable invested capital. Moreover, at critical times the English merchants seemed to exercise an influence so great as to suggest investment in the trade by persons high in authority. On the other hand, if persons interested in western lands were not fewer, certainly they included few home-based English-

---

[42] *Calendar of Virginia State Papers,* I, 303, 320; *Amer. Archives,* III, 1385; Hening, *Statutes of Virginia,* IX, 571; *Col. Rec. of N.C.,* IX, 1122–1125, 1129–1131, 1169–1170, X, 273, 323.

[43] See C. H. McIlwain (ed.), *Wraxall's Abridgment of Indian Affairs* (Cambridge, 1915), p. 221; V. W. Crane, *The Southern Frontier, 1670–1732* (Durham, 1928), pp. 123, 158, 201, 203–204; Alden, *John Stuart.*

[44] *N.Y. Col. Docs.,* VI, 917–918; *Pa. Archives, 1st Series,* VI, 206–210.

men of government circles before Vandalia, and their pressure was presumably in proportion to their investments, which were nominal.

Each of these suggested explanations may to some extent be valid; nevertheless, it seems probable that the essential reason why the trade continued to be nourished and colonization unattempted was fiscal. The question presented was one of immediate cost to the Treasury. The fur trade was a going concern. The land speculators wanted grants that would eventually thrive parasitically on host colonies which the government was expected to establish and develop. A colony, if far inland, would manifestly cost vast sums, and also require abandonment of mercantilistic principles. The fur trade also cost money, but it was impossible to say how much.

Were the costs of maintaining military posts in the West chargeable to the trade or to imperial integrity? The government hesitated for years over this question. One can only say, definitely, that whenever a new expenditure of money was involved, "the determination of any policy relating to the West . . . appears to have been conditioned by its possible effect upon the fur trade. The problem of holding the fur trade for English markets was uppermost in all discussions relative to the West."[45] This fact is, however, open to two interpretations. One is that there was a deliberate preference for the trade, and primary willingness to spend money only for it. The other is that action was controlled by fiscal considerations; that is, by the relative immediate costs of continuing aid to an existing interest or beginning a long-term project to replace that interest. Inaction would appear to have been not a deliberate choice but a continuing necessity.

This alters nothing except judgments of government intelligence. The government's policy has been unqualifiedly denounced. Short-sighted, disastrous, inefficient, sinister, of "incredible stupidity," "one of indecision and obstruction," "a long course of weakness, ignorance, and procrastination"—these are a fair sample of the words that have been used to characterize it.

Except in words, it is not apparent that there was downright stupidity. Certainly there was much ignorance of American conditions, particularly geographical, and sometimes this was ludicrous.[46] Some-

[45] C. E. Carter, *Illinois Country,* p. 134, and *MVHR,* I, 370.

[46] Such as the suggestion in 1725, said to have been seriously considered (V. W. Crane, *MVHR,* VIII, 369), that a strip one mile wide be cleared of woods along the entire back of the colonies to prevent the insults of the

times it actually caused no harm. For example, General Amherst gave orders in 1760 to disarm the French inhabitants of Michigan posts—though somebody prevented it; and General Gage was obliged in 1769 to explain the insanity of such an idea as respected the inhabitants of the French villages in Illinois. Lord Egremont thought in 1763 that Britain had acquired only "desert and useless plains above the junction of the Ohio River with the Mississippi"—which, of course, for the moment they were.[47] When knowledge was available, but unsought or disregarded, lamentable error was invited. Lord Shelburne, for example, declared that colonies in the Illinois Country would be readily accessible "by the vast rivers [not referring to the St. Lawrence] that fall into the Atlantic Ocean."[48]

Ignorance, or disregard of available information, respecting three matters clearly had undesirable effects in administration. Some illustrations of this may be given. One was the belief, if real, that the seaboard colonies had substantial interests in the fur trade.[49] But a vastly grosser error was the assumption that they therefore could and would control it, acting in their own interest, if Britain abandoned control. That information on the first matter was in the hands of the Board of Trade, and elsewhere abundant in London, is certain. Proper legal advice was available there on the second matter. As an illustration of administrative inadequacy, one may note Dartmouth's reference, in 1773, in connection with the Quebec Bill, to the trade plan of 1764: "There is no longer any hope of perfecting that plan of Policy in respect to the interior Country which was in Contemplation when the Proclamation of 1763 was issued."[50] Seemingly, the minister responsible for its application, if possible, did not understand that it was neither enforceable nor capable of being made so. This is suggested—and the fact that nothing had been done with it since 1764 is proved—by its inclusion, unchanged, with Guy Carleton's instructions as governor general of Canada in 1775, notwithstanding that, in considerable part, it was antipodal to

Indians. One colony, proposed in London advertisements in 1763 (the government therefore not involved, J. H. Alden, *New Governments West of the Alleghenies Before 1780,* Madison, 1897), was to stretch from the coast to the Ohio.

[47] *Mich. Hist. Coll.,* XLIII, 41–42, 43; *Ill. Hist. Coll.,* XXVII, 435.

[48] *Ill. Hist. Coll.,* XVI, 20.

[49] *Gage Correspondence,* II, 86.

[50] Shortt and Doughty, p. 485.

what had for years been reported to the Board as desired by the Canadian traders.[51]

Primarily, responsibility for the development of colonial policies rested with the Board of Trade.[52] No doubt the secretaries of the Board, John Pownall and William Knox, knew much of its papers—but only as papers. These were incrusted with bureaucratic practices that embodied imperial dominance. There were only a few secretaries of state—six passed the office back and forth for a dozen years. They manifestly rested, in general, on the record laid before them by the secretaries of the Board. Dartmouth's fresh ideas of 1773–74 were quite exceptional—except in being belated. In general, the casual, unenlightened character of their administration is often strikingly apparent.[53]

Another of its marked characteristics was indecision, over expense or over policy. Prolonged hesitancy over the retention of wilderness posts and over the construction of new ones involved much talk of the fur trade, but no discussion (in published records) of the policy of giving it primacy. Gage alone ventured to question that policy. Issues of policy and expense were similarly involved in establishing colonies in the deep interior. Since such action involved both repudiation of past mercantilism and great expense, even consideration of it seems remarkable, and its approval by Shelburne even more so. However, the final result was a paralysis of indecision.

Vituperation has been heaped on the government for not embarking on the "rapid development" of the Illinois Country.[54] All responsible officials presumably realized the inevitability and desirability of ultimate settlement of the interior country. In 1749 the Board of Trade had expressed the opinion that "settlement of the Country West of the Great Mountains . . . would be for . . . [the] advantage and security of . . . the neighbouring Provinces"; and it reaffirmed that view in

---

[51] *Ibid.*, pp. 614–620.

[52] Basye, *The Lords Commissioners of Trade and Plantations . . . 1748–1782* (New Haven, 1925), pp. 176–178, 157–161, 218.

[53] This is not surprising, considering that at that time even high military rank did not necessarily imply military experience, much less proficiency, and that holding a civil office had no necessary relation either to qualifications or to actual performance of its duties. The relative records of different secretaries in attending Board meetings can be seen, *ibid.*, pp. 220–229.

[54] See Alvord, *Landmark*, VIII, 642, 644; *Illinois Country*, p. 258.

1760.[55] It seems probable, too, that few except the fur merchants could have thought their trade superior in importance to the maintenance of good order among the Indians. To the latter the trade was merely ancillary. John Stuart explicitly so stated his own view; Sir William Johnson less directly, but impliedly on countless occasions, made it the basis of his policy; and General Gage on many occasions expressed without reserve his scant regard for the trade.[56]

It was the opinion of Frederick Jackson Turner that "the conception of the West as an Indian reserve exhibits England's inability to foresee the future of the region, and to measure the forces of American expansion."[57] No doubt few in England could justly have appreciated those matters. It does not follow, however, that if they had been fully appreciated, there would have been no Indian reservation. The United States adopted the reservation system and continued it long after the entire country appreciated the West's possibilities.

Britain, having claimed the West in its sea-to-sea charters, and formally acquired the area by the treaty with France of 1763, has been criticized for failing, within a dozen years, to repudiate her preference for seaboard colonies, and for not beginning interior colonization in expectation of a great future market to replace the petty interest of the fur trade. The first criticism seems unreasonable.[58] The second would have been proof, not of statesmanship, but of the reverse. Statesmanship must be judged with attention to the fact that colonization would presumably provoke continuous war; and therefore with attention to the condition of the Treasury, to the laws restricting English emigration, and to other problems. Britain's financial condition is of crucial importance in judging her western policy.[59] A continuous lament of the costs of military posts and Indian relations, and accompanying preachments of frugality, filled the letters of the secretaries of state. Any large-

---

[55] B. Fernow, *The Ohio Valley in Colonial Days* (Albany, 1890), p. 246; *N.Y. Col. Docs.*, VII, 428–429, 437.

[56] *AHR*, XX, 818, where similar opinions of Lord Barrington and others are cited.

[57] "The Middle West," *International Monthly*, IV (1920), 799.

[58] Britain certainly made vastly greater and far swifter progress in changing economic policies between 1760 and 1825 than the United States in tariff policies between 1890 and 1962.

[59] Shelburne's first instructions in 1766 were based on the King's "insistence" that American expenses be reduced, though he soon took the view "that no expence shall be spared which is really useful" (Carter, *Gage Correspondence*, II, 61; *Ill. Hist. Coll.*, XI, 458).

scale occupation would necessarily have entailed either a vastly increased expenditure for presents or still vaster expenditure for war. The government was so advised by Sir William Johnson and General Gage. The latter believed (correctly, we know now) that continual war would be necessary, and thought the actual policy should be continued "for a century" by purchasing the Indians' good will. Nobody had a stronger conviction than Franklin that the West could be the basis of Britain's greatness and stability, but for its settlement he too allowed at least a century.[60]

Even slow colonization could have been accomplished only by active co-operation between Britain and the seaboard colonies. Emigration from England beyond a tiny dribble was unthinkable, and the seaboard colonies would therefore have furnished the settlers. This was not a new idea—it was in the Proclamation of 1763; however, there is no evidence that Americans were ready to "pour" westward. The years of mass migration were well in the future, under totally altered political conditions. Slow colonization would for some years have necessitated protection by British troops or by colonial militia, and not in small detachments (such as those in the western posts under conditions of postulated Indian amity) but in forces adequate to take the field for protracted hostilities. In both cases such protection was financially and politically improbable. The fate of the proposals of the Albany Congress, and the later unwillingness of Great Britain even to permit intercolonial conferences on Indian problems, are ample evidence to discredit suggestions that the mother country and colonies could together have solved the problem of western expansion, or that anyone had a feasible plan for their doing so.

It is quite clear that the reservation remained and the fur trade was preferred of necessity. There being no free choice, it seems improper to regard government acquiescence in their continuance as mercantilistic policy. Politicians did not prove themselves statesmen by approving plans, between 1763 and 1774, for colonies in the Illinois Country. In rejecting such a plan in 1768, and preferring, instead, the freedom of settlement directly back of Virginia which was secured later in that year by the Fort Stanwix treaty, the Board of Trade evidenced sound judgment. Regardless of the merits or demerits of the preference for seaboard colonies in mercantilistic doctrine, actual interior colonization

[60] Carter, *Gage Correspondence*, I, 277, 278; *Ill. Hist. Coll.*, X, 307; Franklin, *Writings* (Smyth ed.), IV, 55, III, 338.

of the West was an impracticable dream under the conditions of the time. It also seems evident that colonization south of the Ohio, though less difficult to reconcile with the seaboard preference, failed for reasons independent both of that preference and of the merits of colonization *per se*.

There is certainly in the record no great policy, systematically developed, nor can one discover a great statesman with such a policy. There is nothing more than the continuance for a dozen years of a condition left on the government's hands at the end of the French and Indian War. There was much talk of altering it, talk which clearly evinced scant understanding of the situation, and equally little of what was requisite for its alteration. Should the mere continuance of the condition—or the impotence, irresolution, or ignorance causing the continuance—be itself called policy? No matter what the answer, the condition was a fact, and the fact is important history in the West's development. The fruitless plans of land jobbers and speculations regarding the views of British politicians, never realized in action, are of little significance.

CHAPTER 3

The West in War and in Making Peace

IF "THE REVOLUTION" was the resolution to be independent, generated and matured, as John Adams said, in the minds of men —and surely it was just that, and the Declaration merely its publication, and the war which followed merely the means of its realization— then there could have been no "Revolutionary movement" in the West except the extension of the war into it. So prevalent, however, has been the exaggeration of the West's predominance in shaping American history that attention must be given to the ideas that the French villagers in Illinois were revolutionists, and that British management of western affairs for twenty years caused the repudiation of British rule in the colonies.

No social causes can be identified beyond a consensus of opinion, and historians are under no compunction to distinguish, as jurymen must, between causes immediately effective and those less directly or only remotely contributory. It seems clear, however, that these distinctions should be attempted.

West Florida, the only part of the West which existed otherwise than geographically, was not unaffected by the events which presaged the Revolution. The Stamp Act, in particular, had strong repercussions because such a tax was there of peculiar importance.[1] But that colony had not shared in the long experiences in which revolt had generated,

[1] W. B. Kerr, "The Stamp Act in the Floridas, 1765–1766," *MVHR*, XXI (1935), 463–470; Governor Johnstone to Board of Trade, April 1, 1766, in Howard, *The British Development of Florida, 1763–1769* (Berkeley, 1947), pp. 124–126.

and presumably nobody would claim that it shared in the causes of the Revolution. The same is even more clearly true of the western wilderness, whose sole white inhabitants were the French villagers of Illinois. It has even been stated that villagers living in drowsy isolation like seventeenth-century peasants committed "acts of a rebellious character . . . impelled by the . . . same ideas in which the American Revolution had its source."[2]

The administration of the interior reservation was one of repression —particularly prohibition of land grants, prohibition of private purchases of land, prohibition of settlement after 1763. How many Easterners (to whom alone these prohibitions applied) were affected by them? The last is often assumed to have affected, or been resented by, many. One can find statements that good land in the seaboard colonies was already exhausted (which have a mite of truth), and Lord Shelburne argued that giving freedom to spread into the interior would lessen any danger of separation from Great Britain, thereby implying that under past restrictions that danger had existed.[3] No contemporary evidence of such resentment of the restrictions has been cited. In fact, there were no actual restrictions upon migration to produce discontent. Motives of adventure, ambition, democracy, the desire to escape social restraints, taxation, or imprisonment were building border settlements. Even the settlement lines of 1763 and 1768 were paper restrictions only, holding back nobody willing to risk Indian hostilities. The reports of Sir William Johnson were one continual lament over this fact.

In seeking to discover in the West the cause of the Revolution, some writers, stressing as a primary cause the taxation of America, have made much of the fact that the first actual imposition upon the colonies of an expense not for any particular colony's government was for main-

---

[2] C. W. Alvord, *The Illinois Country* (Springfield, Ill., 1920), pp. 292–293. He seemingly adopted unreservedly the view that "the American Revolution" (the revolution in the East) was caused or provoked by, or a "culmination" of, British governmental acts in the West, for the title of his study of those acts—*The Mississippi Valley in British Politics: A Study of the Trade, Land Speculation, and Experiments in Imperialism Culminating in the American Revolution* (2 vols., Cleveland, 1917)—so implies. The implication, however, was not supported by his text, nothing in which goes beyond an assumption. It is extraordinary to suppose that popular resentment in the East could have been aroused by acts in a distant wilderness, and relating solely to foreign war, Indians, and petitions for land grants. Reasons for believing this to be possible have, however, been suggested.

[3] *Ill. Hist. Coll.*, XI, 429.

tenance of the western posts.[4] It is true that the posts constituted no part of colonial government, but they were regarded as protecting the colonies and the trade was British colonial. Nor has it been shown that the proceeds of the Stamp Act were "to pay the bill for the proposed development of the West," or that there was any "proposed development" of it beyond approval by Lord Shelburne (not the government) of the proposal that colonies be established in the Illinois Country. That proposal was rejected and had no special significance. This virtue of a planned "development" has even been attributed to the plan of 1764 for management of an Indian reserve.[5]

The idea that shortcomings in British administration of the West created popular disloyalty in the East must be regarded as baseless. There remains the question whether the affront given to land speculators by the settlement lines of 1763 and 1768, and other restrictions upon land grants and private purchases of land from Indians, were important in causing the Revolution. Washington's judgment that the line of 1763 could only somewhat delay exploitation of western lands was common sense. As regards speculation, no evidence has appeared that settlement lines retarded it. They were merely scorned annoyances. The violent reaction of speculators to the land reforms of 1774, which were very real restraints on speculation, spotlights their indifference to the settlement lines.

The different relations of the British and the Americans to the Indians during the war obstructed for forty years the establishment of good feeling between the two countries. General Gage was urging use of them long before war began, but he claimed that the Americans were already endeavoring to secure them.[6] It may be assumed that it was only from necessity, and with considerable early inconsistency, that the Americans adopted the policy of seeking Indian neutrality; nevertheless it was the more creditable policy. In September, 1775, they made peace, supposedly, with the Six Nations (which were long much

[4] It was stated by Shelburne (*Ill. Hist. Coll.,* XVI, 13) that revenue from the Stamp Act was intended for support of the military and Indian services. The western portion of the military establishment was proportionately the most expensive.

[5] A. T. Volwiler, *George Croghan and the Western Movement, 1746–1782* (Cleveland, 1926), pp. 156, 225; Alvord, *Illinois Country,* p. 258, and *Landmark,* IX (1927), 80.

[6] Shortt and Doughty, p. 583 *et seq.; Amer. Archives,* II, 698, III, 6; A. H. Basye, *Lords Commissioners of Trade,* p. 195; E. Abel in Amer. Hist. Assoc., *Report* for 1906, pp. 263–264; *Ill. Hist. Coll.,* VIII, xviii.

divided in inclinations), Delawares, and Shawnee.[7] The commissioners gave assurances that Americans would not settle north of the Ohio; Congress so voted; Virginia passed a law forbidding settlement beyond that river; and in 1776 the neutrality promises of the preceding year were seemingly confirmed.[8] Of course, these promises of nonexpansion were not fulfilled, but despite them the British gained the active aid of most of the Indians.

The colonials had always encroached upon their territory, the Indian superintendents (despite Croghan's practices) had always denounced these wrongs, and from these officials had come all presents. They continued to come from John Stuart and from Sir William Johnson's deputies (he had died). "Great Pains & Treasure," General Haldimand reported, "were bestowed to bring them to act" with the British.[9] The Six Nations were much divided in sentiment, and ultimately permanently divided by the war, but the conclusive argument that persuaded the Mohawks was some vague guarantee of their hunting grounds.[10] In June, 1776, Congress authorized Washington to use Indians with troops, and to pay bounties for prisoners taken by them.[11] Even that was wholly undesirable, since Indian auxiliaries could not be controlled. John Stuart, although he knew that many Cherokee and Creeks had agreed to neutrality, wrote to Lord George Germain that he nevertheless hoped they would "act for His Majesty's service when deemed necessary," and would "use [his] utmost endeavours to keep [them] in temper and disposed to act when required."

When Governor Galvez proposed to Colonel John Campbell, commanding in West Florida, to renounce alliances which, he said, de-

[7] R. G. Thwaites and L. P. Kellogg (eds.), *The Revolution on the Upper Ohio* (Madison, 1908), pp. 47, 51–54, 61, 68–69, 99, 101.

[8] *Ibid.*, pp. 25–135; Abernethy, *Western Lands,* pp. 175–176, 178.

[9] *Mich. Hist. Coll.,* XX, 663. The yearly cost of maintaining the southern superintendency rose from about £5,000 in 1770 to £14,000 in 1774 to about £20,000 in 1775 and in 1776, and more thereafter. H. L. Shaw, *British Administration of the Southern Indians, 1763–1776* (Lancaster, 1931), p. 83.

[10] Only the Oneida and Tuscarora sided definitely with the colonials, *A.S.P., Ind. Aff.,* I, 546. Compare *Mich. Hist. Coll.,* XX, 178; M. G. Walker, "Sir John Johnson, Loyalist," *MVHR,* III (1916–17), 318–346; W. A. Mohr, *Federal Indian Relations, 1774–1788* (Philadelphia, 1933), pp. 27–29, 37, 45–46; M. Savelle, *George Morgan, Colony Builder* (New York, 1932); *Amer. Archives,* II, 514–518, III, 599; *Mich. Hist. Coll.,* X, 268–270. The guarantee of hunting grounds was repeatedly referred to by Canadian officials, but no copy has been seen. It was doubtless Haldimand's, while commander in chief.

[11] *J.C.C.,* V, 452.

graded more than they assisted, Campbell replied that they would only
be used "against an invading foe" (which events disproved), and that
he had "absolutely forbidden the smallest act of licentiousness, rapine,
or cruelty." Stuart was equally fatuous. The Indians would, he said,
only "assist . . . in distressing the rebels"—which, to Indians, meant
pillage and atrocities. By 1777 he was ordering his subordinates to tell
the Indians they were "principals in the war; that the defense of themselves and their lands [was] one of the greatest causes of it."[12] This
was either gross ignorance or pretense; in Canada it later served for
years as the basis of Britain's Indian policy after 1783.

During the war there were two American campaigns against the
Cherokee. The first was preceded by an ultimatum to the Watauga
borderers sent by Stuart's brother and deputy, and the latter accompanied his wards, the Cherokee—doubtless to save Loyalist borderers,
Indian harassment knowing no political immunity.[13] Responsibility for
Indian atrocities in the Northwest was attributed by the Americans
primarily to Lieutenant Governor Henry Hamilton, who, "painted and
dressed as an Indian, joined . . . in the wild songs and dances" of the
councils he held at Detroit.

Hamilton, Stuart, and the subordinates of both no doubt sometimes
enjoined mercy on the Indians, but that was pure futility. Although
Hamilton reported to his government that he made gifts to those who
should be "proved" to have spared those "incapable of defending themselves," he nevertheless congratulated alike those who took prisoners
and those who took scalps. Many scalps were taken, scalping knives
were supplied in Detroit, and although, one authority says, "it cannot be positively proved that Governor Hamilton offered rewards for
scalps," his successor did pay for them, although less than for prisoners.[14]

George Rogers Clark was a young backwoodsman who had been

---

[12] *Col. Rec. N.C.*, X, 606–608; *Amer. Archives*, IV, 316–317; H. L. Shaw,
Southern Indians, pp. 87, 91, 92, 96, 99, 107, 110.

[13] *Ibid.*, pp. 106, 122, 138–139, 152–153. Stuart is defended by P. M.
Hamer, *MVHR*, XVII (1930), 360. Gage had ordered Stuart, just before
the Watauga troubles, to use the Indians whenever opportune.

[14] Thwaites and Kellogg, *Revolution on the Upper Ohio*, p. 38; *Mich. Hist.
Coll.*, IX, 445, 465, X, 266–269; *J.C.C.*, IV, 395, 452; N. V. Russell, "The
Indian Policy of Henry Hamilton: a Re-Evaluation," *CHR*, XI (1930), 20–37;
J. A. James, *The Life of George Rogers Clark* (Chicago, 1928), pp. 43, 52–
53. Washington, *Writings* (Fitzpatrick ed.), XVI, 68, 272; Jefferson, *Papers*
(Boyd ed.), III, 30, 61, 86, 198.

exploring in Kentucky and along the lower Ohio since 1772. He and Governor Patrick Henry were equally patriotic Virginians and ardent land speculators. They favored rapid settlement of Kentucky and the strengthening in that or any other manner of Virginia's western claims. Moreover, military safety necessitated protection of the West against the British in Detroit. There is no reason to believe that land speculation particularly motivated their actions. In the spring of 1778, Clark assembled some hundred and fifty men on the Monongahela, descended that river and the Ohio, and at Louisville received (May 26) news of the French alliance with the united colonies.

Leaving the Ohio below the mouth of the Tennessee, he marched across country to Kaskaskia, whose commander and citizens were wakened in the night by the cries of the invaders. The French were easily won over by generous offers of freedom to leave if desired, and of religious freedom and citizenship (on taking an oath of allegiance) if they remained. Even more influential, doubtless, was Clark's report of the French alliance. The neighboring villages submitted bloodlessly. The inhabitants of Vincennes also submitted with enthusiasm to two citizens of Kaskaskia sent by Clark, and he then sent one of his captains (Leonard Helm) to command their militia. Before the end of the year emissaries of nearly a dozen Indian tribes from Missouri up to the Miami and northward to Wisconsin and Michigan came to make treaties.[15]

Vincennes was recaptured by Governor Hamilton in December. Like Clark's, his conquest was bloodless; only one French militiaman remained with Captain Helm to man the fort. The inhabitants promptly shifted allegiance to Great Britain.[16] Hamilton settled down to plan a spring attack upon Clark, but the latter did the unexpected. With less than two hundred men he left Kaskaskia in early February on a march of nearly two hundred miles across country. On February 23 he entered Vincennes. Four members of an Indian war party that happened to return with prisoners and scalps were taken prisoners by Clark and tomahawked within sight of the British garrison, to impress the Indians with the powerlessness of the British to aid them. On the 25th Hamil-

[15] Full accounts of Clark's expedition and conquests are given in *Ill. Hist. Coll.*, I; in the Introduction to II by Alvord; and in the Introduction to VIII, pp. lxxxii *et seq.*, by James.
[16] Hamilton's report is in *Ill. Hist. Coll.*, VIII, 174 *et seq.*, and in *Mich. Hist. Coll.*, IX, 489–516.

ton surrendered.[17] His French volunteers were then supplied with boats and provisions by Clark and sent back to Detroit. They departed with huzzas, and the American victory was celebrated for three days in Detroit.[18] Fear of Clark, and belief in his invincibility, long dominated the minds of the Indians.

Clark's exploits have been in various ways disparaged.[19] His conquest was greater in promise because it was not won by force, and he certainly displayed military aptitude.[20] The promise of his deeds was transient for reasons beyond his control, but they alone emblaze the record of the war in the West.[21] The great shortcoming in his efforts was the failure to capture Detroit. Washington had always considered that to be the only certain assurance of western peace. Congress repeatedly planned on it for three years before Virginia acted independently; then, in 1779, when Clark's ascendancy over the Indians was at its highest, voted troops and money for it.[22] But the people of Virginia and Kentucky wanted safety assured by militia when at home, and the discretionary orders given by Washington to the Confederation commander at Fort Pitt enabled him, out of jealousy, to refuse Clark federal troops. In 1780 and 1781 similar conditions, plus the obstacles to recruiting created by the boundary dispute between Pennsylvania and Virginia, again prevented an attempt.[23] Clark believed that he could take Detroit with five hundred men, and it seems certain that he

[17] *Ill. Hist. Coll.*, VIII, 185 *et seq.*

[18] *Ibid.*, lxxxiv, 144, 146, 188–190; Alvord, *Illinois Country*, p. 344.

[19] Alvord, *Illinois Country*, pp. 325–326; *MVHR*, III, 31, citing *Ill. Hist. Coll.*, V, 18 *et seq.*; *MVHR*, III, 33. The amount of resistance in Kaskaskia, and possible aid from spies or others, do not affect the main point: with British troops in Detroit, Washington rejoiced in Clark's presence in Kaskaskia.

[20] To appreciate Clark, compare his feats with the "squaw campaign" of General Edward Hand of the Confederation army, R. G. Thwaites and Kellogg (eds.), *Frontier Defense on the Upper Ohio, 1777–1778* (Madison, 1912), pp. 193, 215–220; and with the Fort Laurens relief expedition of his successor in Confederation command at Fort Pitt, General Lachlan McIntosh. L. P. Kellogg (ed.), *Frontier Advance on the Upper Ohio* (Madison, 1916), pp. 157–185, 203, 207.

[21] Unless one includes that of King's Mountain on the northwest fringe of South Carolina settlement (October, 1780).

[22] *J.C.C.*, VIII, 392, 478, 493, IX, 942–944, XI, 587–591.

[23] *Ill. Hist. Coll.*, VIII, 514, 535, 551, 553, 561, 562, 598. There is a puzzle in Washington's attitude. He was extremely perturbed by state separatism. Virginian as he was, is it possible that he did not favor strengthening Virginia's position in the Northwest? See letters to Jefferson, *Writings* (Fitzpatrick ed.), XV, 401, XVIII, 74, 75; to Brodhead, *ibid.*, XVI, 486–487; XVII, 157, 349; XVIII, 112.

could have done so, for according to the British themselves the French were virtually all pro-American.[24] Occupation of Detroit would presumably have given all Canada to the United States in the peace— whether for good or ill would probably be much disputed today.

In 1778 Virginia had created the County of Illinois, with a county lieutenant and simple courts. The war overwhelmed it with economic ills. Clark bought provisions with depreciated "continental" money, and later with drafts on Virginia with which the Illinois merchants bought fresh supplies in New Orleans. They were soon bought either at great loss to Virginia's agent there, Oliver Pollock, or (after he could no longer maintain her credit) to the merchants.[25]

Meanwhile, a struggle was going on in Congress to induce Virginia to cede her claims to western lands to the Confederation. Her first conditional offer to do so, though not accepted, necessarily altered her military efforts, which subsided into occasional punitive expeditions after major border forays by the Indians. The latter did not cease when Cornwallis' surrender ended the war on the seaboard. "It would be endless and difficult," General Haldimand wrote to London in the autumn of 1781, "to enumerate . . . the Parties that are continually employed upon the back Settlements."[26] There were, of course, horrifying atrocities on both sides.

The Virginia legislature allowed the County·of Illinois to expire in January, 1782.[27] A year later Clark's regiment was disbanded, and the French villages soon relapsed into neglect until the establishment of effective American rule in 1790. The debt of the Americans to them in the war was certainly very great.[28]

[24] *Amer. Archives*, I, 36; R. G. Thwaites and Kellogg, *Revolution on Upper Ohio*, pp. 147–151. Indicating pro-American sentiment: *Mich. Hist. Coll.*, IX, 389, 408, 432, 462, 465; X, 328, 338, 450, 482; *Ill. Hist. Coll.*, VIII, 172, 324, V, 148. Indicating pro-British sentiment: J. A. James, *George Rogers Clark*, pp. 63–64, 256, and Miss. Val. Hist. Soc., *Proceedings*, III, 314; *Ill. Hist. Coll.*, II, 553–563.

[25] C. E. Boyd, "The County of Illinois," *AHR*, IV (1898–99), 623–635; A. C. Boggess, *The Settlement of Illinois, 1778–1830* (Chicago, 1908), pp. 25, 31; J. A. James, "Oliver Pollock the Financier of the Revolution in the West," *MVHR*, XVI (1929), 67–80; *Oliver Pollock: The Life and Times of an Unknown Patriot* (New York, 1937).

[26] *Mich. Hist. Coll.*, X, 517.

[27] Boggess, *Settlement of Illinois*, p. 25, gives correct dates of this and other events.

[28] This was the opinion of Louise Kellogg, *MVHR*, XVIII (1931), 18.

Indian war in the South was a matter of border harassment except in 1776 and 1779. In those years the southern colonies gave remarkable evidence of the possibilities of provincial co-operation. In the Cherokee war of 1776, a force from the Carolinas and Georgia burned the Indians' crops, destroyed their towns, and with typical frontier inhumanity offered many prisoners only a choice between slavery and death. In 1779 the Cherokee again made large-scale forays and again were overrun, this time by North Carolina and Virginia.[29]

The Confederation did nothing, for the seaboard war drained it of every resource. British posts along the Mississippi, particularly Natchez, which was predominantly a settlement of Loyalists and neutralists, weakened Clark's hold on the Northwest and impeded American trade to New Orleans. Pillaging raids on these communities early in 1778 by Captain James Willing, with volunteers collected as he progressed from Pittsburgh to New Orleans, were unauthorized by Congress, but were made under cover of a mission to secure supplies.[30] They had no results beneficial to the American cause except, perhaps, intimidation of the Indians on the lower Mississippi.

Spain's original policy in the war is somewhat obscure. Until war had begun between her and Britain, she could naturally have hoped, by friendly treatment of the Americans, to secure their aid in regaining the Floridas, and this was probably her original idea. She began aiding them in 1775 by supplying powder. In 1776 she increased the amounts and variety of supplies, made a secret loan, opened New Orleans to American commerce. Munitions and great supplies of army clothing were given in 1777, and Governor Galvez greatly favored Americans in the application of prize law at New Orleans.[31] The British made West Florida a special haven for Loyalists, liberalized land grants to attract them, and provided funds for the indigent.[32] But the population was slight, and Indian trade and land speculation were the only interests.

[29] A. Henderson, *Old Southwest*, pp. 261–270, 290.

[30] J. H. Claiborne, *Mississippi, as a Province, Territory, and State* (Jackson, 1880), I, 117–124; J. W. Caughey, *Bernardo de Galvez in Louisiana, 1776–1783* (Berkeley, 1934).

[31] Caughey, *Galvez*, pp. 102–134.

[32] W. H. Siebert, "Dispersion of the American Tories," *MVHR*, I, 184–197; "The Loyalists in West Florida and the Natchez District," *ibid.*, II, 469–470; C. Johnson, *British West Florida*, pp. 144, 145, 202, 204, 205, 207–215.

Reliance for the colony's defense was placed upon the natural strength of Pensacola. In 1776 Congress offered to join Spain in attacking that port, but on conditions—a treaty of alliance, use of the harbor, and free navigation of the Mississippi—which Spain would not consider.[33] By the summer of 1778, these matters and Clark's occupation of Illinois made plain conflicts of interest in the ultimate disposition, if the British should be beaten, of the ports along the Mississippi and possibly of West Florida. When Oliver Pollock and Governor Galvez urged a joint attack on Pensacola in the autumn of that year, Congress was obliged to confess that the undertaking was beyond its powers; but by that time Floridablanca, Spain's secretary of foreign affairs, had plainly shown that he wished the Mississippi valley for Spain.[34]

Galvez received news of Spain's declaration of war (June, 1779) three weeks before it reached Colonel Campbell at Pensacola. Before the latter had word, Galvez occupied Fort Bute and later added Baton Rouge and Natchez (September, 1779). Mobile surrendered without resistance in February, and Pensacola capitulated to a French and Spanish land force and fleet a year later (May, 1781). A third of the garrison were Loyalists from the middle states. The Loyalists around Natchez, who had revolted against Spanish rule, probably under Campbell's urgings, abandoned hope and fled back to the seacoast.[35]

The ends of the united colonies in the war were plain from the beginning. They wanted complete independence—yet, pending victory, could afford sometimes to put greater emphasis upon lesser demands, particularly upon the Mississippi as a western boundary, though that too they sometimes toned down. On both objectives Spain was their inevitable enemy. Rigidly committed to principles of colonial exclusivism—political, economic, theological—she was unalterably opposed for decades to admission of the Americans to the Gulf of Mexico either through New Orleans or Pensacola; therefore, to any genuine rights to navigate the Mississippi or the rivers of Alabama. The safety of her possessions around the Gulf demanded, she believed, the recovery of

[33] *J.C.C.*, VI, 1057 (December 30, 1776). Franklin made the offer in Paris in April, 1777, Wharton, *Dip. Corr.*, II, 280, 282, 304, 308.

[34] *Jour. Cont. Cong.*, XII, 1083 (Oct. 31, 1778); Wharton, *Dip. Corr.*, I, 431 *et seq.*

[35] Shaw, *Southern Indians*, pp. 142–162; Caughey, *Galvez*, pp. 187–214 (Galvez' campaigns), 215–242 (Natchez uprising); Siebert, "Dispersion of Tories," pp. 474–477 (Galvez), 477–480 (Natchez).

the Floridas from Britain and acquisition of the eastern half of the Mississippi valley. Yet her principles would not permit that she ally herself in war with rebellious colonies, even if their objectives had not otherwise been antipodal to her own.

France was therefore placed in a position of extraordinary difficulty when the united colonies sought an alliance. Fundamentally, this arose from her position as the greatest continental power. Harassed as she was by problems of European power politics, she could not desire the addition of an American state to the European group, unless in a wholly subordinate status. Secondarily, her difficulty was increased by her long-time and indispensable ties with Spain, whose navy and whose bullion from the Indies were valuable assets in any war with Great Britain. When they became allies in the European war, it was inevitable that Spain would expect and receive French support of her American claims. What Spain did during the war for the Americans, and in the West for herself, has been seen. The role of France in those actions, and in support of Spain in the negotiations for peace, remains to be examined.

Vergennes, the French foreign minister, repeatedly stated to the French ministers in Madrid and Philadelphia that it was not desired that the United States should grow too much or too rapidly, or "play the part of a great power." France wanted them peaceable, which they might not be if they became "ambitious." Continued British possession of Nova Scotia and Canada would be a salutary cause of anxiety for the Americans. Spain should retain the Floridas, too, and Gérard (minister at Philadelphia) should support her claims, particularly to Pensacola, with all his power, and thus prepare Congress for an ultimate renunciation of American counterclaims (in the peace negotiations). With these British and Spanish possessions as neighbors, the Americans could not be "enterprising and troublesome." Vergennes retained these views to the end, and at least in 1778 was willing to guarantee to Great Britain her possession of Nova Scotia and Canada. Gérard was instructed to applaud plans against them (and even against West Florida), but to give no aid.[36]

[36] J. Jay, The Peace Negotiations of 1782 and 1783: an Address . . . (New York, 1884), pp. 51, 52, 98, 99, 144, 145, 152, 157; Gérard's instructions of March 29, 1778, H. Doniol, Histoire de la Participation de la France à l'établissement des États-Unis d'Amérique (5 vols., Paris, 1886–92), III, 154, 155, 156, II, 556, 557; Wharton, Dip. Corr., I, 436. Pages 144–160, 212, of Jay's address give translated extracts of letters and documents which

Throughout the war these ideas underlay French support of Spain's claims in the West. How Vergennes so worded the treaty of American alliance that this could be done without violating obligations assumed by France to the United States is perfectly clear. He made the alliance with the colonies only after Burgoyne's surrender justified hope that his action would prevent any reconciliation between them and Great Britain—in fearing which he had been encouraged by Franklin. The double objective was their independence and permanent "attachment" (union) to France. He offered them a commercial treaty on a single condition: that they would never renounce independence. A secret treaty of defensive alliance was also prepared, to take effect if Great Britain should declare war on France, and she was incited to do so by making known to her the commercial treaty in a communication beginning with the words: "The United States of America, which are in full possession of independence."[37] Britain responded as desired, and the alliance became effective.

This provided (1) that war should continue until independence should be "formally or tacitly assured"; (2) that neither ally should "conclude either truce or peace with Great Britain without the formal consent of the other first obtained"; (3) that each party should join in military enterprises of the other only "as far as circumstances, and its own particular situation [would] admit"; and (4) that specified conquests (which, of course, did not include Canada, Nova Scotia, the Floridas, or the Appalachian back country), if made by either, should go to it and be subject to a mutual guarantee of territorial possessions. A secret article provided for joinder by Spain in the war.[38]

The above provisions in the American treaty were drafted by Vergennes with this prospective joinder of Spain—and the conflicts be-

---

are to be found in their original in Adolphe de Circourt's translation of G. Bancroft's *Formation of the Constitution: Histoire de l'action commune de la France et de l'Amérique pour l'Indépendance des États-Unis* (3 vols., Paris, 1876), especially III, 307, 310, 312, 320.

[37] Doniol, *Établissement des États-Unis*, III, 154, 155, 156, II, 729; compare *A.S.P., For. Rel.*, I, 572; Wharton, *Dip. Corr.*, I, 259, II, 523–526. Presently prevailing views began with the essays of E. S. Corwin, *French Policy and the American Alliance* (Princeton, 1916), and "The French Objective in the American Revolution," *AHR*, XXI (1915), 33–61; C. H. Van Tyne, "Influences Which Determined the French . . . Treaty with America, 1778," *AHR*, XXI (1915), 528–541.

[38] Hunter Miller, *International Acts*, II, 35–44; on the separate article, pp. 45–47.

tween her interests and those of the united colonies—in mind. Had she joined in the alliance with the colonies, it was to be under "conditions . . . freely agreed to and settled between all the parties." But by no possibility could Spain and the colonies ever have agreed upon such conditions. Joining France alone, the conditions in Spain's treaty with France were not violations by France of the above provisions in her American treaty. Vergennes' letters assumed the impossibility of an American-Spanish agreement. The American negotiators did not and could not protect themselves against the dangers of separate alliances. The situation allowed France to favor Spain freely: her treaty with that nation (April, 1779) did not require such support, in terms, but its interpretation as a Bourbon family compact obviously did. The treaty did state what Charles III expected to gain from the alliance, and Vergennes characterized his expectations as "gigantic."[39]

Long before this Bourbon alliance Vergennes was in every way supporting Spain's American claims. In Gérard's instructions it was emphasized that one matter was of great concern to King Louis: the circumspect negotiation of agreements favorable to Spain.[40] Gérard's letters show that Vergennes was a party in 1778 to Spanish plans to secure "exclusive acquisition of the Mississippi along its whole course," a project which Gérard felt "must be handled with secrecy and dexterity."[41] When giving Gérard his instructions, Vergennes indicated his opinion that Spain's claims to the country back of the Appalachians were superior, and in subsequent letters supporting that view he displayed an ignorance respecting Indian "title," and a disregard of international law and of the cessions by France to Great Britain in 1763, which are astounding.[42] Finally, in April, 1779, he instructed Luzerne, Gérard's successor, that Louis considered it "for the interest of the Con-

[39] It has been said, in particular, that agreement by France in the French-Spanish treaty (of April 12, 1779) to continue war until Gibraltar should be captured was such a violation. On long-prevailing misrepresentations of it (due to the use by George Bancroft of a spurious text), Wharton, *Dip. Corr.*, I, 356–359; Doniol, *Établissement des États-Unis*, III, 620.

[40] *Ibid.*, III, 1 ("les stipulations à ménager en faveur de l'Espagne").

[41] December 22, 1778, Jay, *Peace Negotiations*, p. 146.

[42] Doniol, *Établissement des États-Unis*, III, 154, V, 293–294; letter of July 18, 1779, Jay, *Peace Negotiations*, p. 148. Vergennes wrote of the Northwest lands that "either they belong to the savages or are a dependence of Canada." In 1763 the French had been forced by the Vaudreuil map to admit that whatever land France held east of the Mississippi and south of Lakes Erie and Ontario was part (administratively) of Louisiana, and France had ceded to Britain whatever she owned east of the Mississippi.

gress, as well as a matter of [that body's?] duty to regulate at once, in a manner satisfactory to that power [Spain], the various points which concern it."[43]

It is manifest from the provisions, above noted, of the French-American treaty of alliance that the advocacy of Spanish claims by Vergennes was not a violation of those provisions. The one definite promise by France was to continue war until independence of the colonies should be, "formally or tacitly," not even acknowledged but "assured." Even this was drafted to meet the anticipated attitude of Spain, should she join in the war, although it was explained to the Americans as calculated to meet the possible obstinacy of George III, who might refuse to concede immediate independence, as Spain had done for sixty years in the case of the Netherlands, thirty-nine of them a truce. Spain had barely joined France when she started a mediation with Britain, one part of which was to be a long-term truce with the colonies. Vergennes instructed Luzerne to present the matter to Congress "with all possible caution," lest they "might suspect . . . an intention to stop at a truce." Floridablanca suggested, as the basis of a truce, terms which would have left the St. Lawrence valley in possession of Britain and all the territory between the Mississippi and Alleghenies in possession of Spain. Congress, ignorant of what lay behind the truce proposal, did approve it as permissible if preceded by withdrawal of all British troops from the colonies. But nothing came of the matter.[44]

France was the head of a coalition of four powers; her interests were primarily European. She could give them precedence so far as she was unconstrained by the treaty with the colonies, and that was drafted by Vergennes with extraordinary foresight and astuteness in order to leave him freedom in gaining the aid of Spanish ships and bullion. Of course, France did not treat the united colonies and Spain evenhandedly as separate allies. Whether she violated the mutual pledge in the American treaty to be "good and faithful allies" is another matter, dependent on the terms of the treaty. Whether Vergennes used his foresightedness and astuteness honorably in so drafting it as to insure freedom of action is an inquiry above the norms of politics. After all, the col-

---

[43] July 18, 1779, and January 22, 1781, *ibid.*, pp. 148, 145.

[44] Wharton, *Dip. Corr.*, III, 247; letters of Vergennes, July 18 and September 25, 1779, in Jay, *Peace Negotiations*, pp. 149, 151; Doniol, *Établissement des États-Unis*, III, 395, 472–473, 521–525, 556–559, 593, 596–599, 600–603, 613, 626–636; *J.C.C.*, XX, 618, 651. Wharton discussed this truce episode at length, *Dip. Corr.*, I, index, *s.v.* "truce."

onies did not go to France as a friend, but only as the great enemy of Britain; and they were received as another enemy of Britain. They received the commercial treaty and alliance for which they asked, and accepted the terms. And Franklin, who was constantly wise even if perhaps sometimes mistaken, thought them fair. As Vergennes said, it was unreasonable to expect that the King of France, out of love for the Americans, would subordinate the interests of his uncle, the King of Spain.[45]

France and Spain made their secret alliance in April, 1779, and war between Spain and Britain began in June. As soon as the alliance was made, Vergennes became impatient for the appointment of peace commissioners by Congress.[46] The preparation of their instructions, which was undertaken first, involved momentous problems, and the debates on boundaries speedily revealed the dangers presented by the gratitude of Congress for French aid and its deference to the advice of the French ministers. In 1779 it resolved, after debate, to make the Mississippi as a western boundary, and navigation of it to the Gulf, ultimatums, notwithstanding that a southern boundary at 31° was also given the same status; the navigation claim was therefore obviously independent.[47] Immediately, the French minister urged that "just and moderate terms" be offered Spain, "proper . . . to reconcile His Catholic Majesty perfectly to the American interests" and induce his effectual mediation with Great Britain.[48] In fact, war with Britain had then begun. To this advice Congress answered by insisting on the middle of the Mississippi as the western boundary down to 31°, but it offered to recede from its (assumed) right of navigation below 31° in return for a free port on the river and to guarantee the Floridas in exchange for an alliance.[49]

Meanwhile John Jay had departed for Spain as minister plenipoten-

[45] *Ibid.*, VI, 150. Lecky is one of those who saw that Vergennes never opposed American interests "on any point on which he had promised to support them." W. E. H. Lecky, *A History of England in the Eighteenth Century* (8 vols., London, 1878–1900), IV, 262.

[46] Wharton, *Dip. Corr.*, III, 16, 85.

[47] *Ibid.*, pp. 58–61, 88, 89, 302; *J.C.C.*, XIII, 244, 339–341, XIV, 959–960. Under prevailing law no property right of navigation could extend below 31°.

[48] July 12, 1779, Wharton, *Dip. Corr.*, p. 248.

[49] And on the north a line from its source to Lake Nipissing, thence to the intersection of the St. Lawrence River with the parallel of 45° north (at Cornwall, Ontario). *Ibid.*, pp. 300, 301; *J.C.C.*, XIV, 959 (report of August 19, 1779). Wharton, *Dip. Corr.*, III, 343–344, 373.

tiary, arriving in Cadiz late in January, 1780. Almost simultaneously, Luzerne requested of Congress a precise statement of its attitude toward renunciation of claims west of the Appalachians, toward the propriety of permanent Spanish conquests east of the Mississippi, and toward renunciation of American claims of navigation rights therein, "no territory belonging to them being situated thereon."[50] At that very time Governor Galvez was occupying Baton Rouge and Natchez. Shortly thereafter the Spanish minister of foreign affairs warned Jay that Spain would never mitigate the exclusion of all foreigners from the Gulf of Mexico; that this was the principal objective of the war.[51] Both parties thus made navigation of the Mississippi the crucial issue in their future relations. In the autumn of 1780 Congress reiterated its demand, but offered to guarantee the Floridas in exchange for an outlet to the Gulf through West Florida.[52] The southern colonies, after they were invaded by the British late in 1780, persuaded Congress to relax navigation claims below 31° north if necessary to secure a Spanish alliance. Jay, without disclosing such instructions (which he knew to be impracticable), went no farther than to reduce his claim of right to a hope, a change to which the Spaniards gave no attention, although Congress in May had no doubt that an alliance would follow.[53]

There was no basis upon which the colonies could challenge Spain's conquest of areas admittedly British since 1763, unless they were demonstrably within the limits of those colonies, and none of her conquests was. After the fall of Pensacola, Luzerne demanded (June, 1781) that Congress renounce its ultimatum of Mississippi navigation and instruct John Adams to follow the instructions of Vergennes. Congress did abandon the boundary ultimatum, though preserving its terms as "desire and expectations"; declared insistence on independence and continuance of the French alliance only; and agreed to put American interests

[50] February 2, 1780, *ibid.*, p. 489.

[51] *Ibid.*, pp. 529, 724; IV, 136–137, 145–146; H. F. Johnston (ed.), *Correspondence and Papers of John Jay* (4 vols., New York, 1893), I, 316–326, 424–425.

[52] October-November, 1780, *J.C.C.*, XVIII, 900, 908, 935–947. In this last committee report of October 16, four reasons were given for refusing to renounce the overmountain region to Spain (one entirely acceptable, one wholly otherwise, two highly disputable).

[53] *Ibid.*, pp. 1070, 1121, 1131; XIX, 151–154 (February 15), 554; Wharton, *Dip. Corr.*, IV, 258, 381, V, 760. Congress had, on an earlier day, weakened even more, resolving to renounce the Mississippi boundary claim "if indispensably necessary"; but it never, in instructing Jay, thought it indispensably necessary.

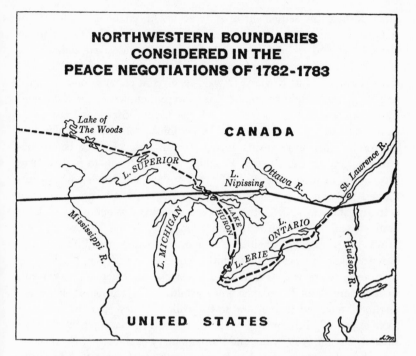

under the control—unqualified and therefore seemingly complete as to all matters—of the French ministry. Our envoy was to "undertake nothing without their concurrence," to be governed "ultimately . . . by their advice and opinion."[54] The peace commissioners (Franklin never doubting) ultimately interpreted this as equivalent to earlier instructions to be guided "by the alliance . . . by the advice of our allies, by . . . our interests, and by your own discretion."[55]

Far more time was devoted to the boundary claims (and other claims attached to them in bargaining) than to other issues. "It would be endless," Franklin wrote to Congress, "to enumerate all the discussions and arguments on the subject."

The course of negotiations was slow, but for reasons external, in

[54] F. Wharton, *Dip. Corr.,* IV, 440 (June 6–14), 471–481.
[55] *Ibid.,* 716–717 (Jay), V, 839 (Adams); for instructions of August, 1779, see III, 302. A final and extremely interesting debate on the danger of allowing France to control the boundary claims, recorded by Charles Thomson, is *ibid.,* V, 645–650.

large part, to the settlement of differences. An enabling act for negotiations was not passed by Parliament until June, 1782. Dissensions in
the cabinet and the death of the prime minister delayed action until
after Lord Shelburne became premier in the first days of July. Dissensions continued, but Richard Oswald received a commission in August
to treat with "certain colonies." Weeks were then devoted to a demand
by Congress that Britain treat "with the United States as free, sovereign, and independent States." The commissioners, in particular Jay,
interpreted this as requiring recognition of independence before negotiating any treaty, whereas Franklin was indifferent to it.[56] A mere
recognition of independence by Britain unilaterally, leaving wholly unaltered the mutual relations of the two powers, would not have been
a treaty, and—in view of the supposed objectives of one party in England—would have been extremely dangerous to the United States.[57]
It was the proposal of Shelburne's opponents, who scorned his policy of
ensuring that independence should be true independence, particularly
of France. Moreover, as Shelburne's peace commissioner pointed out,
such a mere grant of independence would imply "cession of the whole
territory" assigned to the new states while colonies—part of which, it
soon appeared, Britain wished to retain in negotiating peace.[58] Fortunately for the Americans, the Parliamentary enabling act for treating
with the colonies was stated to be one for the settlement of differences,
and thus barred a separate grant of independence.[59] That plan, therefore, was in two ways impossible, and in several dangerous for both
parties. The Americans eventually contented themselves with the courtesy of being called the commissioners of "the United States of America" in the commission given to the British negotiator, together with
an understanding that independence should be granted by the first
article of a treaty.[60] This was late in September, 1782. Only then could
official negotiations begin. However, a great deal had been done unofficially long before.

The acquisition of Canada had been declared by Congress, in its

[56] *Ibid.,* VI, 132.
[57] Wharton, *Digest,* III, 938–942, 945–949 (Jay), 921 (Franklin).
[58] On the difficulties raised, see Lecky, *History of England,* IV, 235; Wharton, *Digest,* III, 933, 943, 945; Wharton, *Dip. Corr.,* I, sec. 109 *et seq.*
[59] Wharton, *Digest,* III, 943.
[60] Other material on the difficulties of the "independence first" idea will be
found in *Dip. Corr.,* II, 425, III, 247, 175–177, V, 613, 748, 779, 805, VI,
131. Also Wharton, *Digest,* III, 905, 943.

final instructions to the commissioners, to be "of utmost importance."[61] In April, 1782, after Franklin and Shelburne had exchanged friendly notes following the latter's joining the Rockingham ministry, Franklin suggested to Oswald that Britain offer Canada as an essential for permanent good relations, rather than have America demand it. Franklin also gave him a memorandum of other points on which he had made suggestions. One was an offer of open trade with Canada free of all duties. Another, that "so much of the vacant land there . . . be sold" as should indemnify both the Loyalists and the victims of British military spoliations.[62] This recognition of Loyalist claims was so inconsistent with Franklin's implacable hostility to them that he did not reveal it to John Adams, as he noted in his diary. In making the suggestion he certainly knew that Shelburne would consider it better to keep lands for the Loyalists than to cede lands and let the Americans judge Loyalist claims. Franklin was clearly giving notice that the Loyalist claims and British spoliations would not be separated by the Americans, yet intimating that the British *could* separate them by assuming the Loyalists' losses. It seemed perfectly safe, for he felt that Britain could not keep all of what was then Canada. Finally, he made very clear to Oswald his anxiety lest France learn of his proposals. It was a matter of exceeding importance, and particularly as regarded the diplomatic problem, because Britain's retention of Canada was basic in French policy; and certainly Franklin knew that perfectly well from Gérard's and Luzerne's communications to Congress.[63]

Here, then, were negotiations between Franklin and Shelburne on the most vital problems of the peace, and Franklin was plainly promising not to make them known to Vergennes. He was asking for separate negotiations.[64] Franklin's suggestion respecting Canada and his memorandum of other points went, of course, immediately before the cabinet. In that, there would presumably have been a basic preference for separate negotiations in order to escape French intervention in a family dispute. There must also have been in all government circles, however,

[61] Wharton, *Dip. Corr.*, III, 302; *J.C.C.*, XIV, 959–960; also XIII, 244, 339–341.

[62] W. T. Franklin (ed.), *The Personal Correspondence of Benjamin Franklin* (8° ed., London, 1817), pp. 133, 134, 135, 143–146.

[63] Wharton, *Dip. Corr.*, V, 538, 541, 547; E. G. Fitzmaurice, *Life of William, Earl of Shelburne* (2nd ed., 2 vols., London, 1912), II, 122. Franklin confessed to Congress that he withheld from John Adams the fact that he even suggested some indemnity to the Loyalists; Wharton, *Dip. Corr.*, V, 540.

[64] Jay, *Peace Negotiations*, p. 52, was depreciatory.

some distrust of Franklin ever since the official denunciation of him to the Privy Council in 1774 as an unscrupulous plotter. And there were divisions in the cabinet. Shelburne was conducting separate negotiations as secretary for the colonies. If joined with the European negotiations, they would be controlled by Charles James Fox as secretary for foreign affairs; and he was believed by some to favor recognition merely of independence, without settlement of other disputes, in order to permit harassment of the new states.

Early in June, Oswald gave Franklin a paper written by Lord Shelburne in which he expressed his willingness to "correspond more particularly with Dr. Franklin if wished" and Britain's willingness to take measures *"conducive to a final settlement of things between Great Britain and America,"* and cautioned Oswald "That an establishment for the Loyalists must always be upon Mr. Oswald's mind, as it is *uppermost* in Lord Shelburne's, besides other steps in their favor."[65]

On May 8 Oswald had thought, Franklin wrote, that the matter of Canada would be settled as the latter desired. After receiving the instructions last quoted, he advised the government to cede the province. Shelburne was not surprised, because he knew Franklin, but it soon became apparent that he was determined to hold the Northwest added to Canada by the Quebec Act.[66]

The British found it extremely difficult to refrain from setting conditions on the independence which the vote of the Commons on General Conway's motion forced them to concede. On June 23 the cabinet instructed Oswald "to insist in the strongest manner that if America was to be independent she must be so to the whole world, and not attempt any connection with France, and to declare that if the negotiation broke off, all the rights of England to America were to stand as before."[67] After these helpless protests, he was further instructed that reparations to America for British spoliations were not to be heard of, and that there could be no recognition of independence unless the Loyalists were "taken care of"—that is, by the Americans.

It happened that at this time news reached London of Rodney's

[65] Lecky, *History of England,* IV, 229, 232, 234, 235, 261, 262; Wharton, *Digest,* III, 894.

[66] Wharton, *Dip. Corr.,* V, 571; VI, 132; Franklin, *Personal Correspondence,* p. 209; Bodley has reported further and abundant evidence of Shelburne's determination in his unpublished papers. *Our First Great West,* pp. 230, 231, 237, 239, 240–241, 268–270, 272, 278.

[67] Fitzmaurice, *Shelburne,* II, 126–127.

destruction of the French fleet in the West Indies. In cabinet council of June 27, conflicting opinions appeared for "independence . . . [not on] condition of a general peace," "negotiation . . . directly, instead of through France," and "independence . . . and . . . restitution of matters to the state of 1763." Oswald showed Franklin a memorandum of the meeting. It left with him an impression that the British would seek to make independence dependent on restoring America to her situation under the peace of 1763. Vergennes and Grenville agreed with him that this referred to restoration of West Indies islands held by France since 1763. "This seems to me," Franklin wrote, "a proposition of selling to us a thing that is already our own, and of making France pay the price."[68] If this was the intent, it would have tied the American and European issues of the peace inextricably together. But if that was the immediate effect of Rodney's triumph upon some members of the cabinet, the British government soon settled definitely on the second plan of separate negotiations.

On July 1 the death of Lord Rockingham dissolved the ministry, and Shelburne soon became the head of a new one. About this time Franklin became ill, although he saw more or less of Jay (Adams was not yet in Paris) and was mentally quite unchanged. Both were consequently left more than before to their own devices. On July 1, also, Franklin abandoned the diary which he had theretofore faithfully compiled for transmission to Congress. On July 9, without informing anybody, he gave to Oswald his ideas of what the peace should be, listing its provisions under the headings "necessary" and "desirable." Having implanted in Shelburne's mind the idea of indemnifying the Loyalists with Canadian lands, it could not have surprised him that the use of the Ohio region should occur to the British as desirable for that purpose. He now warned them off of it by including under "necessary" terms a provision that Canada's boundaries should not exceed those it had before the Quebec Act, and strengthened the warning with three admonitory "desirables"—one of these being a cession of "every part" of Canada. Shelburne knew Franklin well, and could not have misinterpreted the "necessary." It was seemingly acquiesced in by the ministry.[69]

[68] *Ibid.*, 122–128, 132–133; Franklin, *Personal Correspondence*, pp. 161, 164, 168; Lecky, *History of England*, IV, 227–228; Wharton, *Dip. Corr.*, V, 543, 549.

[69] Wharton, *Dip. Corr.*, VI, 132; Franklin, *Personal Correspondence*, pp.

However, be that as it may, the negotiations were never, in consequence, so limited. Nothing whatever was dropped by the British from the field of contention. On July 27, in instructions to Oswald, he was told: "In case you find that the American Commissioners are not at liberty to treat on any terms short of independence, you . . . have our authority to make that concession."[70] And in the same instructions there continued the curious joinder of some terms so illiberal that they would bar any settlement save independence with others offering mutually liberal relations. So, of course, demands for the Ohio area continued. "They wanted," Franklin wrote, "to settle their loyalists in the Illinois Country." And, in their final joint report, the commissioners wrote: "They claimed not only all the lands . . . not expressly included in our charters, but also all such lands within them as remained ungranted by the King."[71]

The negotiations between Franklin and Shelburne—which were not only separate from those with France and her allies but independent of the other American commissioners—fixed the essential framework of the peace. Oswald, in conversation with Franklin, expressed in August the opinion that Franklin's "necessary" provisions "would pretty nearly end the business," dropping or modifying those submitted as "desirable." He reported this as the assurance of a friend of Franklin in England.[72] As a matter of fact the "desirable" articles were all dropped. On September 1, Secretary Townshend sent Oswald the ministry's acceptance of the "necessary" items.

A leading authority has concluded that there never was a chance of getting all of Canada; another, that Franklin, left alone, could have secured it.[73] At any rate let it be noted that the line demanded by Congress from the Mississippi's head to Lake Nipissing, north of all

163, 209, 210. The other "necessaries" were independence and the fisheries; the other "desirables" were mutual equality of trading privileges in the two countries (of immense importance to Britain, and of equal appeal to Shelburne) and indemnity for spoliations by the British army.

[70] Wharton, *Dip. Corr.*, V, 571.

[71] Fitzmaurice, *Shelburne*, II, 165–166, 170, 173. Compare the dates of material noted by Bodley in his unprinted papers.

[72] Wharton, *Dip. Corr.*, VI, 113. He was to demand indemnity for Loyalists, claim New York so far as still occupied, do everything possible "to prevent the United States entering into any binding connection with any other power" (that is, deny them, just preceding acknowledgment of their independence, the quality of independence), yet propose "an unreserved system of naturalization."

[73] S. F. Bemis, "Canada and the Peace Settlement of 1783," *CHR*, XIV (1933), 273; Wharton, *Digest*, III, 919, 929, 930.

the Great Lakes except Superior, stood unchanged until, at the end, by the suggestion of the American commissioners, it was abandoned for a line, better for both countries, through the middle of the Great Lakes.[74] As for the Ohio-Illinois region, various reasons suggested for its release by Great Britain have no support in the record.[75] Shelburne strove to the very end to hold it for the Loyalists, and Britain ceded it because forced to do so.[76] There is no reference in the negotiations to Clark's conquest. Franklin had known of it for three years; no doubt all the Americans had. If Lord Shelburne had believed the British in effective control in 1782 or 1783, surely he would have used that reason to resist cession of the region. Clark's fairly effective military predominance must certainly, therefore, have strengthened the American claims, but the ideas that Clark drove the British from the Mississippi valley, or compelled cession of the Northwest, are unduly extreme.[77]

Spain had hoped to secure consideration of her claims in European-American negotiations, and the Spanish ambassador in Paris, the Conde de Aranda, repeatedly sought interviews with Jay. The latter, however, who had wasted two years in Spain, insisted that negotiations begin with the invariable formality of exhibiting powers, but this would have required recognition of rebellious colonies in Aranda's, and of course they contained none.[78] However, by Vergennes' direction, his undersecretary, Rayneval, prepared a map of Spain's boundary claims (which

[74] *Ibid.*, p. 944.

[75] That she had learned the cost of Indian wars, that the fur trade was decreasing, that it was all shifting to New Orleans, and so on.

[76] Compare Wharton, *Dip. Corr.*, V, 747, and *Digest*, III, 907; Fitzmaurice, *Shelburne*, II, 207. There is therefore no basis whatever for criticizing Franklin for not mentioning the Mississippi in his memorandum (Abernethy, *Western Lands*, pp. 283–284). The Mississippi was never in doubt. Nor is there any trace of evidence to support Abernethy's assertion "that Franklin and his friends in Congress would have been glad to see the Northwest territory [left] in British hands," *Western Lands*, p. 285.

[77] An older view was expressed by Paxson: "Campaigns inspired by the West and directed by its leaders saw to it that when the independence was secured the boundary should not be on the summit of the Alleghanies, but at the Mississippi." *MVHR*, XXI, 376–378. This view originated with Alvord, *MVHR*, III (1916), 34, 37. Compare corrective discussions by J. A. James in Amer. Hist. Association, *Report* for 1917, pp. 315, 329; *Ill. Hist. Coll.*, XIX (1926), lv–lxv; *MVHR*, XVII (1930), 114–115. That Clark's presence saved the Northwest from possibly effective Spanish operations is highly probable; T. C. and M. J. Pease, *George Rogers Clark*, pp. 63–65. But this was of no importance in the peace negotiations.

[78] Wharton, *Dip. Corr.*, V, 321, VI, 25, 28, 45.

were much the same in 1782 as in 1763) and a memoir defending them. They made a slight concession in dividing the West into three zones—British, American, and Spanish, Spain claiming the Southwest below the Cumberland and Hiwasee rivers.[79] This map, seemingly countenanced by Vergennes, greatly alarmed Jay; and when Rayneval slipped off furtively to London, Jay (who was bearing the burden of negotiation while Franklin was ill) sent to Shelburne an agent, a friend of both Shelburne and Franklin, to thwart a suspected intrigue. He overestimated the danger, though he rightly sensed the hostile purpose of Rayneval's trip.[80] That Spain adhered to former claims west of the Alleghenies was fact, and that Vergennes' support of her continued was to be expected. Remarks to that effect by Rayneval in his talk with Shelburne were quite innocuous. Shelburne curtly indicated that he had no interest in Spain's claims.[81] Robert Livingston, American secretary for foreign affairs, had himself suggested to the American commissioners an Indian buffer territory if a deadlock with Spain should arise, but circumstances had excluded that contingency.[82]

Although Jay's fear that Franklin was too inattentive to Vergennes' support of claims dangerous to American interests was exaggerated, the result of his approach to Shelburne was to put the British-American negotiations on a firmer basis. It suggested to the British the possibility

[79] For the memoir, see *ibid.*, 25–28; or *J.C.C.*, XXXI, 546–541; or Johnstone, *Jay Correspondence*, II, 394–398. Vergennes admitted responsibility, Jay, *Peace Negotiations*, p. 156. The memoir does no credit to Vergennes, for it (1) treated the Proclamation line of 1763 as a political boundary; (2) ignored the facts regarding Louisiana's and Canada's boundaries established by the negotiations of 1762; (3) attributed to the southwestern Indians definite territorial locations (contrary to French arguments of 1755). Moreover, it disingenuously treated the buffer areas that Britain proposed in 1754 as suggesting a colonial boundary, although they were nothing but areas within which conflicting claims should be postponed.

[80] Jay's suspicions, Wharton, *Dip. Corr.*, VI, 28–29; instructions to his agent, *ibid.*, 30–32. On Rayneval's trip (inquiry as to sincerity of Shelburne), *ibid.*, V, 607, 612, 616, 855–857, Jay, *Peace Negotiations*, p. 159. Franklin knew the facts, *Private Correspondence*, p. 263, contemporaneous letter; *Writings* (Smyth ed.), VIII, 616, later official report. Rayneval's instructions from and report to Vergennes are in Doniol, *Établissement des États-Unis*, V, 103, 105–106, 121–145; Wharton, *Dip. Corr.*, V, 821–822, I, 361; Jay, *Peace Negotiations*, p. 42.

[81] Doniol, *Établissement des États-Unis*, V, 132–133; Fitzmaurice, *Shelburne*, III, 263; Jay, *Peace Negotiations*, p. 160.

[82] Wharton, *Dip. Corr.*, V, 89.

that the American commissioners might be induced to make peace quite independently of Vergennes, and *that* might make possible satisfaction of the condition which Shelburne attached to recognition of independence—that it must be independence, specifically of France. This, however, could be assured only by making bilateral agreements fully secured against change by a general treaty between Britain and all the allied powers. To that too, it turned out, Vergennes was to make no objection.

A week after the talks with Jay's agent, the cabinet resolved (September 19) to continue the bilateral bargaining and to give Oswald a new commission to treat with the commissioners "of the United States of America." Jay's emissary to Shelburne returned on September 27 to Paris with Oswald, the latter with his new commission and unlimited powers.[83] Official negotiations between Britain and the Americans, and also between Britain and the European powers (until then postponed), could now begin. The question whether Vergennes should be privy to the former immediately arose.[84] Franklin acceded to the desire of Jay and Adams that Vergennes should not be informed of the progress of the British-American negotiations, although he thought this unnecessary, since the essential points had already been settled by his negotiations with Shelburne, and he had no fear that Vergennes would object to any agreements made.

The procedural issue on which they differed was actually of slight importance—but only Franklin could know that. Of no greater importance was the difference in personal characteristics which created the issue. Jay was reserved and unbending, with a lawyer's caution of all loopholes. Adams was excitable and contentious. Franklin was steadily a calm, reflective man of the world. But Congress knew all of them well, and knew the patriotism of all to be absolute. After all was over, Franklin wrote to the Congress:

with respect to myself, neither the letter to Mr. Marbois . . . nor the conversations respecting the fishery, the boundaries, the royalists, &c., recommending moderation in our demands, are of weight sufficient in my mind to fix an opinion that this court [the French] wished to restrain us in obtaining any degree of advantage we could prevail on our enemies to accord. [They

[83] *Ibid.*, V, 747, 748, 778; Wharton, *Digest*, III, 905, 944, 945, 950.
[84] C. F. Adams (ed.), *The Works of John Adams* (10 vols., Boston, 1850–56), III, 336; Jay, *Peace Negotiations*, p. 54; Fitzmaurice, *Shelburne*, II, 183.

might have expressed] a very natural apprehension that we . . . might insist on more advantages than the English would . . . grant, and thereby lose the opportunity of making peace, so necessary to all our friends.[85]

After this decision, progress was rapid. "Preliminary" articles agreed to by Oswald were ready in two weeks (October 8).[86] They were essentially, of course, those made unofficially long before with Franklin. Shelburne sent an additional commissioner to make a last attempt to keep the Northwest for the Loyalists, but Franklin presented the record of spoliations by British troops and both claims were dropped.[87] Congress, early in the month, had formally barred any reparation for the Loyalists, but that action was not needed.[88] Nothing more happened affecting the West, save the change of the Canadian line to the middle of the Lakes at the suggestion of the American commissioners.[89] On November 30 the preliminary articles were signed, to become final when again signed as part of the general treaty.[90]

Did the United States gain anything by dealing separately with the British? It is possible that Britain made greater concessions within the family circle than she would have made to the colonies led by France. What the American commissioners chiefly feared in a general negotiation, however, was French support of Spain's claims of land east of the Mississippi, against which they were united and adamant.[91] Meanwhile, Vergennes knew that the British were contemptuous of Spain's claims, and that he had lost all means of constraining the Americans when the Commons had assured them peace. He could have prolonged negotiations, but only vainly as respected the Americans if they stood

---

[85] The intercepted letter of Barbé Marbois, Secretary of the French Legation at Philadelphia, in which the Frenchman denounced America's claims to the fisheries, caused a stir among the Americans at Paris, particularly John Jay. The letter is printed in Franklin, *Personal Correspondence,* pp. 324–328; on its effect upon other commissioners, pp. 319, 413.

[86] Wharton, *Dip. Corr.,* VI, 47.

[87] *Ibid.,* V, 842, 845, 849; VI, 77–80, 112.

[88] *J.C.C.,* XIV, 563 (September 10); Wharton, *Dip. Corr.,* V, 849.

[89] Wharton, *Digest,* III, 944.

[90] Miller, *International Acts,* II, 96.

[91] Choiseul, in 1762, had been forced to exclude Grimaldi by double-dealing with the British Ministry. Vergennes expressed to the French ambassador in Madrid in January, 1781, his conviction that Spain, in general negotiations, would make her every demand a primary issue, as in 1762. Separate negotiations saved him from useless embarrassments. Later letters emphasized a resolution to ignore Spain. See also Wharton, *Dip. Corr.,* V, 300, 585, 657; VI, 22–25. For Shelburne's part in the preliminaries, see V. T. Harlow, *The Founding of the Second British Empire, 1763–1793* (London, 1952), I, 223–311.

firm. With perfect good will toward the Americans, and in disregard of Spanish claims, Vergennes insisted upon execution of the British-American preliminary treaty before proceeding with the European negotiations. He had not complained to Franklin of the separate negotiations when he first learned of them. When he did, long afterward, Franklin minimized the act as only a discourtesy.[92] If the other allies lost nothing substantial, he was justified. The question is important. Honor certainly required preservation of allied unity so far and so long as required for the protection of substantial interests of an ally. Spain was not an ally of the colonies, because she would not recognize them; she was and had long been France's ally, and to that alliance their hope of taking Gibraltar was of immense significance. Rodney's victory had destroyed one hope for coercion of Britain in the peace, but the siege of Gibraltar had not yet been raised. It was Lecky's opinion that the separate American negotiations saved England that prop of empire.[93]

After all was settled, the American commissioners wrote to Congress: "Since we have assumed a place in the political system of the world, let us move like a primary and not like a secondary planet."[94] Forty years passed before the right of the United States to do that was so undeniable that she could proclaim it to the world and anticipate no challenge.

[92] Wharton, *Dip. Corr.*, VI, 113, 140, 143, 107, 150.
[93] *History of England*, IV, 258–259, 263; C. R. King (ed.), *The Life and Correspondence of Rufus King* (6 vols., New York, 1894–1900), IV, 93.
[94] July 18, 1783, Wharton, *Dip. Corr.*, VI, 568.

CHAPTER 4

Settlement and Separatism in the Confederation Era

WESTERN settlement increased rapidly during the era of the Confederation. There had always and everywhere been a constant border extrusion of adventurers, and after the expulsion of France, and establishment of a semblant British control of the far interior, drifters multiplied in the western wilderness. However, although from then onward substantial and quickening, the migration was slight in comparison with that of Confederation years. Such vivid statements as that squatters' cabins in the decade and more preceding the Proclamation of 1763 "drifted down the western slope of the Alleghenies to the basins of the Ohio, the Cumberland, and the Tennessee," that settlers in the 1760's were "pouring over" the mountains, that there were thousands in the "vicinity" of Fort Pitt by the early 1770's, and that thousands were "swarming" into the area of the proposed Vandalia Colony have some truth; but they are likely to be misleading unless given a prosaic interpretation.[1] There was a steady advance, but one easily exaggerated by imagination.

By 1790 the spread of population beyond the southern Appalachians, and particularly into West Virginia and Kentucky, was far greater than

[1] F. L. Paxson, *When the West Is Gone* (New York, 1930), p. 20; C. W. Alvord, "The British Ministry and the Treaty of Fort Stanwix," Wis. State Hist. Soc., *Proceedings*, LVI (for 1908), 174; T. C. and M. J. Pease, *George Rogers Clark and the Revolution in Illinois, 1763–1787* (Springfield, 1929), pp. 22, 23.

its advance northwest of the Ohio. This was because the relations of the northern and southern Indian tribes to Kentucky, and Sir William Johnson's special relations with the former, had made possible the clearing of Indian claims to lands south, but not north, of the Ohio River.

Considering first the Northwest, some of its early settlements have already been casually mentioned. Those existing in Fayette County, Pennsylvania, in the years 1751–54 were abandoned during the war, re-established after 1758, again abandoned during Pontiac's War, and probably became permanent after 1765.[2] There were other settlements on the Greenbrier and Monongahela rivers in West Virginia and Pennsylvania which may all have begun by 1760.[3] A great increase in them took place in the 1770's. In the portion of West Virginia lying south of Maryland, there were perhaps 4,000 in both 1760 and 1770, four-fifths of them in the larger western section, including the headwaters of the New Kanawha and Greenbrier rivers.[4] By 1780 the population had doubled in the western and trebled in the eastern section. In West Virginia south of Pennsylvania and west of Maryland's westernmost line, which includes the upper Monongahela, there were not over 200 settlers in 1760 nor over 400 in 1770; in the next decade they increased more than thirtyfold.

Consider now western Pennsylvania. If one takes the line of 78° west longitude, which runs through McConnelsburg, the population to the westward in 1760 was perhaps around 3,500, but that number had increased threefold by 1770, fivefold by 1780, and fifteenfold by 1790. By the latter date there were one and one-half times as many settlers in Ohio, along the Ohio River down to Marietta, as there had been in Pennsylvania west of McConnellsburg in 1760. Even up to 1790 the

---

[2] A. P. James, "The First English-speaking Trans-Appalachian Frontier," *MVHR*, XVII (1931), 59, 61.

[3] Settlers dispersed by Colonel Bouquet in 1761 were doubtless on the Monongahela in Pennsylvania, and were those to which John Pownall vaguely referred in 1763 as in "the forks of the Ohio." *Eng. Hist. Rev.*, L, 260.

[4] These and the following statements are based upon the work of H. Fries, "A Series of Population Maps of the Colonies and of the United States, 1625–1790," in *Geographical Review*, XXX (1940), 463–479. In giving total numbers—that is, in interpreting the meaning of Fries's dots in his maps—decided conservatism has been exercised, but in statements of *comparative* growth the dots have merely been counted (using by Fries's courtesy his original large maps). Estimates by speculators were vast exaggerations. A Westsylvania petition of 1776 estimated settlement within Vandalia as not less than 25,000 families (at least 150,000). G. H. Alden, *New Governments West of the Alleghenies before 1780* (Madison, 1897), p. 68.

Allegheny River area of northwestern Pennsylvania had extremely few inhabitants.

There was a great deal of "state-making" in the western country during the Confederation period—that is, the formation of settlements, of varying population and degrees of political organization, which aspired, or allegedly aspired, to be independent of the seaboard states. Some citizens were always ready to move, and land speculators found the weakness of the Confederation and state governments propitious for diverting settlers to areas to which they secured the title and of which they hoped to gain political control.

The only one of these interior "states" that was projected in the Northwest was Westsylvania.[5] It received a death blow from a Pennsylvania law in 1782, but that was six years after a petition to Congress for its recognition as a state.[6] Its bounds would have included land now lying in Virginia, West Virginia, Maryland, and Pennsylvania. It originated in the desires of land speculators, primarily those of George Croghan and the members of the Indiana Company, who sought to protect in this manner claims once believed to be protected by the Vandalia grant. When Croghan became allied with Lord Dunmore and other Virginia speculators, this tied the scheme to all the difficulties arising from the boundary dispute between Virginia and Pennsylvania. Since the success of the plan would have cut from the latter state her southwestern corner, west of the Youghiogheny River, and much land from Virginia, the petition could never have been formally considered by Congress, but it undoubtedly affected the long struggle that secured for the Confederation all of Virginia's claims to territory north of the Ohio.

The first settlers of the mountain valleys of the South came from the north down the Great Valley of Virginia in the 1740's and 1750's, and the earliest settlement of the Virginia and North Carolina piedmont was a continuation of this southward flow.[7] The same is true even down into middle Georgia, a large portion of which was settled by 1784. The

[5] B. Grumrine (ed.), *History of Washington County, Pennsylvania* (Philadelphia, 1882), pp. 187–188; Alden, *New Governments*, pp. 64–68; S. J. and E. Buck, *The Planting of Civilization in Western Pennsylvania* (Pittsburgh, 1939), pp. 170–172; J. P. Boyd, "Attempts to Form New States in New York and Pennsylvania," N.Y. Hist. Soc., *Bulletin*, XII, 257–270; A. T. Volwiler, *George Croghan and the Western Movement, 1741–1782* (Cleveland, 1926), p. 313.

[6] *Amer. Archives,* 4th Series, I, 1061–63.

[7] F. H. Hart, *The Valley of Virginia in the American Revolution, 1763–*

broad pine barrens of that state and South Carolina, which hindered the westward extension of plantation industry, were also unattractive for backwoods farming, so that the tide of pioneers down the great Appalachian valley preceded any settlement of the piedmont from the coast.[8]

The northeastern corner of Tennessee, where it bounds on Virginia, was the site of Watauga, the earliest instance of unofficial statemaking in the West.[9] In 1768–69, pioneers of Virginia and North Carolina under the lead of James Robertson settled on the Watauga and other streams of the Holston area. It was a case of wholly individual migration and settlement. It was also truly democratic in character. Too far removed from the organized county government of North Carolina to be cared for by it, these borderers entered into a compact of self-government (1772) which was modeled on the articles of "association" adopted by the Regulators of North Carolina. Erroneously believing themselves to be within Virginia, they adopted the statutes of that state as models for their legislation (just as the majority of many a state constitutional convention would later honor their natal state), elected magistrates, set up a government, and lived under it successfully and in seeming contentment for about four years. As Lord Dunmore reported to the British government, they managed their own affairs as "an inconsiderable, yet a separate State. A dangerous example to the people of America, of forming governments distinct from and independent of His Majesty's authority."[10] They lived, seemingly, a satisfactorily orderly life, ignoring in 1774 an order of the governor of North Carolina (within whose boundaries their settlement actually lay)

1789 (Chapel Hill, 1942). On squatters in Pennsylvania by 1726, see W. R. Shepherd, *History of the Proprietary Government in Pennsylvania* (New York, 1896), pp. 49–53. Ballagh estimated that squatter holdings comprised two-thirds of the Pennsylvania acreage settled between 1732 and 1740. Amer. Hist. Assoc., *Report* for 1899, pp. 112, 113.

[8] D. H. Bacot, "The South Carolina Up Country at the End of the Eighteenth Century," *AHR*, XXVIII (1923), 682–698; U. B. Phillips, *Plantation and Frontier* (Washington, 1910), I, 78–85.

[9] Accounts rest largely on J. G. M. Ramsay, *Annals of Tennessee* (Philadelphia, 1853), pp. 144–148. Other accounts are in A. V. Goodpasture, "The Watauga Association," *Amer. Hist. Mag.*, III (1898), 103–120; J. W. Caldwell, *Studies in the Constitutional History of Tennessee* (Cincinnati, 1895), pp. 1–33; A. Henderson, *The Conquest of the Old Southwest* (New York, 1920), pp. 187, 197–200, 259; T. P. Abernethy, *From Frontier to Plantation in Tennessee* (Chapel Hill, 1932), Chap. 1.

[10] R. G. Thwaites and Kellogg (eds.), *Documentary History of Dunmore's War* (Madison, 1905), pp. 368, 371.

to remove from the Indian country. Moreover, they plainly evidenced the genuine excuse for their "separatism" in petitioning in July, 1776, to be readmitted under North Carolina's jurisdiction and bear their share of the costs of the Revolution. The settlement thereafter (late in 1777) became Washington County. Yet, when the state of Franklin was organized seven years later as a new state westward of North Carolina, it was Wataugans who took the lead in organizing it, returning finally to the latter state when Franklin had collapsed.

There was no notable westward advance of settlement in Tennessee in that interval save that around Nashville in the bend of the Cumberland River. This was made in 1779 by Wataugans under the lead of James Robertson as an agent of the Transylvania Company. A vast activity in land speculation, particularly in 1783 and thereafter, was largely due to William Blount, but there was little relation between actual settlement and the enormous operations of the land office. There was, nevertheless, a steady growth of these settlements from 1783 onward.[11] The mountain population of eastern Tennessee grew only slowly until a new venture in statemaking occurred.

This was the state of Franklin, the most remarkable of the early West's creations of that character.[12] It was antipodal to Watauga in the factors that dominated its founding. Although Franklin was remarkable for the completeness of its organization, its boundaries were never definite. Its North Carolina founders intended them to take in the valley of the Tennessee down to and including Muscle Shoals, but its width was undefined. Moreover, throughout the period while there was any hope for a legal establishment of the state, it was more or less tied to a project of southwestern Virginians to unite with it several counties of that state and otherwise alter its boundaries.[13] Various local factors co-operated in both its creation and collapse; it is generally agreed that among these land speculation predominated. But basic Confederation policies respecting the public lands entered into its creation, and

[11] The earliest settlement was in 1776 and following. S. C. Williams, *Tennessee During the Revolutionary War* (Nashville, 1944), pp. 100–111; *Col. Rec. of N. Carolina*, IX, 1267–1279; *Amer. Archives*, IV, 546–553; J. W. Caldwell, *Constitutional History*, pp. 34–47.

[12] S. C. Williams, *The Lost State of Franklin* (2nd ed., New York, 1933); Caldwell, *Constitutional History*, pp. 48–72; Abernethy, *Frontier to Plantation*, pp. 64–90.

[13] Abernethy, *Western Lands*, pp. 255, 256, 258, 289–296; *Frontier to Plantation*, Chap. 4.

its ultimate collapse was compelled by the hardening doctrine of state sovereignty.

Under a statute planned and put through the North Carolina legislature by William Blount, that state opened in 1783 a land office for the sale of a great part of its land west of the mountains. Blount was a man of predatory instincts. Perjury, fraud, forgery, misuse of public office, subornation, and corruption of public officials—all were counseled or practiced by him with brazen audacity. Honored by Washington with high office, he was exposed ultimately by his own recklessness. His career evidences the low standards of public life in his time, particularly in the high society of the southern states in which he found associates in his ventures. Under his act, land was set aside for two military reservations, bounty claims to be locatable without reference to "public standards" of survey. Outside of these, all previous entries were nullified; grants were made acceptable regardless of basis or present status, "inceptive or perfected."[14] All Indian treaties and rights of the Confederation and Indians thereunder were disregarded. Surveyors were immediately sent out, and Blount rapidly accumulated enormous holdings in the Cumberland valley.[15]

At this point two relationships between the territory and the Confederation became alternative possibilities under recent actions of Congress. Other states had been ceding their western lands to Congress, which hoped to pay the war debt with the proceeds of their sale. All states were being urged to make such cessions. On June 1, 1784, North Carolina ceded all her lands west of the mountains, subject to two conditions: that all private titles be recognized as valid, and that the offer be accepted within a year.[16] Who would profit by this, if acceptance should constitute literal confirmation of land titles, is obvious. Who would profit by action under another possibility is not so simple. On April 23, 1784, Congress had adopted Jefferson's ordinance for the political organization of the West, North, and South. Jefferson's plan provided that the western territory should be divided into states; that the "settlers" in each should be authorized to form a "temporary gov-

---

[14] *A.S.P., Pub. Lands,* I, 24, 85–86, 91–94; Abernethy, *Frontier to Plantation,* pp. 44–63, 99.

[15] W. H. Masterson, *William Blount* (Baton Rouge, 1954); *A.S.P., Pub. Lands,* I, 24, 85–86, 91–94; Abernethy, *Frontier to Plantation,* pp. 44–63, 99.

[16] *State Records of N. Carolina,* XXIV, 562. Delivery of a properly authenticated copy of the statute was ordered, *ibid.,* XVII, 718. The statute was a present conveyance of the fee, terminable on a condition subsequent.

ernment" under the constitution and laws of such state as they might choose.[17] Now this was much as the Wataugans had done in 1777, and were ready to do again. However, the ordinance referred only to territory already ceded to the Confederation; the states to which it referred were to be formed by Congress within such territory. Still, many persons might assume that the ordinance guaranteed organization as a state to such a community as Franklin. Moreover, one of Jefferson's suggested states could possibly have served as a Procrustean form to which Franklin's sprawling boundaries could be cut.[18]

A plan to secure its admission under the ordinance appeared immediately after North Carolina's cession. On August 23, delegations from the three counties of the Holston basin voted, in convention, to secede from North Carolina and to petition Congress to accept that state's cession and recognize them as a state under the temporary government already adopted. Then, before further organization was effected, North Carolina declared in December a repeal of her cession. That, though technically impossible, was obviously a matter for friendly adjustment. Congress accepted according to the original conditions, yet introduced new complexities by asking for an amendment and for a deed. The first was embodied in a new cession of 1789, and a deed was given in 1790. The Confederation profited little by the cession.[19]

The original creation of Franklin was obviously supported by the Holston inhabitants dissatisfied with North Carolina's government, and advantage was taken of their discontent by the speculators holding land under the act of 1783, who hoped to secure their titles through the condition in the cession to Congress and by control of the new state. Obscurity, however, covers the parties involved after the original steps.

The first Franklin legislature met in March, 1785, and remained in session until November. In this and later sessions taxes were levied, officials were provided for, war was made on the Cherokee, and treaties were made with them for the acquisition of land. There was the semblance of orderly government.

Why it all collapsed is, however, easy to understand. The refusal of

[17] Its character, as compared with the Ordinance of 1787 which replaced it, is fully discussed in *Ill. Hist. Coll.*, XXV, ccl–ccclxiii.

[18] Jefferson's suggested states are shown in J. A. Barrett, *The Evolution of the Ordinance of 1787, with . . . Earlier Plans* (New York, 1891), p. 24.

[19] *State Records of N. Carolina*, XIX, 830–832; XXIV, 678–679; Williams, *Lost State*, pp. 29–34; Carter, *Territorial Papers*, IV, 3; S. C. Williams, "The Admission of Tennessee into the Union," *Tenn. Hist. Qy.*, IV (1945), 291–320; F. L. Owsley, in *MVHR*, XVII, 320–321; Masterson, *Blount*, pp. 291–296.

Congress to intervene was inevitable, since it was asked to dismember two of the old states against their will.[20] In 1782 Pennsylvania had made such a dismemberment (by its squatter inhabitants) an act of treason; Virginia did the same as a result of the action of its south-western counties in the present case; North Carolina was resisting her divisionists. The strength and unanimity of opinion which demanded protection of every state's integrity—from the north, where New York and New Hampshire were quarreling over the Vermont area, to North Carolina—were soon to be manifested in the provisions of a national constitution.

When Congress took no action, North Carolina wore down the sepa-ratists by organizing the dissident counties as a new judicial district. She bought off leaders by appointing them to civil and military offices. The people of Franklin became divided in opinion. Some members of the North Carolina legislature were elected in the Franklin counties, and the right to hold local offices in Franklin was contested between persons asserting claims under different states. In 1786 North Carolina reasserted sovereignty over the Franklinites, but it was not until 1788 (after a few deaths in actual conflict) that resistance to reincorpora-tion definitely ended. The episode's importance does not lie in its ex-hibition of land speculation; it was notable evidence of the political sobriety of which frontiersmen were capable. It ended, substantially, the political challenge of squatter sovereignty to state sovereignty which had been general and conspicuous during the eighteenth century.[21] And, involved as the episode was with grave issues of policy involving Confederation taxation, it also strikingly displayed the conflict between state selfishness and the growing sentiment for stronger federalism which gave greatness to the Confederation era.[22] Despite the great attention which local historians have given to the subject, its details remain obscure.[23]

---

[20] *Pa. Statutes at Large,* XI, 14; W. W. Hening, *Statutes of Virginia,* XII, 41; J. P. Boyd, "Attempts to Form New States in New York and Pennsylvania," N.Y. Hist. Assoc., *Bulletin,* XII, 257–270.

[21] Scattered through Osgood's volumes, many pages reveal squatter philosophy versus vested interests. H. L. Osgood, *The American Colonies in the Eighteenth Century* (4 vols., New York, 1924).

[22] Carter, *Territorial Papers,* IV, 3 and n. 2; S. L. Sioussat, "The North Carolina Cession of 1784 in its Federal Aspects," Miss. Val. Hist. Assoc., *Proceedings* for 1908, pp. 50–62; Monroe to Jefferson, Burnett, *LMCC,* VIII, 145.

[23] Abernethy, *Frontier to Plantation,* p. 89; S. C. Williams, *Lost State,* pp. 5–8, 26–28, 38–39, 122–127; W. F. Cannon, "Four Interpretations of the

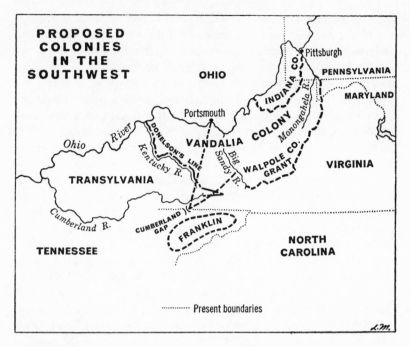

PROPOSED
COLONIES
IN THE
SOUTHWEST

Present boundaries

While the events just narrated had been occurring, many pioneers had moved into Kentucky. The larger part of them, by far, were from Virginia and North Carolina. The reason for Kentucky's preferment, aside from fertility, was the quieting of Indian claims to occupancy east of the Tennessee River by the Treaty of Fort Stanwix. No attention was paid by settlers to the expressed intention of the King that there should be no settlement west of the Kentucky River. Actual settlement was preceded by years of exploration; by 1773 and 1774, various parties were exploring and surveying and making settlements, to Sir William Johnson's alarm, west of the Kentucky.[24] Even Dunmore's War in 1774 failed to interrupt sporadic settlement. Harrodsburg, temporarily settled in that year, was permanently established in 1775.

History of the State of Franklin," East. Tenn. Hist. Soc., *Publications*, III (1950), 3–18; Masterson, *Blount*, pp. 96, 153, 163–164; G. H. Alden in *AHR*, VIII, 271, 274; Caldwell, *Constitutional History*, p. 71; Henderson, *Old Southwest*, pp. 315–317.

[24] *N.Y. Col. Docs.*, VII, 462. All of Virginia west of the Blue Ridge had been made a county (Augusta) in 1745; in 1769 its southwestern portion was made Botetourt County; in 1772 the portion of the latter west of the Kanawha River was set off as Fincastle County.

At this point, however, there intervened one of the most famous of all pre-Revolutionary land companies—the Transylvania Company formed by Richard Henderson. This was vastly more important in its political effects within Virginia than in any influence it had upon the settlement or the political development of Kentucky. It has therefore been referred to in an earlier chapter because it originated in violations of British law and imperial policy; because its purpose was not merely to settle land but to establish a great proprietary colony carved from the western domains of Virginia and North Carolina; because a proprietary colony with a land system of feudal characteristics affronted heavily preponderant American opinion; because the plan compelled Lord Dunmore to publish a proclamation, which he had suppressed, of imperial policies irreconcilable with Henderson's plans, and to enforce orders which he had himself violated; and because all this caused Virginia's convention (assembled to consider the perils of the day) to take steps that paralyzed imperial control, thus channeling the forces which were leading to revolution in that state.

In comparison with its relations to these events, its connection with Kentucky settlement was of negligible importance. Boonesborough was laid out as a Transylvanian outpost in 1775, and laws were there passed for a colony which never became a reality.[25] This Kentucky settlement has been described as the first colony actually established on western lands under an independent government, although even by title it existed only for a day. Moreover, as a self-governing settlement Watauga had long preceded it. The laws framed at Boonesborough were, however, adopted by delegates from four Kentucky settlements, and they may have constituted the first representative body to act governmentally west of the Alleghenies.[26] Henderson's utmost accomplishment, politically, was that the Virginia constitution of 1776 plainly suggested the creation of a new state in her western domains.[27] Even the settlers taken out by Henderson were not permanent, and moreover, as one historian has pointed out, "the Virginians already in Kentucky and others coming to join them greatly outnumbered the Transylvanians, and were little inclined to acknowledge the . . . Tran-

[25] *Amer. Archives,* IV, 545–554; *Col. Rec. of N.C.,* X, 258, 373–376, 1267–1279; Burnett, *LMCC,* I, 306; Henderson, *Old Southwest,* pp. 245–247, 285–286. The boundary description, literally interpreted, was one of the watershed, but the river itself was later regarded as the boundary.

[26] James, *The Life of George Rogers Clark* (Chicago, 1928), p. 22.

[27] Thorpe, *Constitutions.*

sylvania promoters, or to pay them for lands they claimed under the laws of Virginia."[28]

This situation made it possible for George Rogers Clark to organize the settlers against Henderson and induce the Virginia convention to frustrate all his plans.[29] "It was the pioneers" already in Kentucky, led by Clark, who "saved Virginia's claims"; or rather so quickly saved them, for the certainty that Britain never could have approved a feudalistic colony after 1775, and the certainty that under Revolutionary principles it was doomed in its Continental Congress inception, are equally clear.[30]

The main portion of Transylvania, lying within Virginia, was promptly made the county of Kentucky; and after Clark's conquest of Illinois, and a great influx of settlers under the land act of 1779, the county was divided into three, late in 1780. Constant Indian warfare in 1781 and 1782, which were the bloodiest in Kentucky's history, failed to check immigrants coming down the Ohio or overland from the middle and southern states. It seems probable that in 1785 the population was "somewhat less than thirty thousand," and that this was double the population of the rest of the West.[31] In two years, beginning in October, 1786, some 16,000 settlers in more than 1,800 boats passed Pittsburgh.[32] And this was before the organization of the Northwest by the Ordinance of 1787 brought the first rivulets of the flood that would soon cover that territory. In 1790 the national census showed 73,000 inhabitants in Kentucky.

The same year that Henderson founded Boonesborough, Powell's Valley, near Cumberland Gap, was permanently settled, and a wagon

[28] James, *Clark*, p. 23; T. Bodley (ed.), *Littell's Political Transactions in and Concerning Kentucky* (Lexington, 1926), p. 77. See also Henderson, *Old Southwest*, pp. 259, 31, 215, and in *AHR*, XX, 107.

[29] *Ill. Hist. Coll.*, VIII, li–liv, 209–212; James, *Clark*, pp. 23–26; *Amer. Archives*, VI, 1573; *Virginia Hist. Mag.*, XVI, 157–163; *Calendar of Virginia State Papers*, I, 303, 320.

[30] C. W. Alvord, "Virginia and the West; An Interpretation," *MVHR*, III (1916), 29.

[31] In estimates for the Southwest I have relied primarily on A. P. Whitaker, *Spanish-American Frontier, 1783–1795* (New York, 1927), pp. 26, 51, 111, 136; *MVHR*, XII, 163. For the Northwest, see Abernethy, *Three Virginia Frontiers*, Chap. 3. There are some estimates in *Ill. Hist. Coll.*, VIII, xxv, cxv, cxviii; James, *Clark*, p. 104. Estimates of western settlement made for a purpose, as in arguing for the creation of colonies, were wildly unreliable. One by Croghan is cited in J. Winsor, *The Westward Movement . . . 1763–1798* (Boston, 1897).

[32] Carter, *Territorial Papers*, II, 196, 221, 224.

road was being cut toward the Gap, which was soon to become, and for many years remain, the most traveled of all westward routes.[33] However, by 1790, what became Tennessee had less than half Kentucky's population. Undoubtedly, many who started westward went on to Kentucky and some to Illinois.

Down in the Southwest there could have been few inhabitants in what became Alabama and Mississippi. Georgia, in 1790, had a population little greater than Kentucky's, and along with South Carolina was slow in expanding into the piedmont area. The only exception was the later cotton kingdom around Natchez, known since 1763 to be a superlatively fertile region. It was the site of a considerable settlement under the bounty provisions of the Proclamation of 1763, and of Loyalist refugees after 1776.[34]

The above estimates are consistent with the opinions of two historians that by the end of the Revolution the population west of the mountains was probably 25,000; that two years later that of Kentucky alone was from 20,000 to 30,000; and that in 1790 that of the whole West was certainly less than 125,000.[35]

Considering the publicity and magnitude of this great social movement, it seems strange that it should today seem necessary to discuss the question of who settled the West. The necessity arises from a misconception of the role of land speculators.

Land hunger doubtless attacked all landless European emigrants to America, coming from countries wherein economic independence and social status rested on the land. In America, economic advancement sprang from its easy acquisition. Most colonial fortunes were founded on it.[36] The gradual abandonment of entails and primogeniture, and

[33] The settlement was at Martin's Station—a station being a group of cabins forming an imperfect enclosure within an outer stockade. The road was not being cut through the Gap, but built only to Martin's Station, beyond which it remained "a pack-horse trail" until 1792. Thwaites and Kellogg, *Revolution on the Upper Ohio, 1775–1777* (Madison, 1908), p. 2.

[34] W. H. Siebert, "The Loyalists in West Florida and the Natchez," *MVHR*, II (1916), 465–483; L. P. Kellogg (ed.), *Frontier Retreat on the Upper Ohio* (Madison, 1917), *passim;* C. Johnson, *British West Florida, 1763–1783* (New Haven, 1943), pp. 139 *et seq.; A.S.P., Pub. Lands*, I, 257.

[35] For Kentucky, see J. F. Jameson, *The Revolution as a Social Movement* (Princeton, 1926), pp. 68, 69. Channing's extreme allowance was 125,000. His own estimate was 110,000 in *History of the United States* (6 vols., New York, 1905–25), III, 528, although the census gave that many (73,677 plus 35,691) to Kentucky and Tennessee alone.

[36] Alvord (*MVHR*, I, 21) quoted a letter of 1768 from Philadelphia: "It

the evasion of quitrents, increased the salability of land, and British use of rents as insurance of family status and stability gave way to a commercial conception of land.[37] Few Americans could have been interested in it as nutrition for a family tree; only a European could cherish such ideas, as possibly Lord Dunmore did. The distinction was one of many which differentiated Americans and Englishmen before the Revolution. However, men high in British official life quickly succumbed to the American conception when offered partnerships in plans for exploitation of American lands. From an early day every available device had been used in the colonies to amass land, notably by the forgery of headright documents or the corrupt multiplication of headright claims.[38] By the eighteenth century, land speculation was a mania, and in 1754 Peter Wraxall wrote of it in New York: "This hunger after Land seems very early to have taken rise in this Province, & is become now a kind of Epidemical madness, every Body eager to accumulate vast Tracts without having an intention or taking measures to settle or improve it, & Landjobbing here is as refind an Art as Stock jobbing in Change Alley. hence public poverty in the midst of imaginary Wealth."[39] Much earlier (1705) Robert Beverly had described Virginians as "not minding anything but to be masters of great tracts of land."[40]

Early custom in various colonies, north and south, was to make small free grants to actual settlers. Later, in New England, there were free grants to colonizing groups, sometimes on special conditions for protection of the frontier. A natural variation was the sale of land to a group of subscribing townsmen for settlement of a new town, each subscriber having a "right" and the right being transferable.[41] But by the middle

---

is almost a proverb in this neighborhood that 'Every great fortune made here within these fifty years has been by land.'" There was extremely little intercolonial trade.

[37] R. B. Morris, *Studies in the History of American Law* (New York, 1930), Chap. 2; B. Bond, *The Quit Rent System in the American Colonies* (New Haven, 1919); C. Parker, *The History of Taxation in North Carolina during the Colonial Period* (New York, 1928), Chap. 2, 5; L. C. Gray, *Agriculture in Southern United States,* index, *s.v.* "quitrents."

[38] P. A. Bruce, *Economic History of Virginia* (2 vols., New York, 1896), I, 518–20.

[39] C. H. McIlwain (ed.), *Wraxall's Abridgment of Indian Affairs* (Cambridge, 1915), p. 179.

[40] Abernethy, *Western Lands,* p. 2.

[41] R. H. Akagi, *The Town Proprietors of the New England Colonies* (Philadelphia, 1924).

of the eighteenth century the legislatures were selling land to speculators without requiring settlement.[42] By that time Virginia governors
had granted to members of the colonial council, or others politically
powerful, some 10,000 square miles of its back country, and its sheriffs,
and those of North Carolina, were embezzling public moneys to invest
in land-office warrants.[43] Not land scarcity but the high price of lands,
and tax rates without distinction between tidewater lands and back-
country land, were causes of resentment voiced from New England to
the Carolinas. Land forestallment was a notable cause of midcentury
riots in New York and New Jersey, and uniform tax rates were an
important addition to resentment against political subordination and
judicial and shrieval venality in the Regulation upheaval of North
Carolina, and later.[44]

There were two aspects of the land mania. One revealed the irresisti-
ble impulse of the many to live better, or more independently. The
other evidenced the acquisitive impulse of the few to acquire the West
ahead of the emigrant and sell it to him when he got there. For this
reason land-company enterprises were possible stimulants of migration,
or of government policies favorable to migration, if there were any.
But they should not be assumed to be necessarily such; for example,
one reads that "Virginia made vigorous and sustained efforts to promote western colonization."[45] These efforts consisted merely of land
grants to favored individuals (many of them organized as land compa-

---

[42] *Ibid.*

[43] *Va. Mag. of Hist. and Biog.*, V, 175–180, 241–244 (lists of grants and
patents, 1745–69); Abernethy, *Western Lands*, pp. 67–68, and *Three Virginia
Frontiers* (University, La., 1940), pp. 57, 65, 67; J. P. Boyd, "The Sheriff in
Colonial North Carolina," *N. Carolina Hist. Rev.*, V (1928), 152, 159, 168–
169.

[44] Osgood, *American Colonies,* I, Chap. 4. The land policies of the different
colonies had a primary influence on these matters. See I. Mark, *Agrarian Conflicts in Colonial New York, 1711–1775* (New York, 1940), Chap. 2, 4, 5;
C. Spencer, "The Land System of Colonial New York," N.Y. State Hist. Association, *Proceedings,* XVI (1917), 150–164; P. H. Giddens, "Land Policies
and Administration in Colonial Maryland, 1753–1769," *Maryland Hist. Mag.,*
XXVII (1933), 142–171. Not much dependence can be placed on frontier
petitions. Those cited by Henderson (*MVHR*, XVII, 206, 208) were certainly
the voice of speculators, likewise the petition for creation of Westsylvania as a
fourteenth state, as Abernethy says in *Western Lands,* pp. 175–179. For North
Carolina, see J. S. Bassett, "The Regulators of North Carolina, 1765–1771,"
Amer. Hist. Assoc., *Report* for 1894, pp. 150–155; Masterson, *Blount,* pp.
12–18.

[45] Henderson, in *MVHR,* XVII, 193.

nies), plus statutory enticement of Virginian citizens, by promised temporary tax exemptions, to settle on the lands so granted, for the profit of the grantees.[46] The soldiers whose bounty claims were bought up by Washington and others had performed military service, but neither their service nor the purchase of bounty warrants which were its reward settled an acre. Unless by vague reference to the influence of "speculators" in general, nobody, seemingly, has claimed that speculation by single individuals, such as Washington, stimulated settlement—although the activities of William Blount, in the double character of buyer and legislative boss, were very much like those of Virginia just cited. It has been generally said or assumed that George Croghan was a potent influence in western settlement. He was an early explorer, a great trader, an important figure in land speculation, Indian affairs, and the general story of the West—although it is exaggeration to say that by his trading prowess and seduction of the Indians he shook the foundations of the French empire in America.[47] He promoted the organization of various land companies, and he secured from the Indians mythical title to millions of acres of crown lands. But his explorations, as respects settlement, were far too remotely consequential for mention; his trading activity was inimical to settlement; his company activities and title deeds amounted to no more than a prayer that the Empire bring colonists to buy his lands after giving them value by coming. No evidence is offered that anybody went with his aid or that of his companies to the frontier. Nor is there evidence that his acts or talk, or the acts of any of the various land companies of which he was a member, stimulated any individuals to go independently. Within reasonable limits of causation, he contributed nothing to the West's settlement.

For some reason the words "land company" seem to have a magic suggestiveness. The old Ohio Company did have a great influence in bringing on the French and Indian War, because it claimed, by grant of the British Crown, lands France also claimed; but its activities were of trade, not settlement.[48] Nevertheless, it has been said that from the

[46] Henderson cites several such statutes of 1752–54 (the French and Indian War had begun before any of these) and one appropriation of 1754 for the protection of prospective settlers; that is, in fact, of the Ohio Company's interests.

[47] Alvord, in *The Nation*, CXXIV (1927), 182.

[48] M. Savelle, *The Diplomatic History of the Canadian Boundary, 1749–1763* (New Haven, 1940), pp. 154–155.

creation of that Company onward, it and other companies and individuals who followed its example became the "driving power" behind the western movement.[49] A careful reading of the books in which such statements are found will uncover no evidence whatever that supports them. It is not even shown that the Ohio Company made any "definite trial at settlement,"[50] nor that any other pre-Revolutionary company did (in the West we are considering) except the Transylvania Company. Many persons foresaw a future fully-settled West, but the dream did not people it; we have seen that Franklin, Sir William Johnson, and General Gage each allowed a century for its realization.

The land companies, of course, did not wish settlement except on land they owned.[51] Great importance has been attached to the "activities" of the land companies as the predominant or sole "business of" or "on" the frontier. All three words are misleading. Acquisition of the land which every company sought was always a precondition to the company's becoming a functioning entity—sometimes explicitly made so, invariably shown to be so by the company's complete inactivity meanwhile. The niggardly offers made by some companies to colonize land *if* given it have been noted. Very few even made such offers. After getting a grant it was simply held (as by the old Virginia companies) for decades, without any but the most perfunctory efforts at location or survey. It was essentially gambling in futures, on margins mythically slight. There was hardly any advertising, and none (saving again Transylvania) incidental to settlement.[52] In a few instances "shares" (that is, opportunities to enter the partnership) were set aside

<hr/>

[49] Alvord, *Illinois Country*, p. 226. K. L. Bailey, *The Ohio Company of Virginia and the Westward Movement, 1748–1792* (Glendale, Calif., 1939), p. 293, uses virtually the same words.

[50] Though Alvord said it made "the first" (*MVHR*, III, 21). It built a magazine near Cumberland (Md.) for trading goods, and perhaps did some work on what was later Burgoyne's route.

[51] Hence Samuel Wharton's warning to Franklin that it was infinitely more important to secure recognition of the claims of the Suffering Traders (to whom the Indians promised a deed) than recognition of the scheme for a colony in Illinois.

[52] Everything preserved in more than 250 libraries is listed in R. W. G. Vail, *The Voice of the Old Frontier* (Philadelphia, 1949). A. C. Boggess noted some of the publications of the Illinois-Wabash companies in *The Settlement of Illinois, 1775–1830* (Chicago, 1908), p. 11. Most of the items listed were material for lobbying. Of course, Henderson owned Transylvania before he advertised it (Henderson, *Old Southwest,* pp. 219–220).

for use as bribes in securing legislation; in one case, considerable money was spent in lobbying.[53] To designate busyness with such shimmery dreams as "business ventures" or "enterprises" or "economic history" is utterly misleading. The busyness, too, was not of or on the frontier. It was wholly, in early years, far from it, although in later years some speculators did remove to the frontier to facilitate sales.

When applied to the westward movement of later times, there is truth in the statement that "promoters" played a part of some importance in it. But there are assumptions of promotion in the word "promoters." With the exception of the Transylvania Company, there seems to be no evidence that any emigrant parties were organized by them, or guides for them provided; nor that there was any loaning of money, advancement of seed or tools, provision of way stations for food and shelter, or any transportation of goods and persons. These were normal aspects of actual promotion in later years. With extremely rare exceptions, the word "promoted" has been used without indication that something more than paper plans is required to move population.[54]

Land "companies" are generally assumed to have been corporations.[55] Some historians, believing their "stock" to have sold freely on the frontier, have also inferred corporate activity on the frontier.[56] All were partnerships; and since the partners dreamed of a monopolized bonanza, their number was always small and membership exclusive.[57] Transfer of interests (that is, substitution of partners) was frequently

[53] According to Volwiler, the lobbying expenses of the Walpole Company were £20,000; see *Croghan*, p. 272. Contributions to partnership capital were usually (so far as appears) extraordinarily small.

[54] Whitaker is a rare exception in recognizing even the existence of a problem (*Spanish-American Frontier*, pp. 47–48).

[55] The first corporate land company was the Connecticut company of 1796 that received the Western Reserve. J. S. Davis, *Essays in the Earlier History of American Corporations* (2 vols., Cambridge, 1917), I, 289. For the reasons why there were no colonial corporations and joint-stock companies, see *ibid.*, I, 2–29, 91, 96–97, 104–107, 178; II, 4, 5.

[56] Alvord, *Illinois Country*, pp. 340, 385; Bailey, *Ohio Company*, pp. 52, 53, 54, 63, 64, 291.

[57] There were only eight proprietors to divide Transylvania. In companies which made protracted efforts for government recognition, memberships grew with time. There were twenty-two by 1777 (five or six originally) in the Indiana Company, originally forty-two in the combined Illinois-Wabash Company and twice that number (doubled for prospective lobbying purposes) in 1779. The Walpole Company ultimately had about seventy-five members, more than half British—the result of protracted lobbying.

allowed subject to restrictions. But the idea that these interests resembled corporate shares available in a public market is mere delusion.

Settlement of the West was once ascribed to those who went there to live. Those who actively helped them go, even though not themselves settlers (in addition to creditors and legal authorities—sometimes active persuaders), were then added. Later writers added still others whose contributions were only remotely discernible, such as explorers (but not the Indians whose trails they often followed), traders (who were the enemies of settlement), and land speculators. The contributions of the last were quite as immaterial. Importance has presumably been attributed to them as representing economic determinism, but there was nothing economic about them.

Of all the northern companies organized from 1760 onward, not one contributed a trace of activity in the development of the West. This includes the last and greatest, the Walpole Company, in which were joined all older northern interests with sufficient vitality to demand recognition, and some southern. It is quite fair to say of all that so far as regards western settlement, they were only blowing bubbles in the air.[58]

The northern companies merely begged the British government to give them land and, virtually, to settle it. The worst that can be charged (against one) is bribery in lobbying. Little actual settlement was done by the Virginia companies which took crown lands from the Virginia Council, and their claims merely added impediments and expense to Kentucky settlement.[59] The same thing happened to Tennessee because of the plundering of North Carolina's western lands by William Blount and associates. Of even less validity, and therefore even greater nuisances, were the Yazoo grants of Georgia's western lands, so far as they could not be wholly voided, and of all grants of South Carolina's western lands, since they were nonexistent.

It is true, naturally, that when acquisition of cheap land was promised by a company, some borderers could be enticed to move, although

[58] Many writers state or imply a contrary view. Whitaker (*Spanish-American Frontier*, p. 47) says, for example: "The importance of the land speculator in the history of western extension . . . can hardly be exaggerated." And Abernethy has even written that the land speculators helped "to open the way for the West's moving caravan . . . with their spurious grants and dubious titles." *Western Lands*, pp. 368–369.

[59] Making Kentucky the most surveyed state in the Union.

the "vast crowds" advertised by Richard Henderson as flocking into Transylvania amounted only to three or four hundred in a year. It is also true that a prospect of securing cheap land in Georgia's "Bourbon County" in 1785 was soon followed by reports that inhabitants of the southern colonies were "proceeding in great numbers" through the Creek country toward the Mississippi.[60] But some such migration had been going on for years. In 1776 an Indian agent had reported meeting, in the Cherokee country of Tennessee, parties of emigrants from the Watauga and other Holston settlements moving both overland and in boats down the Tennessee River to that same destination.[61] As time passed, such reports became more numerous. Afoot, mounted, in boats, or (later) in wagons, in summer or winter, ambitious, harried, or restless men were forever advancing along the entire border, without benefit of land companies and with scant restraint by proclamation or treaty.

Few men could have been so self-reliant and so desperate as to have braved alone, even briefly, the true wilderness. On the other hand, there were abundant reasons why many men, with or without families, should have removed to the westernmost borders of the old colonies. The search for better and cheaper lands was constant. Personal debts could not be collected pending establishment of effective local government, nor could taxes, until then, be collected. Failures or disappointments could be more easily forgotten in a fresh and perhaps successful start. Social and ecclesiastic restrictions were doubtless less numerous and coercive.

Years ago Frederick Jackson Turner, who initiated the intensive study of the westward movement and frontier life, wrote of the border settlement westward of the Alleghenies (his "Old West"):

The creation of this frontier society—of which so large a portion differed from the coast in language and religion—as well as in economic life, social structure and ideals—produced an antagonism between interior and coast. . . . In general this took these forms: contests between the property-holding class of the coast and the debtor class of the interior, where specie was lacking, and where paper money and a readjustment of the basis of taxation were demanded; contests over defective or unjust local government in the administration of taxes, fees, lands, and the courts; contests over unfair apportionment in the legislature . . . contests to secure the complete separation of

60 Report by Alexander McGillivray, *AHR*, XV, 71, 326.
61 H. L. Shaw, *British Administration of the Southern Indians, 1763-1776* (Lancaster, 1931), p. 100.

church and state. . . . In nearly every colony prior to the Revolution, struggles had been in progress between the party of privilege . . . and the democratic classes, strongest in the West and the cities.[62]

An immense amount of attention has been given to these matters since Turner wrote.[63] His statements overstress geography in economic distinctions and in political issues. There was a "debtor class," of course, throughout each colony. Many border settlers acquired their land as squatters; how enormous was the quantity not owned by Easterners long after independence was shown by William Blount in 1783. Coin was scarce in the colonies as wholes; paper money was issued in vast quantity by their legislatures, not for the borderers only, or because of special border pressure.

There has been more or less emphasis upon border "separatism," using that word, necessarily, with various and indefinite meanings. It is obvious that dissatisfaction of individuals with their place in society or government created a separatism of spirit; that it was constantly expressed in migration of the dissatisfied; and that a desire for more self-government was necessarily central in the conception of better government. The possibility of securing this in the borderland communities referred to in the above quotation from Turner was slight. It was dependent upon securing, by argument or by growth of border population, dominance in the state's government, after conceding—by flight to the border—the impossibility of the former alternative.

[62] "The Old West," Wisconsin State Hist. Soc., *Proceedings,* LVI (1908), 221–222.

[63] His views, in later form, will be found in *The Frontier in American History* (New York, 1920), pp. 110–124. Other essays or monographs include P. Davidson, "The Southern Back Country on the Eve of the Revolution," in A. Craven (ed.), *Essays in Honor of William E. Dodd* (Chicago, 1935), pp. 1–14; M. Farrand, "The West and the Principles of the Constitution," *Yale Review,* XVII (Old Series, 1908–09), 44–58; E. B. Greene, *The Revolutionary Generation* (New York, 1943), pp. 166–168, 407–411. On particular colonies, see J. S. Bassett, "The Regulators of North Carolina," Amer. Hist. Assoc., *Report* for 1894, pp. 150–155, 160, 162–163, 165, 208, 211–212; W. A. Schafer, "Sectionalism and Representation in South Carolina," *ibid.* For 1900, *ibid.*, pp. 324, 353, 400–437; C. H. Lincoln, *The Revolutionary Movement in Pennsylvania* (Philadelphia, 1896), Chaps. 3–4; J. P. Selsam, *The Pennsylvania Constitution of 1776: A Study in Revolutionary Democracy* (Oxford, 1936); Hart, *Valley of Virginia,* pp. 62–65; C. H. Ambler, *Sectionalism in Virginia from 1776 to 1861* (Chicago, 1910), Introduction; A. C. Flick, *History of the State of New York* (10 vols., New York, 1933–37), IV, 175–178; S. C. Williams, *Lost State of Franklin,* pp. 115, 226, 348; E. Stanwood, Mass. Hist. Soc., *Proceedings* for 1907–8, pp. 128–134.

The borderland complaints have been to some extent exaggerated. Some causes of resentment, although not peculiar to our prenational years, were then particularly objectionable. For example, venal administration of local government—very likely less common on the border, where there was less wealth, than in older eastern districts—was particularly resented when coupled with other abuses peculiar to the border. High land prices, though everywhere resented, were particularly obnoxious to those who had hoped, by going to the border, to escape them. Property requirements for voting and holding office were everywhere unwelcome to those who could not satisfy them, but these were relatively numerous in the border countries. Taxes on a given acreage of land were more or less commonly equal, regardless of the land's location, use or value, as the Franklinites particularly complained; but, being fixed by legislatures that Easterners controlled, class favoritism seemed to be added to economic illogic. However, after allowing for such exaggerations it remains clear that there were needed two great and necessary reforms: a liberalized suffrage and the opening of public lands on terms permitting actual settlers to acquire title without prior intervention by speculators. In the next chapter it will be seen that these reforms, which had been impossible in the colonial period, were effected in the 1780's by the Confederation Congress for a federal West to which all prior claims by individual states were renounced.

Some government is needed in the smallest community. The Mayflower Compact is extraordinary only in being an early opportunity for English emigrants to exhibit the effects of long experience in local self-government. Within the broad field of American political history, there is nothing extraordinary in the action of the Watauga settlers. Scores of instances have been collected of similar action by isolated settlers within the United States; many more could doubtless be added from Australia, Canada, and British islands of the Atlantic and Pacific.[64] Drop a few persons of English background on any isolated spot, and history shows that they will hold a meeting, elect a chairman, and frame a plan of government. Illustrations of a related nature have arisen from the associational principle that has been so important in

[64] C. S. Lobengier, *The People's Law* (New York, 1909), *passim*. An instance from Bermuda is discussed in T. M. Dill, "Colonial Development of the Common Law," *Law Quarterly Review*, XL (1924), 227. See *Ill. Hist. Coll.*, XXV, cccxlix–ccclii.

American ecclesiastical organization.[65] The one complaint that runs through all remonstrances, petitions, and representations from all pioneer settlements before and during their organization as territories, from early times to those until recently from Alaska, is that of alleged neglect by distant government.

How much if any extremism in government did the "separatists" of the Confederation period seek to establish? We know little of what they would have done in altering governmental institutions had they been free to attempt it. Retention of their lands would presumably have been their primary concern, and therefore alterations in its taxation and protection. Only in the records of Franklin has evidence survived that desire for constitutional revisions was strong. A popular convention held to draft a constitution met late and broke up in confusion. Another, a month later, voted to elect a legislature immediately under North Carolina laws and framed a constitution for consideration after six months by another convention. This met only after a year (November, 1785); the instructions to delegates showed a "great variety and contrariety of sentiments." A committee, headed by a clergyman, reported a plan politically interesting but eccentric in mingling mundane politics and theology. It was rejected, and the convention then adopted North Carolina's constitution almost without alteration.[66]

There are reasons why a suggestion of political radicalism clings to the last colonial border, despite the absence of evidence to justify it. One is that a somewhat radical doctrine of the right to self-government (derived from English political philosophers of the seventeenth and eighteenth centuries, but inflated with frontier self-confidence) and an even more radical doctrine of "squatter sovereignty" respecting land were current in the colonies.

Jefferson expressed them in 1774 in his *Summary View of the Rights of British America.* Our ancestors, he said (ignoring old, and even contemporary, British statutes), had a right to migrate whither they chose, "and of there establishing new Societies, under such Laws . . . as seem most likely to promote public sentiment. . . . From the nature and purpose of civil institutions, all the lands within the limits which any

[65] Eton, "The Right to Local Self-Government," *Harvard Law Review,* XIII, 441, 638.
[66] The rejected constitution is in *Amer. Hist. Mag.* (Nashville, 1896), pp. 48–63. See G. H. Alden, *AHR,* VIII, 274–275; Williams, *Lost State of Franklin,* pp. 132–133.

particular society has circumscribed around itself are . . . subject to their allotment only."[67] And Richard Henderson, speaking at Boonesborough to the Transylvanians he had led from Kentucky, told them "That we have an absolute right, as a political body (self constituted and subsisting) to frame rules for the government of our little society, cannot be doubted by any sensible, unbiased mind."[68] What he drew up for them, however, were very simple plans of government—for the Transylvanians, for the settlers in Powell's Valley, and for the stations strung along the Cumberland River in Tennessee.[69] All of these were modeled on the county court with which the settlers were familiar in England and later in America, exercising (as had the English quarter-sessions court for centuries) predominantly administrative powers of local government.[70]

The political ideas expressed by Jefferson and Judge Henderson—so far as rights either to migrate or to establish new governments were revolutionary (and both were still horrendously so in contemporary England)—were each by themselves truisms in the colonies. But there was no such acceptance of them in combination, that is, of migration *for the purpose* of setting up a new state. This idea—in effect, political squatter sovereignty—is the purpose which inlanders attributed to the borderers, and sometimes it was in fact, if not in intent, the result of their actions. Mutual distrust and enmity were consequences. The Westsylvania petitioners to Congress for statehood in 1776 declared their right and their will to hold the lands they had settled.[71] They also contrasted their pioneer merits with the absence of these in "the rest of their countrymen softened by Ease, enervated by Affluence and Luxurious Plenty, and inaccustomed to Fatigues, Hardships, Difficulties or

[67] *Writings* (Ford ed.), 1, 429–30, 444. He also said, quite justly: "America was conquered, and her settlement made, and firmly established, at the expense of individuals, and not of the British public."

[68] *Col. Rec. of N. Carolina,* IX, 1267–1269; *Amer. Archives,* IV, 546–553.

[69] Henderson, *Old Southwest,* pp. 252, 285–286.

[70] The governing body in Cumberland (*Col. Rec. of N. Carolina,* IX, 1267–1279; Williams, *Tennessee during the Revolution,* pp. 167–170) was called "court," its members "triers" and "Judges." Was a provision for their removal, and replacement by popular vote in case of dissatisfaction with them (as regards what services being unstated), a case of judicial recall?

[71] In a petition to Congress they proclaimed their desire not to be "enslaved by any set of Proprietary or other Claimants or arbitrarily depriv'd and robb'd of those Lands to which . . . they are entitl'd as first Occupants." *Amer. Archives,* IV, 551–552.

dangers."[72] On the other hand, the people of Franklin were described in the assembly of North Carolina as offscourings of the earth, of whom that state was well rid.[73]

Some of the border problems of the colonial and Confederation eras were ended by approval or by prohibition of border practices by the Constitution of 1788. Some remained little changed in the period covered by this volume. One, in particular, remained almost to the present day in a form more reprehensible than in 1776. Fifty years after independence, one was made basic law for the public lands on all later frontiers. A reference will therefore be later made to these matters.

[72] Alden, *New Governments*, p. 66.

[73] *State Rec., N.C.*, XVII, 602. This was in bitter debate over cession of North Carolina's western lands to Congress.

CHAPTER 5

A National West and New Colonial System

THE organization of the West was a primary problem of the Confederation. Earlier years had revealed the tangled sectional and interstate jealousies which its solution would involve. They were greater in potential consequences for good or evil than anything in the field of international relations. The choices before the Congress were several: of favoring settler or speculator, controlled or unrestricted (that is, compact or haphazard) settlement, immediate or delayed income from the sale of land. But debate of these issues was overlain and confused by the jealousies between states with and without western land claims.

Without attention to these differences, it is impossible to appreciate adequately the immense importance of nationalizing the West, the social significance of competing plans for its settlement, the reasons in 1787 for forever prohibiting feudal fees in the first West (which was extended to all later territories), and, particularly, the immense significance of the unanimity reached on all these points in the Old Congress. These problems all had as a background the extent of land engrossment, as a result of land speculation already discussed.

In 1766, Franklin told the House of Commons, doubtless quite correctly, that the colonies "along the frontier [were] very thinly settled."[1] Of course, too, as General Gage reported in 1770, there was "room for the Colonists to spread within [their then] present limits for a century to come"—even if he regarded the Appalachians as those limits. It is

[1] *Writings* (Smyth ed.); but in V, 519, holdings at high prices by speculators are emphasized.

also true that there was a great deal of unoccupied land within the areas of general habitation—as there is, surprisingly enough, even to-day.[2] But there was not available land at a price poor settlers could pay. In 1700 the governor of Virginia reported that engrossment was causing emigration from Virginia and Maryland. In 1705 the home government disapproved a Virginia law on the ground that under its headright provisions lands "would soon be in the hands of the rich, and not settled." A few years later there was complaint in the Maryland assembly that unexecuted land warrants were preventing settlement of vast tracts. It was said in 1773 that not a twentieth of Georgia's cultivable land, and that only in remote parts, was open.[3] The governor of North Carolina estimated in 1773 that virtually no "good" land was available (only three hundred acres); New York's governor, that there was no demand for tracts of less than a thousand acres; and Georgia's governor, that there was a great scarcity of good land (fit for cotton planting?) along with enormous areas of "waste" land.[4] All this undoubtedly represented the viewpoint of the great planter or speculator. As early as 1763 the Board of Trade advised the King that although "many Colonies appeared to be overstock'd with Inhabitants . . . [it was caused] chiefly by the Monopoly of lands."[5] John Stuart had so reported with respect to the southern states.[6] However well or little understood in London, it was doubtless notorious fact in the colonies.[7]

Before the Revolution this condition was an impediment to the spread of population, and therefore, in popular opinion, to economic justice. The form and amount of engrossment depended to a considerable extent on the land systems of the different colonies.[8] Those, how-

---

[2] Because New Englanders then farmed much land which today is left to forest. Employing a sensible definition of "empty," in 1954 the percentages of such land in seven of the nine states from Pennsylvania to Maine still ran from 21.1 to 67.3. L. E. Klimm, "The Empty Areas of the Northeastern United States," *Geographical Review*, XLIV (1954), 325–345. See Thomson, *Changing Face of New England*.

[3] L. C. Gray, *Agriculture*, pp. 396–397, 401, 403.

[4] *N.Y. Col. Docs.*, VIII, 373; C. H. Laub, William and Mary College, *Quarterly Magazine*, 2nd series, X, 53.

[5] Shortt and Doughty, *Papers*, p. 137; but compare p. 161 and Gray, *Agriculture*, pp. 403–404.

[6] H. L. Shaw, *British Administration of the Southern Indians, 1763–1776* (Lancaster, 1931), p. 21.

[7] Compare *AHR*, XXVIII (1923), p. 685.

[8] C. M. Andrews, "Land Systems in the American Colonies," R. H. I. Palgrave, *Dictionary of Political Economy* (3 vols., New York, 1894–99), II,

ever, were determined in the long run by the pressure of social habits prevailing in different colonies, and the variance between habits of the northern and southern colonials was very great. In one habit there was no difference—namely, in squatting on crown lands, which was universal. Some New England towns prohibited scattered settlement in early years; but there seems to be no evidence that this or any colonial restriction was motivated by a desire to protect the King's lands. Early policy in New England in sometimes granting border land to town groups for protection of the colony satisfied the desire for land and also recognized the value of frontier settlement. Later frontier settlement by wanderers may have enjoyed, therefore, a presumption of desirability. But one striking difference between New England and the South was plain before the Revolution, as William Grayson stated when the land ordinance of 1785 was being debated—namely, that "the Eastern people . . . before the Revolution never had an idea of any quantity of Earth above a hundred acres," whereas in the southern colonies no one wanted less than a thousand.[9]

What is more important, the impediments to recognition of fee-simple title (and all squatters desired to be lords of the land) were less in New England than in the South. There was another great impediment to the easy spread of land ownership in the South. This was the greater prevalence of feudal remnants in land titles.

In all the southern colonies, particularly south of Maryland, official policy and practices favored in every way land engrossment by speculators, the governors and other high officers participating in the gains.[10] In recording proceedings of the Virginia Council, land grants occupied more space than all other subjects combined.[11] That colony's procedure in grants—a warrant of survey, a rough location on land *assumed* to be open, a subsequent survey, a warrant for caveats, and delivery of a patent—was administered with astonishing laxity. Indefinite delay, sometimes for years, particularly before location and before survey, might ensue before the patent issued. Unexecuted warrants for location or survey might be bought and sold among speculators for years, and

---

558; J. C. Ballagh, "Introduction to Southern Economic History," Amer. Hist. Association, *Report* for 1897, 99–129; Gray, *Agriculture,* pp. 372–404; W. R. Shepherd, "The Land System of Provincial Pennsylvania," Amer. Hist. Association, *Report* for 1895, pp. 117–125. See also this volume, Chap. 4, note 44.

[9] Grayson to Madison, Burnett, *LMCC,* VIII, 129.

[10] Gray, *Agriculture,* pp. 396–402.

[11] L. W. Labaree, in *MVHR,* V (1919), 397.

until the land was patented no quitrents were collectible. In every detail the system favored the capitalist and speculator, excluding the would-be settler. The distribution of the colony's greatest resource was characterized by revolting class favoritism.[12]

No doubt there was fraud everywhere, although satisfactory revelations of it are few. Much official fraud—involving not only Sir William Johnson and George Croghan but many others—certainly existed in New York. The best known and most egregious examples are southern. Very likely no single freebooter in South Carolina or Georgia equaled in enterprise William Blount of North Carolina, but the Yazoo frauds were of more towering conception and extent, and some little-known frauds in Georgia are beyond comparison both in their irrationality and in the involvement of the state's governors.[13]

The situation in the middle colonies was nearer that in New England than that in the South. Pennsylvania's economy was markedly agricultural, and since the fertile eastern valleys were relatively settled, a westward movement of squatters on proprietary lands began early. The land system was distinctly favorable to small holdings.[14] New York started with great manors in the Hudson valley, some of them from 400 to 1,500 square miles in area, which were economically akin to English feudal estates.[15] But the economic and political dominance of the manorial group waned, and in the British period feudal estates, even in the masked form of fee grants for quitrents, had little vitality.[16] There were land riots in New York and in New Jersey.[17] There was a

[12] Much of Kentucky was given by the Council to its members in grants of 10,000 to 100,000 acres. W. R. Jillson, *The Kentucky Land Grants* (Louisville, 1925), Introduction. On fraud in the headright system in early Virginia as the basis of grants, see P. A. Bruce, *Economic History of Virginia,* I, 528–532; and later Gray, *Agriculture,* pp. 386–391.

[13] The Yazoo frauds involved speculators of both states. For Georgia, see S. G. McLendon, *History of the Public Domain of Georgia* (Atlanta, 1924), pp. 40–64.

[14] C. Huston, *Essay on the History and Nature of Original Titles to Land in . . . Pennsylvania* (Philadelphia, 1849); A. T. Volwiler, *George Croghan and the Western Movement, 1748–1782* (Cleveland, 1926), pp. 236–240; W. R. Shepherd, *supra,* n. 8.

[15] Maps in O'Callaghan, *Doc. Hist.,* I, 421, 474; compare pp. 249–257.

[16] C. Becker, "Nominations in Colonial New York," *AHR,* VI (1900), 261–262.

[17] J. Mark, *Agrarian Conflicts in Colonial New York, 1711–1775* (New York, 1940). The latest New York riots were against old Dutch manorial dues in 1839–46. D. Murray, "The Antirent Episode in the State of New York," *Amer. Hist. Association, Report* for 1896, I, 137–173; T. J. Wertenbaker,

good deal of land speculation in direct violation or circumvention of royal orders. Speculators resisted grants of the fee, preferring long lease-holds of a hundred or hundreds of years; and as there was no large westward movement of buyers before the Revolution (no settlements west of Utica), the alternative between squatter troubles or small grants in fee was not presented until after federal sales in the Northwest also presented competition.

The land systems of the Carolinas and Georgia were similar to Virginia's. That the social policy evidenced in the southern colonies was truly that of the home government is emphasized by the fact that in the twenty years (1763–83) it held West Florida, when disaffection in the old colonies was rising, it reproduced there everything in the English system that was losing vitality in America.[18]

The Revolution is good evidence that in the political field there was no difference in the Americanism of Northerners and Southerners. It is difficult to find satisfactory reasons why social habits and policies of Southerners should have been nearer than those of Northerners to English practices. Evidence of the difference is found in the distinctly greater prevalence of feudal remnants in land titles in the southern colonies. For vast areas of their land, quitclaim rents (which were a commutation of feudal services) were the purchase price, in substitution for immediate payment for the fee simple. One reason for this may be that northern colonies, particularly Massachusetts, were organized at an earlier date under statutes of their own making.[19] Statutes drafted in England would obviously result in a greater prevalence of feudal titles in the South. A family could be sustained through generations by rents paid under leases for terms of years, or by interest on money for which the fee was sold, as well as by feudal quitrents; and Americans accepted these ideas long before the English—New Eng-

---

Father Knickerbocker's Rebels (New York, 1948). On great grants in middle and western New York to land companies, see R. L. Higgins, *Expansion in New York, with Especial Reference to the Eighteenth Century* (Columbus, 1931), and S. Livermore, *Early American Land Companies* (New York, 1939).

[18] C. Johnson, *British West Florida, 1763–1783* (New Haven, 1943), pp. 30–31, 120–130; C. N. Howard, *British Development of West Florida, 1763–1769* (Berkeley, 1947), pp. 27, 124, 126, and list of grants.

[19] Few of those under which Massachusetts was organized were English, whereas all the South below Virginia had a very large common basis of English statutes. See list in N. Dane, *General Abridgment and Digest of American Law with Occasional Notes and Comments* (9 vols., Boston, 1823–30), VI, 606, 610, 611.

landers possibly no earlier than Southerners. However, one senses that in Virginia there was pressure for a social system based on rents as in England, whereas reports of the practice of long-term leases in New York suggest no motives other than purely economic. This may, of course, be owing to the reporters. Nonetheless, the English system was embedded in the statute books of the southern colonies. This is not meant to imply that primogeniture, quitrents, and entails existed only in the South, since old titles of these types existed everywhere, more or less, in 1775 or 1800 or even later. But there were more such old titles in the South, and the Revolution did not end the creation of them. They fell into desuetude earlier in the North, and their creation was prohibited earlier, speaking generally, in the North than in the South.[20]

Lord Dunmore's characterization of Watauga as a "dangerous example of forming governments distinct from and independent of his Majesty's Authority" became applicable after the Revolution to the projected new states already discussed—particularly to the state of Franklin.[21] It soon became equally a threat to the Confederation. The confiscation and sale of Loyalists' lands during the war had not inured to the benefit of the poorer class.[22] Years of economic depression followed war. For years, too, all the states had been conceding to squatters the favor of pre-emption rights in their open lands. Migration westward inevitably continued on a great scale. Eastern Virginia lost many of its planters to the piedmont; in eastern and middle Tennessee and in Kentucky there was a great growth of farms; everywhere, more or less, wanderers were forming new settlements.

Frederick J. Turner inaugurated serious study of the West's history by emphasizing the fact that the squatterland which constituted the western border of every colony was both socially and politically more democratic than eastern sections of the colonies.[23] For different reasons,

[20] However, only generalities are significant—Jefferson's presence altered the situation in Virginia, the *rarity* of entails might cause their abolition to be late (1851 in Pennsylvania), and so on. See R. B. Morris, *Studies in the History of American Law* (New York, 1930).

[21] April 16, 1774, R. G. Thwaites and Kellogg (ed.), *Documentary History of Dunmore's War* (Madison, 1905).

[22] J. F. Jameson, *The Revolution Considered as a Social Movement* (Princeton, 1926).

[23] "In each colony this region was in conflict with the dominant classes of the coast." F. J. Turner, "Contributions of the West to American Democracy," *Atlantic Monthly*, XCI, 85. Shays' Rebellion of 1786–87 in Massachusetts, the acts of the Regulators in North Carolina between 1754 and 1771 (A. Hender-

economic or political, Washington and other leaders feared such scattering, but there was virtually no governmental opposition to it. It presented two great problems—one of control, the other of social purpose. The first: if its augmented scale and heightened tempo made prohibition impossible, could it be, at least, controlled? And who should control its further progress—the states individually, or all unitedly? The second: should the remaining lands be preserved for actual settlers, only? Or be allowed to pass to them through speculators? These two problems—the first of great political dangers but of immense possibilities for the future of federalism, the second of great social import—confronted the Continental Congress.

The need of centralized control of western lands had long been apparent. The Albany Congress of 1754 had appealed to the King to create a colonial union to manage Indian trade, war, and treaties, buy and settle Indian lands, and temporarily govern such settlements, proposing the creation by the Crown, ultimately, of new states.[24] From 1776 onward there was talk of paying the common war debt with western lands.[25] In the peace negotiations Franklin had that in mind in insisting upon retention of the Ohio-Illinois region. The argument for common enjoyment inevitably centered on the view that the West had been won by all the states joined in war—though Virginia, almost alone, fought it there, even if for her own purposes; and by the treaty of peace, although the latter involved, as will later be seen, an insolvable problem.

That the objectives stated by the Albany Congress would be fundamentals in attempting the later creation of any union of the states was virtually certain. It became clear during the Revolution that fear by the landless states of the power of the landed within any new union would precipitate a bitter struggle. Land meant safety when all were near bankruptcy, and it meant power in any new union. Six northern states—five of them smaller, together, than the smallest of the southern

son, *The Conquest of the Old Southwest,* New York, 1920, pp. 161–189), the land riots of New Jersey and New York, and the armed threats against the legislature of Pennsylvania by the frontiersmen (1763–64) illustrate the truth which Turner first emphasized.

[24] Franklin, *Writings* (Smyth ed.), III, 197–226, particularly 217–222.

[25] *Amer. Archives,* III, 53, 120, 209, 211, 508–509, 788, 827. There was also Silas Deane's proposal of a colony, *ibid.,* pp. 1020, 1051.

states—had definite bounds; three others, of which two were diminutive, had western claims conflicting with Virginia's. The problem faced by Congress when it assumed the task of securing the West for common enjoyment of all the states was that of convincing the landed states that equality in a greater union was more desirable than preponderance in one weakened by inequalities. This was the true and ultimate problem, and success necessarily would depend on common origins and political ideals, and upon the willingness of the landed states to sacrifice land for ideals. The immediate and obvious problems were those of vague and conflicting charter limits, and claims by land companies based on purchases from the Indians.

The indefiniteness and unreality of boundary descriptions were not the only charter problems. How many of the colonial charters had been forfeited is a question open to dispute; what effect forfeiture had upon charter limits is also disputable. Leaving these matters aside, the four southernmost colonies, claiming to the South Sea, had been impliedly acknowledged in the French-British peace negotiations of 1763 to extend only to the Mississippi. New York, often included among sea-to-sea claimants, never claimed even to the Mississippi, but only into the Ohio-Michigan area under a supposed deed from the Iroquois which was utterly worthless.[26] The claims of Massachusetts and Connecticut were visionary, notwithstanding that the latter ultimately received western territory equal to her own area in satisfaction of her claims.[27] Shelburne was quite right in referring to "the nonsense" of the charters. That was true of Virginia's, "from the sea-coast . . . up into the land . . . west and north-west" (seemingly to the South Sea—at least indefinitely). Nevertheless, it was the best, and she had spent blood and money in defending it from 1778 to 1781.[28] Despite conflicting

[26] State of New York, *Report of the Regents of the University on the Boundaries of New York* (2 vols., Albany, 1878, 1884), *passim.*

[27] Under a charter of 1629, but that of 1691 read "towards the South Sea or westward as far as our Collonyes of Rhode Island, Connecticut, and the Narragansett Country." The claims of all the states are stated in T. Donaldson, *The Public Domain* (Washington, 1884), pp. 82, 86–88, but he was not a critical person. Boyd found no evidence antedating 1750 of belief in a South Sea extension. J. P. Boyd (ed.), *The Susquehanna Company Papers* (4 vols., Wilkes-Barre, 1930–33), I, lvii.

[28] Bodley, *Our First Great West* (Louisville, Ky., 1938), p. 69, denies the Crown's right to reduce Virginia's original limits in favor of Carolina, Maryland, and Pennsylvania.

boundary claims of other colonies and without even mentioning such conflicts, the Northwest had been generally treated by Great Britain as Virginia's in the years following 1755.

All attempts to incorporate in the Articles of Confederation congressional powers to secure the West failed. Franklin's draft of confederation articles adopted the proposals of 1754. John Dickinson's draft of articles gave Congress power to fix boundaries and take the West for all the states. It also contained a threat against Virginia in proposing to empower Congress to confirm the claims, which were within her admitted limits, of the Walpole and Indiana Companies.[29] When this draft was revised, only Maryland was willing to give Congress power to fix boundaries, and a proposed appeal to it as a last resort after arbitration was guarded by a provision that no state should "be deprived of territory for the benefit of the United States."[30]

The situation was somewhat similar as respected the land companies and their Indian "deeds." Virginia's position was strong. The West was "Indian lands"—that is, in Indian occupation. Within a few years after the Albany Congress, the increasing number of simulated conveyances of such lands to private persons had led to their prohibition by the Proclamation of 1763. They continued, however, and culminated in the grants to the Illinois and Wabash companies (1773, 1775) and the Indiana Company grant of 1768. The latter, and that to the Walpole Company, were within Virginia's limits. The Revolution had rid her of this last, but the others, as well as Richard Henderson's Transylvania deed, were continuing dangers.

When the claims of the Transylvania Company were denied by the Virginia convention of 1776, it was resolved that no land should thenceforth be purchased within her limits from Indians without legislative authority, and commissioners were appointed to examine into any earlier purchase. The legislature, that year and the following, assured preemption rights to actual settlers.[31] The Indiana Company, late in 1778, submitted an Indian "deed," and protested any Virginia claims west of

[29] *J.C.C.*, II, 197–198, V, 549, XIX, 218; compare V, 682; L. K. Mathews, "Benjamin Franklin's Plans for a Colonial Union, 1750–1775," *APSR*, VIII (1914), 393–412.

[30] August 20, 1776, *J.C.C.*, V, 674–689. This provision was retained in the Articles in their final form. *Ibid.*, XIX, 218.

[31] Abernethy, *Western Lands and the American Revolution* (New York, 1937), pp. 218, 219, 221.

the mountains.[32] The Illinois-Wabash Company, after reorganization to meet new emergencies (with some thirty shares available for use where and when needed), memorialized the assembly and offered land for Virginia's military bounties.[33] Finally, in 1779 those two companies and the Transylvania Company united in a formal presentation of their claims.[34] When the Indiana Company failed, the issue was settled for all—the claim of the Transylvania Company having been again pronounced void in November, 1773.[35] By another act, all Indian grants of land within her borders, and all claims based thereon, were declared void and the Convention resolutions of 1776 were reaffirmed.[36] Consolation grants offered to the three companies were accepted by the Transylvania Company only. When the Indiana Company made known its intent to appeal to Congress, Virginia sent that body a strong protest denying, justifiably, that it had any jurisdiction, although conceding that it might perhaps arbitrate after the Articles of Confederation should be ratified.[37]

As respects the Congress, its discretion was uncontrolled by any provision. Franklin's draft of Articles of Confederation prohibited purchases from the Indians by either private individuals or states. John Dickinson's draft allowed both until state limits should be fixed—therefore throughout the period now being considered. The Articles finally adopted for ratification by the states were silent on the matter.[38]

Congress dealt with the tangled problem with admirable practicality. A fact of great importance, which has seemingly been totally ignored, is that *title* to land was not involved in any "cessions" made to Congress. All the Northwest had been crown land, ungranted and unoccupied, though some claims for military bounty grants had attached to it

[32] The deed had been recorded at Staunton. Abernethy, *Western Lands*, p. 189. Volwiler, *Croghan*, pp. 309, 341; the memorial (October 1, 1776) is in print in a rare volume which he cites.

[33] *Virginia State Papers*, I, 314.

[34] Also the Ohio Company of Virginia, though not of this class; its claims were again ignored.

[35] Henderson, *Old Southwest*, p. 278.

[36] Hening, *Statutes of Va.* Such a policy had first been proclaimed by her in 1754.

[37] *J.C.C.*, XXI, 704, 781, 784, 1057, 1077, 1098, 1113.

[38] *Ibid.*, II, 197–198, V, 549, XIX, 218. Dickinson's draft provided that after state limits should be ascertained, purchases outside them should be by the Confederation for the benefit of all the states.

under the Proclamation of 1763. Acts of the Crown (not, however, that Proclamation) had changed in various ways the boundaries of Virginia and other colonies. Virginia's interest was a mere expectancy that, if no other alterations should be made by the Crown in her boundaries, her government would gradually be extended over the area as it was settled. Similar expectancies of sale or settlement were held by Virginia's rival claimants. All were on substantially an equal basis, and the appeal of Congress was to the patriotism of all equally. It was an appeal to each to renounce its expectancy in favor of all collectively.

Actual title to western lands in both Southwest and Northwest was acquired much later from Great Britain by the treaty of peace. That treaty was made with "the commissioners of the United States of America," and to those states the title must have passed, not to Congress, which was merely their agent in choosing the commissioners, just as it was in securing their individual renunciation, in favor of all, of their separate claims. But did title pass to them, by the treaty, separately or as "united States"—which they were, in a Confederation, when the treaty was made? Embittered controversy over this question delayed (some students have thought it nearly made impossible) the creation of the later federal union of 1788. It cannot, therefore, be ignored merely because, being unanswerable, it was conclusively settled neither then nor later—since it lost significance by adoption of the Constitution of 1788. To settle a controversy in 1802 with Georgia, the United States did, however, concede that Georgia had taken such title directly, and the Supreme Court would not disturb the settlement despite Chief Justice Marshall's disagreement with the concession.[39]

When a second effort to gain for Congress the power to set state limits and take the West for the Confederation was supported by only five states, eight states signed, in July, 1778, a form of ratification.[40] A circular appeal by Congress brought in two more, and only New York, Virginia, and Maryland were left morally uncommitted. Virginia attempted to complete the Confederation without Maryland (by proposing that landed states provide military bounty lands for all landless states that would join), but this failed. The result was a declaration by

[39] *Ill. Hist. Coll.*, XXV, lviii *et seq.* Discussion of these matters, still of vital interest in the law-school years of Justice Story, will be found in his *Commentaries on the Constitution of the United States* (10th ed., 3 vols., Boston, 1833), secs. 198–217, 229–242.

[40] *J.C.C.*, XI, 656, 657, 677; comments in *Ill. Hist. Coll.*, XXV, lvi–lxix.

Maryland (December, 1778) that she would never join until all western lands should be renounced, and in this Connecticut joined her (May, 1779).[41]

Two more years passed before the union was legally established. It was in this period that the land companies pressed their claims, beginning with Walpole and Indiana memorials in 1779. Since a general peace with the Indians was then under consideration, it was proposed that Congress secure from them cessions of land, subject to prior claims of the states, and for the benefit of these to the extent of their proved rights.[42] This proposal was full of absurdities, inconsistencies, legal problems, and dangers.[43] The committee merely recommended that all states suspend sales of unappropriated land during war, and it was so voted, only Virginia and North Carolina dissenting.[44] This was just when sales under the former's land-office act of 1779 were beginning. Manifestly, if the land companies exerted any influence on this occasion, Congress alone profited by it—whether by plan or chance—in putting pressure on Virginia. She answered with a "Remonstrance," but she nevertheless suggested that "one or more of the larger states" might, "for their own Convenience," be divided and claim representation for each part.[45]

An offer by New York in February, 1780, to cede her western claims presented to Virginia the prospect of facing all other northern states as active opponents.[46] During these debates the secretary of Congress

[41] Hening, *Statutes of Va.*, X, 549 (Maryland's declaration, December 15, 1778); *J.C.C.*, XIII, 29, XIV, 617–618, 619–622; *Ill. Hist. Coll.*, XXV, lix–lxx.

[42] *J.C.C.*, XV, 1223–1224, 1229–1230. Congress voted that Indians might "sell" land only to it, or to others with its consent.

[43] (1) If the Indians had title and could cede it, then there would be no prior state claims. (2) If deeds were taken only for land not already ceded to Croghan and the land companies, that would make more difficult successful denial of them in a legal action and (3) contrariwise if Indian deeds were taken for all the Northwest. There seems to be no evidence that the plan was seriously considered. On Indian "title" compare Abernethy, *Western Lands*, pp. 189, 221, 239, 242, 363.

[44] October 30, 1779, *J.C.C.*

[45] December 14, 1779, Hening, *Statutes of Va.*, X, 557–559.

[46] For New York documents, *Report of the Regents . . . on the Boundaries of . . . New York*, I, 149–154. For the deed (February 19, 1780), see correct text in Carter, *Territorial Papers*, II, 3 and n. 8; *J.C.C.*, XIX, 208–213. Final acceptance by Congress on October 29, 1782, *ibid.*, XXIII, 694. Since the distinction between warranty deeds and mere quitclaim deeds of private individuals does not apply, Bodley's strictures upon New York's legislative act (*First Great West*, pp. 176–184) are misconceived.

had reported "a violent inclination in most of the states to appropriate all the western lands to the use of the United States."[47] In September, after approval by Congress of a recommendation that all states should cede such claims, Virginia's delegates moved that all ceded lands not needed for military bounties should be laid out in new states and be "a common fund for . . . members of the Confederation."[48] On October 10 it was agreed that land so acquired should be *"formed into distinct republican states, which shall become members of the federal union, and have the same rights of sovereignty, freedom and independence, as the other states."*[49]

This is the greatest date and act in the history of American federalism—and surely among the noblest acts of Virginia. Its significance respecting political sentiment throughout the country outweighs a hundredfold the monarchical sentiments of a few ultraconservatives whose views were once often cited. Six months before the states had given even legal existence to the frail Confederation, their delegates in the Congress voted unanimously for the creation of a vastly stronger union. Two and a half years before any state owned a single acre of western land, the delegates of all the states recorded in Congress their renunciation of every acre in favor of the greater union to be formed. The states had never given any powers to Congress. They ignored its pleas for troops, for funds. They ignored its efforts to protect common interests by creating auxiliary agencies. But helpless as it was, it had an incomparable knowledge of popular sentiment throughout the country, and on that knowledge it acted confidently and successfully.

A circular letter to all the states, with its unanimous vote for an expanding empire of republican institutions, went out from Congress on the same day as the resolution (October 10). Connecticut immediately voted accession. On January 2, 1781, Virginia's cession was voted, subject to exceptions; on February 2, Maryland's. On March 1, 1781, the Confederation was legally established by the delivery of New York's and Virginia's deeds and Maryland's final signature of the Articles of Confederation.[50]

[47] November 30, Burnett, *LMCC,* IV, 109.
[48] *J.C.C.,* XVII, 808.
[49] *Ibid.,* XVIII, 836, 915, 916.
[50] *Ibid.,* XIX, 138–140, 186, 211–214, 253; Hening, *Statutes of Va.,* X, 564; E. C. Burnett, *The Continental Congress* (New York, 1941), pp. 98–99; S. G. Sioussat, "The Chevalier de la Luzerne and the Ratification of the Articles of Confederation," *Pa. Mag. of Hist. and Biog.,* LX.

It was still necessary to examine the claims of the land companies. Two conditions in Virginia's cession were, first, that Congress should invalidate all private purchases of Indian land and, second, that it should guarantee Virginia's remaining domain—that south of the Ohio. On October 10, 1780, Congress had approved the first of these conditions to the extent of agreeing that no such purchase unratified "by lawful authority" should be "deemed valid or ratified by Congress."[51] This disposed of the Illinois-Wabash purchases, also of the Indiana Company grant included within the Vandalia boundaries.

The second condition covered the sleeping British grant to the Walpole Company and reinforced the test imposed by the first condition upon the grants within Vandalia to the Indiana Company and to Croghan. Twice in 1781, once in 1782 (after Samuel Wharton, long-time lobbyist in London for these associated interests, became a delegate from Delaware), and again in 1783, the pending cessions from Virginia and other states, together with memorials from the land companies, were submitted to committees.

From the first the Walpole grant was disfavored as against public policy, so vast was its extent and so few its beneficiaries. Nevertheless, reimbursement of American partners in that audacious and corrupt foray against the crown lands was recommended from the beginning.[52] As for the claims under Indian deeds, that of the Illinois-Wabash Company was dismissed as without governmental sanction.[53] However, two committees reported favorably on the claims of Croghan and the Indiana Company.[54] A renunciation of land by the Indians in favor of the Suffering Traders of 1763 had, perhaps, been authorized by government, but the deed given in 1768 to the Indiana Company (successor to those Traders) at Fort Stanwix was not approved by the King. As for Croghan, one allegedly made to him in 1749, if actually made, was undoubtedly the only one that was not taken in violation of royal orders with which no one in America was better acquainted than he.

[51] For the conditions, see Hening, *Statutes of Va.*, X, 566; action of October 10, 1780, *J.C.C.*, XVIII, 916.

[52] *Ibid.*, XXI.

[53] *Ibid.* For the ultimate fate of this company, in 1811, see *A.S.P., Pub. Lands*, I, 27, 82, 160, 188.

[54] *J.C.C.* (November 3, 1781, *et seq.*), XXII, 184, 191–194, 223–232, 234, 240, 241, and (May 1, 1782, *et seq.*), 559–563. The first committee said of the Croghan and Indiana Company claims that they had been secured "*bona fide* [which is inconceivable] and for a valuable consideration," which would have recognized no minimum limit under either ethical, economic, or legal standards.

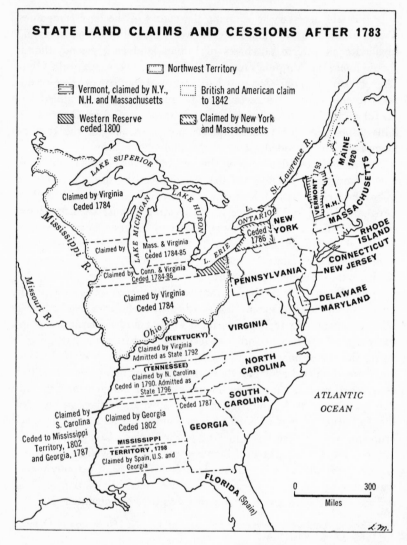

STATE LAND CLAIMS AND CESSIONS AFTER 1783

Northwest Territory

Vermont, claimed by N.Y., N.H. and Massachusetts

British and American claim to 1842

Western Reserve ceded 1800

Claimed by New York and Massachusetts

When the first of these reports in favor of the Croghan-Indiana claims was called up for consideration five months later, Arthur Lee of Virginia moved that, preceding a vote on any state cession, all delegates should declare on their honor whether they were directly or indirectly interested in any land company claiming land in opposition to the claims of a state offering a cession of such land to Congress, and that their declarations should be entered in the journal. This killed that report. When the second report was made, and Lee's motion was substantially renewed, action was several times temporarily, and eventually indefinitely, postponed. The Indiana Company's deed received at Fort Stanwix in 1768 remained a nullity, but perhaps some equity attached to the Company's claims because of Sir William Johnson's negotiations of 1765. All the other claims of the companies were bald illegalities, in view of the prohibition of all private purchases from Indians by the Proclamation of 1763 and by the land plan of 1774, and of the annulment of all earlier purchases proclaimed by General Haldimand under royal orders later in that year. None of the claims was recognized by the United States after 1789.[55]

As Virginia had rightly protested, Congress had no power to decide on the legality of the company claims, which was explained in the course of the controversy.[56] The attention given to the claims by Congress—really very brief, between ever pressing problems of army supplies, finance, and diplomacy—has been exaggerated. Even more exaggeration has been given to the committee reports favoring the company claims based on supposed Indian cessions. They have been treated as attempts to browbeat Virginia, but not by Congress, clearly, for it did not approve the reports.[57] Nor is there discernible any prospective action by Virginia, favorable to company claims, which browbeating might induce her to take or not to take. Eight months before the first

[55] *A.S.P., Pub. Lands*, II, 108–253.

[56] *J.C.C.*, XXV, 561, 562, 563; antecedents, *ibid.*, XXIV, 271, 381, 384, 406–409, 444, note.

[57] Abernethy (*Western Lands*, pp. 239, 245, 307, 365) gives no evidence to support statements that the contest in Congress was "between certain States claiming Western lands for themselves, and those claiming it in the interest of certain land companies," and that "the middle group" of states was "controlled largely by members of the great land companies" (*ibid.*, p. 172). Nor has any evidence been found to support the view that states "like" Maryland were "willing" or "inclined to prefer that Spain should take the West rather than allow Virginia to hold it." T. C. and M. J. Pease, *George Rogers Clark and the Revolution in Illinois, 1763–1787* (Springfield, 1929), pp. 66, 95. It is strange that southern writers, refighting Confederation controversies, should repudiate the nobility of Virginia's cession by accusing her of submission to northern guile and pressure. Bodley's statement that "the great land-grabbing scheme . . . forced Virginia's cession of the Northwest territory" (*First Great West*, p. 194) is a great exaggeration. The statement that "Congress virtually asserted a fictitious claim to the whole trans-Allegheny region"—Bodley (ed.), *Littell's Political Transactions in and Concerning Kentucky* (Lexington, 1926), p. iv—is wholly unacceptable. Britain owned the open Northwest, and until after 1783 Congress never asserted any claims.

of these committee reports was made, she had renounced to Congress all claims to northwestern lands affected by the company claims. Her absolute denial of Indian titles for five years, since 1776, committed her no less irrevocably to denial of company claims south of the Ohio.

As respects state renunciations other than Virginia's, acceptance of any without amendments seemed at first inexpedient, although later New York's was favored on the basis that the Iroquois deed on which it rested had granted (a dodge, but a possibility) "jurisdiction" only— thus evading the issue of Indian title. A year later it was finally accepted.[58] There were some absurdities, such as a report that New York's claim covered all that Virginia offered to cede—this along with another that the latter's bounds had in 1763 (by the Proclamation) been restricted to the Alleghenies.[59] It was only after the peace, and after waiver by Virginia of the two conditions upon her cession noted above, that it was finally accepted on March 1, 1784.[60] After Virginia's cession was accepted, the others needed soon followed. Connecticut offered hers in 1784, but it was only accepted in September, 1786. One meanwhile offered by Massachusetts was accepted some months earlier.[61] After Connecticut's cession the Confederation was in possession of the entire Northwest except a "Western Reserve" (larger than Connecticut) which that state temporarily retained.[62] Cessions in the Southwest will be mentioned in another connection.[63]

ORGANIZATION OF THE PUBLIC LANDS

In framing a land policy for the Confederation the colonies had an abundant experience in the sale, occupation, and attempted control

[58] Committee of June, 1781, *J.C.C.*, XX, 534, 696, 704; Committee of October, 1781, *ibid.*, XXI, 1032, 1057, and *Ill. Hist. Colls.*, XXV, lxxx, *et seq.;* October 29, 1782, *Jour. Cont. Cong.*, xxiii, 694; see Carter, *Territorial Papers,* II, 3.

[59] *J.C.C.*, XXI, 1098.

[60] *Ibid.*, XXVI, 89–90, 112–117; Hening, *Statutes of Va.*, XI, 326–328, 567; Carter, *Terr. Papers*, II, 6–9. But the vote of Congress accepting cession if Virginia would omit one condition was in September, 1783, *J.C.C.*, XXV, 561, 562.

[61] *J.C.C.*, XXVIII, 271–274, 279–283. On October 10, 1780, Connecticut had offered a cession.

[62] *Ibid.*, XXXI, 654–655; Carter, *Terr. Papers*, II, 22–24; III, 84–86.

[63] The total cessions have been variously estimated; compare Donaldson, *Public Domain,* p. 11, and B. H. Hibbard, *History of the Public Land Policies* (New York, 1924).

of their own lands.[64] Surveys were in all necessarily imperfect, primarily because of the undurable character of physical features upon which boundary lines depended. In other matters the chief problem, in view of frontier conditions by 1781, would necessarily be to compromise upon some plan of settlement between the strictly controlled and compact expansion of earliest Massachusetts and the uncertainties of Virginia's lax disorder.

From a governmental viewpoint the former had advantages, which the British government had recognized.[65] To Washington, who knew the West as did few others, a regular and compact settlement seemed a primary consideration.[66] In the spring of 1784 a committee headed by Jefferson drafted a land ordinance which retained considerable of the Virginia practices. After scanty consideration then and a year later it was abandoned, and another plan reported. This was adopted with only one, or no, dissenter on May 21, 1785.[67] According to the committee chairman, William Grayson:

> Some gentlemen looked upon it [the problem] as a matter of revenue only and . . . [thought] it was true policy to get the money [without] parting with the inhabitants to populate the Country, and thereby prevent the lands in the original states from depreciating . . . part of the Eastern Gentlemen wish to have the land sold in such a manner as to suit their people who may chose to emigrate. . . . But others are apprehensive of the consequences which may result from the new States taking their position in the Confederacy. They perhaps wish that this event may be delayed as long as possible.[68]

The ideal of compact settlement, area after area, was abandoned. No title other than a fee simple was ever considered. The plan required a survey of land before sale, sales by public auction, and a deed for each

[64] A. C. Ford, *Colonial Precedents of Our National Land System as It Existed in 1800* (Madison, 1910); H. Tatter, "State and Federal Land Policies During the Confederation Period," *Agricultural History*, IX, 176–186.

[65] Notably, in words in the regulations respecting West Florida. Johnson, *British West Florida*, p. 138 and index.

[66] Jefferson, *Writings* (Ford ed.), X, 303, 306. Washington made a western trip in the autumn of 1784; it evidently confirmed his views, and influenced those of others; see also *Ill. Hist. Coll.*, XXV, cclxiii–cclxvi.

[67] Jefferson's ordinance draft is in *J.C.C.*, XXVII, 446; Grayson's *ibid.*, XXVII, 446, or Carter, *Terr. Papers*, II, 12. Rufus King of New York was the one unyielding opponent of the Ordinance.

[68] Burnett, *LMCC*, VIII, 96.

tract sold. A national surveying plan was adopted which identifies unalterably each square mile of the public domain.[69]

Disputes over the points referred to by Grayson continued for some years, and experience added others on which policy was divergent. Large tracts favored speculators, but promised ready money to pay the war debt. Grayson believed that agreement on any ordinance was made possible only by "the importunities of the public creditors and the reluctance to pay them by taxation."[70] But settlers were bound, as Jefferson said, to be predominantly poor, and sale in small tracts at low prices was bound to become a necessity. So the ordinance started with a compromise: half of each township was to be sold as an entirety, the other half in sections, alternately. When the new Union was established, proceeds of the public lands were pledged for payment of public debts, but a rising national prosperity soon enabled other than financial considerations to dominate the development of the system. The Northwest had been gained from Virginia, and all company claims based on Indian grants disappeared. Of the great Southwest little was secured for the public domain. South Carolina's claims, ceded in 1787, were of questionable existence.[71] Virginia's, and especially North Carolina's, were disappointments. In retaining for herself, soon for Kentucky, the land now within the latter state, Virginia relieved the Union of the stupendous mess of prodigal, unsurveyed, conflicting grants which made Kentucky the most surveyed state of the country and the greatest sufferer from land litigation.[72] Under the terms of North Carolina's cession to Congress of what became Tennessee, it was soon clear that little land would be available for national purposes. After carrying the task and

[69] The plan was once altered in one detail (the manner of numbering sections), but never since then.

[70] *Ibid.,* VIII, 118.

[71] R. S. Cotterill, "The South Carolina Land Cessions," *MVHR,* XII (1926), 376–384; Donaldson, *Public Domain,* p. 11.

[72] The acts of 1779 (Hening, *Statutes of Va.,* X, 35–65, 177–180) had fixed an order of precedence among various types of claims typical of frontier conditions. Excluding reservations for military bounties, etc., warrants had been issued for five or more times as much land as was available for entry. In a quarter-century the Loyal Company had surveyed only one-fourth of its grant of 1,250 square miles; it lost the rest. On Kentucky's heritage of litigation, see W. Ayres, "Land Titles in Kentucky," Kentucky State Bar Association, *Proceedings* for 1909, pp. 160–191; N. S. Shaler, *Kentucky: A Pioneer Commonwealth* (3rd ed., New York, 1886), pp. 49–52; Cotterill, *History of Pioneer Kentucky,* pp. 231–233.

cost of salvage operations for fifty years, the federal government finally renounced, in favor of Tennessee, any possible surplus.[73]

It remained for Georgia to release the remaining claims of states in the Southwest. She did so by an act of 1788, which left open issues over which controversies with the Union continued for fourteen years.[74] In 1785 she had assumedly established county organization around Natchez, thereby asserting rights of jurisdiction. And in 1789 and 1794–95 she made scandalous sales to speculators of enormous areas in what is now Alabama and Mississippi, thereby asserting title to the soil.[75] These claims contradicted claims by the United States to the same area, and violated national treaty assurances given to the Indians of the region; and the actions of the speculators gravely threatened peace with Spain. In truth, Georgia's territory had never extended westward of (substantially) her present limits.[76] However, the United States ultimately secured acknowledged title to that area only by admitting that Georgia had owned it when she made the sales to the Yazoo speculators just mentioned, and by accepting a cession from her—thus becoming financially responsible for sales by those speculators to innocent purchasers.[77]

[73] The state continued to suffer from Blount's legacy. Donaldson, *Public Domain*, p. 83; L. C. Gray, *Agriculture*, pp. 626–627; S. G. Sioussat, "Some Phases of Tennessee Politics in the Jackson Period," *AHR*, XIV (1908), 51–69; citations in Carter, *Terr. Papers*, IV, 3–8, footnotes.

[74] Carter, *Terr. Papers, ibid.;* and Watson, *Digest of the Laws of Georgia*, p. 370. An offer of part of the land made in 1787 had been declined by Congress, *A.S.P., Pub. Lands*, I, 100.

[75] *A.S.P., Pub. Lands*, I, 28–59, 551, 555.

[76] Georgia's western extension was bounded on the south by Florida, the northern line of which was fixed by the Proclamation of 1763 at 31° (in accordance with the commission given Governor Wright of Georgia on June 6, 1764). But a few months later the second commission of Governor Johnstone of Florida moved its north boundary to the Yazoo's mouth, approximately 32° 28'. See *ASP, Pub. Lands*, I, 57. A report by a Senate committee in 1797, *ibid.*, I, 79, overlooked this. Phillips criticized this disregard of the Wright commission, but overlooked Johnstone's. W. B. Phillips, "Georgia and State Rights," Amer. Hist. Association, *Report* for 1901, II, 33. But after that Great Britain, in 1783, ceded West Florida to Spain, and all British rights north of that colony to the Congress. As Georgia had not even an expectancy in the territory, the Confederation necessarily took soil and jurisdiction there for the states collectively.

[77] In creating the territory of Mississippi in 1798 and establishing its government in 1800, the United States declared that these acts should not impair Georgia's alleged rights to soil and jurisdiction. *A.S.P., Pub. Lands*, I, 558, 112; Carter, *Terr. Papers*, V, 142–145; *U.S. Stat. at Large*, I, 549, II, 69. This abandonment of national claims was confirmed in 1802 by a "com-

Plans for settlement had begun long before state cessions of land claims to the Confederation were completed. That explained, in part, the pressure on Congress to provide for sales of large tracts. A first ordinance for government of settlers, passed in 1784, further stimulated preparations for sales. Resolutions of Congress, in 1776 and later, promising lands to soldiers led to an organization of New England officers which ultimately became the Ohio Company of Connecticut. By order of Congress the Board of Treasury sold at New York in the autumn of 1787 one great tract of land and an option on another. The sale was to the Ohio Company for a settlement in the Northwest Territory. While its agent, Manasseh Cutler, was bargaining for one and one-half million acres, he was offered by William Duer, secretary of the Board of Treasury (but primarily a New York speculator), $143,000 for use in the Company's first payment, on condition that the Company take— for Duer and associates, but concealing their identity—an option for purchase of an additional five million acres. Adequately wined and dined, Cutler consented; and he and Winthrop Sargent, a leader of the Company and secretary of the Northwest Territory, received half of the shares of Duer and associates. The prospect of this great second sale carried the Ohio Company's purchase speedily through Congress, various members of which seem to have been of Duer's group.[78] The Ohio Company (it ultimately received slightly less than half the amount for which it contracted) founded Marietta in April, 1788, the first legal settlement in the Old Northwest.[79] The Scioto Company's option (Duer's) was intended, seemingly, to be used solely as one item in a maze of speculation.[80] The Company's Paris agent, instead of selling

---

promise" by which the United States conceded that Georgia had extended in 1789 and 1795 to the Mississippi in the strip north of 31°, Georgia ceded to the United States all her lands west of substantially her present western bounds, and the United States ceded to Georgia whatever right the Union might have "to the jurisdiction or soil of any lands" within Georgia. *A.S.P., Pub. Lands,* I, 82, 113–114, 125, 126. S. G. McLendon, *History of the Public Domain of Georgia* (Atlanta, 1924), pp. 107–116, ignores the boundary problem. The United States, by the compromise of 1802, set aside 5 million acres of the West to settle possible claims against the Yazoo companies. See Fletcher *v.* Peck (1810), U.S. (6 Cranch) 87, in which the company title was held good on the ground, explicitly emphasized, of the compromise of 1802.

[78] *Ill. Hist. Coll.,* XXV, xxxii (n. 70), ccclxiv–ccclxv, ccclxxi (n. 333); Carter, *Terr. Papers,* II, 417, n. 88.

[79] It acquired 892,900 acres out of 1,781,700. B. H. Hibbard, *A History of the Public Land Policies* (New York, 1924), p. 50.

[80] A. B. Hulbert, "The Methods and Operations of the Scioto Group of

shares in an option, contracted with emigrants for land, and the Scioto Company failed in 1792, never having bought any land whatever, or even contracted to do so. Some five hundred Frenchmen, who were thus caused to come in 1790 to Gallipolis (Ohio), were supplied with land and otherwise aided by the Ohio Company, which was never repaid, and which suffered other losses through the cupidity of its agent and a leading member.

A second great sale was made to the Symmes Associates, between the Great Miami and Little Miami rivers. Unlike the Ohio Company's project, Symmes was an ordinary speculator's venture of buying land to profit by eventual settlement. It was not well managed.[81] There was, however, rapid early settlement, Cincinnati and two other towns being started in 1787.

Congress could not stop land engorgement for speculation (it has been said that title to all of Ohio passed through one or more of six hands), but enlightenment proceeded. Every day showed that poor people to whom any taxes were a burden would settle the land, as Jefferson said, "in spite of everybody."[82] Throughout the later history of the public lands, there were no repetitions of sales such as those of 1787.

In 1783 there was, for a time, a hope that the West could be settled compactly, section by section. Alexander Hamilton joined with a Virginia delegate in Congress in moving that it be divided into districts, each to become a state and enter the Union when its population should amount to 20,000. In September, a committee recommended that government be speedily established "in Such District thereof as shall be judged most convenient for immediate settlement and cultivation," and that a special committee should select "the most eligible part" for one or more states. A committee was appointed the next month, with Jefferson as chairman, to prepare a governmental plan. Its report was made on the same day that Virginia's cession was finally accepted by Congress, and after some changes was adopted on April 23, 1784. The plan was one for the entire West. In the original draft, slavery was prohibited after 1800 in all parts, but this was lost before final action. Presumably because settlement could be controlled only within small

Speculators," *MVHR*, I (1915), 505. For details, *ibid.*, I, 502–515, II, 56–73; also "Andrew Craigie and the Scioto Associates," Amer. Antiquarian Society, *Proceedings* (New Series), XXII.

[81] *Ill. Hist. Colls.*, XXV, xxxi–xxxii.

[82] Jefferson, *Writings* (Ford ed.), II, 239–240.

areas, also because Jefferson believed that democracy could thrive only within such, but ineluctably because action by Virginia, by Massachusetts, and by Congress compelled it, new states were not to be larger than 150 miles square—soil, rivers and mountains notwithstanding.[83]

The plan was remarkably democratic. Two years before Vermont, and eight years before the first state in the Union did so, it granted adult male suffrage. It granted also the fullest possible self-government. With excellent sense it allowed the settlers to establish a government, upon their petition or by direction of Congress, under the constitution and laws of any one of the original states. This, of course, did not mean under all its laws, or without alteration, but as the Wataugans had lived—under laws of North Carolina, suitable in number and with such simplifications as suited their condition. Only by an amendment was any provision made for intervention by Congress pending claim by the settlers of the privilege of self-government, and then only, if necessary, for the "preservation of peace and good order." All this was consonant with ingrained practices of American democracy.[84] Adoption of a permanent constitution and government was permitted upon attaining a population of twenty thousand, on condition that in both stages the government should be republican and subject to wise conditions, particularly as respected the public lands. These conditions, although not mentioned in the Constitution, have always been enforced by the Supreme Court as essential to the effective operation of the federal Union.[85] After this, their admission to the Union was to follow upon attaining a population equal to that of the then least populous of the original states.

Such liberties were now to be conceded to the very borderers whom conservatives of the tidewater areas had so recently held in mortal fear. The classes that dominated the Revolution in the states were everywhere framing constitutions and laws of a like radical spirit. Jefferson's plan was a general one, for all territories north and south and the views which it expressed were endorsed by Congress, in adopting it, as a proper basis for a new colonial system. George Bancroft wrote of it that "Next to the Declaration of Independence (if indeed standing

---

[83] *J.C.C.*, XXIV, 385; XXV, 558; XXVI, 277; *Ill. Hist. Coll.*, XXV, ccliv-cclvi; ccxxxi–ccxxxii, cclxxix–cclxxx; cclxx–cclxxii.

[84] *Ibid.*, pp. cclxxxi.

[85] *Ibid.*, pp. ccclxxxii and n. 370; ccxcv–ccxcvii.

second to that), this document ranks in universal importance of all those drawn by Jefferson; and but for its being superseded by the 'Ordinance of 1787,' would rank among all American State Papers immediately after the National Constitution."[86] This judgment of the Ordinance is not extravagant. Of course it expressed in the main the ideals of Congress, and of the country: its main purpose being to give effect to the intent that all western settlements should become equal states in a federal union. That principle, after its adoption by Congress in 1780, had been made a compact with Virginia in 1783; was the basis equally of Jefferson's Ordinance and the Ordinance of 1787; was reduced in 1788 to a mere possibility under the present federal Constitution; and, as respects southwestern lands ceded by North Carolina and Georgia, was made a compact with them.[87] It embodied the ineradicable lesson of our colonial experience and was the repudiation of colonial imperialism, a basic principle of the country's future political life. If our territorial (colonial) system had actually been based on Jefferson's Ordinance this would, as Bancroft also said, have marked "an era in the history of universal freedom."

But the system was not based on it. In two respects Jefferson had gone beyond the principles which—as time proved—Congress was willing to let stand: namely, abolishing slavery in all prospective Territories, north and south, and assuming the fitness for self-government of all their inhabitants from the beginning. It was not to be expected that conservatives would accept Jefferson's trust in the political sobriety of those who emigrated, and they had time to organize because application of his Ordinance was delayed by administrative obstacles. The Ordinance was law, of course, until repealed by the Ordinance of 1787, and it did not go wholly unnoticed on the frontier.[88] However, several impracticable preparatory plans delayed its application.[89] In addition

[86] History of the Formation of the Constitution of the United States of America (New York, 1882), I, 115.

[87] Art. VI, Sec. 1; Ill. Hist. Coll., XXV, c (n. 122), clxvii (nn. 300–302).

[88] The state of Franklin was established consistently with (hardly under) its provisions, and there was talk in the Northwest of similar action. A. B. Hulbert, Ohio in the Time of the Confederation (1918), pp. 95–99.

[89] A land act must first be passed, and a year passed before that was done; a particular district must (it was thought) be selected for the first application of the law; and no settlement could be officially recognized—much less encouraged—until Indian hostilities should abate, which they did not for several years.

to these reasons external to it, there were those inherent in its provisions above mentioned.[90] An authority possessing unrivaled knowledge of the letters of members of Congress and their correspondents concluded that, in the committee ordered to report a plan for territorial organization, "the exclusion of the provision for the abolition of slavery appears to have been one of the reasons why the plan of government lay dormant for more than three years."[91]

Great difficulties arose, also, from the ordinance's allowance of only ten states, of a maximum size of 9,000 square miles. (Rhode Island's was barely 1,000.) Jefferson estimated the area of the Northwest at one-half its actual area, and his reasons for small states included "the nature of things" and the nature "of American character," which would cause large states "to crumble into little ones."[92] Monroe had taken a western trip, and picked up the delusion that prairies were infertile; large portions of the country, he thought, might never support much population, and a small state might never contain that of the least populous of the original states. But most important of all were speculations regarding the effect of new states on the political power of the old. These were speculations on the unforeseeable, based on such intangibles and ignorance as just mentioned, further complicated by misjudgments of and prejudice against the borderer class.

Eastern prejudices had been shown in a committee report to Congress only six months before Jefferson's plan was approved. In this report, referring to the need for "security against the increase of feeble, disorderly and dispersed settlements in those remote and extended territories; against the depravity of manners which they have a tendency to produce . . . or against . . . frequent and destructive wars with the Indians . . ." the committee offered a resolution that government be established as soon as possible "in a district" of the West "for the accommodation of . . . purchasers and inhabitants."[93] Jefferson's plan had been the result of this, but it paid no attention to the "depravity of manners" allegedly characteristic of the frontiersmen, although the land plan later adopted did provide both for "purchasers" and "settlers."

---

[90] These are discussed in *Ill. Hist. Coll.,* XXV, cclxx *et seq.*

[91] Burnett, *LMCC,* VIII, 39.

[92] *Writings* (Ford ed.), IV, 246–248, 227.

[93] October 15, 1783, *J.C.C.,* XXV, 693–694. These "purchasers" were nonresident speculators; compare *Ill. Hist. Coll.,* XXV, cclxxxvii.

James Monroe was long chairman of the committee ultimately charged with consideration of governmental organization of the Northwest. Ten men participated in its work, conservatives clearly predominating. Its reports[94] show very clearly that the prevailing purpose was to repeal Jefferson's ordinance and provide for stronger governments, which would control and not be the creatures of frontier settlers. This was accomplished by steadily increasing the powers of an appointive governor, and making control by Congress direct and close—in other words, by re-creating in the West the system against which the seaboard states had themselves revolted. In all these actions Rufus King of New York was the leader. Monroe finally resigned—chiefly, it would seem, because of three changes made by the conservatives. One was the substitution for Jefferson's population requirement for admission to the Union of another (one-thirteenth the total population of the original states) which, for example, would have kept Wisconsin out until after 1900 and Michigan until after 1880.[95] Under the original plan for ten small Jeffersonian states, this requirement would probably have excluded them forever. Another change was the addition of a requirement that admission be subject to consent by states members at the time. However, the compact between Virginia and the Confederation barred any such requirement as respected states in the Northwest (and equally barred, as respected them, the generally unqualified discretion given Congress by the Constitution). The third change was in increasing the population required before organization of a Territorial legislature—originally 500, to 5,000.

In making these changes the conservatives were, of course, necessarily guided by ideas or prejudices as vague as were the ideas of Jefferson and Monroe. As Nathan Dane later wrote of their efforts: "We wanted to abolish the old [Jefferson's] system and get a better one . . . and we finally found it necessary to adopt the best system we could get." In fact, the conservatives "of the eastern states" achieved, as respects merely government, the re-establishment in the West of the very colonial system from which the eastern states had just escaped.[96]

[94] *Ibid.,* cclxxvi–cclxxvii, cxxviii, cclxxxv; constitutional provisions in Art. VI, Sec. 1, and Art. IV, Sec. 1, Par. 1.

[95] *Ill. Hist. Coll.,* XXV, p. cclxxix, n. 118.

[96] Letter to King, C. R. King (ed.), *The Life and Correspondence of Rufus King* (6 vols., New York, 1894–1900), I, 289. He also wrote: "As the eastern states for the sake of doing away the temporary governments, etc. established in 1784," etc. Burnett, *LMCC,* VII, 636.

In repealing Jefferson's ordinance they in effect repealed the Revolution for others than themselves.[97] In place of immediate self-government they introduced a "first stage" of government by officers appointed by the federal government, under laws to be selected by their judges from the statute books of the states—in practice, old laws of the colonies, deemed suitable to their immature condition.[98] Then, after representative government was secured, this was to be with property requirements for voting and holding office and under the check of a governor with powers of prorogation and absolute veto—in addition to extraordinary executive powers that encroached on the ordinary field of legislation.[99] Election, in the representative stage of government, of a delegate to Congress with power to debate though not to vote was not original with Jefferson but was in his plan, and Dane restored it after it was dropped by Monroe's committee.[100]

Although their initial stage of government was very far from democratic, the inhabitants of the territories were nevertheless assured of a security and liberty thereafter which was likely to end any trace of the disloyalty which the conservatives feared in all migrants; and this may well have been prominent in the objectives of those who framed the Ordinance of 1787. Fears of social disorder, also, naturally soon lessened. Tutelary government, it is true, lasted only until there were five thousand inhabitants, true, but this was sometimes many years—for example, twenty-three for Illinois and thirty-seven for Michigan. However, it is also true that by the time Wisconsin became a territory in 1834, the ungenerous nature of the tutelary stage had been considerably mollified.

Excepting only the Constitution, for at least seventy years the Ordinance of 1787 was the most famous of American state papers. Its authorship, content, and the special reasons for its fame deserve attention.[101] The committee work upon it consisted very largely in omitting from Jefferson's ordinance provisions unacceptable to conservatives. No portion of it was reframed by the committee except that dealing with government. The entire document as presented to Congress for action, except one provision, was written by Nathan Dane; and that

---

[97] *J.C.C.*, XXVI, 279; XXX, 255; XXXII, 343.

[98] *Ill. Hist. Coll.*, XVII, xxvi *et seq.*

[99] *Ibid.*, XXV, ccxc–ccxcii, for further details. A legislative council appeared only in the first committee report.

[100] *Ill. Hist. Coll.*, XXV, ccclxxix.

[101] Authorship is fully discussed in *Ill. Hist. Coll.*, XXV, ccclxiii–ccclxxxvi.

provision—abolishing slavery—was moved by him on the floor of Congress for addition to the Ordinance. Much that his fellow conservatives had dropped was restored by him, and two additions of great importance were wholly his own. Much that gave the Ordinance its fame, though not originating with Jefferson or himself, he also added to the instrument.

One of his personal contributions was a prohibition of any law impairing the obligation of contracts.[102] This illustrated the distrust of borderers in economic matters which aligned him with fellow conservatives in restricting governmental powers. It contrasts sharply with his attitude toward personal liberties, as shown by many other parts of the Ordinance, including his second wholly individual contribution. A Massachusetts lawyer, engaged in compiling the first comparative study of American statutory law, Dane introduced a provision establishing inheritance of land in the Old Northwest on the basis of an unqualified fee simple, and without distinction between the whole and the half-blood—the first such titles, he believed, "in no part whatever feudal" in America.[103] This was a matter of immense social significance. It was, to be sure, a reform already in initial stages in the old states, but by its guarantee to five future states, and by early extension of the Ordinance to additional territories, reform was vastly expedited. It was the first of two great steps taken toward democracy in the disposal of the public lands.[104] The second was taken by Congress in gradually adjusting the law governing those lands to favor a first squatter.

The fame of the Ordinance rested on its so-called compacts, which were not such at all. At most they were, in some cases, legislation. The first and second were mere declarations of personal liberties (such as the right to jury trial or the writ of habeas corpus) which could have been taken from various places, but were actually copied by Dane from the constitution or laws of Massachusetts. The third compact was an exhortation—to citizens or future legislatures—to nourish education, morality, and religion, and be just to the Indians. The fourth, taken from Jefferson's ordinance, proclaimed a number of principles defining the status of the Territories which in fact were later always enforced by the Supreme Court.[105] The fifth "compact," purporting to guarantee the

---

[102] *Ibid.,* p. ccclxxx.
[103] Mass. Historical Society, *Proceedings,* for 1867–1869, p. 477.
[104] *Ill. Hist. Coll.,* XXV, cccxi–cccxii.
[105] *Ill. Hist. Coll.,* XXV, ccclxxxii, n. 370.

admission to the Union of the territories of the Old Northwest, was merely a declaration (or a repealable re-enactment of an earlier resolution) by Congress; the only guarantee was by a true compact between Congress and Virginia. But Dane had a very special reason for his fourth and fifth compacts; namely that the Constitution, then being simultaneously framed (and knowledge of its proceedings and attitudes readily available to members of Congress) does not even mention territories, and provides merely that "New States may be admitted by the Congress." Finally, the sixth and most famous compact, prohibiting slavery, had been in Jefferson's ordinance and was moved by Dane, as already noted, when Congress was considering the Ordinance as reported. That is, it also was legislation.

It is obvious that a committee appointed to draft a plan of government for a specific territory could quite logically have dropped the broad provisions of Dane's fourth "compact," and likewise the sixth. Moreover, like his fellow conservatives, Dane distrusted the personal character, and especially the financial dependability, of wanderers.[106] But it is plain from his draft of the Ordinance that he gloried in the Revolution, ardently believed in federalism and personal liberties, and could tolerate social democracy. His declaration of faith is in the Ordinance. It was also the faith of those who went west, and it gave the Ordinance its extraordinary fame. He has been greatly underestimated.

The debates in the Federal (Constitutional) Convention of 1787 occasionally revealed sharply contrasting opinions among its members respecting the desirable treatment of the West. A few extreme conservatives, echoing the past, would have subjected the West to a new imperial colonialism. They were far outside the current of national opinion. The votes and acts of the Congress reviewed in preceding pages show conclusively that national sentiment was for building English liberties into a federal republic. After years of quarreling over the supposed dangers of western disunion, over the political danger of a settled West to eastern states, over the economic harm caused to eastern landowners by westward migration, the Congress realized that this last could not be checked, that western lands could be sold to pay the war debt, and that the Confederation was safer with new states in it than left outside it. On that basis it had begun its efforts to secure the western lands for common use; had voted unanimously to organize all

---

[106] In his apology of later years (*ibid.*, p. cccxxiv), he ignored his own provision against impairment of contracts.

ceded lands into new states, to be admitted as equals to the union of the old; and had entered into a compact with Virginia so to do. With hardheaded sense it solved the most important of all its problems. Its success virtually assured the prompt establishment of a stable national government. Nevertheless, despite the facts that the Congress did, and the Convention conservatives did not, represent national sentiment, the latter succeeded in excluding from the Constitution any mention of western settlements, colonies, or territories—therefore of their government, or of obligation to admit any as states. It was solely as respected any formed within the Northwest claimed by Virginia that an obligation existed—and only by compact with her; and later, as respects the Old Southwest, by compact with Georgia.

CHAPTER 6

Peace Without Fruits in the Northwest, 1783-94

IN ALL diplomatic problems after 1783, the West played a conspicuous part, completely dominating relations with Spain. It was a predominant factor in Anglo-American diplomacy until well after the beginning of the French Revolution, and then the West assumed great importance in America's relations with France. Only at the very end of the century did commercial problems of neutral rights begin to share an increasingly large part in relations with all these powers. Relations with each were affected at different times by relations with the others, but those with Britain were relatively independent, and will therefore be considered separately. Substantive obstacles to peace arose mainly from new British policies in Indian relations. In form, however, they sprang from variant interpretations of the peace treaty.

It was alleged by Britain that American promises in the peace treaty had been violated, and these alleged violations were the justification most often given for Britain's retention of the territory northwest of the Ohio River. The American government insisted that Congress, representing the Confederation, was the American party to the treaty; that it was the several states which had confiscated Loyalists' estates and barred the enforcement of the claims of British creditors; that Congress could not control the states, and that the peace commissioners could not bind Congress by promises beyond its power to perform. The facts are that the adoption by the Commons of General Conway's motion *compelled* the British to make peace, and that they could not have refused to negotiate with Congress, nor have wished to deal with thirteen states. Negotiations, therefore, had necessarily proceeded on a basis which made continuing disputes virtually certain.[1] At the very end, however, the American commissioners, disregarding their earlier arguments, had ostensibly done precisely what they said they could not do. Of the three articles of the treaty here pertinent, this was true of two, in which it was declared (even imperatively) that creditors "shall meet no lawful impediment to the recovery of . . . bona fide debts" (Article IV), and that "there shall be" no future confiscations or persecutions (Article VI). A third promise Congress did have power to perform—namely, to "earnestly recommend" to the legislatures of the states restitution of estates to claimants of certain classes, and a reconsideration and revision of statutes (Article V). The British negotiators and Parliament were fully informed of the inability of Congress to ensure performance of Articles IV and VI.[2] Hammond, the first British minister to the United States, and Jefferson later agreed upon the foregoing facts as basic in discussion of infractions, the former fully admitting the attempts of Congress to secure full enforcement of its promises by the states. Of these, moreover, "one only . . . refused altogether. The others complied in a greater or less degree." Preponderantly, and to their credit, the treaty was treated by both negotiators as legally conclusive of all issues long before the Supreme Court of the new Union had opportunity to declare it the law of the land.[3] As respects Article IV, it is quite true that "the states refused to repeal their impeditive enactments, and the State courts continued to enforce them."[4] Article VI was also violated. As regards Article V, Congress did more than once recommend to the states the repeal of statutes repugnant to the peace established by the treaty, but with limited success.[5] That the limited nature of the undertaking was not perfectly understood by the British has never been asserted. In view of these facts, there was little ethical basis for British complaint against the Confederation government.

The British withheld all the posts, from Lake Champlain to Detroit

[1] Malloy, *Treaties*, I, 292; Wharton, *Dip. Corr.*, V, 540–542 (compare 476, 548–549), 571–572, 842, 845, 849, 856, 857; VI, 77–80, 112.

[2] *A.S.P., For. Rel.*, I, 189, 193–200, 202 *et seq.*

[3] See Jay's remarks in *J.C.C.*, XXXI, 797 (October 13, 1786).

[4] Moore, *International Arbitrations*, I, 271–299.

[5] Hammond freely recognized what Congress had done. *A.S.P., For. Rel.*, I, 193.

and Michilimackinac. The only reason given in 1786 to John Adams, then minister to Britain, was violation of the debts article.[6] Violations of that and other articles were the reason given in 1791 by Hammond, and no other reasons were ever officially asserted. Many have thought that the safeguarding of the fur trade was the true reason.[7] Its value was, to be sure, utterly insignificant as compared with that of the good will supporting Britain's great trade with the new seaboard states, but financial interest should not be much emphasized since we have seen that it was always undiscussed in maintaining the posts before the war. Several interests successively, each of temporarily predominant influence, probably explained British action and, underlying all, general British opinion that the peace was too generous to rebels.

There was, however, another and more important factor in prolonging bad relations until after 1815. Except in 1790, British-American relations were determined primarily by the respective relations of the two governments to the Indians, and these were determined by the variant positions, *as the Indians understood them,* taken by the two governments toward the rights of the Indians in land northwest of the Ohio River which Britain had ceded to the United States by the peace treaty of 1783. The policy of British officials in Canada originated in ignorance of British law; however, it ensured Indian friendship and was therefore never renounced, but even guilefully defended, by Sir Guy Carleton in particular. Nor did the British ministry ever repudiate this Canadian policy either in its American negotiations or in printed instructions to Canadian subordinates.

The ignorance and helplessness of the Indians were, of course, constant. To begin with, the entire peace treaty was to them incomprehensible. They had never been overrun by the Americans and knew themselves to be therefore unconquered. They knew also that the British in the Northwest had not been overrun or conquered. How, then, could they understand the fact that the Americans were taking everything because *they* were unconquered? And since the Indians regarded

---

[6] For the reason given to Adams, *J.C.C.,* XXXI, 783–784, with specifications of acts of the several states, pp. 784–797, followed by comments of Secretary Jay, pp. 797–874.

[7] Contemporaries in America assumed this. Perhaps 2,000 were dependent on the trade. Whether its products were worth £200,000 on the London market (Davidson, *The Northwest Company,* Berkeley, 1918, appendixes A and E) or only £50,000 (Lord Shelburne, Hansard's *Parliamentary Debates,* XXIII, 408–410) is of slight importance. The question of whose funds were invested in it has seemingly been untouched by researchers.

the land of the Ohio region as their own (not having granted any rights of settlement in it, which to them would have meant total loss), how could the British have ceded that region to the Americans? Yet they were told that the United States had taken, or been given, everything up to the middle of the Great Lakes, and this was true.

The matter was, of course, one of utter simplicity. The United States had taken the British crown title just as the British had held it—subject to the necessity of buying the right of settlement and peaceful enjoyment from the Indians. The Indians had lost nothing, and their misunderstandings could have been easily dispelled. This was not done, at first, because of the misapprehensions of the governor of Quebec, Sir Frederick Haldimand, a Swiss soldier of fortune who was an honest man but was totally without comprehension of the facts and the law. Others revealed the treaty's provisions to the Indians—although evidently unable or unwilling to explain them. Sir Frederick kept them secret so far and so long as he could.[8] Embarrassing assurances had been made to the Indians by military headquarters (doubtless by Haldimand while commander in chief at the beginning of the war) of certain British victory, and that the Indians would not lose "their" lands.[9] It was necessary, Haldimand wrote, to reconcile the Indians "to a measure for which they entertain the greatest abhorrence," meaning their supposed loss of the Ohio-Illinois region; "it will be a difficult thing to convince them of our own good faith"—that is, in his promising they should not lose their lands, again assuming that they *had* lost them. The Americans, he said, "had the impudence to assert a claim," in consequence of the treaty, to "Indian lands," thus revealing his ignorance of the distinction between ownership and use for hunting as respects the Indians. The "Indian country" was merely that which, being unsettled by whites, was hunted over by the Indians. Haldimand wrote to Lord North that the Indians had no idea, though some Americans had "insinuated it," that the King "either has ceded or had a right to cede their territories" to the United States.[10] Of course, as Lord Shelburne

---

[8] *Mich. Hist. Coll.*, X, 458.

[9] Haldimand wrote that they were "Thunder Struck" by the terms of peace, "so far short of their Expectation from the Language that had been held out to them." *Ibid.*, p. 663, and compare p. 57.

[10] *Ibid.*, pp. 178, 458. He volunteered an opinion that the Northwest should be "considered entirely as belonging to the Indians"—that is, forever. See letters printed *ibid.*, XX, 57, 110, 116, 117, 118-120, 122, 123, 128, 131-132; other letters printed, quoted, or summarized in A. L. Burt, *The U.S., G.B., and*

said, "the soil [was], and [had] always been acknowledged to be the King's."[11] To ignore crown title is to ignore the creation of the colonies and masses of facts in their territorial history.[12] Lord Shelburne long resisted cession of the Ohio country—as British, not as Indian, land. Evidently, Haldimand had not the slightest comprehension of the difference between the political boundary through the Great Lakes fixed by the treaty of peace and the white settlement line along the Ohio fixed by agreement with the Indians.

Sir John Johnson—son of Sir William, and now superintendent "of the Six Nations and of those in Quebec"—arrived at Detroit early in 1783, and in a council with the Indians used language indicative both of understanding and of a desire for removing the Indians' misconceptions: "You are not to believe . . . that by the [treaty] line . . . it was intended to deprive you of . . . country, of which the right of soil . . . is in yourselves . . . as far [southward] as the boundary [settlements] Line . . . established . . . in the year 1768 at Fort Stanwix."[13] Substituting for "right of soil" the words "of excluding American settlers"—which the Indians could have understood and which was the truth—the statement was acceptable. It was quoted in a grand council later in the year, when the Indians were urged to cease hostilities unless and until their hunting grounds should be invaded.[14] Sporadically, too, this advice was given in later years. But there was no repetition of Sir John's *words,* and he was undoubtedly muzzled. Three obstacles stood in the way of the calm to which his assurance might have led. First, the Indians, in view of past assurances, insisted upon denials that anything had been ceded by Britain. Second, the Americans, by errors of judgment, increased the Indians' fears and prolonged misunderstandings between them and the Indians. Third, the British government (probably following the lead of Sir Guy Carleton, who dominated transitory secretaries of state) gradually formed territorial plans inconsistent

---

British N. America to . . . *1812* (New Haven, 1940), pp. 88, 92, 93; and in N. V. Russell, *British Regime in Michigan* (Northfield, Minn., 1939), pp. 232, 238, 239.

[11] E. Fitzmaurice, *Life of William, Earl of Shelburne* (2nd ed., 2 vols., London, 1912), II, 194.

[12] It is ignored throughout Burt's volume.

[13] Portions are quoted in Burt, p. 89–90, and in *Mich. Hist. Coll.,* XX, 177.

[14] Joseph Brant, speaking for the Six Nations to all the other tribes, said (*ibid.,* p. 179) that "Sir John assured us that the boundary Line lately agreed to, did not deprive us of our lands."

with anything except the original denials of the Canadian officials. As respects the third obstacle, a speech made in 1791 by Carleton (by then become Lord Dorchester) will be considered after giving attention to wars and treaties preceding that date. The second obstacle may now be disposed of.

The problem before the United States was simple. It was necessary, first, to explain to the Indians that, as the British king had earlier replaced the French,[15] so now Congress replaced him, up to the Great Lakes, as their Great White Father, for the purposes of trade, presents, and treating for land; and, second, to repeat the assurances given at the opening of the Revolution that the Indians should continue, as always before, in the enjoyment of their hunting grounds except as they should renounce them by treaties, as in the past. This the Indians would have understood perfectly.

What Congress actually did was remarkably inept. But, impolitic as it was, it was honest, and Washington's recommendations were partly responsible for it. His contempt for what he considered wrong in past British policy led him to undervalue what was useful in Sir William Johnson's methods. Congress knew that no land could be actually occupied without compensating the Indians, intended to do so, *and so declared*—as Washington advised. But he felt that the Indians should be made to understand that they were a conquered people, that as British allies they had forfeited any claims to leniency (both policies declared by Congress since 1779), and that any received by them would be out of mercy only. However, although precedents for punishing them might have been found in contemporary practices of war, punishment would not have been morally justifiable, as Congress admitted, since the Indians had been only helpless dependents of the British. Moreover, even such preachments would necessarily lacerate Indian pride, upon respect for which their inattention to the fact of crown title was dependent.[16] The preachments were nevertheless embodied in a foolish ordinance of Congress (of October 15, 1783) for the regulation of Indian affairs, and commissioners duly repeated them to the Indians in various would-be peace councils.[17] Congress made other true but useless decla-

---

[15] And as was then explained to them. A. T. Volwiler, *George Croghan and the Western Movement, 1741–1782* (Cleveland, 1926), p. 162.

[16] *J.C.C.*, XV, 1320; Washington, *Writings* (Kirkpatrick, ed.).

[17] *J.C.C.*, XXV, 680–693. The committee's phraseology had the usual imperfection in referring to "lines of property for dividing the settlements of the citizens from the Indian . . . hunting grounds."

rations in justification of a declaration that a cession must be made, and the settlement line demanded was specified.

In 1783, commissioners of Congress made attempts at Niagara and Detroit to talk with the Indians, but were prevented from doing so.[18] Two attempts in 1783 and 1784 by Congress to secure access to the posts, or recognition of the promise to evacuate them, were wholly fruitless. Since there were no orders from England, the action of Canadian officials was recognized as correct.[19] This explains the ordinance of October, 1783.

Gradually, contacts with the Indians were established. Since 1779 there had been an impractical plan of dealing with all in one treaty. Congress soon learned that the Indians were forever divided by disparate interests and mutual distrust. During the following years this fact was to operate unfavorably both to British policies and to American. After some vacillation, Congress made a series of treaties which fixed a settlement line approximately as demanded in the ordinance of 1783.[20] The proceedings of the councils in which these agreements were made—at Fort Stanwix in October, 1784, at Fort McIntosh in January, 1784, and at Fort Finney in January, 1786—amply illustrated tribal disagreements.[21] They also exhibited the unwisdom of the ordinance of Congress, and the extreme vagueness of Indian land claims.[22] In making these treaties presents were given in amounts seemingly adequate for satisfaction of the Indians. The treating and the agreements were novel in three respects. Unlike all of Sir William Johnson's (with the single exception of that which closed Pontiac's War), the agreements entered into were stated separately and definitely. The proceedings also

[18] *Ibid.*, XXIV, 251; *A.S.P., For. Rel.*, 1, 190–193, 206–207, 225–227; Washington, *Writings* (Kirkpatrick ed.), XXVI, 398, XXVII, 61, 63, 133–140, 285–287, 350–351, 353–354; *Mich. Hist. Coll.*, XIX, 378, XX, 136–139, 145–147, 149, 158, 161, 165–168, 230, 236–239.

[19] Washington, *Writings* (Kirkpatrick ed.); *Mich. Hist. Coll.*, XX, 141–145, 161, 165–168, 230, 238–239. Attempts to trade with the Indians were also thwarted, *ibid.*, pp. 158–159.

[20] *J.C.C.*, XV, 1320; XXXVI, 153, 258.

[21] *A.S.P., Ind. Aff.*, I, 10; Kappler, *Indian Affairs*, II, 3–4, 4–5, 16.

[22] At Fort Stanwix some of the Five Nations renounced lands in New York and Pennsylvania over which western Indians asserted conflicting claims, thus necessitating the Fort McIntosh treaty. But in that treaty the western tribes, having no definite claims, did not know with what claims by what other tribes theirs conflicted, and merely ceded all lands "not yet ceded by the Indians."

lacked the side arrangements ("jollifications"—that is, rum drinking—separate conferences, and special gifts to chiefs of special influence) of Sir William's councils. And there was no taking of deeds. Peace was made and land was opened, for a price, to settlement.

Even before the first of these treaties was made, a "confederation" of western and some southern tribes had been formed by the Canadian officials and the Mohawks. The chief of that tribe was now Joseph Brant, brother of one of Sir William Johnson's housemates. Treated by Sir William as a ward, relatively educated and familiar with both Philadelphia and London (where much had been made of him and his Indian dress), he was of great importance in the events of the next dozen years, before the end of which he regretted the British alliance. In a grand council in September, 1783, it was agreed that no cession by any tribe would be recognized unless approved by all.[23] The undesirability of thus tying British policy to Indian desires, which were never common to more than a small group and never stable beyond a brief time, is obvious. Its ineffectiveness was displayed in the treaty negotiations of 1784 and 1786.

In December, 1786, in grand council at Detroit, the confederation sent an address to Congress. It complained of the omission of the Indians as parties to the treaty of peace at Paris; declared ratification by the confederation indispensable to the validity of any cession; asked for a revision of the three treaties made since 1783 and for a withdrawal of the surveyors then busy in the new federal Territory north of the Ohio. The detailed guidance of the British was manifest in the first complaint and in another that Americans took no deeds for lands the Indians relinquished. The British, who had rarely taken even ostensible deeds since 1755, were characteristically taking none at this time for lands in Upper Canada on which to settle the American Loyalists—but such was the simplicity of the Indians that the British could nevertheless thus give color to their denial that they had ceded the Ohio country to the United States by the peace treaty.[24]

---

[23] *Mich. Hist. Coll.*, XX, 174–183. The three American treaties had disregarded this demand. Downes, *Council Fires on the Upper Ohio* (Pittsburgh, 1940), pp. 290, 293, and Burt, *U.S., G.B.*, p. 86, have denounced the American procedure, and Downes imagined the American treaties to be therefore invalid. The British, when at war with the Indians, had followed the rule of *divide et impera* even to the point of repeatedly encouraging intertribal war. It was an important part of Sir William Johnson's Indian policies.

[24] Brant's correspondence with Lord Sydney is in Stone, *Life of Jos. Brant*

These complaints by the Indians were laid before Congress in July of 1787 only after organization by Congress of the Northwest Territory. Money was voted for another treaty, but the anticipated inauguration of government under the new Constitution delayed action. The appropriation for the new treaty was to be used for extinguishing Indian claims, whether in lands already ceded by the treaties of which complaint was made or in additional lands if procurable. General St. Clair was charged with negotiation of the new treaty. He was instructed to secure a better boundary and to make every exertion to defeat confederations and combinations.[25] There was little need of the last admonition.[26] A preliminary council with the tribes revealed little agreement and much jealousy among them, which, he wrote, "he was not willing to lessen by appearing to consider them as one people. . . . It would not be very difficult, if circumstances required it, to set them at deadly variance."[27] These circumstances made it easy to make two treaties (at Fort Harmar, January, 1789).[28] One, with the Six Nations, was identical with the Fort Stanwix treaty of 1784 in its essential terms. The other, with the western tribes, was identical in essentials with the Fort McIntosh treaty. The Indians merely received additional presents. A provision that no lands (within American boundaries) might be relinquished to any other power than the United States merely stated what had always been implicit in English law. Another provision repudiated the fictitious hegemony of the original Six Nations over the Ohio tribes by transferring it, as respected the Shawnee, to the Wyandot. No deeds were taken from the Indians for the lands relinquished.

In all these years following 1783, sporadic Indian wars had been nearly continuous. Some of the years were the bloodiest in Kentucky's history; 1786 was perhaps the most confused of Ohio's. The Indian confederation, alleging unity where none existed, only impeded peace when that was locally desired. Occasional Indian victories encouraged

(2 vols., Albany, 1838), II, 250–255 (in early 1786); letter of Secretary Knox to Brant, July 23, 1787, *ibid.*, p. 266; complaints of the council of December, 1786, to Congress, *A.S.P., Ind. Aff.*, I, 6.

[25] *J.C.C.*, I, 8 and 9 (no. 2).

[26] Stone, *Brant*, II, 278; Downes, *Council Fires*, pp. 301–305.

[27] W. H. Smith (ed.), *The St. Clair Papers* (2 vols., Cincinnati, 1822), II, 109–113; *A.S.P., Ind. Aff.*, I, 10 (no. 2).

[28] *St. Clair Papers*, I, 156–158, II, 108–113, 622–630. The treaty with the Six Nations (other than the Mohawk) is in *A.S.P., Ind. Aff.*, I, 5–6, 54 (no. 3); with the western tribes, *ibid.*, 6–7. The two treaties are in Kappler, *Indian Affairs*, II, 18–23, 13–18, respectively.

1. Immigrants on the way westward

From Roux de Rochelle, *États-Unis d'Amérique*, Paris, 1837

2. Chicago in 1820

From H. R. Schoolcraft, *Information Respecting the . . . Indian Tribes . . .*

3. SIR WILLIAM JOHNSON

From *Papers
of Sir William Johnson*

4. DANIEL BOONE

From a painting
by Chester Harding

5. Joseph Brant

Engraved from a painting
of G. Romney

6. General Sir Guy Carleton

7. Dorton's Fort, near Nickelsville, Virginia,
built by Robert Killgore in 1790

(Courtesy, Virginia Historical Society)

8. Ground plan of Fort Defiance

From J. W. Monette, *History of . . . the Valley
of the Mississippi*

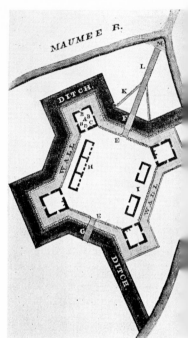

9. Fort Sackville in Vincennes, Indiana, 1779

10. Fort Harmer

(Courtesy, The Historical Society of Pennsylvania)

11. Campus Martius, initial settlement of Marietta, Ohio, 1788

From J. W. Monette, *History of . . . the Valley of the Mississippi*

12. GEORGE ROGERS CLARK
as a young frontiersman, 1778

A statue in Quincy, Illinois

13. The Saucier House, the first courthouse of the Old Northwest

(Courtesy, Illinois State Historical Library)

14. WILLIAM HENRY HARRISON, *ca.* 1812

Painting, probably by John Wesley Jarvis, and owned by the Francis Vigo Chapter, D.A.R., is in the Harrison Mansion, Vincennes, Indiana.

15. Medical College of Ohio, Cincinnati

From Drake and Mansfield, *Cincinnati in 1826*

16. Public landing in Cincinnati, Ohio. Part of these buildings antedated 1830

From *Centennial Review of Cincinnati,* edited by J. W. Leonard

17. Major General Arthur St. Clair
After a painting by C. W. Peale

18. Anthony Wayne
n C. Moore, *Under Three Flags*

19. The first floating mill on the Ohio

From Hildreth, *Memoirs of the Pioneer Settlers of Ohio*

(Courtesy, The Historical Society of Pennsylvania)

20. Sketch of a flat-bottom boat used on the Ohio and the Mississippi

(Courtesy, The Historical Society of Pennsylvania)

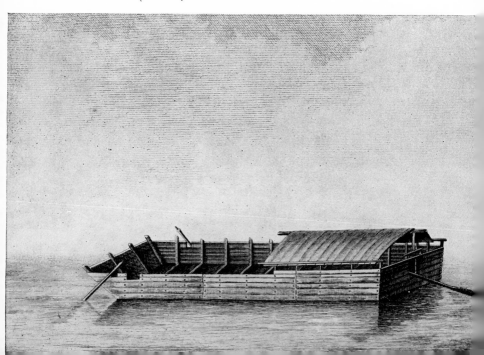

21. The Detroit River front in 1794

(From a contemporary drawing in the Burton Historical Collection,
Detroit Public Library)

22. An American log house

(Courtesy, The Historical Society of Pennsylvania)

23. Grease lamp—the up-to-date lamp of 1818

From S. J. Buck, *Illinois in 1818*

24. Printing Press

(Courtesy, Illinois State Historical Library; original in Missouri Historical Society)

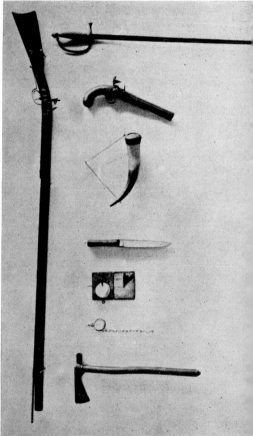

25. The rifle, tomahawk, watch, pocket compass and sundial, hunting knife, powder horn, pistol and sword of General George Rogers Clark, articles owned by Col. R. T. Durrett, Louisville, Kentucky

From A. B. Hulbert, *The Ohio River*

26. Flatboat, family boat and steamboat on the Mississippi
Lesueur Print. (Courtesy of American Philosophical Society)

27. Interior of *The Philanthropist,* probably mealtime and inspection
Lesueur Print. (Courtesy of American Philosophical Society)

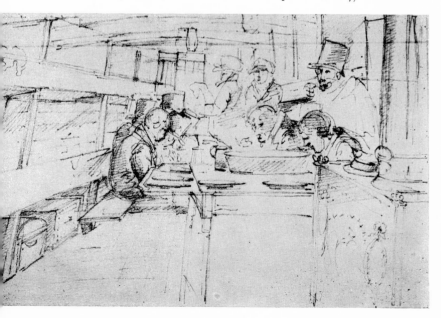

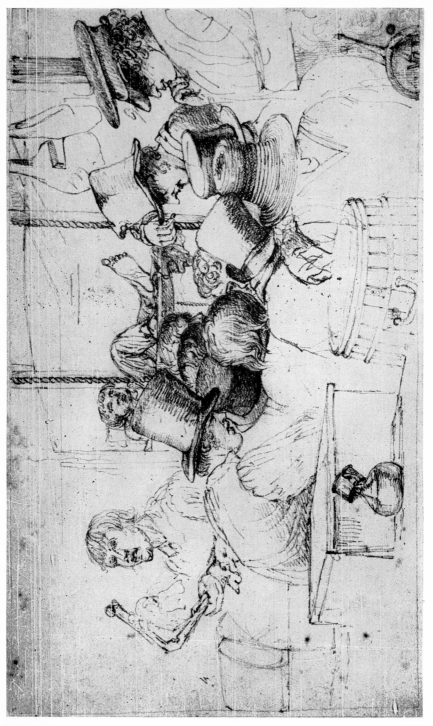

28. Scene on steamboat

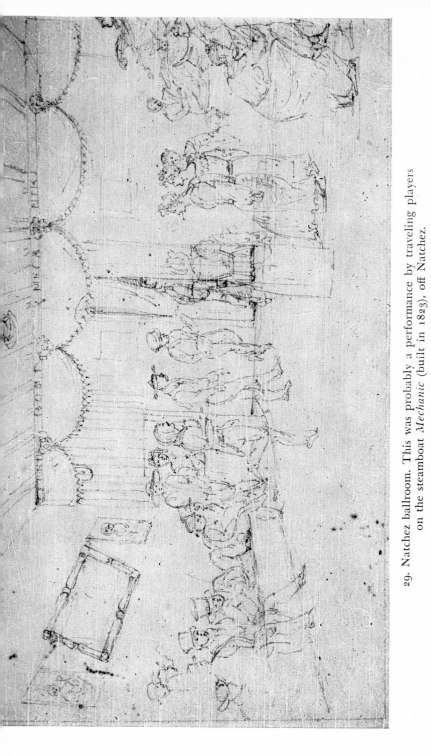

29. Natchez ballroom. This was probably a performance by traveling players on the steamboat *Mechanic* (built in 1823), off Natchez.

Lesueur Print. (Courtesy of American Philosophical Society)

30. A typical Indian village

British planners, and also created some Indian idealists—such, in later years, as Tecumseh and his brother The Prophet.

Although the acts of Canadian authorities had long suggested a definite government policy, it seems doubtful whether such a policy existed in London prior to 1791. In the debate in Parliament in December, 1783, the secretary of war in Lord North's ministry had declared that the government intended to convert the American war into a "war of posts": "His idea was . . . to keep no regular army in the field; but in keeping the posts we had, we might add others whenever . . . [possible]: thus affording . . . the means of doing it with success."[29] If one looks for any steady and conscious policy during the next half-dozen years, this one of simply holding the posts for opportunistic advantages seems best to fit the case.[30] All the facts fall within it; none less loosely opportunistic will cover them.[31] However, although dislike of the peace might explain long inaction by the London government, no evidence has appeared that the conduct of Canadian officials was in pursuance of orders.

There were ample reasons why Canadian officials would have welcomed retention of the posts. Relations with the Indians were extraordinary. "Great Pains & Treasure were bestowed," Haldimand wrote, to secure their aid; the cost of the alliance which originated in this "necessity of bringing them to act" became "enormous," and to lose it would present incalculable dangers: "They have so perpetually harassed the Enemy that they Cannot look for Reconciliation upon any other Ground than Abandoning the Royal Cause."[32] Peace left them and the British mutually dependent in an extraordinary degree. The Indians were in a dangerous mood after learning of the promise to surrender the posts, which were their guarantee of rum, guns, powder, occasional

[29] G. O. Trevelyan, quoted by S. F. Bemis, *Jay's Treaty* (New York, 1923), p. 91.

[30] Douglas Brynner, director of the Canadian Archives, was a leader in affirming a definite British policy to withhold the posts, Canad. Archives, *Report* for 1890, p. xxxi. O. E. Leavitt, "British Policy on the Canadian Frontier, 1782–92; Mediation and an Indian Barrier State" (Wis. State Hist. Society, *Proceedings* for 1915, pp. 151–185), put early emphasis upon the border project.

[31] The withholding, and therefore reasons for it, may possibly have been judged by some to be of little importance; see Oswald's curious ideas in 1782. W. E. Stevens, *Northwest Fur Trade* (Urbana, Ill., 1928), p. 73.

[32] *Mich. Hist. Coll.*, X, 663.

refuge, and charity; and the posts had always been virtually at their mercy. The Indians did not fully understand this, since few matters could be simplified sufficiently to make them understandable.

All that is mere background. Visible and primary facts were that the British had committed themselves morally, and inconsistently, with the Americans and the Indians. In London they ceded the Ohio country to the United States as crown land. In Canada they promised the Indians to help them hold it as "Indian land."

Early in 1783 Governor Haldimand wrote to Major De Peyster (at Detroit) that every possible aid would be given to the Indians to "secure and defend their own," and De Peyster accordingly instructed Colonel Alexander McKee of the Indian service. McKee, since he had long been a deputy of Sir William Johnson, knew the truth about Indian lands, but he was decidedly not one to spread knowledge of the truth. General MacLean (commanding at Niagara) contemporaneously assured the Indians that although "the States . . . never would . . . go to war about some miles of a desert," yet, "if such an attempt was made . . . all the King's troops, should stand by them." Repeatedly they were told that they would be given all possible aid in defending "their property."[33] However, with a unanimity that must have been due to orders (or to concerted acquiescence in Governor Haldimand's misapprehensions), it was left to the Indians to judge what their "property" was. They were often told, also, to keep the peace unless and until their "rights" were invaded, in which event they were assured of British military aid, but the rights were never defined.[34] In doing this the Canadian officials nurtured Indian misconceptions. To the extent that they spoke honestly, they promised war in defense of them.

The home government neither disapproved of the actions of its Canadian officials nor removed the misconceptions that caused them. In the spring of 1786, Lord Sydney instructed Lieutenant Governor Simcoe that to give the Indians no aid would not be "consistent with justice

[33] N. V. Russell, *British Regime,* p. 235 (Haldimand, February 14, 1783); *Mich. Hist. Coll.,* XI, 359 (De Peyster, April 20, 1783); *ibid.,* XX, 119–120 (MacLean, May 18, 1783).

[34] For example: "Ye are the best Judges of the Rights, by which you hold your lands; the King of Great Britain . . . can do no wrong, whatever land he bestowed to his children [the Americans] when he gave them Peace, he had no doubt a right to do. Your country you say has not been given away, you cannot then be blamable in being unanimous to defend it." *Mich. Hist. Coll.,* XXIV, 137. This same attitude underlies dozens of speeches from 1782 onward. Compare *ibid.,* X, 660, XI, 342, XX, 150, as samples.

or good policy"—which was true as respected all needs for hunting; that "at all events in the present state" of England, "open and avowed assistance" should be avoided; that "active assistance would . . . be extremely improper." Was this for ethical reasons? When Lord Dorchester, going back a little later to Quebec as governor (for the second time), sought more precise instructions, he was told to supply the Indians "in a way the least likely to alarm the Americans."[35] These instructions were followed in the autumn of 1787 by orders to hold the posts at all costs and to recapture them if taken.[36]

Up to this time, the retention of the posts might have been attributed merely to dislike of a treaty overly generous to rebels, or to nonperformance of a condition on which the cession of the Northwest was allegedly contingent, or to Canadian fear of the Indians, or to Governor Haldimand's ignorance of crown title. By 1791, at least Canadian official policy, so far as it could independently exist, was a repudiation of crown title and therefore a denial of any cession. The change was a consequence of events of 1790 and 1791, and those factors were operative in shaping the new policy.

As a matter of opportunism, merely, self-interest during the Confederation period might not have counseled a British policy favorable to peace between the Indians and the United States. In all those years it was questionable whether the states would fall asunder. Disputes between three of them over the Vermont area, a bitter clash in Congress in 1784 between the New England and southern states over Mississippi navigation, alleged disloyalty thereafter in Kentucky and Tennessee, financial troubles and Daniel Shays' armed rebellion in Massachusetts in 1786–87, were sufficient to balance hopes raised by steps taken toward stronger union and stability. There was ample reason to await definitive developments.

One special reason for so doing had long existed in Canadian relations with Vermont.[37] The international boundary, west of New Hamp-

---

[35] Burt, *U.S., G.B.,* pp. 102, 103.

[36] Bemis, *Jay's Treaty,* p. 17.

[37] F. J. Turner (ed.), "Documents: English Policy Toward America in 1790–1791," *AHR,* VII, 700–735; VIII, 18–86; S. F. Bemis (ed.), "Documents: The Relations between the Vermont Separatists and Great Britain, 1789–1791," *AHR,* XXI, 547–560. Also, A. C. Flick (ed.), *History of the State of New York* (1933–37), III, 307–324, V, 3–28; G. Lanctot, *Les Canadiens et leurs voisins du sud* (New Haven, 1941), pp. 127–130, 133–135; G. S. Graham, *British Policy and Canada, 1774–1791; A Study in . . . Trade Policy* (New York, 1930), pp. 118, 122, 128–130.

shire, ran across northward-running valleys that had long been channels of intercourse between the two countries. Claimed by both New Hampshire and New York, independent of both Canada and the Confederation, Vermont flirted with the British even during the Revolution, more ardently thereafter.[38] Of necessity, Montreal was the market of northern Vermont. In 1786 and 1787, Dorchester put the trade "upon the most liberal and friendly footing." But even Dorchester felt he lacked authority to make a treaty with Vermont, and the Privy Council—suggesting that "he might perhaps think it would be offensive to the United States . . . which . . . [might] consider [Vermont] as a part of their territory" (an instructive disregard of the peace treaty's line)—approved of that view.[39]

This was at the moment when the second factor which compelled definition of British policy was in its most dangerous stage of development—the Nootka Sound incident. War over Spain's assertion of paramount rights over the Pacific Ocean seemed certain, and the growing radicalism of the French Revolution, presaging the end of the long alliance between France and Spain, heightened the threat of a general European war. At the same time the United States struggled to establish internal stability by agreement upon the future character of the national government (involving the ending of western unrest and accord upon disposition of western lands), and to strengthen its international security by ending controversies with Spain and Britain while maintaining friendly ties with France. Members of Washington's cabinet held variant and divergent opinions.[40] Anything seemed possible.

The Vermont flirtation and Britain's enormous trade with the states had seemingly raised a hope that Britain might regain all the interior country, and the prospect of war with Spain greatly augmented the possibility of its realization. To judge the future of the Confederation, Dorchester had earlier sent agents (of little worth) to New York and Kentucky.[41] Instructions given him in 1789, presumably in consequence

[38] Led by the three Allen brothers. On the boundary issue, see *Report of the Regents,* I, 77–86; O'Callaghan, *Doc. Hist.,* IV, 224–230.

[39] *AHR,* VIII, 82.

[40] However, Hamilton, the most friendly to Britain, warned Dorchester's agent that the United States looked forward to the acquisition of New Orleans. Canadian Archives, *Report* of 1890, pp. xxxviii, 149, 164–165; Bemis, *Jay's Treaty,* pp. 69–79; for Jefferson's views, *Writings* (Ford, ed.), V, 225–231, 216–218, 224.

[41] Bemis, *Jay's Treaty,* Appendix I; Canad. Archives, *Report* for 1890, pp. 97, 103, 107–117, 156–158. On one of them, Dr. John Connolly, see T. Bodley

of his reports on those of his agents, throw a revealing light upon the knowledge of the states accumulated in London offices after long administration of the colonies, and the slight aid of Dorchester and his agents. He was instructed that the western settlements should be "kept" distinct from the United States and connected with Great Britain.[42] However, when Lord Grenville asked whether the United States was likely to demand the northwest posts, either after or without making an alliance with Spain, Dorchester had little to report.[43] Grenville was cultivating Levi Allen, then in London, in the hope of controlling Vermont in case of war. Since the government was considering the incitement of revolts in the Spanish colonies, and had never ceased to regret its renunciation of New Orleans in 1763, Grenville also suggested to Dorchester that he hold out to the Americans (only "particularly to the Kentucke and other Settlers at the back of the old Colonies") that opening the Mississippi was "at least as important as the possession of the Forts, and . . . much more easily attainable" by aiding Britain against Spain than with Spain's aid against Britain.[44] The Americans were not so stupid as so grossly to miscalculate the relative generosity or weakness of the two powers.

While war with Spain was likely, the Board of Trade reported its views (April 17, 1790) of policies which should be followed respecting the West. They were based on the Vermont experience. Having "repeatedly" considered the question, it reaffirmed past advice that cross-border trade was commercially and politically desirable, and likewise trade on the Great Lakes "or through the Rivers emptying into them."[45] And it added that it was commercially desirable to secure treaties with "Kentuck and all other Settlements" forming in the interior—although the lords commissioners manifested a perfect understanding that Kentucky was a portion of Virginia.[46] Hamilton discouraged Dorchester's

---

(ed.), *Littell's Political Transactions in and Concerning Kentucky* (Lexington, 1926), pp. lxiv–lxvii; A. P. Whitaker, *The Spanish-American Frontier* (New York, 1927), p. 143; Canad. Archives, *Report* for 1890, p. 124. Reports of another agent, Pierre Allaire (Bemis, *Jay's Treaty*, pp. 19 and 72), in *AHR*, VII, 719, 724–726, show how very little there was in Kentucky, even of gossip, to report.

[42] F. J. Turner, in *AHR*, X, 256, citing unprinted sources.

[43] Canad. Archives, *Report* for 1890, pp. 107, 108, 131, 133, 147, 152, 162, 106, 138.

[44] Carter, *Gage Correspondence*, I, 276, II, 108–110, 122–123, and index; Canad. Archives, *Report* for 1890, pp. 132, 133.

[45] F. J. Turner (ed.), *AHR*, VIII, 78–80 (quotation, p. 80).

[46] *Ibid.*, p. 84.

hopes of getting New Orleans.[47] When Spain came to terms with Britain six months later, these plans lost much of their possibilities.

This vision of a vast possible trade in the continental interior was the third factor operative in causing the British in 1791 to deny a cession in 1783 (and then to insist upon negotiation of a new treaty to replace that of 1783). The above instructions of the Board of Trade, if considered alone, merely suggest that commerce was a primary objective of British policy. However, as regarded even the sole trade then existing, the fur trade, Britain had always striven to maintain exclusive control of the Indians. Obviously, complete control of midcontinent trade would also require exclusive control of the Great Lakes. Secretary Hamilton assured Dorchester's agent in New York (Major Beckwith) that reports of American plans to attack the posts were false. But he also made it plain that Indian relations required American troops in the Northwest. Major Beckwith reported these assurances as disclaiming any desire of "having possessions further to the Northward than our present boundaries" (as defined in Quebec? or in New York?)—that they "would be esteemed an incumbrance, with an exception to the Forts."[48] What Hamilton disclaimed was any desire to hold possession of anything north of the settlement line except the posts. However, events led to military action against the Indians in 1790 and 1791 which emphasized American insistence upon the recognition of its sovereignty up to the treaty boundary. These moves precipitated counteractions by the British which manifested with equal clearness the two branches of their policy mentioned above.

The military weakness of the United States was suggested in the autumn of 1790 by the Indians' defeat of General Josiah Harmar on the Maumee in territory which the British jealously guarded.[49] Following this, the appalling weaknesses of the quartermaster's department, inadequate training of regular troops, and complete unreliability of militia without months of training were all displayed in a campaign in 1791 by General Arthur St. Clair. His defeat, again in the Maumee

[47] Canad. Archives, *Report* for 1890, pp. 163, 164; and Dorchester's other informants agreed (*ibid.*, pp. 134, 137, 145, 160).

[48] *Ibid.*, pp. 138, 146, 161. Was this poor reporting? Or was it the calculated speech of a subordinate to one who did not tolerate unwelcome truth? Compare *ibid.*, p. 170, and G. M. Wrong, *Canada and the American Revolution* (New York, 1935), pp. 228–229, 342–343.

[49] *A.S.P., Ind. Aff.*, I, 104–106, 166; *Mil. Aff.*, I, 20–36.

country (November 4), was one of the three most disastrous in American Indian wars of more than a century.[50]

In 1790 and 1791 there were striking manifestations of Dorchester's Indian policies, and of the misunderstandings that underlay them. In 1790 Secretary Hamilton suggested to Major Beckwith that Dorchester might aid in establishing Indian peace by recommending a peaceful course to the Indians.[51] No doubt Hamilton did assume that the British were sustaining war (all supplies of the Indians came from the British), and perhaps he felt that they were encouraging it. However, he contemplated a friendly communication to both parties when next in council. Lord Dorchester took the suggestion as one for a formal international mediation. He accordingly instructed Sir John Johnson to ascertain the terms on which "the Confederated Indian Nations" would make peace, "together with the grounds of equity, justice, and policy, of their claims." Necessarily, Hamilton explained to Beckwith his inability even to "submit such a paper to the President's consideration."[52] However, the incident presumably caused irritations. In July, 1791, a number of tribes, encouraged by St. Clair's defeat, agreed to demand alterations in the settlement line across Ohio fixed by the treaty negotiated by St. Clair at Fort Harmar in 1789. Their agreement was laid before Dorchester shortly before he started for England (for a full two-year stay) in September. In a speech to assembled Indians, he used these remarkable words:

But . . . [1] this line . . . even supposing the treaty had taken effect, could not prejudice your rights. [2] The King's [only] rights with respect to your territory were against the nations of Europe: [3] these rights he resigned to the States. But [4] the King never had any rights against you, but to such parts of the country as had been fairly ceded by you yourselves . . . by public convention and sale; how then can it be said that he gave away your lands?[53]

---

[50] Near Greenville, Ohio, For prior notifications to British authorities, see *ibid.*, pp. 96, 99, 101, 172, and *Mich. Hist. Coll.*, XXIV, 191, 288; W. H. Smith (ed.), *St. Clair Papers* (2 vols., Cincinnati, 1882), II, 258–267, 275, 277–278, 281–300; *A.S.P., Ind. Aff.*, I, 136–138 (St. Clair's report), 172–174 (his instructions); *Mil. Aff.*, I, 36–44 (reports of congressional committees); *Mich. Hist. Coll.*, XXIV, 98–99, 137, 287–288; Canad. Archives, *Report* for 1890, pp. 320 *et seq.*

[51] Canad. Archives, *Report* for 1890, pp. 163, 169.

[52] *Ibid.*, pp. 168–169, 171.

[53] Bemis, *Jay's Treaty*, p. 116.

Here were four statements of alleged fact and one rhetorical question. The first statement was true, since the Indian "right" (power to bar settlement until paid for permitting safe enjoyment) was unaffected by the King's cession. But if Dorchester knew that, then he knew that the other three assertions, either as stated or as intended to be understood, were not true. The fourth denied crown title explicitly. The second denied it implicitly, by deceptive implication of the word "only." The third was only partly true, since it included the false implication of the second. The whole concoction was only an artful misconstruction of all Indian treaties since 1755, and disregarded scores of facts in the creation and later history of the colonies.

Dorchester's decades of American service preclude any possibility of ignorance of crown title. He had been responsibly associated with Canada for thirty years, and was then for the second time its governor. He must have known considerable of the French seigniories there created, as also of the military bounty lands granted in the Northwest by the Proclamation of 1763.[54] It is surely proper also to assume his knowledge of the fact that Virginia's charter limits extended far into the Northwest, where he was executing royal orders through Lieutenant Governor Simcoe, resident in Detroit. Yet his speech and all British policy (1) denied original British title to that area and (2) assumed the nonexistence of Indian cessions of it; therefore denied any basis for establishment by the Crown of his own governorship. Dorchester's speech cleverly capsulated in 1791 the policy of British officials in Canada after 1783, but he knew that it was spurious.

The policy had originated in a Swiss soldier's natural ignorance of the problem. But some of his subordinates, particularly Alexander McKee, the head of the Indian bureau (who had long been a deputy of Sir William Johnson), knew perfectly well that Dorchester's doctrine contradicted earlier colonial procedure.

Dorchester's pronouncement of 1791 was inconsistent with Canadian practice in the years shortly preceding and following it. It was true that there had never been any Indian cessions of the country beyond the Lakes, either to the French or to the English. As commander in chief

<hr>

[54] W. B. Munro, *The Seignorial System in Canada* (New York, 1907), *passim;* W. B. Munro (ed.), *Documents Relating to the Seignorial Tenure in Canada, 1598–1854* (Toronto, 1908), *passim;* also G. C. Patterson, "Land Settlement in Upper Canada, 1783–1840," Ontario, Dep't of Public Records and Archives, *Report* No. 16 (Toronto, 1921), p. 18.

in New York at the end of the Revolution, Dorchester (then Sir Guy Carleton) had necessarily been familiar with the plans (and unplanned facts) respecting the establishment of Loyalists in Ontario—perhaps 10,000 of them by 1784, and many more later.[55] A Canadian investigator, who had evidently been taught that "the British government always [had] recognized the title of the Indian tribes of Canada to the lands which they occupied," naturally assumed that the history of Ontario lands should begin with Indian cessions. However, in the provincial archives he found no "deeds" and an extraordinary paucity of information: "scarcely a record . . . was used," he reports, by those managing Indian lands.[56] There are maps, of course, in unofficial publications of what are labeled "cessions," but such official or semiofficial records as exist seem to be lists of "claims"—that is, claims of Indians —to British lands![57] Indians as well as Loyalists were settled on land to which "claims" were relinquished. Even Joseph Brant, chief of the Mohawks, chief aide of the British in organizing Indian "confederations" to oppose the Americans, was assigned a tract on the Grand River, and later had a dispute with the British over his right to it.

Not only Canadian authorities but the ministry in London ignored the treaty cession of 1783, despite the King's explicit act, the Crown's title, and long-continued colonial practices. The ministry had another cause for inaction. Its basis was reasonable in nature, but the action based on it was less so.

As early as the spring of 1790 Pitt, in conversation with Gouverneur Morris about the northwestern posts, had "admitted that it was perhaps the idea of the ministry to negotiate a new treaty rather than carry out the old one, and that there was a possibility that Great Britain might desire to retain the posts."[58] This had probably, ever since the signing of the treaty, been the hope, if not the plan, lurking behind

[55] Burt, U.S., G.B., pp. 50–62; Patterson, "Land Settlement," p. 21.

[56] Ibid., p. 219. Finding no evidence of cessions, instead of rejecting what he had been taught (seemingly under constraint), he assumed that the evidence was either lost or had never existed.

[57] Maps with dates of "cessions," ibid., p. 220, and Mich. Hist. Coll., XIX, 382.

[58] A.S.P., For. Rel., I, 123. Inasmuch as Secretary Hamilton had assured Beckwith that the United States "would not go to war over the question of the posts, even should Spain and Britain come to grips" (AHR, XXI, 551), Dundas naturally treated that question as negligible. See also J. P. Boyd, No. 7 (Princeton 1964).

the government's nonperformance of the treaty. It now became overt policy. It is to be noted that after Harmar's repulse in the autumn of 1790, the Indians showed a strong inclination to move beyond the Mississippi unless promised British military aid, and the question was officially raised how far removal would be consistent with British interests. The fur merchants, on the other hand, wanted the Indians to "listen to peace."[59]

When Dorchester sailed for England in 1791, new instructions were dispatched to Canada from a new secretary of state for American affairs, Henry Dundas. These instructions revealed that the government had basically changed its position since 1786. Troubles would not end, said Dundas, "if the Americans continued to assert their claims to the Indian lands." The Indians should be urged to accept any reasonable proposition, but

the chief object . . . will be that of securing to them the peaceful possession of . . . their [present] hunting Grounds, and such others as may enable them to procure a comfortable subsistence. . . . If the Indians are either extirpated from their countries, or rendered insecure in the possession of them, our trade in that quarter, and which Your Lordship and the merchants of Montreal state to be so valuable, must be much injured, and the enjoyment of it rendered altogether precarious. The subject of the Posts . . . is unfortunately connected with what I have just adverted to. The measures taken for securing the possession of those Posts, as well as . . . [all the lands along the treaty line] are fully approved.[60]

He hoped that the Americans would refrain from acts which might compel Dorchester to use force to stop them. Lord Grenville in September had earlier warned the United States minister in London that Britain "could not be indifferent" to a "total extirpation" of the Indians.[61] This reads like the oldtime magnification of the fur trade, but it was that and much more.

By the middle of 1792 the plan was plainly to gain access to the Mississippi to permit competition for the Valley's trade and control.[62]

[59] Mich. Hist. Coll., XXIV, 387, 426, 306; O. E. Leavitt, "British Policy on the Canadian Frontier, 1782-92," Wis. State Hist. Soc., Proceedings for 1915, p. 116.

[60] September 16, 1791, Canad. Archives, Report for 1890, pp. 172, 173–174; compare Mich. Hist. Coll., XXIV, 305.

[61] Bemis, Jay's Treaty, p. 92; W. E. Stevens, The Northwest Fur Trade, 1763-1800 (Urbana, Ill., 1928), pp. 169–170.

[62] Bemis, Jay's Treaty, pp. 107, 122, 239–242.

And with this went another plan to exclude the United States from the Great Lakes by creating an Indian reservation south of them on British land to be taken back from the States. The new plan as described by Dundas to Hammond (March 15, 1792) was to use mediation between the United States and the Indians to create an Indian buffer territory extending "along the whole line of His Majesty's Dominions, and that of the United States of America."[63] With this idea was coupled another of "rectifying" New York's boundary around Lake Champlain, so as to make Canada less vulnerable to attack. This entire reservation was to be taken out of American territory. "The price Britain would have to pay was the surrender of the posts."[64] They were to be returned but destroyed, and settlers excluded from a neutralized reservation. Moreover, it soon appeared that special commercial concessions in the interior were also desired. Several grand councils of the Indians were part of the maneuvers for realization of this grand plan in one or another of its stages. Hammond, from Philadelphia, had earlier asked the Canadian authorities to induce the Indians to make a "spontaneous" petition for British intervention in order to secure a neutralized Indian buffer reservation. These Indian councils again revealed the Indian pupils under British instruction.

The ultimate burden, however, of giving reality to the ministry's dream fell on Hammond. Even before the last-quoted instructions from Dundas had left London, the latter had Hammond's report that no mediation would be possible while the posts were retained; yet the instructions were not altered, and Hammond was urged to carry them out (April, 1792). The proposed new buffer strip included land in New York and Pennsylvania long since released by the Indians and much of it settled, also land in Ohio released by the Fort McIntosh and Fort Harmar treaties. Hammond took advantage of the discretion allowed by his general instructions, and raised the question only informally with secretaries Jefferson, Knox, and Hamilton. The first two brushed aside any relinquishment of territory. The last, far the most friendly to Great Britain, declared "briefly and coldly . . . that any . . . cession of territory or . . . allowance of any other Power to interfere in the disputes with the Indians would be considered . . . as absolutely . . . inadmissible."[65] The matter was out of the way by early summer of 1792.

Vain efforts were made by the United States in 1792 and 1793 to come to agreement with the Indians on a basis for peace. In 1792 their answer was a demand for the expulsion of all settlers north of the Ohio,

[63] *Ibid.*, pp. 117–118. Compare Dorchester (in London) to Dundas, *Mich. Hist. Coll.*, XXIV, 386–389.

[64] Burt, *U.S., G.B.*, p. 119.

[65] Bemis, *Jay's Treaty*, pp. 92, 117–122. It is easy to believe that a secretary of state could be ignorant of such facts, but not Dorchester, and he was in London.

where occupation rights had already in large part been twice paid for. They justified this repudiation of these treaties "without repayment [of the purchase price] by balancing it against the abandonment of their claim for lands stolen from them on the other [south] side of the river" Ohio—that is, by the treaty of Fort Stanwix in 1768 made with Sir William Johnson.[66] Grenville, in charge of foreign affairs, was still hoping to get all the Northwest and more as an "extremely small" setoff against British losses in consequence of American infractions of the treaty.[67] One wonders if he shared the views of Dundas, who wrote about the same time to Simcoe of the Americans, "those Gentlemen . . . pretend to call the Indian Country their Country: and the Privileges [reoccupation of the posts?] granted on conditions they never performed, their undoubted Rights; and the Line designated in the Treaty their acknowledged Boundary; affecting to consider our reoccupying a Post at the Rapids of the Miamis [Maumee] as War itself."[68]

In fact, every pretense here falsely charged to Americans was the reverse of an actual one by the British. So far as a treaty can be judged by law, cession of title to the midline of the Great Lakes was not made conditional upon prior or concurrent performance by the United States of any counterpromise. However, as a matter of political ethics, Britain was free openly to treat evacuation of the posts as conditional (for example, upon payment of debts to British merchants)—and chose to do so. Various Americans thought this just, among them John Jay. Resort to pretended excuses was unnecessary.

In 1793 the American government—willing at last to regard as ill-timed any negotiations for clearing land in advance of imminent settlement—authorized its commissioners to offer either the return of the land ceded at Fort McIntosh and Fort Harmar (except that already sold to the Ohio Company and the Symmes Associates) or $50,000 plus an annuity of $10,000 for another confirmation of the original cessions. The commissioners were long delayed at Niagara by Lieutenant Governor Simcoe before being allowed to go westward to the meeting place, and were not allowed to meet the Indians—merely Indian deputations. Eventually, the Ohio was again demanded "as the boundary

---

[66] Their demand was made in council at the mouth of the Auglaize in October, *A.S.P., Ind. Aff.*, I, 322–324. Brant visited Philadelphia in the summer (Stone, *Brant*, II, 321–329) and did not attend the council. For the quotation, see Burt, *U.S., G.B.*, p. 126.

[67] Grenville to Hammond, April 25, 1792, Bemis, *Jay's Treaty*, p. 121.

[68] *Mich. Hist. Coll.*, XXIV, 689.

between your people and ours." The American commissioners replied that it could not be the settlement line. However, presumably hoping to gain good will, the commissioners, in effect, apologized for the treaties of 1784 to 1789. Their predecessors who negotiated those treaties, they said, had "put an erroneous construction" on the British-American treaty of peace, and they adopted and repeated Dorchester's sophistical speech of 1791.[69] This groveling (adopted because the Secretary of War and some others believed that the Indians would never accept the truth) accomplished nothing.[70] Nor could an earlier adoption of the untruth have prevented war, since it would not have altered American needs for land, or British attachment to the fur traders, or British promise that Indian occupancy of the Ohio area should be unaltered.[71] Its resumption was inevitable because the British had made the meeting with the Indians an insult and a futility.

Back from England, Dorchester in February, 1794, made a speech to an Indian assemblage in which he declared: "There is no line between [the Americans] and us"; predicted war and, if necessary, the fixing of a boundary by the Indians and the King's troops.[72] In this speech he also restated Dundas' theory of conditional (postponed) cession of the Northwest, and a week later ordered Simcoe to re-establish an abandoned British fort at the Maumee rapids (Miamis). This was while General Anthony Wayne was advancing northward from Cincinnati to attack the Indians. So far as Simcoe was concerned, in his plans the fort's erection was the beginning of a conquest of the states.[73] On the other hand, the secretary of state, on the theory of merely ethical retention of the posts, charged the British minister in Washington with an

[69] *A.S.P., Ind. Aff.,* I, 340–360 (instructions, pp. 340–342; exchanges with Indian deputations, pp. 350–357; quotations, pp. 353, 359); Stone, *Brant,* II, 338–356; *Mich. Hist. Coll.,* XX, 320; XXIV, 579–592.

[70] *J.C.C.,* XXXIV, 124; *A.S.P., Ind. Aff.,* I, 12–14.

[71] Burt was a native of the Loyalist country in Ontario, and believed (*U.S., G.B.,* pp. 130–131) that "if the American government . . . from the beginning" had "come round to the British position that what had been transferred had not been the title to the Indian territory but merely the exclusive right to acquire it from the natives," there need have been "no Anglo-American entanglement over the posts, nor any Indian war in the Northwest."

[72] E. A. Cruikshank (ed.), *Simcoe Papers,* II, 149–150; *A.S.P., For. Rel.,* I, 462, Waite, *State Papers* (2nd ed.), II, 60–61.

[73] Order to rebuild fort, *Mich. Hist. Coll.,* XXVI, 642; Dorchester's speech, *ibid.,* XX, 331, 336, 343, XXIV, 656; Simcoe's strategic plan, *ibid.,* pp. 658–659; Simcoe's general views, *ibid.,* XI, 378, XXV, 2–4.

act of "hostility" itself; and John Jay, in London, similarly warned the British government.[74] It admonished Dorchester (avoiding the main issue) that the fort was not "within the Limits of the Post at Detroit, the immediate protection of which, as well as the Posts in our possession . . . is the only object to be attended to."[75]

The new campaign against the Indians had been authorized in October, 1793. A year before that Wayne had taken command of the remnants of St. Clair's troops, and since the spring of 1793 he had been consolidating a force of regulars with frontier riflemen and cavalry, and thoroughly training them. In the battle of Fallen Timbers, perhaps two miles from the new British fort at Miamis, the Indians suffered a defeat (August 20, 1794) as overwhelming as St. Clair's had been in 1791. The fleeing Indians (and some Canadian militia) were followed very nearly to the British fort, within which some presumably took refuge. Aside, however, from mutual irritations by letters and some show of martial readiness, the two commanders avoided hostilities.[76] Up to the last moment active aid from the British had been expected by the Indians—not unreasonably.[77] Wayne destroyed the storehouses of various British traders and the headquarters of Alexander McKee, devastated the cornfields and villages of the Indians, established Fort Wayne, and withdrew for the winter to give the Indians time to prepare, as was their custom, for a peace council.

In June the ceremonial fire was lighted at Fort Greenville. More than a thousand Indians gradually gathered, and in August, 1795, a treaty was concluded with twelve tribes.[78] It opened much of Ohio for settle-

[74] *A.S.P., For. Rel.,* I, 333.

[75] *Mich. Hist. Coll.,* XXIV, 680.

[76] For Wayne's reports, *A.S.P., Ind. Aff.,* I, 487–495, 547–548, 571, 574; also *Mich. Hist. Coll.,* XXXIV, 341–733, at 544 *et seq.* For McKee's accounts, *ibid.,* XX, 364, 370–371; letters of Wayne and commander of British fort, XXV, 16–23; *A.S.P., Ind. Aff.,* I, 490.

[77] Some British had fought with the Indians in an earlier attack on Fort Recovery, a small contingent of British militia fought at Fallen Timbers, and the military stores at Detroit were exhausted in aid of the Indians in 1794. *A.S.P., Ind. Aff.,* I, 488, 491; *Mich. Hist. Coll.,* XX, 355, 364. In January, 1796, Brant wrote to a British officer (*ibid.,* XX, 434): "this is the second time the poor Indians have been left in the lurch & I cannot avoid lamenting that they were prevented at a time when they had it in their power to make an Honorable & Advantageous Peace"—presumably 1783 or 1793.

[78] Kappler, *Indian Affairs,* II, 30–34; *A.S.P., Ind. Aff.,* I, 547–548, 562–563; with documents, 563–583.

ment except for a broad strip south of Lake Erie between the Maumee and the Cuyahoga.[79] Within the remainder of the British cession, left in Indian occupancy, the United States reserved the old settlements of Vincennes and of southern Illinois, and various strategic points, all with rights of way to them over reservation lands. The United States again distributed presents and engaged to pay annuities. It also promised trade under a new system of government control which had been inaugurated that year among the southern tribes.

Who was responsible for British action? Both Dorchester and Simcoe had a notable share of the arrogance which characterized Britain's foreign relations between her two imperial victories of 1763 and 1815. Both fought in the American Revolution; each, seemingly, felt that he could have altered its end. Ten days before Wayne's victory, Simcoe suggested to Dorchester an attack on, and dismemberment of, the United States. Each had desired to control diplomatic relations with the states—much as by a nonresident minister. To a considerable degree Dorchester, who secured the higher post, seemingly did control them as a result of his masterful spirit, long visits in England, and prestige.

American historians have generally blamed the superior officials in London for nothing more than occasional indiscreet words as individuals. But discretion in orders to Canadian agents was less important than oversight. Considering what actually happened, it may be fairly said that the price of peace was fixed by the Canadian officials, and it amounted to American renunciation of the Northwest. Indian relations were the basis of Canadian policy, and all American difficulties with the Indians arose either from the acts of the Canadian Indian agents or from the misrepresentations respecting Indian rights in the land which were made, more or less innocently, by Canadian officials and army officers. Various historians have approved the view that those authorities can be absolved of blame if one makes "a sharp distinction between inciting the Indians to warfare and taking pains to preserve their attachment" to Great Britain.[80] This is too charitable. It totally ignores the misrepresentations respecting "Indian land" and crown title.

[79] The line ran from the mouth of the Kentucky River to Fort Recovery, thence to the Muskingum River and site of former Fort Laurens (near Canton, Ohio), thence up that stream to the Cuyahoga portage and down the Cuyahoga to Lake Erie.

[80] A. H. Abel, in Amer. Hist. Association, *Report* for 1906, p. 261. Their purpose was to keep the Northwest.

It also ignores the point that what was said to the Indians is not to be judged as addressed to us, but to them. The question is, What was *their* understanding? The chief of the Wyandot answered this in the Fort Greenville council of 1795; the British, he said, gave him the tomahawk to be planted in the head of General Wayne. The home government never corrected the repudiation by its Canadian representatives of crown title, from which resulted the minor acts that ran counter to pacification. The reason, too, seems perfectly plain. Britain was holding the Northwest, and the ministry tolerated anything which held the Indians for the fur trade and for substitutional defense of the posts.

Meanwhile, diplomatic negotiations had begun in London, and were in progress during Wayne's campaign. John Jay, whose manifest integrity had won British confidence in 1782 and appointment as the first chief justice of the United States Supreme Court, had been selected to represent the United States. There were only three things which the United States could ever have gained by a treaty: termination of controversy over debts to British merchants, a commercial treaty, and evacuation of the posts. The Constitution of the new Union promised the first by giving those creditors access to the federal courts. Wayne was in the field, and if his victory should be decisive that would weaken relations between the British and Indians, and greatly aid in recovering the posts. For reasons unconnected with the West, the possibility of a commercial treaty became scant long before Jay's appointment, and during Jay's mission was rendered quite impossible by American action.[81] Jay's instructions were, therefore, to secure the posts, disarmament on the Great Lakes, and an agreement that neither party should interfere with the Indians.[82]

Jay could not have effectively pressed the issue of the posts because, as has been noted, he had officially committed himself in 1786 in favor

[81] Hammond had had no powers to negotiate in Philadelphia on either commerce or the posts. British trade with the states was already satisfactorily immense, but Americans were threatening to raise customs and tonnage duties. Schuyler, *American Diplomacy and the Furtherance of Commerce* (New York, 1886); J. B. Moore, "The Contest with Commercial Restrictions," *Harper's Magazine* (1904), pp. 459–468. The secretary of state, Edmund Randolph (a Republican), had included in Jay's instructions an admonition to consider joining the Armed Neutrality. Bemis, *Jay's Treaty*, pp. 192–196, 246–247, 210; but on that possibility Hamilton quieted Grenville's fears. *Ibid.*, pp. 199–202, 221–229, 231, 246–251, 260, 269.

[82] *Ibid.*, pp. 210–217.

of the British position—as the British knew.[83] He was therefore given freedom in his instructions to act as self-respect required.[84] However, it seemed to be agreed from the beginning that they should be evacuated. Britain had reason to believe that her interests would not suffer in so doing. Two years before Jay's mission, Hammond had reported that secretaries Jefferson, Knox, and Hamilton all agreed that if the posts should be returned the United States would be willing to reduce the garrisons, agree to mutual limitations of armament on the Lakes, and consent to whatever measures the Canadian authorities might judge necessary for protection of the fur trade on the Lakes and the "communications" between them. Hammond also believed that the United States might be willing to raze the forts, and also consent to "such a regulation of the northwestern boundary as would afford a free and effectual communication with the Mississippi."[85] This encouraged British hopes of controlling the continent's interior trade. When Grenville prepared his proposals to be made to Jay, he quite naturally included all these proposals in favor of Britain, but omitted limitation of armaments on the Lakes. He left it to Jay to demand mutuality of rights in the fur trade and interlake communications.[86]

It has been stated that Jay's instructions included one—it was said, "one from which the United States will not willingly depart"—that the Indians within the peace treaty's boundaries should not be interfered with by the British government.[87] President Washington had justly declared this to be the main cause of all the government's troubles in the West.[88] A minimum attention to self-protection would seem to have required removal of this before making any concessions to Grenville. On the contrary, before Jay submitted any proposals to protect the United States, it was agreed that the subjects of each party might freely cross the boundary by land or inland waters for purposes of trade.[89] Britain rejected Jay's proposals later made that neither of the parties, in case of war between them, should take the Indians as allies;

[83] *Ibid.*, p. 236.
[84] *Ibid.*, pp. 207, 215; compare 45, 75, 196–197, 205.
[85] *Ibid.*, p. 122.
[86] *Ibid.*, p. 253.
[87] *Ibid.*, p. 213.
[88] "All the difficulties we encounter with the Indians, their hostilities, the murders of helpless women and innocent children along our frontiers, results from the conduct of the Agents of Great Britain in this Country." August 30, 1794, *Writings* (Kirkpatrick ed.), XXXIII, 484.
[89] Bemis, *Jay's Treaty*, p. 237; for treaty provision, p. 322.

that neither should make treaties with Indians within the other's territory; that each should "restrain" its Indians if they were at war with those of the other and not supply them arms or ammunition.[90] Likewise rejected were proposals to prohibit armed vessels on the Lakes and to withdraw military forces. Jay, in turn, did refuse one concession that Grenville desired—an adjustment of the northwestern boundary, in order to assure British access to the Mississippi.[91] Instead, the treaty provided for a joint survey to ascertain the facts.

There was one great gain by the treaty: the debts, illegal British captures and condemnations, access to the Mississippi, and the northeast boundary were all submitted to fact-finders or to arbitration, giving the treaty an honored place in that field of international good sense.[92] As regards the posts, Britain rid herself of a useless expense, and American pride was flattered. Cross-boundary trade was mutually desirable. The British could continue their use of the Indians as an instrument of policy, but American growth soon made it inconsequential. That the British, after being given half of the Great Lakes in 1783, would fortify and seek to control them wholly was plain; but by 1817 that too would be ended by American growth. Clearly it was Grenville's treaty rather than Jay's: it was Grenville who agreed or did not agree. To be sure, nobody, seemingly, has considered Jay's concessions in the West as vital. They are emphasized to make clear the British inflexibility on western interests. But it was national growth that made the concessions harmless.

The treaty was signed on November 19, 1794, and ratifications were exchanged a little less than a year later.[93] In the meantime the Senate had confirmed it by precisely the two-thirds vote required by the Constitution, after one of the bitterest battles in the Senate's history; and the House of Representatives had voted, by a margin of only three votes, an appropriation for its performance. There was not much to have been expected from any negotiation. Whether the expectation was

[90] *Ibid.*, pp. 243–244, 261–262.

[91] It was not then known that this would have transferred to Britain a large amount of American territory as defined by the treaty of 1783.

[92] Moore, *International Arbitrations.* The ultimate financial balance against Britain (illegal captures over debts) was nearly $9 million.

[93] The correspondence of the mission is in *A.S.P., For. Rel.,* I, 470–525; the treaty, in Malloy, *Treaties,* I, 379–397; Miller, *International Acts,* II, 245–267; with notes, 267–274. Statements (e.g., in Bemis, *Jay's Treaty,* p. xiii, Mr. Hunt) that Washington so disliked the treaty that he withheld it are corrected by Miller, p. 269.

lessened by the choice of the negotiator is highly disputable, for possibly no other could have gotten any treaty whatever, in which case new recriminations would doubtless have been added to the old. Washington could best judge. No other negotiator could have been more patriotic, none more acceptable in personality to the British. Presumably, he secured all possible concessions and read the future accurately.

On July 11, 1796, American troops occupied Detroit and the British fort at Miamis. Michilimackinac, the last to be surrendered, was taken over in October.

CHAPTER 7

The Southwest and European Relations to 1798

THE policies toward the American West which controlled France and Spain in the peace negotiations continued with no substantial changes for many years. It was inevitable that European powers should consider how much strength they would willingly see pass to a new nation already with a great commerce and starting with a territory four times the size of France. Vergennes' successor, the Comte de Montmorin, faced that problem in 1787, in drawing up instructions for the French minister to the United States, the Comte de Moûstier. In case there should be talk in Congress of securing an open Mississippi for the western settlements, he was instructed to "remark that the King would regret to see the United States become embroiled with Spain over a matter in which principle is in favor of the latter power. . . . As respects consideration of a new constitution, His Majesty . . . feels that it is desirable for France that the United States shall remain in their present condition, for if they should acquire the coherence of which they are capable, they would soon gain a strength and power which they would probably be eager to misuse."[1] France wished, decidedly, to maintain the American alliance, but with a dependent, not a strong, United States. She expected the dissolution of all union between the states, and would not regret it. She had "never pretended to make of

[1] E. H. Bourne (ed.), "Correspondence of the Comte de Moûstier with the Comte de Montmorin, 1787–1789," *AHR*, VIII (1903), 709–733, and IX (1903), 86–96. Quotation of October 10, 1787.

America a useful ally," but had "no other object than to deprive Great Britain of that vast continent."[2]

Still less was there change in the purposes of Spain. Jay's two-year assault, before the peace, upon the postulates of her colonial system had been a complete failure. But equally futile had been Floridablanca's rejection of the American arguments based on natural law. The forty-year contest now began anew. All of Spain's policies respecting America were substantially policies of fear, particularly fear for the mines of Mexico. So extravagant was that fear that other governments used it for their own advantage: the French throughout the 1700's up to 1763, the British in then making peace, France again when she regained Louisiana in 1800, even McGillivray of the Creeks.[3] In fact, for decades it underlay the American policy of waiting—waiting while the frontiersmen pushed deeper into the back country where Spain hoped to hold them. Looking out from Pensacola's wooden "citadel" and the island stronghold of New Orleans into the endless forests where American backwoodsmen were threatening the Indian barrier upon which Spain relied, her officials sedulously collected gossip, facts of trade and travel, and rumors of the moment, and recorded them in their reports (thus becoming the first and indispensable historians of the old Southwest). But they ignored the obvious facts that the various American settlements forming in the West were hundreds of miles apart, and that the nearest was hundreds of miles from Pensacola or New Orleans. "There is no time to be lost," wrote Martín Navarro (able intendant at New Orleans in 1787): "Mexico is on the other side of the Mississippi, in the vicinity of the already formidable establishments of the Americans."[4] And a few years later, Carondelet, the governor of Louisiana, imagined hordes of American frontiersmen "of unmeasured ambition . . . hostile to all subjection, advancing and multiplying . . . with a prodigious activity."[5] Along with such basic atti-

---

[2] Instructions of August 30, 1787, to Minister Otto in G. Bancroft, *History of the Formation of the Constitution of the United States* (2 vols., New York, 1885), II, 438–439. For other letters emphasizing the importance of maintaining the treaty tie, see *AHR*, VIII, 710, 711, 712, 728.

[3] *Ill. Hist. Coll.*, XXVI, xiii, 157; M. S. Fletcher, "Louisiana in French Diplomacy from 1763 to 1800," *MVHR*, XVII (1931), 374; A. P. Whitaker, *The Spanish-American Frontier, 1763–1795* (New York, 1927), p. 34.

[4] *Ibid.*, p. 27.

[5] C. E. R. Gayarré, *History of Louisiana* (4 vols., New York, 1851), *Spanish Dominion*, 183. For another similar letter of Carondelet, see J. A. Robertson, *Louisiana . . . 1785–1808* (2 vols., Cleveland, 1911), I, 294.

tudes as these of France and Spain toward the new American state went their uncertainties of the latter's viability. It was highly questionable whether its new federal form would be a workable political system. Moûstier, when he first arrived as minister in Philadelphia, found the Confederation equally weak internally and externally, and of no value as an ally.[6] But, watching with bewilderment the events of 1786–87, he reported to his government that he could express no opinion on the future of the new country.[7] By the spring of 1788 Montmorin concluded that the government had been transformed from a phantom into a power theretofore unforeseeable. European states, he wrote, "ought now, it would seem, to be concerned with adjusting their political policy [*conduite*] to an event which will give the United States the coherence and vigor of a firm and powerful government."[8] This was written before the new Union actually existed.

It was also uncertain whether the strength of the new system would be adequate to dominate the sectionalism of the Confederation era and to hold the West until incorporated as states into the Union. The influence of this uncertainty upon the policies of foreign governments was intermittently important through more than a decade. Closely associated with it, of course, was the uncertain future of the adjoining Spanish colonies, acquisition of which, by conquest or cession and by one or another power (including the United States), was repeatedly expected as their relations with Spain shifted between war and peace. Britain was very near war with Spain in 1789–90; their relations again became strained in 1795, and war followed in 1796. France and Spain were normally Bourbon allies; the former was possibly pondering acquisition of Louisiana earlier than 1795, when its cession was refused. In 1793 the two countries were at war, and in 1795 again allied. In 1790 the United States weighed the desirability, in case of war over the Nootka Sound incident, of joining Britain or joining Spain or acting independently to protect American interests in the Mississippi—but actually doing nothing. Similar problems were presented by every later European crisis and the government adhered to the policy of watchful waiting while time might act. This policy was not compatible with the policies of land speculators or the temperament of Americans. Sometimes generated by these crises as they successively arose, sometimes

---

[6] *AHR*, VIII, 715, 719, 726.
[7] *Ibid.*, pp. 714, 725.
[8] *Ibid.*, pp. 716 (February 8, 1788), 727.

merely contemporaneously with them, intrigues and bizarre rumors disturbed the West. Mere chronology is only one bond between these episodes; however, it seems probable that chronological review of them will best reveal the realities and unrealities, the tensions and turmoil of the period, and make international negotiations more understandable.

The immense possibilities of American westward expansion were realized by many observers in the Revolutionary era, and predicted by some. The first notable incident in western history which tested the power of the Confederation to control expansion was a revival by the state of Georgia—after Virginia's cession of the Northwest to the Confederation, and before the organization of federal territory by Congress —of the problem whether Britain had ceded the West to the states severally or collectively.

As a result of a survey made under the land act of 1783, William Blount learned that the Big Bend of the Tennessee, long known for its rich lands, was in Georgia or South Carolina. Two of his partners immediately bought the Indian claims. Blount then secured permission from the Georgia legislature to colonize the area above the Bend in present-day Alabama, which was organized as a Georgia county.[9] This raised the question between the United States and Georgia of title to lands westward of the settled areas of that state to the Mississippi.[10] In 1783 an act of her legislature had defined her boundaries as the 31st parallel on the south and the Mississippi River on the west. In 1785, on petition of Thomas Green and other settlers at Natchez, she organized that area as Bourbon County and sent out various justices.[11] However, the neutralists and Loyalists of that community were of decidedly divided sentiment, many desiring independence, which even one of the Georgia justices urged. Governor Miró of Louisiana put various malcontents in irons and banished others. When Spain protested to Congress, the latter expressed disapproval of Georgia's acts, but had no power to do more—its right to do more being in dispute with Georgia.

Rumors had reached Spain's officials that a military attack was a part of Georgia's plans. George Rogers Clark was a chief supporter of

9 W. H. Masterson, *William Blount* (Baton Rouge, 1954), pp. 71, 72, 79, 80–83, 89–90.

10 *Ill. Hist. Coll.,* XXV, lviii *et seq.*

11 See E. C. Burnett (ed.), "Papers Relating to Bourbon County, Georgia, 1785–1786," *AHR,* XV, 66–71, 297–353; T. M. Green, *The Spanish Conspiracy . . . in the Southwest* (Cincinnati, 1891), p. 75.

Green, and it is said that Georgia's permission was sought for military occupation of the Natchez region by a force to be led by him.[12] A spectral regiment, ready to march under his command hither and yon, remained a steady unreality in western romance for more than a decade.

Britain had no political interest in the Indians of the Southwest after taking Florida in 1783, and though trade was virtually in British goods alone, it was a monopoly of a single British firm. Spain's interest in the Indians was exclusively political, and she sought their control through this firm and through subsidizing Alexander McGillivray, the chief of the Creeks. The United States wanted merely to occupy Indian hunting lands when needed, but also, inconsistently, wanted peace.

Since Spain was adamant in claiming title to the entire Appalachian back country, attempts by the United States to clear land of Indian claims was regarded by Spain as hostility. Even the making of any treaty was regarded as a wrongful use of "her" Indians. American countercharges were far less unreasonable: that Spain made land grants of disputed territory, sought attachment of the Indians for political purposes, and dissuaded them from observing peace treaties made with the United States.[13] Only very rarely, however, did Spanish officials incite attacks upon British or Americans.[14] General Gage conceded in 1772 that their object seemed "only to preserve Peace universally."[15] They merited the good will of the Indians, but lacked means of using them. McGillivray had a mind decidedly his own, and the Panton firm, which paid well for its monopoly, regarded trade as independent of politics.[16] This monopoly of British traders and British goods continued the influence of British administration in some degree from 1763–83, and during the period of the present chapter it sug-

---

[12] J. A. James, *Life of George Rogers Clark* (Chicago, 1928), p. 372; Green, *Spanish Conspiracy*, pp. 385–386.

[13] If Gayoso (governor of Natchez) advocated (1793) joint regulation of Indian affairs by the two countries—J. M. Berry, "The Indian Policy of Spain in the Southwest, 1783–1795," *MVHR*, III (1917), 473—it was utterly impractical.

[14] Whitaker, *Spanish-American Frontier*, pp. 39, 42–43, 60; Berry, "Indian Policy of Spain," pp. 463, 474.

[15] *Johnson Papers*, VIII, 552.

[16] Whitaker, *Spanish-American Frontier*, pp. 40 *et seq.*; also *Documents Relating to the Commercial Policy of Spain in the Floridas* (Deland, Fla., 1931), xxxii, lii.

gested to three adventurers—William Bowles, James O'Fallon, and John Chisholm—the enlistment of British political interest in bizarre plans of western empire.

American relations with the southern Indians were of extraordinary complexity, resulting from conflict between state and federal action, and from control of the former by land speculators. Under the Articles of Confederation, regulation of Indian relations was entrusted to the Union. No difficulties arose from this in the Northwest after Virginia's cession to the Confederation. In North Carolina, however, speculators had bounty warrants and other inchoate titles for enormous holdings, and by them, as well as by their fellows in South Carolina and Georgia, federal claim of title to the Southwest was more feared than Spain's claims.

William Blount's "land grab" of Tennessee in 1783 has earlier been referred to in its relations to the Indians and the national land system. Georgia, North Carolina, even the state of Franklin, made treaties with various tribes after 1783, and in all these treaties land speculation played a large part. A treaty made by Congress in 1784 at Hopewell (South Carolina) with the Cherokee, which left Transylvania and the Cumberland settlements outside Indian territory, was wholly disregarded by Blount's land act of 1783.[17] This also treated much of the state of Franklin, including its capital, Greenville, as in Indian territory. In 1790 McGillivray was induced to go to New York, was flatteringly entertained by the government, and a treaty was made with him for the Creeks.[18] This cleared considerable land of Indian claims; permitted federal troops on the border to repress hostilities between Indians and borderers; and, by a guarantee of other Indian hunting land (until needed), offered hope of checking land speculation. Georgia and North Carolina both complained of the Hopewell treaty, and the secretary of war was soon warning against shameful violations of it.[19] Efforts after 1783 by Blount to secure a foothold in the Great Bend of the Tennessee,[20] grants there by Georgia in 1789, and rivalry between

[17] Kappler, *Indian Affairs*, II, 8–11 (November, 1784); also in *A.S.P., Ind. Aff.*, I, 43–44; Masterson, *Blount*, pp. 103–105, 186.

[18] The treaty was made on August 7, 1790. See Kappler, *Indian Affairs*, II, 25–28; *A.S.P., Ind. Aff.*, I, 81; Miller, *International Acts*, II, 344.

[19] Blount's protest is in *A.S.P., Ind. Aff.*, I, 44; later developments to 1789, pp. 45–54. On probable military conflict, see *J.C.C.*, XXXIV, 476–479.

[20] Masterson, *Blount*, 71–73, 81–83.

groups of speculators interested in the region greatly complicated the differences between Georgia and the Union over cession of her western claims. They were not lessened by another federal treaty which, in revising the Hopewell treaty, pushed the line of white settlement farther down the Tennessee toward the Bend.[21]

Great changes had come to the West since Spain's first aid to the revolting colonies. Among them were her relaxations in enforcement of her colonial system, made in the hope of protecting herself against American expansion. That danger was most tangibly presented in the claim of the American government for an open Mississippi and in the illicit British trade around the Gulf which had been particularly great up the Mississippi while England held the Floridas.[22] Spain's officials in Louisiana, knowing that a continuance of these irregularities was essential to Louisiana's prosperity, tolerated them when circumstances permitted independent action, and had the courage to recommend their approval by the home government.

Such approval in Spain, despite occasional relapses into standard mercantilism, seems truly astonishing. Spain's colonial commercial system had long been simple: Spanish products in Spanish ships trading between special ports of Spain and the colonies. As for the first requirement, Spain could not produce what the colony particularly needed, and other colonies were better sources than Louisiana for what Spain desired. As respects the second requirement, the *sole* port for colonial trade was Cadiz until 1778, when that tenet was liberalized by confirming special relaxations allowed Louisiana since 1768.[23] Simultaneously with this act of the home government, the colony's governor reported that only "free trade with the French colonies and with France itself" could give the colony the market and imports needed for prosperity.[24] In 1780 its intendant urged a more radical remedy: "a general,

[21] Treaty of Holston (Knoxville, Tenn.), July 2, 1791. Kappler, *Indian Affairs*, II, 31; *A.S.P., Ind. Aff.*, I, 53, 544, 628.

[22] The treaty of 1783 gave them entry by the Mississippi from the Gulf, and, as they could moor at will, they unloaded whatever was desired as they ascended the river. Whitaker, *Commercial Policy of Spain*, ix, xxii (n. 4), xxiv–xxv, 5, 17. British dominance up to 1779 was complete—C. Johnson, *British West Florida, 1763–1783* (New Haven, 1943), pp. 193–198—and the Spanish intendant was voluble on its benefits to the colony. Robertson, *Louisiana*, I, 244, 245, 246.

[23] Whitaker, *Spanish-American Frontier*, pp. 35–36.

[24] Whitaker, *Commercial Policy of Spain*.

free, and common trade with any national whatsoever . . . [under] any flag."[25] The government in 1782 adopted the governor's suggestion, with some limitations, one of which led to much illicit trade between the colony and the United States.[26]

For the duration of the Revolution Louisiana's trade had already been opened to French ships, and the Mississippi had been opened to Americans. However, without regard to the actual results of all these relaxations, a royal order of June, 1784, closed the river to all but Spanish ships; that is, theoretically, as necessities allowed.[27]

Spain had realized that the Revolution, if successful, would compel some disposition of the Appalachian back country. By her conquests in British West Florida, she had improved her bargaining position and had put relations with the Americans on a friendly basis by aiding them. It has been seen that she lost any chance to utilize those gains in the peace negotiations, and was now forced to negotiate with the United States under far more difficult conditions. Before relating their opening negotiations, two matters should be put aside: one because logically irrelevant to the problems to be negotiated; the other because, although relevant, it was certain to be excluded by Spain from immediate consideration. This last refers to the relaxations in Mississippi navigation. No matter how significantly they bore on the disputes of the future, they had been made for Spain's own special purposes, and she could not be expected to recognize American demands for their continuance without adequate compensation.

Wholly irrelevant, logically, to the rights of the parties, although often treated as relevant, was a secret article in the provisional treaty between Britain and America of 1782. This provided that 32° should continue to be the northern boundary of West Florida if by the final European treaty Britain should retain the colony, but 31° if the colony be ceded to Spain. The United States, in exchange for renunciation by

[25] Robertson, *Louisiana*, I, 252–255; Whitaker, *Commercial Policy of Spain*, p. 226, n. 22, where he gives the true date of the document as September 24, 1780. Navarro's "Political Reflections" is a sarcastic paper: the colony would be in good condition *if* some dozen matters were different—various of them sufficient, each alone, to keep it worthless (*ibid.*, pp. 251–252).

[26] *Ibid.*, pp. xxix, 30–38, 67, 234 (n. 11). The opportunity in the islands for good fellows to get together was compulsive; see J. A. Jameson, "St. Eustatius in the American Revolution," *AHR*, VII (1903), 683–708.

[27] Whitaker, *Commercial Policy of Spain*, p. xxvi. On local orders respecting Mississippi trade, see James, *Clark*, p. 360.

Britain of all other claims west of the Appalachians, renounced in favor of Britain, in the contingency stated, any claim to the one-degree strip.[28] The article dealt, on a contingency never satisfied, with mere conflicting claims of Britain and the United States. It could not affect any of Spain's claims in any manner or American claims as against Spain's, and Congress—very sensibly—did not even express any opinion on the matter.[29] It is true that Lafayette believed that in 1783 he secured Spain's agreement to abide in negotiations with the United States by the boundary of West Florida thus agreed upon as between Britain and the colonies. Lafayette's understanding, however, was not legally binding upon Spain.

As respects the joint declaration by Britain and the United States in their final treaty of 1783 that the navigation of the Mississippi should forever remain free to both from its source *to the Gulf,* the legal standing of the italicized words under dominant contemporary international practice is quite clear. They had no legal effect whatever. At that time few international conventions had altered the status of an interstate river from that of any intrastate stream. The right of a riparian owner (power or individual) to navigate a river passed as part of the land title. On the other hand, a riparian power could give to a nonriparian by treaty, *at most,* a contractual right to share its appurtenant navigation rights so long as it should remain a riparian owner. Britain owned, from 1763 to 1783, two sections of the Mississippi's east shore: one down to the north boundary of Florida, and below that one down to the mouth of the Iberville—beyond which the boundary of West Florida ran through that creek and Lakes Maurepas and Ponchartrain. Britain, in words, ceded both sections to the United States in 1783, and they carried Mississippi navigation rights—above but not below the mouth of the Iberville. Below that, Britain had held seeming acquisition of the latter below 31° by the words of her treaty of 1763 with France, which had been nullified by the latter's destruction of her own appurtenant right by prior transfer of Louisiana to Spain. This was deliberate: in 1762, King Louis XVI had declared himself indifferent

---

[28] Wharton, *Dip. Corr.,* VI, 117, 567–568.

[29] Miller, *International Acts,* II, 101. Spain had an older claim through exploration than had France or England. (Confusion has arisen from discussing her "quasi title" by military occupation; compare L. Houck (ed.), *The Spanish Regime in Missouri . . . Documents* (2 vols., Chicago, 1909), I, 237.

as respected how much land he ceded to Britain, provided only it be rendered worthless to her. All he ceded east of the Mississippi was made worthless, in his judgment, by the prior cession to Spain of all west of the river and of both banks at New Orleans. What Britain could give to the United States in 1783 was manifestly nothing more below the mouth of the Iberville than a contractual right to use that gully and the Lakes while Britain should retain West Florida—and by the final treaty of 1783 she ceded it to Spain. Years later, Lord Lansdowne (Shelburne) explained that the ostensible grant was inserted when Britain still expected to retain Florida, and was inadvertently retained when that intention was abandoned.[30]

At that time international law (practice) was in a state of transition on various matters. In championing the doctrine that upper riparians have interests that could not be ignored by a power holding a river's mouth (as in championing change of nationality, and neutrality on land and sea), the United States proclaimed doctrines of great importance. Some of "the rights claimed by the United States were laid down as a part of the public law of Europe by the Congress of Vienna, but the credit of having first proclaimed them belongs to the United States alone."[31]

In 1784, Diego de Gardoqui arrived in Philadelphia as Spain's chargé d'affaires. John Jay, secretary of foreign affairs, was instructed under no condition to waive the right to navigate the Mississippi.[32] But Spain, despite the urgings of Lafayette, had refused with equal

[30] For the King's views, *Ill. Hist. Coll.*, XXVII; see for the treaties of November 3, 1762, and March 10, 1763, and further information, H. Miller, *International Acts* (2nd ed.), I, 17, 33; *A.S.P., Pub. Lands*, II, 209; C. R. King (ed.), *The Life and Correspondence of Rufus King* (6 vols., New York, 1894–1900).

[31] E. Schuyler, *American Diplomacy and the Furtherance of Commerce* (New York, 1886), p. 266. Gradually, through the nineteenth century, various straits and rivers of Europe and the two Americas were opened to commerce. P. S. Reinsch, *Public International Unions . . . a Study in International Administrative Law* (2nd ed., Boston, 1916), *passim*. It was, for example, only in 1872 that the United States acquired the right to navigate the St. Lawrence, in exchange for Britain's to navigate Alaskan rivers to and from the sea.

[32] *J.C.C.*, XXVII, 529 (June 3, 1784). Fearing that instructions of August 7, 1782, had not wholly revoked those of February 15, 1781 (Wharton, *Dip. Corr.*, VI, 826), which had ordered Jay to *recede* from earlier orders (of September 29, 1779, and October 4, 1780) that insisted on rights of navigation and deposit, Congress on May 31, 1784 (*ibid.*, pp. 489–490, 530), explicitly revoked the old rescission, and ordered assertion of those rights "in the strongest terms."

finality to concede that right in 1783, and long before Gardoqui arrived it was learned that he was under similar orders.[33]

The United States was now enjoying a booming commerce with Spain on the most-favored-nation basis. Spain offered its continuance, a defensive alliance, and a mutual guarantee of territories. After nearly two years, no progress having been made on the issues of Mississippi navigation and western boundary, the negotiators discussed waiver by the United States of navigation rights for a term of years, perhaps twenty-five. The offer in exchange was a commercial treaty satisfactory to the New England and the Middle states. The southern states looked upon the development of the West as their own development, and regarded an open Mississippi as its indispensable basis. From late spring onward (1786) the issue held the sharp attention of the country. The old questions whether westward emigrants would be "lost" to the Confederation, whether emigration would lower the East's wealth and value of its land, how it would alter the political power of different states or sections, became involved with fears of each party that the other was willing to sacrifice the Confederation.[34] Jay defended his views ably in Congress in support of a waiver for twenty-five or thirty years, and after three weeks that body—by a strictly geographical vote of seven states to five, with the Potomac as the dividing line—empowered him to act as he judged best.[35] However, since approval of any treaty required nine states, and bitter feeling barred any compromise, negotiations necessarily ended.

A slight softening in Spain's policies in 1787 came when the Continental Congress was moribund.[36] In July, 1788, it voted to leave the problem of Spanish relations to the new government, with a last resolution that the western settlers had a clear and essential right to navigation of the Mississippi.[37]

Was there actual need of an open river? Jay thought that there would be none for fifty years, but the later development of the river trade shows his view to have been a gross underestimate. On the other

[33] *Ibid.*, XXXI, 542–543; *A.S.P., For. Rel.,* I, 250–251. Gardoqui's orders came from Havana, see James, *Clark,* p. 364.

[34] More fully discussed in *Ill. Hist. Coll.,* XXV, cclxxiv–cclxxvi.

[35] Speech of August 3, *J.C.C.,* XXXI, 473 *et seq.,* particularly 489–490, 530; speech of August 28, 29, *ibid.,* 565–570, 574–596. The ultimatums revoked were of August 25, 1785.

[36] Whitaker, *Spanish-American Frontier,* p. 84.

[37] *A.S.P., For. Rel.,* I, 251; *J.C.C.,* XXXIV, 530–534.

hand, in the West the need was vastly exaggerated. But even there economic needs and political sensitivity are difficult to separate. The river was never actually closed, since smuggling and special permits were always possibilities. Much as the Spaniards heard of George Rogers Clark as an enemy, he, for example, received a permit in 1786 for shipment of 1,500 barrels of flour from the Monongahela.[38] Contraband trade to the eastern coast via the West Indies, under cover of exceptions in the Spanish laws, was great.[39] There was in fact a flourishing circular trade from the Northwest to New Orleans, and through the West Indies to Philadelphia and Baltimore.[40] An opinion may perhaps be reasonably hazarded that the Mississippi was open, on reasonable terms, to all those who were actually in a position to utilize it.

The arguments in the East were predominantly political. Washington hesitatingly upheld Jay because he felt trade to be the only way to hold the West, and closure of the Mississippi desirable until direct trade could be developed between West and East; Richard Henry Lee agreed, likewise Madison.[41] Political considerations were dominant in a powerful argument by Charles Pinckney against Jay's proposed waiver.[42] Rufus King's opposition was not based merely on the supposed harm that westward emigration would do to seaboard economic interests. He emphasized loss of man power and depreciation of eastern lands, but he also feared that every westward emigrant would be "lost to the union" —the political argument.[43] The opposition of Gouverneur Morris rested on political miscalculations that were wildly speculative.[44] On the whole, what was lacking was economic facts. The debate "was little short of ferocity"; there was talk of breaking up the Confederation.[45] The Virginia assembly unanimously declared that any renunciation of the navigation right would be destructive of the Confederation's "peace, safety, happiness, and duration" (November, 1787). Neverthe-

[38] James, Clark, p. 382.
[39] Whitaker, "The Commerce of Louisiana and the Floridas at the End of the Eighteenth Century," HAHR, VIII (1928), 198.
[40] Compare Canad. Archives, Report for 1890, pp. 141–142, for a description of it in 1790.
[41] Washington, Writings (Fitzpatrick ed.), XXVIII, 460, 484, 256, 207; J. C. Ballach (ed.), Letters of Richard Henry Lee (2 vols., 1911–14), II, 424; Burnett, LMCC, VIII, 381 (Lee), 203, 424 (Monroe); Madison, Writings (Hunt ed.), VI, 67, 130, 262.
[42] AHR, X, 817–827.
[43] Burnett, LMCC, VIII, 380, 458.
[44] Wharton, Dip. Corr., II, 807, III, 159.
[45] E. C. Burnett, The Continental Congress (New York, 1941), pp. 655, 658.

less, it was a squabble over speculative issues, and in addition it ignored patent realities which it had already recognized as the basis for ensuring the West's retention. It was insanity to suppose that frontiersmen dissatisfied with distant government from New York could imagine themselves happy under government from Madrid. The idea that products of East or West could not be transported over the Alleghenies was perhaps pardonable in 1784. But the sole realities in the great debate were the fears which eastern political conservatives and landowners entertained of those who had become Westerners to escape conservatism and find cheaper land. It has already been seen that when all these were presented in 1780 as a problem of national policy demanding action, neither the economic fears (though they proved to have had some basis) nor the political speculations had prevented Virginia's cession of her western lands, provision by Congress for the sale of all western lands, and unanimous adoption of a law for the creation, government, and admission of new states to be organized therein.[46]

Agitation against Jay's proposal was made in Kentucky. Kentucky delegates in the Virginia convention held to consider ratification of the new federal constitution voted against it.[47] James Wilkinson, and others long associated with him in what is known as a "Spanish Conspiracy," were active in this Kentucky agitation against Jay.[48] While the navigation issue was before Congress, Gardoqui had received suggestions that Kentucky emigration to Natchez should be stimulated by slight concessions in Mississippi navigation, and that free navigation of the river might induce Kentucky to join Spain.[49] The former was accordant with views already given effect by Louisiana officials; the latter was new western politics. Before the Spanish government made its choice it also had before it a memorial from Wilkinson—soon to be set out. As a result of all, the King instructed the Council of State to "take advantage . . . whenever the opportunity presents itself" of the fact (one of Wilkinson's "facts") that "leading people" of Kentucky, "in case the free navigation of . . . the Mississippi should be denied to them, might wish to separate themselves from the United States and place them-

---

[46] *Ill. Hist. Coll.*, XXV, cccxxxiv, where the whole matter is discussed.

[47] Green, *Spanish Conspiracy*, pp. 387, 389.

[48] *Ibid.*, pp. 389–391 (memorial to Virginia), 109–112 (Wilkinson group); Bodley, *Littell's Political Transactions*, pp. 79–80 (resolution of Virginia assembly), 78–79 (Wilkinson group).

[49] The latter suggestion was from James Brown, a representative of North Carolina in Congress. Whitaker, *Spanish-American Frontier*, pp. 78–85, 88.

selves under the protection of Spain."[50] This order (of November 20, 1788) states the policy to which Spain (not so exactly her colonial officials) adhered throughout the following years, with no change before 1798.

Before the navigation debate in Congress, dissatisfaction in Kentucky had centered on the scarcity of desirable land, and on alleged neglect by the distant and supposedly indifferent Confederation government.[51] Separation from Virginia was a political issue by late 1784. Beginning in November of that year, eight conventions—selected or popular—were held in Kentucky in four years. Wilkinson, Harry Innis, and Benjamin Sebastian, all elected to a popular convention of May, 1785, were already the core of a group which augmented and guided for more than a decade agitation over the Mississippi in aid of intrigue for personal gain with the Spanish officials in New Orleans. The first popular convention petitioned Virginia's consent to separation as a preliminary to Kentucky's admission to the Confederation. In the course of all the conventions, there was never a vote against such union; only once a vote against application for admission.[52] Twice, on generous terms, Virginia agreed to separation subject to such admission.[53]

Wilkinson, whom these proceedings brought back into American history, was one of the most colorful public figures that the period produced. He was well educated, unquestionably able, adroit, a good judge of men. His military career had been exceptionally creditable.[54]

[50] Whitaker, *Commercial Policy of Spain,* pp. 63, 229 (n. 59), 231 (n. 80); *Spanish-American Frontier,* pp. 101–102. The King approved the order on December 1, 1788.

[51] Abernethy, *Western Lands and the American Revolution* (New York, 1937), pp. 304–305, 308–309, and "Journal of the First Kentucky Convention," *Jour. of Southern History,* I (1935), 75.

[52] A full account, with documents, is in Bodley, *Littell's Political Transactions.* The conventions are reviewed in James, *Clark,* pp. 373 *et seq.,* and in Abernethy, *Western Lands,* pp. 303 *et seq.*

[53] Hening, *Statutes of Va.,* XII, 45, or Bodley, pp. 72–76. A later act (Hening, XII, 40) authorized separation at any time chosen by Kentucky and approved by Congress.

[54] In two years he rose to a brigadier generalate through staff appointments, equally unusual, under Arnold, Greene, and Knox. F. B. Heitman (comp.), *Historical Register and Dictionary of the United States [Army]* (Washington, 1890), p. 1037. No charges whatever were brought against him in connection with two army scandals mentioned by his implacable detractors. Washington presumably knew as much as anybody did about them, and it was he who, as President (with Knox as secretary of war), was responsible for Wilkinson's readmission to the army as a lieutenant colonel in 1791. This, be it also noted, was after abundant rumors of Wilkinson's Spanish connections. Note also that

In 1787 he loaded several flatboats with products of Kentucky and sent them down the river by an agent, whom he followed after an interval allowed for advertisement of his coming. He was well received, as his former high military rank, his education, and personal charm entitled him to be. Besides, he had two special claims upon the good will of the Spanish authorities. He had fostered a belief that he had thwarted alleged plans of the Bourbon County expansionists to launch a military attack in 1785, under command of George Rogers Clark, on the Spanish colonies. And in 1787 he had directed an inquiry by the Kentucky legislature (wholly extralegal, although the governor of Virginia acted on its findings) into Clark's confiscation in 1786 of the goods of three Louisiana traders in Vincennes—an act of violence, in a time of border anarchy, that is variantly interpreted by historians.[55] He spent three months in New Orleans; prepared a *First Memorial* (August 21, 1787), in which he described conditions in Kentucky, and advised his new friends (Estevan Miró, governor, and Martín Navarro, intendant) on the policy which they should pursue; and took an oath of allegiance to Spain (August 22).[56]

Although recognized as a leader in agitation for free navigation of the Mississippi or separation of the western country from the seaboard colonies, Wilkinson actually did not take so extreme a stand at this time. His immediate request was merely a monopoly of Kentucky trade for himself.[57] Moreover, he recommended continued closure of the Mississippi, except for similar concessions to other men of influence in Kentucky (whom Wilkinson might select), to "cheer the People to the

Jefferson had certainly, at least once, earlier discussed with Washington the charges against Wilkinson's loyalty, that he retained the confidence of both, and that Hamilton, in 1798, chose him as second in command, under himself, in case there should be war with Spain.

[55] On precedence by his agent on first trip, Daniel Clark, in *Annals of Congress*, 10th Cong., 1st Sess., pp. 2732–2733; Bodley, *Clark*, p. 312; W. R. Shepherd, "Wilkinson and the Beginnings of the Spanish Conspiracy," *AHR*, IX (1904), 503, n. 3. On his actions against Clark, Whitaker, *Spanish-American Frontier*, p. 97; Shepherd, "Wilkinson," p. 495; Bodley, *Littell's Political Transactions*, p. xliii; Green, *Spanish Conspiracy*, pp. 387–388. On Clark's acts in Vincennes, G. Thornbrough (ed.), *Outpost on the Wabash, 1787–1788* (Indianapolis, 1957), pp. 7, 12, 13, 14; C. W. Alvord, *Illinois Country, 1688–1820* (Springfield, 1920), p. 342, and *Ill. Hist. Coll.*, V, 367–368; James, *Clark*, pp. 341–343, 354 *et seq.*, 376–380.

[56] The *Memorial* was actually presented September 5, and is in Shepherd, "Wilkinson," pp. 498–503; also in Bodley, pp. cxix–cxxxix.

[57] On his later shipments, see Whitaker, *Spanish-American Frontier*, pp. 97, 128; James, *Clark*, pp. 383, 395, 396.

hope of a free . . . intercourse." He also recommended a simultaneous encouragement of American immigration, especially at New Madrid—which was already Spanish policy. Finally, he held out two terminal possibilities. He declared that Kentucky was "on the eve of establishing herself as a free and independent state," and predicted that, once independent, she would demand an open Mississippi, after which some "connection" between her and Spain must (of course) be negotiated. Alternatively, he predicted a federation of western states, and that unless Spain should give them free navigation of the Mississippi, they would get it with the aid of England—and Britain would get New Spain.[58]

However, Wilkinson did make obeisance to the wish of her "leading characters" to open immediately negotiations for "admission to [Spain's] protection as subjects with certain privileges in political and religious matters," and *promised* that he would use all his powers "to compass this desirable event." Spain was already permitting the settlement of Americans in Spanish territory, provided they promised orderly behavior and obedience to local authority, and received in return "protection as subjects"—not as *being* subjects, but as subjects were treated. Miró and Navarro recommended Wilkinson to their superiors in Madrid, and the decision of the Council has already been noted.

Wilkinson's oath of allegiance to Spain had the significance, legally, of blank paper. As a testimonial of good faith, given to Miró and Navarro, they alone could judge it. In view of the furor caused by British impressment of "American" seamen, every American might be expected to know that, under the international practice ("law") then prevailing, nationality was fixed irrevocably at birth. It is also an aid to fair judgment to remember that service by nationals of one country in the armies of others (as General Haldimand served Great Britain) —or even in high offices of state—was common. The prominent historian who first revealed this oath thought it disloyal—a vague word. It seems probable that most of the many historians who have thought of Wilkinson as a "traitor" have at least included this oath as evidence of, if not *per se,* treason. It was totally ineffective, and would have remained so under our law until 1920 (when we were frightened by defectors to Russia).[59] Miró probably knew the law. Wilkinson's entire

[58] *AHR,* IX, pp. 498, 499, 501.
[59] American law was altered by an Act of 1920. See, in general, Moore, *International Law,* III, secs. 431, 455, 468, 464 *et seq.,* 717.

Memorial shows knowledge and caution. To the Spanish government it could have been only an assurance of good faith.

Other American leaders outside Kentucky tried to gain favors from the Louisiana and Florida officials—particularly James Robertson and John Sevier (unlike Wilkinson, still regarded as frontier heroes), but they were clumsy and their expectations extraordinarily naïve.[60] Both men sought the aid of Gardoqui; both were reported by his intermediary as eager to transfer their allegiance to Spain; and Gardoqui was reported as "very favorably inclined" to protect the state of Franklin.[61] Sevier even wrote letters emphasizing his own desire to give allegiance to Spain and declaring that "the principal men" of the state were equally ready to do so.[62] And in this case, unlike that of Kentucky, there was no condition that separation from North Carolina should first be secured.[63] However, to treat such matters as serious disloyalty is to misrepresent the conditions of the time, reading into them our own nationalism nearly two centuries later.

Wilkinson left New Orleans, it is assumed, in Spanish pay as an agent to give information to Miró. So far as the record shows, he gave the Spanish officials only such information as today would be available in newspapers. To advise foreign officials what to do or not to do has, of course, never been illegal. Such advice is given constantly today by the pundits of radio and magazines of opinion.

The Mississippi was opened to all westerners, duties reduced from an ad valorem duty of 25 to 15 (later, 6) per cent.[64] And the government—in desperation, and with pitiable innocence—continued, with emphasis, its liberal immigration policy (since 1782), but with American immigrants in place of French, to save New Spain from American frontiersmen. Subject to an oath of loyalty, actual settlers were assured

[60] Whitaker, *Spanish-American Frontier,* pp. 108–111.

[61] A. Henderson, *The Conquest of the Old Southwest* (New York, 1920), pp. 328–334, and "The Spanish Conspiracy in Tennessee," *Tenn. Hist. Mag.,* III (1917), 229–237; Whitaker, "The Spanish Intrigue in the Old Southwest: An Episode, 1788–1789," *MVHR,* XII (1925), 158–162.

[62] The same three writings at, respectively, pp. 339–346, 237–243, and 162–176; also, Masterson, *Blount,* p. 153.

[63] It is said that after the Federal Union was organized, Gardoqui repeated to Kentuckians that if Kentucky became independent she could expect favorable arrangements at New Orleans. Green, *Spanish Conspiracy,* p. 168; Bodley, *Littell's Political Transactions,* pp. xxv–xxxi. Of course she could, in trade.

[64] Whitaker, *Commercial Policy of Spain,* pp. 63, 229 (n. 59), 231 (n. 80); Shepherd, "Papers Bearing on James Wilkinson's Relations with Spain, 1787–1789," *AHR,* IX (1904), 749.

of land grants (relatively, and creditably, well protected against speculative accumulation) and of the commercial rights of Spanish subjects, including an open Mississippi. Nor was such treatment of immigrants limited to Roman Catholics.[65] These were astoundingly great and liberal deviations from old colonial practices.

But Spain had waited too long; that was the vice of her administration. Many colonies of Americans were proposed (including one by Wilkinson), but none attained even a puny reality except George Morgan's at New Madrid, and that ended in dismal failure.[66] Although the Spanish offers were liberal, the plan proved chimerical because the entire' Northwest was about to open to settlement under the Ordinance of 1787. Even had self-government been assured, no Spanish colony could have survived. It would have had no time to develop; "the American hive was too near, the advance of its swarms too rapid."

The Confederation was displaced on July 2, 1788, by the present Federal Union, although Virginia did not enter it until two months later—with Kentucky still part of it. Wilkinson felt it necessary, some months later, to make secure his position in New Orleans. He complained to Miró of Spain's generous new policy, "because every motive of discontent [in Kentucky] having thus been removed, the political agitation has subsided, and today there is not one word about separation. . . . Many who loudly repudiated all connection with the Union, now remain silent. . . . I fear that we can rely on a few only of my countrymen, if we cannot make use of liberal donations."[67] This letter emphasized the problem of separating Kentucky from Virginia *and* keeping it out of the new Union. His purpose was to convince Miró that he was maintaining excitement in Kentucky and keeping her an ostensibly free agent. When another Kentucky convention assembled in November, 1787, a motion for separation and admission was tabled.

---

[65] On terms of settlement in Missouri, see Houck, *Spanish Regime in Missouri*, pp. 275, 279, 284, 286–289; M. Savelle, *George Morgan, Colony Builder* (New York, 1932), pp. 206, 209, 227; *Ill. Hist. Coll.*, XXV, cccxxxi–cccxxxii. Immigration into Upper Louisiana had been encouraged since 1778. Houck, I, 152; on very slight immigration after Morgan abandoned his attempt, pp. 319–321, 327.

[66] On those proposed by professional speculators—Wilkinson, George Rogers Clark, James White, George Morgan, John Sevier, James O'Fallon—see Savelle, *Morgan*, pp. 215–225; *AHR*, IX, 757; and particularly Houck, *Documents*, I, 359–368; James, *Clark*, pp. 392–396; Whitaker, *Spanish-American Frontier*, 128–129.

[67] C. Gayarré, *Spanish Dominion*.

Wilkinson then read supposed portions of the *First Memorial* demand-ing an open Mississippi, and thanks were voted him.[68] He then went again to New Orleans and submitted a *Second Memorial* (of Septem-ber 24, 1789).[69] In this he emphasized the old canard that American immigration would bar "usurpations" by Britain and the United States. He renounced abandonment of his plan, never before announced in writing, of "immediate" incorporation of Kentucky into the Spanish dominions, but he promised "to employ all indirect means to cause the separation of this section of country from the United States, which would likely be followed by a connection with Spain to the exclusion of any other power."[70] However, as in his *First Memorial* so in this one, he carefully guarded both himself and his Spanish friends. He warned Miró that Spain would profit more by an alliance than by having Kentuckians as subjects (repeating a warning given by letter seven months earlier).[71] By "indirect means" he meant that he would work only through popular sentiment—thus carefully excluding the possibility of treasonable acts. His emphasis upon that was beyond mis-understanding: "whenever the people of Kentucky withdraw from . . . the United States," "if the people of Kentucky were to withdraw from the United States," "whenever the western settlements assert their in-dependence." But he wanted Spain to act at once, "to anticipate the intentions [not stated] of Congress and to overthrow the present de-signs of Great Britain."[72] This would have eliminated altogether the need of action by himself. However, pending decisive developments, he suggested twenty-two Kentuckians who should be pensioned.[73]

The parts played by the different actors—Spain, Kentucky, and Wilkinson—in the transactions just reviewed must be sharply distin-guished. There was never any bargaining by Spain; it was always plain that independence of Kentucky must precede any negotiations by her. As for Kentucky, her conventions had voted separation from Virginia only as a step preliminary to statehood in the Union, old or new.

[68] Bodley, *Littell's Transactions*, pp. lvi–lxv, 99 *et seq.*

[69] This was fifteen months after creation of the new federal Union. It is printed in W. R. Shepherd, "Papers Bearing on James Wilkinson's Relations with Spain, 1787–1789," *AHR*, IX (1904), 751–764.

[70] *Ibid.*, pp. 752, 753, 754.

[71] Gayarré (February, 1789), *Spanish Dominion.*

[72] *AHR*, IX, 751, 752, 753, 755 for quotations.

[73] *Ibid.*, pp. 753, 755, (list) 764–765. Bodley has suggested that Wilkinson sought to strengthen his position in Kentucky, those recommended by him being friends, enemies, and neutrals. *Littell's Political Transactions*, pp. lxiv–lxvii.

Those who have denounced Wilkinson have been quite undiscriminating. It should be pointed out that to call him a traitor for any acts attributed to him *after* July, 1788, ignores the constitutional definition of treason, the very purpose of which was to rid us forever of the dangers of its loose employment as in the state trials in England. Absolutely nothing that Wilkinson could have done in service of Spain could have been treason before 1898.[74]

Granted that Wilkinson labored to separate Kentucky from Virginia while the latter was a member of the Confederation. In that, the states were sovereign, and his act could have been treasonable.[75] Pennsylvania and Virginia passed laws making treasonable the creation of new states within their borders without their consent. However, in all the Kentucky proceedings, Virginia's consent was sought and given.[76] There are statements that Wilkinson *talked* revolutionary separation[77]—but mere talk has no legal significance. It has also been urged that he intended his plan to be understood by others as one to make Kentucky completely independent, which, assuming him a villain, would be poor evidence that this was his intent.[78]

Let us consider Wilkinson's promise to "employ all indirect means" to bring about Kentucky independence. By this he evidently meant, by arousing public opinion. In his *Memoirs* he denied that he even did this, declaring the charge to be "as absurd as the idea of reducing [Kentuckians] to the vassalage of Spain"—which latter he characterized (surely quite reasonably) as "absurd," "ludicrous," "vain and chimerical," "a monstrous extravagance."[79] The charge, however, was proper, and could be avoided only by pleading that he violated his written promise; but belief that it could have been performed would

[74] "Treason against the United States, shall consist only in levying war against them, or in adhering to their enemies," meaning, in war, "giving them aid and comfort."

[75] Some interesting material is in C. H. Van Tyne, "Sovereignty in the American Revolution: An Historical Study," *AHR*, XII (1908), 525–545, and D. H. Chamberlain, "State Sovereignty before 1789," *Yale Review*, II (1894), 248–263.

[76] *Ill. Hist. Coll.*, XXV, cccxlvi, n. 111; Hening, *Statutes of Va.*, XII, 45, 240. Agitators for separation from Virginia had been prosecuted for spreading of false news (Bodley, *Clark*, pp. 263–264). North Carolina proceeded against John Sevier, for the organization of the state of Franklin, as for the crime of high treason. Henderson, *Old Southwest*, pp. 336–337.

[77] Green, *Spanish Conspiracy*.

[78] *Ibid.*, pp. 85, 128–130, 155–157, 160, 204–206, 247–249.

[79] *Memoirs of My Own Time* (3 vols., Philadelphia, 1816), II, 113.

seem to be as absurd as Wilkinson pronounced the charge. All these questions retained interest in Kentucky politics for a century, and no evidence appeared of acts in performance of the promise in the *Second Memorial*.

There was nothing whatever in Wilkinson's two *Memorials* harmful to the United States. As regards his statements respecting western conditions and probable actions, he merely repeated opinions expressed since 1783 in Congress and in constitutional conventions by eastern conservatives. His predictions in the *First Memorial* respecting the West's future, and encouragement of Spanish hopes based thereon, were identical with the pessimistic fears of such conservatives as Rufus King, Richard Henry Lee, and Charles Pinckney. Overemphasis to Spain of danger was better service to her than underemphasis. Of course, the advice he gave ensured his pension. Nor had he any belief in the western disaffection upon which he encouraged Spanish reliance. His views respecting the West were identical with Jefferson's. But one cannot believe that the New Orleans officials would have believed assurances of Kentucky's loyalty; for years, the Spanish agents in New York had believed the contrary. Wilkinson's cupidity was certainly plain to the Spanish officials (and sometimes a matter of jest among them in later years) from the first moment when he asked for a personal trading monopoly instead of an open Mississippi. However, for some years they continued to pay him money—for his tobacco, his information and advice, possibly at first for his cautious promises. He continued to receive money after he re-entered the army in 1791, and even after he became its head. Several investigations failed to reveal precisely how much he received.[80] That conflicts of interest might have arisen after 1791 is manifest; the only one known will be considered later.

Much space has been given to this first "Spanish Conspiracy," and in particular to Wilkinson's role in it, although neither his unofficial character, nor his acts, nor their discernible effect upon events could justify the emphasis. As a part of national history, these Kentucky incidents

---

[80] Some have guessed $30,000 to $40,000. Official papers are in *A.S.P.*, *Misc.*, I, 936–939, II, 79–127; *Annals of Congress*, 10th Cong., 1st Session, pp. 1360 *et seq.*, 2306, 2730 *et seq.* One may compare Whitaker, *Spanish-American Frontier*, pp. 117, 157; Green, *Spanish Conspiracy*, pp. 323–324, 327–335; Abernethy, *Burr Conspiracy*, pp. 11, 12, 13; I. J. Cox, "General Wilkinson and his Later Intrigues with the Spanish," *AHR*, XIX, 794, 795, 800, 801, 803–804, 806.

have little importance. The leading authority on the Old Southwest has sensibly appraised the actions of the few Kentuckians and North Carolinians involved as "on the whole an attempt to discover what their southern neighbors could do for them with respect to their three principal interests—commerce, land speculation, and the Indians."[81] Detailed discussion has been necessary only because craving for romanticism in history has encouraged historians in crying "treason," and because of preoccupation with this they have overlooked differences between the Confederation and the Federal Union, have ignored the Constitution, and have failed in judging Wilkinson to remember the lesson of the impressment issue of 1812. Wilkinson manifestly knew these things.

Late in 1789, when war between Spain and Great Britain over the Nootka Sound incident seemed certain, the Georgia legislature contracted to sell to three land companies nearly half of present Alabama and Mississippi.[82] The undisturbed occupancy of this land had been guaranteed to the Indians by treaties with the United States; and, in particular, the South Carolina Company's purchase in the Yazoo region was certain to offend Spain, with whom diplomatic negotiations had just begun. That Georgia used the land speculators, or they used Georgia, to challenge national claims to the West at that particular moment was doubtless in expectation of a temporary paralysis of power in the region. The action taken by the Carolina Company was manifestly precipitate. Instructions to its chief (or sole) agent in the field, James O'Fallon, were to seek friendship with the Indians, "occupy" the Company's grant (of nearly 8,000 square miles) "immediately," and assure the Spanish officials of the Company's ardent desire for their friendly relations with the "independent state" it was determined to establish. O'Fallon was a presumptuous braggart, with no military force save on paper, and swung easily from one irrational plan to another, since none had other substance than words. His state was to be independent and allied with Spain; it was to be conquered from Spain; it was to be formed on Indian lands—permission to buy which he solicited from President Washington, plus recognition and alliance in exchange for a promise to conquer New Orleans.[83]

81 Whitaker, *Spanish-American Frontier.*
82 The Georgia statute is in *A.S.P., Ind. Aff.,* I, 114. Estimates of the price vary from eight-tenths of a cent to one and a half cents per acre. See S. G. McLendon, *History of the Public Domain of Georgia* (Atlanta, 1924), Chap. 3.
83 Whitaker, "The South Carolina Yazoo Company," *MVHR,* XVI (1929),

It unduly dignifies these maneuvers to call them an intrigue or a plot. Their irrationality suggests insanity. The government made a satisfactory treaty with the Creeks, and the Spaniards built a fort near Vicksburg (at Walnut Hills). In two proclamations Washington warned the western people against seduction, and ordered legal proceedings against O'Fallon. None were ever brought; he sank into obscurity in Kentucky.[84]

It was soon evident that Americans were pushing their border westward, without accepting the offers of religious and political privileges made to such settlers in Upper Louisiana (Missouri). That their increase since 1780 in Tennessee, Kentucky, and Ohio—claims to which Spain had not yet officially renounced—was, in itself, a danger as real as their military potential (which in Governor Carondelet's imagination was perhaps quadrupled)[85] was clear to both him and Gayoso (governor of Natchez), but their policies were different. Early in 1793 Carondelet (who was also intendant) had reduced the duty on imports from Kentucky from 15 per cent, fixed by the royal order of 1788, to 6, and made other concessions to American trade.[86] It happened that this enlarged opportunities for contraband through the West Indies; nevertheless, the realism of Carondelet's action is creditable to his judgment.[87] Strangely contrasting with it was Gayoso's advice that rights of western Americans to navigate the Mississippi—and only above New Orleans—should no longer be accorded them "as a part of the United States." Secret negotiations with them must first secure "their entire

---

383–394; J. C. Parish, "The Intrigues of Doctor James O'Fallon," *ibid.*, XVII (1930), 230–263; *A.S.P., Ind. Aff.*, I, 115–117; L. P. Kellogg (ed.), "Documents: Letter of Thomas Paine, 1793," *AHR*, XXIX (1924), 501–505. On the other two companies, see *A.S.P., Ind. Aff.*, I, 112; Masterson, *Blount*, pp. 199–200, 214; Carter, *Terr. Papers*, IV, 83–84, 105; *A.S.P., Pub. Lands*, I, 133, 168.

[84] *A.S.P., Ind. Aff.*, I, 12; *For. Rel.*, I, 281. Compare *Ind. Aff.* I, 12; Richardson, *Messages*, I. Letters of the Company were in Wilkinson's hands before O'Fallon went to the West. He informed Miró.

[85] Robertson, *Louisiana*, I, 297–298.

[86] The duties were 15 per cent on imports, 6 per cent on exports except on specie or produce exported to purchase Negroes (the only purpose for which specie was allowed to leave legally). Whitaker, *Commercial Policy of Spain*, p. 177, notes 171, 172, and p. xl; also "The Commerce of Louisiana and the Floridas at the End of the Eighteenth Century," *HAHR*, VIII, 198, n. 26.

[87] Whitaker, *Spanish-American Frontier*, p. 193, and *Commercial Policy of Spain*, pp. xlviii, 205, 234 (n. 117). He also recommended, as Navarro had done in 1780, that New Orleans be opened to the shipping of all countries.

separation from the other states."[88] Gayoso knew this to be nonsense, and was very likely in accord with Wilkinson in desiring to discredit Carondelet, whose actions revealed stupidity. Carondelet reported to his government that Louisiana would within a few years surpass the American West in wealth, and that Spain would possess in it a "warlike, energetic people" for the defense of Cuba and Mexico. And this although in the same letter he warned the government that the advancing American settlers would "unquestionably force Spain to recognize the Missouri as their boundary within a short time, and perhaps pass that river"—unless, to be sure, his plan of defense be adopted. He admitted that he could take no offensive action with his own forces; his reliance was upon the southern Indians.[89] He was greatly impressed by St. Clair's defeat in 1791. An Indian "confederation" was formed, as in the Northwest, and Carondelet informed his government that Louisiana would be protected by the Indians "whenever incited by presents and arms."[90] He negotiated a treaty with the Creeks that purported to nullify their treaty of 1790 with the United States and mutually guaranted the possessions of the parties; then sent an agent to persuade them to drive Georgians out of territory ceded in 1790, but this order was countermanded by the captain-general in Havana.[91]

These inanities of Carondelet, and the bellicism they inspired in the Spanish commissioners in Philadelphia, made war a serious probability. Jefferson thought it inevitable as early as 1792.[92] To cap the climax, a second part of Carondelet's plan, upon which he relied to save Louisiana, was a renewal of the intrigue with Wilkinson, notwithstanding that Kentucky since 1792 had been a state of the Union. To this last stupidity attention will be given later. The dangers of his earlier misjudgments were greatly increased by serious controversies in 1793 with France.

[88] *Ibid.*, p. 287.

[89] From 1791 to late 1794, he spent nearly $300,000 on defenses (including Indian cessions and Kentucky negotiations). Robertson, *Louisiana*, I, 293 *et seq.;* cf. *AHR*, II, 474–505. Yet he estimated $607,000 as still needed. *Ibid.*, I, 344 (n. 151); Amer. Hist. Assoc., *Report* for 1896, I, 975–977, 998–999. He had 700 soldiers in New Orleans, 921 in scattered posts. *Ibid.*, p. 996.

[90] Whitaker, *Spanish-American Frontier*, pp. 166–168, 177–179, 215; see C. D. Harmon, *Sixty Years of Indian Affairs, 1789-1850* (Chapel Hill, 1941), pp. 41–53, on war in the Southwest, 1789–96.

[91] Whitaker, *Spanish-American Frontier*, p. 168. The captaincy-general included command of Louisiana and the Floridas.

[92] Jefferson, *Writings* (Ford ed.), VI, 315–316, 321–324.

In a somewhat strange manner the policies of the French government were entangled with the interests of the Yazoo land speculators when Edmond Genêt was sent in 1793 as minister to the United States. In January, 1793, a report had been ordered on the possibility of an expedition against the Spanish colonies, initiated by an offer by George Rogers Clark to lead an expedition against Louisiana. The offer was communicated by James O'Fallon (now Clark's brother-in-law) to Thomas Paine, a member of the French Legislative Assembly. The government had approved this plan before Genêt left France. According to Paine, it was part of the French plan, in case of war with Spain, to treat as a conquest of Spanish territory the territory included in Georgia's Yazoo grants and also claimed by the United States, and to confirm claims of actual possessors even if the territory be not Spanish. Genêt was instructed that if the United States should be timid in establishing an intimate concert for extension of liberty, he should propagate "the principles of liberty and independence" in Louisiana and other colonies "neighbors of the United States," such as Kentucky.[93] The choice of agents to revolutionize Louisiana was naïve: two Americans, Joel Barlow and Stephen Sayre (a poet and—incredibly—a banker who was an adventurer) and two Frenchmen, one (Lachaise) long resident in Louisiana who was either blind to obvious facts or ignored them to secure the appointment. Every aspect of the undertaking attests ignorance of American conditions.[94]

The landing, at Charleston, South Carolina, was suitably near to Florida and Louisiana, and also obviously promising for the interests of the South Carolina Yazoo Company. Genêt immediately organized

[93] If we believe this, what should we say of the "loyalty" of Clark and Paine as compared with Wilkinson? L. P. Kellogg (ed.), "Letter of Thomas Paine," *AHR*, XXIX (1924), 501–505; E. C. Burnett (ed.), "George Rogers Clark to Genêt, 1795," *AHR*, XVIII (1913), 780–783; F. J. Turner, "The Origin of Genêt's Plan," *AHR*, III (1898), 650–671. For his instructions, see Amer. Hist. Assoc., *Report* for 1896, pp. 958–967; for a "View of Genêt's Conduct," by an agent of a later ministry, *AHR*, III, 505. The general idea was to seek a treaty inseparably uniting (*confondant*) the political and commercial interests of the two countries.

[94] The full original sources (aside from citations in the preceding note) are in the "Correspondence of Clark and Genêt," Amer. Hist. Assoc., *Report* for 1896, I, pp. 930–1107; "The Mangourit Correspondence in Respect to Genêt's Projected Attack upon the Floridas, 1793–94," *ibid.*, for 1897, pp. 569–679; correspondence of French ministers to the United States, *ibid.*, for 1903, II; F. J. Turner (ed.), "Documents on the Relation of France to Louisiana, 1792–1795," *AHR*, III (1898), 490–517; Houck, *Spanish Regime*, II, 59–99.

military expeditions—on paper only—against both Spanish colonies.[95] Upon reaching Philadelphia, he began his correspondence with Clark, commissioning him as "Chief of the Independent and Revolutionary Legion of the Mississippi."[96] He also sent various agents to Louisiana and Kentucky, where "Democratic Societies" were organized and gave him some support.[97] Support in *what* it is impossible to say; there was an exhibition of popular self-confidence, in part bombast, in part a lean but promiseful expression of popular ideals.

It has been assumed that Clark's plan failed only for lack of money. No evidence is given in support of this view—that the frontiersmen were not interested in liberty, but only in money; that many recruits were available for money; or that the Spaniards were, militarily, negligibly weak. His contribution in this as in other frontier uprisings was mythical. Early in 1793 he wrote that four hundred men could clear Upper Louisiana (Missouri) and eight hundred capture New Orleans; but at that moment he was advertising for recruits;[98] a year later, that more than two thousand men waited with impatience to enter Louisiana, and that there was "universal Applause of the People throughout those back Countrys in Favour of the Enterprise, the arristocratical party excepted." But the latter seemingly prevailed in number, for again he was appealing at the moment in the press for volunteers, and he ultimately asked pay for only a hundred men for two months as actually in service.[99] The President issued a proclamation of neutrality

[95] Amer. Hist. Assoc., *Report* for 1897, pp. 575–679.

[96] *Ibid.*, pp. 967–974, 986, 1007. But Clark preferred to style himself "Field-Marshal of the Armies of France and Commander-in-Chief of the French Legions on the Mississippi," or other variants. *Ibid.*, p. 996; Houck, *Spanish Regime*, II, 26.

[97] The chief agent was André Michaux, a botanist; for his instructions, see Amer. Hist. Assoc., *Report* for 1896, pp. 990–995. Four others are named in *A.S.P., For. Rel.*, I, 455. On August Lachaise, see *AHR*, III, 511–515; *A.S.P., Misc.*, I, 931. Lexington (Ky.) resolutions of May 24, 1794, on Mississippi navigation, Amer. Hist. Assoc., *Report* for 1896, pp. 1056–1058. Other documents of the Democratic Societies, *ibid.*, for 1903, II, 500–502; *Wm. and Mary Qy.* (New Series), II, 239–256; and *A.S.P., Misc.*, I, 931. On the Democratic Societies, generally, E. P. Link, *Democratic-Republican Societies, 1790–1800* (New York, 1942); M. Coulter, "The Efforts of the Democratic Societies of the West to Open the Navigation of the Mississippi," *MVHR*, XI (1915), 376–389.

[98] Amer. Hist. Assoc., *Report* for 1896, pp. 971–972.

[99] *AHR*, XVIII, 781; on troops, Amer. Hist. Assoc., *Report* for 1896, pp. 1095–1096; on advertising, James, *Clark*, p. 426.

in April, 1793, and Governor St. Clair of the Northwest Territory had issued another, and Anthony Wayne (who was training an army in Clark's vicinity which within a few months showed its good quality at Fallen Timbers) thought that the steps taken by him to preserve the law would be "effectual."[100] In March, 1794, Clark's commission was revoked by Genêt's successor, Fauchet.[101] "The frontiersmen were marching," it has been said by Turner—twenty thousand, twelve thousand under Elijah Clark, smaller numbers, but oftener, under George Rogers Clark—and all imaginary.

The true importance of the Genêt episode was in the great contribution made by Jefferson to the law of neutrality.[102] The West was, to be sure, the occasion for that contribution. But it affected the West's development only in so far as, in its minor applications, it increased the West's tranquillity. The general frontier doctrine was that a free American was free to carry a gun, and free to carry it anywhere. That his purpose could restrict the lawfulness of the latter act the ordinary frontiersman had, doubtless, not the slightest idea. Significantly, Governor Shelby of Kentucky, a dyed-in-the-wool frontiersman, had no realization that neutrality was such a restraint, until so admonished by the secretary of state.[103]

It is quite possible that Lafayette, pleading for good relations between Spain and the United States in 1783, received a promise (which, of course, was not binding) that she would abide by the north boundary

[100] The President's Proclamation is in Richardson, *Messages*, I, 157 (April 22); St. Clair's in W. H. Smith, *St. Clair Papers: the Life . . . with Correspondence* (2 vols., Cincinnati, 1882), I, 201–203, II, 321; Wayne to Governor Shelby, *A.S.P., For. Rel.*, I, 458.

[101] March 6, 1794, Amer. Hist. Assoc., *Report* for 1897, p. 629; compare Clark's later letters, *ibid*. for 1906, p. 1095, *ibid*. for 1903, II, 567; and *AHR*, XVIII, 780–783.

[102] "The policy of the United States in 1793 constitutes an epoch in the development of the usages of neutrality. . . . It represented by far the most advanced existing opinions as to what those obligations were; and in some points it even went further than authoritative custom has up to the present day advanced. In the main, however, it is identical with the standard of conduct which is now adopted by the community of nations." W. E. Hall, *Treatise on International Law* (8th ed., Oxford, 1924), p. 707. Jefferson showed no favors to Genêt; see Amer. Hist. Assoc., *Report* for 1896, pp. 984–985, 1005; Jefferson, *Writings* (Ford ed.), I, 235–236; VI, 259, 316, 322; *A.S.P., For. Rel.*, I, 458.

[103] *Ibid.*, I, 456–457; compare Clark in Amer. Hist. Assoc., *Report* for 1896, pp. 1007, 1008.

of West Florida fixed in 1782 by Britain and the United States in case Britain should retain that colony (which she did not).[104] This would have required Spain to evacuate posts indisputably above 31° north latitude. However, since she had no assurances to lessen her fear of American encroachments or blunt the issue of Mississippi navigation, she retained the posts as a guard on both these points—as Britain retained those in the Northwest.

In 1789, Gardoqui—probably as much baffled as Moûstier by the progress made toward creation of a strong new government, settlement of the Northwest, and the agitation in Kentucky—returned to Spain. That power, as the British had calculated, never considered, during the Nootka Sound crisis, an alliance with the United States. It had, however, come to realize the possible necessity of boundary concessions to the Union.[105] The intensification of European war, which made it impossible for France or Spain to satisfy Louisiana's needs, counseled improvement of relations with the United States.[106] Gardoqui, who shared that opinion and became director of Spain's colonial commerce, recommended concessions respecting both boundaries and Mississippi navigation (August, 1791). Floridablanca, the minister of foreign affairs, decided to attempt a comprehensive settlement of differences.[107]

Discussions during the Nootka Sound crisis had shown that all of Washington's cabinet hoped to secure peacefully at least free navigation of the Mississippi. Jefferson had firmly adopted the view that was to guide him (and Madison) thenceforth—that Spain's colonies were safest in her hands, for ultimate American acquisition. He was even willing to guarantee her possession of Louisiana and the Floridas.[108]

In August, 1790, before notice had been received of Floridablanca's willingness to negotiate, Jefferson had given William Carmichael, chargé in Madrid, instructions both blunt and presumptuous. He was to request immediate conversations respecting navigation of the Mississippi, provided Spain was ready to cede it, and negotiate respecting a port of deposit. Jefferson expected Spain to be at war with Britain before the letter could be received. "It is impossible," he wrote, "to

---

[104] A.S.P., For. Rel., I, 253 (February 22, 1783).

[105] Whitaker, Spanish-American Frontier, p. 206.

[106] Whitaker, Commercial Policy of Spain, pp. 102, 114, xliii.

[107] Whitaker, Spanish-American Frontier, p. 148.

[108] Jefferson, Writings (Ford ed.), IV, 188; V, 199. All relevant documents are collected in W. C. Ford, The United States and Spain in 1790 (Washington, 1890).

answer for the forbearance of our western citizens." Somewhat inconsistently, both with this covert threat and other records, he also wrote
that it was not our interest to cross the Mississippi "for ages."[109]
Through William Short, chargé d'affaires in Paris, the influence of
France was sought for the same ends, and even for a cession of New
Orleans.[110] After receiving word of Floridablanca's willingness to negotiate, new instructions were sent, Short joining Carmichael in Madrid. Recognition of the boundary of 31°, recognition of American
right to navigate the Mississippi, and reasonable privileges to use the
shore, including a right of deposit, were made indispensable conditions
of a treaty. But Jefferson felt that these points should be argued, and
for this he had no basis in law or logic. He made the usual misconstruc-
tions of the treaties of 1763 and 1783, treating them as giving navigation rights to the Gulf; then claimed the shores, treating riparian rights
as dependent on rights to use the stream, which was the reverse of law.
In effect, there was only a claim of natural right, or justice—of fair
dealing. Though logic and law upheld the American case as respected
the secret article of the British-American provisional articles of November, 1782—and Spain had had knowledge of it for at least seven years
—Jefferson instructed our commissioners to deny knowledge of it.[111]
They did not reach Madrid until March, 1793, and that month Jefferson sent additional instructions. With reference to reports of French
plans against Spain on the Mississippi (Spain and Great Britain had
become allies in 1792), they were instructed to offer Spain no guarantee.[112]

Gardoqui had been named to act for Spain. For years, in negotiations
with Jay he had steadily rejected all the arguments and demands that
the American commissioners could advance. Moreover, he was still for
prohibiting all trade between Louisiana and all foreign countries of
Europe and America. The Americans arrived in Madrid a few days
after the execution of Louis XVI, an event unpropitious for negotiations by republicans. The French republican minister in the United
States was openly threatening conquest of Louisiana, and the Amer-

[109] Jefferson, *Writings,* V, 216–218, 220; *A.S.P., For. Rel.,* I, 247. Of Spanish
claims north of 31° he wrote: "They never merited . . . an answer . . . it
has been admitted at Madrid that they were not to be maintained."
[110] Jefferson, *Writings* (Ford ed.), p. 220; *Amer. Hist. Rev.,* X, 258.
[111] March 18, 1792, *A.S.P., For. Rel.,* I, 252–256. Cf. Whitaker, *Spanish-
American Frontier,* p. 11.
[112] Jefferson, *Writings* (Ford ed.), VI, 206; *A.S.P., For. Rel.,* I, 433, 434.

icans offered Spain no aid. Gardoqui procrastinated; the American commissioners did the same. When compelled by direct instructions to proceed, no progress was made, and after some months Carmichael left Spain.[113]

The failure of the negotiations left to Spain, and in large degree to her colonial officials, the problem of saving Louisiana when both she and France were at war (temporarily with each other), when the United States was taking over the carrying trade of Europe, and when the supposed threat of American frontiersmen was unlessened. However, the United States fared very well at New Orleans. A royal order of June, 1793, authorized trade *thence* with all friendly nations "having treaties of commerce" with Spain—which last excluded the United States.[114] This, however, did not alter their navigation rights on the Mississippi under earlier orders that were unrepealed.

The country escaped involvement in European wars only to face western problems anew in another assertion by Georgia of title to her back country. In January, 1795, her legislature sold to four Yazoo companies, for half a million dollars, some 35 million acres of land—well over half the acreage of the present states of Alabama and Mississippi.[115] Every member of the legislature with a single exception (according to him) was bribed. Of twenty partners, only one gave more than £2,000.[116] Various grand juries protested the grants. The legislature of 1796 repealed the statute and solemnly burned the origi-

[113] Whitaker, *Commercial Policy of Spain*, pp. 117 *et seq.*, 233 (n. 109), for Gardoqui; *A.S.P., For. Rel.*, I, 433–444, for negotiations. From 1790 to 1792, and again in 1799, Spain had to deal in Florida with a bizarre adventurer named William Bowles. Beyond being a local nuisance, he had no importance. Materials in F. J. Turner, "Documents: English Policy toward America in 1790–1791," *AHR*, VII, 717–735; discussion in Whitaker, *The Mississippi Question, 1795–1803* (New York, 1934), pp. 162–175.

[114] Whitaker, *Commercial Policy of Spain*, pp. 177 *et seq.*, xl–xliii, xliv, xlv. A vote of the Council of State of May 3, 1793, had declared for such trade with all "allied and friendly" nations (*ibid.*, pp. 173, xlvii).

[115] *A.S.P., Pub. Lands*, I, 28–59, 144, 156, 157. *Laws of the United States*, I, 512–541—testimony submitted in January, 1796, to the House of Representatives by Georgia; *A.S.P., Ind. Aff.*, I, 114–117; T. Donaldson, *The Public Domain: its History, with Statistics* (Washington, 1884), p. 84. Basic accounts are in C. H. Haskins, "The Yazoo Land Companies," Amer. Hist. Assoc., *Papers*, V (1891), 61–103; McLendon, *Public Domain of Georgia* (Atlanta, 1924), map, p. 70.

[116] S. E. Baldwin, "American Business Corporations before 1789," *AHR*, VIII (1903), 463.

nal. The legislative action of which it had been the result was expunged from the state's legal records, and the rescinding act was incorporated in a subsequent constitution of Georgia (1798).[117] The purchase price paid by the companies was also repaid to them. Even if Georgia had had title, it was therefore seemingly cleared of all claims of these companies. However, because by a compact between Georgia and the United States in 1802 the latter acknowledged that title *had* been in the state when the grants were made, and because conveyances given by the companies before repeal of the statute were ultimately acquired for value by innocent transferees, the claims of these innocent purchasers were paid by the United States out of a portion of the price paid by the government for the lands ceded to it by Georgia.[118]

In the summer of 1794 it was intimated to the United States that renewal of negotiations would be welcome to Spain. For her to make peace with France (as she did at Basle in July, 1795) would mean certain war with Great Britain, and Manuel de Godoy, Spain's prime minister, doubtless felt that a settlement of disputes with the United States would greatly lessen the dangers to Spain of a British war. In August, the Spanish commissioner in Philadelphia informed the government that Spain was prepared to treat of commerce, boundaries, Indian relations, or anything essential to good relations.[119] After assurances that negotiations could be expected to proceed without interruptions, General Thomas Pinckney was transferred from London (where John Jay was negotiating as special plenipotentiary) to Madrid. He arrived late in June, 1795. It soon appeared that Spain wanted a mutual guarantee of territory and an American alliance with France and Spain, and would not treat of commerce or of rights on the Mississippi. Upon this recurrence of old delays, Pinckney demanded his passport. Three days

[117] J. Randolph in *Annals of Congress,* 9th Cong., 1st Sess., p. 910 (March 29, 1805); Constitution of Georgia (1798) in Thorpe.

[118] McLendon, *Public Domain of Georgia,* pp. 98–106. In all, the United States paid about $6,200,000 to such claimants and for "Yazoo scrip." No official records remain in Georgia (*ibid.,* p. 74), but the journal of the lower house of its Assembly is in *A.S.P., Pub. Lands,* I, 144; the report to the U.S. Senate on claims under the companies is found *ibid.,* p. 133; and Jackson's report in the Georgia Assembly on the corruption by which the grants were secured is in McLendon, pp. 74–98.

[119] If proper representatives be sent. W. H. Trescott, *The Diplomatic History of the Administration of Washington and Adams* (Boston, 1857), pp. 238–245, prints this interesting letter. There were reasons for requiring "proper" representatives and full powers, *ibid.,* pp. 243, 244.

later (October 27) a treaty was signed which established as boundaries the parallel of 31° north and the middle of the Mississippi "from the northern boundary of the said states," and granted free navigation of it from its source to the Gulf and a right of deposit at New Orleans.[120] Navigation was to be restricted to the two powers exclusively, unless Spain should later concede it to others; and the right of deposit, given for three years, was to be either then renewed or another one substituted. Disputes arose later over both these provisions.[121] No commercial treaty was made. Military forces were to be withdrawn by Spain from posts within American limits within six months after exchange of ratifications, which was effected on April 25, 1796. Commissioners were to survey the line of 31°.

The treaty was not won by arguments; Pinckney's were mere repetitions of the old assertions of natural right and misinterpretations of former treaties. The United States gained what she demanded because Godoy wanted the good will of the greatest neutral carrier of foodstuffs, and to guard against a possible future alliance between Britain and the United States that might be fatal to Spain's colonies. The decisiveness with which the states had checked Genêt's acts directed specifically against Spain must also have influenced him. The end, said Gayoso, was to "do anything to keep the United States in a perfect neutrality."[122] Pinckney himself believed Godoy's motive to be the

[120] A.S.P., For. Rel., I, 533–549, for negotiations (Pinckney's memoir on boundaries, pp. 537–538); the treaty is at 546–549, and in Malloy, Treaties, I. For additional information, see Miller, International Acts, II, 318–338; with notes, 338–345. The subject is exhaustively treated in S. F. Bemis, The Pinckney Treaty (New York, 1926). Whitaker's opinions, in brief, are in his Spanish-American Frontier, pp. 184, 205 et seq. The first approach toward peace with France was made by Spain through James Monroe, American minister at Paris, and gave rise to a great controversy in the United States. Trescott, Diplomatic History, pp. 236–238; J. Monroe, "View of the Conduct of the Executive in Foreign Affairs," Writings (Hamilton ed., 7 vols., New York, 1898–1903); B. W. Bond, The Monroe Mission to France (Baltimore, 1907).

[121] In 1783 the United States gave Great Britain a contractual right to share American littoral rights down to the Iberville (worthless for lack of access from Canada), in return for similar rights below the Iberville if Britain retained Florida in the peace—which she did not. On May 4, 1796, American and British representatives signed a statement that British rights under these agreements were unaffected by American and Spanish agreements in Pinckney's treaty. This was true, but unimportant. However, it displeased Spain and caused her temporary retention of her Mississippi posts. See Whitaker in AHR, XXXV (1930), 804–810, "Godoy's Knowledge of Jay's Treaty."

[122] June 17, 1796, Gayoso to Daniel Clark, Annals of Congress, 10th Cong.,

avoidance of any American alliance with Britain.[123] Jay's treaty (published in Philadelphia in July) had temporarily and conditionally lessened the bad relations between the two powers, and performance of its provisions, including those left to arbitral commissions, had dangerous possibilities, even of ultimate alliance.[124] It was wisdom to grant to Americans navigation rights which officials of Louisiana, and experimental royal orders, had long recognized as essential to the colony's prosperity. And it was wisdom to satisfy the United States instead of permitting irritations to be constantly renewed. Various colonial officials had doubtless realized that Spain must ultimately yield, for a consideration, to the facts of American expansion. The captain-general of Cuba, Las Casas, had so advised Godoy.[125] In Godoy, Spain had at last a minister willing to live with facts. The treaty was a great departure from orthodox Spanish colonial policy, but it was far from a sudden departure.

Orders for the execution of the treaty were sent by him to Louisiana at various times up to the end of October, 1796, when delay was ordered on the basis of inconsistency in the American treaties with Britain, France, and Spain, but was then ordered again a year later.[126] Long before that, however, other reasons had intervened to delay actual transfer of the ceded territory.

The fact is that Godoy acted too late. France had failed to secure Louisiana. She was enraged by the concessions in Jay's treaty to British restrictions of neutral rights, and Monroe's mission to pacify her was a failure.[127] Secretary Pickering found the basic cause of the Pinckney treaty's nonexecution in the expectation of war between France and

---

1st Sess., p. 2730. The influence of the government's curb upon Genêt was emphasized by G. L. Rives, "Spain and the United States in 1795," *AHR*, IV (1898), 75–77. It has been inadequately emphasized.

[123] *A.S.P., For. Rel.*, I, 535; II, 16.

[124] Whitaker, *Spanish-American Frontier*, pp. 184, 205–207, 244 (n. 10). In the minutes of two crucial meetings of the Council of State, there was no mention of the Jay treaty. *Ibid.*, p. 206.

[125] May 19, 1795, that in time the demand for an open Mississippi must be granted, and that the United States would absorb Louisiana. James, *Clark*, p. 428.

[126] Whitaker, *Mississippi Question*, pp. 53, 54, 55, 56, 57, 65. Jay's surrender to the British on the subject of neutral rights had indeed greatly worsened relations with France.

[127] This was the view of Henry Adams, *History of the United States*, I, 350–351, and seems now to be general; F. J. Turner, in *AHR* (1904) X, 275; G. L. Rives, *ibid.*, IV (1898), 78.

the United States, and undeclared naval war between them did in fact begin simultaneously with execution of the treaty.[128] Rumors of British plans against Louisiana were certain to cause pressure by France against evacuation of the Spanish posts, and it was soon discernible.[129]

There was justification for suspicions of British plans. Three days before Pinckney's treaty was signed, "most private and secret" orders had gone to Governor Simcoe of Upper Canada to make connections with leaders in western American settlements to secure aid against Spanish colonies if war should come with Spain.[130] An expedition was conditionally contemplated, and war did come (in October, 1796). George Rogers Clark, too, received and rejected overtures from Simcoe to attack the Spanish colonies.[131] The rumors steadily thickened. By March of 1797 a French general traveling in the West[132] was writing to the Spanish minister in Philadelphia of a contemplated British attack, the British minister was writing home of "the Probability of the Cession of Louisiana to the French," and the Spanish minister was demanding enforcement of America's new neutrality law. In May, the rumors of a British attack (with William Blount's name now associated with it) were so strong that Carondelet issued a proclamation against it and suspended survey of the Florida boundary.[133] Naturally, too, he delayed evacuation of the Spanish posts, and at Walnut Hills stopped the puny military troop destined to accompany the American surveyor, Andrew Ellicott.[134] The latter and Governor Gayoso suspected

[128] B. W. Bond, *Monroe Mission;* Bemis, *Jay's Treaty* (New York, 1923), pp. 150 *et seq.,* and "Washington's Farewell Address: A Foreign Policy of Independence," *AHR,* XXXIX (1934), 250–268.

[129] *A.S.P., For. Rel.,* II, 79.

[130] Printed in *AHR,* X, 575–576.

[131] James, *Clark,* p. 434. Carondelet wanted aid, naturally, against the danger to Louisiana. Cf. Houck, *Spanish Regime,* I, 413–414, I, 4, 9, 23, 59–99. In January, 1794, he appealed to Simcoe for aid against the attack by Clark planned by Genêt, and from the Maumee (where he had gone to rebuild a fort notorious in the Northwest's annals). Simcoe answered (April 8) that he must be cautious. A. L. Burt, *The Old Province of Quebec, 1760–1791* (Toronto, 1933), p. 364.

[132] Some of his reports are in *AHR,* X, 580–583.

[133] All the rumors of the time are customarily, but misleadingly, referred to as the Blount Conspiracy. A bibliography by F. J. Turner is in *AHR,* X (1904), pp. 272, 274. The most important documents are in Turner (ed.), "Documents on the Blount Conspiracy, 1795–1797," *ibid.,* pp. 574–606. See also Whitaker, *Mississippi Question,* pp. 108–115; W. H. Masterson, *William Blount* (Baton Rouge, 1954), pp. 302–323. For Carondelet's proclamation, see *A.S.P., For. Rel.,* II, 82; Gayoso issued another on June 14, *ibid.,* p. 85.

[134] For Ellicott's instructions, see *Annals of Congress,* 11th Cong., Part 2,

each other, chiefly because of Gayoso's secret pledges to the Indians that the Spaniards would not leave.[135] Wilkinson's presence was also a disturbing factor. President Washington verbally instructed Ellicott to watch him, in order that rumors of his Spanish connection, "perhaps ill-founded," might not increase.[136] Talk against the British government stirred the considerable British and American loyalist element in the Natchez settlement. Representatives of the Yazoo land companies were busy there with land titles, and were naturally suspected of being accomplices of Blount. A situation developed that was near to localized war.

Blount's plan had nothing to do with Spain's retention of the Mississippi posts; that was caused by earlier events, rumors, and fears. His "conspiracy" grew out of a smaller plan of one John Chisholm, a rare character, one-time British soldier, frontiersman by choice and affection, Indian interpreter by calling; in his infinite self-confidence, he was as colorful an example as can be found of the old frontier. The plan was to capture East Florida for Great Britain; that, he thought, two dozen of his like could accomplish—perhaps with some Indians added. He went to Blount, his employer, and the latter, insolvent and desperate, went to Liston (British minister) with an enlarged proposal to unite frontiersmen, Indians, a Canadian force, and a British fleet in taking the whole Southwest. Liston thought the plan sufficiently worth consideration by his government to hunt Chisholm out in Philadelphia's grogshops and spirit him away to London.[137] The English government did nothing for him, but the American minister in London did, and received his whole story. The Senate, of which Blount was a member, expelled him on the basis of a letter written by him to another confidant, in consequence of which a later attempt to impeach him neces-

---

p. 2306; for his letters, *A.S.P., For. Rel.*, II, 20–27, 78–87, and *Annals of Congress*, 10th Cong., 1st Sess., Part 2, pp. 2736–2742; for his deposition respecting Wilkinson, *A.S.P., Misc.*, II, 89–90. His journal (a rare volume) is summarized in Amer. Hist. Assoc., *Report* for 1893, pp. 331–366. Gayoso withheld the posts under secret orders from Madrid of October 29, 1796; see Whitaker, *Mississippi Question*, p. 57. On Yazoo agents, see Masterson, *Blount*, pp. 305, 308; Whitaker, *Mississippi Question*, pp. 65, 109, 114.

[135] Though Spain was postponing delivery, the territory was, he knew, not hers, yet he made a treaty with the Choctaw and Chickasaw by which they were promised continued occupation. Robertson, *Louisiana*, I, 279–281.

[136] *A.S.P., Misc.*, II, 89.

[137] *A.S.P., For. Rel.*, II, 71. That he approved of them seems highly probable; cf. *AHR*, X, 588, 593.

sarily failed.[138] He returned to his land jobbing, seemingly little lowered in the esteem of his frontier constituents.

The entire complex of impending war, possible alliances, contingent objectives, and rumored conspiracies was a typical frontier phantasm.

In January, 1794, Wilkinson advised Carondelet that the time had come for Spain to make a final decision respecting the western country. That was quite true. Wilkinson knew that a settlement between Spain and the United States must soon be made; and knew, too, that if any more money was to come from New Orleans, the last opportunity was at hand. Wilkinson's success with the Spaniards had resulted from presenting the problem of the West to them, truthfully, as one involving several unknown quantities. As they had no means of resolving these, they simply waited (as the governments of the two countries waited), taking Wilkinson's advice when worried. He may occasionally have caused them to worry, in order to advise them, as was now done with Carondelet. However, there was always cause for worry, and perplexity in Philadelphia was as real and constant as in New Orleans.

In the course of 1794, the government of the United States dealt energetically and successfully with Genêt, and likewise with the Whisky Insurrection in western Pennsylvania; Jay went to London to settle differences with Britain; Anthony Wayne demolished the Indian "confederation" in the Northwest. It was a year which demonstrated both the strength of the government and the complete absence of dangerous disaffection in the West. To believe, in the face of these events, and in disregard of evidence accumulated since 1787, that the West could be enticed to desert the Union was imbecility. But there had been time since 1791 for Wilkinson to learn that Carondelet had that qualification.

He relied, seemingly, on old papers in the New Orleans archives. "I have shown incontestably," he wrote (repeating Wilkinson's old assurances), "in several secret despatches . . . that the whole power of the

[138] *Annals of Congress*, 5th Cong., pp. 2365–2369. His testimony is in *AHR*, X, 595–605; see C. R. King (ed.), *Life and Correspondence of Rufus King* (6 vols., New York, 1894–1900), II, 217–218, 253–258. The letter that was Blount's undoing is in *A.S.P., For. Rel.*, II, 76–77; general materials, 71–103. Fuller materials are in *Annals of Congress*, 5th Cong., pp. 2339 (the letter), 2369–70 (Chisholm), 2388–2393 (deposition), 2319–2323 (impeachment articles). Liston ventured the opinion that the American government would have welcomed the execution of "the plan" if rapidly effected; see *AHR*, X, 593. As regards Blount's plan, in the proper sense, this seems impossible, since the government had in 1790 recognized the unlikelihood of profiting by a British fleet's capture of New Orleans.

Atlantic States is insufficient to subject those of the west." The latter were "determined to procure by force" free navigation of the Mississippi, and if opposed by the eastern states would become independent, or join Canada.[139] Quite inconsistently, he was also assuring the government (on the basis of other old misconceptions) that the Indians could at any time hold back *all* Americans. Ignoring that, he took the old assurances of Wilkinson from the archives and sought salvation from Kentucky. But the first clear step in the intrigue was taken by the Kentuckians.[140] Harry Innes initiated a cipher correspondence with Gayoso, asking for the conditions offered by Spain for action by the Kentuckians, and for assurance of indemnity for losses which they might suffer.[141] Carondelet wrote to Godoy that he would negotiate with Wilkinson for the independence of the West if the latter kept his promise to come to New Orleans.[142] A year later he offered pensions to Wilkinson's associates, and asked for negotiation by Kentucky's agents with Gayoso on opening the Mississippi.[143] This was a complete departure from all earlier Spanish policy, and the contemplated end was Kentucky's secession. Carondelet received the truthful reply that his correspondents had no power to appoint such agents and a warning that peace could not long continue unless the river be opened.[144] Gayoso, it was learned, could offer nothing free of customs dues.[145] Godoy had the good sense

---

[139] Robertson, *Louisiana*, I, 299.

[140] Wilkinson and Harry Innes had earlier assured Carondelet that Clark's rumored expedition for Genêt would collapse. This, or some unrecorded communication, may have been the initial step; Whitaker, *Spanish-American Frontier*, p. 195. Benjamin Sebastian, member of Kentucky's highest court, had long had a Spanish pension; likewise, Harry Innes, judge of the United States court, district of Kentucky. George Nicholas was a Kentuckian of high standing. On Innes, see following note; on Sebastian, see Houck, *Spanish Regime*, II, 24; *Annals of Congress*, 10th Cong., 1st Sess., pp. 1373, 2729-2734, 2744-2745; Green, *Spanish Conspiracy*, pp. 336-339, 349; Bodley, *Littell's Political Transactions*, ci-cix.

[141] *A.S.P., Misc.*, I, 922-934; Whitaker, "Harry Innes and the Spanish Intrigue, 1794-1795," *MVHR*, XV, 236-248, printing Innes' letters at 245 *et seq.*

[142] Amer. Hist. Assoc., *Report* for 1896, pp. 1069, 1081.

[143] Bodley, *Littell's Political Transactions*, p. lxxx; Green, *Spanish Conspiracy*, p. 344. Carondelet had been liberal as respected navigation of the river, reducing duties from 15 to 6 per cent. Whitaker, *Commercial Policy of Spain*, pp. xliii, xlviii, 241 (n. 171), 242 (nn. 172, 173), and *Spanish-American Frontier*, pp. 176, 193; Daniel Clark (April, 1798) on commerce at New Orleans, *Annals of Congress*, 10th Cong., 1st Sess., pp. 2731-2736.

[144] Bodley, *Littell's Political Transactions*, p. lxxxi.

[145] *Ibid.*, p. lxxxiii.

to disregard Carondelet's reports on this intrigue; in the minutes of two crucial meetings of the Council of State, they were not even mentioned.[146]

However, as other causes prevented performance of the Pinckney treaty, Carondelet clung to his hopes, probably in part because he was under the delusion that the Indians would never permit American occupation of the ceded territory.[147] When, at last, Carondelet made a direct offer of money if his correspondents would lead Kentucky to independence, all of them unequivocally refused to consider secession from the Union.[148] The game being over, Wilkinson pronounced the whole project futile since Pinckney's treaty. That same year (1796), however, he collected some thousands of dollars in pension arrears.[149] There is no reason to believe that he or the others had any objective other than to prolong their Spanish pensions.

[146] Whitaker, *Spanish-American Frontier*, p. 206.

[147] See his letter of June, 1796, in *Annals of Congress*, 10th Cong., 1st Sess., pp. 2730–2731. In October, 1796, Carondelet wrote to Gayoso that in Godoy's opinion, since the signing of the Pinckney treaty, it was "now useless to treat separately with Kentucky." *Ibid.*, p. 1361.

[148] His financial offers for securing Kentucky independence exceeded $200,-000. Green, *Spanish Conspiracy*, pp. 351–352, and Bodley, *Littell's Political Transactions*, p. lxxxvi (note), print the letter. *Annals of Congress*, 10th Cong., 1st Sess., pp. 1370–1371. By October, Ellicott had knowledge of the outline of the plan; *A.S.P., Misc.*, II, 89.

[149] *Annals of Congress*, 10th Cong., 1st Sess., pp. 1259–1260; *A.S.P., Misc.*, II, 89; Whitaker, *Spanish-American Frontier*, p. 195.

CHAPTER 8

Acquisition of Louisiana and the Floridas

WHEN in 1763 Britain shoved France out of North America except around New Orleans, no British statesman, seemingly, had a broader thought of peace than satisfaction in lessening by one the fronts on which the seaboard colonies must be defended. In that year, to Britons "of empire and of glory," broad ideals of trade and peace were confined to men like Adam Smith and Immanuel Kant—and, to some extent, the idealists in Congress who framed the model treaty for peaceful friendship and unhampered trade. By 1783, Lord Shelburne and Franklin realized the possibility of permanent peace within a free-trade area, but the idea was lost in British past, and American immediate, unwisdom. The British lacked time to identify and repeal the maze of laws in which past mercantilism was embodied. The Americans, in the first treaty by which a European power accepted their model treaty, also entered into an alliance with France which tied them to the whirligig of European wars and territorial exchanges.

It was not unusual for France to warn Spain of British designs against Spain's colonies, or for Britain to warn her of French designs, and for years France gave her counsel against dangers from the United States. But there seems to be no evidence that either of them had a policy, until late in the century, of securing Louisiana for itself. A contrary view respecting France had strong support fifty years ago.[1] It was

[1] Instructions by the British foreign office to its representatives in Paris, long assuming a continuous French policy of regaining her American empire, were mere office routinism. See S. Pargellis in *AHR*, XLI (1935), with citations to L. G. Wickham Legg. F. J. Turner followed an older view in *AHR*,

pointed out earlier that France's actual policy in allying herself with America in 1778 was to seek revenge for the humiliation of 1763, and that for some years following she sought to hold in balance the conflicting claims of Spain and the United States in order to retain both as allies.[2]

Jay's treaty made plain to France how very difficult this would be, and it also presented grave problems to Spain, but not because its terms could have suggested to either France or Spain any immediate alliance between the two parties to it. What was alarming was the great concessions which each had made to avoid imminent war: Britain's willingness to abandon the northwestern forts and arbitrate other galling difficulties, and America's abandonment (as against Britain) of the doctrines of neutral rights proclaimed in the French alliance of 1778. When Spain had made peace with France at Basle (July 22, 1795), she knew that this would carry her into war with Britain. In making the Pinckney treaty to secure (*inter alia*) the aid in that war of American neutral trade, she was immediately presented with the danger of a British-American reconciliation. At the same time French-American relations were alarmingly worsened by the concessions against neutral rights in Jay's treaty. The necessity of preventing any closer relations between its parties became the immediate objective of French policy, but underneath the surface the problems persisted which ultimately culminated in undeclared naval war with the United States in 1798. The West, and Louisiana in particular, soon became a central part of the story. There seems to be no indisputable evidence of any effort by France to secure a recession of Louisiana until she asked for it at Basle, and she accepted Santo Domingo in its place.[3]

X (1904), 249; see M. S. Fletcher, "Louisiana as a Factor in French Diplomacy from 1763 to 1800," *MVHR*, XVII (1930), 367–376; J. A. James, "Louisiana as a Factor in American Diplomacy, 1795–1800," *ibid.*, I (1914), 44–56; A. P. Whitaker, *Documents Relating to the Commercial Policy of Spain in the Floridas* (Deland, Fla., 1931), pp. xlvi, xlix–l. P. C. Phillips, *The West in the Diplomacy of the Revolution* (Urbana, Ill., 1913), and E. S. Corwin, *French Policy and the American Revolution* (Princeton, 1916), introduced now-accepted views.

[2] E. W. Lyon, *Louisiana in French Diplomacy, 1759–1804* (Norman, Okla., 1934), attempted, but failed, to show early desires to secure a retrocession of Louisiana. Fletcher, "Louisiana," p. 369, dates this objective from 1789. Whitaker (*HAHR*, XI, 485) doubts continuity of policy antedating 1795.

[3] Fletcher, "Louisiana," pp. 367–369; Amer. Hist. Assoc., *Report* for 1903, II, 567.

Circumstances soon gave emphasis to Louisiana. George Rogers Clark was assuring the French government of sympathy in the West for France; a friend of Clark in Paris, seeking remuneration for his past military services, was doing the same in 1796.[4] Fauchet, the French minister in Philadelphia, had urged his government to put pressure on the American government by forming a party in the West. His successor, Adet, sent General Victor Collot in the spring of 1796 to descend the Mississippi and report on the Spanish posts on its east bank, and on Louisiana. He reported the posts valueless unless held together with the territory eastward to the mountains—therefore valueless without an alliance with the western states of the Union. He reported, also, that one country should hold both banks of the river.[5]

Although Spain refused to cede Louisiana to France in July, 1795, she offered it to her late in the year to regain Santo Domingo (which was at that time of far greater demonstrated value) and six months later signed a treaty promising retrocession to France, which the latter did not ratify.[6] She then allied herself with France for the impending war with Britain, and necessarily became a puppet in French diplomacy.

War began in the autumn of 1796. A possible exchange of Louisiana for Santo Domingo, coupled with rumors of French plans to conquer Canada, were reported late that year to President Adams,[7] who, with his experience of 1782 and Genêt's recent mission in mind, was convinced that France desired a protectorate over the United States.[8] He adopted a policy of strict neutrality. In March, 1797, France severed diplomatic relations by refusing to receive an American minister. The events which followed that act, to some extent its consequences, constitute one of the most turbulent, impassioned, and irrational chapters—in part creditable, in part discreditable—in American history. The President then sent three commissioners to Paris to negotiate a settlement of differences. Talleyrand attempted to collect a bribe as the price of negotiating (the XYZ affair). The report of this, which was immediately published by

[4] J. A. James, *The Life of George Rogers Clark* (Chicago, 1928), pp. 429–430, 432, 436, 437.

[5] *AHR*, X (1904); more clearly in G. H. Victor Collot, *A Journey in North America* (Paris, 3 vols., one of maps, etc., 1826).

[6] A. P. Whitaker, *The Mississippi Question, 1795–1803* (New York, 1934), pp. 53, 183.

[7] Adams, *Writings* (Ford ed.), II, 21, 31 (n.), 128.

[8] *Ibid.*, p. 132.

the President (March, 1798), caused a prodigious uproar.[9] Congress immediately voted funds for an army and navy; an undeclared naval war soon began against French vessels which, under French rules of neutral trade, seized goods on American vessels.

Thousands of French and British fugitives and Irish radicals had become refugees in the United States. The implacable bitterness between friends of Britain, with whom the Federalist party of President Adams was bracketed (in political controversy), and the friends of France, bracketed with the Democrats led by Jefferson, is incredible. Under the Alien and Sedition Laws, which embodied the animus of the Federalists, George Rogers Clark was saved from deportation, when he refused to resign his French commission, only by the intervention of the Spanish minister, and even when back in Kentucky was again saved only by forceful rescue and flight to St. Louis.[10] Americans have in later years repeatedly revealed a high emotional potential, but never since 1798 have they exhibited, as a whole, the irrationalism of that year.

In the meantime, the British government was weighing the possibilities of co-operating with Francisco de Miranda, the Venezuelan revolutionary, in freeing the Spanish colonies—or, perhaps, making some her own.[11] The United States, with similar temptations, was as wary of British occupation of New Orleans as it was of French. Unless France would allow Spain absolute neutrality, some Americans favored force to exclude other powers. Alexander Hamilton, chosen by Washington to be next to him in command of the army (1798), had grandiose dreams of great conquests in the Spanish colonies.[12]

While this turmoil shook and weakened the United States, Talleyrand was seeking to induce Spain to surrender Louisiana, urging the old bogeys of Canadian and American attacks, and that France could, better than Spain, protect Mexico against them. Nevertheless, in September, 1798, he sent word that new American commissioners would be properly received. On October 1, 1800, a treaty was concluded between France and the United States.[13] The same day, in Spain, the

[9] A.S.P., For. Rel., II, 157.

[10] James, Clark, pp. 445–446; see his letters to the French government, ibid., pp. 511–55.

[11] W. S. Robertson, Life of Francisco Miranda (1929) I, 168–187.

[12] Works (Lodge ed.).

[13] Malloy, Treaties, I; Miller, International Acts, I.

treaty of San Ildefonso was signed between France and Spain, providing for the retrocession of Louisiana.[14]

This treaty, as in 1796, promised the retrocession after France should have provided a certain territorial establishment in Italy for the son-in-law of the Spanish king. In the following year, referring loosely to the former treaty as one by which Spain "cedes" to France "possession" of Louisiana, the treaty of Madrid provided that "the contracting parties agree to make the provisions of that treaty effective, and to exercise their respective rights thereunder while the difficulties referred to in it shall be in process of adjustment."[15] Even after that, however, King Charles delayed, desiring a pledge that France would never alienate Louisiana. European peace was re-established by the peace of Amiens (March 25, 1802), but new plans for national aggrandizement, certain to renew international suspicions, immediately took form. On July 22, 1802, the French minister gave the pledge that Spain desired.[16] Only after that did King Charles order (October 15) delivery to France of actual possession—that is, occupation.

It was once believed that Napoleon had neither title nor right to convey (as he was later to do) to the United States; and that the latter, in acting on an alleged transfer of title, were "accomplices of the greatest highwayman of modern times."[17] However, Spain did make an unconditional cession to France, and therefore the United States did receive perfect title from her. Napoleon's *promise* not to convey it could not affect the title or his power to transfer it. Spain's long delay in giving orders for transferring occupation of the province was, of course, equally irrelevant.[18]

[14] J. A. Robertson, *Louisiana under Spain, France, and the United States* (2 vols., Cleveland, 1911), II, 92; *A.S.P., Pub. Lands*, II, 576.

[15] Treaty of March 21, 1801. *Ibid.*, 336; *A.S.P., For. Rel.*, II, 511; confirmation in July, 1802, *ibid.*, p. 569.

[16] Copy in Robertson, *Louisiana*, II, 77; compare *A.S.P., For. Rel.*, II, 569.

[17] E. Channing, *History of the United States*, III, 79. "Louisiana at that time did not belong to France. . . . Nor could Napoleon, had Louisiana belonged to France, have sold it without consent of the French. That consent was not even asked, and the United States took title from a man who had neither the legal nor the moral right to dispose of it." John Bach McMaster, in Amer. Hist. Assoc., *Report* for 1905, I, 62–63.

[18] Equally misleading is an assurance, said to have been given by Talleyrand in May, 1803, to Spain "that the cession [by Spain] was but nominal, and that she [Spain] might still retain *possession*." J. Bécker, in *La España Moderna* (May, 1903).

The President had learned within six months of the first promise to cede the colony.[19] From that moment three thoughts were in his mind: the first, the threat to American trading rights on the Mississippi existing since 1795; the second, the purchase of West Florida—if Spain still had it (in fact, she had refused to cede it with Louisiana); the third, an alliance with England. "The day that France takes possession . . . of New Orleans," he wrote to our minister to France, "we must marry ourselves to the British fleet and nation."[20] That minister, Robert Livingston, had already spontaneously waved before his Spanish colleague in Paris the two bogeys always available against Spain—the danger to Mexico of a French military colony, and the likelihood of a British-American alliance.[21]

In October, 1802, a new danger threatened the United States. This was the suspension of the right of deposit at New Orleans by the intendant, Juan Ventura Morales.[22] Assuming adherence to the Pinckney treaty, obviously there could be no suspension of trade, nor any indefinitely long delay in assigning another place of deposit. The intendant had made the suspension in obedience to a secret royal order of July 14, 1802 (eight days before the French ambassador gave France's pledge never to alienate the colony), and also attempted to justify his act by an interpretation of the Pinckney treaty.[23] In the latter he was logically weak, resting upon words that had been ignored during nearly two periods, each of three years, and no action had been taken in Spain or in New Orleans at the end of the first. Under predominant international practice (as already noted, repeatedly stated by France respecting the Mississippi, and recognized by Spain in the case of the Tagus) all American rights of navigation below the southern limit of the American littoral, under her treaty of 1795 with Spain, had automatically ceased when Spanish title to the river's banks below that limit had passed to France sixteen months before the order of July 14, 1802—leaving to the United States, of course, claims against Spain for compensation. On July 15, Spain also notified France of her decision

[19] G. Chinard, *Thomas Jefferson, Apostle of America* (New York, 1929), p. 410.

[20] April 18, 1802, Jefferson, *Writings* (Ford ed.), VIII, 145.

[21] *A.S.P., For. Rel.*, II, 518, 531.

[22] Robertson, *Louisiana*, II, 29 n., printing the decree in part, and as of October 16; *A.S.P., For. Rel.*, II, 469, with date of October 18. Whitaker gives a chapter to the subject, *Mississippi Question*, pp. 189–199 (dating it October 18).

[23] Robertson, *Louisiana*, II, 91.

to transfer actual possession of the colony, although this was again post-poned until October.[24]

Spain had good reason for doing this; it would ensure the safety of the Floridas. And France also had a reason for the closure of the deposit. Until the United States should learn the date of the change of sovereignty, revocation of the deposit right would be attributed to Spain, and this would postpone American irritation while protecting the legal right of France despite her pledge to execute treaties "in accord with the existing condition of affairs."[25] Existing when? King Charles's reluctance to give the order of July 14, and his attempts to revoke it, clearly suggest that it was dictated by France, and the order was necessarily sent to the prospective French intendant, Laussat, through the French minister at Washington.[26] General Victor, who was to be the French captain-general of the colony, was told in his secret instructions that "the captain-general must, on his arrival, limit himself to tolerating what he shall find established," and (this immediately following) report fully respecting English and American navigation of the Missisippi. The instructions continued: "It is clear that the Republic, as sovereign of the two shores of the Mississippi at its mouth, holds in its hands the key to its navigation. That navigation, moreover, is of the highest importance to the western states of the federal government."[27] One need hardly ask what France would gain—complete subordination of American policy to her own, provided she could reduce the United States to submission in war if that became inevitable. And the regaining of Louisiana as a means of putting pressure on the United States was precisely what Fauchet, the French minister in Washington, had been urging on Napoleon.[28] Spain would gain complete assurance that she could hold West Florida against American pressure, already threatening. Complete security, also, against American demands for navigation to the Gulf on the rivers flowing through West Florida. Naturally, then, when Spain had expressed willingness to give France possession, she

[24] *Ibid.,* II, 33.

[25] The instructions are *ibid.,* I, 367–373; also in Adams, *History of the U.S.,* II, 5–12.

[26] Some months earlier King Charles had expressed a desire to have the deposit reopened, and Morales was ordered to tolerate its use. Whitaker, *Mississippi Question,* p. 230; Villiers du Terrage, *Les dernières années de la Louisiane française* (Paris, 1903), pp. 367, 369.

[27] *A.S.P., For. Rel.,* II, 511, 543; Madison, *Writings* (Hunt, ed.), VII, 23. Jefferson and Madison fully recognized the right of closure exercised by France.

[28] *Amer. Hist. Rev.,* X, 265–266.

had also asked for the promise (received on July 22) that France would never alienate Louisiana. All this meant the nullification of Pinckney's treaty, victory on all points against American ambitions.

Incidentally, the instructions to Victor again evidence the persistent influence of European ignorance respecting American conditions. Referring to the jealousy with which the American government would see France occupy Louisiana, they recognized that the American western population (never the eastern) "[might] be an enemy to be feared," then added that Indian alliances were essential—Spain's old, delusive policy. "But," the instructions ended, "everything that would occasion . . . quarrels with the United States must be avoided." There was serious danger of a quarrel. The Mississippi trade of the western country had become considerable in amount and importance, and the angry protests from that area were loud and genuine.[29]

Louisiana was not a thoroughly patriotic colony, French or Spanish. For forty years it had enjoyed, legally or illegally, special commercial privileges. There was reportedly a general expectation of American annexation—perhaps likely to be welcomed. At least there was a strong sentiment, based on experience, for local autonomy. In December, 1802, President Jefferson informed Congress that the retrocession called for a change in the country's foreign relations. Privately, he had declared that "it completely reverse[d] all the political relations of the United States." Two million dollars were promptly provided for undefined purposes, and James Monroe was appointed minister extraordinary to France. The British minister in Washington was told that even at the cost of war the United States would never renounce navigation of the Mississippi—hinting desire for alliance with Britain. The French minister, now Pichon, was told that the Floridas and Louisiana were essential to the American settlements above them, and that two or more million dollars could be had for them. Monroe reached Paris on April 12, 1803. In a private letter, Jefferson had written to him, "on the event of this mission depend the future destinies of this republic."[30]

[29] "Documents: Despatches from the United States Consulate in New Orleans, 1801–1803," AHR, XXXII (1927), 801–824; XXXIII (1928), 331–359; Daniel Clark to the Secretary of State, April 18, 1798, in Annals of Congress, pp. 2731–2736; A. P. Whitaker, "The Commerce of Louisiana and the Floridas at the End of the Eighteenth Century," HAHR, VIII (1928), 190–203, and Mississippi Question, pp. 86–95, 130–154; "Daniel Clark, Jr.," in J. T. Adams (ed.), Dictionary of American Biography.
[30] Writings, VIII, 191.

On March 1 another royal order had instructed Morales to reopen the deposit on the original terms of 1795. This however, settled nothing, since France had held title since March 21. Jefferson knew of this when, in April, he authorized Monroe and Livingston, should France force war, to make a British alliance binding both parties to make peace only in common.[31]

It is obvious from Victor's instructions that Talleyrand and Napoleon realized that closure of the deposit might cause grave trouble with the United States. Their representatives in America knew that in politics the West was Republican; that closing the deposit was offensive to friends of France and also bound to irritate the Federalists who had supported the naval war of 1798.[32] Yet Laussat (waiting to take possession of the colony for France) thought re-establishment of the deposit would be "most dangerous."[33] On the other hand Pichon, in transmitting American protests, had himself protested to Morales the irregularity of his action.[34] These American difficulties confronting France were real, but others, as judged then, were doubtless considered far more important by France. The occupation of Santo Domingo, instead of being a formality, became a formidable military problem. In September, 1802, General Victor's sailing orders were postponed.

There was no basis for the rumors that Spain would resist transfer to either France or the United States, the latter acquiring title by agreement of May 2 (antedated to April 30), 1803. Misunderstandings arose from the difficulties of intercontinental correspondence, or from administrative laxity. Irujo's personal opposition and advice to his government that it resist transfer were seemingly due to ignorance of the treaties it had signed and of its willingness to perform them.[35] Actual transfer of possession was made at New Orleans before he received a copy of the royal order (sent through the captain-general of Cuba) for that action.[36] But, before either, he had concluded that, as a neighbor, the Americans would be preferable to a French mili-

[31] A.S.P., For. Rel., II, 555.
[32] Ibid., II, 525.
[33] Ibid., II, 552–554; Adams, Hist. of the U.S., II, 40; Miller, International Acts; M. Farrand, "The Commercial Privileges of the Treaty of 1803," AHR, VII (1902), 494–499; E. W. Lyon (ed.), "Documents: The Closing of the Port of New Orleans," AHR, XXXVII (1932), 280–286.
[34] Letters of November 4 and 5, Robertson, Louisiana, II, 109.
[35] All Irujo's letters are ibid., pp. 61–135.
[36] The order was of October 15. Ibid., p. 91.

tary colony.[37] After transfers to French control (November 30, 1803) and then to American (December 20), Spain gave notice in Madrid and Washington disavowing rumors of her continuing opposition to American title.[38]

As respects French settlement and specifically French profit, Louisiana had never been a successful colony. It had been no more profitable to Spain except as a protection of New Spain, and the costs of its administration had been a burden·in each case upon the mother country or upon other colonies.[39] Hopes for improvements in these respects must have entered into Napoleon's plans for the management of the regained colony—just as western interest in Mississippi navigation affected American policy. But the economic influence was seemingly wholly contingent and subordinate. The efforts of France through years to secure the colony, and equally Napoleon's sudden relinquishment of it, were moves in the game of European power politics that centered in the rivalry of France and Britain.[40] Louisiana was purchased by the United States to secure safety on its border from European politics. Its acquisition was jubilantly approved by the West, but to say that the purchase "was called out by"—implying then existing—"frontier needs and demands" is manifest distortion.[41]

It was soon made clear that in the plans of the President the land acquired was not, for a generation or more, to be open even for settlement. The constitutional power of the federal government even to acquire the territory had been denied by many and doubted by more.[42] Jefferson believed a constitutional amendment necessary for acquisition of foreign land, and also that other amendments were necessary before

[37] *Ibid.;* p. 118.

[38] *Ibid.,* pp. 215–221, 225; *A.S.P., For. Rel.,* II, 572–583. Upper Louisiana was delivered on March 9, 1804.

[39] W. R. Shepherd, "The Cession of Louisiana to Spain," *Political Science Qy.,* XIX (1904), 439; Robertson, *Louisiana,* I, 178–179, 211 n., 215 n. 49; Villiers du Terrage, *Dernières années,* pp. 368–370; Whitaker, *Mississippi Question,* pp. 177–178.

[40] Different writers have given variant emphasis to the economic factor: A. P. Whitaker, "France and the American Deposit at New Orleans," *HAHR,* XI, 485–491; Fletcher, "Louisiana," pp. 369–371; L. Pelzer, "Economic Factors in the Acquisition of Louisiana," Miss. Val. Hist. Assoc., *Proceedings,* VI, 109–128.

[41] F. J. Turner, *The Frontier in American History* (New York, 1920), p. 214.

[42] For reasons discussed in the *Collections* of the Ill. State Hist. Library, XXV (1950), lviii *et seq.*

it could be utilized for the creation of Territories and states. In several pages of print, he partially expressed essential constitutional changes, but the Congress decided that the best procedure was to take the land and leave questions of power to the future.

Amendments proposed by Jefferson would have enabled Congress (1) to clear lands west of the Mississippi of the occupancy rights of western Indians, and to settle these lands with eastern Indians; and (2) to exchange eastern lands, after clearing them of Indian rights of occupancy, for lands west of the Mississippi already occupied by whites north of 31°. These things done, all Indians would have been concentrated beyond the Mississippi; the compact of 1802 with Georgia would incidentally have been performed; and Jefferson would have accomplished his original plan to make all Louisiana an Indian reservation for an unspecified period of time. This period, he believed, could be ended, and Territories organized for whites, only by another amendment of the Constitution. This would have provided: "The legislature [Congress] shall have no authority to dispose of the lands of the province otherwise than as hereinbefore permitted, until a new Amendment of the Constitution shall give that authority. Except as to the portion . . . South of the latitude of 31°."[43] By thus suspending the constitutional power of Congress to deal with "territory" of the United States, almost certainly for at least some decades, the Indians would have been assured of unhampered occupancy.[44] And these were the views of a great friend of frontier èxpansion! Congress ignored Jefferson's ideas, except for a provision, in the law of 1804 which organized the Territory of Orleans, for removal of eastern Indians to lands west of the Mississippi.[45]

The Federalists had bitterly denounced this purchase of a "wilderness." It has been suggested that Jefferson perhaps conceived his plan as a means of answering that charge by using the land for a desirable

[43] *Writings*, VIII, 241–249. See E. S. Brown, *The Constitutional History of the Louisiana Purchase* (Berkeley, 1920). Jefferson's proposed amendment showed an astoundingly narrow view of existent governmental powers. For example, it would have authorized the exercise of police power over non-Indians, and the power to maintain military posts and to explore the territory's geography and resources.

[44] Art. IV, Sec. 2, Para. 2. Bitter division of opinion on various sectional and political problems—with that on slavery less than two decades in the future—justifies this assumption. As Secretary Robert Smith pointed out, the Indians would have had constitutional rights instead of a mere revocable license of occupancy. Jefferson, *Writings* (Ford ed.), VIII, 241–242.

[45] March 26, Sec. 15. *U.S. Statutes at Large,* II, 283, or VII, 78; Carter, *Terr. Papers,* IX, 212.

national purpose.[46] But his acts were not political; they were based on convictions. Irujo believed that only evil could come to the United States from the purchase; that "to add a new world of woods" to an extent of territory "already burdensome" was "a kind of madness."[47] Later he came to ascribe extraordinary statesmanship to the government, in part because of its trans-Mississippi policy. After reading a pamphlet written, he believed, by Madison (secretary of state), he expressed to his government his conviction "that we can do no less than cast aside all doubt as to the good faith of this government when it assures us that it will try to prevent settlement on the right side of the Mississippi."[48] The Spanish minister of foreign affairs read the pamphlet in part to the King, and thanked Irujo for His Majesty.

The purchase removed a dangerous enemy, secured all rights in the Mississippi, and greatly limited in the field of overseas trade the danger of embroilment in the Napoleonic wars. It vastly extended the area within which Anglo-American political institutions could freely develop, and was also a stimulant to American self-confidence, soon to be expressed, with more thought for acreage than institutions, in the cry of manifest destiny. Boundary disputes with Canada and Spain were latent in its provisions. One of these arose almost immediately.

In conferring powers which it would be difficult to detail, it was common practice to use a catchall phrase. Lord Dorchester, for example, was granted all powers "which unto the said Offices respectively belong and appertain or of Right ought to belong and appertain." Examples of similar precaution could presumably be found in many treaties ceding title to territories.[49] In the retroceding of Louisiana to France, the promise was that, upon performance of conditions stated, Spain would cede Louisiana "with the same extent which it now has in the hands of Spain and which it had when France possessed it, and such as it should [may] be since the treaties made between Spain and

[46] A. H. Abel, "The History of Events Resulting in Indian Consolidation West of the Mississippi," Amer. Hist. Assoc., *Report* for 1906, I, 244.

[47] Robertson, *Louisiana,* II, 73, 75. The disparity between population and area was doubtless greater in various Spanish colonies, if not all.

[48] *Ibid.*

[49] They were necessary because, without such precaution, mistakes would easily be made in dealing with unknown territory. The instructions to General Victor described Louisiana as bounded "on the east,"—instead of west—"by the River Bravo." Robertson, *Louisiana,* I, 362. See T. M. Marshall, *Western Boundary of the Louisiana Purchase* (Berkeley, 1914), pp. 46–70.

others states."[50] It is obvious that France gave Louisiana to Spain in 1762 as it was when France then (last) possessed it, and equally obvious that the retrocession of France was of Louisiana as Spain then (last) held it, subject possibly to rights acquired in it by other countries during Spain's tenure. When France ceded it to the United States, Monroe and Livingston had a copy of the Spanish retrocession treaty. It was natural and proper to employ the same formula in the three treaties, instead of using merely the word "Louisiana." The boundary problem was one of fact: What were the eastern bounds of Louisiana? On that, varying views might be possible, and Jefferson's—surely perverted by national interests—were maintained by the United States for twenty years. But it is astounding that diplomatic representatives of the United States found the words of grant puzzling, or could have argued that the quoted words of grant evidenced, in themselves, a grant of West Florida. No boundaries, save near New Orleans and along the Mississippi, were precisely known. The description used in the three treaties was more exact than any other that could be given, and at the same time pledged the good faith of the successive grantors as respected the area conveyed.

What passed from France to the United States was what France had received from Spain—and France, wrote Vergennes, could take possession of nothing except "between the right [west] bank of the Mississippi and New Mexico." In no Spanish, French, or American document did any reference to Louisiana suggest its extension east of the Iberville. No such reference was made in the ceremony attending its transfer to French occupation, or to American.[51]

Confusion possibly arose from the fact that in 1763 Great Britain had insisted that France cede to her "the river and port of Mobile, and everything which he [His Christian Majesty] possesses or ought to possess" east of the Mississippi channel except the island of New Orleans (the earlier transfer of that to Spain being unknown to Britain). France did have broad claims southward from the Great Lakes, and some vague claims between the Pearl and Perdido rivers. Spain, like France,

---

[50] Martens, *Recueil des Traités*, VII, 708; or Villiers du Terrage, *Dernières années*, p. 375; similarly in the agreement of March 21, 1801, Martens, *Recueil des Traités*, VII, 336.

[51] Robertson, *Louisiana*, II, 87. I. J. Cox, *The West Florida Controversy, 1798-1813* (Baltimore, 1918), pp. 81, 82, 84, found the description both "indefinite" and "puzzling."

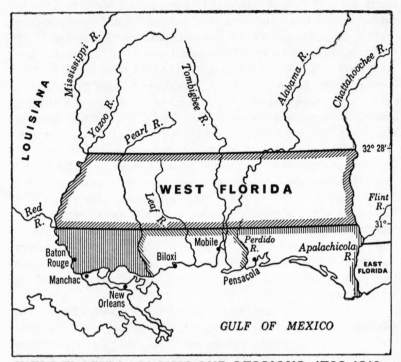

WEST FLORIDA: CLAIMS AND CESSIONS 1763-1819

Areas ceded by Spain and/or France to Great Britain in 1763; all British territory north of 31°—contingently, north of 32°28′, if Britain should retain West Florida (which she did not)—was ceded to the United States in 1783.

Claimed by Spain, 1783-95; renounced by her by treaty of 1795; southern boundary survey completed in 1799.

Predominantly settled by Americans by 1803, was thereafter claimed as part of the Louisiana Purchase; was occupied by U.S. in 1810 and administered with Territory of Orleans, 1804-12; part of the state of Louisiana after 1812.

Claimed by U.S. in 1812, occupied in 1813.

Admittedly purchased from Spain in 1819, by treaty in which Spain also renounced her claims to the other areas.

was compelled to cede to Britain "all that she possesses to the east or southeast of the river Mississippi."

These claims were mentioned in order to destroy them. Such of them as had then no relation to the title of West Florida merged in British claims west of the Alleghenies, relinquished in 1783 to the United States. But if any affected the title of Spain to West Florida, then, when Britain acquired the former from France and the latter from Spain, they merged in and perfected that title, leaving Louisiana limited to the line of the Mississippi and Iberville (save from New Orleans to the Gulf).[52] Louisiana and West Florida under Spain were distinct colonies with different governors, both subordinated to the captain-generalate of Cuba. Even if, while one was French and one Spanish, governors of Louisiana occasionally acted administratively in West Florida west of the Pearl River (a district reached from Pensacola only with extraordinary difficulty), these were trifling administrative irregularities, matters of momentary convenience, of no importance.[53]

About three weeks after the cession to the United States was signed, Robert Livingston advised Madison to claim West Florida to the Perdido as part of Louisiana.[54] Monroe thought that this view was subject to no doubt, and Madison instructed him and Livingston to collect evidence to sustain it. Jefferson adopted it as a settled policy for years. The contrary views of Rufus King, Timothy Pickering, and others who, equally with himself, had had diplomatic experience, and of American officials in Louisiana, had no effect upon him.[55]

The four parts of which West Florida had once been composed had had very different histories. The northern belt between 31° and 32° 28' north has been repeatedly mentioned. Of the rest of the colony, the portion east of the Perdido River, although it included Pensacola, the

---

[52] T. C. Pease (ed.), *Anglo-French Boundary Disputes in the West, 1749–1763, Ill. Hist. Coll.*, XXVII; Whitaker, *Mississippi Question*, pp. 307–308.

[53] Henry Clay referred to these matters in 1810. *Annals of Congress*, pp. 43–45.

[54] *A.S.P., For. Rel.*, II, 563. He sought from the French government removal of a supposed ambiguity in the recession to France and in her cession to the United States (*ibid.*, p. 561). An intimation by the French negotiators that "the Americans might interpret the treaty to suit themselves"—which was justifiable jesting—has sometimes been taken seriously, as in Cox, *West Florida Controversy*, pp. 81–82.

[55] *A.S.P., For. Rel.*, II, 242, 245, 627; C. King (ed.), *Life and Correspondence of Rufus King* (6 vols., New York, 1894–1900), IV, 329–332, 363, 554, 555. Gallatin, at first opposed, later accepted Jefferson's view. *Writings*, I, 151; Monroe, *Writings* (Hamilton ed.), IV, 503.

administrative headquarters, had had a scanty history aside from Indian trade and relations. The portion between the Perdido and the Pearl rivers included Mobile toward the east and Biloxi toward the west. American settlement in the Mississippi Territory, just north of Mobile, was already considerable, and transportation down the Alabama and Tombigbee rivers (which joined to form the Mobile in a tangle of channels just above 31°) had for some years caused international disputes. Finally, in the portion west of the Pearl, migration of Americans southward from Natchez had long since become important. In settlement, agriculture, and trade it was essentially polynational.

In November, 1803, a bill was introduced in Congress to put Louisiana under American law. One section annexed to the revenue district of Mississippi Territory "all navigable waters . . . lying within the United States which empty into the Gulf of Mexico east of the Mississippi River"—which was proper enough; another authorized the President to form a separate revenue district so defined as would have been objectionable, but this was not done. The President made Fort Stoddart the port of entry and clearance for the revenue district of "Mobile." This indicated no intent to control elsewhere than strictly at the American terminus, therefore attempted nothing improper, and satisfied the Spanish minister, Irujo.[56]

The representatives of France and Spain in Louisiana at first protested against transferring it, but ultimately did so without public protest, and without mention of West Florida.[57] The United States, in a similar acceptance of realities, did not demand West Florida or occupy it. But the claim had an unfortunate influence upon the country's foreign relations. Coupled with diplomatic efforts to gain East Florida, it remained a problem until 1819.

The entire Florida problem seems superficially simple, since the colonies obviously would ultimately be more valuable to the United States than to Spain. But the history of their acquisition is extremely complicated. For this there were various reasons. Jefferson's view that the mere intrusion of Americans into both Floridas would bring them into the Union would have been as true as it was simple—*if* the test could have been made apart from the complexities of European politics. These made governmental inaction by the United States impossible, and by Spain difficult; for although her hold on them was precarious because

56 Adams, *History of the U.S.*, II, 260–263; Gallatin, *Writings*, I, 182.
57 Robertson, *Louisiana*, II, 168 *et seq.*

Britain or France might seize them, they might also be traded to either for support if threatened by the United States. For two reasons they had no substantial values, each considered alone. Attitudes toward Louisiana and Florida had no effect upon the general policy of any country—excepting the United States. The former were, rather, determined by the latter, and changes of policy in adjustments between peace and war therefore resulted in great and repeated inconsistency in the lesser matter. For another reason, inconsistency in this was inevitable. The basis of a colony's valuation must have been either economic or military. Excepting some West Indian colonies, few had any estimative economic value. Military values shifted with changing political alliances. East Florida was indispensable to Spain while she could hope to exclude foreign ships from the Gulf of Mexico; losing that power, Louisiana retained some value in guarding New Spain. For these reasons colonies had long been pawns in international peace settlements. In 1762, for example, France offered Louisiana to Britain in order to save the Floridas to Spain.[58] Whatever the speculative value to Napoleon of Louisiana's economic development, it was outweighed by the military value to him of the price paid by the United States and prevention of the colony's seizure by Britain.[59] For similar reasons Britain had offered it to the United States in 1802 if the latter would acquiesce in its seizure.[60] Presidents Jefferson and Madison, the members of their cabinets, and their diplomatic agents abroad (who expressed their individual opinions with extraordinary freedom in negotiations) were divided in opinion respecting ethics, strategy, and the relative values of Louisiana and West Florida. These circumstances caused confusion—although countercircumstances made much of this harmless— and gave the Florida story its wearying detail. From the beginning of American negotiations for the purchase of Louisiana, utter disunity of opinion was constant respecting the relative values of Louisiana and the Floridas. When Robert Livingston, in Paris in 1802, believed that Spain had ceded to France all three colonies, he suggested to Joseph Bonaparte that France return Louisiana to Spain and give New Orleans with the Floridas to the United States to settle American spoliation claims.[61] Just before Louisiana was ceded to the United States, he

[58] Shepherd, "Cession of Louisiana," p. 449.
[59] He so declared to Barbé-Marbois, according to the latter's (in some respects discredited) *History of Louisiana*, pp. 263–264.
[60] Cox, *West Florida Controversy*, 121.
[61] *A.S.P., For. Rel.*, II, 525.

assured Talleyrand that the United States did not desire it; and advised Madison that if acquired, it be exchanged for the Floridas.[62] Yet the instructions from Secretary Madison appraised East Florida, West Florida, and Louisiana (virtually "the island of New Orleans") in the ratios of 1, 2, and 12.[63] James Monroe, however, two weeks after acquiring Louisiana, likewise advised Secretary Madison to exchange it for the Floridas.[64] Charles Pinckney, in Madrid, had made an offer to buy the Floridas and guarantee Spain's possessions west of the Mississippi.[65] Spain's officials in America were similarly divided in opinion. Irujo did not regard the retrocession of Louisiana as a loss to Spain; there was little commerce with it, its administration was expensive, it was too large to be militarily defensible. The Floridas, he thought, were more valuable for checking contraband in the Gulf and for war with the United States.[66] Spanish officials in Louisiana had variant opinions, but probably not after receiving from Wilkinson a memoir in which he advised them that Spain would do well to exchange the Floridas for everything west of the Mississippi and, in addition, assume the debt of the United States.[67] In 1805, after the problem of the Texas boundary had arisen, Spain twice suggested that the United States take both Floridas in exchange for part of Louisiana.[68]

It was stated by the Spanish governor at Natchez, Manuel Gayoso de Lemos, that most of the inhabitants of northern Louisiana in 1792, "from Baton Rouge to Illinois," were already Americans.[69] The inhabitants of what is now Louisiana were almost wholly French; August Lachaise, a longtime French resident, declared in 1793 that there were "not four" Spaniards, soldiers and sailors excepted, in the colony.[70] The portion of West Florida west of the Pearl River was the most favored in soil, and consequently in settlement. It has been estimated that there were perhaps 3,000 inhabitants near the Mississippi in 1774,

---

[62] May 18, 1803, ibid., p. 552, 553.

[63] Ibid, p. 544; Madison, Writings, VII, 28.

[64] May 18, 1803, Writings (Hamilton ed.), IV, 24.

[65] February 17, 1803, Cox, West Florida Controversy, p. 77.

[66] Robertson, Louisiana, II, 70.

[67] Ibid., pp. 325–347; I. J. Cox, "General Wilkinson and His Later Intrigues With the Spaniards," AHR, XIX, 798 n., also West Florida, p. 91.

[68] Ibid., pp. 123, 131.

[69] Robertson, Louisiana, I, 384; Houck, Spanish Regime, I, 410–412. The governor of Louisiana from 1791 to 1796 was the Baron de Carondelet; Manuel Gayoso de Lemos was governor of Natchez until he succeeded Carondelet.

[70] AHR, III, 496.

and that the number had perhaps doubled by 1779.[71] In 1783, the British peace treaty brought the American boundary in what is now southwestern Mississippi within thirty miles of Baton Rouge, and seventy-five from New Orleans, by air. That this boundary was not accepted by Spain until 1795, nor its survey to the Apalachicola River completed until 1799, made no difference as respected the intrusion of American settlers. In 1794 the first two government factories for conduct of Indian trade were established above and near the Florida border, in what became, in 1798, Mississippi Territory.[72] Before 1800, Americans predominated along the Mississippi and the mouths of its tributaries from St. Louis to the Florida border, and probably in the neighborhood of Baton Rouge. That district continued to grow most rapidly of all in the colony. In 1809 John Adair estimated that five-sixths of the inhabitants of the entire colony were west of the Pearl, and that nine-tenths of the latter were Americans. The Baton Rouge district had three times the population of Mobile and Pensacola combined.[73]

It was not in population alone that American encroachment was visible. From the first years of the colony, as has been pointed out, large land grants had been notable in its administration. Daniel Clark, long acting and then official consul of the United States in New Orleans, was prominent among the speculators, but certainly no more so than Spain's intendant, Morales. Such activities probably encouraged the idea that some of West Florida was part of Louisiana. Governor Claiborne of Louisiana put an end to Morales' activities, but Casa Calvo, the former Spanish governor (left to act as boundary commissioner), secured Claiborne's pledge that *he* would make none.[74] John Smith of Ohio and John Adair of Kentucky (senators of the United States until later forced to resign by their associations with Burr) were merely prominent among a host of American speculators, most of them settled in the colony. There were echoes of its land mania even in Paris.[75]

West Florida was decidedly one part of the West to which one could not attribute a general sober steadiness. It was not a slow, natural,

[71] C. Johnson, *British West Florida, 1763–1783* (New Haven, 1943), pp. 135–140, 146–148, 149, 153–154.

[72] O. B. Peake, *History of the United States Indian Factory System, 1795–1822* (Denver, 1954), p. 10 (map) and index.

[73] Cox, *West Florida Controversy*, pp. 28, 59, 151, 212, 316, 327, 580 (only one family in 1810 between the Pascagoula and Mobile), 582.

[74] Cox, *West Florida Controversy*, index *s.v.* "Morales."

[75] With British and Spanish speculators earlier involved in the XYZ affair; Cox, *West Florida Controversy*, pp. 73, 269.

native outgrowth of the seaboard colonies. Its first British governor, in a letter to the Board of Trade, declared it planned "to rise from the refuse of the Jails of great Citys, and the overflowing Scum of the Empire."[76] Army deserters and fugitives from justice moving between the colony and Louisiana˙ troubled General Gage as well as Governor Johnstone.[77] Later, after some years of troubles, Governor Claiborne wrote of its society that "a more heterogeneous mass of good and evil was never before met in the same extent of territory."[78] Others, if not Claiborne, included among the evil elements the "border ruffians" and filibusterers who resisted with violence Spanish rule and organized American pressure for the government's intervention.[79]

In the summer of 1804 what has been called an insurrection occurred in the Pearl River district. Two factors were doubtless of great background importance—one as a cause, the other in the timing, of the trouble. The former is, of course, the Americanization of the Baton Rouge area. The influence of land speculation in creating the situation out of which the immediate problems arose is plain. Spanish export taxes on the cotton exports of American settlers were doubtless also of influence in encouraging dissatisfaction. The timing of the disturbances was presumably set by the fact that war or peace between Spain and Great Britain was an open question during much of 1804. If Spain joined France, might not Great Britain seize the Floridas before the United States could seize at least West Florida as part of Louisiana? Such was the common fear that she would do so that the British and Spanish ministers in Washington (war between their countries began in the autumn) secured a declaration in London that Spain would not release West Florida, or otherwise weaken her control of the Gulf to the detriment of Spain or Great Britain.

John Smith obtained from Captain Grand Pré, the commandant at Baton Rouge, an order for the removal of members of the Kemper family (prominent for years in frontier unrest and disturbances of the peace) from land Smith claimed—that is, after some kind of a trial. After a local *alcalde* with Spanish militia drove the occupants off the land and into American territory, a small force returned, made captive

[76] C. N. Howard, *The British Development of West Florida, 1763–1769* (Berkeley, 1947).

[77] Carter, *Gage Correspondence*, I, 215–216.

[78] Cox, *West Florida Controversy*, p. 507.

[79] Some of these—notably the Kemper brothers and the Caller brothers (see Carter, *Terr. Papers*, V, index)—became local American officials.

several Spanish officials, and proclaimed the independence (August, 1804) of just what territory is unclear and unimportant.[80] But the prevailing state of opinion was indicated by the fact that on Grand Pré's call 150 volunteers swept Kemper's marauders out of the district. In 1805 the Kempers were seized in their home in American territory and delivered to the Spaniards, but captives and captors were retaken and delivered to American authorities. The territorial judge, Thomas Rodney, released the Spaniards and bound the Kempers to keep the peace.[81] There was correspondence between American authorities in New Orleans, Fort Adams, and Washington; between Governor Folch in Pensacola and officials in New Orleans and the Pearl River district; between the Spanish officials and their superior, the captain-general of Cuba; between the American and Spanish governments. It was a tempest in a teapot, which in some aspects seems ridiculous, but it was the quintessence of the old southwestern frontier, and was recorded as few small incidents ever could be.

The local authorities all lacked power, perhaps fortunately. Grand Pré offered to pardon the Kempers if they and their fellow marauders would leave West Florida. The United States sent no troops to New Orleans until after the crisis passed. When it did send them, and somewhat more than first was announced, this caused decided apprehension, but the attitude of the government was (at this time) in all respects correct.

In the long run it was trade, not international politics, that determined the fate of the Floridas. It was seen in the preceding chapter that the wars terminated in 1763 and 1783 caused great relaxations by Spain's officials in New Orleans of her traditional colonial system, which changes were in large part sanctioned in Madrid. In the relations between Spain and the United States, they were matters of mutual concern economically, but relatively inconsequential politically until France, in 1793, began the wars which ultimately led to the destruction of Spain's colonial empire. In 1791 Gardoqui (who had become the director of colonial commerce) had recommended the opening of Louisiana trade "with all friendly nations with which Spain had a treaty of com-

---

[80] The proclamation was attributed to Edmund Randolph of Pinckneyville, a partner of Daniel Clark. Grand Pré believed them to be responsible for the revolt because of their extensive interests in the Baton Rouge region. Cox, *West Florida Controversy*, pp. 155, 158.

[81] W. B. Hamilton (ed.), *Thomas Rodney, 1744–1811. Anglo-American Law on the Frontier* (Durham, 1953), pp. 77–78.

merce,"[82] and the United States had none. Whether the words of qualification were used conjunctively or disjunctively was not tested. However, a royal order of 1793 opened commerce with Louisiana to "all
friendly and allied nations," and the colonial officials treated this disjunctively. Under it Louisiana's economy was revolutionized.[83]

In October, 1798, they established the deposit, opened the river to
"neutrals" (that is, virtually, Americans), and ignored positive orders
to revoke this action, pleading that to do so would cause "utter ruin
or insurrection." This situation continued until the intendant (Morales)
prohibited all foreign trade and closed the deposit in October, 1802.[84]
The connection between this action and the negotiations between
France and Spain for the colony's acquisition by France were discussed
in the preceding chapter. The colony's subsequent commerce is of interest only so far as related to American trade with West Florida.

Three factors shaped the specific problems which arose in the latter
colony in the remaining years of Spanish rule: the rapid increase of
American settlement in the Mississippi Territory, with increasing need
of open commerce on the Mobile River, and the continuance of European wars which steadily lessened Spain's control of her colonial policy
and officials. The last factor was displayed through some six years in a
quarrel, after Spain lost Louisiana, between her longtime intendant of
that colony, Morales, and the longtime governor of West Florida, Vi-
zente Folch. Each claimed the powers of intendant in the latter province. Each issued orders contradicting or purportedly nullifying acts of
the other. Despite appeals to Madrid, and a decision by the captain-
general of Cuba upholding Morales, Folch maintained a margin of
predominance in commercial realities, and he was far more friendly
than Morales both to Americans and to the desire on both sides of the
border for liberalized trade across it.

In December, 1803, Daniel Clark (Junior) reported from New Orleans to Secretary Madison that Louisiana procured pitch, tar, timber,
lime, fish, "etc.," from West Florida, and sent in return to the inhabit-

---

[82] A. P. Whitaker, *Commercial Policy of Spain in the Floridas* (Deland,
1931), p. xlv. It is official regulation, from Madrid or locally, that is dealt
with in this volume. Some aspects of West Florida commerce are dealt with
in Cox, *West Florida Controversy*, pp. 169–186, 216–222.

[83] Whitaker, *Commercial Policy*, pp. xlv, xlvii–xlix, 241 (and n. 177), 205,
and Document XXVI; and "The Commerce of Louisiana and the Floridas at
the End of the Eighteenth Century," *AHR*, VIII (1928), 190–203.

[84] Whitaker, *Commercial Policy*, pp. xl–l, 244.

ants and garrisons of Baton Rouge, Mobile, and Pensacola "their supplies . . . They absolutely depend on us for their existence."[85] The first act of Morales earlier that month had been to prohibit such trade under the United States flag, and impose a 6 per cent duty on it under the Spanish flag.[86] Governor Folch had earlier abolished duties on such imports in Spanish or neutral vessels, and although this act was reversed by royal order in September, 1805, Morales himself renewed the abolition in March, 1806, and his action was confirmed by royal order in November.[87] Dates are of no importance except to illustrate the fact that what was law at any particular time was rarely certain—even as respects distinctly Spanish interests.

The same uncertainty was more certain to exist because of the different attitudes of the two Spanish officials toward American interests, when such were involved. When Morales (with concurrence of the Board of Treasury) had—as just stated—restored in March, 1806, Folch's abolition of customs dues on American products imported under Spanish flag, they had prudently opened the colony to commerce with *all* neutrals (which they knew meant, practically, the United States), and subject, "pending the . . . development of such trade," to no duties.

Trade on the Mobile River between the Tombigbee settlements of Mississippi Territory and Pensacola was of great importance to both parties. Governor Folch had given the Americans trading privileges in 1804 subject to duties on export and import, and Natchez had similar privileges.[88] Morales stopped the trade in 1806, Folch reopened it, and when their superior in Havana directed decision by the War Board (*Junta de Guerra*) in Pensacola, naturally it did nothing. When the Embargo Act cut off trade from New Orleans, the Treasury Board in Pensacola abolished duties on imports from the Tombigbee for the duration of the embargo, and offered a drawback of all duties paid at Mobile on any goods for the Tombigbee settlements that should come back to Mobile.[89] This was "to save the province . . . from starvation." The extension of the Embargo Act to inland waters (in March, 1809) greatly increased the colony's difficulties, already heightened by the French occupation of Spain.

[85] *AHR*, XXXIII, 356–358.
[86] Whitaker, *Commercial Policy*, p. liv.
[87] *Ibid.*, pp. lv, lvi, 215, 217, 219 (and n. 99).
[88] *Ibid.*, pp. lvii, 203, 245 (and n. 94).
[89] *Ibid.*, pp. lviii, lix.

The United States had no treaty rights in the Mobile. The concessions made by the local Spanish officials were probably as important and welcome to the Americans as the Spaniards. From the time Fort Stoddart was established in Mississippi Territory, the Spanish authorities had shown courtesies to the United States as respected passage of government ships and government supplies for the garrison. The United States had no treaty rights on the Mobile River, and such concessions as were made by the Spanish to the American settlers of Mississippi Territory were pure favors, no matter how helpful to the bestowers. However, the United States conferred no favors in return. Notably, it did not grant the Spaniards drawbacks of duties collected on goods imported at New Orleans (after it became American) when shipped out to Baton Rouge and Mobile; and Gallatin, to defend this practice, offered the explanation that the Treasury Department "consider[ed] territory in Spanish possession as Spanish" for revenue purposes no matter what the American political claims.[90]

The Embargo Act was an expression of exaggerated self-esteem, calculated to coerce European powers, and, as such, a failure. Its extension in March, 1809, to inland waters was offensive to immediate neighbors, and as respects West Florida it was not merely without gain but mutually harmful. The "insurrection" of 1804, which has been earlier referred to as illustrating the importance of American settlement and influence in the Baton Rouge area at that period, had, of course, some connection with the economic troubles of the colony, the weakness of control from Spain, and the quarrels between Folch and Morales just reviewed; and was also very important in connection with the "Burr conspiracy" discussed in the next chapter. President Jefferson's denunciations of Spanish policy in the colony in 1804 and 1805[91] were extremely biased, echoing warlike bluster among the Tombigbee borderers.[92] In the region of Baton Rouge there was another disturbance in December, 1808, somewhat similar to the earlier one.[93] The threat was to the Spanish government and the movement was led by Americans. A memorial was sent to the captain-general in Havana which hinted the need of "quieting the public mind." Public meetings were held to

---

[90] *Ibid.,* pp. lv, 217; *A.S.P., For. Rel.,* II, 675; Robertson, *Louisiana,* II, 188; Cox, *West Florida Controversy,* pp. 168–171.

[91] Messages of December, 1804 and 1805, Richardson, *Messages,* I.

[92] Cox, *West Florida Controversy,* pp. 169–170.

[93] *Ibid.,* pp. 314–324.

discuss its perturbation. "Roving bands" called for reorganization of the militia. As West Floridians, they protested the embargo as an ungenerous and unneighborly act; as Americans, they hinted, in a memorial to the captain-general in Havana, that "these people" (so singularly composed of diverse elements) might—if "affronted" (by a Spanish government unappreciative of their co-operation?), or if "opposed in [their] good dispositions"—turn to the United States.[94] Both the "insurrection" of 1804 and the "movement for independence" of 1808 have an artificial aura. The documents have a decidedly Spanish style, but Americans plainly led the demonstrations.

The events just considered—and the conditions of trade and American settlement from which they derived—were obviously such as would make diplomatic negotiations between the American and Spanish governments extremely difficult. For nearly twenty years they were unpleasant, fruitless, and in detail drearily monotonous. One reason for this was American insistence for many years upon the delusion that part of West Florida was acquired as part of Louisiana. Another was the increasing likelihood, as Napoleon's conquests spread and finally engulfed Spain and extinguished the Spanish monarchy, that either Britain or France might seize one or both of the colonies, that Spain might cede one or both to Britain, or that the United States might seize one or both. As already noted, the views of the President, members of his cabinet, leaders in Congress, and diplomatic representatives differed on all these matters, and the President was sometimes hesitant, sometimes inconsistent, in the resolutions he adopted.

In 1804 James Monroe was sent as minister extraordinary to Madrid, where Charles Pinckney seemed ineffective. Monroe's instructions were to perfect the supposed grant of West Florida to the Perdido as part of Louisiana. This would avoid recognition of later Spanish land grants in that area and permit discretion as respected British and later American claims. Further instructions were to settle disputes over the western bounds of Louisiana, and to offer $2 million for the rest of West Florida and East Florida. Before his departure, the Perdido line was made a *sine qua non,* and equally Spain's renunciation of "all" Texas.[95]

---

[94] *Ibid.,* pp. 314–324.

[95] January 11 and July 29, *A.S.P., For. Rel.,* II, 616, 628, 630. The instructions authorized a provision that there should be no settlement west of the Mississippi for *x* years. Cox, *West Florida Controversy,* pp. 102–138, covers this mission in great detail.

He reached Paris in October, 1804. While there, he joined John Armstrong, newly appointed minister to France, and Robert L. Livingston, the former minister, in pressing France to support the claim to the Perdido line. Nothing was secured beyond a suggestion that money given in Paris might secure a satisfactory settlement; however, a complete condemnation of the American boundary claim by Napoleon presumably preceded Monroe on the road to Spain.[96]

In Madrid, when he asked for a specification of Spain's "rights" in Louisiana (that is, specification of boundaries), Monroe received the reply that the original rights were those of France.[97] American puzzlement respecting a description entirely correct was justly treated as a joke in Paris. Pessimistic, Monroe took the extraordinary step of sending to Napoleon his entire correspondence with Cevallos.[98] Back came the comment: "Spain is right on every point of the controversy."[99] After Spain refused to confirm navigation privileges on the Mobile as rights, which her colonial officials had conceded as privileges, Cevallos renewed a suggestion that West Florida be ceded in exchange for an equivalent west of the Mississippi, to which Monroe replied with his final offer: that Spain cede both Floridas, and the United States accept the western Colorado River as the western boundary of Louisiana, some American spoliation claims to be renounced and others arbitrated.[100] The offer was declined. Surely the United States was a gainer by the impasse, although Monroe's mission was a failure (May, 1805).

Nevertheless, the failure was viewed with anxiety in Washington and likewise in the Southwest. With the exception of Gallatin, who regarded the American claims as unfair and certain to injure the country's prestige if insisted upon, and the Floridas not worth a war, the members of the cabinet, leading diplomatic representatives of the United States, and even the President exhibited a fractious bellicosity over Monroe's rebuff in Madrid.[101] Some were for seizing both West Florida and Texas, some—presumably convinced of the insubstantiality of the Per-

[96] Monroe, *Writings*, IV, 294; Adams, *History of the U.S.*, II, 310–314.

[97] *A.S.P., For. Rel.*, II, 644 *et seq.*, 653–657.

[98] Only a month earlier he had written to Armstrong (Cox, *West Florida Controversy*, p. 123): "The United States must go ahead and depend less on other nations."

[99] *Ibid.*, pp. 129–130; Adams, *History of the U.S.*, IV, 54–55.

[100] *A.S.P., For. Rel.*, II, 667; Cox, *West Florida Controversy*, pp. 123, 131, 134–135.

[101] H. Adams, *History*, III, Chap. 3.

dido claim—for seizing Texas only, which had long been the policy favored by John Armstrong, the American minister in Paris. Monroe adopted it after his failure in Madrid, and at least for a time so did Jefferson—perhaps only if allied with Britain or assured of her good will, but Britain's hardening policy against neutral carriers soon removed that possibility.[102] In the course of the year the American garrisons in New Orleans and Mississippi Territory and the Spanish in Pensacola were somewhat strengthened, though still remaining puny; Morales was forced by Governor Claiborne to leave New Orleans; and a few Spaniards seemingly dreamed that Kentuckians could still be detached from the Union and, with their aid, the Southwest be overrun.[103] On the other hand, President Jefferson contemplated offers of land bounties to volunteers who would settle strategic frontier points and give part-time military service.[104] By the end of the year, however, the policy of the government settled on renewed negotiation through France for purchase of both Floridas, somewhat relaxing claims respecting the boundaries of Texas if that should be necessary.[105] The French government, despite advice by its minister in Washington that it seize both Floridas and Cuba to thwart the United States, decided to aid the American commission.[106] Perhaps because of past experience, it was anticipated in Washington that part of any purchase price paid through France would never reach Spain, and Jefferson balked both at the necessary subservience and the expected bribe.[107] He sent to Congress in December an Annual Message which implied a strong and definite policy, possibly war; but also sent a secret message which reviewed relations with Spain since 1803 without stating any definite policy.[108] That is, in effect he left to Congress the burden of decision. A bill was introduced in the House of Representatives to increase army forces on the southern border, and to exchange American "claims" west of the Mississippi for Spanish "claims" east thereof. The confusion of American attitudes was further illustrated by the fact that although the House struck out the military provision, leaving acquisition of the Floridas

---

[102] Cox, *West Florida Controversy*, pp. 129, 227, 229.
[103] *Ibid.*, pp. 173–175.
[104] Jefferson, *Writings* (Ford ed.), VIII, 442.
[105] Adams, *History*, III, 101–102.
[106] Cox, *West Florida Controversy*, pp. 85–86.
[107] *Writings*, VIII, 397–402.
[108] Messages of December 3 and 6, Richardson, *Messages of the Presidents*, I, 384, 388.

the bill's sole purpose, it refused to substitute "east of the Perdido" for "east of the Mississippi."[109] Fear of war was greatly increased by the President's Annual Message, but soon lessened.

If Spain should refuse to "acknowledge and confirm to the United States, West Florida and cede to them forever the same and East Florida" (which would have invalidated Spanish land grants in West Florida after 1803), the American commissioners were empowered in their final instructions to accept the phraseology "Spain cedes and confirms forever to the United States East and West Florida."[110] It was also indicated that in order to retain "[part of] West Florida" and "obtain" East Florida, some concession could be made on the east boundary of Texas.

Talleyrand, in a report to Napoleon, pronounced the Perdido claim untenable. The American representatives, he said, should drop it with both Spain and France—otherwise, France should take "formal" action against it; also, the United States should deal directly with Spain. The interests of the United States in the Floridas he considered, however, far greater than Spain's; they might take the colonies by force, and Napoleon should consider whether it was wise to leave unsettled so dangerous a situation, perhaps favoring American interests in the Floridas, unless he wished them for France or for use in ulterior negotiations. It would seem that Napoleon disavowed such desires, and favored American sovereignty, for Talleyrand advised in a later report (Godoy having indicated a preference to leave all to Napoleon) that the United States should drop both the spoliation and West Florida claims, buy both Floridas, and settle the west boundary of Louisiana reasonably.[111] However, Spain desired no negotiations, leaving any action to France, and in the summer of 1806 Napoleon suspended negotiations.

Accounts of the negotiations have been cluttered with supposed plans of unofficial actors in the background hopeful of fees in American money or land for expediting the Florida sale, but there is no evidence that they in any manner affected the negotiations.[112]

War was again expected—indeed, it seemed virtually inevitable during much of 1806. In July the French minister informed Madison that neither Spain nor France recognized American claims in West Florida

[109] Cox, *West Florida Controversy*, pp. 234–235.
[110] *A.S.P., For. Rel.*, III, 539, 540.
[111] Cox, *West Florida Controversy*, pp. 249–251.
[112] *Ibid.*, pp. 246–248, 258–259.

and that interference with Spain's colonies would meet with their united resistance.[113] By that time the West was abuzz with rumors of Burr's supposed plans, involving a probable attack on Mexico. By the end of the year Wilkinson had ended that possibility, brought Burr to the verge of ruin, and had established (November 5) with the Spanish commander in the field a provisional eastern boundary of Texas which on that matter long proved satisfactory. But other causes for fear and threats soon appeared.

In 1807 the French occupied Spain; in 1808 Napoleon's brother became her king; in the same year the Embargo Act (of December, 1807) threatened West Florida with ruin when that colony, had it been generously provided with foodstuffs, might have asked occupation. Jefferson would not relax the Act, and thought that Spanish favors of navigation on the Mobile merely balanced her treaty rights on the Mississippi. In August, 1807, in Paris, Madison made a suggestion—by then amounting to a threat, in view of the French occupation of Spain —that both Floridas be seized if Britain become allied with Spain.[114] The Act of 1805 for purchase of West Florida would expire at the end of 1808. West of the Pearl River, there had been the "insurrection" of 1804 and the exhibition of vague disquiet in December, 1808. These manifestations of popular disquiet, together with the great growth of economic interdependence, justify an assumption that American occupation would have been less resented than British or French, but they do not justify an assumption that any foreign occupation was desired while hope of Spain's recovery of independence remained. No overt acts during the the disquieting months of the Burr "conspiracy" had revealed any desire for American annexation.

Jefferson had twice assured Spain that he would not use force to secure the Floridas. In October, 1808, the cabinet again agreed to a policy of waiting unless Great Britain should threaten occupation of the colonies.[115] Napoleon had already made known both in Paris and in Washington that he could not approve occupation, even under those circumstances, unless Spain consented.[116] But when Jefferson transmitted the cabinet resolution to Governor Claiborne of Louisiana, it was with authorization to repeat it to Spain's local officials, and Jefferson

[113] Cox, *West Florida Controversy*, p. 257.
[114] *Ibid.*, p. 277.
[115] October 22, Jefferson, *Writings* (Memorial ed.), XII, 186.
[116] Cox, *West Florida Controversy*, pp. 279, 280.

added: "We consider their interests and ours the same and that the object of both must be to exclude all European influence from this hemisphere."[117]

This implied a suggestion of annexation and asked the officials of West Florida to join in excluding all European powers, Spain included. Even before the Cabinet's decision, Jefferson, in a letter to Someruelos, the captain-general of Cuba, assured him that the United States would not even press the West Florida claim, would seize no other territory, and would resist any interference by any power in either Florida. However, when Wilkinson, who had delivered Jefferson's letter, went on from Havana to Pensacola (April, 1809) and to Louisiana, he urged upon the new secretary of war (Madison having become President) the immediate occupation of both Floridas. The secretary replied: "It is the continued wish and instruction of the President that no interference of any kind in the affairs and territories of Spain should take place, or be encouraged, or permitted, by any person or persons, whether civil or military belonging to or under the authority of the United States."[118]

Madison had Gallatin explain to the French minister, General Trudeau, that the President did not desire the Floridas, that the United States was not involved in popular meetings in West Florida, and that it would not take Cuba as a gift.[119] All this was presumably said as a pledge not to seize the colonies by force unless necessary in protection of American claims.

Napoleon's brother Joseph, as King of Spain, retained varying authority for five years while French, British, and Spanish armies fought for control of the country. Each suspected the policy of the others, and all suspected that of the United States respecting the Spanish colonies. Governor Folch, always an understanding official respecting American interests in the Floridas, had told Wilkinson that it was premature to divide Spain's colonies while she lived, but appeared willing, otherwise, to deliver the Floridas—as he later officially offered to do.[120] Wilkin-

---

[117] Jefferson, *Writings* (Memorial ed.), XII, 186.

[118] *Annals of Congress,* 11th Cong., 3rd Session, App., p. 1254; J. Wilkinson, *Memoirs of My Own Time* (2 vols., Philadelphia, 1816), II, 344–349, 357; Cox, *West Florida,* pp. 297, 299, 300; *Amer. Hist. Rev.,* XIX, pp. 811–812.

[119] Adams, *History,* V, 37, 38; Jefferson, *Writings* (Memorial ed.), XII, 240, 273, 277; Madison, *Writings,* VIII, 53; *A.S.P., For. Rel.,* II (May 1, 1809). Jefferson, of course, hoped that they would seek incorporation.

[120] *A.S.P., For. Rel.,* III, 398.

son's deviation from Jefferson's policy of patience was doubtless caused by assurances received in New Orleans that the Spanish-American conglomerate was ripe for revolt. The judgment was soon proved sound.

The demonstration, however, was again given by the population west of the Pearl.[121] Early in 1810, Governor Holmes of Mississippi Territory characterized the situation there as one of anarchy: the Spanish authorities inactive, volunteer militia ineffective, the inhabitants divided into nationalistic factions. Even earlier, a former associate of George Rogers Clark in French service, now become adjutant general of West Florida's militia, had offered to Madison his aid in annexing it. To Madison, this could only mean, at least officially, the occupation of what was already claimed by the United States as part of Louisiana. Governor Claiborne of Louisiana won the President's acceptance of this plan. The latter wanted, however, a declaration of independence and a petition for annexation, and he authorized an official of Claiborne's government to secure these habiliments of virtue. Petitions were then circulated; assemblies held of local *alcaldes* and syndics, officers of militia, and other prominent citizens; and agitation over defects of local government was employed to deprive the local Spanish commander, De Lassus, of everything except title and salary. Several "popular" conventions maneuvered the colony toward independence. One sought information of Madison's policy from Governor Holmes of Mississippi Territory, but Holmes had no instruction. Another asked for immediate annexation by him, and for a general amnesty for onetime Loyalists, army deserters, and fugitives from justice. Finally, an assembly took revolutionary action. The fort at Baton Rouge was occupied, and on September 26, 1810, independence was declared, a constitution adopted, and annexation again petitioned. Under government instructions of July, Holmes had been "diffusing impressions" favorable to annexation.[122] The President issued a proclamation (October 27) to justify intervention, and instructed Claiborne to take possession of the area as part of the Territory of Orleans, organize militia, establish courts, and use force against armed resistance, but not to attack the almost nonexistent places held passively by the Spaniards.[123] In November a territorial government was organized.

---

[121] Cox, *West Florida Controversy*, pp. 328–436; *Annals of Congress*, 11th Cong., 3d Session, App., pp. 1254 *et seq.*

[122] Of July 12 and 17, Cox, *West Florida Controversy*, pp. 332–333.

[123] *A.S.P., For. Rel.*, III, 396–397.

Eventual revolution had been certain for years. It immediately appeared, however, that there had been no interlocking of plans. Governor Skipwith of West Florida resented the form of the government's action. The revolutionists, he complained, had asked annexation as a state. They were now ordered to submit to armed force, their state ignored. They had wished to save the government from embarrassment by offering it a sound title based on accomplished revolution; but the President's proclamation once more reasserted the claim of cession in 1803. By appropriate salutes to the West Florida flag, by assurances that Floridians would never be returned to Spain by the friendly negotiations promised with that power, and by an amnesty to deserters and others, this internal dissidence was finally overcome.[124]

American occupation was not then extended beyond the Pearl. Much trouble arose in the Mobile district.[125] A temporary re-establishment there of Spain's navigation restrictions increased American anxiety to occupy it, and agitation for attacks upon the town was, for a time, at least countenanced by the American military officers. However, one of the federal judges, Harry Toulmin, with the support of sober citizens, compelled the cessation of hostilities and quiet was established by the beginning of 1811. In that year there were fruitless negotiations between Folch and the American government for the colony's surrender.[126] Finally, an act of Congress of February 12, 1813, provided for occupation of the area, which was completed by the end of June.[127] In West Florida itself, in Washington, and in Europe the action aroused resentments which only an honorable treaty with Spain could end.

There was no possibility of negotiations for such a treaty until after the Napoleonic wars. Meanwhile, a jealous rivalry arose between the Mississippi Territory and the Territory of Orleans (about to become the state of Louisiana) over the Baton Rouge area. After the creation of Louisiana (1812), its legislature approved an act of Congress (April 14, 1812) which divided the area west of Pearl River between that state and Mississippi Territory. There had probably never been any intent, or willingness, to make title to that portion of West Florida the subject of "friendly negotiation" with Spain.

[124] Cox, *West Florida Controversy*, pp. 432–436, 487–505.
[125] *Ibid.*, pp. 437–486.
[126] *Ibid.*, pp. 481, 509–510, 521–525; *A.S.P., For. Rel.*, III, 394–395.
[127] Originally of the "Floridas," but East Florida was later omitted. Mobile was occupied on April 15, 1813, and in June occupation was extended eastward to the Perdido.

After the Napoleonic wars, with wars for independence then long under way in Spain's South American colonies, negotiations for the purchase of the Floridas became possible on a basis of reason, and began in 1815.[128] The parties repeated old arguments, the Spaniards even asking for consideration of the old American proposal to exchange most or all of Louisiana for the Floridas.[129] Finally, in 1819, a Spanish minister was empowered to negotiate the sale of both Floridas. John Quincy Adams, secretary of state, again defended the claim of cession to the Perdido in 1803, but the words of cession employed in the treaty (approved by the French minister as intermediary) were that the Spanish sovereign ceded "all the territories which belong to him eastward of the Mississippi, known by the names of East and West Florida."[130] This successfully "covered"—that is, hid—the views of both disputants.

There is nothing in this Florida chapter of our history in which an American can take satisfaction—unless it be Spain's stubborn self-respect.

[128] Great Britain had protested American actions in West Florida. This matter was excluded from the British-American peace negotiations of 1815, when the British became convinced that it would merely delay peace without profit to them.

[129] Negotiations are in *A.S.P., For. Rel.*, V, 425 *et seq.*

[130] *Ibid.*, pp. 452 *et seq.*; Jefferson thought it superb, *Writings*, X, 132. *A.S.P., For. Rel.*, VI, 619–624; both parties had ratified (Spain first) by February 22, 1821.

CHAPTER 9

Burr's Conspiracy and Nationalism

THE acquisition of Louisiana at once greatly increased the Union's potential power and gradually facilitated its political isolation. As respected the attainment of self-consciousness and self-sufficiency, the acquisition was also of immense importance. Nevertheless, the West, being only half American, was long beyond satisfactory American control, and the growth of the Union in resources and power did not greatly lessen the dangers of the situation. The Embargo Acts proved that the United States could not isolate itself commercially. The Burr "conspiracy" presented the question whether the West was truly and self-consciously a part of the Union.

The Territory of Orleans (the present state of Louisiana) was given what many members of Congress denounced as a military government —and certainly one far removed from a democratic one; but that was because of doubts concerning the "fitness" of its inhabitants for English institutions. It is important for present purposes to note that New Orleans, for this and other reasons, was seething with discontent.[1] The fitness of the French, Spanish, and American inhabitants of upper Louisiana (Missouri) for self-government was wholly problematical. Jefferson deliberately planned a military government for it, and for that reason appointed General Wilkinson to supervise its organization and report upon the feasibility of Jefferson's plans for the region's future.

In a message to Congress in January, 1803, Jefferson proposed the

[1] Carter, *Terr. Papers*, IX, 262–265, 309, 348.

exploration of Upper Louisiana. For twenty years he had been gathering information of the region, and had more than once proposed its exploration. His present suggestion was the germ of the great expedition of Lewis and Clark.[2] Two other expeditions, sent out by Wilkinson as governor of the District of Louisiana, to Santa Fe and to the headwaters of the Mississippi, were geographical in purpose. The former (Pike's, 1806) had also, to be sure, military importance in case of war with Spain.[3] Other objects were to lay the basis for resettlement of the eastern Indians, as already seen, to extend the system of Indian trading houses begun in 1795, and to ascertain how many settlers were removable from territory north of the Territory of Orleans.

This would delay performance of, but not violate, the promise exacted by France in the treaty ceding Louisiana. However, as respected that, although the new territory was a part of the United States in a geographical sense, could it constitutionally become a part of the Union of federal states?

Jefferson drafted amendments of the Constitution, assuming their necessity, to overcome that and other difficulties. The problems presented were debated in the Senate with the fervor and acumen which they merited.[4] In the end, however, the government proceeded without changes in the Constitution.

The original plan for a purely military government of Upper Louisiana was altered; the pre-existing Spanish laws were established as a basis for its government. Although modifiable by the officers of the Indiana Territory (sent briefly to St. Louis for the purpose), there was no organic connection between the two territories. Wilkinson was appointed governor of the Territory in March, 1805.[5] To those who have believed in a Burr-Wilkinson conspiracy it has doubtless seemed significant that Senator Jonathan Dayton, a friend of Burr who was later arrested for complicity in the latter's supposed unlawful plans, but not

[2] Richardson, *Messages*, 1, 353; Jefferson, *Writings* (Ford ed.), II, 92–93; VII, 192–202.

[3] Like all other events of the time in the West, this has been generally treated as related to the Burr conspiracy. It had nothing to do with it. Amer. Philosophical Society, *Proceedings*, XCI (1947), 447–456.

[4] *Ill. Hist. Coll.*, XXV, lvi (and n.) *et seq.*, clxviii *et seq.* The debate is reproduced in part in E. S. Brown, *Constitutional History of the Louisiana Purchase* (Berkeley, 1920), pp. 121–127.

[5] Act of March 26, 1804, *U.S. Statutes at Large; Ill. Hist. Coll.*, XXI, cv, n. 3; "Messages and Letters of William Henry Harrison," *Ind. Hist. Coll.*, VII, I, 170–171.

tried, was one of those who denied any authority in the Constitution to legislate for Upper Louisiana. Said he: "That Country is a purchased territory and we may govern it as a conquered one. A military government is the best and the only government you can prudently establish. . . . I hope we shall prevent the settlement of Upper Louisiana, not only for the present, but forever. If that country is settled, the people will separate from us—they will form a new empire—and become our enemies."[6] A great land speculator, Dayton doubtless knew that Senator John Smith, who was also one (and another confidant of Burr), was right in declaring that no law and no government could long *prevent* settlement. Temporary military government, however, was both inevitable and highly desirable, for undoubtedly it was planned by Jefferson and Wilkinson (who was the commanding officer of the army) to attack Mexico in case of war with Spain—which from 1804 through 1806 seemed highly probable. In January, 1806, the latter wrote to a confidant that he had "reserved those places"—the Santa Fe region—"for [his] own triumphal entry." There is no reason to doubt that, and good reason to surmise that it was for such purposes that he and Burr (as one-time fellow officers, and both then hoping for official appointments in the West) were studying Spanish maps in the winter of 1804–5, as was Wilkinson's manifest duty both for military and civilian reasons, and certainly entirely proper as respects Burr. For years Jefferson, too, had been puzzling over trans-Mississippi geography.

The supposed Burr conspiracy has received an attention which—aside from what it reveals of the West, the conspiracy's setting—has greatly exceeded its importance.[7] That exceptional aspect was unnoticed

---

[6] Brown, *Louisiana Purchase,* p. 123.

[7] A complete bibliography would be immense. McCaleb's book, *The Aaron Burr Conspiracy* (New York, 1903), initiated (largely in vain) a critical attitude toward supposed western disloyalty, but assumed a conspiracy. Abernethy, in *The Burr Conspiracy* (New York, 1954), is exhaustive in his survey of materials, but preserves the old traditions respecting the conspiracy without clarification as respects its nature or parties. He agrees that the "conspiracy" is now generally regarded "as a minor incident in American history. As far as actual results are concerned, that, he says, "is a correct view of the affair, but its potentialities were so portentous that . . . next to the Confederate War it posed the greatest threat of dismemberment which the Union has ever faced." *Ibid.,* p. 274. The words "potentialities" and "posed" assume an actual conspiracy. If an actual conspiracy threatened disunion, Wilkinson precluded disunion, and should receive credit, but receives none from Abernethy. Cox has written that "the Burr Conspiracy was destined to exert an influence on American frontier problems [upon writing about those problems] out of all proportion to the real peril alleged." *West Florida,* p. 187.

until stressed by one student sixty years ago, but even then not as an exception, for he believed in the conspiracy—*some* conspiracy. For that reason, and because no conspiracy whatever can be proved, the story must be stated with sufficient fullness to make clear both the causes for misjudging it and its true importance.

Before narrating the acts of Burr and Wilkinson, their significance can be clarified by stating that there were two offenses of which Burr ultimately was accused. One was treason, which the Constitution defines as consisting "only in levying war" against the United States, or "giving . . . aid and comfort" to its enemies (that is, during war); and for conviction of treason it requires "the testimony of two witnesses to the same overt act."[8] That is, treason can be proved only by proof of one or more overt acts, each proved by at least two witnesses. The other offense was the statutory misdemeanor of an act of war against a power with which the United States was officially at peace. Peace with Spain, though precarious, was unbroken throughout the period of Burr's western activities. The misdemeanor was therefore a possibility. Whether treason could exist if acts of war against Spain were coupled with an intent to occupy New Orleans and overthrow the federal government therein was a question not presented by the facts.

The very broad possibilities of guilt or innocence covered by Burr's actions have been briefly stated as follows: "The probable foreclosure of Burr's future political preferment in the United States, at least in the eastern part, induced him to turn his thoughts to the West, where he might gain a seat in Congress as a representative of one of the western states or territories; or become the leader of a new nation to be formed out of the western states or the Spanish territories; or at least lead a party to where there was plenty of cheap land upon which to found a settlement."[9] This last possibility refers to Burr's acquisition of an equity (by a small payment down to two American members of the Mexican Association in New Orleans) in a great tract of land on the Washita River in Arkansas, a portion of a grant originally made to a Baron Bastrop by a colonial official, but never validated by the Crown.[10]

That both Burr and Wilkinson had western plans—one should per-

[8] Art. III, Sec. 3, Para. 1.

[9] C. E. Carter, "The Burr-Wilkinson Intrigue in St. Louis," Mo. Hist. Soc., *Bulletin* (1954), 447.

[10] Carter, *Terr. Papers*, IX, 294–295, 479–480; *A.S.P., Pub. Lands*, III, 53–54; J. Q. Mitchell and R. D. Calhoun, "The Maison Rouge and Bastrop Spanish Land Grants," *La. Hist. Qy.*, III (1957), 289–462.

haps say hopes—is clear. An army officer in Missouri (Major Bruff) of whose testimony much has always been made, patriotic and honest but clearly lacking in logical sense, reported that Wilkinson questioned him about the political attitudes of the French population (as was obviously wise), praised military government for that territory, declared that Jefferson planned to depopulate it, hinted at an expedition against Santa Fe, and breathed vaguely of a grand scheme to make the fortunes of himself and others.[11] It is also true that one of the territorial judges, Rufus Easton, a young protégé of Burr, stated that Wilkinson "often talked in a dark, mysterious manner about a western empire," and that Burr made the witness "proposals which . . . astonished and confounded him so that he was struck dumb."[12] Doubtless Wilkinson did talk mysteriously—of necessity in this case; but there could be an "empire" won without any emperor. Wilkinson's inquiries respecting the capacity of his subordinates to lead a military expedition were also proper, and necessary. There was no war, no campaign against Santa Fe; dreams of rank or wealth remained dreams. What is their pertinence as evidence of a Burr-Wilkinson conspiracy to levy war against the United States or attack a friendly power?[13]

Very soon after the expiration of his term as Vice-President, Burr had started for the West. On his way down the Ohio he met Senators John Smith and Jonathan Dayton, spent some days with Wilkinson at Fort Massac, then proceeded to New Orleans, where he hobnobbed with the members of the Mexican Association, returning in September to St. Louis for a week's visit and from there to the East. In the following year he started westward in August; visited Herman Blennerhassett (who was to lend him money) on his island in the Ohio; again met John Smith and also Gardoqui's old western agent, John Brown of Kentucky, now one of her senators; and visited all of her larger towns. During this time he secured some suitable river boats, arranged for others, procured some recruits and also agricultural implements, and

---

[11] *A.S.P., Misc.*, I, 571 *et seq.*

[12] *Ibid.*, p. 573; *Ill. Hist. Coll.*, XXI, cclxxvii, n. 83. Politics plainly appears in Easton's attitude.

[13] The facts that Burr sought the governorship of the Territory of Orleans, that his stepson was made a judge there, and that his brother-in-law was made secretary of the District of Louisiana are primarily evidence that territorial appointments were politically valuable, and Burr still politically influential. But such appointments could have no other significance without proof of a sinister conspiracy.

contracted for large supplies of flour and other supplies (some more needed on the Washita, clearly, than in New Orleans).

If there were any plans of Burr and Wilkinson respecting the Mississippi valley, action was necessarily left to Burr. Whether Wilkinson was in any way actually involved in them will be considered later. As for Burr's acts, it is obvious that had he intended merely to settle the Bastrop grant, it could have been done without arousing comment. If, on the other hand, he planned to seek a new political career in the West, he needed to do more. Some startling stroke was necessary to gain political support. It seems quite clear that Burr contemplated nothing except honors to be won in war with Spain for Mexico or Florida. Andrew Jackson wrote that Burr, in talking (during two visits) with him, "always held out the idea of settling Washita, unless a war with Spain; in that event . . . an appointment [in the army]; and if he did [secure that] he would revolutionize Mexico."[14] Most of the rumors and irresponsible talk later presented against Wilkinson in congressional reports are consistent with that same intent.

However, some policy on which to organize a following was needed by Burr while awaiting war. That it must be one respecting the West is obvious, and circumstances selected West Florida, since the President was claiming part of it as already ceded to the United States. An insurrection in its western portion had just shown that its population was divided in opinion between maintaining independence and seeking annexation by the United States. Burr's advisers, Senators Smith and Adair, had long been investing in its lands. It was in fact the chief political topic of the day. Moreover, at least some Spanish officials then dreamed that, in case of war with the United States, they could seduce Kentuckians and with their aid divide the West.

War between Britain and Spain began in the autumn of 1804. Before Burr returned to Washington in 1805, Dayton (for Burr) asked the English minister in Washington, Merry, for the aid of British ships in support of "a projected revolt . . . [in] West Florida." Merry and the British government believed that Burr wanted money. Yrujo was asked for money, but his government would not consider even a fourth of the sum requested, although the request was accompanied by a warning that Britain might give aid first. Yrujo was also told that Burr planned "to seize the Floridas, revolutionize the western states, and possibly in-

[14] Quoted by McCaleb, *Burr*, p. 260, from J. Parton, *The Life and Times of Aaron Burr* (15th ed., New York, 1859).

vade Mexico." Naturally, he sometimes feared the last (though he considered it "ridiculous") and sometimes believed the second.[15] The curious thing is that we know no more today—because neither Wilkinson nor Burr knew. When the former moved down the Mississippi in the late summer of 1806, he did not know whether there would be war, nor whether in case of war he should attack Spain through West Florida or through Texas.[16] And Burr—likewise having no complete plan controlled by himself—was really without any plan.

Under these conditions the supposed conspiracy grew by itself in the Mississippi valley. Even before Burr met Wilkinson at Fort Massac in the spring of 1805, Kentucky newspapers published items which aroused suspicions in Major Bruff of the St. Louis forces by alluding, as he said, "to the old plan to form a separate government west of the Allegany . . . [ascribing] it to General Wilkinson, and doubting whether that scheme had been abandoned."[17] This publication presumably resulted from Burr's meeting with Smith and Dayton at Cincinnati on his way to Fort Massac to see Wilkinson. Dayton, returning to the East, then began in Washington the feelers above referred to. A vast excitement spread through the Mississippi valley. Newspaper comment had begun in Philadelphia and Richmond when Burr had barely left New Orleans in 1805, and wild rumors were circulating in that city by the time he had left St. Louis.[18] Early in 1806 the United States Attorney for Kentucky (Joseph H. Daveiss) sent to President Jefferson a list of persons whom he suspected of sympathizing with plans for independence of the western country. The old controversy over the Spanish conspiracy which had raged before the end of the century was by then raging again in Kentucky, and Daveiss' list (which, ridiculously, included William Henry Harrison and Henry Clay) was essentially part of that local controversy. The President sensibly ignored it.[19] What a "conspiracy"!

[15] McCaleb, *Burr*, pp. 54–58, 65, 67, 69, 93; I. J. Cox, *The West Florida Controversy, 1763–1783* (Baltimore, 1912), pp. 185–190. McCaleb (p. viii) thought money was Burr's objective, for an attack on Mexico. In 1806 Burr was still assuring Merry that the Louisianians wanted independence under Great Britain, so much so that Burr anticipated a bloodless revolution, the American garrison being too weak to resist, "should it not, as he had good reason to believe enlist with him."

[16] J. Wilkinson, *Memoirs of My Own Time* (3 vols., Philadelphia, 1816), App. LX.

[17] *A.S.P., Misc.*, I, 57.

[18] Abernethy, *Burr*, pp. 32–35.

[19] *Ibid.*, pp. 91–95; Jefferson, *Writings* (Ford ed.) VIII, 467.

Not only the people of the West but those of the East, the government in Washington, and the ministers of foreign powers (with early invitations) were watching its production.

An attack on Mexico was possible so long as war between the United States and Spain was possible. At various times in 1806 both Burr and Wilkinson expressed to confidants a belief that there would be no war. Only once and very briefly did Wilkinson, just before his success in preventing it was complete, believe war inevitable—and seemingly welcome it.[20] Nevertheless, a threat of war was present on the Texas border throughout 1806 up to late October. In March the President called the danger to the attention of Congress. Wilkinson had barely been confirmed as governor of the District of Louisiana (March, 1806) when his transfer to New Orleans was ordered. Late in 1805 the Spanish had occupied a post (Bayou Pierre) east of the Sabine, had withdrawn under protest, then reoccupied it in July, 1806. After receiving his transfer orders in June, Wilkinson tarried in Missouri for three months, then moved slowly down the Mississippi, reaching Natchitoches on September 22.[21] While tarrying in St. Louis he made pacific overtures (which were not received, however) to the Captain-General of the Interior Provinces, Salcedo, whose headquarters were at Chihuahua. He also ordered his subordinate at Natchitoches to avoid hostilities, although both had orders from Washington to drive the Spaniards back. Had he *wished* war, therefore, he could safely have had it, notwithstanding the fact that Governor Claiborne, at New Orleans, had already been assured by the Spaniards that they would occupy no posts in the disputed area pending negotiations. Salcedo had already given orders to the officer in occupation of Bayou Pierre to leave the disputed area and not attack the Americans if they entered it. Wilkinson suggested that the territory between the Sabine and Arroyo Hondo (about seventeen miles west of Natchitoches) be made a neutral zone, at the same time informing the Spaniards of Burr's projects. On November 5 the agreement was made at Wilkinson's camp, and was observed until all disputes with Spain were definitely settled by the treaty of 1819.[22]

[20] *Ibid.*, pp. 37, 40, 41, 44, 46, 50, 55, 143.

[21] Governor Harrison of the Indiana Territory, with three judges of its court, was in St. Louis until December, 1804, drafting basic laws for the District of Louisiana and holding a court therein. This, therefore, did not enter into justifications for Wilkinson's delay. Citations in *Ill. Hist. Coll.*, XXI, cv (n. 1), cxcix, xxiii.

[22] Documents relating to the territorial dispute are in *A.S.P., For. Rel.*, II,

With war between Spain and the United States eliminated as a possibility, Burr—if he contemplated any action under those circumstances —had none left save invasion of Florida or occupation of New Orleans (peacefully or forcibly) as a base from which to attack Mexico. The latter could have been considered only by a bewildered mind.[23] New Orleans had a population of something over a thousand whites, and there is no reason to believe that Burr could have enrolled more than a very few men, as was the case in Kentucky.[24] There is no evidence that any substantial aid in money and shipping would have been contributed by the Mexican Association. Andrew Jackson had warned Governor Claiborne in November in the strongest terms to prepare defenses against internal enemies, and Claiborne issued a proclamation (a month later) against persons associated to overthrow the possessions of Spain.[25] Wilkinson then made Burr's supposed plans hopeless by assuming the necessity of martial law—which Claiborne refused to proclaim—and by virtually establishing it in defiance of the courts. Hundreds of soldiers were brought from Natchitoches and Mississippi Territory. Six associates of Burr were arrested and held in defiance of writs of habeas corpus, and five were shipped to the East. The legislature refused to suspend the writ, but all but one of the cases of its disregard had preceded this action. To Governor Folch of West Florida, and to Jefferson, Wilkinson reported Burr's forces in thousands, up to fifty times the true number, Burr's insignificant and harmless band, the size of which he knew almost exactly. He described the threat, to Jefferson, as "a deep, dark, and dangerous conspiracy" of Burr—with whom? (With Senators Dayton, Smith, and Adair, the writer believes, if with anyone). It was a histrionic but masterful performance, full of the martial blare and color needed for the moment and the place. The Presi-

---

803 *et seq.* Assuming, seemingly, that Wilkinson's border negotiations were manifestly unpatriotic, Abernethy reprints them, *Burr*, pp. 47–53, 138–155. Jefferson's message of December 2, 1806, relates to the border settlement. Richardson, *Messages*, I, 405.

23 Abernethy, *Burr*, p. 60.

24 To the governor of West Florida and in scaring the citizens of New Orleans, Wilkinson put the number in thousands. Abernethy, *Burr*, pp. 175, 127. To the viceroy of Mexico, he put it on November 17 at 129 (*AHR*, IX, 534); that is, told the exact facts, thus proving, at least, that the money for which he later asked was not for ending the danger of attack by Burr.

25 *A.S.P., Misc.*, I, 563 (November 12); Carter (ed.), *Terr. Papers*, Vol. IX, contains the official record in detail.

dent credited the defeat of what he believed to be Burr's plans to the judgment "of the commander in chief in promptly arranging the difficulties . . . on the Sabine, repairing to meet those arising on the Mississippi, and dissipating before their explosion plots engendering there."[26] To conspiracy believers this was Wilkinson's "betrayal" of Burr.

The passage of statutes in Kentucky in November, 1806, and in Ohio in December, aimed at Burr's activities, and two attempts in Kentucky to secure his indictment, followed by the seizure of additional boats on the day set for their delivery to him, caused the abandonment of Blennerhassett's Island in the night of December 10–11 by all of Burr's recruits there gathered. This party reached the Mississippi with nine boats and about one hundred men and boys, horses, agricultural implements, provisions, some lead, and personal arms. Before the end of the month President Jefferson's proclamation against the allegedly unlawful enterprise presaged its collapse. On January 6, 1807, Burr reached Mississippi Territory. He assured Governor Meade that his destination was the Washita lands—which, by then, he very likely hoped it to be. An indictment was sought (at Washington, the seat of territorial government), but the grand jury found no bill and was discharged. When Burr was nevertheless still held, improperly, under his recognizance, he finally fled (probably toward West Florida), only to be recognized and arrested, returned, and sent on to Richmond for trial.

Tried there before Chief Justice Marshall, sitting with the circuit judge, on an indictment for treason, he was held not guilty.[27] In the indictment of Burr the act of treason was charged to have been committed at a certain time on Blennerhassett's Island. The Chief Justice ruled that the war referred to in the Constitution's definition of treason is actual war ("an act of public notoriety," "a visible transaction, and

[26] *A.S.P., Misc.,* I; Carter, *Terr. Papers,* IX, 172–174, 489, 618, 660–661, 683–684, 686, 688–689; Richardson, *Messages,* I, 429.

[27] The Burr trials were reported by D. Robertson, *Reports of the Trials of Aaron Burr* (2 vols., Philadelphia, 1808). J. J. Coombs presents the trials with comment on subsequent legal precedents, useful to one interested in the law's development rather than in Burr. Documents remitted by Jefferson to Congress at various times are in *A.S.P., Misc.,* I, 468–645, and in *Annals of Congress,* 9th Congress, 2nd Session, pp. 1008–1019; 10th Congress, 1st Session, Part I, 385–778. The material in the *A.S.P.* and *Annals* is not at all in the order of the trial, and contains only a little of the trial proceedings—notably Wilkinson's testimony—*A.S.P., Misc.,* I, 539–556, with documents therein referred to, pp. 557–567. See also R. B. Morris, *Fair Trial* (New York, 1953).

numbers must witness it"), not merely a planned and prospective war; that Burr must therefore have done some overt act essential to the prosecution of an actual war at the time and place stated; and, Burr having actually been far away from the island, that he could not be held to have been constructively present if united with those on the island merely through a conspiracy to make war.[28] After the prosecution presented all witnesses who could testify of direct knowledge respecting acts and conditions on the island, further evidence was excluded. The Chief Justice then charging that no act of war had been proved by even one witness, the jury gave a verdict of not guilty (September 15, 1807). Burr was next tried on the charge of high misdemeanor, and more than fifty witnesses were heard. After allowing much testimony that was technically inadmissible, the defense objecting to more, Marshall ruled that legal testimony must tend to show that the defendant performed some act specifically charged in the indictment, or that the expedition was military or was directed against Spanish dominions. Thereupon the prosecution abandoned the case (a nol-pros being sought but not permitted), and a verdict of not guilty was given.[29]

It was said at the outset that the importance of the conspiracy was long greatly exaggerated. It is still greatly exaggerated, save in one respect which is important but generally ignored. Two obstacles confront one who attempts to decide what actually occurred.

The first is that the sources respecting the actions of the two chief parties are of the poorest quality—a few ciphered letters that are suspect as to purpose,[30] and a vast mass of common talk or gossip. Much of this was collected by John Graham, a competent person who followed Burr around in the West for Jefferson, under instructions which went beyond the law for the collection of evidence of treasonable acts.[31] When this failed to prove actual war (despite ample time later to gather proof of it, if it existed), the President complained of "Mar-

[28] Moreover, even if the contrary were true, previous conviction of one on the island for commission of an overt act of war would have been indispensable for conviction of him who procured or advised its commission. If the actor were not guilty, the procurer could not be.

[29] Robertson, *Trials of Burr*.

[30] *A.S.P., Misc.,* I.

[31] Graham testified that his instructions were "to consider the moving down the Ohio as a violation of the law," *A.S.P., Misc.,* I, 528–532. Irujo also sent agents to gather information, but they seem to have realized (Abernethy, *Burr,* p. 77) that all they collected was rumors.

shall's tricks to force trials before it is possible to collect the evidence."[32] And when Burr had been cleared of all charges, Jefferson insisted that still more "testimony" be collected and recorded. This explains only partially why various committees in Congress made additional compilations of testimony. Some of these were compiled by persons who believed Wilkinson to have been the real traitor and submitted the compiled evidence to the President (without conclusions of their own) for his action. The evidence in these reports was not submitted to the law's tests of relevance and truth. Congress, on the other hand, ignored Jefferson's request that it decide, as respected Burr, whether "the defect" of his escape was "in the evidence of guilt, or in the law, or in the application of it."[33] He wished to attack the judiciary through Congress. The committees sought to embarrass him politically for protecting Wilkinson—who, at his own request, successfully met the test of a court-martial.

The second obstacle is that although history is here concerned with alleged conspiracy to commit treason or violate a statute—that is, with purely legal matters—historians, predominantly, have not treated them as such. The true facts in a legal case are necessarily to be ascertained by law, and are necessarily the historical facts *within the field of law,* such as that here involved. Jefferson realized this as a lawyer, but as an emotional human (and politician) it caused him to make rancorous comments on Marshall. The view, still more or less accepted by historians, that the case before Chief Justice Marshall was not decided "on its merits" means that the protection given by legal rules to the defendant in a court of law may be disregarded in establishing "historical" truth.[34] It presumably arises from a belief that rejected evi-

[32] April 20, 1807, *Writings* (Ford ed.), IX, 42; See McCaleb, *Burr,* pp. 310–312. On April 1, Marshall had held that the failure to prove war made it impossible for him to commit Burr for trial on a charge of treason. He was indicted by a jury.

[33] The verdict of not guilty of treason was rendered on September 15. On September 4, Jefferson wrote that the object was "not only to clear Burr, but to prevent the evidence from ever going before the world. But this . . . must not take place. It is . . . indispensable that not a single witness be paid or permitted to depart until his testimony has been committed to writing. . . . These whole proceedings will be laid before Congress that they may decide whether the defect has been in the evidence of guilt, or in the law, or in the application of it." *Writings* (Memorial ed.), XI, pp. 187–191.

[34] "So sensational was the trial—though it was not decided on the merits of the case—that it has tended to overshadow the conspiracy itself . . . even

dence disclosed a "moral" guilt that should predominate in "history" over legal facts in a legal problem. In using the great collection of testimony, it is essential to eliminate, particularly, hearsay—of which there are abundant and gross examples.[35]

After Burr was found not guilty of either treason or misdemeanor by the Circuit Court at Richmond, a motion was made to commit him for trial in Ohio. In support of this, the government was allowed to introduce almost any evidence it wished, and in any order, including all that Wilkinson had to offer. Marshall held him on the charge of statutory misdemeanor, but again refused to do so as respected treason, saying: "There is not only a failure to prove that such a design [to dismember the Union] was communicated to or undertaken by the men who were assembled at the mouth of the Cumberland [where Burr had joined the men who left Blennerhassett's Island on December 10], but the . . . United States have adduced several witnesses belonging to that assemblage who concur in declaring that they heard nothing, that they suspected nothing hostile to the United States."[36]

The government considered the indictment of Wilkinson, but solely for misprision of Burr's assumed treason—which the Court pronounced nonexistent. To the government lawyers the evidence suggested no

---

historians . . . have frequently seen Burr as a shining example of injured innocence." Abernethy, *Burr,* p. 234.

[35] Carter, assuming *some* intrigue, has arranged in an article on "The Burr-Wilkinson Intrigue in St. Louis," Mo. Hist. Soc., *Bulletin* (1954), pp. 448–464, the facts respecting its St. Louis incidence. Specific evidence cited by him (pp. 458–459) and by Abernethy (*Burr,* p. 24) is that A, being in Natchez, was told by B, who came from St. Louis, that in St. Louis he was told by X (whom he refused to name) that Y, an "agent" of Burr (unnamed, but assumed to be Colonel de Pestre, "Burr's chief of staff" and "sent" by him), had unsuccessfully attempted to induce "prominent" persons to engage in a revolutionary conspiracy, and that C, offered a commission, "attempted" to burn it. If no intrigue between Burr and Wilkinson is assumed, the question becomes whether such evidence as the above should be disregarded in seeking the truth. The mere statements of fact, even more so the assumptions, manifestly do not prove that Burr had a military staff, that de Pestre was its chief, had commissions, and so on—although vast sums of money are lost yearly by persons who believe a man is who and does what he says he is and does. There is no commission extant, no oath taken or record written by C. Naturally, one of Wilkinson's confidants in Missouri gave him this story, and he used it (outside the law) in destroying Burr (Abernethy, *Burr,* p. 158).

[36] *A.S.P., Misc.,* I, 645. Marshall committed them for trial on the charge of misdemeanor, but at the time set for trial the defendants did not appear and no further action was taken.

wrongful compact or relationship between Wilkinson and Burr. Historians have simply assumed a conspiracy, but without definite commitment on objectives. "Conspiracy" has been merely a title for the narrative of events. Some additional consideration is therefore necessary of the events and of the actions of the parties already narrated, within which, if it existed, some conspiracy was concealed. They require no addition. In different accounts of the "conspiracy" details are merely rearranged, emphasis shifted, or irrelevant bits of gossip added.

War with Spain was expected by Jefferson and the Cabinet much of the time from 1804 to 1807. The Vice-President and the head of the army, fellow soldiers in the Revolution and both hoping for employment in the West (Burr in Louisiana), studied western geography together in the winter of 1804–5, and doubtless each encouraged the hopes of the other. Doubtless, also, each appraised the other. The evidence seems to show that they had wholly independent plans, each to be a part of war with Spain, and that neither contemplated action (excepting a subordinate phase of Wilkinson's plans) if peace continued. Quite probably Wilkinson gave Burr reason to hope for aid in securing a military appointment, and quite probably without intent to give aid, for his own ambition would have been for a solo performance. From the early summer onward, his letters to the Secretary of War emphasized a campaign against the Interior Provinces (of New Spain) led by himself.[37]

Immense confusion obscures the views of those who assume *some* unlawful conspiracy between Burr and Wilkinson. Assuming an unlawful conspiracy to attack a friendly power, they should regard Wilkinson's border peace in the national interest as a "betrayal" of Burr. This embarrassment is avoided by another theory: that Wilkinson made peace because of fear that Burr's continuance, with inadequate forces, with their plan (whether a plan to force war on the border or some other conspiracy is never stated) would arouse investigation that would reveal their relations. What these were is never made clear. These tangled theories ignore letters of Burr which indicate lessening hope of war between Spain and the United States.[38] Moreover, one of Burr's assist-

[37] Abernethy (*Burr*, p. 35) regards these letters as showing how early "coolness" began in his attitude toward Burr. Seemingly, he assumes an earlier conspiracy and this coolness the germ of betrayal.

[38] Abernethy, *Burr*, pp. 67, 68, 71. "He and Wilkinson . . . had always

ants in whom President Jefferson had confidence testified that Wilkinson's troops were not expected to aid Burr (in what was unstated) unless individually; but that no interference by them was expected.[39] There is also evidence that, actually, Wilkinson intended to take under his command, in case of war, whatever forces Burr might raise in the West.[40]

Vastly exaggerated attention has been given to a few ciphered letters. In one to Burr, Wilkinson referred to "our project," and in another and ciphered letter wrote, "I am waiting for you." In another, to Adair, he wrote of Burr, "he reckons on you . . . visit me and I will tell you all." And in introducing Burr to Daniel Clark (and so to the Mexican Association of New Orleans) he referred Clark to Burr for "many things improper to letter." There is nothing in all this inconsistent with mere common hopes for glory in a campaign against Mexico. Wilkinson merely had a coat-and-dagger epistolary style—and, also, was (the writer believes) merely hoaxing Adair.

No more deserving of attention than the preceding letters was one from Burr to Wilkinson in cipher, somewhat variantly translated. It was written in the East on July 29, 1806, just before Burr started for his second western trip, and stated as mere matters of fact that British *and American* naval forces would co-operate (unless officially this would imply insurrection), a British admiral meet the expedition on the Mississippi, and Burr descend by mid-November to the Falls of the Ohio with a first contingent of 500 to 1,000 men.[41] Now (1) to avoid the above absurdity, this assumed or involved war with Spain, therefore excluding the statutory offense of attacking a power at peace with the United States; and the participating naval forces being official,

---

looked upon war with Spain as a necessary condition for the carrying out of their plans," *ibid.*, pp. 37, 43, 59 (this removes the basis for much of Abernethy's volume) ; McCaleb, *Burr,* pp. 73–75.

[39] *A.S.P., Misc.,* I, McCaleb, *Burr,* pp. 337–339.

[40] On October 21, in a letter to the President (peace not yet obtained and highly doubtful, but Burr on his way down the Mississippi), Wilkinson suggested that, if war came, the reported revolutionists should be diverted against Mexico under Wilkinson's command. Abernethy, *Burr,* p. 152. At that time he was assuming (to alarm the President) 8,000 or more men under Burr, *ibid.*, p. 150; and in slightly earlier letters, 7,000. McCaleb, *Burr,* pp. 145, 162, 163.

[41] *A.S.P., Misc.,* I, 473; II, 112–113; McCaleb, *Burr,* pp. 73–75, 217; Abernethy, *Burr,* pp. 51, 59. Jefferson, in 1820, attributed belief in this to Wilkinson. *Jefferson* (Federal ed.), XI, 148.

that is evidence against any plan to detach the West from the Union. But (2), if Burr and Wilkinson were partners in conspiracy, and Burr honest with his partner, then Wilkinson knew of Burr's failure only a year earlier to gain even British consideration of such a plan. Without other and precedent evidence, Wilkinson would not have taken it seriously. Moreover, (3) whether they were or were not co-conspirators, Burr knew that any agreement of the two countries on joint action would immediately have been reported by the Secretary of War to Wilkinson. Was the letter, then, intended as a joke? The writer believes it to have been just that, and one directed against Adair or others of Burr's hangers-on. Hope, hallucination, intended deceit, or joke, the letter was no evidence of conspiracy and deserved no attention.

To justify (after Chief Justice Marshall's decision respecting a conspiracy to attack Spain's colonies) continued talk of *any* conspiracy, it is necessary to seek it in connection with western disunion, which was not even mentioned in the President's proclamations. As a matter of fact, the reports of John Graham to Jefferson showed that there was virtually no disaffection in the West—as Jefferson had predicted that Burr would learn. Graham found no significant unfriendliness to the Union, no talk of secession, much talk of Mexico and of Miranda's plans against other Spanish colonies.[42]

One cannot, then, find in western sentiment for disunion evidence of a conspiracy between Burr and Wilkinson, because there is no evidence of disunion sentiment—and no other evidence of a conspiracy. One can find in the *absence* of such sentiment, however, evidence of both Burr's political bankruptcy and the cause of his ruin by Wilkinson.

As respects the former, did Burr actually believe in the spring of 1805 that the West was disloyal, and plan to use its disloyalty to secure a political base for political rehabilitation? If not, why did he not denounce, in the West and in the East, Senator Dayton's acts in attributing that plan to him? Since he did not, it has been assumed by the writer that at least he was willing to accept the consequences of the attribution. If this was because it allayed the burn of Jefferson's refusal to appoint him to political office in the West, then vanity was his undoing. If one rejects this reasoning as excluded by his proved ability and political experience, then he was the victim of irresolution. There

[42] Graham's testimony is in *A.S.P., Misc.,* I, 529–530.

is abundant evidence to support that. For months he delayed and wandered, waiting for war with Spain, obviously totally out of touch with his supposed co-conspirator, until war was excluded by Wilkinson's border peace with the commander of the Mexican forces. Only after Burr belatedly learned of that did he begin his descent of the Mississippi, with his boatload of equivocally equipped followers, with no convincing evidence of peaceful plans, with Wilkinson loudly denouncing him and Wilkinson's agents ready to arrest him. For months his conduct had been one of irresolution and inconsequence to the point of madness.

As respects a reason for Wilkinson's ruining Burr, it seems clear. Wilkinson had known for many years that the idea of detaching the West from the Atlantic states was an absurdity. Jefferson was so sure of it that he completely ignored the contrary report of the United States attorney in Kentucky.[43] Nevertheless, Burr's western tour of 1805 had opened with an attribution to himself (through an obvious agent, first in Ohio and then in Washington) of a plan to detach the West from the Union, and described as a revival of Wilkinson's one-time plan—although, as has been emphasized in the last preceding chapter, there is no evidence that it had ever been Wilkinson's plan.[44] However, having himself for political purposes once fostered rumors of western infidelity, what would have been Wilkinson's reaction to Burr's revival of those rumors for political ends?

Manifestly, Wilkinson served, in some way, very personally, in Burr's plans; and in a way supposedly unknown to Wilkinson, for Burr wrote to his daughter: "Wilkinson and Brown [Burr's brother-in-law, secretary of the District of Louisiana] will suit most admirably as eaters and, I believe in other particulars."[45]

Wilkinson's abilities have been as much underestimated as his offenses have been exaggerated. That he could appraise men and circumstances with sagacity is clear from his entire career. One may surmise that Burr planned to use Wilkinson, that the latter knew it and resolved to be, himself, the puppeteer, if any; but there was time to wait for de-

[43] I. J. Cox (ed.), "Joseph H. Daveiss, View of the President's Conduct Concerning the Conspiracy of 1806," Hist. and Philos. Soc. of Ohio, *Quarterly Publication*, VII (1917), 72–74.

[44] That he later dangled the delusion before the French government (in 1810, Cox, *West Florida*, p. 311) merely shows how desperate his situation then was in exile. But perhaps he was as desperate in 1806.

[45] Quoted by Abernethy, *Burr*, p. 22, from Parton.

cision. This does not require one to date "betrayal," since no assumption is made of a conspiracy. The many who assume conspiracy and betrayal have not defined the first or made clear the second. Not a shred of evidence supports the idea that Burr and Wilkinson conspired; and if Burr "conspired" with Dayton and Adair and talked about western disaffection for political purposes, it was of no significance.

There is only one enigma in the "Burr conspiracy." It is the question of Wilkinson's reasons for ruining Burr. Abundant reasons may be given as probable. A first group of these were wholly personal and not discreditable: because of long agreement with Jefferson in politics, particularly in opinions and policies respecting the West; because of dislike of Burr for his reported intrigues with the Federalists, his near defeat of Jefferson for the Presidency; because of gratitude for the President's confidence in him and for his appointment to organize the Territory of Louisiana in accordance with the President's plans (an appointment with which Jefferson remained extremely satisfied);[46] and finally, because of Burr's offensive revival of the old charges of Wilkinson's disloyalty, re-examination of which by congressional committees was to plague him for the next five years.

A second conceivable reason for ruining Burr would also have been wholly personal, but also wholly discreditable, although it has been largely overlooked by Wilkinson's detractors: that he made a mere border armistice, instead of attempting a great conquest, because he planned to seek pay from Spain for not making that attempt. The fact is that after making the peace he asked of the Viceroy 121,000 pesos as "reimbursement" for "expenditures" which may be disregarded.[47] Was it for abstaining from a conquest of New Spain—assumed to be possible? Or for serving the best interests of both countries—assuming a right to judge that matter? It was a fair peace, seemingly satisfactory

[46] In May, 1806, he wrote (after the House of Representatives had debated the union of civil and military power in the government of the District of Louisiana): "Not a single fact has appeared which occasions me to doubt [believe] that I could have made a fitter appointment than Genl. Wilkinson. . . . I considered it not as a civil government, but merely a military station." Carter, *Terr. Papers,* XIII, 504. And he later wrote that of all his appointments he was still best satisfied with that of Wilkinson.

[47] W. R. Shepherd (ed.), "Wilkinson to Iturrigaray, Nov. 17, 1806," *AHR,* IX, 533–537; H. E. Bolton, "General James Wilkinson as Adviser to Iturbide," *HAHR;* I. J. Cox, "General Wilkinson and his Later Intrigues with the Spanish," *AHR,* XIX (1914), 794–812.

to both parties, and if we have renounced the ethics of 1846, who would say he was wrong *except* in asking for money?[48] It was an early case of conflict of interests—and on that the consciences of our representatives in high offices still require vast improvement.

[48] Wilkinson is entitled to a fair presentation of facts. They do not support F. J. Turner's dictum that he was "the most consummate artist in treason that the nation ever possessed" (*AHR*, III, 652). There is no evidence whatever that he was a traitor. The writer believes that exaggerated self-esteem made him abnormally histrionic, and led him to envy and circumvent or dupe superiors or rivals. This applies to parts of his army career, but only subordinately to the extraordinary hostility exhibited in the case of Burr. Nothing but rancorous personal animosity can explain the fact that although he told the truth about Burr to the Viceroy, his lies respecting him to Jefferson were prodigious —and inconsistent with the mutual reliance which characterized their relations through many years.

CHAPTER 10

The West in Relations with Canada and Britain, 1795-1830

RELATIONS between the United States and Canada after the Revolution and down to 1830 were explainable in large part by two influences. One was the independence of the former and the continuing colonial status of the latter as affecting direct relations between them. The other was a carryover in London offices, in dealings with both Canada and the United States, of attitudes fixed during the colonial period of the states. So far as possible, Great Britain continued to enforce restrictions upon trade between the States and Canada which were essentially those of the old colonial system, and to govern the colony as the states had been governed in the early stages of their colonial development. A distinguished Canadian historian has written: "It is often assumed that the American Revolution resulted in a changed outlook in . . . colonial policy. In fact it did not make the attitude of the governing class more sympathetic to colonial self-government. On the contrary it served as a warning that colonial liberality might encourage . . . [revolution]. After the American Revolution the non-tropical countries were more strictly controlled."[1] This statement referred particularly to the government of Canada. As another Canadian authority has said, "all the issues in Canadian history"—particularly in the period before 1837—"find their political bedfellows" in the history of the thirteen southern colonies.[2] However, much the same was true of trade.

[1] George M. Wrong, in *CHR*, VI, 4.
[2] W. P. Kennedy, *CHR*, VI, 255, reviewing H. L. Osgood's *The American Colonies in the Eighteenth Century* (4 vols., New York, 1924).

The United States were dedicated by their Declaration of Independence to the cause of freedom in government, and their commercial treaty of 1778 with France was a clarion call for free commerce both in peace and during war.[3] There were many in Britain, even in Parliament, sympathetic to both causes. Between the implications of mutual citizenship (which David Hartley advocated in Parliament)[4] and the desire of Charles Fox to acknowledge independence without removing any of the bitter differences between the two countries created by the war or by colonialism, there remained some opportunities for creating generously friendly relations. They were in the field of commerce. The Americans wanted the freedom stipulated in the French treaty. The British—at least many, Shelburne evidently believed—would satisfy American desires if the terms could virtually ensure retention of the American market and break the French alliance.

The negotiations were conducted between Shelburne and Franklin on a plane of high statesmanship. The commercial view upon which they framed the treaty, already illustrated in relations with Ireland, was very much like the principles drafted by the Continental Congress as a model treaty and already substantially embodied in treaties with France and Holland.[5] Josiah Tucker and Adam Smith had already argued that Britain would gain by freeing the colonies and then making a treaty establishing commercial relations with them on a basis of mutual interest.[6] The peace negotiators accepted that principle wholeheartedly.[7] Even British merchants realized, to some degree, the necessity of the change.[8] Pitt had introduced a bill in Parliament to establish commercial relations between the two countries on a principle of complete equality, as between two parts of one country, with a provision

---

[3] J. B. Moore, "Beginnings of American Diplomacy," *Harper's Monthly Mag.* (1904), pp. 497–500, and "The Contest with Commercial Restrictions," p. 459.

[4] W. T. Franklin (ed.), *Private Correspondence of Benjamin Franklin* (8° ed., 2 vols., 2nd ed., London, 1817), II, 358.

[5] G. L. Graham, *British Policy and Canada, 1714–1791* (New York, 1930), p. 50. Franklin, in his first personal note to Shelburne, asked for adoption of this principle. See Wharton, *Dip. Corr.*, V, 132; E. Schuyler, *American Diplomacy and the Furtherance of Commerce* (New York, 1886).

[6] R. L. Schuyler, *The Fall of the Old Colonial System: A Study in British Free Trade, 1760–1870* (New York, 1945), pp. 38–55.

[7] Franklin, *Private Correspondence*, II, 347–354, 356–358, 360–363, 376–397, 432–434.

[8] E. C. Burnett (ed.), "Observations of London Merchants on American Trade, 1783," *AHR*, XVIII (1912), 769–780.

for repeal of all laws inconsistent with equality.[9] "Rarely can the future be so completely unburdened of the past. Britain wished independence only if it should be impossible to form with them any political league of union or amity to the exclusion of other European powers."[10]

The plan failed. Time was lacking to tear apart the labyrinth of hundreds of statutes in which were embedded the navigation system and the incapacities of aliens.[11] Pitt's bill was doomed when he and Shelburne lost office to the North-Fox coalition. The new ministry at once secured an act, repeatedly renewed down to 1797, empowering the King in Council to regulate trade with the former colonies, and there began a series of such orders which contributed to the controversies that ultimately led to another war. Lord North called on William Knox, a bigoted mercantilist long a secretary of the old Board of Trade, to draft regulations of commerce between the two countries. He accepted on the understanding that they should be based on "the principle . . . that it was better to have no colonies at all, than not to have them subject to the maritime strength and commercial interests of Great Britain."[12]

The explanation seems clear. The seaboard colonies were not settled and developed by the British government, but—as Jefferson said—by individual citizens. They had been governed by Britain, with considerable concessions of self-government to keep them quiet; but the only other policy exhibited in their control was to exploit them under the restrictive principles of mercantilism. There was no evidence of a rational positive policy, either political or economic, for their self-serving development.[13] What followed Shelburne's failure was inevitable. The Revolution, the French treaty, and the peace had challenged every principle of trade, politics, and empire entertained by Britain's ruling

[9] E. C. P. Fitzmaurice, *Life of William Earl of Shelburne* (2nd and rev. ed., 2 vols., London, 1912), II, 186.

[10] Oswald's general instructions, July 31, 1782, *ibid.*, 169; Wharton, *International Law*, III, 934.

[11] See Governor Pownall's report of February 2, 1783, in G. L. Graham, *British Policy and Canada;* also Fitzmaurice, *Shelburne*, II, 203.

[12] Quoted from Graham, *British Policy and Canada*, p. 63. On Fox, see Wharton, *Dip. Corr.*, I; also Wharton, *International Law* (2nd ed., 3 vols., Washington, 1887), III, 898, 899, 900, 943, 953.

[13] In the political field the one great opportunity offered the government was by the Albany Congress, and the response showed that the colonials were more than a century ahead of the mother country in their thinking. After 1763 there was no time, nor was there good will after 1770.

class. We have seen that Spain, while vowing she would never relax her colonial principles, and in form never doing so, did in fact greatly relax them. France did so in formal treaty with America. Britain was too hidebound in her mercantilism to do so, her rulers too bitter to reason. They conducted their relations with the states for another thirty years with sullen disdain.

Provisions for government of Quebec in 1763 had no practical relation to the West, Canadian or American, and there was neither time nor money to change anything between 1763 and 1776.[14] Those made for the Illinois Country by the Quebec Act had scarcely any practical existence.[15] So far as respected western Canada, the Quebec Act was repealed by the Constitutional Act of 1791, which divided the distinctively English portion from the distinctively French (eastern) portion of the province of Quebec as enlarged in 1775. It thus created the provinces of Upper and Lower Canada, and relieved the early settlers of the former, who were very predominantly transplanted American Loyalists, of the French law and the Roman Catholic Church which had been conceded to the old French province.

It soon became apparent in the conduct of Canadian trade that the policy of the British government would be little affected by loss of the older colonies. It has been suggested, and is possible, that the British government—believing Quebec's loyalty in 1776 was expressive of gratitude for retaining old French law and Catholicism—felt that the American Loyalists would be equally satisfied to retain a system against which they had not rebelled.[16] The only modification of policy, if there was any, resulting from loss of the thirteen colonies was distinctly reactionary.

Before the Revolution, the restrictions upon shipping which virtually excluded their vessels from the British West Indies had been to Amer-

[14] V. Coffin, *The Province of Quebec and the Early American Revolution* (Madison, 1896), pp. 326–327, 330.

[15] Shortt and Doughty, pp. 600–601, 607 (sections 15, 31 of Carleton's instructions of 1775); W. R. Riddell, *Michigan under British Rule: Law and Law Courts, 1760–1796* (Lansing, 1926); W. E. Stevens, *The Northwest Fur Trade, 1763–1800* (Urbana, Ill., 1928), 37 n., 38.

[16] Graham, *British Policy and Canada,* p. 65. The governor general of Canada was supreme throughout the colony in both civil and military matters. The lieutenant governor (in Upper Canada) was allowed virtual supremacy there in civil matters. An appointive legislative council checked an elective assembly of very limited powers.

icans the most objectionable of all features of mercantilistic doctrine. When the Quebec Revenue Act was passed in 1774, the only economic interest in the Canadian West was the fur trade, and the most nearly indispensable item in the trade, after firearms, was rum. An attempt was made by that Act to replace the seaboard colonies with Canada in the West Indian trade. The plan was to organize a triangular trade: Canada to supply lumber, staves, naval stores, and provisions to the islands; they to send molasses, sugar, rum, and coffee to England; and she to send her manufactures and duty-free rum to Canada. The practical weaknesses in this scheme included the puniness of the fur trade and Canada's slight population, climate, and extremely limited capability of producing foodstuffs. Nevertheless, after the war the experiment was launched. This policy in Canada did not harm the United States; however, its disregard of ordinary commercial considerations is almost inconceivable: in the late 1780's the states were taking from Great Britain approximately nine-tenths of all their imports, and were exporting thither more than a hundred times as much as Canada.[17]

There is another and more bizarre illustration of British policies. Franklin and Shelburne, in negotiating peace, had early agreed that the two countries should have equal trading rights in the continental interior, and equal use of the Mississippi and St. Lawrence rivers.[18] Even submission of such plans to Parliament was impossible because time was lacking to identify statutes that must be repealed. Nevertheless, this dream which could not be made part of the treaty became, as seen in an earlier chapter, part of the basis for nonobservance of the treaty as actually made. Naturally, there developed an important transboundary American trade, in large part illegal. Despite explicit contrary orders to the governor, and an ordinance of the Quebec council, the introduction of American goods was greatly increased in consequence of action by Lord Dorchester from 1787 onward. In the East

[17] A. M. Whitson, "The Outlook of the Continental American Colonies on the British West Indies," *Political Sci. Quart.*, XLV (1930); Graham, *British Policy and Canada*, Chap. 6, deals with this system; also F. L. Benns, *The American Struggle for the British West India Carrying Trade, 1815–1830* (Bloomington, Ind., 1923); R. L. Schuyler, *Old Colonial System,* pp. 80 *et seq.* In 1830 the United States accepted conditions under which Britain had opened her West Indies to all nations in 1825.

[18] Wharton, *Dip. Corr.*, VI, 603. In the articles submitted on October 8, 1782, Article 4 gave equal rights of navigation "in all rivers, harbors, lakes, ports, and places" of the two countries; *ibid.*, pp. 469, 470.

this trade was through Vermont, and was declared in 1790 by the Board of Trade to be commercially and politically desirable.[19] It was manifest that Upper Canada must be so supplied, legally or illegally. The limited time during which the St. Lawrence was open, and the long and enormously difficult water route westward, made every border crossing one for smuggling.[20] In 1787 Dorchester ruled that prohibition of American imports applied to seaborne importation only. This plainly disregarded protection of British goods and encouragement of British shipping, the purposes for which the navigation laws existed.[21] The London government acquiesced. Jay's treaty was the next step. It provided that British and American citizens, and Indians, living in either country, might freely trade in either, and navigate lakes and rivers for that purpose. Portages on both sides of the boundary were opened equally to all traders.[22] This return to the friendly policy of the peace negotiations was creditable, even though it only legitimized what, in general, was certain to happen in the wilderness.

Even before 1763, the construction of boats for use on the Great Lakes had begun at Niagara and at Detroit. The British posts north of the Lakes had always been provisioned by water. The fur trade is the only reason revealed for ignoring the treaty boundary through the Lakes, for occupying the land south of them, and for thus monopolizing their navigation—as the British did in early years. American access to Lake Erie by the land route south of it was eventually (after 1825) to give American traders a great advantage in time over Canadians delayed by the St. Lawrence rapids.[23] But until after the War of 1812, British use of the Lakes was virtually uncontested.

Private commercial navigation was prohibited, after the Revolution began, until 1785, and for three years longer preferences were given to boats engaged in royal service.[24] The control was complete, and it was

[19] Graham, *British Policy and Canada*, pp. 55, 132; Shortt and Doughty, A. L. Burt, *The United States, Great Britain, and British North America* (New Haven, 1940), p. 64.

[20] The old-time difficulties, now overcome by the Seaway, are indicated in *Mich. Hist. Coll.*, XVI, 505.

[21] Shortt and Doughty; Burt, *U.S. Gr. Britain and Br. No. America*, p. 64; R. L. Schuyler, *Old Colonial System*, pp. 294, 295.

[22] Miller, *Treaties*.

[23] W. E. Stevens, *The Northwest Fur Trade*, pp. 97, 100.

[24] N. V. Russell, *The British Regime in Michigan and the Old Northwest, 1760–1796* (Northfield, Minn., 1939), pp. 163–188, and "Transportation and Naval Defense in the Old Northwest during the British Regime, 1760–96," in University of Michigan, *Historical Essays*, XI (1937).

the deliberate policy of the London government.[25] The smuggling of furs into the United States was thus prevented—but because furs were involved, not because of any objection to smuggling, which was constant and notorious, and, especially between Vermont and Montreal, was British policy.[26] In less than one year, however, after Simcoe became lieutenant governor of Upper Canada, he reported to the home government that he considered the fur trade "on its present foundation to be of no use whatever to the colony." He wanted Upper Canada (as his later actions showed) to be a colony of homes, not a fur preserve; the trade was hostile to settlement, and particularly to agriculture, his steady objective. Indeed, his ultimate objective was that of Shelburne in 1782, which the governments succeeding his followed— namely, commercial domination of the continental interior.[27] Although his superior, Lord Dorchester, did not urge this policy, and although the home government's policy continued to be expressed, generally, in terms of protecting the fur trade, it seems sensible to assume that the broader policy was the long-range objective of the government.[28] The connection between the two policies was plainly indicated by the Board of Trade in 1790, in a report in which it expressed the opinion that, "in order to have full command of [the Indian trade]," vessels transporting over the Great Lakes, "or through River's emptying into them," goods needed in that trade

should . . . belong to British subjects only, and that the posts which command the Entrance of these Lakes, and which are best situated for securing the Navigation of these Rivers should be retained by His Majesty (if other important Considerations will so permit) and be Garrisoned. . . . For there can be no doubt that the various Settlements which are now forming in the interior parts of America, afford the prospect of a most Extensive and valuable Commerce to those Nations who can secure . . . it.[29]

[25] *Mich. Hist. Coll.,* XXIV, 189–191.

[26] G. Lanctot, *Les Canadiens et leurs voisins du sud* (New Haven, 1941), pp. 133–135; M. W. Hansen, *The Mingling of the Canadian and American People* (New Haven, 1940), pp. 73–75.

[27] F. Landon, *Western Ontario and the American Frontier* (New Haven, 1941), pp. 6–7.

[28] The habit of referring in official documents to miserable frontier posts as "in an advanced stage of cultivation and settlement," in adulation of the Crown, concealed the truth from those higher officials who had never been in the West, or even in America.

[29] April 17, 1790, Bemis, *Jay's Treaty.*

This was seven years after the treaty of peace, if given effect, would not "so permit."

Several disputed interpretations of provisions in Jay's treaty, none serious individually, were doubtless irritating at the two extremes of the fur traders and the foreign offices, but none could have been a matter of popular knowledge or influence.

One issue was the collection of American customs duties at portages not involving merely a brief and incidental crossing of an international water boundary. This was the case, particularly, at Grand Portage, which led into a great area of American territory with no British territory (other than that just left) except far away. Acceptance by the British government of American protests compelled abandonment of Grand Portage—which was all that its name implied.[30]

The second issue (allied to Grand Portage trade) arose over the right claimed by British fur traders to hunt on the Missouri and Mississippi rivers, and to navigate the Mississippi. The last matter has already been discussed. If Britain had any *property* right in the river it was (after 1783) only above the Canadian border, in case the river rose farther north. If she had any right below the border, it was a contractual right to share enjoyment of the property rights of the United States as owner of the east bank down to the Spanish border, fixed at 31° in 1795. This right was confirmed by Jay's treaty of 1794 and the Bond agreement of 1795.[31] But Jay's treaty also granted mutual trading rights "in the respective territories and countries of the two parties" in North America. If this applied to Louisiana, they could trade on the Missouri and Mississippi and navigate the latter. After the United States acquired Louisiana, the British right would have been extended to the Gulf—provided these earlier agreements were extensible by changes in the circumstances existing when the agreements were made, although such an extension was not then stipulated. In addition the British right of access would have been vastly extended, subject to two assumptions: first (extension in nature), that a right to navigate included a right of access to the river; second (extension in application), that access was permissible from any point in Canada over any route to the river.

---

[30] *A.S.P., For. Rel.,* II, 588, III, 163. The words of Jay's treaty, exempting goods carried over portages "on either side of the line," referred to travel on boundary waters, interruption of transit along which might briefly necessitate carriage, at different points, from one to the other country.

[31] Malloy, *Treaties,* I, 379, 395.

There was one group of persons for whom these theoretical questions had practical importance—the fur traders. The Canadian traders long traded wheresoever they wished in Louisiana, using whatever routes they desired. Spanish traders were, of course, doing the same without any treaty. Both were competing with American fur companies trading from St. Louis.[32] The problems of treaty interpretation were settled incidentally to the trade dispute. General Wilkinson, while governor of Upper Louisiana in 1805, issued a proclamation barring British traders from access to the Mississippi. He was unquestionably correct, and this position was ultimately acquiesced in by the British government.[33] Such a decision, naturally, had little effect for a considerable number of years upon what was actually done in a wilderness. However, the theoretical settlement of the access issue made all other questions of Mississippi navigation insubstantial because by then it was generally realized that the river's source was south of the border.

Indian relations had been a constant source of irritation since 1783. Up to the negotiation of Jay's treaty, they had continuously embittered relations between the two countries. The slightness of American population in the Northwest up to that time, though it incited Indian hostilities, had lessened the danger of a war between the two countries, but these favorable conditions soon deteriorated. The Census of 1790 ignored the slight number of settlers save Kentucky's 73,000. In 1810 there were nearly 700,000 in the states of Kentucky and Ohio, and the organized territories of Indiana and Illinois.

The Indians seemingly had little of which they could complain. They were paid liberally for allowing whites to settle in the Old Northwest; paid, indeed, two or three times for permitting occupation of a very large part of it. This was vastly more generous than the British had been in taking most of the eastern half of the country. Canada had no Indian problem up to the end of our period (1830), when upper Canada had only (perhaps) 100,000 inhabitants.[34] The Canadians, however,

[32] A mass of correspondence on these matters is in A. P. Nasatir, *Before Lewis and Clark; Documents Illustrating the History of the Missouri, 1785–1804* (2 vols., St. Louis, 1952).

[33] *A.S.P., For. Rel.,* III, 126, 147, 152–153, 163. Burt (*U.S., G.B.,* p. 201) remarks that even if the treaty had explicitly excluded territory later acquired, "still the Canadian merchants would have had a grievance, for by prescription they had prior rights in the country just taken over by the United States." This is an extraordinary distortion of both equity jurisprudence and international law in attempting to unite them.

[34] M. W. Hansen, *The Mingling of the Canadian and American People*

were overwhelmingly preponderant in the Indian trade. The Indians naturally turned to them as friends, and to some extent the old-time irritations of the years preceding 1795 were revived.

On the whole it appears that the American policy of continual land treaties, to keep the line of permissible settlement well ahead of immediate need, was wise, for it lessened the likelihood of war. William Henry Harrison, however, who became in 1800 governor of Indiana Territory (then all the Old Northwest beyond Ohio), soon began to extend accessions with unwise rapidity and aggressiveness.[35]

It is not surprising, therefore, that as early as 1805 tribes were seeking, at Malden (where the headquarters of the Indian Department of Upper Canada were located), British assistance against this pressure.[36] It was two other factors, however, which brought about a renewal of the old relationship of virtual alliance. One was a crisis in the trouble over neutral rights in Atlantic trade—the *Chesapeake* affair of 1807, reparation for which was demanded of Britain by President Jefferson. The British called the northwestern tribes to Malden, and from then until well after the War of 1812 they were abundantly supplied for subsistence and war. This was not out of mere charity; writing in 1808 to the governor general,[37] Lieutenant Governor Simcoe—manifestly expressing the views of subordinate officials in Upper Canada—expressed the opinion that large reductions in presents to the Indians after 1795 were explainable by its having been "thought little probable that we should ever have occasion for their assistance again; and they have therefore been much neglected." The gifts were enormous in 1808–9.[38]

(New Haven, 1940), pp. 89–90; A. Dunham, *Political Unrest in Upper Canada, 1815–1836* (New York, 1927), pp. 5–6.

[35] His policy is discussed in D. B. Goebel, *William Henry Harrison* (Indianapolis, 1926), pp. 97–117 and in *Ill. Hist. Coll.*, XXI, lx–lxiii (the judgments in which the writer now feels were unduly severe).

[36] *Mich. Hist. Coll.*, XXIII, 39.

[37] Burt, p. 246. Burt accepted that view. Lieutenant Governor Gore having suggested in 1807 the possible desirability of an Indian alliance (*ibid.*, p. 249), the Superintendent of Indian Affairs sounded out the Indians early in 1808 (*Mich. Hist. Coll.*, XV, 44–45) and reported to Gore that those presumably available for aid were not more than 1,500 and "very backward" (*ibid.*, pp. 47–48).

[38] $129,083; for 1808–16, $180,120; and for 1810–16, $51,440. C. B. Peake, *The United States Indian Factory System, 1795–1828* (Denver, 1954), p. 131. On the goods distributed at Malden in 1811, see *A.S.P., Ind. Aff.*, I, 797–804.

This, too, is not surprising, for the United States had for years been paying its treaty obligations in annuities, and they were large.[39]

The other cause was the activity of the Prophet and of his brother Tecumseh.[40] The former preached renunciation of the white men's dress and goods, of firewater, of war in aid of either British or Americans. He adjured the Indians to devote themselves to agriculture. It is said that by 1807, Indians were gathering from afar to hear him. But he also advocated, with Tecumseh, the revival of Joseph Brant's Indian confederation. His purpose was to check Indian cessions by having the tribes claim all lands in common; Tecumseh's, by having them battle the whites together. Both of these objectives had been advocated by Brant's earlier alliance. The appeals of both leaders were spread throughout the West, north and south. After various fruitless conferences Harrison finally marched against the Indians in 1811, and crushed them at Tippecanoe, their headquarters from 1809 onward (November 7). Tecumseh, then proselyting in the Southwest, fled to the British. This ended efforts for a confederation, but assured Indian participation in the coming war.

During the earlier wars of the French Revolution, Jefferson had written, "Our object is to feed and theirs to fight. If we are not forced by England, we shall have a gainful time of it."[41] They did, indeed, but England did "press." It is not pertinent to a discussion of the West's development to refer, beyond an indispensable minimum, to the harassment of American trade by France and Britain, and to American complaints against the latter over impressment of American sailors, which were partial causes of the War of 1812. Nor may more be said of the nonimportation and nonintercourse acts of 1806, antedating and surviving the Embargo Act of December, 1807.[42] This last was repealed in March, 1809. Quite aside from violations of it in foreign and coastwise trade, there was abundant violation on the southwestern and northwestern frontiers. Smuggling took place on a great scale along the Canadian border, and also, as already seen, in the Southwest, where American officials, in attempting to enforce it, showed a disregard of

[39] Peake, *Indian Factory System*, p. 130.

[40] The primary source is Dawson, *Civil and Military Services of William Henry Harrison* (Cincinnati, 1824).

[41] *Works* (Federal ed.), VI, 89.

[42] On this there are exhaustive quotations of his letters in L. M. Sears, *Jefferson and the Embargo* (Durham, N.C., 1927), Chap. 1.

Spanish rights on Lakes Pontchartrain and Maurepas and in the adjoining Spanish territory very similar to that shown by British officials in Upper Canada to American rights in the Great Lakes.[43] A supplementary act, designed to cut off border trade by land and water, passed in 1808.

Continuing fruitless efforts, after the Embargo's repeal, to secure settlement of disputes with Britain may be passed over. The President, acting on indirect assurances (accepted as a fact) that France had withdrawn hostile decrees, proclaimed a reopening of trade with her, and, despite some hostile French acts thereafter, trade with her remained open. Diplomatic relations with Britain were terminated in February, 1811. War was declared on June 18—just two days after the British ministry, harassed by debate in Parliament, had agreed to suspend its orders in council.

In the last century, historians recognized nothing save the violation of American rights of trade and navigation as a cause of the War of 1812. Since F. J. Turner's emphasis in 1893 upon the West's role in American history, and Professor Beard's emphasis somewhat later upon economic determinism, writers have underscored the desire to annex West Florida and Canada, and the need for new markets.[44] There is little logic to support some of these suggestions. Much of West Florida had long been occupied; the remainder, economically considered, was already pretty much a part of the United States. War with Britain was certain to bring—and did bring—what had long been feared: British warnings in behalf of Spain respecting Florida. It is certain, too, that if the West needed markets (not, of course, to be found in the Cana-

---

[43] *Ibid.,* pp. 67, 77, 90–95, 194 *et seq.;* I. J. Cox, *The West Florida Controversy* . . . (Baltimore, 1912), pp. 221–224.

[44] The West had a sixth or seventh of the country's population. Differences there with Great Britain seem less likely than British offenses against New England shipping to have inflamed national public opinion. But Alvord thought "the true issues of the War" were in the West. C. W. Alvord, *The Illinois Country* (Springfield, 1920), p. 440. Beard in *The Rise of American Civilization* (one-vol. ed., New York, 1930), I, 393, wrote that the war was in reality conceived primarily "in the interests of [western] agriculture. . . . The men who voted in 1812 for the declaration of war . . . represented the agrarian constituencies of the interior and their prime object was the annexation of Florida and Canada." The assumptions underlying the emphasis upon agrarian voters are very large ones. Admitting that almost *all* the country was rural, (1) what proportion of citizens were controlled by agrarian interests? And (2) what proportion would favor war to protect American ships?

dian wilderness), it was because of British repression of neutral trade.[45]

The *Chesapeake* affair of 1807 caused immense resentment. Local associations in favor of war were formed in many localities, and from then on talk of war was a commonplace. The shipping interests, however, were not for war; despite great losses, neutral trade was profitable.[46] Shippers were more than willing to write off losses and insults together as business risks, but the citizens, patriotically, made no distinction between nation and commercial class and were for war. It is a fact that, as time passed, perhaps there was more bluster in the West. In case of war, there could be no possible attack upon Britain except in Canada. Its easy conquest was expected by President Madison and Jefferson.[47] An assumption of its occupation runs through the congressional debates of 1809 and 1811. A group of extraordinarily able young men, ardent for war (the War Hawks), entered the Lower House of Congress in 1811, and dominated its proceedings.[48] When the vote on war or peace was made, the East was much divided, the interior less so, the frontier West, north and south, least of all. As F. J. Turner said, the West "turned the scale," but might the same be said of any other block of votes?[49] Long before the War Hawks appeared, war sentiment had been widespread and intense. The cause of it was plain. The United States was in truth contemptibly weak, but resented the arrogance with which the British had treated them since 1783. The War Hawks spoke partly for politics, and partly in rebuke of coastal communities that opposed war even in defense of the country's honor.

A scholar whose researches directed special attention to the causes

[45] Beard put the cause for war in the West—desire for Canadian land. Craven left it in the East, but based western resentment on losses caused by British closing of markets abroad. See D. R. Fox (ed.), *Sources of Culture in the Middle West* (New York, 1934), p. 48. The violations of neutral economic interests were flagrant, continuous, and contemptuous. So great had British arrogance grown since 1759 that, as respects her rules for war at sea, she allowed her allies on the Continent no greater freedom than the Americans to discuss them. J. H. Rose, *Life of Napoleon* (New York, 1902), II, 389.

[46] A. C. Clouden, *American Commerce as Affected by the Wars of the French . . . 1793–1812* (Philadelphia, 1932), *passim*.

[47] Jefferson, *Writings* (Ford ed.), VIII, 450; Madison, *A.S.P., For. Rel.*, III, 172.

[48] Notably, Henry Clay (who was immediately made speaker) from Kentucky, Felix Grundy from Tennessee, John C. Calhoun and Langdon Cheves from the northwestern corner of South Carolina.

[49] *Atlantic Monthly*, LII, 293. The vote in the House was 79 to 49; in the Senate, 19 to 13.

of the vote in Congress concluded that without the maritime issues and also "without the peculiar grievances and ambitions of the West there would have been no war."[50] However, this illumines nothing. The "but for" formula throws no light whatever on the relative importance of causes; it was not the last straw, but all, that broke the camel's back. The West undoubtedly had ambitions, but her grievances, if she had any, were certainly highly "peculiar" and difficult to define.[51] In the diplomatic problems above noted, only fur traders were interested—in one case, American.

That it was the West which wanted land, and therefore wanted Canada, seem equally to be myths. It was Easterners who wanted land: speculators, who were few, and would-be settlers, who proved during the next few years to be millions. Everybody expected Canada to be acquired in case of war, but Westerners—that is, Easterners who had gone west for land and had acquired it—knew best that the West was not crowded, that Canada was not needed.[52]

Military operations being inept (in the West less than elsewhere), no more land was added to the Union. Governor William Hull of Michigan Territory, a Revolutionary patriot grown old, upon whom command was virtually forced, marched north from Dayton toward Detroit in May, 1812, assembling troops, repairing defective guns, cutting a road through the wilderness to Detroit. He reached Detroit on July 5 before knowing war had been declared, and a week later crossed the river to conquer Canada. Colonel Isaac Brock, hearing first of the war, had hurried in boats down Lake Erie. He had, like George Rogers Clark, an instinct for the initiative and a gift for bluffing. Hull's supply line had already been cut three times at Monroe, at the west end of Lake Erie, by the Indians. Despite his superior forces he retreated before Brock, immured himself in Detroit, and on July 16, without one

---

[50] J. W. Pratt, *The Expansionists of 1812* (New York, 1925), p. 14.

[51] The government was quieting Indian hunting claims in land far beyond immediate need, and all beyond the Mississippi was untouched. Beard (*American Civilization*, p. 411) overestimated the Indian "barrier," and his figures for Indians under Malden's influence were exaggerated.

[52] Beard, for example, characterized the West as "vibrant with prospects of great agricultural enterprise"—surely that was well in the future. He characterized those "with the largest imagination" as the social element "prepared for imperial enterprise" (*American Civilization*, pp. 394, 395)—a reference to war or to economics? He also romanticized the West by phrases suggestive of a general social restiveness (*ibid.*, pp. 394, 410). The writer believes that relative satisfaction characterized the frontier despite the toil and sobriety of life.

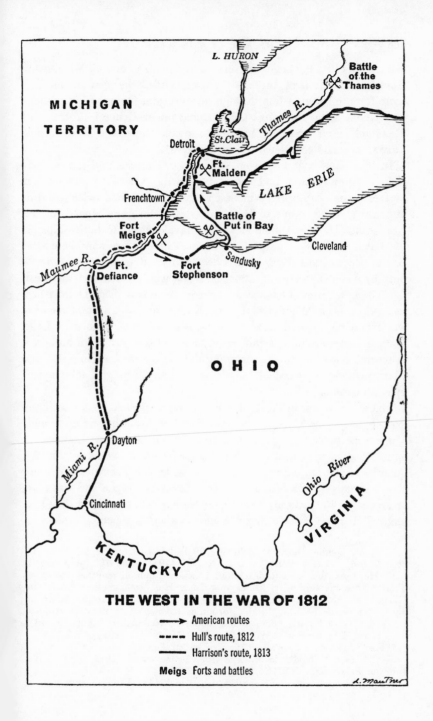

THE WEST IN THE WAR OF 1812

→ American routes
---- Hull's route, 1812
— Harrison's route, 1813
Meigs Forts and battles

cannon shot into the besiegers, surrendered that fort and all Michigan.[53] Governor Harrison of Indiana Territory ended the year in building more forts to secure a line through northwestern Ohio, and in maneuvers which compelled retreat of a force under General Procter and Tecumseh. Four American failures to invade Canada at Niagara and Lake Champlain completed the record of 1812.

In 1813, land operations were entrusted to Harrison and James Winchester. After Monroe had been taken by the Americans and retaken by the British (capturing Winchester), and Procter had twice failed in attempts to capture one of Harrison's forts,[54] fortune changed for the Americans. The government had sent naval officers to build ships on the Lakes, and a fleet under Commodore Oliver Perry annihilated the British fleet on Lake Erie.[55] Harrison then moved an army to Amherstburg by water. Procter retreating, Harrison won a decisive victory near the Thames River (October 5), where Tecumseh died. Detroit had meanwhile been abandoned by the British, and this virtually ended warfare in the western area. A few raids on settlements north of Lake Ontario had no military significance, save that the burning of buildings in several Canadian towns, including the Parliament buildings in York (Toronto), set a precedent for the subsequent burning of the Capitol in Washington.

The war was lost in the East, where operations, save for the brilliant exploits of the navy, were a muddle of failures from beginning to end. There was, indeed, one weakness from which all others sprang—the administrative inadequacy of the War Department. Weak in military qualities as the militia everywhere were, at least it was shown by Harrison's success in 1813 (and had been shown by Wayne and was soon to be shown by Jackson) that under leaders they respected they had mettle.[56] It is regrettable that Canadian success in repelling attacks by

---

[53] M. M. Quaife, "General William Hull and His Critics," *Ohio State Archaeological and Historical Quarterly*, XLVII (1932), 168–182, ably defends Hull. He was condemned to death, but President Madison remitted execution. Shortly after his surrender, his nephew Isaac Hull, commanding the frigate *Constitution*, defeated Britain's *Guerrière* in the most spectacular American naval victory of the war. In this fortuitous balance of family and national fortunes, Charles Francis Adams found comfort: "Wednesday, August 19, 1812, 6:30 p. m.: The Birth of a World Power," *AHR*, XVIII (1912), 513–521.

[54] Fort Meigs, at Wayne's battlefield of Fallen Timbers.

[55] R. Neeser, "The Battle of Lake Erie, September 10, 1813," U.S. Naval Institute, *Proceedings*, XXXIX (1913), 921–930.

[56] Amos Kendall wrote of Kentucky militia of 1814: "The soldiers are under

a country vastly stronger in population and resources should have been tarnished by the alliance with the Indians, whose aid was insignificant, and who were guilty—in addition to ordinary border barbarities—of two gruesome massacres of prisoners.[57] The United States had sought Indian neutrality, as in 1783.[58] The reason for their employment given by British authorities was not their value as allies for defense, but, in the words of the governor general of Canada, their destructiveness as enemies—which meant, for burning homes, pillaging, and massacring.[59] As in earlier years, the British alliance was with the tomahawk and torch. The Indians were used as allies, but without either the rights or liability of allies. It was, in fact, another way of exploiting them as a backward race.

After Harrison's victory and Tecumseh's death at the Thames, Indian hostilities died down, and a general peace with northern tribes was made in August, 1814.[60] Another Indian war had meanwhile begun in 1813 with the Creeks.

This had nothing to do with the War of 1812 except that, being simultaneously waged, each increased the difficulties of the other. It was rooted in land questions long existing in the Southwest, though action by the Creeks was stimulated by the exhortations of Tecumseh. Although both Britain and Spain had ample reason to consider its possible contribution to their future advantage, and the former had a military officer in Florida during the war, no part was played in its initiation by either power aside from British encouragement to Tecumseh, and encouragement of his ideals was proper.[61] Hostilities began with an

---

no more restraint than a herd of swine. Reasoning, remonstrating, threatening, and ridiculing their officers, they show their sense of equality, and their total want of subordination."

[57] One was of combatants and noncombatants taken when Fort Dearborn (Chicago) surrendered. M. M. Quaife, *Chicago and the Old Northwest* (Chicago, 1913), pp. 215–216, 230–236. The other was west of Monroe on the Raisin River, when Procter defeated Winchester in January, 1813. It was charged that Procter pledged protection, but withdrew.

[58] *A.S.P., Ind. Aff.*, I, 745–746; compare *Mich. Hist. Coll.*, XV, 196–198.

[59] Burt records the hesitations of the governor general at length (*U.S., G.B.*, pp. 246–254, 302–304), but on the assumption that in using the Indians a distinction was feasible between defense and offense (pp. 249, 252, 302, 304). After eighteen months, "Castlereigh sanctioned Craig's policy of cultivating the Indians, echoing his own statement that the important consideration was not the use of the natives as allies but their destructiveness as enemies" (p. 267).

[60] August 4, Kappler, *Indian Affairs*, II.

[61] Spain had, naturally, hoped to use the Creeks if the United States at-

attack by Tombigbee settlers.[62] Andrew Jackson, leading frontier volunteers, crushed the Indians at Horseshoe Bend (March, 1814), and crushed them further with the Treaty of Fort Jackson (August 9), by which they ceded a freeway between Georgia and the Mississippi Territory, rights to establish army posts and Indian trading factories, and twenty million acres of land. He took this, too, from both hostile and friendly Creeks, and despite orders to take no more than should suffice to pay the costs of the campaign; nor did he grant indemnities which, he conceded, had been promised by the commissioners who had negotiated the treaty.[63] A show of military force secured submission to the boundary, and a final treaty (October 15) then confirmed that of Fort Jackson. The war afforded the United States both an opportunity and a need to occupy West Florida up to the Perdido River, its eastern boundary, and this territory, as already seen, was held until Spain consented to sell it. In this manner, although there was at first a prospect that he would be recalled and censured, Jackson became a frontier hero.[64]

The negotiations for peace were as curious as the war.[65] They were, in fact, in large part a projection on the conference table of the war's changing fortunes. Early in 1813, Czar Alexander of Russia offered mediation, and the United States accepted. The instructions to the American commissioners show that the government was then (April) still buoyant with the hopes with which war was begun. The commissioners were to demand various concessions to neutral rights, refuse renewal of the interior-trade provisions of Jay's treaty (particularly on rivers wholly within the United States), secure removal of limitations on American rights in the Great Lakes, and secure mutual restitution of conquests.[66] More confidently, it was soon suggested that the boundary from the Lake of the Woods be amended and that Upper Canada,

---

tacked Pensacola. I. J. Cox, *The West Florida Controversy* (Baltimore, 1912), pp. 612, 627–629.

[62] *Ibid.*, p. 629.

[63] G. D. Harmon, *Sixty Years of Indian Affairs . . . 1787–1850* (Chapel Hill, 1941), pp. 143–148.

[64] Soon to become a greater one: great numbers of the Creeks joined the Seminoles in Florida, with whom war began in 1817.

[65] *A.S.P., For. Rel.,* III, 621–622, 695–742; C. M. Gates, "The West in American Diplomacy, 1812–1815," *MVHR,* XXVI (1940), 499–510; Miller, *Treaties.*

[66] April 23, *A.S.P., For. Rel.,* III, 695–700.

or even all Canada, be ceded in order to assure future peace.[67] However, Britain having declined Russian intervention, new instructions were prepared in January, 1814. This was after Harrison's decisive victory at the Thames and gave some basis for repeating, in general, the earlier instructions, suggesting again the cession of all Canada. Before any meeting of the commissioners of the two countries, however, the government, warned by its own, authorized silence even respecting the fisheries.[68]

At the first meeting of the commissioners it was agreed to exclude consideration of neutral rights; the Americans had been long enough in Europe to know that British public opinion was adamant on that point. The British commissioners made known, also, that gratuitous enjoyment of the fisheries would not be longer conceded; that they wanted general revision of the American-Canadian boundary, including the northern limits of Louisiana as acquired from France, also renewal of the interior-trade provision (Article III) of Jay's treaty; and that, in particular, it was a *sine qua non* of any treaty that a permanent buffer Indian territory be created in the Northwest.[69] At the next meeting it was added that neither country should ever acquire part of this territory, and that the Treaty of Greenville line of 1794 should be the buffer's southeast boundary, the United States renouncing sovereignty within the reservation. It is clear, however, that it was not intended to alter the international boundary through the Great Lakes, for the British further demanded American disarmament in the northwest and a new line from Lake Superior to the source of the Mississippi. The British were doubtless expecting good military news from America (August), for they warned that, were these terms rejected, others might be worse.[70] The Americans rejected them, however, declaring that there could absolutely be no unilateral disarmament, suggesting a prohibition of trade by the nationals of either power within the territories of the other, and offering peace on the *status quo ante bellum*.[71]

[67] Amer. Hist. Association, *Report* for 1913, II, 227–228; Miller, *Treaties*.
[68] January 28, *A.S.P., For. Rel.*, III, 701–704; Amer. Hist. Association, *Report* for 1913, II, 263–264. A line from the Lake of the Woods directly to the source of the Mississippi was suggested to make possible British navigation of that river. It was trading privileges under Article III of Jay's treaty that the United States would not recognize.
[69] *A.S.P., For. Rel.*, III, 708; Amer. Hist. Association, *Report* for 1913, II.
[70] *A.S.P., For. Rel.*, III, 708–710.
[71] *Ibid.*, pp. 711–713. This was August 24.

The Americans had lost hope of conquering much of Canada. Perhaps the British still hoped for additions to it by military victories far from the Northwest. There, at any rate, the British ministry began to weaken. The idea of an Indian reserve had come from the colonial office, and it has every mark of the old Board of Trade and its fur-trade policy.[72] The ministry ceased to insist upon it as an ultimatum, and now demanded only (1) that the Indians be "included" in the peace and (2) that the treaty restore their rights as of 1811. This last may well have had the laudable purpose of protecting them against an American threat to exterminate, or drive beyond the Mississippi, tribes allying themselves with the British. Actually, some of the Indians had already, by a treaty they made in August, been pacified without extermination or expulsion, but the American commissioners sensibly accepted the second demand (made an ultimatum), which in fact restored the Indians to their rights as of 1811 only provided they desisted from hostilities and kept their agreements. The British action was in performance of a pledge. Legally, and historically, it was wholly without basis.[73]

The Indian problem was hardly out of the way when news came of Governor General Prevost's retreat, with his army of European veterans, after the Americans destroyed his fleet on Lake Champlain. The British were then in possession of Michilimackinac, Niagara, and much of Maine, and they offered, after accepting a line from the Lake of the Woods to the Mississippi, to settle boundaries otherwise on the principle of *uti possidetis*. The Americans, though they had once suggested that, now insisted, of course, on a return of all conquests. An American draft of a treaty was then taken under consideration, and became the treaty of peace after omission from it of everything except the declaration of peace, provision for the immediate return of occupied territory, the Indian article, and provision for various boundary commissions and ratifications.[74]

No settlement of any issue relating to the West was effected. Even the agreement on a line from the Lake of the Woods to the Mississippi

[72] Gates, "West in American Diplomacy."

[73] *A.S.P., For. Rel.*, III, 713–724 (September 24–October 13). The Indians were living in American territory, where they had lived when it was British territory. Britain had, of course, always demanded that "her" Indians be free from French interference.

[74] Ratified by the Senate, February 17, 1815. See Moore, *International Arbitrations,* and Miller, *International Acts,* for account of commission reports, etc.

was deleted, because the British offered an amendment giving them free navigation of the river and free access to it with goods from Canada. Notably, the British rejected an article binding each party to restrain its Indians from committing hostilities against the other, and binding each to refrain from using them against the other in any future war.[75] Jackson's overwhelming victory at New Orleans over British veterans from Europe had earlier given satisfaction to Americans.[76]

Trade with Britain was active by early autumn. Aside from spoliations in raids north of Lake Ontario in 1813, Upper Canada had suffered chiefly, and only temporarily, for lack of provisions, which high prices brought in large supply from the United States, through reopened smuggling channels, in the first winter of the war.[77] The American West, except southeastern Michigan, had suffered little; there, destruction and privation were great.

The effects of the war were greatest politically. Proof positive of the imperfection of American nationalism was afforded by the refusal of state militia to cross the state line in two attacks at Niagara and one at Lake Champlain. On the other hand it has been emphasized that at least from 1806 onward there was always a large portion of the population that demanded action to protect the country's honor. That nationalism had greatly grown by 1815 was evidenced by the fact that the Federalist party was destroyed by its antinational policy during the war.[78]

In Upper Canada there was a great strengthening of British sentiment. In the population of that province, despite its original settlement

[75] Inviolability of neutral trade in noncontraband goods was not mentioned in the treaty. Articles on impressment, blockade, and mutual indemnification for spoliations were dropped. The fisheries having become tied to Mississippi navigation in argument, no reference was made to either. The Senate immediately ratified the treaty, February 16, 1815.

[76] January 8, 1815, with several smaller and three introductory engagements (since December 23) which should have warned the British commanders. In the main battle the British killed or wounded (the latter, few) totaled 2,100; the American, 21.

[77] F. Landon, *Western Ontario and the American Frontier* (New Haven, 1941), pp. 39–40. The reference in the text is not to such matters as inflation of the currency and land speculation (A. Dunham, *Political Unrest in Upper Canada, 1815–1836,* New York, 1927, p. 37), and other indirect effects of the war, or perhaps of government inefficiency.

[78] It has been said that the Republicans in 1793, like the Federalists in 1812, opposed the policy of their government in time of crisis. But in 1793 the Republicans aligned themselves with a power to whom much was owed, and not one virtually at war with their country.

by American Loyalists, later immigrants from the United States had become preponderant, and great fears were entertained of their loyalty from 1807 onward.[79] Nevertheless, out of the fervor of war, fostered in part by irritations between the two groups of Americans, there was born an exalted loyalty to Britain.[80]

Like the disagreements between the two countries between 1783 and 1815, all later arisings up to 1830 sprang from, or were accentuated by, Canada's colonial status.

Nevertheless, the differences now arising (or continuing) did so despite factors favorable to permanent good relations which were in operation after 1815. None of these was immediately obvious. The cessation, with Britain's triumph over Napoleon, of affronts to American sovereignty proved to be permanent. This is not to be attributed exclusively to a change in Britain. Long before any serious new problem arose in the relations between the two countries, the growing power of many states had compelled recognition of neutral rights.

A second factor conducive to peace showed how quickly Britain could adopt a new policy favorable to her interests. This was her now unqualified recognition of the principle that reciprocal profit is the basis of all desirable trade. The entire system of mercantilistic restrictions was repudiated.[81] The hundreds of statutes in which it was imbedded, and which had balked Lord Shelburne in 1783, were repealed under the lead of William Huskisson. The old differences with the United States, such as those over West Indian trade, disappeared as economic interests were freed of political entanglements.[82] The third factor for permanent peace, the most potent for mutual understanding, was the increasing settlement of Americans in Canada and, to a lesser extent, of Canadians below the border.

As in 1783, so as respects the Treaty of Ghent, the Indians could not understand it, and doubtless many British citizens, civilians and army officers, understood it no better. In words virtually identical with those used by Governor Haldimand and others three decades earlier, a prom-

[79] Dunham, *Political Unrest, passim.*
[80] Which has always continued. Incidents of Goldwin Smith's career illustrate its strength up to his death in 1910.
[81] Progress much more rapid than that away from American protectionist policies from 1890 up to 1960.
[82] See A. L. Lingelbach, "William Huskisson as President of the Board of Trade," *AHR,* XLIII, 759–774, and R. L. Schuyler, *Old Colonial System,* index, *s.v.* "Huskisson."

inent fur trader wrote to the governor general: "It will be extremely difficult, if at all practicable, to persuade the Indians that Government have not at the Peace broken faith with, and left them, in the power of their implacable enemies."[83] This covered the old delusion respecting "Indian" lands. The British commander at Michilimackinac, a lieutenant colonel, repeatedly expressed to the acting governor general the opinion that the establishment of American posts at Prairie du Chien and Green Bay in Wisconsin, they being "in the Indian Country," violated the treaty provision restoring the Indians to "all their Possessions . . . as . . . enjoyed before the War." "Their Boundary then," he said, "ought to be their boundary now"—as, of course, it was.[84] The fur traders, too, had been bitterly disappointed in Britain's not acquiring the Upper Lakes and the upper Mississippi Valley,[85] and their understanding of the treaty was on a level with that of the Indians: "The Northwest Fur Company declared that their trade with the Indians was on the verge of annihilation unless the stipulation in the treaty meant the exclusion of all military posts and custom houses of either nation from their territory."[86] With the fur traders and responsible army officers so uninformed, it was inevitable that the Indians would repeat the laments of 1783: "Father when you went to war with the Big Knives you sent the Tomahawk to us demanding our assistance . . . you told us that we . . . would get back again our old French lines . . . you told us . . . we should be recompensed for anything we might lose."[87] Unlike authorities of earlier years, the new governor general, Sir John Sherbrooke, and the new minister at Washington, Charles Bagot, promptly corrected the misapprehensions underlying such complaints.[88]

The United States made many new Indian treaties in 1815 and 1816 with tribes in the Old Northwest and along the upper Mississippi and Missouri; established various army posts in northern Illinois and Wisconsin; reopened old or established new Indian trading factories at

[83] William McGillivray to Sir George Prevost, March 28, 1815, *Mich. Hist. Coll.*, XVI, 67.

[84] *Ibid.*, p. 509 (August 7, 1816), but compare his remarks, pp. 510–511.

[85] The idea was more or less prevalent that there was a failure to *retain* these; that they were "in British hands."

[86] E. A. Cruikshank, "The Negotiation of the Agreement for Disarmament on the Lakes," Royal Soc. of Canada, *Proceedings and Transactions*, 3rd series, XXX, sec. II, 171.

[87] *Ibid.*, p. 471, June 19, 1816, at Amherstburg.

[88] *Ibid.*, 522; *A.S.P., Ind. Aff.*

various locations.[89] By the new treaties the Indians acknowledged the protection of the United States, "and of no other power whatsoever." In addition, a law was passed in 1816 requiring all foreign traders to secure a license from the President; in practice, from the American district Indian agents.[90]

This law, which Bagot anticipated would "amount to a total exclusion of British subjects," was of great importance in lessening irritations beyond the Mississippi.[91] However, the fur trade continued, and therefore the distribution of presents at Malden and British influences over the tribes continued; and not only American Indians of Michigan but others from Illinois and westward went regularly to profit by British policy. In all this there seems to have been nothing of which the United States could properly complain.[92] It was doubtless true that despite British liberality "not a winter [passed] without many lives being lost from want of cloathing & ammunition to procure food."[93] The charity came properly from the supporters of the fur trade, because it was that which had degraded the Indians and kept them in poverty.

It was not alone in the field of Indian relations that the animosities left by war were strongest in the West, ignorance of elementary principles of public law there most extraordinarily exhibited, and the recklessness of officials most extreme. Colonel James, commanding at Amherstburg, proceeded, as he explained, on the understanding that Great Britain was made by the Treaty of Ghent the protector of the Indians.[94] He assumed British jurisdiction to exist over an island in the St. Clair River near to the Michigan shore, demanded punishment of the alleged murderer of an Indian at that point, and offered a reward for his apprehension. After pointing out that the situs was in American territory and jurisdiction exclusively in American courts, Governor Cass (of Michigan) issued a proclamation ordering citizens to repel by force any

[89] The key treaty is that of Spring Wells, near Detroit, *ibid.*, II, 12–25. The others follow. All are also in Kappler, *Indian Affairs*, II, 117–119 *et seq.*
[90] *U.S. Statutes at Large.*
[91] Cruikshank, "Negotiations," p. 171. It resulted in a reorganization of western fur companies to the profit of John Jacob Astor.
[92] A great deal has been made of it. Its extent is discussed by A. C. McLaughlin, in Amer. Hist. Association, *Report* for 1888, pp. 78–79; Quaife, *Chicago and the Old Northwest*, pp. 263–264; and many details in *Mich. Hist. Coll.*, XVI, 36–37, 523, 524, 525, 537, and index.
[93] *Ibid.*, p. 510.
[94] *Ibid.*, pp. 363–64, 367.

attempt by British citizens to apprehend anybody in Michigan.[95] This proclamation was doubtless really caused by a more reprehensible case, just decided by the Michigan court, in which the evidence showed the invasion and search of houses, with threats of force and refusal to release a deserter taken in one of them.[96]

There were other incidents of less significance.[97] Perhaps, of all incidents likely to prevent good relations, the search of American vessels on the Lakes was most serious. In answer to American objections at Ghent to unilateral disarmament on the Lakes, the British had proposed that all of them be held by one power.[98] The right of vessels of each power to navigate its portion of each lake sprang from property and sovereignty defined by the treaty line of 1783; no new treaty reference to it was needed. But, the line not being marked, it was common sense to treat all of each lake as navigable by both parties, regardless of any treaty provision—which on that point was lacking. Searches of either American vessels or British were designed to prevent smuggling or to capture deserters. For various reasons American offenses were few, British relatively numerous—and mainly on Lake Erie.[99] The government in London, by the summer of 1816, was willing to adopt any reasonable system to reduce expenses and lessen controversy. It was agreed in Washington, after cessation of all work on American vessels, that the British fleet should not be enlarged during negotiations, and the governor general was instructed by London to discourage, by every means in his power, actions prejudicial to good relations.[100] Inquiries

[95] *Mich. Hist. Coll.,* XVI, 313, 362, 365–366 (proclamation of October 27, 1915).

[96] Blume (ed.), *Transactions of the Supreme Court of the Territory of Michigan, 1805–1836* (6 vols., Ann Arbor, 1935–40); *Mich. Hist. Coll.,* XVI, 238–241, 247–249, 321–350. The name appears as Vidal except in a letter of the defendant (*ibid.,* p. 350) and in the court record. The statement of facts in A. L. Burt, *U.S., G.B.,* is not in accord with the evidence printed in these two sources.

[97] Blume, *Transactions,* pp. 354, 363 (stolen horses), 474, 500 (deserters).

[98] "That the whole [all the] Lakes should belong to one party," C. F. Adams (ed.), *The Memoirs of John Quincy Adams* (12 vols., Philadelphia, 1874–77), but not meaning some, as a whole, to each country.

[99] *Mich. Hist. Coll.,* XVI, 496–521, 529, 534, 546, 551, 552. Full discussions are in J. W. Foster, *Limitation of Armament on the Great Lakes* (Washington, 1914), written in 1892; E. A. Cruikshank, "Negotiation," pp. 151–182.

[100] Bagot to Monroe, July 26, and to Commodore Owen, August 14; Bathurst to Sherbrooke, September 16. *Mich. Hist. Coll.,* XVI, 502, 517–518, 529.

into the actual armament of each power and discussion of virtual disarmament were both initiated by the American government, but were carried forward with equal good will by both parties. In February, 1817, after Monroe had become President, the suggestions earlier made by him to Bagot were accepted: save for a total of four small and lightly armed vessels to be used for revenue purposes, the frontier between the two countries was totally disarmed. The agreement was embodied in official notes between the British minister and the secretary of state.[101] The good will developed during Bagot's extremely impartial service made possible the settlement of another, much older boundary problem.

The peace treaty of 1783 fixed the boundary between Canada and the United States as running from the Lake of the Woods due west to the Mississippi, although most contemporary maps did not show the river as running that far north, and Lord Shelburne was warned by fur traders that in their opinion it did not.[102] The British later adopted the view that the treaty grant to them of the right to navigate the Mississippi sufficiently justified a demand that the boundary be redrawn to make it meet the river. In the Jay negotiations of 1794, however, although Britain asked for one of two suggested rectifications of the boundary for that purpose, neither of these would in fact have satisfied the objective. In 1802 a convention fixing a line between the Lake of the Woods and the nearest source of the river failed to become effective. A minor reason for its abandonment was a belief that the proper northern boundary of Louisiana (just acquired by the United States) was latitude 49°, and that the suggested line would lie wholly within American territory and add some of it to Canada. Finally, in 1818, the boundary was fixed as a line from the northwesternmost point of the Lake of the Woods southward on the meridian of that point to the parallel of 49° and westward on that to the Rocky Mountains. It was identical with an article as framed in 1803, 1807, and 1814, but for different reasons not then adopted.[103]

The negotiations of the convention of 1818 covered a wide range of other matters left unsettled in earlier years, but none of these concern us except a last effort to secure navigation of the Mississippi, and access

---

[101] Of April 28 and 29, Miller, *Treaties*.

[102] S. F. Bemis, "Jay's Treaty and the Northwest Boundary Gap," *AHR*, XXVII (1922), 465–484; Miller, *Treaties*; Moore, *International Arbitrations*.

[103] Miller, *International Acts*.

to it with goods from Canada on terms that would have made reality of the old dream of a British inland commercial empire. The American commissioners absolutely excluded discussion of access to the river.[104] The extraordinary thing about these negotiations was the mutual good will with which they were conducted during nearly four years.

There was an explanation for much of this. George III had expressed for his government in 1783 the hope that "Language, Interest, Affections . . . [might] prove a bond of permanent union" between Britain and her long-time colonies. Those factors for abiding peace had been slowly altering relations between the United States and Canada, and ill will along the border had largely disappeared by 1817. Both in the East and in the West, the two countries were growing together in understanding.[105]

Loyalists were the first American settlers in Canada. In the East, they sailed to the maritime provinces, or simply crossed the New England boundary; in what became Upper Canada they were settled by the government. Most of those in the maritime provinces, if they remained in Canada, eventually moved westward in search of better land. Even in original settlements in Nova Scotia and Upper Canada, some betrayed a "republican" or "mutinous" materialism in objecting to taking land allotted to them without choice.[106] In Upper Canada, the constitutional act of 1791 had established representative government, and land titles were free of all feudal incidents. Land was abundant and cheap, and government grants to encourage permanent settlement were liberal. It is important, too, to remember that all of the southern portion of Ontario, up to the latitude of Toronto, lies east of southern Michigan up to Saginaw, and that all of New England below the middle of Vermont and New Hampshire is in the same geographical belt. The westward migration route south of the Great Lakes, or later by boat on Lake Erie, was the direct route alike to northern Ohio and to Upper Canada. By 1812, the western end (as far eastward as Toronto) of

[104] *A.S.P., For. Rel.,* IV, 391, 395.

[105] Lanctot, *Canadiens,* pp. 124, 130–133, 137, 139; Hansen, *Canadian and American People, passim.* The latter cites an estimate (p. 75) that on the Vermont frontier 15,000 Americans had settled across the border by 1807, and 20,000 by 1812. In M. Wade, *The French Canadians, 1760–1945* (New York, 1955), it was estimated that there were some 2 million persons in the states who were of Quebec or Acadian origin (55 per cent of the number of French Canadians in Canada).

[106] Hansen, *Canadian and American People,* pp. 66–90, 91–94; Dunham, *Political Unrest,* pp. 8–9; Landon, *Western Ontario,* pp. 33–39.

what is now the province of Ontario was considerably settled, and the majority of its inhabitants were Americans.

The fact that these were of two elements, the Loyalists and the mere land-seekers, affected Canadian history greatly in the War of 1812, and hardly less for two decades after that. In the western portion of the area then settled, the temper of society and politics was democratic. In the region around Lake Ontario's western end, Loyalism was strong and British social and political influence were more in evidence. The controversy between Great Britain and the states over neutral rights opened rifts in Canadian opinion which appeared to the authorities to amount to divided loyalties after 1807. When war came, nothing worse appeared in Lower Canada than an uneasy neutralism. In Upper Canada Americans had long been dominant in the General Assembly, the elective lower house of the legislature, and three of its members (then or earlier) chose the American side.[107] The Executive Council decided, the Assembly refusing to join, on a general oath of allegiance, and to expel men claiming exemption from military service. However, little enforcement resulted.[108] Hundreds who left the province were sufficiently important to be listed by the government; hundreds more are believed to have left. It was clearly Loyalist militia and British regulars who prevented occupation of Upper Canada by American invaders. In judicial proceedings of 1814, fifteen inhabitants were sentenced to death for treason (one admitting guilt), and eight were hung. Estates of nearly thirty, accused but not apprehended, were forfeited. Naturally, some of these last led raids against Canada during the war.

This intermingling went on and on, contributing to mutual understanding between the two countries. The problems were part of Upper Canada's development, not of the American West's. But the reasons that made them problems in Canada were reasons that had very greatly therefore—intermingling, problems, and causes, particularly the last—affected the development of the American West since 1760. All three, must be briefly considered.

When war ended, Canada needed more than ever an increase of population, and taxes adequate for the opening of roads. But, although

[107] Burt cites authority (p. 183) for the statements that in 1812 two-thirds of the assembly were natives of the United States; and that but for a proclamation by the governor "making it treason for any one to attempt to cross the line," half the population would have left. That the governor could do this is the most significant of these facts.

[108] Landon, *Western Ontario,* pp. 33–34.

a vast westward migration in the states began in 1815, the flow into Canada, blocked by the unfriendliness which had been engendered, never again attained the relative proportion of earlier years. Emigration from the northern states through the Mohawk Valley of New York moved straight ahead into Illinois and Iowa. A small part moved north into Michigan, its size increasing after the opening of the Erie Canal made it possible to avoid the bad roads of northwestern Ohio and to transport household goods by boat up Lake Erie. But, had American migrants considered Canada, the actions taken after the war against those already there would have checked the thought. An equally notable change was the beginning of British immigration into Canada in 1814. Under the mercantilistic system Britain did not allow more than a trickle of her subjects to go to her colonies.[109] In particular, artisans were not allowed to go until 1824.[110] In 1814, however, some "distressed" persons were allowed to migrate to Canada in troopships sent for British soldiers. Thereafter, as her commercial liberalism increased so did emigration, although it is estimated that more than half of those who went to Canada went on to the United States.[111]

Questions of great importance arose immediately after the war respecting the political status of provincial residents of American origin, and the discussion of these questions aroused bitter controversy. In 1815 the London government ordered (1) that no more land grants should be made to them, and (2) that, if possible, the entry of additional Americans should be prevented. Businessmen and land speculators strongly opposed the latter order, preferring the Americans to "pauper"

[109] Joshua Child estimated that he was in a minority of one to one thousand in favoring emigration. *Cambridge History of the British Empire*, I (1929), 564–565. Josiah Tucker estimated that from 1759 to 1777 an annual average of the "enormous, and almost incredible number" of 6,000 had gone to America. G. L. Graham, *British Policy and Canada*, p. 62. William Knox, a shell-crusted mercantilist, felt that the loss of the thirteen colonies would benefit England; that it would "prevent emigration to America." *Ibid.*, p. 53. More fully, on Tucker's views, R. L. Schuyler, *Old Colonial System*, index, *s.v.* "Tucker."

[110] Discharging soldiers who were handicraftsmen in America was a matter for General Gage's attention in 1768. C. E. Carter (ed.), *The Correspondence of General Thomas Gage with the Secretaries of State* (2 vols., New Haven, 1931). In 1794, ports were still being watched to keep them at home, and it was another thirty years before the restriction was removed. Bemis, *Jay's Treaty*, p. 214; Schuyler, *Colonial System*, p. 120; S. C. Johnson, *Emigration from the United Kingdom to North America, 1763–1912* (London, 1913).

[111] Hansen, *Canadian and American People*, pp. 97–101; Dunham, *Political Unrest*, p. 12.

immigrants.[112] The entire land policy of the colony, which had been
exceptionally improvident and in several respects objectionable, was
attacked in the General Assembly, and conflict over it between that
body and the Executive Council widened into one over the entire field
of government policy. Meanwhile, the other instruction was so applied
that it raised the questions, who were "illegally" occupying land, and,
were "aliens" occupying land?

The attempt to exclude American immigrants was gradually abandoned. The details of the controversy may be ignored, but its large
features are important. The issues were legal, but there was no law to
settle them. There were, of course, no British statutes on naturalization
(its possibility not being admitted), but only laws relative to voting,
officeholding, and privileges of British subjects. These had been ignored
in Upper Canada, because assumed to be inapplicable to a colony. But
if not ignored, the majority of its inhabitants had no rights to the privileges they were enjoying. Controversy on these matters continued for a
decade. The solution, characteristically, was a statute of Upper Canada
(1) dictated by the London government, which (2) indicated what
inhabitants should enjoy the privileges of British subjects, but (3) did
not even mention aliens or naturalization, and (4) provided solely for
Americans already resident in the colony, with no mention of those
who might later enter.[113] This was no temporary solution of the alien-
age-naturalization problem; it was merely an evasion of it—although
there had been forty-odd years to think about it since the peace of 1783
and the impressment problems preceding the War of 1812 had shown
its importance.[114]

In connection with aspects of colonial administration elsewhere noted,
here again are the ignorance and incuriosity of high provincial officials
respecting British law applicable to the colony, and equal ignorance in
London respecting what provincial officials had for years been doing.
Again, it is amazing that city archives of 1827 reveal that such matters
as dog taxes and fire prevention "in the several police towns" of Upper

[112] On the trades and occupations in which Americans were prominent, see
Hansen, *Canadian and American People,* p. 77, and Landon, *Western Ontario,*
pp. 50–53.

[113] The best discussion is in Dunham, *Political Unrest,* pp. 67–78.

[114] That is, there were persons in Canada whose presence suggested that
problem. The new statute removed them from within its compass for legal
purposes; so to speak, it hid them.

Canada were dealt with by authorities in London.[115] Such matters have nothing to do with the development of the American West beyond indicating the probability that causes for poor relations between it and Upper Canada would presumably continue. The American Northwest was developing with extreme rapidity. Ohio, Indiana, Illinois, and Missouri were members of the Union by 1820; Michigan was being, at last, rapidly settled. In all local affairs they were free of distant government, free to experiment in local legislation. They played, too, a part in national affairs that was already important in 1812 and steadily becoming more so. American political practices were increasingly bound to influence Canadian thinking. Agitation there for popular participation in local government had begun strikingly in 1817. By 1825 two popular leaders had appeared to rouse debate not only over the policies of provincial government but over its basis. One, silenced under a statute passed *ad hoc* for disturbing public tranquillity, left Canada. The other carried agitation onward toward the reforms of 1837.

[115] G. C. Patterson, "Land Settlement in Upper Canada, 1783–1840," Province of Ontario, Department of Records, 16th *Annual Report* (Ontario, 1921), p. 4. Local government in general was exercised by the judges of general quarter sessions, appointed by the lieutenant governor.

CHAPTER 11

Removing Indians and Selling Public Lands

REMOVAL of the Indians was a formidable problem. It was in the Northwest that heavy settlement was foreseen, and there the relations established in the Revolution between the Indians and the British made progress exceedingly difficult. It has been seen that great land sales were made in Ohio in 1787, and the first settlement, at Marietta, was made in 1788. However, until British evacuation of the Northwest in 1796, all policies were entangled with diplomatic problems. Before discussing further the survey and settlement of that section, it seems desirable to consider the entire problem of removing the Indians east of the Mississippi.

Reference has been earlier made to Jefferson's plan to reserve Louisiana for the Indians in return for their removal from lands east of the Mississippi. The Act passed in 1804 for the government of the Territory of Orleans (the present Louisiana) empowered the President to do this, and one condition in assignments of western land to Indians was that they might not sell it "to the citizens of the United States."[1]

In 1806, Jefferson reported to Congress the willingness of western Indians to move in order to make room for various tribes of the Northwest.[2] The latter, at least in part and in times of depression, had long been tempted to move beyond the Mississippi; some had, indeed, removed there before and immediately after the Revolution. No doubt this was often caused by personal restlessness, but often, too, fear and

[1] Section 15 of the Act of March 26, 1804, Carter, *Terr. Papers*, IX, 212.
[2] February 19, 1806, Richardson, *Messages*, I, 398.

politics were involved.[3] The superintendent of Indians in Upper Canada in 1790, Alexander McKee, reported their inclination to do this (notwithstanding their defeat, then recent, of United States forces under General Harmar) unless assured of British aid. McKee submitted to his superior the question how far their removal "would be consistent with our [British] Interest."[4] In 1793, with permission of the Spanish authorities, part of the Shawnee and Delawares did remove to Cape Girardeau, Missouri.[5] Although Madison and Monroe thoroughly agreed with Jefferson's policy, nothing was done until 1817 beyond what Governor Harrison of Indiana Territory was able to accomplish by various purchases. By that time the westward flow of emigrants necessitated a national plan, and great areas of territory in the Southwest had been acquired in terminating war with the Creeks. A proposal of removal made in 1817 to the northwestern tribes was accompanied by an offer of land for life, with full title to their children, to such of the Ohio Indians as should choose to remain. Many did remain, and twelve tracts were allotted to them.[6] Thereafter, by treaties of 1818 and 1819, enormous areas were secured in Indiana and Illinois from tribes that were moved westward.[7] It has been authoritatively estimated that by 1824 some 8,000 had been moved into southwestern Missouri.[8] Michigan and Wisconsin tribes were removed by later treaties, but none of the tribes was removed intact at one time. Indians were exceedingly individualistic in this as in all other matters. They moved in small groups or even individually, more or less simultaneously with other groups. After their first settlement in Missouri, the Shawnee and Delawares, for example, continued to make other moves, and many of those who had originally elected to remain in Ohio, Indiana, and Illinois also moved.[9] No doubt many bands wandered westward "be-

[3] The Peoria of Illinois about 1780, and the Shawnee immediately after the Revolution. G. Foreman, *Indians and Pioneers . . . the American Southwest before 1830* (New Haven, 1930), pp. 216 n., 217 n. Emigrants of many tribes, including Cherokee, collected there. *Ibid.*, p. 31 n.

[4] *Mich. Hist. Coll.*, XXIV, 140. McKee believed removal not consistent with British interests.

[5] *U.S. Statutes at Large*, VII, 397.

[6] Kappler, *Indian Affairs*, II.

[7] *Ibid.*

[8] A. H. Abel, "The History of Events Resulting in Indian Consolidation West of the Mississippi," Amer. Hist. Assoc., *Report* for 1906, I, 233 *et seq.*, esp. 287–295, 362.

[9] Foreman, *Indians and Pioneers*, pp. 214–215.

cause . . . homeless, stronger factions having ceded the land they claimed as their own."[10]

Despite these removals, it was estimated by the secretary of war that at the end of 1824 more than 12,000 Indians remained in Ohio, the lower peninsula of Michigan, northern Indiana, and northern Illinois, whose removal was planned—to Wisconsin, it was then proposed.[11] By 1830, Ohio was almost clear, and both Indiana and Illinois save for a small area south of Lake Michigan. Despite the great lag of Michigan behind the more southern states in settlement, nearly half of its area was likewise cleared. Many scores of treaties are involved in the Northwest.

An authority who devoted many years to the study of Indian cessions gave a special account of those within Indiana's borders.[12] There were fifty-four "cessions," many of these being concurred in (once or more times) by other tribes in other treaties. Sometimes, after a cession by one tribe and a recession to it, the United States took cessions of the same land from one or more other tribes. Seemingly, by 1830 just twenty-one cessions were clear—with no overlapping cessions, no confirmations to follow. Tribal claims were not wholly extinguished until 1872.[13] Similarly, as respects Illinois, "The United States, in order fully to extinguish the Indian claim, actually bought it twice, and some portions of it three times."[14] The number of overlapping claims in that state is, indeed, amazing.[15] Seemingly, no tribe—north or south, at any time—renounced claims to any land where, in its wanderings, life had been pleasant—not, at least, while the United States would give annuities for the claim. This is not to say that they received more than they deserved; the point is—accepting as inevitable the policy of gradual displacement of a backward race—that the government obviously strove to be just.

[10] Abel, "Indian Consolidation," p. 295.

[11] Secretary Calhoun's report of January 24, 1825, as in *A.S.P., Ind. Aff.,* II, 542.

[12] Maps of cessions in each state, prepared by C. C. Royce, will be found in the 18th *Annual Report,* Part II, of the Bureau of American Ethnology, *Indian Land Cessions in the United States* (2 vols., Washington, 1889); Volume II contains the maps.

[13] C. C. Royce, Bur. of Amer. Ethnology, *Ann. Report,* I (1881), 257–262.

[14] On Illinois, *ibid.,* pp. 254–256, quotation, p. 256.

[15] As the writer understands the data, of eighteen treaties by nine tribes, each of eight cessions was overlapped by one other; each of three, by two others; each of two, by three others; each of two, by six others; each of two, by seven others; and one, by eight others.

As respects the tribes of the Old Southwest, the difficulty of postu-
lating the inevitability of a removal policy is far greater. Moreover,
removal was forced upon these Indians. However, though necessarily
executed by the federal government, the execution was also forced upon
it by a compact made by it with Georgia in 1802, already mentioned.[16]

Though all Indians were nomads, in the north their nomadic habits
had undoubtedly been greatly weakened by the dependence upon the
whites for food and clothes which was a consequence of the fur trade.[17]
In the Southwest, the adoption of the white man's manner of living by
many of the Creeks and Cherokee had a similar but greater influence.[18]
However, one should not assume that the Civilized Tribes, because civilized, remained at home. Some, attached to the French, crossed the
Mississippi after 1763, and the Cherokee settled in Missouri in 1795.
After Jefferson adopted a removal policy, he caused Indian delegations
to inspect the trans-Mississippi area, and held other conferences to com-
pose their differing opinions. Doubtless this stimulated unofficial and
impermanent removals. By 1815 perhaps 2,000 Cherokee were living in
Arkansas, and they were a powerful element in the wars of the trans-
Mississippi region.[19]

These migrants, in the main, had moved without formal agreements
and were only tentatively western settlers. Even though they had made
some considerable cessions to the United States, they had made no
agreement to remain in the West, and had received no western land.[20]
In 1817, however, the government agreed to give them as much land
there as they had abandoned in the East. Two years later, nearly one-
third of the Cherokee had moved or agreed to move, but the rest were
opposed to removal.[21] On that policy the Lower Creeks (in Georgia)

[16] An account of the dispute, by an ardent friend of the Indians, is in H. R.
Schoolcraft, *Information Respecting the . . . Indian Tribes of the U.S. . . .*
(6 vols., Washington, 1851–57), VI, 395–446.

[17] Although regulation of it, or the welfare of the Indians, sometimes *caused*
tribes to be moved.

[18] The debates in Congress in 1830 are full of data on these matters.

[19] Foreman, *Indians and Pioneers,* pp. 14, 26 n., 30 n., 32, 33, 39, 43, and
Pioneer Days in the Old Southwest (Cleveland, 1926), p. 27; Abel, "Indian
Consolidation," pp. 252, 256.

[20] A report by a House committee on the civilized tribes is in *A.S.P., Ind.
Aff.,* II., 457–460; other reports, chiefly on extinguishment of Indian claims
("title"), follow.

[21] Foreman, *Indians and Pioneers,* p. 171; C. C. Royce, "The Cherokee
Nation of Indians . . . ," Bur. of Amer. Ethnology, *Report* of 1887, pp. 121–
378, particularly 218, 227–228. The estimates were by the governor of Tennessee.

and the Upper Creeks (on the Alabama River and its tributaries), the Georgia Cherokee and the Tennessee Cherokee, were divided in opinions; and each group was, in less degree, similarly divided.[22]

From 1817 onward the compact of 1802[23] dominated the problem of removal—strictly speaking, of Indians in Georgia only, but virtually of all the southwestern tribes. The matter became, then, primarily a chapter in constitutional history. Congress, by an Act of 1830, finally enforced removal in accord with Jackson's views. The removal policy, in its general basis and ideal, was sound. It had one great weakness: that it was too late even by 1805 (as Governor Wilkinson of Upper Louisiana had then warned Jefferson) to remove the whites already west of the Mississippi, or to exclude others. President Monroe's belief was that the success of removal depended upon assuring the Indians three things: adequate land, permanent security of occupancy (he said "title"), and some system of self-government. The first could easily have been satisfied by a steady policy of government; the Quapaw, for example, though only a few hundred in number in 1803, claimed the land between the Red and Arkansas rivers for several hundred miles westward.[24] In all the Missouri-Arkansas region there could hardly have been 5,000 warriors of all tribes.[25] The third desideratum had been satisfied in a small degree for the Cherokee by their adoption of a constitution in 1827. But, as the second could not be realized in Georgia, at least, the old idea of an independent Indian state could not have been possible east of the Mississippi. That it was seriously contemplated as possible (1823–25) west of that river there is no doubt; but for various political reasons (including southern prejudices based on color), even the idea of an exclusively Indian territorial government was abandoned, and military supervision of a reservation, which was originally a necessity, was made permanent by inertia.[26] This "solution" had, in fact, been taking form ever since 1803, and in it were repeated most of the wrongs and errors of earlier times until the Indians were given a region definitely their own (for a time).

[22] U. B. Phillips, "Georgia and State Rights," Amer. Hist. Assoc., *Report for 1901*, II, 68; the lands of the Creeks are discussed at pp. 39–65, those of the Cherokee at pp. 66–86.

[23] G. Foreman, *Indians and Pioneers,* p. 14.

[24] According to data accepted *ibid.,* pp. 14, 26 n.

[25] *A.S.P., Ind. Aff.,* II, 543.

[26] Foreman, *Indians and Pioneers,* pp. 210–226; President Adams's message, Richardson, *Messages,* I. Secretary Barbour's later plan was to form it from volunteer individuals, disregarding tribes. Abel, *supra,* n. 8, 365–367, 453.

The difficulties preventing any permanent and logical solution of the problem were not all in the minds and acts of the whites only. Indians who practiced agriculture were derided as "fieldmakers"—and menaced—by warlike tribes. War was constant; and sometimes, when the civilized tribes first penetrated far beyond the Mississippi, it was between those with guns and others with only bows and arrows, as it had been when the Iroquois shattered the Hurons a century and a quarter earlier.[27] New times, and equally the childlike quality of all Indians, are illustrated by the complaint of the Osage that the Cherokee "had insulted them by bringing spoons in their pockets" to a conference called by the Osage.[28] As respects relations between whites and Indians, there were, naturally, some signs of change for the better. In one treaty, for example, land was acquired from the Indians at approximately 1,200 acres for a dollar, but was appraised at six dollars per acre when given in settlement of a trader's claim against them. The Indians, too, were undoubtedly tamer. In the Old Northwest, surely no woman would have wished, as did the widow of an agent with the Cherokee in Arkansas, to remain alone among them; she charmed them with her piano playing.

Great steps, in moving more and more tribes out of Missouri, and then in 1824 to 1828 out of and westward of Arkansas, prepared the way for the creation in 1834 of a true Indian Country, which for some fifty years realized the promise made in a treaty of May 6, 1828, that the Indians should have "a permanent home . . . which shall . . . never . . . be embarassed by having extended around it the lines, or placed over it the jurisdiction of a new territory, or a state, nor be pressed upon [by] the extensions of the limits of any existing territory or state."[29]

Removal beyond the Mississippi of the 77,000 so listed in 1824 was far from complete in 1830. The Removal Act of 1830, passage of which was forced by Georgia, expedited performance of the task; by 1840 it was substantially completed.[30]

[27] *Ibid.*, p. 268; Foreman, *Indians and Pioneers*, pp. 24, 45.
[28] Kappler, *Indian Affairs*, II, 147 (1824); Foreman, *Pioneer Days*, p. 36, and *Indians and Pioneers*, p. 83 (relying, for the spoon incident, on Nuttall, 1819).
[29] Kappler, *Indian Affairs*, p. 206.
[30] George Catlin's map showing Indian locations in 1833 should be compared with his map of locations in 1840. In 1830, approximately 12,000 square miles of Alabama were still occupied by Chickasaw, Choctaw, Cherokee, and Creeks.

The cessions of their western claims to the Old Congress by the several states created one of the greatest administrative problems of the Confederation and the federal government—disposition of the public lands. Its performance was obviously one of the greatest factors in the West's development, so far as that was affected by governmental influences. Some treaty requirements, some past declarations of public policy, and some inveterate habits of citizens and of government seemed certain to affect administration in the outset.[31]

The first—a requirement that must be honored—was the recognition of foreign titles that had originated in earlier periods of foreign rule. There were such provisions in the treaty of 1783 with England, and later in those of 1803 with France and of 1819 with Spain. But recognition was required only of titles, after due consideration of title claims. The bulk of contested or questionable claims—in West Florida, Louisiana, Missouri, the Illinois Country, and the Detroit area—was very great. So far as they rested on grants made by local authorities (such, in the Illinois Country, as Virginia's county lieutenants and the magistrates of the French villages, or Lord Dunmore in Kentucky), they were without legal basis.[32] Conditions in Missouri were presumably much the same as in Illinois, many of the same speculators operating, in early years of American control, in both. Both, too, in earlier years had been under the same administration, from New Orleans. General Gage proposed to annul all French grants in the Northwest, but seemingly found none.[33] References have been earlier made to land speculation as a prime activity in West Florida from 1763 onward. A demand that land titles be left undisturbed was a condition which quali-

[31] Few aspects of western development have been more adequately discussed than that of the public lands. Statistics in great detail are given in T. C. Donaldson, *The Public Domain: Its History, with Statistics . . .* (Washington, 1884). P. J. Treat, *The National Land System* (New York, 1910), covering all aspects; B. H. Hibbard, *A History of the Public Land Policies* (New York, 1924), far broader than its title; and R. M. Robbins, *Our Landed Heritage: The Public Domain, 1776–1936* (Princeton, 1942), are the other most important books. C. F. Emerick, *The Credit System and the Public Domain,* and A. C. Ford, *Colonial Precedents of Our National Land System . . .* (Madison, 1908), opened vistas for later work.

[32] Louisiana authorities made grants in the Illinois Country; example in M. M. Quaife (ed.), the *John Askin Papers* (2 vols., Detroit, 1829–31), I, quarto edition, frontispiece. Valid grants in Canada could be made only by the authorities in Quebec.

[33] Carter, *Gage Correspondence,* I, 307, 348; on Detroit, N. V. Russell, *British Regime in Michigan,* pp. 101, 116, 120.

fied the desire of its prominent inhabitants for annexation by the United States. In Louisiana, the extent of private claims was enormous.

Claims against governments, sure to carry liberal interest, are never renounced; great numbers of all these private land claims—all necessarily ancient—were unsettled in 1880, and even later.[34] They presented puzzling differences in the extent to which they covered the area of different states. These are not consistently explainable by geographic location, and certainly not by the variant intensity of speculation. They illustrated, presumably, official favoritism, qualified by other considerations.[35]

Only in Illinois Territory were all claims of title scrupulously examined by competent officials.[36] Their reports revealed illegalities of stupendous extent—fraud, perjury, subornation, and forgery—and the complete record was published.[37] There is no evidence that the commissioners who performed the task were actuated by politics; that charge was merely the cry of those unmasked.[38] There is every reason to believe that the situation was everywhere as uniform as its causes— land lust and opportunities for chicanery. Politics was manifestly involved to prevent similar investigations in other territories.

The private claims thus confirmed amounted ultimately to an area exceeding 50,000 square miles.[39] There can be no doubt that they were considered with the greatest possible allowance for equities.

A second initial control on administration, which was involved in rejecting some claims of foreign title, was the policy of refusing recognition of any claim originating in a private purchase from the Indians.

[34] Donaldson, *Public Domain* (to 1880); table (giving data down to 1904) in Hibbard, *Public Land Policies*, p. 29.

[35] In Illinois, the private claims amounted to only .51 per cent of the state's land area; in Michigan, which was surely less accessible from Quebec than Illinois from New Orleans, to 1.36 per cent. Every state offers difficulties.

[36] The British had cleared up doubtful French and Spanish titles in West Florida by simply giving British titles if others were renounced. C. Johnson, *British West Florida, 1763–1783* (New Haven, 1943), p. 31; C. N. Howard, *British Development of West Florida, 1763–1769* (Berkeley, 1947), p. 31. In Michigan the American judges reported that there were "only eight legal titles to land" (*A.S.P., Pub. Lands*, I, 283). As title, they therefore recognized occupation and cultivation since July 1, 1796, when American occupation began.

[37] The situation there is thoroughly discussed by the writer in *Ill. Hist. Coll.*, XXI, xxiv–xxxvi, lxv–c.

[38] Which C. W. Alvord faintly echoed in *The Illinois Country, 1678–1818* (Springfield, 1920), p. 421.

[39] They totaled 52,250.75 square miles up to 1904. Hibbard, *Public Land Policies*, p. 29.

Congress adhered firmly to the policy of the Continental Congress, which followed the British policy constantly proclaimed from 1763 onward. Nevertheless, the problem was again presented by British titles originating in private purchases in the Northwest after 1783 while withheld with the northwestern posts. After re-establishment of American sovereignty, attempts were made to secure American recognition of enormous purchases of this nature.[40]

A third policy that was certain to operate in administration of public lands was that much of them would be given away—perhaps not to speculators (although the start in 1787 left that a decided possibility), but to others whom precedents had suggested as proper objects of favor. Many American soldiers had received land bounties for service in the French and Indian War; Congress and the states had given land during the Revolution to stimulate enlistment and reward British deserters. Twice as much—more than the combined areas of Delaware and Connecticut—would later be given to soldiers serving in the second war with Britain; and though that would be all within the period of this volume, it would be a bare beginning.[41] There were colonial precedents, too, for gifts of land in aid of education, and these were to be followed on a grand scale.[42]

Finally, a fourth basic rule of practice was bound to operate in all fields as it did in the consideration of the private claims above discussed. This was the consideration of all equities in individual cases. Squatters had been a considerable portion of the population of every colony, and each one had perforce dealt more or less liberally with them. In many cases they were undoubtedly simply given title; in par-

[40] *Debates and Proceedings in the Congress of the U.S.* (hereafter, *Annals of Congress*), 9th Cong., 2nd Session, pp. 1027–1028. John Askin and associates purchased a million acres south of Lake Erie between Cleveland and Sandusky ("the Cuyahoga Purchase") for a minuscule sum, and went as high as Secretary Hamilton in seeking recognition of the title. Quaife, *Askin Papers*, II, 5–8, and *Burton Historical Leaflets*, No. 7, reprinted in F. C. Bald, *Detroit's First American Decade, 1796–1805* (Ann Arbor, 1948), pp. 12–14; further history, 233–234.

[41] Donaldson, *Public Domain*, pp. 82, 209–213, 232–237, 210; Hibbard, *Public Land Policies*, Chap. 7, especially p. 132. Military bounties in form of transferable scrip were decidedly not sound public policy. Henry George, *Our Land and Land Policy* (New York, 1901), p. 15.

[42] E. W. Clews, *Educational Legislation and Administration of the Colonial Governments* (New York, 1899). The Ordinance of 1785 reserved section 16 of every township for schools and four other sections for later disposition by Congress. *J.C.C.*, XXII, 446; Carter, *Terr. Papers*, II, 12.

ticular, the allowance of pre-emption rights had been liberally accorded to them.[43] When Virginia passed a general land act in 1779 to lessen the muddle produced by her past loose practices in Kentucky, she found it necessary to adjust the relative equities of bounty holders, of settlements before or after certain dates in her legislation, of pre-emption rights for actual settlement before or after a stated date, of a settlement later in date but of longer duration, for raising a corn crop, for building a "hut."[44] This was merely the application of the basic principle of ethics, in law as in common sense—that circumstances alter cases.

After gaining independence, Massachusetts, New York, and the four southern states held large amounts of unsold land. Kentucky and Tennessee were virtually outside the federal system; South Carolina and Georgia would be completely so unless and until they should make cessions to the Congress—which were postponed for years. When the land ordinance of 1785 was adopted, it was anticipated that all of these states, by selling their lands, would obstruct Confederation policy of selling their common lands in the Ohio region. But state policies of land management had little influence upon the federal system except in some details in much later years.[45]

In fact, the federal system had great advantages. Some of these, however, could not be appreciated by the ordinary citizen, or in the early years of the system's operation. The removal of all feudal incidents from land title was a vast improvement in social organization under law, but such incidents were in course of obsolescence before the Revolution, and the ordinary citizen doubtless had no understanding of the importance of the simple rules of inheritance established by the Ordinance of 1787. The enormous ultimate economic gain from a system of rectangular units—forever free, also, of doubts respecting monuments and bounds—was also at first unappreciated, largely because of imperfect surveying instruments and inadequately trained surveyors.[46]

---

[43] H. Tatter, "State and Federal Land Policy During the Confederation Period," *Agricultural History*, IX (1935), 176–186; R. M. Robbins, "Preemption—A Frontier Triumph," *MVHR*, XVII (1932), 331–349.

[44] Early statutes in various states repudiated the rule of common law in protecting the "occupying claimant" who made improvements on another's land.

[45] R. S. Cotterill, "The National Land System in the South, 1803–1812," *MVHR*, XVI (1930), 495–528.

[46] This had colonial precedents; see Ford, *Colonial Precedents*, Chaps. 1–4.

On the other hand, if one considers what the main characteristics of settlement would initially be, some seeming disadvantages of the system must have worked in its favor. It was clear that early settlers would be predominantly poor. By 1785 it was also clear—to Washington, to Grayson (who reframed Jefferson's land ordinance), and to others—that settlers could not be held back, and settlement could not be systematic. A policy favoring poor settlers obviously called for sales of small tracts, and at low prices if not on credit. A policy aimed at large immediate revenue called for sales of great tracts for cash, at prices so low as to interest capitalists in tying up large investments. Debate over the relative merits of settlement policy and revenue policy continued. The failure of the speculators who made the Scioto purchase in Ohio,[47] the lesser tribulations of the Symmes Associates, and the success of the Ohio Company's plan of immediate settlement by the subscribers of capital taught a plain lesson. Speculators would turn to state lands, and at least some states would go incredibly far in co-operating with them.

Ohio was a problem state for initiation of the public land system. Six regions with special problems totaled nearly half of the state's area. With the largest of these, Virginia's military reserve, the federal government never had anything to do, save for a small portion in much later years. Connecticut's Western Reserve (as large as Connecticut) soon passed to the United States, and thereafter presented no problems. The Seven Ranges and the Ohio Company's purchase were the first to lose identity by sale. A great federal military reserve in the center of the state had a longer existence and special difficulties, and its purchase by the Symmes Associates, between the Great and Little Miami rivers north of the Ohio, presented tangled issues of law and ethics. No grant being ever made to the Scioto Associates, they have no memorial in Ohio's geography. However, the government did grant land to deluded French settlers of Gallipolis, who had bought, as land, shares in that partnership's option expectations.

The first Land Act passed by the Congress of the new Union, in 1796, provided for sales in the Seven Ranges at auction by townships—

The utter undependability of ordinary monuments is strikingly proved by the testimony of C. C. Royce, *Indian Land Cessions*. Most worthless of all were supposedly "blazed" lines.

[47] A. B. Hulbert, "The Methods and Operations of the Scioto Group of Speculators," *MVHR*, I (1915), 502–515; II (1915), 56–73.

alternately as entireties and by sections of one square mile (640 acres). The minimum price was two dollars an acre, and though 10 per cent was taken off for cash, or credit allowed up to one year (not enough to ensure even a first crop), the penalty for default in any payment was total loss of past payments and of any claim.[48] The act definitely established the rectangular system of survey and reserved four sections in every township for disposition by Congress. However, none of the provisions were in any way favorable to poor emigrants, and in operation it was a failure, since neither speculators nor settlers bought land. Settlers bought of the Ohio Company or Symmes, or lands in Connecticut's Reserve, or became squatters.[49]

A second Act, of 1800, drawn by William Henry Harrison, though intended to be a frontiersman's act, left the price at two dollars (unless paid in cash), made a half-section the minimum purchasable area (outside of the Seven Ranges), and allowed credit of four years on three-fourths of the purchase price.[50] This Act, too, was unsatisfactory. Establishment of a land office in each land district, by lessening objections to weeks-long auctions away from home, was a permanent improvement. However, if large-scale speculators were not operating through agents, it was plain that many buyers of limited means were speculating, since much land that was bought was not cultivated. A speculator buying with evidences of the public debt, which were held almost exclusively by wealthy men, was on exactly the same footing as a settler paying cash.[51]

Gallatin, secretary of the treasury, still adhered to Hamilton's revenue objective, but believed its success depended on sales of small tracts. In another law, of 1804, therefore, in accordance with his ideas, the minimum tract was made a quarter section, the cash price was slightly reduced, no interest was taken until after default, and small tracts were made grantable to actual occupants and improvers.[52]

Under these three early laws some results became clear. State com-

---

[48] May 18, 1796, *U.S. Statutes at Large,* I, 465. The price was set at two dollars, although "much state land was selling for from thirty cents to a dollar," "in order to shut out speculators and increase the revenue." Hibbard, *Public Land Policies,* p. 76.

[49] Less than 50,000 acres were sold. *A.S.P., Pub. Lands,* I, 73.

[50] May 10, 1800, *U.S. Stats. at Large,* II, 73.

[51] Hibbard, *Public Land Policies,* p. 77.

[52] *A.S.P., Pub. Lands,* I, 149; the Act, of March 26, 1804, *U.S. Stats. at Large,* II, 181.

petition presumably held sales down; certainly, if true, to the comfort of those who cherished the old fears that a westward drain of settlers would lower land values in the thirteen states.[53] But how much they actually delayed migration and frontier sales is wholly speculative. Much more certain is the conclusion that auctions did not raise prices, and—if without that supposed merit—were in every way undesirable.[54] The most serious defect in actual operation of the laws was their credit provisions; but it must be remembered that credit was a necessity because it had not yet been learned what prices should be set for immediate settlers, and how to exclude all others. Up to 1811 nearly a fifth of the entire sum due for sales in the Northwest and Southwest was in arrears.[55] Between 1806 and 1820, a dozen statutes in relief of such debtors extended time for payment. However, as this was done haphazardly with respect to the land offices, years, and situations to which successive statutes applied, they were no bar to many forfeitures.[56] When exports dropped and hard money disappeared during the embargo years, when problems of paper money and banking became acute during the War of 1812, when speculation became universal, when migration westward became a flood following that war and the government's acceptance of paper money for land pushed speculation to fantastic extremes, the debts due it for land rose from $3 million to $17 million in the years 1815–18.

Upon that situation fell the panic of 1819. Since 1812 some petitions had come from the frontier for free land, or for a nominal price. From 1812 or earlier, congressional committees had recommended abolishment of the credit system. At the end of 1819 the unpaid balance due the government for lands north of the Ohio was $9,868,295, which was reduced by the end of 1820 to $6,610,924; in the Southwest, where speculation had been far more frenzied, the arrears at the later date were still $14,602,426.[57]

[53] Hibbard, *Public Land Policies*, pp. 58–61, 67, 71, 74, 76, 78, 101. Much state land was selling cheap—but what land? Sales by Massachusetts of Maine water and timber at 17 cents per acre were not competitive with even poor land in Ohio. Those sales, too, were to great speculators; see A. B. Hulbert, "Andrew Craigie and the Scioto Associates," Amer. Antiquarian Society, *Proceedings*, XXIII (1913). This was true of much eastern land.

[54] Hibbard, *Public Land Policies*, pp. 105 *et seq.*

[55] *Ibid.*, p. 88.

[56] *Ibid.*, pp. 93–94.

[57] Donaldson, *Public Domain*, p. 205; R. C. Buley, *The Old Northwest* . . .

In 1820 an Act was passed which abolished the credit system.[58] It was not, perhaps, primarily the injustice of forfeiture that caused this change; the age was one of very little sympathy for debtors. But the forfeiture provision would not work—it was very difficult to get a defaulting tenant off the land in order to resell it.[59] It was still more difficult to collect arrears from a debtor whose only means of payment was taken from him. Congress had aimed from the beginning to exclude speculators, yet had left open the way to nationwide, frenzied speculation. It now closed that way, reduced to $1.25 the price per acre, and reduced to eighty acres (an eighth of a section) the minimum acreage purchasable.

A series of relief acts cleared up the $21 million owing to the government under the credit system when it was abolished. Defaulters were allowed to settle for cash at the price, fixed for the future, of $1.25, which was the predominant result in the Northwest; or allowed to relinquish land, applying past payments to any part retained, which was the preferred solution in the Southwest; or to continue with a final extension of credit. Within half a year the debts were reduced some 40 per cent, but it was twelve years before all were liquidated.[60] The Act of 1820 carried the government some distance toward the final policy of disposing of the public lands.

That goal was reached through the pre-emption system. A pre-emption right was the right to settle on unappropriated public land and buy it, without competition, at the minimum government price. It would not "destroy all competition,"[61] but substitute competition in settlement for competition, rowdyism, and intimidation at auctions. Manifestly, the statutes theretofore in force conflicted in principle with recognition of squatters, and a choice between principles was unavoidable. Pre-emption was a reward to squatters, and therefore anathema to such Easterners as harbored the old-time fears of eastern depopulation, industrial decay, and subornation of officials.[62] Misjudgments

---

1815–1840 (2 vols., Indianapolis, 1940), I, 125; Hibbard, *Public Land Policies,* pp. 82–100.

[58] April 24, 1820, 3 *U.S. Statutes at Large,* 566.

[59] Neighbors would not bid on the land; speculators were not interested in such fortuities.

[60] *A.S.P., Pub. Lands,* III, 645; Hibbard, *Public Land Policies,* pp. 94–96, 99, 100.

[61] The quoted words were used in reports adverse to pre-emption.

[62] Robbins (*MVHR,* XVIII, 341) quotes a report of Richard Rush (1827),

of pre-emptioners were grossly unjust, for land-squatting had been a main factor in creating Americans. Such misjudgments were also associated with wholly fallacious ideas of English law. An illustration of this is found in views expressed in 1824 by a committee of the House of Representatives: "It cannot be perceived by what principle persons having no color of title should . . . [when on lands] known to belong to the United States at the time of . . . settlement, claim in it pre-emption rights. . . . [This encourages settlement] with little respect for the rights either of the Government or their Indian neighbors."[63] Public land was involved; but as for "having no color of title," it had been English law for over seven centuries that a wrongful possessor of private land (or chattels) would be protected by the courts against all the world (was owner against everybody) except a claimant showing a higher title—one of right *or an older one of wrong*. This was law in every American state. Law is a social product, created to protect or advance social interests. The squatter had never been punished as a wrongdoer, except when denied aid if an intruder on Indian hunting grounds. The government wanted to sell its lands promptly, and to actual settlers. Why should it not adopt the view governing private lands, at least to the extent of giving squatters a right to buy as against a stranger to the land who might later bid at an auction? Of course, too, the squatter would be entitled under common-law principles to legal protection against a "claim jumper" who ousted him to usurp his pre-emption right—and that too was ultimately recognized. Meanwhile, outside all law, squatters joined each other in self-protection by force.

These were the issues of substance in the question of pre-emption. All the states had given the squatter a legalized status. Its substantive content varied, but generally included pre-emption rights—they, too, of varying nature. Long before Virginia had ceded the Northwest to the Confederation, her county lieutenant in Illinois had reported

secretary of the treasury: "the creation of capital is retarded, rather than accelerated, by the diffusion of a thin population over a great surface of soil." *A.S.P., Finance,* V, 630, at 638. Pre-emption, then, to hasten settlement, would be desirable. Foot's Resolution, to consider the expediency of limiting sales of western lands (1829), the Webster-Hayne debate, and the pre-emption act of 1830 arose from discussion of the view Rush expressed—that any law would be salutary that counteracted the diffusion produced by the laws regulating western lands.

[63] *A.S.P., Pub. Lands,* III, 619.

"Land jobbers from the South side of the Ohio . . . making improvements (as they call them) upon Lands on this [the north] side of the River."[64] "Settlement rights" and "improvement rights" were property interests at least in the southern states, freely bought and sold, and collected by speculators along with the warrants of survey extravagantly issued by Virginia and North Carolina.

Emissaries and petitions from the frontier urged recognition of squatter rights from an early date. From 1791 onward, motions and committee reports in Congress revealed a continuing conflict. Preemption rights were granted, as already noted, in many claims under foreign titles after 1804.[65] They were granted to would-be purchasers from the Symmes Associates of lands outside the Symmes purchase.[66] They were given to settlers who built gristmills or sawmills; to a host of squatters on the land ceded in 1803 by Georgia to the United States before that was opened in 1806 for sales; to white squatters in Arkansas who were compelled to leave lands ceded to eastern Cherokee.[67] In 1821 and 1830 they were given to defaulting land buyers who were compelled to relinquish part of their claims under the option allowed by the law of 1820 that abolished the credit system. Moreover, in 1806 Congress had begun a practice of issuing indemnification "scrip" to claimants whose claims were confirmed but could not be located because of conflicting claims or surveys.[68] Such action presumably often involved mere occupants who claimed foreign titles.

During the entire period from 1789 to 1830, Congress passed only one statute "to prevent settlements . . . until authorized by law"— and that, seemingly, only to protect public property in two peculiar cases.[69] But until nearly 1830 no favor was shown to squatters. In 1828 the Committee on Public Lands of the House of Representatives reported in favor of pre-emption: "It is impossible to prevent settlement on the public lands. . . . It is right and proper that the first settlers who have made roads and bridges over the public lands at their own

[64] Chicago Historical Society, *Collections,* IV, 188.

[65] Treat, *National Land System,* Chap. ix.

[66] By Act of March 2, 1799 (three others later, required to adjust consequences of his irregular acts).

[67] U. B. Phillips, in Amer. Hist. Assoc., *Annual Report* for 1901, I, 29–37; Treat, *National Land System,* pp. 356–359, 362–366; Foreman, *Indians and Pioneers,* pp. 266, 267.

[68] Donaldson, *Public Domain,* pp. 236, 289.

[69] 2 *U.S. Statutes at Large,* I, 5; *Opinions of the Attorneys General,* I, 471, 475.

expense . . . should be allowed a privilege greater than other purchasers."[70] In 1830 the legislatures of three states petitioned Congress
to adopt pre-emption. It did so that year,[71] by an Act which, being for
one year only, was four times renewed, and then replaced by a permanent act of 1841.

Despite the ethical element of improvements, some historians have
regarded the committee pronouncement just quoted as embodying a
revolutionary or illegal doctrine.[72] Congress merely made a choice of
public policy in declaring the occupation of public land to be lawful.
The choice was a wise change in the law for two reasons. One is that
it was accordant with American practice since 1607. No law flatly contradictory of contemporary customs and belief is living law—because
it cannot be enforced. Squatters were certainly a very considerable
fraction of early Westerners, and undoubtedly they contributed a corresponding portion of western leaders.[73] The other reason is that it
was a great step toward attainment of the land system's primary objective, which, all agreed, was to sell the land to bona fide settlers. Under
the original system the government held an auction, hoping that a
buyer would come, settle, pay, and remain on the land. Abolishment
of sales on credit removed the third of these uncertainties, but the last
could never be removed.[74] The pre-emption system removed the first

[70] *A.S.P., Pub. Lands*, V, 401.
[71] May 5, 1830, 4 *U.S. Statutes at Large*, 420.
[72] Notably, Robbins, *MVHR*, XVIII, 332, 342, 343, 344, 345. Although not
erroneous, it implies a narrow interpretation to say that "agrarianism was
successful in tearing down an aristocratic land system and in dictating the
democratic basis for a new system." It was not merely, nor even primarily,
agrarianism. It was practicality (quicker settlement), and also legal consistency.
Congress extended to some public property, because it judged the extension to
serve public interest, the rule which since 1100 (it was ancient Germanic law)
had governed private property, land and chattels, in English law. If the pre-
emption system was "democratic," so was that ancient property rule. Robbins
denounced the law because of frauds practiced by speculators in its application.
Any law (seemingly) may be used for evil purposes.
[73] According to Joseph Schafer, it was on good authority that "it was reported in the United States Senate in 1837 . . . that the . . . Territory of
Wisconsin had a . . . legislative body made up, in a large majority, of men
who were squatters." *Social History of American Agriculture* (New York,
1936).
[74] The great uncertainty today is in keeping owners on the land, instead of
tenants. C. L. Stewart, *Land Tenure in the United States with Special Reference to Illinois* (Urbana, 1916); P. W. Gates, "Land Policy and Tenancy in
the Prairie Counties of Indiana," *Indiana Magazine of History*, XXXV (1939),
1–26.

two. The best way to catch a settler was after he so made himself—and he was likely to remain, having already made a choice of land, if he affirmed it with money.

The influence of early sectional fears, interests, or politics upon the public land system's development has several times been noted. Its vagueness may induce one either to exaggerate or unduly to minimize its influence. Before 1830 suggestions of drastic character were made to alter the system for political or economic purposes. Making political issues anew of old arguments over sales for revenue or sales for settlement, suggestions were made of graduating prices to fit the qualities of lands sold. The governor of Illinois, Ninian Edwards, a former senator and politically ambitious, proposed in 1826 (and again in 1828) that the public land within each state be forthwith ceded to it. In 1828, Senator Thomas Hart Benton introduced a "graduation" bill to reduce land prices annually down to 50 cents, then offer to actual settlers, gratis, all not yet sold, and a year after a last reduction to 25 cents donate any remainder to the states. Louisiana and Indiana officially asserted their rights to such land.[75] A committee of the House of Representatives went no farther than to recommend annual distribution of all profits to the states. All of these matters entered into a great and famous debate on Foot's Resolution, but only the proposal to distribute proceeds had any chance of approval. This had been earlier suggested than the more extreme suggestions already mentioned, and its consideration outlasted that given to the others, their lack of vitality being conclusive evidence of their purely political character.[76] A bill for distribution of proceeds was finally passed in 1833, but vetoed by President Jackson—for reasons that need not be mentioned beyond saying that some went back to the interstate compacts which created the public domain.[77]

The proceeds from sales of lands were not profits. Up through 1830 the cost of buying foreign lands, of buying peace from the Indians, and of administration exceeded by more than $19 million the income

[75] Several decisions of the Circuit and Supreme Courts established national title to public lands within the states.

[76] Benton's bill passed the Senate, but was tabled by the House, in which the greater population of the states without public lands could be effective.

[77] The matters referred to in the above paragraph are fully discussed in R. G. Wellington, *The Political and Sectional Influence of the Public Lands, 1828–1842* (Boston, 1914), and in Hibbard, *Public Land Policies*, Chap. 7 (pp. 171–184).

from sales.[78] In that respect, moreover, the situation did not improve with time but steadily worsened, as the cost of opening Indian lands, and of land gifts in aid of education and other social benefits, steadily mounted.[79]

[78] Relying on Donaldson, *Public Domain,* pp. 13, 17, 18, 20. Administration after 1812 was by the General Land Office, then created.

[79] By 1880 the cost of foreign land purchases had risen to $88.15 million, of payments to Indians to $187.32 million, of expenses of sales to $46.5 million. As the total of proceeds from sales was only $200.7 millions, the over-all deficit had become $121.33 million. These are Donaldson's figures, *Public Domain,* pp. 20, 21. Special land grants to individuals and worthy causes, which began before 1830 (*ibid.,* pp. 209–213), vastly and steadily increased, particularly for canals, roads, and railways, and for education (*ibid.,* pp. 223–239, 255 *et seq.*). Complete statistical tables on the land system's operation, compiled by A. B. Hart, are given in the *Quarterly Journal of Economics,* I, 252, 253.

CHAPTER 12

The Great Migration

THE rapidity with which the American people spread toward the Mississippi in the opening decades of the 1800's was phenomenal. An account of the movement is not accomplished by merely reciting statistics which prove the swiftness and magnitude of the movement; something must be said of the routes over which it moved, of the manner and costs of travel, and of the motives which impelled it. Nor was settlement accomplished merely by arrival in Ohio, Kentucky, or Alabama and Mississippi—the word implies, basically, fixation. It was by the farming of land and the prosecution of varied industries that a permanent society was established. This account of westward migration must be supplemented by a discussion of the West's economic and social development.

Various river and cross-mountain trails used by early fur traders and adventurous wanderers had no relation to mass migration and settlement, with which alone this discussion is concerned. Two facts controlled the early settlement of both the Southwest and Northwest. The first was that the Appalachians shut off most of the colonies from the interior. The borderers to whom reference has been frequently made were stragglers through the nearer valleys of the mountain barrier. The second dominating fact was the existence in its midst of a great central valley running from New York across Pennsylvania between mountain ranges (in Virginia the Blue Ridge and Alleghenies) down to the piedmont region of the southern colonies.

Only across New York was there a low and open way to the West, and there, also, were valleys for easy travel to the north. However, although the valley of the Mohawk was geographically open, it was politically closed by the military and trading policies of the Five Nations and the Dutch, which the British continued in Sir William Johnson's wardship of the Six Nations. Of enormous importance for that reason in the pre-Revolutionary straggler period, its aftereffects upon massive western settlement, in union with New York's land disposal policies, were great for four decades following the Revolution. Western New York remained a wilderness until long after Kentucky had various towns and thousands of inhabitants, and Rochester was "founded" in 1802, but it had only one house in 1811.[1] Only thin and very scattered settlements permit one to recognize even a frontier as existing east of its western border.[2]

Down the Great Valley, beginning in the mid-1700's, thousands of early migrants moved from western Pennsylvania into Virginia and western North Carolina before 1770. Some became the Wataugans. Much later, great numbers passed out of the Valley's southern end onto the piedmont of South Carolina and Georgia. Running across the mountains, the Potomac, Rappahannock, and James rivers facilitated entry of migrants into the Valley. Although the Appalachian streams were virtually impassable for household goods, unburdened emigrants —and their goods too, if they could be gotten up by land into the Great Valley—could pass by it down to the headwaters of the Greenbrier and Kanawha, and to the Cumberland Road at Cumberland Gap. All these were routes by water or road to the Ohio.[3]

By 1750, westward travel through Pennsylvania was virtually confined to two routes.[4] One was confined to a packhorse trail (the Forbes Road) between Philadelphia and Pittsburgh, which was improved as a military road by General Forbes in 1758. The other (the Cumberland Road) was a route up the Potomac and across southwestern Pennsylvania to Redstone Fort on the Monongahela. This was likewise an old Indian path, improved in 1755 for the transportation of General Brad-

---

[1] F. L. Paxson in *Mich. Hist. Coll.*, XXXVIII, 144.

[2] R. Higgins, *Expansion in New York* (Columbus, 1931), placed its frontier in 1800 at that point, instead of regarding the scattered settlers as stragglers beyond the frontier.

[3] A great amount of information respecting Indian trails and portages, emigration roads, and canals is in A. B. Hulbert, *Historic Highways* (16 vols., Cleveland, 1904), and a brief account is in his *Paths of Inland Commerce: A Chronicle of Trail, Road, and Waterway* (New Haven, 1920).

[4] Hulbert, *Historic Highways*, I, 133–134.

dock's cannon. These were two of the most used and most famous roads in western history. The latter, after half a century of deterioration but steady service, attained even greater fame, and far more importance, when—with minor changes of route—it was rebuilt from 1811 onward as the National Highway. Access to this road from Virginia and Maryland long involved the use of wagons, canoes, and small boats, and so many transshipments as made the route impractical for many travelers or any great amount of freight. Despite considerable improvements, its defects became the reason for the building of the Chesapeake and Ohio Canal.

If Indian hostilities or other reasons made the Pennsylvania routes undesirable, as was often the case both in very early years and after the Revolution, emigrants from Philadelphia and Baltimore could reach the Wilderness Road by entering the Great Valley at Wadkin's Ferry on the Potomac. Emigrants from Richmond gathered at Fort Chiswell, near the head of the Great Kanawha (Wyeth, Virginia). The Wilderness Road may perhaps best be regarded as starting at the Long Island in the Holston River, near Cumberland Gap, which was virtually unknown to whites until 1769. At the Gap, emigrants from the Carolinas gathered. From there the road ran up into Kentucky, dividing at Rockcastle Creek into two branches, of which the northern became the more important in western emigration. This ran to the Ohio River at Louisville.

The worst part of this route was in the wilderness where it started. The states lacked the money to construct good roads, and south of the Ohio there was no public domain which the United States could give to the states to finance road building. In 1793 Harry Toulmin advised emigrants that roads and accommodations were "tolerably good to the borders of the Wilderness," through which it was "hardly possible for a carriage to pass."[5] Most of the scores of thousands who settled in Kentucky before 1790 probably traveled by this route. Other thousands, however, emigrated by cross-country routes from Maryland and Pennsylvania as early as 1779–80, and great numbers in the 1780's

[5] H. Toulmin, *A Description of Kentucky . . . [also] Observations Respecting the United States* (Lexington, 1945), p. 96. R. C. Thwaites and G. P. Kellogg (eds.), *Revolution on the Upper Ohio* (Madison, 1908), p. 2, state that there was a wagon road to Powell's Valley, and beyond that, "until 1792," only a packhorse trail. In 1795 Virginia appropriated £2,000 to improve the eastern end, and Kentucky made the western part, legislatively, a wagon road. It never became a good road.

were entering from the Ohio River.[6] It has been said of the Cumberland Road that "it was by far the most difficult way" to the Old Northwest. However, the same authority also said that Boone's Wilderness Road was "the longest, blackest, hardest road of pioneer days in America."

The greatest problem in establishing a stable, self-sustaining western society was transportation—of families, household goods, farm crops, and eastern manufactures.[7] In the colonial era roads were few because inland trade was discouraged, and slight. Ferries were few, floating bridges fewer, fixed bridges virtually nonexistent.[8] This condition was everywhere the same up to 1783. Pennsylvania's two early military roads were in rough and difficult terrain. The Forbes Road, however, was the only fortified highway into the West, was built for heavy traffic, was maintained in relatively good repair, and was for a long time the safest and best road into the West. The carrying capacity of any road was limited by the character of the roadbed and the size of freighters that could use it. For this reason the Wilderness Road was displaced by the Pennsylvania roads before 1790 even in the settlement of Kentucky.

Wagons were abundant and rather cheap by 1790. Metal tires must have been used early, for in 1778 a wooden cannon wrapped with them was used in defending Boonesborough.[9] Narrow wheels cut even the best roadbeds so badly that broad-tired vehicles were ultimately charged lower (or no) tolls on the National Highway. Any wagon might be broken by ruts or stumps. Endless repairs, delays, and losses called for constantly better wagons; increasing freight and more numerous emigrants required larger ones. By about 1790 the "Conestoga wagon" had assumed the form which it retained to the end of the emigrant days east of the Mississippi. Long experience with rocky roads and mountain grades dictated every detail of its form.[10]

[6] T. P. Abernethy, *Western Lands and the American Revolution* (New York, 1937).

[7] The most notable specific study of this is still, perhaps, that of W. L. Wilgus, *The Role of Transportation in the Development of Vermont* (Montpelier, 1945).

[8] According to Jefferson, of eight rivers between Charlottesville and Washington, there were neither bridges nor ferry boats on five—H. B. Adams, *History of the United States . . .* (9 vols., New York, 1889–91), 1, 14.

[9] A. Henderson, *The Conquest of the Old Southwest* (New York, 1920), p. 276.

[10] The bed slanted upward toward each end; a brake could be operated

Beginning about 1795, the whole country built roads with frenzied energy. Many were turnpikes—the roughest of these being the bumpy corduroy roads of crisscross tree trunks laid in swampy lowlands. They introduced the turnpike era, with its passenger coaches and wayside inns; made possible larger Conestoga wagons and freighters; lessened the delays and uncertainties, the hardships, monotony, and loneliness of travel; and literally changed the face and tempo of the country. The first corporations chartered in the country were to build these roads. To some extent they were initiated to meet the needs of westward settlement, and they in turn enormously increased these needs. By a compact made with Ohio when she entered the Union in 1803, the national government assumed the obligation to build a road to her border. Pennsylvania dictated the route, by requiring that any road built within her borders must pass through Uniontown and Washington (Pennsylvania). The Cumberland Road, therefore, became the National Highway. Construction did not begin until 1811, but the entire road was opened in 1818 when it reached the Ohio border at Wheeling. The new macadamizing process was adopted. Four rods wide, slightly crowned, with drainage ditches at the sides, its bed a varying mixture of earth, crushed stone, sand, and gravel, with sound bridges, and no grade exceeding 5 per cent, the road was a freighter's dream come true—and an emigrant's. It was, moreover, constantly improved.[11]

Despite the excellence of Pennsylvania's roads, however, she lost primacy to New York in bringing emigrants to the West. Two turnpikes between the Hudson and Buffalo were completed by 1802. Buffalo, situated above the rapids of the St. Lawrence, was obviously destined to be the freight and travel center of the Northwest. After years of agitation, New York in 1817 also began the Erie Canal, which was

---

from either the ground or the driver's seat; the sides of the body flared outward; the wheels had broad tires, and the heavy spokes were "dished" and "toed-in" with strong nails; hoops supported a canvas cover.

[11] The United States was to build the road with 2 per cent of the proceeds from sales of public land within Ohio, and Ohio to spend 3 per cent on roads within the state. The cost for the most expensive portions averaged $13,000 per mile. The road was extended by Ohio to Zanesville by 1826, and to Columbus by 1833. Of various books describing the road, perhaps the best is that of A. B. Hulbert, *The Old National Road . . . American Expansion* (Columbus, 1901). The schedule of toll rates for 1831 (pp. 64–65) allowed for tires exceeding eight inches in breadth, but any above four inches were undoubtedly rare.

completed in 1825. Not wide or deep, nearly four hundred miles long, running through river valleys with virtually no grades, its boats—although slow and cramped—offered greater safety, less discomfort, and cheaper passage for freight and emigrants than the turnpikes.[12] Its carrying charges for household goods and other freight were far less. It was aided by Pennsylvania's reconstruction of the old French military road between Presque Isle and French Creek (Erie and Waterford)—the first good road ever opened in the Northwest.[13]

In the settlement of the Southwest, roads played either an obscure or a less important part. Of others than the Wilderness Road, there is little to say. In very early years travelers to the Cumberland settlements in Tennessee used the Wilderness Road until turning southward over an Indian trail north of Nashville. A direct road between Knoxville and Nashville was opened, however, in 1788.[14] These roads were important in the settlement of Tennessee, but not otherwise.

In connection with the settlement of Kentucky, something has been said of settlers entering from north of the Ohio. Even before 1780, squatters along that river were numerous from Fort McIntosh (Rochester, Pennsylvania) to the Muskingum, and up some of the Ohio's northern affluents. In 1785 a military force attempted to dislodge them for seventy-five miles below Pittsburgh—that is, well toward Wheeling.[15] Some of the settlers even posted a call for a constitutional convention. The government issued futile orders to prevent intruders from entering the Northwest from West Virginia and Kentucky, but St. Clair's efforts in 1785 were as fruitless as those of Bouquet in 1761. In 1788 the first forty-nine of the Ohio Company's members came west over the Forbes Road, and in April founded Marietta, where a government was instituted in July. Late that year, the establishment of Fort Washington marked the beginning of Cincinnati. By 1790, Lord Dorchester's agent in Philadelphia reported emigration to Kentucky and the Northwest as beyond the bounds of credibility, yet daily increasing, particularly from New England.[16] But all this was of uncertain perma-

[12] It was 363 miles long, cost $7 million, and its income the first year was $1 million. The present New York State Barge Canal (its successor) is still of importance.

[13] There is some account of it in Hulbert, *Historic Highways*, IX, 74–75.

[14] The Natchez Trace (R. S. Cotterill, "The Natchez Trail," *Tenn. Hist. Mag.*, VII [1921], 27–35) was of slight importance in emigration.

[15] W. H. Smith, *The Life and Public Service of Arthur St. Clair . . . With his Correspondence* (2 vols., Cleveland, 1882), II, 1–5.

[16] Canadian Archives, *Report* for 1890, p. 103.

nence because of the Indian wars. The Indians clamored for the annulment of the treaties by which they had renounced claims to part of Ohio, and the British were occupying Michigan. After St. Clair's defeat in 1791, settlers fled to Pittsburgh, Wheeling, and Louisville, and to the new military posts—Fort Harmar, at Marietta, and Fort Washington. After Wayne's victory in 1794, the Indian menace ended. Settlement began in the Virginia Military District on the·Great Miami; far in Ohio's northeast, Cleveland was started in 1796; and from then on settlement was on an assumption of permanence. A steady and swelling flow of emigrants had begun over the various routes already described, and it was not to cease but to grow up to and beyond 1830. One notable increase followed the War of 1812; one temporary decline followed the business depression in 1819. During the War of 1812 the attention of the country was centered on the West, where much of the military action took place and great expectations withered. Scores of thousands of militia of different states served brief terms in western campaigns, and the possibilities of a fresh start in life in that region presumably attracted many. At any rate, a vast acceleration of migration followed.

The conditions of travel somewhat changed, but not greatly except in the improvement of roads. In 1793, Harry Toulmin, then living in Kentucky and writing for English readers, advised emigrants that, although inns were available and their charges "remarkably reasonable" for "the whole distance on the different roads," they should preferably sleep in their wagons, buying fodder for their horses and provisions for themselves along the way.[17] Another intelligent Englishman, who traveled some hundreds of miles among them twenty years later, Morris Birkbeck, described them for us sympathetically: "A cart and single horse frequently afford the means of transfer, sometimes a horse and pack saddle. Often the back of the poor pilgrim bears all his effects, and his wife follows, naked-footed, bending under the hopes of the family." At a cost small to those who had any money, one could travel very differently: "A small wagon (so light that you might almost carry it, yet strong enough to bear a good load of bedding, utensils and provisions, and a swarm of young citizens—and to sustain marvellous shocks in its passage over these rocky heights), with two small horses; sometimes a cow or two, comprises their all; except a small store of hard-earned cash. . . . The family are seen before, behind, or within

[17] Toulmin, *Kentucky,* p. 36.

the vehicle, according to the road or weather, or perhaps the spirit of the party."[18] Another traveler of the same year on the same road described the passage of wagons over the mountains as "a continuance of miracles," for which he eulogized the drivers.[19]

The best time to travel, when roads were best, was in April or September. The speculators were no longer idle seekers of land grants, doing nothing. They had bought government land, with other first-comers, and were everywhere waiting for sales to late-comers, for whom they everywhere advertised, and whom they occasionally aided. Their activities in Connecticut after the war have been described: "Newspapers were again filled with land advertisements by the New York and Ohio land agents. Western correspondents' letters were published along with articles descriptive of the West. . . . Widely circulated guides, gazetteers, and books of travel played their share in this general education. The omnipresent agent was nowhere inactive. Young men who built roads in New York or worked further west during the dull season returned, praising the soil and climate. The New England peddler brought back his usual store of information concerning the new country and its opportunities."

The chief cause of migration in Connecticut was the lure of Western lands—at a fifth of the price of her own much poorer land, and for prices that specially favored actual settlers. But "equality and social democracy" were also a real cause of migration, and there were special efforts to attract "men of standing who were already freeholders." "The movement was sufficient to arouse misgivings." As shown by the censuses of 1800, 1810, and 1820, in many of her towns there was no increase in population in thirty years; some in 1790, more in 1800 were larger than in 1820.[20] The loss in Connecticut was, in large part, the gain of Ohio—what was once the Connecticut Reserve.[21] What is said of Connecticut applies to the rest of New England, at least as regards the causes of migration and its general magnitude. Connecticut, then decidedly a farming state, probably suffered most.[22]

[18] M. Birkbeck, *Notes on a Journey in America from Virginia to . . . Illinois* (Dublin, 1818), p. 35.

[19] B. F. Fearon, *Sketches of America: A Narrative of a Journey . . .* (London, 1818), pp. 191–192.

[20] R. J. Purcell, *Connecticut in Transition, 1775–1818* (Washington, 1918), pp. 146–147, 143, 150, 151, 152, 154.

[21] A. Mathews, *Ohio and Her Western Reserve* (New York, 1902).

[22] L. K. Mathews, *The Expansion of New England to the Mississippi River*

Emigrants from all the New England states, traveling through Connecticut, gathered with those from New York at Albany. Others gathered similarly at Philadelphia, Baltimore, and down the Valley of Virginia at the towns or concentration points earlier mentioned.

Three thousand freighters were busied in 1820 in the western trade.[23] Stagecoaches began running regularly to Pittsburgh in 1804. A passenger described those he saw as carrying twelve persons, with leather shades to let down if weather required. Few had springs; the bodies of most were carried on heavy leather belts. Ten miles an hour was ordinary speed. Fearon, who rode in one (when not by choice or necessity walking) from Chambersburg to Pittsburgh, tells us that "though the pain of riding exceeded the fatigue of walking, yet . . . it refreshed us by varying the weariness of our bodies."[24] The number of stages, Conestoga emigrant wagons, and travelers by horse or foot can only be imagined. Stages were booked ahead, but to have a reserved seat was not necessarily to have one at all. Routed by way of Hagerstown and across country to "the great turnpike from Philadelphia," Birkbeck's road, stage line, and rights all ended at McConnelsburg. He walked most of the way beyond. "We find ourselves," he wrote, "in the very stream of emigration. Old America seems to breaking up, and moving westward. We are seldom out of sight, as we travel on this grand track towards the Ohio, of family groups, behind and before us. . . . Add to these the numerous stages loaded to the utmost, and the innumerable travelers on horseback, on foot, and in light wagons, and you have before you a scene of bustle and business, extending over three hundred miles, which is truly wonderful."[25] In the Ohio villages across

---

(Boston, 1909); G. I. Cross, "The New England Migration," Worcester Hist. Society, *Publications*, II, 129–137; H. F. Wilson, "Population Trends in Western New England, 1790–1830," *New England Quarterly*, VIII, 276–306, with map.

[23] On page 39, *Notes on a Journey*, Birkbeck wrote: "About 12,000 waggons passed between Philadelphia and Baltimore in the last year [1816], with from four to six horses (each) carrying from thirty-five to forty cwt." This presumably meant wagons bound for Ohio. He continues: "The cost of cargo is about seven dollars per cwt. from Philadelphia to Pittsburgh, and the money paid for the conveyance of goods on this road exceeds £300,000 sterling." According to Hulbert, one of five commission houses in Wheeling unloaded 1,081 wagons in 1822, and paid $90,000 freightage over the National Highway alone. *Old National Road*, p. 37.

[24] Hulbert, *Old National Road*, pp. 83–86; Fearon, *Sketches of America* pp. 95–96.

[25] Birkbeck, *Notes on a Journey*, pp. 35, 40. Curious onlookers in the East

Ohio to Illinois through which he rode, Birkbeck counted the emigrant wagons daily passing, just as they were counted in Connecticut. The children particularly interested him. "The wagons," he wrote, "swarm with children. I heard today of three together, which contain forty-two of these young citizens." He himself passed one wagon with twenty passengers.[26] Activity ceased only at night. Although no reference is here made to freight wagons, they were always in the stream of traffic. The whole image is suggestive of the endless belts of today's industrial world.

The trip from Philadelphia or Baltimore could be made on horseback in eight days, or much less in case of emergencies.[27] By wagon, over the Forbes Road, sixteen to twenty days were required from the same towns. Over the Cumberland Road, before its improvement after 1811, twelve to fourteen days were required for the trip from Baltimore to Redstone on the Monongahela.[28]

The cost of the trip was not great. Harry Toulmin estimated the price of a good horse at $17, of a satisfactory wagon at $14, although that was very far below other estimates.[29] The cost of provisions bought along the route, given by him in detail, was low. F. J. Turner cited the costs of a Maryland family of ten members with five slaves as averaging only one-third of a dollar daily per person, for a trip of three hundred miles in fifteen days.[30] After migration became heavy,

---

counted the westbound wagons passing daily through their towns. In Pittsburgh, already industrial and smoky, where wagons from several roads united, forty to fifty wagons often passed westward in a day by 1816. *Miss. Val. Hist. Rev.*, XIV, 141–142.

[26] Birkbeck, *Notes on a Journey,* pp. 64, 67.

[27] Birkbeck instances men and women averaging forty-five miles daily, *ibid.*, p. 58. In 1812, General Hull, in military haste, made the trip from Baltimore to Pittsburgh in four days. News of the treaty of Ghent reached Detroit from Washington in six days. A horseback traveler in 1804 rode from Philadelphia to Pittsburgh in eight. Amer. Hist. Association, *Ann. Report* for 1904, p. 154.

[28] Toulmin, *Description of Kentucky,* p. 96.

[29] Toulmin's extraordinary inconsistencies (pp. 41, 94) in giving the values of British money make his financial data of doubtful value. Fearon, *Sketches of America,* p. 184, gives surprisingly high prices. The many thousands of emigrants seem sufficient evidence that costs could not have been high. For a coach ride of 140 miles Fearon paid $14 (p. 187). He passed 20 small "family wagons" (p. 190), his price for which type is given as $70–$90 (p. 184). It is not believed that general prices were so high.

[30] *AHR*, XI, 312; this was in 1835, over the National Highway to Wheeling. The trip was in a four-horse wagon, and the cost of forage (if any) was seemingly included in the total expense of $75.

taverns were established in great numbers, at least along the main highways across New York and Pennsylvania. The cost of freighting household goods from Philadelphia to Pittsburgh was perhaps from $100 to $175 per ton from 1790 onward.[31] A western promoter put it in 1790 at not above a guinea per hundredweight, "a mere trifle," as he said (whatever a guinea might then have been), "in fine goods"; assuredly so if a wife were so freighted, as she sometimes was.[32]

By whatever route emigrants might travel, their goal was the Ohio—directly or from Redstone down the Monongahela. At the edge of the wilderness they were to people and develop, the great roads dropped them and their belongings. From Redstone, Pittsburgh, or Wheeling the vast majority were carried by water to the localities, north or south of the Ohio, in which they chose to make a home. The distribution point for Kentucky was Maysville (then Limestone)—terminus of Zane's Road across Ohio from Wheeling—and a reputedly "large and very good carriage road" led to Louisville.[33]

At the end of the overland journey, travel conditions became much the same as they had been a century earlier. Each party planning on a common destination bought one of several varieties of boats with which to float down the Ohio, and poles with which to avert wreckage on the islands, sandbars, rocks, and tree snags with which that crooked and turbulent stream abounded. All these boats were of shallow draft, mere variations of precursors of the 1700's, as all of those had been variations of the birchbark canoe.[34] The boat purchased would be of

[31] Birkbeck, *Notes on a Journey,* p. 39 (he reported the yearly expenditure for freight over the Forbes Road as above £300,000); Toulmin, *Description of Kentucky,* pp. 41, 96; W. F. Gephart, *Transportation and Industrial Development in the Middle West* (New York, 1909), p. 44; F. Lippincott, *A History of Manufactures in the Ohio Valley . . . to 1860* (Chicago, 1914), pp. 67, 97. Lippincott puts the average at $100 to $150, and states that in 1784 the rate from Philadelphia to Erie (Presque Isle) was $249. O. B. Peake, *A History of the United States Indian Factory System, 1795–1822* (Denver, 1954), pp. 89, 90, 93 gives a general view of freighting problems beginning after 1794.

[32] Canadian Archives, *Report* for 1890, p. 142; Hulbert (*Historic Highways,* IV, 199) cites a case of 1796.

[33] Canadian Archives, *Report* for 1890, pp. 118, 119. Redstone (Brownsville) was the crossing point of the Monongahela on the National Highway, and Wheeling its terminus, because they combined for emigrants the Road's accommodations for travelers and freight with the certainty of navigable water at its terminus.

[34] A birchbark canoe might be as long as thirty-five feet and four to five feet wide. A pirogue was a "dugout," heavier. A batteau was an extra-large

the "flatboat" type, large enough for living quarters, provisions, household goods, possibly some livestock; and when thus made a houseboat, it was often called an ark. It was essentially a floating box of rough wood, at least partly roofed, which could be maneuvered down, but not upstream, and it was intended to be broken up at journey's end. Purchased at so much per foot of length ($1.00 to $1.25) or per ton of estimated cargo, it might cost fifty to one hundred dollars; and unless its passengers chose to risk its navigation, a crew to do that (usually four men) could be cheaply hired.[35] There was always open water from May to November, and even in midsummer sufficient for a flatboat of forty tons—a common size. However, except in high water, navigation was difficult for some seventy-five miles below Pittsburgh. From there on down the Ohio and the Mississippi there was adequate water (for a flatboat) except at the Falls (Louisville), where the river fell twenty-six feet in two miles over jagged rocks. To pass these, three-fifths of the flatboats needed experts (such pilotage costing $3). Beyond that, descent might be slow or dangerously rapid, according to the season. Eighty miles in a day, or a week from Pittsburgh to the Falls, was very rapid; ten days to the Falls was probably faster than average travel.[36] Our English reporter Birkbeck, who seems not to have used a boat himself, described them as providing "on the whole, when navigation [was] good . . . pleasant and cheap traveling."[37] This doubtless expressed the general opinion.

It has been estimated that in the early 1820's 3,000 flatboats annually descended the Ohio.[38] Their number steadily increased because of the mounting quantities of farm and industrial products transported, in addition to passengers. The first steamboat, built in 1811, was followed by hundreds—most of them short-lived. About four hundred were operating in 1830. They played a secondary part to the flatboat except in what was then luxurious travel, particularly in travel up the Mississippi from New Orleans; and their subordination in early

---

and sturdier canoe, which might carry fifteen or sixteen tons. The ark and the keelboat (similar, but with a keel) were "flatboats."

[35] A typical flatboat would be about forty feet long and fifteen feet wide, with sides about six feet high. Details in Hulbert, *Historic Highways,* IX, 119; Gephart, *Transportation,* p. 97.

[36] Hulbert, *Historic Highways,* IX, 93, considered ten days a quick passage.

[37] Birkbeck, *Notes on a Journey,* p. 49.

[38] Gephart, *Transportation,* pp. 71, 97.

years, as today, to the lowly barge in the carriage of freight was complete.

Some generalities respecting the distribution of population seem desirable. One fact, already adverted to, which influenced the course of northwestern settlement, and in particular American relations with Canada, was that geography forced all New England emigration to be southward through Connecticut and then westward along New York's Mohawk valley, so that Buffalo, the terminus of travel by canal and favored turnpikes, lay well north of Detroit and of the settled British population of Canada. Many emigrants therefore entered Upper Canada at Niagara and proceeded by land, north of Lake Erie. Others either took to Lake Erie, entering either Canada or Michigan at the western end, or spread southwestwardly south of the Lake through the Connecticut Reserve and northern Ohio into Indiana and Illinois. There were other circumstances that delayed the settlement of Michigan. The watershed between northern tributaries of the Ohio and the southern tributaries of Lake Erie runs east to west in far northern Ohio. This was very convenient for portages in canoe travel, but it created various difficulties in the construction of roads, particularly an immense Black Swamp south of Toledo, which was the cause of infinite problems in military campaigns and in road travel south of Lake Erie, for decades virtually preventing access to southern Michigan from Ohio. By 1828, on the other hand, emigrants could go by stage in four days from Niagara to Detroit, and even earlier could go by ship or (after 1818) by steamboat.[39] Even if access to Michigan had been easy, however, the condition of land titles would for some years have made settlement impossible. The first American judges of the Territory found only eight legal titles to land. In Illinois no dependable titles could have been given until after 1810, and sales began in 1812.[40]

In the period of this volume, a large proportion of the settlers of southern Illinois and Indiana came from the southern states (notably, from Virginia and North Carolina, with Tennesseeans and Kentucki-

[39] M. L. Hansen, *The Mingling of the Canadian and American Peoples* (New Haven, 1941), pp. 105–106.

[40] As respects Michigan, *Ill. Hist. Coll.*, XXI, xciii n. 2; and as respects Illinois, *ibid.*, lxxxi *et seq.*

ans). As respects Illinois, settling began in the Revolutionary and Confederation periods. The northern sections of both Illinois and Indiana, and much of all Ohio, were predominantly settled by New Englanders. Michigan drew some of its early population from Upper Canada and Ohio. Substantial settlement followed the opening of the Erie Canal and traffic on Lake Erie, and New Yorkers were heavily predominant in this later development. Ohio drew notably from New England, with a particularly large contribution from Connecticut. No appreciable immigration from abroad, except from England, occurred before 1830.

Settlement of the Southwest was peculiar in more than one respect. No southern road has been mentioned except the Wilderness Road, and that settled the Northwest about as much as it settled Tennessee and Kentucky. The settlement of Alabama and Mississippi—and, to a decidedly less degree, West Florida—was substantially a mere pushing out of South Carolinians and Georgians into the piedmont and the pine forests. No particular roads were involved, although old trading routes through the Creek lands, and to the Chickasaw and Choctaw lands, were abundant. The most remarkable feature of southwestern settlement was that the plantation system was everywhere in competition with the small farmer's desire for good land. Speculators were in the Northwest as in the Southwest, but they aroused more animosity in the latter, for there the possible prizes were greater (until agriculture ceased to be dominant in the North).

Details respecting the distribution of population are matters of local history only. As settlement in the seaboard colonies had spread, for obvious reasons, up the river valleys, so it did in the West. But as roads of real utility became available, settlements also clustered along them, as they did along the Wilderness Road,[41] up the Missouri from St. Louis, and along Zane's Trace from Wheeling to Zanesville—which became Ohio's first respectable road. It has already been noted that the economy of West Florida, until at least after the War of 1812, was exclusively dependent on the Mobile River.

Settlement of the West beyond Ohio up to 1830 may at this point be dismissed in few words. Louisiana, whose population was very slight after six decades of French rule, had increased perhaps fourfold be-

---

[41] According to Judge Toulmin in *Description of Kentucky*, there was once no habitation for two hundred miles along the Road, but when he wrote no more than half of it retained that character.

tween 1762 and 1803, and greatly increased between then and 1810.[42] A large American addition to the population of Missouri began in 1803. Some French of the Illinois villages, fearing to lose their slaves under the Ordinance of 1787 (which they misunderstood), moved across the Mississippi.[43] Some Americans had been induced by Spain's policies during the Revolution to settle there. The Tennessee-Kentucky current of migration after that war had carried far more pioneers across the Mississippi—including Daniel Boone in 1799. By 1804 settlement was continuous for some forty miles up the Missouri, by 1810 the inhabitants doubled in number, and by 1816 immigration was described as an avalanche.[44] The few American squatters on the Arkansas River in Arkansas, for whose sake the United States had removed many Cherokee to Oklahoma, had had only slight additions to their number. The importance of the trade with the Indians in Oklahoma led, however, to the establishment of Fort Smith, where the Arkansas River cuts the west boundary of the state, in 1817. Five years later a steamboat first ascended the river that far, but in 1826 steamers were traveling it to the head of navigation, near Muskogee, some six hundred miles from the Mississippi. In 1819, population required the organization of Arkansas Territory. The fact that nothing more was heard after 1803 of Jefferson's idea of reserving the Louisiana Purchase for the Indians was undoubtedly due to Wilkinson's report from St. Louis in 1805 that the number of American squatters below that town along the Mississippi was already too great to permit of their removal.

In other portions of the West there was virtually no settlement before 1830. There were two old and small settlements in Wisconsin—at Green Bay and Prairie du Chien—and an army post in Minnesota, at the site of Minneapolis. Trickles of settlers into Iowa would begin by 1832.

The following table gives the population of eleven western states from the time of their organization as a territory or (in the case of Kentucky only, admitted as a state), as found by the federal censuses

---

[42] The various estimates are collected in J. A. Robertson, *Louisiana Under the Rule of Spain, France and the United States, 1785–1807* (2 vols., Cleveland, 1911), pp. 149, 150 n. 3; and A. P. Whitaker, in *HAHR*, VIII, p. 196 n. 24.

[43] *Ill. Hist. Coll.*, XXI.

[44] So great was travel by night that, long before the torrent of migration following the War of 1812, an Ohio law of 1809 required stagecoaches to be lighted at night, forbade driving by drunken drivers, and imposed fines for leaving an unhitched team untethered.

Censuses	1790	1800	%	1810	%	1820	%	1830	%
Ohio	73,677	45,365	199.8%	230,700	452.6%	581,434	152 %	937,903	61.3%
Kentucky	35,691	220,955	195.8	406,511	83.9	564,317	38.8	687,417	21.8
Tennessee		105,602		261,727	147.8	422,823	61.5	681,904	37.6
Mississippi[a]		8,850		40,352	355.9	75,448	89.7	136,621	81.0
Indiana		5,641		24,520	334.3	148,178	500.2	343,031	61.3
Michigan[b]				4,762		8,896	86.8	31,639	255.6
Louisiana				76,556		153,407	100	215,739	40.6
Illinois				12,282		55,211	349.5	157,445	185.1
Missouri				19,783		66,586	236.5	140,455	110.9
Alabama						127,901		309,527	142
Arkansas				1,062		14,273	1243.9	30,388	126.9
								3,672,069	

[a] Contained Alabama from 1798 to 1817.
[b] Of which 3,000 are said to have been in 1830 in what is now Wisconsin.

of 1790 to 1830, with the percentage increases in successive decades.
All save Arkansas and Michigan were states by 1830. The population
of all in that year was more than 28 per cent of the entire country's.
It fell little short of that of the thirteen original states in 1790.

One may say that there were many specific reasons, or that there
was one basic reason, for the vast shift in American population which
has just been described. It took place for precisely the same reason
which explains why there is today no state in the Union in which
native-born citizens constitute more than nine-tenths of its population,
and why, in seven western states, at least half the citizens are immigrants—the overwhelming part of them from other states.[45] One word
covers the cause: discontent, dissatisfaction with a former home. The
cause of discontent, passing or permanent, may be, of course, of many
forms. It may range from mere restlessness or boredom or desire for
novelty to a physician's order, a journey for matrimony, or flight from
a sheriff. Of one thing we can be certain: excluding the recklessness or
caprice of youth, no one faced the dangers of the old frontiers for
trivial reasons. Imprisonment for debt was universal, universally illogical and unmerciful. The struggle to remain solvent, or attain solvency,
doubtless prompted many thousands to emigrate, and the fear of imprisonment for actual debt doubtless prompted other thousands. Quarrels over the established church in Virginia, and over the social restraints of a theological hierarchy in Massachusetts and Connecticut,
were undoubtedly of more or less influence. Dissatisfaction with taxes,
or with the local administration of government, undoubtedly alienated
many citizens. Dissatisfaction with their place in society was doubtless
as general as today—and probably more so, for they had less opportunity to improve it.

[45] In 1890 an economist, Richmond Mayo Smith, wrote that "Our public
land has been our great safety valve, relieving the pressure of economic distress and welfare." Unquestionably, it is a fact that it did, for countless individuals. As respects the quoted statement alone: (1) This is no statement
that all discontent in a community is a pool, so that taking out X persons
discontented over taxes would lower the discontent of industrial workers or
church dissenters. (2) It is also an incontestable fact that many artisans (and
also many persons with "aptitudes" for development into skilled artisans) did
go west. (3) Whether the public lands were ever used by the friends or the
enemies of labor to affect labor depressions or controversies in the East are
questions of fact, and the writer thinks it unnecessary to refer further to the
"safety-valve theory" up to 1830.

There is no mystery about these dissatisfactions. They were those of the hundreds of thousands of borderers—using that word literally—along the sides of the colonies from New Hampshire to South Carolina. Much has been written of their grievances, and of the complaints against them made by·the colonial governments, nor is there any mystery as to the remedy which they sought for their grievances. As Lord Dorchester emphatically reported to the government, it was an uncontrollable passion for land, as the basis of economic safety, of the rights to vote and hold office, and of respectability in society. Few of them, however, while they remained under the government of the old states, attained more than the first of these objectives.

It may be well to emphasize again, as respects the availability of land, that what was lacking in the old states was good land at a moderate price. Although there was a tremendous increase in population in the two decades following the French and Indian War, it seems unlikely that it was "this cumulative demand," *so caused,* "for territory which accounts in large part for the dramatic suddenness with which an agricultural frontier . . . was forced across the Appalachians."[46]

There were good reasons, and obvious, why the great westward migration came when it did. It could not come earlier, nor could it have been longer postponed. It is clear that the colonies could not prevent but would not encourage migration. While they remained colonies, too, overmountain settlement increased Indian unrest and stimulated the British government's policy of restricting it. When the colonies became independent, there was at first no policy except their separate preferences. A policy was required—therefore some goal and incentive—that would override the limited interests of the individual states, and a political support for it that was sufficiently strong to break the influence of the seaboard landed interests. Only then could any great mass of the population begin a westward shift. That policy, already discussed, was provided by the almost powerless, but farsighted and magnificently audacious Continental Congress. It happened, coincidentally with the preceding events, that a vast disorganization of trade and finance, greatest in the South, and a general unrest in society, followed the tensions of the Revolution.[47] This situation, possibly as much as the

46 G. E. Howard, *Preliminaries of the Revolution,* p. 20; on population, see E. B. Greene, *Provincial America.*

47 J. F. Jameson, *The Revolution Considered as a Social Movement* (Princeton, 1924), *passim.*

specific discontents of individuals, loosened the framework of society. It was the necessities of the hour that inspired the Continental Congress. In effect, the westward movement of the following decades precisely fitted Birkbeck's description: Old America *was* breaking up. The War of 1812 gave the breaking an accelerative impulse. These are the reasons why the westward movement came when it did.

Its enormous scope and spontaneity, however, were seemingly due to something whose very existence as late as Burr's "conspiracy" has been denied by some and doubted by more: nationalism. Those who migrated accepted with reasonably good will the temporary illiberalities of territorial government, but they did not so accept them because in the territories they became nationally minded. They migrated because they were already nationally minded, because they were dissatisfied with their states. The federal government, too, assured them self-government as soon as they should number 5,000. It offered full satisfaction of the three desires predominant in the complaints of the borderers of the old colonies. Nationalism was not acquired by living in the West, although it was doubtless strengthened by time, which fulfilled its promises. Westerners were nationalists from the beginning.

There was seemingly no essential difference in migration into the Northwest and into the Southwest. It has been suggested that whereas the former was of discontented classes, the latter, at least after 1820, was "a social expansion of contented portions of the older communities." This may be true of the cotton planters, but surely the small coast farmers who sought western land did so because of discontent. Moreover, they could not have been content in Alabama or Mississippi in competing with planters and speculators. Many therefore migrated farther, or into the Old Northwest. Eroded or worn-out lands, emphasized by other writers as a cause of southern emigration, and New England lands poor by nature, were alike in creating discontent.[48]

[48] Compare Wertenbaker, "The Molding of the Mid-West," *AHR*, LIII, 226–227.

CHAPTER 13

Settling Down: Industry and Trade

I T REMAINED for the thousands of emigrants, whose course we have just followed to the West to buy and occupy land, to develop the means of individual subsistence and communal economy, to adjust their social life to the conditions of a new land and their political interests to the government provided by the Ordinance of 1787. Only in thus settling down could they become true settlers. The vast majority undoubtedly did so; only a very few adventurers moved onward with the fringe of frontier settlement. These aspects of permanent settlement must be briefly considered.

Land was the emigrant's prime objective, and farming (with occasional hunting for food or to protect crops) was at first his sole activity. It was necessarily a matter of manual labor by the members of the family; sometimes, as isolation lessened, with the air of neighbors. Except in the northern parts of Illinois and Indiana, the forest was everywhere. The colonials probably took from the Indians the practice of girdling and burning trees; wasteful as was this destruction beyond satisfying necessities, their removal was in large part unavoidable.[1] So far as waste was unnecessary, it was partly due to a delusion—which

---

[1] Bear, wolves, buffalo, and deer were more or less common up to 1815 or later. A. C. Boggess, *Settlement of Illinois,* Chicago Hist. Soc. Coll., V, 14; Ohio Experiment Station, *Bulletin* 326 (1918), p. 26. Wild turkey and pigeons were innumerable. Regarding girdling and burning trees, see Bidwell and Falconer, *Agriculture,* I, 8; J. Schafer, *Social History of American Agriculture,* (New York, 1936), p. 60; B. Shimick, "The Pioneer and the Forest," *Miss. Val. Hist. Assoc., Proceedings,* III, 96–105; H. Muelder and D. N. Delo, *Years of the Land* (New York, 1943).

originated in colonial times, and on which the pioneers acted from New Hampshire to the Illinois prairies—that treeless land was infertile. This led them, as a New England agriculturist protested in 1760, to choose "the worst land for their Improvement." Certainly they chose the hardest to bring into cultivation.[2] A petition of 1805 from Indiana represented prairie lands as worthless.[3] James Monroe, in a western trip of 1784, picked up this delusion respecting lands west of those he visited in Ohio, and it fundamentally affected his policy respecting the West in estimating the probable duration of first-grade government for the Northwest Territory.[4] George Croghan, however, had recognized the fertility of the prairies in 1765, and others, like Governor St. Clair, continued to do so, so that by 1817 the truth had spread so far that settlers were advised in a western gazetteer to seek access to wood and water but avoid "clearing" land.[5] They had begun to do so in Illinois by 1814;[6] nevertheless, Governor Coles of that state wrote in 1821 that a great proportion of immigrants from forested states were "still from the force of habit . . . preferring the laborious task of clearing lands, and cultivating . . . crops in the midst of stumps and roots, to cultivating lands already cleared." Although the belief that this required less capital than prairie farming has found acceptance, Governor Coles had tested the theory and rejected it.[7] It required perhaps a winter's work to clear four acres.[8]

The prairies also, as they were treated, presented great obstacles. It might cost as much to break the sod, using oxen and a heavy sod plow, as to buy the land, and a year for the turf to rot, and that was not the end of troubles.[9] The only essential tools in cultivating were a

[2] Bidwell and Falconer, *Agriculture*, II, 9–10, 157–158.

[3] J. P. Dunn, *Indiana Hist. Coll.*, II, 485.

[4] He wrote to Jefferson, of lands he never saw, that large areas near the Great Lakes and the Mississippi were "so miserably poor" that they would never support any considerable population. *Writings* (Hamilton ed.), I, 40–41, 117.

[5] *Ill. Hist. Coll.*, XI; Carter, *Terr. Papers*, II, 246 (compare VII, 125); Gray, *Agriculture*, p. 866.

[6] C. W. Alvord, *The Illinois Country, 1678–1818* (Springfield, 1920), p. 416. But he also says, p. xvi, that prairie farming was "beginning" in 1824.

[7] Compare *Ill. Hist. Coll.*, XV, 255–257, with Bidwell and Falconer, *Agriculture*, p. 159.

[8] J. Schafer, *History of Agriculture in Wisconsin* (Madison, 1922), p. 77.

[9] R. C. Buley, *The Old Northwest . . . 1815–1840* (2 vols., Indianapolis, 1950), I, 170–174. Governor Coles, though stating as prevalent the idea that at least four horses were required, found a pair of horses or oxen sufficient.

hoe and a shovel: "A single shovel plow was the most common horse hoe," and scouring plows were unavailable until after 1830.[10]

In the early West only actually planted lands were fenced, and early laws put on the landowner the burden of keeping livestock off his land. In early statute books, those laws dealing with brands and other marks of hogs and cattle are conspicuous.[11] All livestock increased prodigiously, feeding on farm products and the forest's mast. Hogs and cattle, running wild, were easily collected. Until after the introduction of farm machinery, the heavy work of field and transportation was very largely done by oxen instead of horses. The livestock industry of the West with which we are concerned merely reproduced the earlier history of the cowpen regions of the Southwest of the late 1600's and 1700's. Beginning in 1804, great numbers of hogs and cattle were driven eastward to Baltimore, Philadelphia, and New York, and, in later years, many sheep. By 1810 the annual drive of hogs was estimated at forty thousand.[12] By 1817 the opportunities of this eastern cattle market were used in advertising the advantages of settlement in the Western Reserve.[13] Droving over the Wilderness Road and through Pennsylvania and New York continued until long after 1830.

Corn was the pioneer's first crop. It was palatable to humans, and for livestock it was by far the best food. It ripened early, yielded abundantly. It was the crop on which the pioneer relied to make himself an independent landowner.[14] Wheat, whose yield was lighter, displaced corn because of changes in labor conditions and markets. It was a crop which required much labor and developed specialists—as sicklers (later

---

Compare L. Rogin, *Introduction of Farm Machinery in Its Relation to . . . Labor in . . . Agriculture* (Berkeley, 1931), pp. 3, 4, 7, 8, 19, 21, 31; R. J. Pool, "White Man versus the Prairie," *Science,* XCI, 53–58.

[10] Ohio Agricult. Exper. Station *Bulletin* No. 326, p. 50; Buley, *Old Northwest,* I, 170–174.

[11] *Ill. Hist. Coll.,* XXI, cxxiii, 210, 244–245, 294–297, 344–347.

[12] Bidwell and Falconer, *Agriculture,* pp. 177–178; Ohio Agricult. Exper. Station *Bulletin* No. 326, pp. 66–68; W. F. Gephart, *Transportation and Industrial Development in the Middle West* (New York, 1909), p. 84. Morris Birkbeck gave the purchase price of oxen in *Notes on a Journey* (Dublin, 1818), p. 66.

[13] R. J. Purcell, *Connecticut in Transition, 1775–1818* (Washington, 1918), p. 148.

[14] Judge Toulmin advised emigrants that it could be done, without incurring debts, with three crops. H. Toulmin, *A Description of Kentucky . . . [and] Observations Respecting the United States* (Lexington, 1945), pp. 98–99. But in Ohio (A.E.S. *Bulletin* No. 326, p. 44), the estimate was three to five years.

cradlers), binders, and shockers.[15] Few families could supply the necessary labor; neighbors who also grew wheat or other small grains could not aid; dependence upon an impermanent supply raised the economic and social problems of cash crops and itinerant harvester crews.[16] In addition to all this, the labor of threshing and winnowing the grain and clearing the field remained as an immense winter task until threshing on treading floors by horses or cattle became common in the late 1820's.[17] Although by 1830 Ohio was becoming one of the great wheat-producing states of the country, wheat ultimately moved, following corn, across and out of the Northwest as that ceased to be "the frontier."[18] Other crops require mention only in connection with manufactures.[19]

Through the period up to 1830, agriculture in Kentucky followed very nearly the same course as in Ohio. The cultivation of tobacco, stimulated by speculative prices after the War of 1812, was important until after 1830. Droving of cattle to the eastern markets and of horses to the southeast seaboard and New Orleans was important by 1800, and both this and other types of trade with western Georgia and Alabama and Mississippi grew greatly after the Creek War.[20] Missouri showed little variation from the states north of the Ohio.

The rest of the West fell more or less preponderantly into the plantation economy of the South—eastern and southern Arkansas; all of Louisiana, Alabama, and Mississippi; middle (and after 1830, west-

---

[15] As the sickle or scythe cut the grain, it fell in orderly handfuls on several wooden slats parallel to the blade. This "cradle" came into use about 1815. There are pictures of it (and other farming tools) in Rogin, *Farm Machinery,* p. 69; Bidwell and Falconer, *Agriculture,* p. 209; L. C. Gray, "Agricultural Machinery," *Encyclopaedia of the Social Sciences,* I, 551–554; and in Buley, *Old Northwest* (see index).

[16] Ohio A.E.S. *Bulletin* No. 326, pp. 51–52; Schafer, *Agriculture in Wisconsin,* pp. 81, 84, 87, 95, and *Agriculture* (New York, 1936), pp. 80–81, 128, 197; Rogin, *Farm Machinery,* pp. 125, 126–127.

[17] Buley, *Old Northwest,* I, 181–182, estimates ten acres to have been a man's winter task. Ohio A.E.S. *Bulletin* No. 326, p. 52, estimates that the threshing of fifty man-days was done in one day by horses on a trampling floor.

[18] B. Schmidt, "The Westward Movement of the Corn Growing Industry across the United States," *Iowa Journal of Hist.,* XXI, 121–144, and "The Westward Movement of the Wheat Growing Industry . . ." *ibid.,* XVIII, 396–412; E. C. Brooks, *The Story of Corn and the West* (Chicago, 1916).

[19] Cotton, rice, and tobacco were all grown more or less successfully for a time in the Old Northwest. Ohio A.E.S. *Bulletin* No. 326, pp. 55, 56, 59; Gephart, *Transportation,* pp. 59, 85, 89; Schafer, *Agriculture,* pp. 140–141.

[20] Gray, *Agriculture,* pp. 861, 868, 876–877.

ern) Tennessee. All this was predominantly cotton area, and cotton was from the beginning a cash crop of immense value. It became the greatest commercial crop of the country well before 1830 and, in value, by far the greatest article of its exports.[21]

However much plantation economy may have affected the South-west of our period, economically and in government, "the great majority of the Southern people lived on small farms and worked with their own hands."[22] They constituted a society which preserved its pioneer features much longer than any portion of the Northwest retained them, but very little has been written about them with the exception of the two regions where old customs, old speech, household industries, and other characteristics of frontier isolation and family self-sufficiency lingered longest—in the Ozarks and in the highlands of eastern Kentucky and Tennessee.[23]

Salt licks considerably affected the course of early migration both north and south of the Ohio. Reservation of national salines in early grants and sales of public lands were a notable feature of early frontier policy. Following 1806, supplies from West Virginia, and from the Muskingum and Scioto valleys of Ohio, gradually ended all shortages. In early years the price of a barrel of salt was long above $6, sometimes $12; by 1825, it had fallen to 37½ cents.[24]

Coal, although early known to be abundant in Ohio (as well as in Pennsylvania and Kentucky), was little used even in industry until after 1830; and this was so despite its known superiority to wood for steam engines.[25] The greatest of the Ohio mines, those of the Hocking Valley, were opened only in the late 1820's.

Shortly after the Revolution Tench Coxe proved the vast amount of home manufactures by studying small scattered areas.[26] Harry Toulmin reported in 1793 that linen and woolen cloths, and leather goods including shoes, were made in Kentucky homes. But he also reported that "all the trades necessary to . . . new settlements" were practiced there: those of the carpenter and joiner, blacksmith and gunmaker,

21 *Ibid.*, pp. 684, 687, 688, 689, 695, 878, 880, 892.

22 *Ibid.*, ii, vi.

23 Particularly interesting is J. C. Campbell, *The Southern Highlander and his Homeland* (New York, 1921).

24 Lippincott, *Manufactures in the Ohio Valley;* Gephart, *Transportation,* pp. 85–86.

25 *Ibid.*, pp. 86–87; Buley, *Old Northwest,* I, 546–547.

26 Tench Coxe, *View of the United States* (Philadelphia, 1794).

wheelwright and millwright. He reported many gristmills, sawmills, fulling mills, linseed-oil mills, and papermills.[27] In 1795 hatters, coopers, a clockmaker, a skin dresser and tanners, and other artisans, thirty-seven in all, were reported in Pittsburgh, and it was a small town.[28] By 1817 Morris Birkbeck thought that there were more artisans than materials for their employment, but he specified only leathermakers.[29] English artisans were doubtless coming in, through Canada, years before England repealed her statutory prohibition against their emigration. In 1818, even in Michigan, the thinnest-settled part of the Northwest, Detroit had a Mechanics Society and Ypsilanti had a Working Men's Society. It seems highly probable that the entire frontier was well supplied with more or less skilled artisans who emigrated as such, and as industry grew their numbers were increased by local additions.

Home industry was characteristic of the primitive frontier. By 1823, manufactures were reported from over three-fourths of Ohio's counties, but only in small amounts from other states and territories of the Northwest, and in proportion to their age of settlement.[30]

The grains, the livestock, and the timber of the farm all gave rise to industry and trade. Flax supplied linen, and mixed with wool furnished the linsey-woolsey universally used on the frontier. Linseed-oil mills were numerous. Hemp, in addition to its use in textiles, became so important in connection with shipbuilding that in 1810 Kentucky's production of cordage was exceeded by that of Massachusetts only. Kentucky supplied the South with cordage, burlap, and rough clothing textiles used on the plantations. Papermills, chiefly in Kentucky, supplied various newspapers, particularly after 1800, and ultimately a large amount of other publishing.[31]

As soon as grain production became large, homemade grinders became worthless, and even "horse mills" were very soon inadequate. Gristmills, which were very expensive, were of enormous importance, and mill sites were the sure basis of stable communities. Governor Reynolds of Illinois, one of its earliest immigrants, believed that the lack of mills "retarded the improvement of the country in early times more than all other" causes. Needless to say, the laws carefully regulated rates

[27] Toulmin, *Description of Kentucky*, p. 89.
[28] Lippincott, *Manufactures in the Ohio Valley*, pp. 83–84.
[29] Birkbeck, *Notes on a Journey*, p. 66.
[30] *A.S.P., Finance*, IV, 447–458.
[31] Ohio A.E.S. *Bulletin* No. 326, pp. 54, 55; Lippincott, *Manufactures in the Ohio Valley*, pp. 109–112; Gray, *Agriculture*, p. 871.

and penalized overcharges and discrimination among customers.[32] A floating mill was in operation on the Muskingum in 1791, and by 1814 there were some steam mills in different parts of Ohio for grinding grain, but in 1820 there were still no mills in almost half of Ohio's counties.[33] The early lack of water power was a cause of the early introduction of steam engines. The early inadequacy of milling facilities, and the fact that cheap grain (corn, in particular), ground or not ground, could not bear transportation costs, were chief causes for the conversion of enormous quantities of grain into whisky.[34]

One industry of considerable importance developed from the abundance of hogs on the frontier—meat packing. Ham and salted pork became prominent items in trade down the Mississippi in very early years. Packing had become a distinct industry (combining slaughtering, curing, and packing) by 1818, and Cincinnati was long called Porkopolis.[35] Dairying became important at an early date in the Western Reserve.

As respects the forest, there was almost no social return for its destruction. This is not surprising, for what legislation there had been in the states on preserving or cutting timber had been little concerned with the public interest.[36] Out of the vast bonfires of stricken trees there came only potash and pearl ash, substantial commercial articles of frontier trade.[37] Many houses must have been built of boards, since sawmill sites were greatly prized, and Governor Harrison's home at Vincennes testifies to their good products. One encounters, however, only rare

[32] *Ill. Hist. Coll.*, XXI, cxxiv, and see index, *s.v.* "mills." "A gristmill was the first institution, save the school, in which all settlers had an interest." Schafer, *Agriculture in Wisconsin*, p. 71.

[33] Gephart, *Transportation*, p. 102.

[34] The majority of mills were on the Muskingum, Scioto, and Miami rivers. The valleys of the last two were also the great corn and livestock areas, and three-fourths of the 552 distilleries reported in the Census of 1820 were in the same two valleys. Ohio A.E.S. *Bulletin* No. 326, pp. 52–55; Lippincott, *Manufactures in the Ohio Valley*, pp. 88–89.

[35] Gephart, *Transportation*, pp. 84–85.

[36] The usual objectives were to prevent trespass and conserve timber, presumably with little or no thought of public interest, but that was necessarily involved in laws prescribing lumber inspection. J. P. Kinney, *Forest Legislation in the United States Prior to . . . 1789* (Ithaca, N.Y., 1916), pp. 363, 371, 381; and *Development of Forest Law*, pp. 20–23.

[37] The immense amount of timber burned in clearing land, used in buildings, for fences, for heating homes, as fuel in manufacturing establishments; and simply wasted was horrifying to General Collot in 1797. G. H. V. Collot, *A Journey in North America* (3 vols., Paris, 1826), II, 199–200.

references to timber conservation and sale.[38] Log cabins were vastly
more common than frame houses for several decades.[39] In Michigan,
whose settlers in 1830 were scattered in villages far apart in virtually
unbroken woodland, there were already hundreds of mills.[40] Lumbering was there a major industry from the beginning. In Ohio local needs
seem to have absorbed supplies.[41]

Although shipbuilding was a notable industry from 1790 onward, the
tonnage of ships was small. Twenty-six built before 1812 at Marietta
were of 120 to 350 tons, and few of those later built there or elsewhere
up to 1830, including steamships, exceeded 400 tons. This is true of
those that plied the Great Lakes. Many of these vessels went to the
West Indies and some to Europe, even to Russia.[42]

The iron industry was important to the entire West from the beginning of the 1800's. Primary materials abounded in western Pennsylvania, and after 1825 in Ohio. High freight rates on eastern iron
enabled the industry to develop quite independently, and it was the
first western industry to become important in national production. The
first demand was for household utensils, such as pots, kettles, fireplace
fixtures, flatirons, and ovens. The workmen who satisfied this demand
were blacksmiths, many of great skill in making tools for house and
farm work, and some—such as gunmakers and clockmakers—were
master craftsmen. Even the frontier ax, in the hands of the skilled, was
a tool of versatility and marvelous effectiveness. However, in this there
was no special relation to the western frontier, for the needs were everywhere the same, and likewise the role of the blacksmith. What might be
called manufacturing for a market seems to have begun about 1790 in
western Pennsylvania. The second most important demand was for
nails, wire, crowbars, and other simple tools. Furnaces for the casting

[38] G. C. Wing, *Early Years on the Western Reserve* (Cleveland, 1926), de-
scribes such an area.

[39] In the youth of persons now or recently living, many log cabins were
standing in southern Indiana, and many have been preserved elsewhere. They
were everywhere except in localities where large-scale lumbering began early in
the period of settlement. Schafer, *Agriculture in Wisconsin,* pp. 67–68.

[40] M. M. Quaife and S. Glaser, *Michigan: from Primitive Wilderness to Industrial Commonwealth* (New York, 1948), p. 219, give an estimate of 400 by
1837.

[41] There was also, seemingly, some reliance upon outside supply.

[42] The frames of these short-lived freighters, destined to sink on river snags
or in the seas, were of black walnut, and their "furniture" of walnut, birch,
and cherry gave elegance to cargoes of flour, iron, and pork. Hulbert, *Historic
Highways,* XII, 132–136.

of cooking pots and the like, and for the production of wrought nails and tools, existed in Pittsburgh, Lexington, and then in Ohio in the early years of the century. They were, however, extremely few. Cincinnati had no foundry in 1815, nor had St. Louis any in 1821. Blacksmiths were still making kitchen utensils. After the discovery of large and rich iron deposits in Ohio and across the Ohio River in Kentucky in 1825, the industry greatly expanded. Pittsburgh had become a great iron center before 1830, and Cincinnati and several lesser Ohio towns became moderate producers.[43]

By 1825 Cincinnati had become the greatest distributing center of the West, and next to Pittsburgh the greatest in industrial production. A list of Cincinnati's manufacturing establishments in 1826, giving the number of some three thousand employees as distributed among them,[44] shows that seven-tenths of them were workers in the building trades, in textiles, in wood (excluding carpenters), in leather, and in iron. A surprising number (135) worked in the paper and printing fields—including a papermill, type foundry, and bookbinding. There were various specialists making plows, combs, brushes, sashes, and sieves; milliners; workers (108) in silver, copper, brass, and tin; one cutler; copperplate engravers (3); one organ builder and two piano "factories." Some home furnishings indicated comforts in the home: clocks (eighteen makers), mattresses, upholstery, and wallpaper.

The agricultural and industrial production just described presupposes trade, and therefore means of transportation. Communal isolation characterized the whole country after 1783; its diminution proceeded everywhere with great rapidity, and nowhere more strikingly than in the West. Nowhere was the role of transportation in social development more conspicuously illustrated.

Adequate outlets for distant trade were available over Pennsylvania roads and the Mississippi. The problem was one of local roads to reach

---

[43] Gephart, *Transportation*, pp. 60–61; Lippincott, *Manufactures in the Ohio Valley*, pp. 96–109.

[44] B. Drake and E. D. Mansfield, *Cincinnati in 1826* (Cincinnati, 1827). Various specialists, such as gunsmiths, were not separately enumerated. In tailoring and clothier shops, there were 467 women and 132 men workers. Similar data for Pittsburgh, Chillicothe, Steubenville, Zanesville, Vincennes, and Hamilton are given in Gephart, *Transportation*, pp. 90, 91 and 92, and Buley, *Old Northwest*, I, 554. The latter gives $350–700 as the cost of "cabinet pianos," p. 551.

these outlets, and to reach the Ohio for distribution within the Northwest.[45]

The federal government built various post roads, particularly in the Southwest, but also in the Northwest, notably (1801) between Pittsburgh and Cleveland.[46] Various others were built as military roads. Of these a very important one was from Detroit around the end of Lake Erie to the Maumee Rapids, then on through the Black Swamp (fifteen miles of corduroy) to Lower Sandusky (Fremont).[47] Another, known as the Chicago Road, ran from Detroit to Chicago. Throughout all the West, up to 1830 and thereafter, the national government continued the building, by soldiers, of roads more or less desirable for military use.

In 1805, in his second inaugural, Jefferson recommended that surplus revenue be devoted to canals, roads, manufactures, education, and the arts. It soon developed that prevalent interpretation of the Constitution would prevent the direct use of federal money for internal improvements within the states. However, in 1806 Congress authorized the National Road, and enlarged its agreement of 1802 with Ohio for the latter to use, in building roads within the state, three-fifths of the proceeds from public lands sold therein, on condition that no state tax be levied for five years on the lands sold.[48] This system ultimately proved of vast significance in the West's economic growth.

Despite these contributions by the national government, the main burden fell upon the states and turnpike companies. Territorial statutes were ambitious and enlightened from the beginning in requiring wide roads, and for their maintenance by adjoining owners, though

[45] Detroit lacked dependable agriculture, and aid from Illinois was occasionally imperative. N. V. Russell, *The British Regime in Michigan and the Old Northwest, 1760–1796* (Northfield, Minn., 1939), p. 120; Alvord, *Illinois Country*, p. 359. Middle Tennessee was dependent on Kentucky; see Gray, *Agriculture*, pp. 869–870, 880. The first American store in Kaskaskia had a branch in Nashville.

[46] One ran from Lake Pontchartrain (Madisonville, Louisiana) across Mississippi and Alabama to a point north of Muscle Shoals, a distance of 392 miles. By 1820, some 700 miles of post roads had been built in Arkansas.

[47] This road was supposedly completed before 1819, *A.S.P., Misc.*, II, 596. The Black Swamp, heavily timbered, covered a wide belt from the Maumee Rapids to its mouth in Sandusky Bay. Except in winter, this swamp virtually prevented passage from Detroit around the Lake, and in the War of 1812 was an immense obstacle.

[48] Details on laws and funds thus raised are given in B. H. Hibbard, *History of the Public Land Policies* (New York, 1924), pp. 84, 86.

realities necessarily lagged far behind provisions.[49] In Illinois, where Indian traces across the prairie had been the only roads, and two-wheeled carts without tires, hauled by an ox, had been the only freighting wagons, there was time for preparation. In Ohio, the problems were immediate. By the ending of the War of 1812, its important towns were connected by relatively good roads.[50] There were notable bridges at Zanesville, Dayton and Shawneetown, and an exceptionally good road connected Louisville, Vincennes and Portland.[51]

None of these roads, however, is to be imagined good by modern standards. The requisites for them were understood, but the labor force and money needed for their realization were lacking. In Indiana there was no stone or gravel on any important road until after 1830. As regarded Illinois prairie, the more an unsurfaced road was "worked," the more easily it became muddy when rain came. As regarded forest states—and such were all the others of the Old Northwest and (in lesser degree) the Southwest—to remove stumps cost much labor and much money. All local roads wound around hills, if not in wooded districts. To drive through woods, straddling stumps, required less time than to drive around a large wood, and less magic than to drive around trees. In Indiana, nine-tenths of the National Road ran through timber, and the specifications for its construction permitted stumps (so "rounded and trimmed" as to present "no serious obstacles to carriages") nine or fifteen inches high according as their diameter was less or greater than eighteen inches.[52] Morris Birkbeck thought some Ohio roads better "attended to" than those in Virginia or western Pennsylvania, but surely the last presented the greatest problems.[53] Until after 1830 even the army-built road from Detroit to the Maumee Rapids and Fremont seems to have remained a route of extreme difficulty for wagons, although it was a stage road after 1826.[54] Harriet Martineau described the ruts, mud, stumps, bumps, jolting, tipping, and imminent overturnings presented by a ride on the Chicago road in

[49] *Ill. Hist. Coll.*, XVII, index *s.v.* "roads"; XXI, xiii–xiv, cxxiv, and index *s.v.* "road labor," "roads," and "ferries"; XXX, II, index *s.v.* "roads," "ferries."

[50] Buley, *Old Northwest*, I, 449 *et seq.*; Gephart, *Transportation*, gives a map as of 1810.

[51] Meyer and MacGill, *Transportation before 1860*, pp. 31–32, 46, 47, 48; Gray, *Agriculture*, p. 869.

[52] Buley, *Old Northwest*, p. 463.

[53] Birkbeck, *Notes on a Journey*, p. 65.

[54] G. N. Fuller, in *MVHR*, II, 43.

1836.[55] Often, on coaching roads, the only way to avoid mud was to leave the road (hence, wide roads). It was also common for passengers to walk, more or less, to help the horses on hills. Nor were the locations of the first roads likely to be permanently desirable; a county seat or market town might become even a more important terminus than a mill. One road with a ferry would displace several with none.

The decade of 1820–30 was one of enormous activity in roadbuilding throughout the country, by the states, the Union, and private turnpike companies.[56] In 1825, of all local laws passed in Ohio, 44 per cent dealt with roads and 22 per cent of general acts dealt with transportation. In 1826, 55 per cent of all statutes dealt with transportation, primarily by road.[57] Public lands were granted to Ohio and Indiana for construction of several particularly important roads. Before 1830, Ohio and Indiana each received at least 500,000 acres, and Illinois more than 200,000. (Ultimately, they and others fared much better.)[58] Probably none of these roads (except the National Road west from Wheeling, the Maumee roads, and those around a few important towns) were praiseworthy as compared with the "turnpikes," which were, in general, both macadamized and toll roads, though their name indicated neither fact. Ohio began these in 1809, and after the War of 1812 they rapidly multiplied. There were 110 "free turnpikes" in the period before 1830.[59]

After the success of the Erie Canal became foreseeable, the West turned to canals. Talk of them—at first as aids to river navigation—had begun by 1812. Gradually the idea grew that canals uniting Lake Erie with the Ohio River might carry all eastern manufactures, and

[55] Fuller, *ibid.*, p. 44, quotes her description of these terrors. Various writers give instances of passengers shifting logs in corduroy roads, or otherwise aiding drivers. Buley cites (*Old Northwest*, p. 461) a stage coach ride out of Detroit that required eighteen hours for thirty miles in 1837.

[56] Only one business corporation was created in the United States before 1793. Before 1801 there were more than 300, nine-tenths of them created before 1789. Of these, the great majority were for the construction of roads or canals. See J. S. Davis, *Essays in the Earlier History of American Corporations* (2 vols., Cambridge, 1917), II, 6, 8, Appendix B (listing corporations, 1781–1800).

[57] Gephart, *Transportation*, p. 140.

[58] T. C. Donaldson, *The Public Domain: its History . . . to 1883* (Washington, 1884), pp. 236, 258, 260; see also W. J. Donald, "Land Grants for Internal Improvements in the U.S.," *Jour. of Political Economy*, XIX (1911), 405.

[59] Gephart, *Transportation*, pp. 141–144.

even European imports, to the Old Northwest and Kentucky. Engineers from the Erie Canal recommended various routes, but conflict between the interests of competing sections, between towns on different rivers, and between present needs as against hopes compelled compromises. Agreement was reached by 1824 on two routes: one of these, the Ohio Canal, was to run from Cleveland to Portsmouth down the Cuyahoga and Scioto valleys; the other, the Miami Canal, was to connect Cincinnati and Toledo. Both were formally begun in July, 1825, in which month, also, the President and Vice-President of the United States formally announced, near Wheeling, the resumption of work on the Cumberland Road as a National Highway. Much of the Ohio Canal was completed before 1830, the whole by 1833; the Miami Canal was open to Dayton in 1829, and only slightly extended thereafter.[60] One canal was also initiated in Indiana, and partially completed, before 1830, and one of very great benefit was initiated in Illinois, but not actually begun until 1836.[61] Up to 1830, a total of 2,586 square miles of public lands was given by Congress to aid the canal projects of Ohio, Indiana, and Illinois.[62]

The contribution by roads and canals to economic development was spectacular. Low, irregular, and fluctuating prices of produce characterized the early years, and transportation costs made surplus products in some localities worthless. They were estimated in Indiana in 1818 at 50 cents per hundredweight every twenty miles and at 16 cents every nine miles, which meant that corn could not be profitably hauled even if produced at no cost, nor wheat be hauled farther than forty or fifty miles.[63] Wheat at Sandusky might be worth more than twice its value at Columbus or Chillicothe.[64] The influence of the canals was enor-

[60] *Ibid.*, pp. 110–128, and E. L. Bogart, *Internal Improvements and State Debt in Ohio* (New York, 1924).

[61] The former was the Wabash and Erie Canal, to connect the Wabash River with Lake Erie. Two land grants were made in Illinois for the canalization of the Chicago-Illinois River portage route, which proved to be of immense importance.

[62] Donaldson, *Public Domain*, p. 258. A grant to Alabama for river improvement was the equivalent of road and canal grants for any state in the Northwest. G. R. Taylor, "Prices in the Mississippi Valley Preceding the War of 1812," *Jour. of Econ. and Business History*, III (1930), and "Agrarian Discontent in the Mississippi Valley, Preceding the War of 1812," *Jour. of Political Economy*, XXXIX (1931).

[63] Many details for various years are in Bidwell and Falconer (I, pp. 870, 181), Gephart, Lippincott, Gray, and Buley.

[64] Buley, *Old Northwest*, I, 534.

mous. Freight rates from New York to Pittsburgh for typical goods fell to $2.25 per hundredweight; to Sandusky, $1.25; and by all-water route (after 1830) to Dayton, $0.875. The value of wheat and corn in the interior of Ohio more than doubled between 1825 and 1832. This influence of cheapened transportation extended over a belt of "at least one hundred miles on either side of the canals."[65]

On the other hand they contributed greatly to the instability of the financial system of every state in the Northwest—with least harm to Ohio, already the strongest economically. However, the errors there were typical. On all sides exaggerated expectations precluded caution. Routes were affected by politics. Even trifling taxation was resented. Caution and effective control were lacking in estimates, contracts, and construction.[66] Nevertheless, the canals were disappointments, primarily, only because they very soon faced railroad competition, and had to rely merely upon local patronage.

During the French Revolution, Louisiana became completely dependent on American trade. There were some advantages for the Northwest in continuing this trade, such as abundant supplies of Spanish wool and direct trade with the Mississippi-Alabama region. It long remained, also, a cheap route for heavy European goods competing with American. Swedish iron long competed in Cincinnati even with Pittsburgh's products. Moreover, in early years it was also a cheap route for western trade with the Atlantic states, and for trade, licit or illicit, with the West Indies. Corn, cornmeal, wheat, flour, hemp, tobacco, smoked and salted pork products, lard, bacon, dried beef, whisky, potatoes, apples, cider, butter, cheese, beeswax, feathers, "country" linen, shoes and other leather products—all these went down the river in early years. In later years, glassware, cast-iron utensils, and other products became important.[67]

Specific statistics have little meaning. What were the total shipments down the River each year—what their ultimate destinations? There are no records to show. At what points in Ohio, Missouri, or western New York (for some did come from there) did the shipments originate?

[65] *Ibid.*, I, 534, 535.
[66] Gephart, *Transportation*, pp. 125–126, 128.
[67] Gray, *Agriculture*, p. 882; J. A. Robertson, *Louisiana . . . 1785–1807* (2 vols., Cleveland, 1911), I, 93, 220 n. 63, 221. The amount of trade in various years (subject to the doubts stated in the text) can be found in *A.S.P., Misc.*, I, 354–356, and *ibid.*, *Finance*, II, 56; Bidwell and Falconer, *Agriculture*, pp. 172, 173; Gray, *Agriculture*, p. 870; Turner, in *AHR*, XI, 324.

Only steamboat freight was registered; of the enormous bulk of flatboat cargo, there was no record.[68] It seems certain, merely, that almost
everything that went down the River originated in Ohio and Kentucky,
since Indiana, Illinois, and Missouri were little developed, and it seems
improbable that after the earliest years anything east of Pittsburgh
would have been sent south if intended for the East.

Keelboats and barges—freighters—increasingly filled the lanes of the
Ohio up to and beyond 1830; the houseboats of early days declined.[69]
Until a canal was opened in 1828 around the falls at Louisville, these
were a cause of tremendous losses in wasted wages, extra labor charges
and pilotage, damages to perishable cargo and boats, occasional losses
of a favorable market, and liabilities to shippers.[70] Up to 1829 most
produce went to New Orleans in keelboats or barges only because
steamboat rates were higher.[71] But both plied inland rivers long after
1830, and to a lesser extent the Ohio and Mississippi.

Fifteen days from Pittsburgh to the Ohio's mouth was very good
time; as much was often consumed in getting to Maysville, and ten days
might be lost at the Falls. A month to New Orleans was excellent time,
and three months, or even four, might be required for the upward
trip, which was no better than in colonial days.[72] Two or three round
trips could be made in a season.

All this was greatly altered by the steamboat. The first on the Ohio
appeared in 1811, and made a demonstration trip to New Orleans. By
the end of 1827, 251 had been built.[73] They were water skimmers—the

---

[68] Lippincott, *Manufactures in the Ohio Valley,* pp. 65, 89; Gephart, *Transportation,* p. 119. There are some figures in *A.S.P., Finance,* II, 56. Ernest
Bogart, who gave much attention to western economics, thought that 80 per
cent of the incoming commerce of New Orleans in 1816 ($8,062,540) came
from Ohio and the upper Mississippi.

[69] The keelboat predominated on the Upper Ohio. The barge was larger
and more maneuverable (often with sails to supplement setting poles or tow-
line in warping the boat around corners or shallows), and predominated on the
Mississippi, particularly in upriver traffic. Terminology and statistical statements
on some matters, are irreconcilable: Hulbert, *Historic Highways,* IX, 106, 109,
110, 113–120, 125–127, 139, 140; Buley, *Old Northwest,* I, 428.

[70] Gephart, *Transportation,* pp. 107–110, 113; *A.S.P., Misc.,* I, 419, 453,
479. The time of arrival at New Orleans was important because its market was
seasonably bare or glutted.

[71] By $1 per barrel, Gephart estimated, *Transportation,* p. 96. Steamboats,
carrying greater cargoes, thereafter enjoyed primacy until themselves displaced
by engined "tugboats" (which were always or soon became pushboats).

[72] Gephart, *Transportation,* pp. 61, 63; Alvord, *Illinois Country,* p. 213.

[73] The number built yearly is given in Gephart, *Transportation,* p. 79; pp. 69

Ohio had many extremely shallow places until 1900; the Mississippi had countless submerged trees. The steamers were therefore glorified keelboats in design: long, narrow, of no deeper draught either unloaded or loaded.[74] But they were more powerful. Although very soon seen on the Missouri, Cumberland, Tennessee, and Allegheny, their full possibilities were not realized until after 1830. This was partly because of litigation between patentees, which even involved states, and partly because until 1828 they could pass on the Ohio beyond Louisville, in either direction, only in high water.[75] They reduced the travel time between Pittsburgh and New Orleans to one month. By the mid-1830's they had very largely displaced barges in the upward traffic of the Mississippi.[76]

By 1835 it was clear that some products that formerly went to New Orleans were going through the Canal.[77] On the other hand, supplying the Northwest with heavy products was still cheaper by the sea.[78] It was the railroads that first—and later—presented the Mississippi with effective competition.

In 1817, Morris Birkbeck tells us, local storekeepers went East each year to buy their stock, with which, doubtless, they returned.[79] The value of the trade is evidenced by the fact that as early as 1800, in order better to compete with New York's turnpikes, Pennsylvania began improvement of the old French military road between Lake Erie and the Allegheny River.[80] Later, after the War of 1812 ended exclusive British navigation of the Great Lakes, and after the Convention of

---

et seq. trace the history of early years. Drake and Mansfield, Cincinnati in 1826, pp. 72–75, name 233 built through 1826, sixty of them built in Cincinnati. They were short-lived; some were lost on snags, some in collisions, some by fire, many were merely "worn out," some simply disappeared.

[74] Two and one half feet and four feet, respectively, Hulbert, American Highways, pp. 140–141.

[75] The first steamer on the Ohio, Nicholas Roosevelt's, was built under Fulton's patent, which received the support of Louisiana. Gephart, Transportation, pp. 70–77, gives details.

[76] Buley, Old Northwest, I, 427. Between 1800 and 1816, freight rates to New Orleans are said to have been cut by half, but compare Gephart, Transportation, pp. 71, 93.

[77] Ibid., pp. 118, 119.

[78] Possibly increasingly so, for in 1815 some goods theretofore "wagoned" eastward were shifted to the New Orleans route, ibid., p. 79. Probably, too, upriver freightage fell, in competition between barges and steamers.

[79] Ibid., pp. 92, 94, 95, 96, 97; Canadian Archives, Report for 1890, p. 142; Birkbeck, Notes on a Journey, p. 104.

[80] Between her forts at Presque Isle and Le Boeuf, now Erie and Waterford.

1817 ensured friendly co-operation of the two countries in trade, this old road made cheap transportation available to Upper Canada, Detroit, and the Maumee section south and west of Toledo, which last had long been isolated and undeveloped.[81] From then onward, Lake Erie became important in trade between the states and Upper Canada, and very important to the former in trade through the Erie Canal. The first steamboat (*Walk in the Water*) was built on the Lake in 1818, and inaugurated a nine-day passenger schedule between Buffalo and Detroit. By 1820 the time had been reduced by half. By 1830 fourteen steamers and at least 250 other ships, British and American, were operating on Lakes Erie and Ontario. Within a few more years the Erie Canal and steamers on Lake Erie were carrying thousands of settlers into Michigan,[82] and commerce over the lake was an addition to the great system flowing down the Erie Canal and over the roads of Pennsylvania and New York. Pearl ashes, whisky, hemp, pork products, lumber products, and wheat and flour in great quantities, in later years some iron and glass products from Pittsburgh, were noteworthy exports. As early as 1806 western wheat was being sold in New England.[83] The Erie Canal, despite three portages, was a great factor in increasing the volume and value of this commerce. A shipment from Philadelphia to Columbus at $5 per hundredweight, and requiring thirty days in transit before the Canal opened, was deliverable thereafter in twenty days for half the former freightage. Flour priced at $3.50 in Cincinnati, if sent by road to New York at the rate of $4.50 per hundredweight, could be sent by the Canal for $1.70.[84] Pennsylvania continued to spend millions on a canal to compete with New York's, but with little success.[85]

[81] In 1804 Cleveland's imports had a value of only $50, and in 1809 the Maumee area's exports were of bear, coon, and mink skins worth $3,000.

[82] *Walk in the Water* was of 330 tons, with a passenger capacity of 200. Buley, *Old Northwest*, I, 420–421; Fuller, in *MVHR*, p. 39; Gephart, *Transportation*, pp. 67, 80–81; A. Dunham, *Political Unrest in Upper Canada* (New York and Toronto, 1927), p. 14. Boats of more than 350 tons were few up to, at least, 1827.

[83] Purcell, *Connecticut in Transition*, p. 147.

[84] Buley, *Old Northwest*, I, p. 534; Gephart, *Transportation*, pp. 118, 113. The three portages between New York City and Pittsburgh were from Albany to Schenectady (fifteen miles), around Niagara Falls (ten miles), and from Erie to Waterford (fifteen miles).

[85] By 1826 she had expended $16 million on roads, bridges, and a canal from Philadelphia to Pittsburgh. By 1834 the latter was complete save for a thirty-six-mile gap where a portage railway was inserted, with alternate levels and

Not merely improved transportation but great advances in commercial organization underlay the expansion of trade just described. For commerce on a large scale it was essential to find capital and establish the mechanism of a credit system. The Northwest had no product which, like the South's cotton, ensured credit wherever exported, and there were long lacking, also, not only banks but all the agencies which, by assembling, warehousing, and selling products, assure control of the time and place of marketing, and protection of buyers and sellers. Shipping centers were developed, banks established, and in the course of widening business transactions there were created the instrumentalities of a credit system adequate for business transactions between different parts of the country. The transformation began with the village stores—the number of which in isolated towns is one of the West's surprises.[86] The farmer could sell a little produce to newcomers, or at the tavern, or perhaps sell to or barter with neighbors, or he could sell it at an open market in the village. Or it could be taken to the village store, or to a river trader, and bartered for household or farm necessities, such as needles, crockery, or clothing. Such barter, or of labor for goods, or of raw materials for finished products, was common until long after 1830, and prevailed that late even at some cotton and woolen factories.[87] But the storekeeper might do other things. He might store pork, grain, or flour for future disposition. Indeed, it is said that "pork houses were kept in connection with all the stores"; and that after being salted and packed in barrels and stored for a time, they would be shipped.[88] At the very least, the storekeeper was here a warehouseman. He might, however, have bought the products for himself, as a speculation; if not, in addition to acting as a warehouseman, he may have sold them for the owner for a commission.[89] Inasmuch as grain and flour were very often similarly treated,

---

inclines. Gephart, *Transportation,* p. 118. Nothing resulted from companies chartered in Ohio to construct canals that would connect with the Pennsylvania system.

[86] There were twenty in Detroit in 1778; Russell, *British Regime,* p. 109. There were eighteen "stores of merchandise" in Vincennes in 1817, together with four "groceries" and two "market houses"; Buley, *Old Northwest,* I, 554.

[87] Gephart, *Transportation,* pp. 89, 90; Lippincott, *Manufactures in the Ohio Valley,* pp. 63, 75; Buley, *Old Northwest,* I, 234.

[88] Ohio A.E.S. *Bulletin* No. 326, p. 67.

[89] Bidwell and Falconer, *Agriculture,* p. 174, indicate that all these things were done; similarly, L. E. Atherton, "The Services of the Frontier Merchant," *MVHR,* XXIV (1937), 53–70.

it is clear that a commercial mechanism for trade in general was certain to develop speedily. There were commission houses at an early date. Sellers organized "exporting companies" to secure the advantages of large shipments and sales, beginning in 1803. By 1813 there were wholesale houses in various cities.[90]

There was also a banking system. Ohio had begun hers in 1808; by 1814 she had five banks, by early 1818 twenty-four, including various unincorporated concerns theretofore functioning as banks.[91]

The West of our period, like the colonies, never had sufficient metallic money; Congress minted none for the country from 1806 to 1836.[92] In the West there was little save the Spanish dollar, and what accumulated could not be prevented from draining eastward in trade.[93] The framers of the Constitution, realizing that popular opinion favored inflationary practices, and warned by the excesses of the Revolutionary era, followed the example of Parliament in prohibiting the issue of bills of credit by the states.[94]

This did not prevent financial recklessness. As in the past (since the days when a beaver skin was the frontier's monetary unit), all sorts of substitutes for official money were used as mediums of exchange: warehouse orders and receipts, notes of trading firms, even tickets signed by individuals—anything which promised redemption in something generally desired, such as grain, whisky, or dry goods.[95] All this facilitated

90 Gephart, *Transportation*, pp. 99, 557; Buley, *Old Northwest*, I, 557.

91 *Ibid.*, pp. 568, 571, 572. The operation of unincorporated banks ceased when the Second Bank of the United States came into existence in 1816.

92 Coin soon accumulated in the hands of the storekeepers, who sent it east. Even in much later years, collecting and exporting coin was at times a remunerative business. Illustrations are in Gray, *Agriculture*, pp. 220, 221, 870. The situation was even worse in Upper Canada; a British statute of 1820 made British, Portuguese, Spanish, French, and American coins legal tender there. Dunham, *Unrest in Upper Canada*.

93 It was habitually cut into eight bits (corresponding to the *ryal* or "real"), whence the use today of the expression "two bits."

94 The colonies issued bills of credit until Parliament prohibited the practice. The Revolution was financed by paper promises, some of which depreciated to a ten-thousandth of the face value; details in A. S. Bolles, *Financial History of the United States* (New York, 1894).

95 "At Zanesville more than thirty kinds of paper money were circulating" in 1815. An Indiana law of 1815, passed to prevent swindling, recognized the right of individuals to issue notes if their names were printed thereon. Buley, *Old Northwest*, pp. 571, 576; see B. W. Barnard, "The Use of Private Tokens for Money in the United States," *Quarterly Journal of Economics*, XXXI (1917), 601–634.

trade so long as belief continued that those who issued the tokens would redeem them; for so long, they had value.

Unfortunately, irrational conceptions were prevalent respecting banks, money, and credit. So strong was the inflationary spirit that the issue of notes was regarded as the chief purpose of a bank. In addition to this, the mercantilistic delusion that bullion was the only wealth had been displaced by another that was far more dangerous: that anything which would pass as money was capital. A stockholder in a bank could buy stock with his promise to pay money; to that extent, the bank's capital was not savings seeking investment, but promises. When the bank made a loan, it handed out its notes, promises to pay money.[96] Thus far there was no actual investment. Often, too, no sound investment was contemplated. In 1816, Secretary Calhoun attacked the state banks as circulating their notes on a reserve of less than 9 per cent of their obligations. The banks, he said, were incorporated, not because capital sought investment, but because men without capital, and unable to obtain loans from "individuals having real capital and established credit," wanted loans.[97] Later authorities have supported this criticism.[98]

A main reason for the eastward drainage of metallic currency at the time was plain. The branches in Cincinnati and Chillicothe of the Second Bank of the United States (1816–36) were notably active, partly because business in general was booming in Ohio and partly because of the great activity of the land office. Great amounts of land were paid for in notes of the local banks, and these were deposited in the branches of the national Bank. That was slow to use the power of its creditor position, but when used it was quickly effective. In 1818 the

[96] "Country banks made most of their loans in the form of notes. . . . In the cities the deposit account subject to check was extensively used. Even in the cities, however, this means of payment was less used than notes." W. B. Smith, *Economic Aspects of the Second Bank of the United States* (Cambridge, 1953), p. 61.

[97] *A.S.P., Finance,* III, 494.

[98] More than a hundred banks (but none in New England) suspended specie payments in 1814. The main causes were excessive note issues and the financing of speculations. E. R. Taus, *Central Banking Functions of the United States Treasury, 1789–1941* (New York, 1943), p. 25. In 1816 the currency outside New England consisted very largely of bank notes "of varying degrees of depreciation" (Smith, *Second Bank*). Until much later days, "state banks often began to operate before subscriptions had been paid. Stockholders borrowed from the bank, using the stock as collateral in the process of paying for it" (*ibid.*, pp. 28–29, 59).

Cincinnati branch was instructed to grant no further credit to Ohio banks pending payment of balances already due, whereupon three Cincinnati banks suspended specie payments. Business houses failed. Foreclosures put the federal branch banks in possession of great amounts of land. The Ohio legislature put a heavy tax on each branch of the Bank of the United States in that state, and a state officer seized money in its Chillicothe branch. In the end, the Supreme Court held, of course, that an agency of the national government could not be so taxed by the states.[99]

It was by economic developments that the West was definitely settled. It was trade that made it inseparably part of the country, as Washington (speaking of the Southwest) said it would. How completely it had become an integral part of the country was, in fact, dramatically illustrated by its contribution to the depression of 1819 and by its suffering from it. The West has often been treated as causing the depression, but the part played by it, causatively, is in large measure indistinguishable from that played by other parts of the country. Everywhere there had been a great increase of state banks, and in the mass they had issued an immoderate amount of notes.[100] The situation in the West, however, was peculiar in the relatively large number of banks, in their rivalry when co-operation was desperately needed, and in the fact that their stockholders and directors and depositors were all in large part speculators. Selling prices of farm products fell so low that, as in early years, transportation costs equaled or exceeded them.[101]

By 1819, if not by 1815, the West had seemingly lost all apartness from the rest of the country—had ceased, outwardly, in any significant sense, to be a "frontier." However, in one respect of great importance this was not true. A vast disorganization threatened the community because so many were debtors and so few were solvent. The state legislatures gave relief by passing "stay laws" and "relief laws" which vio-

[99] Buley gives many details, *Old Northwest*, I, 125–129. The average receipts of the land office, 1800–1813, were $735,392; in 1814 they rose to $1,784,560, and continued rising until in 1819 they were $14,645,547. Further details are in *A.S.P., Pub. Lands*, III, 420; *Finance*, III, 431.

[100] The total number was 88 in 1811, 208 in 1815, 307 in 1820, 329 in 1830; Taus, *Central Banking*, App. VI. Kentucky, Tennessee, Indiana, Illinois, and Michigan had a total less than Ohio's. "The behavior of the state banks varied so much from state to state and from time to time that satisfactory generalization about them is almost impossible." Smith, *Second Bank*, p. 59.

[101] *A.S.P., Finance*, III, 718.

lated the federal Constitution, for they compelled creditors either to accept bank notes in settlement of debt or (in disregard of contract) give extended credit.[102] Various laws were also passed which assured favoritism to debtors in the appraisal of property attached by creditors. This disregard of communal integrity shows that in 1819 the Old Northwest was not a fully integrated part of the country. Indeed, it shows—since later frontiers showed a similar mercy for debtors—that in 1819 that first national Territory was still a "frontier."

[102] "No state shall . . . pass any . . . law impairing the obligation of contracts," Art. I, Sec. 10, Para. 2.

CHAPTER 14

The West as a Frontier Society

W E HAVE seen how the West originated as a colonial entity; the part it played, for the most part passively, in peace, war, and diplomacy; the manner in which it was settled and politically organized; and how it grew into the political and economic organization of the Union. Little has been said of its inhabitants as a society, respecting which erroneous ideas have been long and widely entertained, and still less of the interrelations between it and the older East by whose discontented citizens it was settled. It remains to consider these hitherto neglected matters.

Little information seemingly exists respecting settlers of western colonial borderland earlier than those of the Revolutionary generation, to whose economic and political discontents reference has been made in recounting their migrations. As respects later emigration evidence is abundant, and respecting its causes there is no disagreement. Timothy Dwight's *Travels in New England and New York* was published (1821) when many citizens of Connecticut were greatly alarmed by the past and continuing migration of its inhabitants to the West. Dwight was in some ways exceptionally well qualified to judge. Not the least, for us, of reasons to credit his opinion of the leading causes of migration was his contemptuous opinion of "restless inhabitants . . . who are delighted with innovation . . . who have nothing to lose, and therefore expect to be gainers by every scramble."[1] Despite this attitude, how-

[1] Timothy Dwight, *Travels in New England and New York* (4 vols., London, 1823), II, 441.

ever, he wrote of New England's departing citizens: "Those who are first inclined to emigrate, are usually such as have met with difficulties at home. These are commonly joined by persons who, having large families and small farms, are induced, for the sake of settling their children, to seek . . . cheaper lands. To both are always added the discontented, the enterprising, the ambitious, and the covetous. Many of the first, and some of these classes are found in every new American country [community], within ten years after its settlement has commenced. From this period, kindred, friendship, and former neighborhood prompt others to follow them."[2]

These statements are consistent with what one finds in on-the-spot descriptions of the old Northwest. However, as respects the "foresters or pioneers" who were, in Dwight's terminology, the first to migrate—and who ought, therefore, to be the individuals referred to in the first of the above quotations—his description of them was utterly inconsistent with what is known of actual life in the Old Northwest.[3] The reason is obvious. The discontents, ambitions, and covetous spirit which led to migration were "difficulties at home" only because Dwight (and others of like mind) regarded those holding them to be of "noxious disposition" because they complained of New England's social order. Dwight described such persons with a contempt which is evidence of the social prejudices of his time and class.[4] The variety of these discontents, many of them amply justified, has been discussed in other connections.

Everything known of westward migrants, after migration became distinguishable from mere local extrusion of population on the fringe of old settlements, is contradictory of uniformity in those migrating, except as respects the personal qualities of character above mentioned, which all who migrated presumably possessed: discontent, ambition, initiative, and courage. Even these greatly altered as new frontiers followed each other. The threat of torch and tomahawk to borders of early colonial times was vastly greater than any faced by settlers of the Old Northwest. The hazards of reaching each new frontier became diminishing hardships; the dangers of living there became diminishing inconveniences.

---

[2] *Ibid.*, p. 439.

[3] *Ibid.*, pp. 439–441. Namely, as leading an "irregular, adventurous, halfworking and half-lounging life," "hating sober industry and prudent economy," and so on.

[4] *Ibid.*, p. 443.

How real, and how great, were the differences between frontier society and that of the states from which the frontiersmen came? With few exceptions before the 1820's migration, and even more uniformly settlement, was of individuals or families, not of large groups unified by locality of origin, or otherwise. In general, therefore, individual migration and promiscuous settlement made impossible any massing of groups similar in racial, natal, political, religious, or educational characteristics, or united by a similar training other than that of farming. With that exception the pioneers seemingly came from everywhere, had done everything, and were of a great variety of beliefs and prepossessions. Nor was there much similarity in cultural level, unless in the earliest migration through Kentucky from North Carolina and Virginia. Of his companions of 1817 in the great migration through Pennsylvania, Morris Birkbeck (an intelligent Englishman) tells us that from the Virginia coast to the heart of the Alleghenies "we have not for a moment lost sight of the manners of polished life. Refinement is unquestionably . . . rare . . . but so is extreme vulgarity."[5]

It is virtually certain that the early West, as compared with the East, had relatively fewer of the rich or of the very poor. It had decidedly more, proportionately, of the uncultured; illiteracy was very high. It may have had more of the rude-mannered, but there is no reason for assuming this, or other lack of refinement. One obvious fact is that the frontier was not without a variety of social types similar to those of the East. Every territory numbered among its residents, permanent or temporary, representatives of distinguished families, men who had been or were in high government service at home or abroad, and many more were well educated.[6] There were also many educated foreigners.[7] Arthur St. Clair and Albert Gallatin (both long residents of southwestern Pennsylvania), Harry Toulmin (English Unitarian, friend of Jefferson), Robert and David Dale Owen of New Harmony, are merely well-known examples. In Alabama there was a colony of Napoleonic exiles.[8] It was said that ten settlers of Gallipolis had been members of

---

[5] *Notes on a Journey in America from* . . . *Virginia to* . . . *Illinois* (Dublin, 1918), p. 40.

[6] Joseph Schafer goes so far as to say that "Highly educated and cultivated Europeans were to be found in every community." *Social History of American Agriculture* (New York, 1936), p. 209.

[7] D. R. Fox, *Ideas in Motion* (New York, 1935), p. 27.

[8] Canadian Archives, *Report* of 1890, p. 147.

the National Assembly of France.[9] But quite aside from cultured Americans and Europeans, the West managed to produce, early, its own famous sons such as Clay and Jackson. The army and the government civil service contained an abundance of cultured men, and many, like William Henry Harrison, Ninian Edwards, and Henry Schoolcraft, served the West in varied fields. Read Samuel Hildreth's *Pioneer Settlers,* or any of the diaries and letters which describe journeys in the early West (scores of which have been printed), and the sharpest impression is that of the variety of backgrounds.

In the original colonies the ownership or nonownership of land (in Europe, after family, the straightest and most solid road to enduring status) was very early destroyed, as a basis of social cleavage, by the practice of squatting on public land. On the other hand, social divisions based on family connections, official services, professions, varying economic occupations, and success in accumulating wealth became more or less definite and enduring cleavages. In these older communities, indiscriminate social mixing of persons of sharply variant backgrounds could not be natural or common. On the frontier, it was a continuous necessity.

There was, of course, for limited purposes, some recognition of social classes. High civil officials, military officers, the richer merchants, and the larger landholders constituted the upper class; varying numbers of travelers or other exceptional residents might be added. They gave the balls and skating parties which, in Detroit, filled the winter months with festivity.[10] In earlier years, the wives of French officers in the Illinois villages had sought, it is said, to follow the fashions of Paris. One of the invaluable early diarists of British years tells us that the ladies of Detroit and Miamis dressed as though their parents "possessed the greatest dignities in the state," and the men, in the opinion of Governor Henry Hamilton, dressed "beyond their means" at the post balls. It is gratifying, however, also to read that deprivation of one lady's society was "an intellectual famine."[11]

[9] A. B. Hulbert, "Methods and Operations of the Scioto . . . Speculators," *MVHR,* I (1915), 510, 515. And the intent of Brissot de Warville, revolutionist and humanitarian reformer, to become an American citizen was defeated by the guillotine.

[10] Many of the original sources cited in N. V. Russell, *The British Regime in the Old Northwest, 1760–1796* (Northfield, Minn., 1939), particularly pp. 145–147, 151, are worth reading.

[11] *Ibid.,* pp. 141, 142, 144.

Aside from extraordinary occasions, class lines did not preclude mixing. Nationality meant nothing, race almost nothing. A Quaker visitor in Detroit in 1793 thought the inhabitants "as great a mixture . . . as ever [he] knew in any one place. English, Scotch, Irish, Dutch, French, Americans from different states, with black and yellow, and seldom clear of Indians of different tribes in the day time."[12] More or less similar conditions prevailed in all the older posts and trading centers of the West. In these western posts race meant little more in ordinary life than nationality did. The Illinois villages and Detroit, particularly, contained numerous French-Indian families—unions between soldiers or fur traders with Indian squaws—which were occasionally sanctioned wholesale by the church but were in general ignored, and their irregularity was not regarded as a social stigma.[13] Illiteracy constituted, of necessity, no social handicap. "Colonel" George Croghan, for example, had long been the powerful subordinate of Sir William Johnson, and had represented him in London. He was phenomenally illiterate, but he lived in comparative luxury, and was for years the leading citizen of pre-Revolutionary Pittsburgh. Before American migration, illiteracy was nearly universal, and schooling—aside, of course, from family instruction—was completely lacking. Kaskaskia had no school until 1817.[14] It was said in 1788 of Detroit that the people were "wholly illiterate, and if we except five or six Canadian families . . . there will not be found twenty people nor perhaps that number, who . . . can even write their name or know a Letter of a Book."[15] There would have been no demand for a reduction of this illiteracy if the emigrants to the West had not included considerable numbers of educated and cultured individuals. In every western colony and later territory there was this leavening fraction.[16]

Peddlers from New England were doubtless the first salesmen of books in the Northwest, supplying Bibles, spellers, dictionaries, and favorite English classics along with household "notions" of great variety.

12 *Mich. Hist. Coll.*, XVII, 639.
13 On Detroit, F. C. Bald, *Detroit's First American Decade, 1796–1805* (Ann Arbor, 1796–1805), pp. 36–37, 88, and Governor Hull in *Annals of Congress,* 9th Cong., 2nd Sess., p. 1027; C. W. Alvord, *The Illinois Country, 1688–1818* (Springfield, 1920), pp. 219–220.
14 Alvord, *Illinois Country,* p. 455.
15 *Mich. Hist. Coll.*, XI, 642.
16 There were educated military officers in all posts. On West Florida, see C. Johnson, *British West Florida, 1763–1783* (New Haven, 1943), pp. 168–169.

English and American novels, or other popular publications, were available in the West within three or four months. Even in remote Kaskaskia, advertisements made known the availability of old favorites such as Young's *Night Thoughts* and the current literary sensations in London. After the War of 1812—that is, at least contemporaneously with the beginning of the great migration to the Northwest—towns such as Zanesville, Detroit, and Cincinnati had newspapers which carried advertisements of books. Detroit had a small press as early as 1809 to serve the needs of Catholic parishioners. From early dates newspapers served that town, Kaskaskia, Shawneetown, St. Louis, and some others.[17]

One surprising feature in frontier government is the youth of important officials, suggesting emigration of the ambitious and talented in early years. High political and legal offices were held, state constitutional conventions were dominated, political crises were surmounted by men in their twenties.[18]

Self-sufficiency of the family, individually and as a unit, was characteristic of the pioneer period of settlement. It was a quality which had been necessitated by isolation of all frontier life since the early 1600's. It had made the average man a jack-of-all-trades, and given women equal versatility in all household arts.[19] Common in our period to both Northwest and Southwest, this frontier influence and competence survived in portions of the latter in large areas until recently.

Various traits of personality were emphasized by travelers, foreign and American. One was the great informality of manners noted by foreigners and conservative Easterners. What they report was doubtless merely the friendly equality assumed by one frontiersman in greeting another, but, when addressed to strangers, questions respecting their homes, travels, plans, and opinions naturally seemed to them impertinent.[20] In the main, the questioning merely revealed the innocent curi-

---

[17] Buley, *The Old Northwest . . . 1815–1840* (2 vols., Indianapolis, 1950), I, 554, 555, 556, 559; M. M. Quaife, *Pictures of Illinois One Hundred Years Ago* (Chicago, 1918).

[18] For example, Steven T. Mason became secretary of Michigan Territory when nineteen years old, and the first governor of the state when twenty-four.; Elias Kent Kane was the leader in the constitutional convention of Illinois (1818) when only twenty-one.

[19] Buley, *Old Northwest*, I, 165–166, lists the many household utensils made by men of ordinary skill.

[20] It is pleasant to know that one British naval captain, Basil Hall, found the

osity of isolates. Deriving from the two primary characteristics of youth and self-sufficiency were traits of self-reliance and self-confidence, with, of course, their extremes of recklessness and boastfulness. The near equality of economic conditions, and the compulsive restriction of each family's social relations to a small neighborhood, necessitated a general tolerance of the opinions and manners of others.

There was also relative equality of opportunity. A general spirit of individualism, and equally one of optimism, pervaded society. The self-made man was predominant in fact, and was not merely respected but idealized. This is presumably what is generally referred to as the democracy of the frontier—a general approbation of almost unrestricted individualism. No trait has been, or is, more pronounced in Americans than the freedom allowed everyone to believe what one will, and to say or do anything not manifestly a legal wrong to another. There was no political democracy either on the frontier or in the East, beyond the fact that there everywhere prevailed—though probably more generally and in more unqualified form in the West—a belief in the competence of almost any citizen to hold office, or (if that statement be too strong) at least to judge the worthiness of any candidate for office.

Frederick Jackson Turner was doubtless right in ascribing to frontier life the development of various traits of personality which are (or at least were long said to be) characteristic of Americans. He credited this, however, solely to the first frontiers west of the Alleghenies, saying: "The colonial tidewater was in close touch with the Old World, and soon lost its western aspects. . . . In the middle of the eighteenth century . . . along the upper waters of the tributaries of the Atlantic . . . the West took on its distinguishing features."[21] It is astounding that he should have attributed miraculous influences upon American society by successive frontiers beginning with the Old Northwest (the later ones not even meriting the name), yet dismiss for fallacious reasons earlier frontiers through a period longer than all the later ones

---

Westerners understood his jokes, which was hardly ever true of eastern Americans, in whom he found "frigid and uninviting formality." *Fragments of Voyages and Travel*, III, 355.

[21] *Atlantic Monthly*, LXXVIII (1896), 289; similarly, Wis. State Hist. Soc. *Proceedings*, LVI (1908). On this point F. L. Paxson finally abandoned Turner, saying, "It was on the English frontier, washed by tide-water in the seventeenth century, that the American was made." *When the West Is Gone* (New York, 1920), p. 22.

together, and those the ones on which life was by far the most isolated, hard, and dangerous, demanding complete self-reliance in defense and self-support. Compared with their lonely settlers, little courage and self-sufficiency were required of the hosts that migrated to the Old Northwest. Surely, the temper of border society, the behavioral characteristics of its members, their basic attitudes toward individualism and social demands, were developed east of the Alleghenies long before 1776. In that long period Americans had become different from Englishmen not merely in individual personality but in social organization. Two differences in particular—one political, the other economic—sharply distinguished them.

One reason why democracy developed on the frontier was that Englishmen had acquired a devotion to local self-government, notwithstanding the shriveled and aristocratic roots of the local courts and gentry by which it was administered.[22] As Charles Beard pointed out, local administration gave rise to an assumption that liberty was promoted by local autonomy, and English emigrants brought this idea with them to America.[23] Another reason was of vast importance: that the political controversies in England preceding and during the Civil War and incidental to the framing of the Bill of Rights constituted probably the greatest popular debate ever joined on the issues of civil liberties. They were part of the spiritual baggage of English emigrants, a portion of the solid basis for American democracy. And third, "a salient fact in the history of the British empire, as well as [in] the beginning of American [legal] democracy was the establishment of representative government in Virginia in 1619."[24] These reasons account for the vast political difference that gradually developed between Englishmen at home and in America.

Emigrants to America had, however, learned in and about the hundred and county courts, and in the thousands of courts baron and courts leet which then existed in England, much more than an appreciation of local self-government. They were equally familiar with medieval social ranks, and had some consciousness of the medieval land law

[22] Compare the present writer's prefatory note to S. Ames (ed.), *County Court Records of Accomack–Northampton, Virginia, 1632–1640* (Amer. Hist. Assoc., *American Legal Records,* VII (Washington, 1954), pp. xiv–xv.

[23] Article "Centralization," A. C. McLaughlin and Hart (eds.), *Cyclopedia of American Government* (3 vols., New York, 1914), I, 238–239.

[24] A. C. McLaughlin, *Steps in the Development of American Democracy* (Abington, Conn., 1920), pp. 1–2.

which dominated the country; and although serfs had almost disappeared before 1600, their long existence had influenced the national mind in its attitude toward labor. These serfs, tied to the land, had performed the menial tasks of the countryside. They had cared for the livestock, cleaned the barns, manured the land, cultivated the crops, dug ditches, trimmed hedges—done everything that American farmers have always done. Finally, all our English immigrants knew through the local courts of the centuries-old vagrancy laws which prevented English laborers from leaving their villages to seek either work or adventure, and of the parish administration, from whose control no indigent Englishman could escape. Of "personal liberty" as Blackstone defined it in 1758 to students at Oxford—liberty "of changing situation [employment], or removing . . . to whatever place one's own inclination may direct"—there was for centuries virtually none in England until reformatory legislation began in 1762.[25] The Webbs tell us that for centuries "the property-less man [five-sixths of the population] . . . under the law of settlement found himself, at the discretion of the Overseers of the Poor, legally confined to his parish for the term of his natural life."[26]

From all this, Britons in America were relatively free from 1607 onward, not because they were free from transplanted compulsory labor laws, either in the colonies or in the early Territories, but because these laws were comparatively little enforced, and because escape from them was possible for many through flight, as it was for debtors.[27] The callousness of the old colonial laws re-enacted in the Old Northwest, and

[25] Sir William Blackstone, *Commentaries on the Laws of England,* any modern edition, index, *s.v.* "liberty." In the best edition, W. C. Jones, ed. (2 vols., San Francisco, 1915), the quoted passage, and others relevant, are in I, 4, 211, 240, 374.

[26] Sidney and Beatrice Webb, *English Local Government from the Revolution to the Corporations Act [1689–1835]; The Parish and the County* (London, 1906), p. 4. "For over seven hundred years . . . the statute book abounds in laws of ever-increasing severity against vagrants whether as . . . beggars or rogues . . . or as labourers who abstracted themselves from their obligations to the manor or parish to which they belonged, as well as from the service of the 'Master' to whom it was assumed that they owed their Labour." Webbs, *English Local Government: English Poor Law History: Part I: The Old Poor Law [to 1834]* (London, 1927), p. 23 (pp. 23–28, on migration of laborers). "Wandering in search of employment" was conspicuous from 1700 onward. The law bore most harshly on agricultural laborers, such as all who farmed in America. By 1788 there was "great freedom," *ibid.,* pp. 344–341.

[27] See R. B. Morris, *Government and Labor in Early America* (New York, 1946), pp. 1–13.

to some extent of their enforcement, was extreme. But opportunity to escape was also extremely great, and its importance equally so.

British emigrants to America saw here limitless stretches of unoccupied land with only a few roving Indians enjoying it, and nobody to prevent its occupation by themselves, with inconceivable freedom from the restraints that bound them in England. This created a land mania of one type, which gave squatters economic independence, before the possibility of securing Indian "grants" created a second mania of land speculation. Both flourished and powerfully influenced the history of the seventeenth and eighteenth centuries. It was proved, following 1763, that land squatting was wholly beyond control of the British government. Following 1783, it equally defied restraint by the American government. It was simple fact, as General Gage wrote, that "it was the passion of every Man to be a Landholder, and the People had a Natural Disposition to rove in Search of good Lands, however distant."[28] Lord Dunmore's excuse to the government in 1774 for his failing to enforce its regulations was the same:

I have learnt from experience that the established Authority of any government in America, and the policy of Government at home, are both insufficient to restrain the Americans; and that they do and will remove as their avidity and restlessness incite them. They acquire no attachment to Place: But . . . for ever imagine the Lands further off, are Still better than those upon which they are already Settled. . . . Proclamations have been published from time to time to restrain them: But impressed from their earliest infancy with Sentiments and habits, very different from those acquired by persons of a Similar condition in England, they do not conceive that Government has any right to forbid their taking possession of a vast tract of Country, either uninhabited, or which Serves only as a Shelter to a few Scattered Tribes of Indians. Nor can they be easily brought to entertain any belief of the permanent obligation of Treaties made with those People, whom they consider as but little removed from the brute Creation. These notions . . . I by no means pretend to Justify. I only . . . State matters as they really are.[29]

No doubt the vast majority of squatters merely knew a good thing when they saw it, and took it for safety or economic gain. But no doubt, also, they showed others how foolish it would be to pay feudal rents to the Crown's grantees, and as they spread by thousands annually

[28] C. E. Carter, *Gage Correspondence,* I, 277.
[29] R. G. Thwaites and Kellogg (eds.), *Documentary History of Dunmore's War* (Madison, 1905), p. 371.

over Crown lands, even quitrents became uncollectible, and feudalism
lost all life.[30] Gradually, too, as state and federal pre-emption laws
turned these squatters into lords of the land, all on an approximately
equal footing economically, they became democratic socially and in
their political thinking. That this thinking was nationwide in 1787 is
shown by the action of the Continental Congress in banning feudalism
from national territories, however great might be the problem of eradi-
cating it from the colonial statute books of the states.

All the basic problems of the West's development in the period of
British'rule and of our Spanish relations up to 1819, as discussed in
earlier chapters, were an outgrowth of the migratory habits of Americans. "They will settle the lands in spite of everybody," Jefferson
wrote.[31] "You might as well," wrote Washington, "attempt to prevent
the reflux of the tide . . . within your rivers."[32] Various provisions in
the bills of rights included in early constitutions of the states attest the
importance then ascribed to the "natural and inherent" rights of (1)
migrating and (2) of forming new states. These disappeared only because the first was fully protected in the federal Constitution of 1788,
the second protected with qualifications by the same, and the enjoyment of both fully provided for both in the territorial system established by the Continental Congress, under compacts between the states,
and under the Constitution by its confirmation of those compacts.[33]
No differences between Britons and Americans in 1776 were greater

[30] Edward Channing pronounced Dane's addition to the Ordinance of 1787
more valuable than all the rest; J. F. Jameson, *The American Revolution Considered as a Social Movement* (Princeton, 1926). Jameson did not sufficiently
emphasize for most readers the social change involved, and the same may be
said of Charles Beard in *New Republic,* XCVII, 360, col. 2. Compare Gray,
Agriculture, I, 382–385.

[31] *Writings* (Ford ed.).

[32] *Writings* (Fitzpatrick ed.).

[33] Pennsylvania, in its constitution of 1776 (Declaration of Rights, sec. XV)
and Vermont in its constitution of 1777 (Declaration of Rights, sec. xvii) proclaimed the first right as "natural and inherent." Vermont reiterated both
rights in her constitution of 1786 (Declaration of Rights, sec. xxi). Pennsylvania and Virginia, by their treason statutes of the 1780's, limited the
second right as within their territories. The provisions of the federal Constitution of 1788 are in Art. IV, Sec. 2, Par. 1 (migration), Art. IV, Sec. 3,
Par. 1 (new states), and Art. VI, Sec. 1. These were a confirmation of Confederation compacts, which, although literally limited to lands ceded to the
Confederation by Virginia, never were given, geographically, any restricted
meaning. See *Ill. Hist. Coll.,* XXV, clix–clx, clxxxix–cxci.

than these. The basic economic and social differences here in question, accompanied as they were by the eradication of feudalism and the inculcation by frontier life of national characteristics of personality, created the American. He was an Englishman—but one divested, a century or two earlier than his compatriots in the homeland, of various social prejudices and restraints of medieval root, and with impulses toward popular government which American conditions fostered, while those in the homeland blunted and repressed the democratic impulses of the 1600's.

It was not merely on the "Atlantic" frontier but long before settlement of the western portions of that area that the visible characteristics of Americans were created. It was in that area east of the mountains that nationalism was developed; by it, primarily, that nationalism was made secure by the Revolution, and—again primarily—that the West was pledged to expanding federalism. The borderers on the western edge of the Appalachians did not support the Revolution until bought, after earlier legislative reforms, with the radical constitutions of 1776–77, promising them the representation and fair government which they had long been denied (and which, in 1964, the Supreme Court is finally giving to the entire country).[34] By these constitutions the governing class (freed of the Loyalists) purged its hypocrisy—with new hypocrisy.

If one seeks opinions of western society in the writings of contemporaries, an estimate of the judges' prejudices may be as undependable as an independent estimate of the society. However, the prejudices are in some cases quite manifest. There was sometimes no other basis for them than a distrust of discontented rovers entertained by persons socially content. For example, when Chancellor Kent was on circuit near Lake Champlain in 1800, he wrote that "jurors and people looked rude in their manners and dress and gave me an unfavourable opinion of

[34] W. C. Webster, "Comparative Study of the State Constitutions of the American Revolution," *Annals* of the Amer. Academy of Political and Social Science, IX; A. Nevins, *The American States During and After the Revolution, 1775–1789* (New York, 1924), especially Chap. 5 (pp. 117–170). There were eight constitutions in 1776, three in 1777. The radicals did not gain much. In five states constitutions adopted during the Revolution gave suffrage to taxpayers after varying periods of residence. For officeholding, property requirements were higher. The preambles were eloquent of popular sovereignty, the equality of men, freedom of election, majority rule, and so on.

the morals of the country."[35] To this emotional confusion of external appearance with morality, he added a contemptuous reference to "squatters, insolvent emigrants, and demagogues" in which prejudice heavily predominated over reason. Without further examples of mere prejudice, one may quote the warning of Timothy Flint—churchman, Harvard graduate, and western missionary with an unsurpassed knowledge of the West—with which he dismissed the misjudgments of President Dwight: "The people of the Atlantic States have not yet recovered [1828] from the horror, inspired by the term backwoodsman. This prejudice is particularly strong in New England, and is more or less felt from Maine to Georgia."[36]

Some reference should also be made to inconsistent judgments—inconsistent because prejudices varied. In 1817, on the Forbes Road, Morris Birkbeck heard repetitions of old reports that the inhabitants of Indiana were "lawless, semi-barbarous vagabonds, dangerous to live among." He found, on the contrary, the laws "respected, and . . . effectual," and the manners of the people "kind and gentle."[37] The neighborhood in question was that of Vincennes, the territorial capital from 1805 to 1813. The charges were an echo of those made in 1770 by General Gage, with no basis whatever even then except his exasperation against French fur traders operating from Vincennes. And "Vagabonds," an English statutory designation of wandering laborers, was British military vituperation in the same period against intruders (French fur traders or American squatters) into the western wilderness. One Englishman found the "impudence, ignorance, and laziness" of Indiana's inhabitants an unpleasant change from the hospitality and politeness of Kentucky. Another was happy to leave "the spitting, gouging, drinking, duelling, swearing, and staring" of Kentucky.[38]

If credence be given to miscellaneous reports, as some historians have done, the West was full of criminals.[39] For more than one reason this is not believable. The first is that the evidence supporting it is poor. Every such contemporary statement seen by the writer is easily discredited by circumstances. For example, Andrew Ellicott admitted to a

[35] J. T. Horton, *James Kent: A Study in Conservatism* (New York, 1939), p. 126.
[36] *Recollections of the Last Ten Years* (1826, repr. 1932), p. 170.
[37] *Notes on a Journey*, pp. 93, 96.
[38] Buley, *Old Northwest*, I, 29.
[39] A.·B. Hulbert, *Historic Highways of America* (16 vols., Cleveland, 1904), IX, 159, 176–188 (esp. 177).

committee of the United States Senate that he had "declared a large proportion of the inhabitants of the Mississippi Territory to be a set of the most abandoned, malicious, deceitful, plundering, horse-thieving, rascals on the continent."[40] But he said it at Natchez in 1797, in a time of excitement and fear, and any member of any of the five factions then tense with mutual suspicions in that center of international suspicions would doubtless have expressed an opinion equally derogatory and unconsidered of the group he most distrusted. A government agent to the Cherokees in Arkansas, newly arrived among them in 1813, wrote of the earlier white settlers there, who were contesting their displacement by governmental resettlement of the Cherokee, "I am here . . . among the worst banditi: all the white folks, a few excepted, have made their escape to this country guilty of the most horrid crimes."[41] In addition to the manifest reason for exasperation, this agent was surely a tenderfoot who had been spoofed by jokers. As a final illustration, consider a statement by a committee of Congress in 1800 that the Northwest Territory was an asylum for "the most vile and abandoned criminals." This was made in a report seeking money for more courts.[42] In the absence of supporting evidence, it would be absurd to give credence to such statements.

The nature of different crimes gives us considerable aid in judging charges of frontier wickedness. Crimes common in the West were those "natural" to the character of the frontier. Horse thieves were undoubtedly numerous. The Indians had always stolen horses from the borderers, the latter from the Indians, and doubtless to some extent from each other. For obvious reasons, this crime remained the frontier's characteristic crime down to the end of the frontier. The theft (or careless appropriation) of cattle and hogs, both running more or less wild around all settlements, was equally common. The laws against these thefts go back in all states to the frontier period. One of the earliest acts in West Florida (1764), the earliest new frontier of the period covered in this volume, required any seller of beef to hang the hide, hair out, "on his stockade fronting the street for four hours in the day."[43] Laws requiring marks and brands on all livestock, and punish-

[40] *A.S.P., Misc.*, II, 88.
[41] G. Foreman, *Indians and Pioneers . . . the American Southwest before 1830* (New Haven, 1930), p. 39.
[42] *Ill. Hist. Coll.*, XXI, clxxxiii.
[43] Johnson, *West Florida*, p. 28.

ing their alteration, are to be found in the statute books of every state in its frontier era, at least in the period covered in this volume. Another class of wrongdoers possibly numerous in the West was that of fugitive debtors. It is to be hoped they were numerous, for imprisonment was allowed for incredibly paltry sums, and many jails were inhuman beyond present-day conception.[44] The criminals of various types who prey on the commerce and accumulated wealth of old and settled communities would certainly never, unless as fugitives, have gone to a poor and rough frontier (unless, in later years, to gamble on Mississippi steamers); and for most of them, as fugitives, it would have offered the least possible concealment. Those guilty of crimes of violence might, however, have sought its cover.

There were doubtless much vulgarity and swearing, some dueling, much rowdyism, and more or less truculence. The last was shockingly manifested in biting, gouging, and other acts of mayhem upon opponents in brawls and even in wrestling contests. These acts were crimes in many older communities from which visitors and settlers came, but although they were not such in the West until made so by statute, refined observers would earlier have so regarded and reported them. In the Northwest Territory profanity became a crime in 1788, gambling in 1790, maiming in 1798, dueling, and even challenging to "fight," in 1799.[45] There was virtually no enforcement of such statutes so far as extant records show.[46] And as Richard Hooker had said long before, "laws they are not," practically speaking, ". . . which public approbation hath not made so." It is quite impossible to determine the extent to which the laws passed were necessary. It is manifest that the authorities charged with their enforcement did not so regard them, and that predominant public opinion in early days was indifferent. However, law-abiding travelers and settlers would nevertheless have denounced as criminals not merely persons adjudged as such but also those whose reputed actions were forbidden, or should in their opinion be forbidden, by the law.

But no matter how few or how many "criminals" there may have been, by any definition, the vast majority of the population were of course law-abiding citizens. On circuit in 1802 in the Genesee Valley,

---

[44] J. B. McMaster, *The Acquisition of Political, Social and Industrial Rights of Man in America* (Cleveland, 1903).

[45] *Ill. Hist. Coll.*, XVII, XXI, indexes.

[46] *Ibid.*

Chancellor Kent wrote in his journal: "They are a rude, fierce people, very democratic and licentious, and there is little government among them."[47] So they were, presumably, if one strips "licentious" of moral and political connotations beyond mere unruliness. Nor would they, in that case, have objected to the description.[48] They *were* unrestrained in fact and unruly by desire, and their attitude toward all laws restricting behavior was simply that of extreme individualists. The prejudice of Chancellor Kent, like that of President Dwight, was mere social prejudice. It was common in the East, as we know from its rebuttal by Timothy Flint, already quoted.

Aside from the possible objectives of a few speculators in land or politics who were active in creating the state of Franklin and in the plans for the creation of Westsylvania and Transylvania, there is nothing in the history of the early frontiers that involved any "separatism" other than the separatism of spirit which induced all migration to the frontier. An assumption has nevertheless seemingly been widespread that only a doubtful attachment to the federal Union, or even actual disloyalty, characterized the early West. For this reason much attention has been given to the "Spanish conspiracies" of James Wilkinson, James Robertson, and John Sevier, and to Aaron Burr's supposed reliance upon southwestern disaffection in 1805. Our greatest authority upon the Old Southwest has dismissed the "Spanish" conspiracies (without definiteness as to Wilkinson) as being for the purpose of possible gains in land or trade.

He has also referred, however, to "the turbulence, the lawlessness, the violence of the . . . frontiersmen and land speculators."[49] Undoubtedly these qualities were there, in some places and in some degree. They are not matters of disloyalty, although the two could well have been united in some land speculations. But even as respects the characteristics mentioned, it is also not stated that they characterized any considerable portion of the inhabitants, or any considerable number of the land speculators. The important question is whether, any-

---

[47] Horton, *James Kent,* p. 127.

[48] A committee reported in 1789 to the House of Representatives, one committee member, a Pittsburgher, stating that "forming settlements . . . upon the frontiers . . . requires men of enterprising, violent, nay, discontented and turbulent spirits. Such always are our first settlers in the ruthless and savage wild." Quoted in B. F. Hibbard, *Public Land Policies* (New York, 1924), p. 57. But the committee wanted funds for courts.

[49] Whitaker, *Spanish-American Frontier,* p. 19.

where in the West up to 1806, events actually occurred which indicated decided social instability or suggested general disloyalty. Nothing should be accepted as evidencing either fault except events embodying popular action or receiving popular approval. Between the Revolution and Burr's conspiracy, various incidents in the West, already noticed, had involved lawlessness or turbulence, military action or lesser violence, and had roused suspicions, started rumors, excited fears, or agitated governments. This was particularly true of nine incidents.[50] Of these incidents four were closely centered in Natchez, and two others little less so.[51] Its population—of pre-Revolutionary British and Spanish, later of refugee Loyalists and other Americans—ensured factionalism and suspicions, invited intrigues and rumors, and its strategic location was a choice one for their dissemination. There seems to be no evidence that in any of these nine incidents of southwestern history the people of the West, otherwise than in a very local sense, exhibited lawlessness, violence, or turbulence in a special degree; and as respects such of the incidents as affected public opinion in both East and West, there appears to have been in its expression nothing to distinguish western from eastern society.

[50] (1) Willing's raid down the Mississippi in 1778; (2) the Natchez insurrection of 1781; (3) the vote of Congress in 1786 authorizing Jay to renounce temporarily the claim of right to navigate the Mississippi; (4) the Bourbon County episode of 1785; (5) James Wilkinson's agreements following 1787 to stimulate discontent in Kentucky; (6) the Georgia land grants of 1789 and 1795; (7) James O'Fallon's bluster, bluff, and backdown in 1790–91; (8) Citizen Genêt's appeals to the West to attack Louisiana in 1793; and (9) the several matters chronologically associated in 1797 with William Blount's conspiracy.

[51] The Natchez incidents were items 1, 2, 4, and 9 of the preceding list; the two others were 6 and 7. The first two incidents were acts of war. The Bourbon County episode (No. 4) was the act of a state, controlled by land jobbers. Acts of violence were done by McGillivray and Spain. Local lawlessness, if any, and turbulence were forced by outsiders. The same was even more obviously true of whatever unrest was manifested in the West as a result of the grants to land companies (Nos. 6, 7). O'Fallon's only important acts seem to have been done in uninhabited pinewoods. Further, considering the publicity and character of acts by American and Spanish officials at Natchez in 1797 (No. 9), and the presence there of Easterners who were supposedly Blount's agents, the behavior of the citizens seems to have been satisfactorily restrained. As regards lawlessness or violence in the other episodes, none beyond talk was manifested in the West over the Mississippi issue in 1786 (No. 3), or provoked by Wilkinson on that issue in 1787–89 (No. 8), or aroused by Genêt in 1793 (No. 5). And, as regards turbulence, agitation was certainly as high in pitch in 1786 in Congress as in the West; and public excitement was surely as great and widespread in the East as in the West over Genêt.

Assuming provisionally the correctness of these opinions, the question arises why contrary views so long prevailed. There are, seemingly, three reasons. One was the romanticism ascribed to the West in the early years of the Romantic Movement. For forty years the West was the object of international suspicions or ambitions. Rumors of colonial cessions were constant. Every strange traveler was suspected of being a foreign agent. The Floridas and Louisiana being always available as prospective spoil in imaginary alliances, fantastic rumors of wars and alliances recurrently circulated through the Mississippi Valley. Most of these fantasies presumably originated in western taverns. Their absurdity at the time of Genêt's mission—when, if ever, some truth in them was to be expected—has already been noted. The extraordinary credulity with which they were received and circulated is illustrated by the fact that Laussat, in the same letter in which he reported the coming of an army of 80,000 down the Mississippi, also wrote that boats from Tennessee and Kentucky landed daily and reported those states quiet. "Their interest," he said, "was in crops and prices."[52] These frontier phantasms have nothing to do with the West's development beyond conclusions respecting the interest and character of the inhabitants. The report just mentioned (of 1802, following termination of the right to deposit at New Orleans) certainly represents the homely interests of the vast majority of settlers.

Another explanation of misjudgments of the West was the persisting prejudice against borderers, which has already been discussed. From this second explanation of misjudgments follows the third. Outside the narrow scope of occasionally truly original research, the process of historical writing is compilatory. The facts used are within the public domain; they quickly become part of established tradition; and when facts are repeated, the traditional views with which they are associated —and the prejudices with which they are incrusted—will cling to them unless carefully considered. There can be no doubt that a general tradition of American history has fostered the idea of a disloyal West. False views of the political character of the Revolutionary generation, running through conservative histories, were astonishingly prevalent at

[52] In the Old Northwest, various similar rumors of dangers and disloyalty were current in 1797–99; none was supported by a trace of substantial evidence. Houck, *Spanish Regime,* II, 259, 285–91, W. H. Smith (ed.), *Life and Public Services of Arthur St. Clair* (2 vols., Cincinnati, 1882), II, 417–420; Carter, *Terr. Papers,* II, 597, 611; *A.S.P., Pub. Lands,* II, 224; *Ill. Hist. Coll.,* XXV, cccxxx.

the end of the last century, when they were relied upon in university instruction. The loss suffered through the exile of the Loyalists, as a conservative check on democracy, was grossly magnified by writers then in vogue, and the remaining classes of society were lumped as riffraff,[53] very much as the tidewater governing class had always characterized the border element of colonial society.[54] This accords with and may partially explain the perdurability of the idea that frontiersmen were lawless—that is, scofflaws—for they were often of necessity without immediately enforceable law (as, indeed, despite all our courts, we often are today).

Other influences than romance, prejudice, and repetitive writing have entered into the persistence of the view that the early West was at least weak in national feeling. Historians occasionally introduce novel explanations of why events happened or why they "needlessly" happened. Sixty years ago, when the influence of geography upon history was being emphasized, one prominent historian wrote: "When the United States was in its infancy, all conditions, geographical, political, social and economic pointed toward the formation of two confederacies, one along the Atlantic seaboard, the other along the Mississippi."[55] Various cases could be cited to illustrate the unsatisfactory character of such reasoning.[56] Geography alone, apart from the other factors, must

[53] "The Revolution . . . had unsettled society . . . destroying one of the balance-wheels of society. The aristocratic, wealthy, and conservative class had been almost entirely swept away. . . . One of the principal barriers against anarchy had been destroyed, and free scope and full encouragement were thus given to the most pernicious and extreme errors of democracy." H. C. Lodge, in *North American Review* (1876), p. 123. "The anarchical elements which had existed in the pre-Revolutionary agitation" began to make themselves felt "as soon as the dangers of the war were past." W. G. Sumner, *Alexander Hamilton* (New York, 1890), p. 122. "In the States, then, the elements of revolutionary dissolution and decay began to work . . . the Union was from the start at war with the turbulent, anarchistic elements which the Revolution had set loose." *Ibid.,* p. 13. These books (and others by Lodge and others in the same series as Sumner's) were relied on in university instruction of the writer's day in the late 1890's.
[54] The General Assembly of the State of Franklin, in 1785, resented such references to Franklin settlers by members of the North Carolina legislature as "offscourings of the earth; fugitives from justice." G. H. Alden, in *AHR,* VIII, 277.
[55] W. R. Shepherd, "The Cession of Louisiana to Spain," *Political Sci. Qy.,* XIX (1904), 458.
[56] Did the common language and institutions of England and America, their common use of the Great Lakes, the nearness of the American border to the St. Lawrence, the true economic interests of both countries, "point" to union—or

obviously be ignored. Economic and social factors pointed away from the conclusion stated, and the political were contradictory. The passage quoted is one of scores which rest (aside from illogic) on an exaggeration of the importance of Mississippi navigation in early years. If these conditions were conducive to dismemberment of the Confederation or early Federal Union, not only countervailing but dominating factors of unity must have existed. These important factors, which prevented dismemberment, were in the minds or in the settled habits of citizens.

There was another episode of the same years as the supposed Burr Conspiracy which gave even plainer evidence of western loyalty, notwithstanding the fact that of all examples of early frontier "turbulence" it was the greatest, unless the Whisky Insurrection of western Pennsylvania be so adjudged. This was the insurrection in West Florida. The French minister in Washington wrote to Talleyrand, in 1805, "that continual vagabondage . . . that system of allowing the population to scatter . . . is perhaps, for the government of the Union, one of the surest methods of conquest. . . . Those private takings of possession form collectively . . . a taking of possession for the state."[57] So, indeed, they did, *on one condition:* namely, provided one attributes an abiding nationalism to these wanderers. Spain's officials in Louisiana did not; they counted for years on making them content under Spanish rule. On the other hand, it was Jefferson's basic belief that if American backwoodsmen occupied the Floridas, these would fall, like ripe fruit, into the Union. Events proved how right he was.

Following constitutions of Pennsylvania and Vermont adopted in the Revolutionary era, the Federal Constitution of 1788 affirmed the right of unrestricted migration; affirmed the right to form new states—subject, if formed within an existing state, to its consent; and guaranteed admission of new states to the Union—thus retrospectively approving such statemaking as that of Watauga.[58]

Political, economic, ecclesiastical, and other causes of separatism of

---

even to early common use of the St. Lawrence? As respects even the latter, fruitless pointing continued until 1870 in right, until 1959 in fact. Dozens of such questions could be put, to other assertions, to reveal the insecurity of such reasoning. Moreover, it is obvious that "geographical" conditions must be active primarily through "economic," that "social" conditions must largely be dependent on economic, and that the latter could be effective only through "political."

[57] Robertson, *Louisiana,* II, 142.

[58] Art. IV, Sec. 2, Par. 1; Art. IV, Sec. 3, Par. 1; and Art. VI, Sec. 1; *Ill. Hist. Coll.,* XXV, clix–clx, clxxix–cxci.

spirit were all plain and strong in the prenational period of western development. With gradually lessening importance of the political element which had in so small part always prompted migration from the eastern states, and with relatively slight change in other elements, all these causes of migration remained powerful throughout the period covered by this volume. Their "apartness" rooted in one or another discontent—in political or economic disappointment, in adventuresomeness, idealism, or mere fiddle-footedness—emigrants in theological restraints poured westward into the new "apartments" of the territories, and added state after state to the Union.

This phenomenon of continual social displacement did not end with the Confederation era, nor even with the disappearance of an identifiable "frontier" by 1890. Even today ten million citizens move each year from one state of the Union to another; settling down, they constitute at least 10 per cent of the population of every state. Nor are the past and the present tied together solely by the existence of this type of separatism. Some of the causes of it in the Confederation era continued to operate not only throughout the years considered in this volume but much later. Indeed, there was one cause of resentment against government two centuries ago which had long existed in England in far more flagrant form than in America—namely, unequal representation in the legislature; and this has remained a part of the American political structure, in which it is vastly more common and more monstrous today than in the Confederation era. After 1788 all frontiers (geographically considered) were territories (successively created by Congress in the West) substantially free of the defects just mentioned, and the primary purpose behind demands for increased local government was to secure what attention was possible, under the territorial system, for peculiarly local needs (and leaders).

Nothing has thus far appeared which suggests why there could have been more than superficial differences between American society in the West and in the East. The West was merely passing (in successive territories) through a stage through which the Atlantic states had earlier passed. Excepting the southern plantation area, the entire country was one of little farms; urban population was insignificant; farming and home industries characterized both East and West, although communications, trade, industry, and a financial system were everywhere developing.[59]

[59] In various respects, in this period the whole country was "primitive" in the

spects the second quotation, there were in fact some striking examples of this, such as mining customs in the Far West, and the ultimate accordance of legal primacy to the claim of a first squatter on government land. It is true that, in the latter case, frontiersmen, to protect the right of such a squatter, had—before his primacy became legal—combined in unlawful acts to prevent bidding against him at government auctions.[69] But this is the only example appearing in Turner's writings of a frontier "custom" that became law. He heartily approved, however, of various acts by frontiersmen, such as lynching, which never became, but in his opinion should have become, lawful.[70]

Turner could never even have read the Ordinance of 1787—not, seemingly, before 1899. At least he wrote in that year—hesitantly, gropingly, as in the dark:

The West was a field in which new political institutions were to be produced. It offered a wide field for *speculative* creation and for the [speculative] adjustment of old institutions to new conditions. The study of the evolution of western institutions shows how slight was the proportion of [even] actual theoretic invention of institutions; there was abundant opportunity for the study of the sources of the institutions actually shown [not so as respects laws], the causes of the selection [even less so], and the new institutions actually produced by the new environment [neither here nor elsewhere named because nonexistent].[71]

This was never published until after Turner's death. It was a confession which would have necessitated enormous alterations not only of

behind have in each generation been forced to remodel themselves upon the newer growth beyond." This is a fantasy unsupported by any evidence ever cited by Professor Turner or by the follower quoted, F. L. Paxson, *When the West Is Gone* (New York, 1930), p. 47.

[69] B. H. Hibbard, *History of the Public Land Policies* (New York, 1924), pp. 198, 218; Joseph Schafer, *Agriculture in Wisconsin* (Madison, 1922), p. 73.

[70] Turner only vaguely, if at all, admitted their illegality. He and others excused such acts as lynching, and not merely the combined action of squatters to prevent bidding by "claim jumpers," who entered upon land to which a first squatter was eventually given a pre-emption right. These excuses were based on the view that law was absent, or courts distant, which, even when true, was irrelevant, for there was ample opportunity to seize and hold alleged wrongdoers. *Minn. Hist. Bull.*, III, 400; (*Atlantic Monthly*, LXXVIII, (1896, 292); XCI (1909), 88. Compare Turner in McLaughlin and Hart, *Cyclopedia*, II (1911), 62.

[71] *Early Writings*, p. 289. Months would be necessary to identify the sources of the laws selected by the judges acting as as legislature.

There was, however, one vast difference: Congress (at first, in literal accord with the Ordinance of 1787, by 1834 with moderate liberalizations) did not permit those who moved into a territory to live there under such laws as had governed them before leaving. Their political sobriety was perhaps doubted because they left, and their moral responsibility likewise. The governor and judges of the Northwest Territory were appointed by the national government and constituted, together, the territorial legislature in its first (nonrepresentative) stage. In other words, in the land of their hopes, settled by their courage and hardihood, they were denied self-government: in Ohio for ten years, in Indiana for sixteen, in Illinois for twenty-three, in Michigan for twenty-eight, and in Wisconsin even longer.[60] As respected problems involving merely adjustment to physical environment (Indian relations, militia, roads, bridges, common fields, enclosures, strays, brands), it was natural that the governor and judges should have selected, as they did, laws from the statute books of the colonies when these had been in an early stage of settlement—notwithstanding that better ways must have developed in dealing with some of those problems. But as respects laws regulating basic social interests (the family, vice, crimes and punishments, courts and attorneys, debts, attachments and executions, guardians, poor relief), it was clearly illogical, and most undesirable, that the statutes selected should also have been, *as they were,* a century and more old.[61] Why should emigrants from states with better than those early laws not have been given them in the Northwest Territory? Governor St. Clair had lived for years in western Pennsylvania, holding official offices in communities whose members were doubtless indistinguishable from the migrants into the Northwest Territory a few miles westward. Manifestly, the predominant opinions respecting rovers, of those who framed the Ordinance of 1787, were closely akin to the opinions expressed a generation later by New York's most eminent judge and by the president of Yale, already quoted. Manifestly, too, similar opinions were allowed to control the choice of laws for the Northwest Territory in its nonrepresentative stage of government. However, justi-

sense of "backward"; compare J. B. Clark, Introduction to J. R. Commons *et al., Documentary History of American Industrial Society* (10 vols., Cleveland, 1910–11), I, 34. Or, as respects transportation of persons, for thousands of years before Henry Ford and fast trains; or, as respects house lighting, before Edison.

[60] See *Ill. Hist. Coll.*, XXV, index, s.v. "territories," "legislatures."

[61] See Preface to *Ill. Hist. Coll.*, XVII.

fication for distrust was not wholly on the side of the Union's wards; the Union had some defense.[62]

Estrangement between frontiersmen and stay-at-homers was inevitable, however little written evidence of it may survive. The self-eulogy of their own hardihood voiced by the rovers of Westsylvania, their disdain for the weaklings who stayed at home, have been quoted; likewise the contempt voiced in the North Carolina legislature for the settlers of Franklin. In a milder form of mutual distrust such estrangement presumably affected national politics until well after the period of this volume.

In considering the West's development, we started with Great Britain pondering what to do with a country which Lord North characterized as "the habitat of bears and beavers"—plus a few thousand Indians. At its end, the question inevitably arises, What contributions, before or during the period covered by this volume, were made by the West to the identity of Americans, to their basic social institutions, or even in a permanently unique manner to their history?

The writings of Frederick Jackson Turner elaborated a view that the West's contribution was immense. In his theory, ordinary Easterners, merely moved to the West, miraculously and repeatedly regenerated (with the aid of Grecian and anthropological mythology) the political and other "institutions" and the ideals of American society, both of the West and the East. It is impossible here to do more than state very briefly his leading theses, and the objections to which they are obviously open.

After using "frontier" in either a lineal or areal sense, or in both, he adopted as its meaning "a form of society, determined by the reactions between the wilderness and [settlers on] the edge of advancing settlement"; more specifically, "a democratic, self-sufficing, primitive agricultural society in which individualism was pronounced."[63] His

[62] "Within less than twenty years after the formation of the new state [of Ohio] it denied the authority of the National Government and passed acts of nullification that indicated less respect for Federal authority than did those of South Carolina a dozen years later. . . . The acts of nullification were not [however] because the people of Ohio believed in states' rights. They believed in individual rights and resented the authority that attempted to interfere with such rights." I. F. Patterson, *Constitution of Ohio* (1912), p. 16.

[63] In his most famous paper (an address before the American Historical Association in 1893), Turner defined frontier as "the outer edge of the [population] wave . . . the hither [western] edge of [occupied] free [non-feudal] land."

asic ideas were that "American society has been repeatedly "b ing over again at the outer edge of settlement," and "developin each area . . . out of the primitive conditions of the frontier, the plexity of city [small town] life."[64] The settlers' "most fundam traits, their institutions, even their ideals were shaped," Turner clared, "by this interaction between the wilderness and themselve The settler burned trees, plowed land, planted seed; the land yie crops and inspired thoughts. But neither thankfulness for its nonfe title (to which Turner sometimes attributed everything above cred to the "interaction") nor any other "interaction" could alter any portant institution.[66] That word has been used to include almost social practice or contrivance from potash or other outhouses thro cattle branding, roof-raising parties, and quilting parties to const tional conventions and constitutions. The sod-breaking plow seem be the only frontier "institution" created in the Old Northwest by teraction of pioneer and wilderness.

As for important institutions of social organization or activity, all created and regulated by law, and every immigrant into the Old Nor west from 1788 onward lived under laws required to be approved Congress. Yet Turner wrote that "the evolution of American politi institutions was dependent on the advance of the frontier," and t "in all America we can study the process by which in a new land soc customs form and crystalize into law."[67]

As respects the first of these two assertions, the long deprivation all legislative power suffices to prove its absurdity. It was long a shown by one critic of Turner that in the Old Northwest public opi ion did ultimately "somewhat . . . accelerate . . . manhood suffra and the popular election of executive and judicial officers."[68] As r

[64] McLaughlin and Hart, *Cyclopedia* II, 61, col. 1; *Atlantic Monthl* LXXVIII (1896), p. 289; similarly, *ibid.*, XCI (1908), 93; "The Old West, Wis. St. Hist. Society, *Proceedings*, LVI (1908), 186.

[65] "The West and American Ideals," *Washington Hist. Quarterly*, V, 24 289.

[66] *Atlantic Monthly*, XCI (1909), 86, 91.

[67] *Early Writings*, p. 213; *Minn. Hist. Bulletin*, III, 400.

[68] B. F. Wright, "American Democracy and the Frontier," *Yale Review* XX (1930), 349–365, and "Political Institutions and the Frontier," in D. R. Fox (ed.), *The Middle West: Backgrounds Versus Frontier* (New York, 1934). A follower of Turner has written that "The controlling influence of the frontier in shaping American problems has been possible because of the construction of civilized governments in a new area, unhampered by institutions of the past [such as the supreme courts of state or Union?]. . . . The settled lands [states]

his earlier publications but of those he continued to publish in later years.

The treatment of ideals is as unsatisfactory as that of institutions. He seemingly never specified others than the "squatter ideal" and "equality," and no reference by him to a humanitarian ideal has been noted by the writer.[72] In the eastern states great progress was made between 1775 and 1789 in respect to religious freedom, feudalism, slavery, penal law, and education.[73] As respects slavery and feudalism, the eastern states had excluded these from the Northwest by the Ordinance of 1787. This provision was violated in Indiana, Illinois, and Michigan Territories, and no outcry or punishment was thereby provoked.[74] A revolting injustice characterized the treatment of the Indians.[75] In the old colonial laws adopted for the Northwest Territory, "the jail, the lash, and compulsory labor . . . were part and parcel of family government, of township government, and even of the laws respecting the weak and poor."[76] Laws for the relief of "poor, old, blind, impotent, and lame persons" permitted their indenture for service and farming out at auction, and insane persons as well as poor children were thus auctioned. Not only Negroes but whites indentured themselves for periods so long as to mean for life. Long indentures in Indiana Territory were often merely disguised slavery. And all these indenture laws were of the representative stage of government. They were not imposed on the frontier society; they were its choice, representing its ideals—which, according to Turner, were regenerating the East.

[72] "The West and American Ideals," *Washington Hist. Quarterly*, V (1914), 245.

[73] See Allen Nevins, *The American States . . . 1775–1789* (New York, 1924), pp. 420–469, regarding religious freedom, feudalism, slavery, penal law, and education.

[74] See *Ill. Hist. Coll.*, XXI (1930), index, *s.v.* "slavery."

[75] Dawson, *Civil and Military Services of William Henry Harrison* (Cincinnati, 1824), pp. 7, 10, 31, 45, 73, 97, 178. Sir William Johnson had repeatedly noted the impossibility of securing justice for them in the court; *Johnson Papers*, VIII, 472, 493, 496, 512, 514, 551, 640. So did General Gage; Carter, *Gage Correspondence*, I, 91, 152, 157, 163, 165. Governor St. Clair proposed that a heavy fine be imposed on any county in which an Indian was murdered, and lesser fines for lesser offenses. Carter, *Terr. Papers*, II, 543.

[76] *Ill. Hist. Coll.*, XXI (1930), cxxxiv, with abundant illustrations on all the matters here discussed, cxxxiii *et seq.* See also, for general conditions in the eastern states, J. B. McMaster, *The Rights of Man in America* (Cleveland, 1903), pp. 36–40, 48–49; J. P. Dunn, *Indiana: A Redemption from Slavery*, pp. 234–251.

Prohibition of an act is not evidence of its occurrence, but it is evidence that its occurrence seemed likely; and a prescribed brutal penalty is evidence of the legislators' ideals. When the territories acquired self-government, they did not reform the old laws. One of the few changes made in them when Indiana Territory in 1807 revised the colonial laws selected for the parent territory was the addition of a law which required gamesters, wife deserters, and (using old English statutory language) "other idle, vagrant and dissolute persons, rambling about without any visible means of support" to be apprenticed if minors, hired out if adults, or lashed if nobody would hire them.[77]

That Turner's frontier was totally unreal is evident. The question remains, What were the sources from which it was derived? The essential element was primitivism, which was the catalyst that provoked the "interaction" between wilderness and frontiersman. But whence came primitivism? In the basic lexicological sense, the first Americans created by frontier life *were* primitive Americans. However, Turner never referred to this lexicological source of primitivism, and his idea that Easterners were made primitive merely by living briefly with fewer household conveniences and lessened social life is another obvious unreality.

The literature dealing with our truly first Westerners offers a clue to Turner's theories. Examples have been given of the extraordinary influence upon history attributed to geography at the turn of the last century by leading historians, including Turner. Ever since Montesquieu a great and indefinite influence in shaping civilization had been attributed to environment. Henry Buckle had attempted to explain much of English history by it in a work published contemporaneously with Turner's birth, and the latter may well have read it in youth and his thinking been strongly influenced by it.[78] When he went to Johns Hopkins he evidently took no interests in the attempts which German and English scholars had made to trace some English ideas of self-government to the Germanic tribes that occupied the island. He spurned such laborious scholarship in a passage typical of his own reliance upon environment and mythology, writing: "American democracy came

---

[77] *Ill. Hist. Coll.,* XXI, cxxxi and 566.

[78] H. T. Buckle, *The History of Civilization in England* (2 vols., London, 1857, 1861). The writer read it when out of school for a year and compelled to browse in the family library, and it seems likely that any youth specially interested in history might have done likewise.

from no theorist's dreams of the German forests. It came stark and strong and full of life out of the American forest, and gained new strength each time it touched a new frontier," as Antaeus did each time he touched the earth in his combat with Hercules.[79] There was another myth, current among anthropologists of the late 1800's, which —it is suggested—Turner had heard or read, and had accepted without question because without knowledge of its technical limitation.[80] This myth, generally abandoned by the early 1900's, was that the "culture" of a "primitive" people was entirely shaped by its environment; "primitive," as used by anthropologists, meaning "retarded" in progress toward "civilization," and American Indians being an example.[81] Turner wished to make the frontier the agency for ennobling all American society. He used environment, first, to reduce civilized Easterners to primitivism. The same environment then (on anthropological authority) created their entire "culture," including ideals and institutions— and to all these Turner simply attributed nobility. Through relation back upon the East, by methods equally vague and imaginary, the institutions and ideals of that section were equally remade and ennobled. Every individual being unique, and all variations of individuals being everywhere mingled, how often was this regeneration accomplished? Turner's answer was "once in a generation," evidently employing that word in the usual sense of approximately thirty years. This manifestly should have made nonsense to Turner himself of any claim for magic frontier influence. In thirty years from the first settlement Ohio had been twenty-two years in the Union, Indiana fourteen, and Illinois lacked only two years of admission.

[79] "The West and American Ideals," *Washington Hist. Qy.*, V (1914). Charles A. Beard seems to have shared contempt for such Germanic origins. *New Republic*, XCVII (1939), p. 139, 245; similarly, *AHR*, XI, 304.

[80] Discussions of this delusion will be found in R. L. Lowie, *Culture and Ethnology* (New York, 1917), pp. 47–66; Clark Wissler, *Man and Culture* (London, [1923]), pp. 314–320; A. A. Goldenweiser, *Early Civilization* (New York, 1922), pp. 292–301, and in his *Introduction to Primitive Anthropology* (New York, 1946), pp. 443–454.

[81] On p. 1 of A. C. Kroeber's *Cultural and Natural Areas of Native North America* (Berkeley, 1939), he wrote of "the old environmentalism which believed it could find the causes of culture in environment," that "[cultures] are no more produced by . . . [that piece of nature in which they occur] than a plant is produced by the soil in which it is rooted"—without seed. "The immediate causes of cultural phenomena are other cultural phenomena." On p. 3, he adds: "For a generation American anthropologists have given less and less attention to environmental factors . . . a healthy reaction from the older naïve view."

What seems to be a fair appraisal of the frontier's influence is a dull substitute for Turner's fabulous tribute. Frontier isolation and self-dependence doubtless did contribute to outward characteristics of speech and manners, as all travelers noted. No doubt they did encourage democratic types of social and political behavior. However, it is possible that the influence of the frontier in this respect has been exaggerated. It became evident more than a century ago, when "nativism" became a political issue in the Old Northwest, that although individual opinions and practices in matters of mere utility in living were greatly and easily altered in frontier competition, this was not true of politics, which involved groups and passion. Also, individual traits of character attributed to frontier life may have been exaggerated. Charles Beard thought, for example, that frontier "individualism" has been over-stressed.[82] As respects the early colonial borderlands this seems improbable, but as respects the last frontier it would be an absurdity to attribute such influence to it.[83] Again the meaning of words is involved. It has been pointed out that unless "liberty" and "equality" be clearly defined, conflict is inevitable between them—and how can such definitions be framed, or applied?[84]

When James Bryce expressed in 1888 the opinion that "the West [was] the most American part of America," this is excellent evidence that the effects of frontier living were still distinct. Sometime between then and now they have certainly weakened—at least in the Middle West. In particular, the perdurance of personal traits that derived from the self-sufficiency of frontiersmen must have depended upon how enduring were the social conditions which had necessitated self-sufficiency. From the moment transition began from a household-subsistence economy to one resting on cash crops, the farm was linked to trade and the family income to the village store and artisan, and necessarily the manifestation (at least) of self-sufficiency diminished. This change, it has been seen, was in large degree effected in Ohio within two decades.

[82] *New Republic,* XCVII (1939).

[83] Railroads carried household goods near to intended homes. The town in which the writer spent five years as a boy in north-central Nebraska was one of neat frame houses, with various stores and a moderately adequate school. In various homes there were fair libraries, to say the least. In some, the *Atlantic Monthly, Nation, Forum, Arena,* were read. There was a Shakespeare Club, of which at least two members traveled to Omaha to see Booth and Barrett.

[84] By Richard Shryock, *AHR,* XLIX (1945), 734.

Later areas of frontier settlement started with succsively increasing conveniences for living.

The necessity for actual self-sufficiency had ceased long before the years of the last frontier. It can be assumed that there resulted a corresponding decline in ability; and if this had diminished, one may assume a change in the traits of personality which it engendered. "The significance of the decay of the household manufactures can hardly be exaggerated . . . there went with it long-established habits and traditional . . . ways of thinking and of living. The self-sufficient economy emphasized the virtues of self-reliance and independence . . . it concentrated attention upon the interests of the family group."[85] Such a change seems the more probable because the decline of household industries was accompanied by, and connected with, the growth of internal trade, which has likewise been regarded as of immeasurable social importance.[86] Neither of these changes originated in the West. The first began long before the Revolution, but vastly increased thereafter; the second began, notably, immediately after it—both of them in the old states of the East.[87]

Turner's theory of repeated re-creations of frontier primitivism avoided the problem of heritability. Some of his adherents, on the other hand, have assumed the heritability in the Old Northwest even of "southern" manners or customs. There are obvious difficulties in any suggestion of inheritance. The first one is that the Germanic tribes that became part of the English people had for centuries been fighting their way back and forth through forests. What was their contribution, if there be anything heritable, to the English settlers of America? A biologist of international repute, Julian Huxley, has written of the American frontier much as American historians have done as respects the creation of personal characteristics—assuming a preselection of emigrants from Europe, and successive later selections of emigrants to the West, "for restlessness, initiative, adventurousness, and the qualities making up the pioneer spirit." More specifically he has added: "The easily contented, the unadventurous and the timid, were pre-selected

[85] P. W. Bidwell and J. I. Falconer, *History of Agriculture in the Northern United States* (Washington, 1925), pp. 251–252.

[86] G. S. Callender, "The Position of American Economic History," *Amer. Hist. Rev.*, XIX (1913), 91–92.

[87] Professor Turner credited "the Old West" with beginning internal trade—Wisconsin State Hist. Soc. *Proceedings*, LVI, 219.

to remain behind. So, too, on the average, must have been those with artistic, philosophic, literary, or mathematical gifts. . . . Once the immigrants were established in the country [on the frontier] selection continued . . . so long as there was open physical frontier to the west, and an open economic frontier in the more settled regions."[88] More specifically as a biologist, Huxley added that the American frontier since 1607 is "a classic example" of "opportunities for the expression of human traits which may be destined to become dominant at a future stage."

Another writer, having in mind the single characteristic which in the pioneer's mind dominated all others—namely, hope—has said that "the East" was "where people had achieved satisfaction with their mode of life, and when satisfaction with a mode of life should have crossed the country, permeating every part, the distinction between East and West [would] be gone."[89] Perhaps it is gone, but dissatisfaction remains; we move from everywhere to everywhere, for all the reasons for whose protection the Constitution guaranteed the right to do so. Perhaps the greatest privilege, and reciprocal contribution, of the frontier was to satisfy the hope of millions for a hundred years with cheap land when land was the surest guarantee of family security.

[88] If not taken from a businessman turned historian—J. T. Adams, *Epic of America* (Boston, 1931), index, *s.v.* "frontier" (particularly pp. 122–123)—these ideas could have been. See comments on Adams by Carl Becker in *AHR,* XXXVII (1931), 558–561. Huxley's first expression of them was in the *Eugenics Review.* That philosophers, literary men, mathematicians, and artists are easily contented (financially or otherwise), inadventurous, or timid seems extremely doubtful, and a mere assumption that they are seems oddly unscientific.

[89] J. C. Parish, in J. T. Adams, *Dictionary of American History,* pp. 184, 187.

Abbreviations

As respects almost all citations, a complete description has been given in each chapter when a book is first cited, and abbreviated citations given thereafter. However, as regards a few publications of the United States or various state governments—not readily available in other than research libraries and some of them habitually cited in extremely abbreviated forms—the first citation in any chapter is made to the list below. Abbreviations for a few much-used journals are also given.

SHORT TITLES	FULL TITLES
AHR	*American Historical Review*
Amer. Archives	*American Archives, Fourth Series* (6 vols., Washington, 1837–46)
A.S.P., For. Rel.	*American State Papers, Foreign Relations* (6 vols., Washington, 1834–61)
A.S.P., Ind. Aff.	*American State Papers, Indian Affairs* (2 vols., Washington, 1832–34)
A.S.P., Mil. Aff.	*American State Papers, Military Affairs* (7 vols., Washington, 1834–61)
A.S.P., Misc.	*American State Papers, Miscellaneous* (2 vols., Washington, 1834)
A.S.P., Pub. Lands	*American State Papers, Public Lands* (8 vols., Washington, 1834–61)
Annals of Congress	*Debates and Proceedings in the United States Congress* (42 vols., Washington, 1831–56)
Bidwell and Falconer,	P. W. Bidwell and J. I. Falconer, *History of*

Short Titles	Full Titles
Agriculture	Agriculture in the Northern United States (2 vols., Washington, 1925)
Burnett, LMCC	E. C. Burnett (ed.), Letters of Members of the Continental Congress (8 vols., Washington, 1921–36)
Carter, Terr. Papers	C. E. Carter (ed.), Territorial Papers of the United States (Washington, 1934—)
CHR	Canadian Historical Review
Col. Rec. of N. Carolina	W. L. Saunders et al. (eds.), The Colonial Records of North Carolina (10 vols., Raleigh, 1886–90, with a supplement of state records in Vol. XI)
Carter, Gage Correspondence	C. E. Carter (ed.), Correspondence of General Thomas Gage with the Secretaries of State, 1762–1775 (2 vols., New Haven, 1931–33)
Doniol, Établissement des États-Unis	Henri Doniol, Histoire de la Participation de la France à l'Établissement des États-Unis d'Amerique (5 vols., Paris, 1886–92)
Gray, Agriculture	L. C. Gray, History of Agriculture in the Southern United States to 1860 (2 vols., continuously paged, Washington, 1933)
HAHR	Hispanic American Historical Review
Hening, Statutes of Va.	W. W. Hening, The Statutes at Large of Virginia (13 vols., Richmond, 1809–23)
Ill. Hist. Coll.	Collections of the Illinois State Historical Library
Johnson Papers	J. Sullivan et al. (eds.), The Papers of Sir William Johnson (11 vols., Albany, 1921–53)
J.C.C.	W. C. Ford et al. (eds.), The Journal of the Continental Congress, 1774–1789 (34 vols., Washington, 1904–37)
Kappler, Indian Affairs	C. J. Kappler (comp.), Indian Affairs, Laws and Treaties (2nd ed., 2 vols., Washington, 1904)
Malloy, Treaties	W. M. Malloy, Treaties and Conventions Between the United States and Other Powers (Washington, 1889)
Meyer and MacGill, Transportation	B. H. Meyer and C. MacGill, History of Transportation in the United States Before 1860 (Washington, 1917)

SHORT TITLES	FULL TITLES
Mich. Hist. Coll.	*Michigan Pioneer and Historical Collections* (40 vols., Lansing, 1877–1929)
Miller, *Treaties*	Hunter Miller, *Treaties and Other International Acts of the United States* (8 vols., Washington, 1931–48)
Moore, *International Arbitrations*	J. B. Moore, *History and Digest of International Arbitrations to Which the United States has Been a Party* (6 vols., Washington, 1898)
Moore, *International Law*	J. B. Moore, *Digest of International Law* (8 vols., Washington, 1906)
N.Y. Col. Docs.	E. B. O'Callaghan (ed.), *Documents Relating to the Colonial History of the State of New York* (15 vols., Albany, 1853–57)
O'Callaghan, *Doc. Hist.*	E. B. O'Callaghan and E. B. Fernow (eds.), *Documentary History of the State of New York* (4 vols., Albany, 1851)
Richardson, *Messages*	J. A. Richardson (comp.), *Messages and Papers of the Presidents, 1789–99* (10 vols., Washington, 1898–99)
Shortt and Doughty	A. Shortt and A. G. Doughty (eds.), *Papers Relating to the Constitutional History of Canada, 1759–1791* (2nd ed., Toronto, 1918, 2 vols., continuously paged)
Thorpe, *Constitutions*	F. N. Thorpe (comp.), *The Federal and State Constitutions, Colonial Charters, and Other Organic Laws* . . . (7 vols., Washington, 1909)
Dip. Corr.	F. Wharton, *Diplomatic Correspondence of the American Revolution* (6 vols., Washington, 1889)
Wharton, *International Law*	F. Wharton, *Digest of International Law* . . . (2nd ed., 3 vols., Washington, 1887)

Appendix

Affairs of the West have been discussed in five chapters of this volume as involved in relations between the United States and Great Britain, in two chapters as involved in relations with France and Spain, and in seven as presenting special problems in, or particularly contributing to, the development of the United States. A proper bibliography for these fields of study would require a listing and discussion of materials for which the pages allotted to that purpose are wholly inadequate. The editors have therefore decided that the citations in the footnotes will suffice for students in starting further reading, and to devote the space thus here made available to further discussion of Professor Turner's views respecting the frontier.

FURTHER COMMENTS ON THE TURNER THESES

In emphasizing western problems of the Revolutionary era, in services as a member of a commission which gathered from foreign archives great quantities of materials pertinent to American history, in editing some of these for publication, in writing various articles based upon them, and above all in stimulating study of the western borderlands of the late colonial period, Frederick Jackson Turner rendered great services to American historiography. But he undertook the far more difficult task of explaining American history, and that attempt is the only matter here in question.

This attempt was made in various articles on the role supposedly played by the frontier in American history, and in a famous book that is a reprint or condensation of those articles, *The Frontier in American History* (New York, 1920 and later prints). He did not, in these, *write* American history; did not assemble, interpret, and illuminate historical facts. He did not even refer to more than very few. The only way to reconcile his writings with the integrity universally attributed to him is to assume his early conviction that the essence of our history was a constant progress in social ideals and institutions, and it is only of that postulated epitome of our history that his frontier thesis offered an explanation. But even then his explanation is totally unacceptable. He based this explanation—for no other discernible cause than attachment to the colorful history of the area where he was born—upon the frontier, to which he attributed repeated regenerations of society, each bringing higher ideals and better institutions not only to the West but to the East. As stated in Chapter 14, he specified no ideal save equality, and no institution whatever, and it must be assumed that he never consulted the laws in which the truth respecting both institutions and ideals was imbedded.

He explained how this regeneration was accomplished by making two additional assumptions. The first was that eastern Americans who moved to the West were made a "primitive society"—regardless of their character, education, or experience—by subjection to the "primitive conditions" of the environment. The second assumption was that the same environment then raised them to a higher culture than they had ever before attained.

There are two ways of approaching these propositions. Were they intended as statements of historical fact? If so, how could Turner possibly have believed them? The idea that individuals whose ancestors had for centuries constituted one of the great civilized countries could lose their civilization, and become a "primitive" society—regardless of their individual character, education or experience—merely by congregating in an isolated territory where they lacked for a few years some of the aids in field and household labor, and some of the social life enjoyed in their earlier homes, was manifest absurdity. One immediately suspects that Turner did not use "primitive" as meaning a lack of civilization. Even more absurd was the idea that those thus decivilized were so ennobled by thoughts of the wilderness about them (the least absurd conception of their "reaction" to it) that in each generation they remade and elevated the country's ideals and institutions.

It is not positively necessary to answer the question whether Turner believed these statements. There are two reasons why the answer is not necessary. The first is that one who has sufficient faith needs no evidence to support beliefs, for faith takes the place of evidence. Turner's doctrine of frontier salvation was to him like the individual salvation found in a frontier revival tent. It was faith, not evidence, that underlay his idea that American ideals and institutions were recurrently purified in the simplicity of frontier living. The other and sufficient reason (permitting his faith) is the assumption suggested in Chapter 14 that Turner was unaware, when he first read of "primitive people," that the scholars (anthropologists) who wrote about such peoples used "primitive" with a specialized meaning.

It should be mentioned that if one agrees with Turner that "the American" was made—because his basic personal characteristics were made—on the frontier, then those first Americans were truly primitive Americans in the lexicographical sense. But they were certainly made on the pre-Revolutionary borders between 1607 and 1776, and those borders were ignored by Turner. Nevertheless, they may have suggested to him the idea of primitiveness which he attributed to frontier settlers of the Old Northwest.

The important fact is the astonishing lack of evidence that Turner gave any thought to the basis of his various conceptions. To begin with this matter of primitiveness, his scores of references to frontier society as primitive are inadequately informative as to why it was such. We are accustomed to characterize as primitive anything crude, awkward, or old-fashioned in objects or methods. Turner's language sometimes suggests this: that the society was primitive because characterized by or made primitive by "primitive" housing, utensils and furniture, poor roads, and meager social structure. At other times, for example in describing the society as "a democratic, self-sufficing, primitive and agricultural society," primitivism appears to be an independent quality (Wis. Hist. Soc., *Proceedings,* LVI [1908], 219). However, such passages are in turn offset by many references to the changes involved "in developing out of the primitive economic and political conditions of the frontier, the complexity of city [small town] life" (*Early Writings,* p. 186, the famous "Significance" article of 1893, and compare *Atlantic Monthly,* XCI [1901], 91, regarding "the old historic democracies"). The only definite conclusion one can draw from many such passages is that he never critically examined his conceptions. The important idea in his mind, the idea which dominated all others, was that in a primitive society, no matter what it might precisely be, no matter how it might be created, all its civilization ("culture"), all its institutions and their underlying ideals, were created by the physical environment.

The conception of the "frontier" was likewise never critically considered by Turner. In his famous address of 1893 on the significance of the frontier in American history, he defined the frontier (doubly) as "the outer edge of the [population] wave . . . the hither [western] edge of [occupied] free land." *Early Writings* (Madison, 1938), p. 187. The effect of the wilderness, however, was not confinable to this "edge." Wilderness surrounded all settlers. Neither can one accept the definition of the frontier as a form of society "determined by the reactions between [sometimes "interaction between"] the wilderness and the [settlers at] the edge of expanding settlement." American Geogr. Soc., *Bulletin* XLVI (1914). There was no mutuality of action capable of aiding in regenerating society; the settlers merely burned trees, plowed and cultivated land. The only reaction conceivably capable of affecting society would be the effect of "wilderness" surroundings on the life and minds of the pioneers. The point of criticizing mere words is that Turner's words, after expounding his theory for virtually thirty years, suggest no thought of a problem.

More important are the questions: What was the extent of a "frontier"? How long did one last? How many frontiers were there? Turner always assumed a plurality. The environment ("wilderness") acted on individuals—immediately (we must assume) and wherever settled, each of them (we know) unique; and it continued to act until the "society" was "regenerated." Not because of their varying susceptibility to regenerative magic, but because they spread with varying speed, Turner suggested separate frontiers for workers in fishing, farming, and other industries as late as 1914. McLaughlin and Hart, *Cyclopedia of American Government* (3 vols., New York, 1914), II, 626; compare *Early Writings,* p. 199. His followers adopted this absurdity and added many more groups; e.g., F. L. Paxson, *When the West Is Gone* (New York, 1920, pp. 26–27). When were enough of each group regenerated to make a "society"? Turner suggested "once in a generation"—not as a joke, but presumably meaning about thirty years. However, as earlier noted, that would extend the frontier period far beyond attainment of statehood by Ohio and Indiana.

It seems evident that Turner never seriously considered questions essential for the definition of an actual frontier. Of course there was a "pioneer era" of rude conditions wherever new settlement began (estimated as one of fifteen years in Wisconsin by Joseph Schafer, *Agriculture in Wisconsin,* Madison, 1922). But in any other sense there was only one frontier until its outward characteristics were lost by merger with the western states about 1890. Within the years covered by this volume, the advance of westward settlement may have averaged two to three miles yearly.

Then and thereafter there was one uninterrupted advance, accelerated by the development of railroads; at times affected by special acts of Congress, such as the Pre-emption Act, the Homestead Act, and the opening of Oklahoma to whites; sometimes slowed by fears of Indian wars.

Sometimes Turner substituted "free land" for "wilderness" as the factor in regenerating society. In thus emphasizing the importance of the public lands, he had many predecessors. Jefferson, in preparing his land ordinance for Congress, and the Continental Congress in passing it, realized their vast importance, perhaps particularly in excluding feudal titles. For that Daniel Webster had repeatedly lauded them. Various others, notably Henry George, had emphasized the role of cheap land. Six years before Turner's address of 1893, Albert Bushnell Hart had written: "For a century, our political, economic, and social relations have been sensibly affected by the nearness, accessibility, and cheapness of government land. The population of the country has at last overtaken our unsettled domain." *Qy. Jour. of Economics,* I (1887), 169.

Turner accepted these ideas to some extent, but not to the extent of abandoning his main idea of environmental magic. For example, he wrote that the West was "the region where social conditions result[ed] from the application [subjection] of social institutions and ideas to the transforming influences of new land." *Atlantic Monthly,* LXXVIII (1896), 289. And again he clung to pure magic in writing that "the fundamental fact in regard to this new [western] society was its relation to land. . . . By the very fact of the task set forth [replacing "reaction"], far reaching ideals of . . . society have evolved in the West . . . the fundamental traits of the man of the interior were due to the free lands of the West" *(ibid.,* p. 292). By fundamental traits, he meant, doubtless, simply democracy and equality *(ibid.,* XCI [1909], 86, 91).

The preceding were not the greatest of his inconsistencies and silences respecting the frontier. He dismissed colonial expansion east of the Appalachians because, he said, the area east of them had been "in close touch with the Old World." In fact, of course, that of the Old Northwest with the East was vastly closer. Inconsistently, however, by 1906 he admitted that a frontier "pushing back the Indian" had existed since early colonial times *(AHR,* XI [1906], 303), and by 1914 even admitted that "American society [had] been beginning over again at the outer edge of settlement from the earliest colonial days onward" (McLaughlin and Hart, *Cyclopedia,* II, 61). Yet, notwithstanding this, all who went to the West after 1787 were as imperfect as in 1607 or 1620. And this was because they had not enjoyed the successive "rebirths" that began in the Old Northwest. These too, unfortunately, were only for a brief time effective: the "West" included the "frontier" and the more populous zone adjacent (presumably just behind it) which was "still influenced by pioneer tradition" (after, the text indicates, only a few years) and "reacting" on the East. *Atlantic Monthly,* LXXVIII (1896), 289; *ibid.,* XCI (1908), 93; *Sections in American History* (1925), p. 23.

Turner's objective was, of course, plain: to glorify the frontier as the birthplace of social "equality" and "democracy." There seemed to be, to travelers early and late (as late as Lord Bryce's visits in Turner's youth), a freshening of those qualities in each area of new settlement. No doubt there was—and this was Turner's "rebirth" of society. Wilderness environment made life difficult and, in Turner's conception, "primitive"; therefore made the pioneer primitive, and thus society. He then applied to this society his anthropological theory of environmental influence respecting uncivilized peoples. It was a theory adopted early in life (compare his *Early Writings*), and never corrected. And to the last he remained uncritical respecting what was sufficiently primitive to effect miracles. "We are hardly a generation removed from the primitive conditions of the West," he wrote in 1899 in the *Atlantic Monthly,* XCI (1899), 93. So we were if kerosene and gas in homes of the cultured and gas light in city streets could make us "primitive."

Turner's thesis, if one includes under that description various matters which have been confused with it in controversy, has had an extraordinary history. One must consider his own role in its creation and exposition, and the writings of his critics and those of his protagonists. He never offered it as more than an explanation of an assumed frontier ennoblement of American ideals, especially of democracy, and of institutions. So far as we have possessed these, they must greatly have affected our history, but they are not, *per se,* history. He may never have learned whence he derived his idea of the efficacy of primitivism—if that derivation has been correctly surmised. To his credit, he never supported (at least not in print) the assumption by followers that the thesis was a summation of American history. For a quarter of a century he repeated it in the West to university auditors whose grandparents or great-grandparents had been among those ennobled by the wilderness—and he continued to call them "primitive."

Moreover, he remained to the end utterly obscure respecting the meaning and characteristics, and mode of action, of "the frontier." Its process of regeneration was obscure and its effectiveness was incomplete. All regeneration by colonial frontiers left the inhabitants in need of improvement, and the regenerations under Turner's theory were also imperfect. His language occasionally hinted limited durability on the spot, and although he repeatedly stated that each frontier regeneration also effected, "by relation back" upon the East, ennoblement of eastern institutions and ideals, nothing suggests that the newcomers from the East were ever without need of the frontier's new salvation. The printed evidence leaves the thesis as an example of "playing freely with facts and ideas," as one of the "novel ideas carelessly thrown out" which characterized him in the classroom. Carl Becker, *Every Man His Own Historian,* pp. 199, 198, 192.

However, he included in his 1920 volume some materials emphasizing other formative factors than the frontier in American history—particularly sectional interests—and these materials produced new forms of Turnerism. Students would naturally assume the frontier materials to be part of, or explanations of, the history; and their teachers seem to have shared the misconception. Turner's followers have never been united in stating his views. One of them, after decades, characterized them as a thesis, although obviously they were a concatenation of theses. Another summarized them as "composite race and Americanization, social re-creation in the light of the frontier experience, and nationality." F. L. Paxson, "A Generation of the Frontier Hypothesis." MVHR, XVIII (1931), 219.

Charles Beard stated Turner's "conception" as containing "twelve major elements." *New Republic,* XCVII (1939), 360. The fact is that without the anthropological key to their meaning, Turner's theses could not be understood, and in addition they were indistinct and complicated. They were therefore, after a couple of decades, largely ignored, and the difference between his followers and critics came to be regarded as merely one of differently estimating the West's contributions to the development of the country, and then one (on which disagreement ceased) respecting the influence of the public lands. Thus, long before Turner's death, swirling fog covered the meaning—and discussion—of the frontier thesis.

It was to become worse. In 1927 Carl Becker wrote (*Every Man His Own Historian*, p. 213): "He deals only with . . . the experience of the American people within definite space and time limits, and so [with] the evolution of a particular society." The first of these statements is inaccurate; although primarily interested in the Old Northwest, Turner used that only as an example of what was true of all frontiers westward (he assumed plurality), and later admitted that the same process had been going on east of the Alleghenies since some early colonial period. The second statement is therefore equally inaccurate. Both of them contradict the title given by him to his volume of 1820. The contrary of both of them was assumed by all his followers for three decades after his address of 1893 before the American Historical Association. Even more objectionable is the use of the word "evolution." In Turner's theory successive Societies were individually ennobled in their ideals and institutions, and what each then laid aside is a complete and independent entity, for another to develop; nor was there in his words any suggestion of distinct stages in this process as respects time, order, or nature. Those are essential characteristics of evolution in the biological sense (as well as in the contruction of steel office buildings). Turner did not suggest his frontier hypothesis as a biological evolutionary process. This is important because that was one stage in the burial of the hypothesis.

It was not, however, the first stage. That was, naturally, various articles in which an attempt was made to define the meaning of Turner's vague words. Assuming that Turner was merely emphasizing the influence of geography, one scholarly critic showed that he ignored such essentials as aridity or humidity, variations of altitude and fertility, presence or absence of obstacles to transportation, and so on. (G. W. Pierson, 1940). The same critic, assuming that Turner was explaining American character but confining discussion to "institutional results" and ignoring law, emphasized Turner's amazing shortcomings in that respect (article of 1942, inadequately emphasizing them). Charles Beard's interpretation of Turner's "Frontier" as meaning "class configurations" and "social and economic arrangements" (article of 1939) merely replaced plain words with Beard's own mental prepossessions. And only an assumption that Turner was attempting to epitomize American history can explain Beard's criticism of Turner's inattention to eastern industrialism, to the South's plantation system, and to the conflict between capitalism and labor.

By the mid-thirties the idea of "evolutionary" development was popular. Turner's editor (Fulmer Mood, 1936) lauded the "extraordinary ability which Turner showed" in "expounding historical developments in terms of an evolutionary principle." Seemingly acting on Becker's suggestion that Turner's thesis dealt with the experience of the American people only "within definite space and time limits," he has been welcomed into what appears to the uninitiated to be a new field of philosophy (J. C. Malin, "The Turner-Makinder Space Conception of History," in *Essays on Historiography*, Lawrence, Kan., 1946; R. F. Berghofer, "Space, Time, Culture and the New Frontier," *Agricultural History* XXXVIII [1964] 21–30). According to the latter, Turner's "triumphant thesis" originated in an "organismic theory of society," which postulated "a constant adaptation of the whole organism to its external environment of soil, climate, and other physical factors of contact" (pp. 21–22). As already noted, Mr. Pierson could find no evidence that Turner gave any attention to such factors. It is also evident that the only "whole organism" exposed to the environment was man, and no adaptation to his environment of man, as a physical entity, was asserted by Turner.

Turner's thesis was simple, was plainly stated, and was wholly acceptable, *modus operandi* excepted, if restricted in operation to social democracy and the personal characteristics of Americans. Its fame caused it to be misinterpreted in illogical and exaggerated claims of reference or relevance to other matters. Reference has been made above to some of a series of articles, in the same periodical, in which the thesis was applied in the troubled field of sociology. The series ended, still under a title assuming pertinence to the Turner thesis, with a mere bibliography of census publications on the westward movement of population! Since this was contributed by the editor of Turner's papers, it seems particularly significant. Sometimes, on the old frontier, when it was necessary to bury a member of a hunting party, his comrades sought to prevent profanation of the body by burying it beneath the campfire site, then strewing matter over that which they thought would make impossible any suspicion of a burial.

Much of the preceding comment may be regarded by some readers as petty faultfinding with language merely imaginative and extravagant. History, however, cannot be based on one fact, particularly a suppositious fact; and imagination, Greek mythology, and an attractive style are fitter as decoration than as foundation. Therefore, another and very important matter is involved. Beard expressed the opinion that Turner's address of 1893 had "a more profound influence on thought about American history than any other essay or volume ever published." *New Republic*, XCVII (1939), 359. It introduced, he said, an era in American historiography. That it immensely stimulated study of the West and of expansion problems is not to be doubted, but to what extent the discussion it provoked raised critical standards is doubtful.

In the writer's opinion, guild amities unduly stifled professional judgments, a matter understandable to anyone who will read Carl Becker's recollections of Turner in *Everyman His Own Historian*. Conflicting judgments produced, however, some two to three dozen decidedly valuable books or articles, some of which may be mentioned. Everett E. Edwards, in his *References on the Significance of the Frontier in American History* (U.S. Dept. of Agriculture, *Bibliographical Contributions*, No. 25, Washington, 1939), includes an article on the Great Wall of China and many items on "frontiers" of opportunity in science. Fulmer Mood, "Concept of the Frontier, 1871–1898," *Agricultural Hist.*, XIX (1945), 24–30, and "Notes on the History of the Word Frontier," *ibid.*, XXII (1948), deals with side issues. A few citations to articles which throw light on Turner's concepts and the state of American historiography are given below. The writer suspects that Dixon Ryan Fox realized that Turner's "primitive" was borrowed from the anthropologists, but the articles he wrote or edited merely illustrate how arts and crafts are spread in civilized societies by "carriers" or practitioners, and contain no direct criticism of Turner. Most of the items mentioned in the foregoing discussion are not included below, and likewise items earlier mentioned in Chapter 14 of the text.

Almack, J. C., "The Shibboleth of the Frontier," *Historical Outlook,* XVI (1925), 197–202

Beard, C. A., "Culture and Agriculture," *Sat. Rev. of Literature,* V (1928), 272–273

———, "The Frontier in American History," *New Republic,* XXV (1921), 349–350; XCVII (1938), 359–362

Benson, Lee, *Turner and Beard,* Glencoe, Ill. (1960)

Crane, V. W.; Webb, W. P.; and Harlow, V. T., "The Frontier in British and American History," London University, Institute of Historical Research, *Bulletin* XVI (1938), 112–116

Craven, A., "The 'Turner Theories' and the South," *Jnl. of So. Hist.,* V (1939), 291–314

Farrand, M., "Frederick Jackson Turner," Mass. Hist. Soc., *Proceedings,* LV (1940), 432–440

Fox, Dixon R., *Ideas in Motion* (New York, 1935), containing "Civilization in Transit"; also in *Amer. Hist. Rev.,* XXXII (1927), 753–768; "Culture in Knapsacks"; "Refuse Ideas and Their Disposal"

——— (ed.), *Sources of Culture in the Middle West* (New York, 1934)

Freund, Rudolph (ed.), *The Middle West: Backgrounds Versus Frontier* (New York, 1934)

Hayes, Carlton J. H., "The American Frontier—Frontier of What?" *Amer. Hist. Rev.,* LI (1946), 199–216

Hofstadter, Richard, "Turner and the Frontier Myth," *Amer. Scholar,* XVIII (1949), 433–443

Kane, Murray, "Some Considerations on the Frontier Concept of Frederick Jackson Turner," *Miss. Val. Hist. Rev.,* XXVII (1941), 389–400

Macdonald, William, "Some Observations on the . . . American Frontier," Colonial Soc. of Mass., *Publications,* XXVI (1926), pp. 165–180

Pierson, George W., "The Frontier and Frontiersman of Turner's Essays," *Penna. Mag. of History,* LXIV (1940), 449–478

――――, "The Frontier and American Institutions: A Criticism of the Turner Theory," *New Eng. Qy.* (1942)

Sizer, T., *et al., Aspects of the Social History of America* (Chapel Hill, 1931)

Taylor, George R., *The Turner Thesis,* New York (1956)

Wilson, Woodrow, "The Proper Perspective of American History," *The Forum,* XIX (1895), 544–549

Wright, B. F., "American Democracy and the Frontier," *Yale Review,* XX (1930), 349–365

Index

Act of 1805, 229
Act of 1820, 297, 299–300
Adair, John, 219; and Burr, 239, 242, 248–249, 251
Adams, John, 53, 136, 203–204; and peace negotiations, 68, 71, 73, 77
Adet, French minister, 203
Agriculture, 372; corn, 324, 328, 334–335; cotton, 325–326, 339; wheat, 324–325, 334–335, 338; tobacco, 325; grains, 327–328, 339
Alabama, 123, 166; settlement, 31, 91, 303, 316, 321, 346; Indians, 288, 289n; crops, 325–326
Albany Congress of 1754, 1–2, 14–15, 46, 51, 110, 112, 255n
Alexander, Czar of Russia, 270
Allen, Levi,. 147
Amherst, General Jeffrey, 14, 48
Aranda, Conde de, 75
Arkansas, and Indians, 287, 289, 299; and land, 299; crops, 325–326
Arkansas Territory, 317, 319
Armstrong, John, 225, 227
Askin, John, 292n
Atkin, Edmund, 2

Bagot, Charles, 275–276, 277n, 278
Banking system, 341–343
Barbé-Marbois, François, 77, 217n; intercepted letter, 78n
Barbour, James, 288n
Barlow, Joel, 187
Bastrop, Baron, and Burr, 237, 239
Baton Rouge revolts, 220–221, 224–225
Beard, Charles, 264n, 265n, 266n, 351, 372; and War of 1812, 264

Beckwith, Major George, 148–149
Benton, Sen. Thomas Hart, 301
Beverly, Robert, 92
Birkbeck, Morris, 309, 311–312, 314, 321, 327, 332, 337, 346, 356
Blennerhassett, Herman, 238
Blount, William, xii, 99, 107, 166, 168, 196–197, 360n; and state of Franklin, 84–85; as speculator, 94, 97
Bond agreement of 1795, 260
Boone, Daniel, 89–90, 102, 306, 317
Boundaries, 39, 40, 59, 82, 196; Miss. R. as, 62, 166, 173, 271–272, 278; and Revolution, 66–69, 74–75, 77–78, 219; and Jay's treaty, 161, 194; W. Fla., 170–171, 189–190; Mo. R. as, 186; and Spanish negotiations, 189–191; and La. Purchase, 212–216, 225–226, 228; with Canada, 270–272, 278
Bounties, land. See Land bounties
Bounties, for prisoners, U.S., 56; British, 57
Bouquet, Colonel Henry, 3, 9, 308
Bowles, William, 168, 192n
Braddock, General Edward, 304–305
Brant, Joseph, 138n, 141, 151, 263
Brissot de Warville, 347n
Brock, Colonel Isaac, 266
Brown, Senator John, and Burr, 238
Bruff, Major, 238, 240
Burr, Aaron, xii, 239, 359–360, 363; in west, 219, 224, 228–229, 238–239; "conspiracy," 234–236, 247–252, 321; motives and plans, 237–238, 240–242; arrest, 243–246

Calhoun, John C., 265n, 341
Caller brothers, 220n
Camden-Yorke opinion, 42–43, 45
Campbell, Colonel John, 56–57, 62
Canada, 199, 203, 257; and Revolution, 60, 63–64, 70–74; and U.S. relations, 253, 256–261, 264, 274; and War of 1812, 263–266, 268, 270–273; and fur traders, 275; and boundary, 270–272, 278; and Miss. R., 279; and settlement, 279–283, 315
Canals, 307–308, 331, 333–336, 338
Carleton, Sir Guy, 48, 136, 138–139. See also Dorchester, Lord
Carmichael, William, 190–192
Carondolet, Baron de, 164, 185–186, 196, 198–200, 218n
Cessions (land), to Confederation, 111, 113–116, 118–120, 127, 132–133, 290
Charles III, King of Spain, 65, 67, 175–176, 205, 207, 212
Cherokee, 10, 22, 26, 29–30, 32–35, 45, 56–57, 61, 168, 317, 357; and state of Franklin, 86; and removal, 285n, 287–289; in Arkansas, 299
Cheves, Langdon, 265n
Chickasaw, 22, 289n
Child, Joshua, 281n
Chisholm, John, 168, 197–198
Choctaw, 289n
Choiseul, Louis César, Baron de, 78n
Claiborne, William C. C., 219–220, 227, 229, 231; and Burr, 241–242
Clark, Daniel, 219, 221n, 248
Clark, Daniel, Jr., 222
Clark, Elijah, 189
Clark, George Rogers, 45, 58n, 90, 166, 174, 177, 187–189, 196, 203–204, 231, 266; and Revolution, 57–62, 75
Class structure. See Social structure
Clay, Henry, 240, 265n, 347
Coal, 326
"Conestoga wagon," 306–307, 311
Connecticut, 111, 115–116, 120, 294; settlement, 310, 312, 315–316, 319, 344
Connolly, Dr. John, 40–41
Constitution, U.S., Ky. against, 175;

and La. Purchase, 210–211, 235; and internal improvements, 331
Constitutional Act of 1791, 256
Convention of 1817, 337–338
Conway, General Henry, 72, 134
Cook, James, 25
Cotton, planting, 105
Coxe, Tench, 326
Credit system, for trade, 339–343
Creditors, British, 134–136, 155, 159, 161
Creeks, 10, 56, 164, 167–168, 185–186, 270; and war, 269, 285, 325; and removal, 287–288, 289n
Croghan, George, 10, 15–16, 26–28, 31, 40–43, 56, 82, 94, 107, 117–118, 323, 348
Cumberland Road, as route west, 304–307, 312, 334
Currency, 98–99, 296, 340–343
Cutler, Manasseh, 124
"Cuyahoga Purchase," 292n

Dane, Nathan, 129–132, 354n
Dartmouth, Lord, 36, 37, 48–49
Daveiss, Joseph H., and Burr, 240
Dayton, Sen. Jonathan, and Burr, 235–236, 238–240, 242, 249, 251
Deane, Silas, 43n
Delawares, 3, 22, 25–28, 30, 41, 56; and removal, 285
Democrats, 204
de Pestre, Colonel, and Burr, 246n
De Peyster, Major, 144
Depression of 1819. See Panic of 1819
Dickinson, John, 112–113
Disarmament, on Great Lakes, 159–161, 277–278; War of 1812, 271
"Distribution," 301
Dorchester, Lord, 308, 320; in Canada, 145–152, 156–158; and Canada boundary, 212; and trade, 257–259. See also Carleton, Sir Guy
Duer, William, 124
Dundas, Henry, 152–156
Dunmore, Lord, 37–41, 43–45, 82–83, 89, 92, 109, 290, 353
Dunmore's War, 41n, 88
Dwight, Timothy, 344–345, 356, 359, 365

East Florida. See Florida

Easton Indian Treaty of 1758, 3n
Easton, Rufus, 238
Edwards, Ninian, 301, 347
Ellicott, Andrew, 196–197, 356
Embargo Acts, 223–225, 229, 234, 263–264 ·
Engrossment, of land, 104–106
Entail, 91, 109
Erie Canal, 307–308, 315–316, 333–334, 337–338
Erie and Waterford Road, 308, 337n, 338

Fallen Timbers, battle of, 157, 189
Fauchet, Minister, 189, 203, 207
Federalists, 204, 209, 273; and La. Purchase, 211; and Burr, 251
Fee-simple title, 106, 108, 121, 131
Feudalism, 104, 106, 108, 354–355, 367, 369
Five Nations, 304
Flint, Timothy, 356, 359
Florida, 164, 167, 172, 196, 264; East Florida: created, 4, 6; and Blount, 197; U.S. interest in, 216–218; U.S. - Spanish negotiations, 228; West Florida: 37, 56, 290, 357; created, 4, 6; settlement of, 7–8, 219–221, 316; and Revolution, 53, 56, 61–63, 68; land system, 108; and boundary, 170–171, 189–191; and Gt. Br., 172; secret U.S.-British article, 170–171, 191; U.S. interest in, 206, 217–218, 220, 230–233; and La. Purchase, 213, 215–217; U.S. trade with, 222–223; and Embargo Act, 224–225, 229; U.S.-Spanish negotiations, 207, 225–226, 228; Act of 1805, 229; and Burr, 239; and War of 1812, 264; and Creek war, 270; insurrection, 363
Floridablanca, Conde de, 62, 66, 68, 164, 190–191
Floridas, 64, 67, 169; and Spain, 207, 218, 225–229, 233; U.S. desire for, 208, 230; and Gt. Br., 220; and trade, 221–222
Folch, Governor Vicente, 232, 242; and W. Fla. trade, 221–224, 230
Foot's Resolution, 298n, 301
Forbes Road, 304–306, 308, 312, 356
Fort Finney agreement, 140

Fort Greenville, treaty of, 157–159
Fort Harmar treaties, 142, 149, 154–155
Fort Jackson, Treaty of, 270
Fort McIntosh treaty, 140, 142, 154–155
Fort Stanwix, Treaty of (1768), 24, 30–33, 41–42, 51, 117–119, 138, 155; cession under as cause of war, 34–35, 37–38; and Ky. settlement, 88
Fort Stanwix agreement (Oct., 1784), 140, 142
Fox, Charles James, 72, 254–255
France, 187–188, 195–196, 263–264; and west, 1, 8, 22, 163, 165; and U.S. alliance, 58–60, 64–65, 67–69, 72, 77, 146, 163, 201–202; U.S. commercial treaty and trade, 64, 67, 253–256; and Spanish relations, 165, 169, 192–193, 202, 225, 229; and La., 201–208, 213, 216–217, 290; treaty with U.S., 1800, 204
Franklin, Benjamin, 14, 16, 27–28, 36n, 42, 51, 95, 104, 110–113, 201; and peace negotiations, 64, 67, 69–79; and British trade, 254, 257
Franklin, State of, 84, 109, 168, 179, 359, 362n, 366; settlement of, 84–87, 100–101, 103
French and Indian War, 1, 52, 94, 292, 320
Fur trade, 136, 148, 152, 156, 159–160, 287, 356; under English, 17–21, 38–39, 46–51; and Canada, 257–261; legal rights, 260; and War of 1812, 272, 275–276, 278

Gage, General Thomas, 6, 8, 12–14, 16n, 17–21, 27, 33, 35, 43–44, 48–51, 95, 104, 167, 220, 281n, 290, 353, 356; and use of Indians, 55, 58n
Gallatin, Albert, 215n, 224, 226, 230, 346; and land disposal, 295
Galvez, Governor, 56, 61–62, 68
Gardoqui, Diego de, 172–173, 175, 179, 238; and U.S. negotiations, 190–192; and La. trade, 221
Gayoso de Lemos, 167n, 185–186, 194, 196–197, 199, 218

Genêt, Edmond, 194, 198, 203, 360, 361; and Yazoo frauds, 187–189
Georgia, settlement, 82–83, 91, 98, 114, 177, 304, 316; land system, 105, 107–108; and cession, 123, 127, 133, 166–169; and Yazoo frauds, 184, 192–193; and Indians, 287–289; and land, 293, 299; land grants of 1789 and 1795, 360n
Gérard, Conrad Alexandre, Chevalier, 43n, 63, 65, 71
Ghent, Treaty of, 274, 276–277
Godoy, Manuel de, 199–200, 228; and Jay's treaty, 193–195
"Graduation," of land prices, 301
Graham, John, and Burr, 244, 249
Grand Ohio Company, 35–36
Grand Pré, Captain, 220–221
Grayson, William, 106, 122, 294
Great Britain, law re west, 21–26, 42; and U.S. relations, 134–137, 143–148; and Spanish relations, 146–148, 165, 191, 193, 239; and U.S. trade, 146–147, 159–161; and west, 164, 166–167, 169–171; and Nootka Sound incident, 184; and W. Fla. boundary, 189–190; and war in west, 196; and La., 201, 217; and Jay's treaty, 202; policy toward Spanish colonies, 204, 225; U.S. alliance, 206, 208–209; and French relations, 220; American trade policy, 254–257, 274; and smuggling, 258; Canadian trade policy, 259–260; and Indians, 262–263, 276, 284; and War of 1812, 264–265, 269, 271–273; and Canadian boundary, 278; and Canada settlement, 281–282
Great Lakes, 258, 264; and War of 1812, 268, 270; as boundary, 271; disarmament, 277–278; for transportation, 329, 333–334, 337–338
Green, Thomas, 166–167
Greenbrier Company, 32, 40
Greenville, Treaty of, 271
Grenville, Lord, 73, 147, 152, 155, 160–161
Grimaldi, Jerónimo, Marqués de, 78n
Grundy, Felix, 265n

Haldimand, Sir Frederick, in Revolu-

tion, 43, 56, 60, 119, 178; as governor of Quebec, 137–138, 143–145, 274
Hall, Basil, 349–350n
Hamilton, Alexander, 125, 204, 295; and relations with England, 147–149, 151n, 154, 159n, 160
Hamilton, Lt. Gov. Henry, 57–59, 347
Hammond, George, British minister to U.S., 135–136, 153–154, 159n, 160
Hard Labor, Treaty of, 32, 40
Harmar, General Josiah, 148, 152, 285
Harrison, William Henry, 240, 262, 285, 328, 347; and War of 1812, 263, 268–269, 271; Land Act of 1800, 295
Headright, 92, 105
Hemp, 327
Henderson, Richard, 45, 112; and Transylvania Co., 89–90, 98, 102
Hillsborough, Lord, 6, 12, 18n, 20–21, 31, 35; resigns, 36
Holston, Treaty of, 169
Hopewell, Treaty of, 168
Horseshoe Bend, battle of, 270
Household manufactures, 326–327, 372
Hull, Isaac, 268n
Hull, William, 266–268
Hurons, 289
Huskisson, William, 274

Illinois, 130, 283; settlement, 1, 91, 315–317, 322–323, 327, 334, 336, 365; and Indians, 285–286; land jobbing, 298–299; and roads, 332–333
Illinois Company, 16, 27–28, 42, 112
Illinois Country, 16, 18–19, 41, 48–49, 51, 55, 74–75; and Quebec Act, 256; land titles, 290
Illinois Territory, 261, 291, 369
Illinois-Wabash Company, 113, 117
Immigration, 179–180, 316, 346–347, 351–356, 373
Impressment, of American seamen, 178, 184, 263, 282
Imprisonment for debt, 319, 358
Indian buffer territory (reservation), 154, 271–272
Indian confederation, 263
Indian neutrality, 269

Indiana, as state, 283; and Indians, 285–286; and settlement, 315–316, 322–323, 334, 336, 356, 365; and roads, 332–333

Indiana Company, 28, 31, 35, 40–41, 82; claims, 112–113, 115, 117–119

Indiana Territory, 235, 268, 369–370; settlement, 261–262

Innes, Harry, 176, 199

Internal improvements, 331–332

International law, re Miss. R. navigation, 171–172; re nationality, 178

Iowa, 317

Iron, 329–330, 335

Iroquois, 111, 120, 289

Irujo, 209, 212, 216, 218

Jackson, Andrew, 268, 270, 273, 347; and Burr, 239, 242; and Indian removal, 288; and "distribution," 301

Jackson, Richard, 21

Jay, John, 63–64n, 155, 164, 198; and peace negotiations, 67–68, 70, 73, 75–77; and Jay's treaty, 157, 159–162, 195; and Miss. R., 172–175, 360n; and Spanish negotiations, 191–193

Jay's treaty, 159, 161–162, 195, 202, 260–261; and Canadian trade, 258; and War of 1812, 270–271; and Canada boundary, 278

Jefferson, Thomas, ordinance adopted, 85–86; and Summary View . . . , 45, 101–102; and Ordinance of 1784, 121, 125–130, 294; and land sales, 122; and Ordinance of 1787, 131–132; and views on west, 183; and Spanish relations, 186, 190–191, 224, 226–227; and La. Purchase, 206, 208–211, 213, 215, 217, 235; and Fla., 206, 216, 229–231; and Territory of Orleans, 234; and Lewis and Clark expedition, 235; and Upper La. government, 236; and Burr, 238, 240, 242–245, 247–251; and War of 1812, 262, 265; Indian policy, 284–285, 287–288; and internal improvements, 331

Jefferson's Ordinance. See Ordinance of 1784

Johnson, Sir John, 138, 149

Johnson, Sir William, 2–3, 6, 9–13, 15–16, 19, 21, 24, 34–35, 41, 43, 50–51, 54, 56, 81, 88, 95, 107, 119, 138–141, 144, 150, 155, 304, 348; and new settlement line, 25–33; and Fort Stanwix treaty, 30–33

Johnstone, Gov. George, 10, 220

Kemper family, 220–221

Kent, Chancellor James, 355, 359

Kentucky, 346; settlement, 31, 58, 80–81, 88–91, 97, 109, 185, 261, 303–306, 308–309, 313, 315–317, 356; as county of Va., 46, 90; land surveys, 122; and Indians, 142; and loyalty to Confederation, 145–147; and Miss. R., 175–184, 190, 199–200; and trade, 177, 185, 336; and Federal union, 180, 186; and neutrality, 189; and separatism, 227; land titles, 290; land policy, 293; products, 325–327, 330; transportation, 334

Kickapoo, 22

King, Rufus, 129, 174, 183, 215

Knox, Henry, 154, 156, 160

Knox, William, 49, 255, 281n

Lachaise, August, 187, 218

Lafayette, Marquis de, 171–173, 189

Land, cultivation of, 322–324

Land Act of 1783, 166, 168

Land Act of 1796, 294–295

Land Act of 1800, 295

Land Act of 1804, 295

Land bounties, 4, 15, 94, 113–114, 116, 168, 227, 292–293; claims, 40, 85

Land cessions. See Cessions (land)

Land companies, 15; character and role in settling west, 93–97; first, 96n; and claims, 111–112, 115, 117, 119–120; activities during Confederation, 124–125; and Yazoo frauds, 184. See also under individual companies

Land forestallment, 93

Land hunger, 91–92

Land jobbing, 52, 92, 198, 299, 360n

Land Ordinance of 1785, 121–122, 293

Land plan, of 1774, 43–45, 119

Land policy, during Confederation, 100, 104, 110, 120–122, 124–125, 132

Land, price of, 105, 294–297, 301–302, 310, 320, 345

Land reforms of 1774, 55

Land riots, in N.Y. and N.J., 107

Land systems, 105–109, 316; national, 168

Land titles, 315; federal policy, 290–294, 297, 299–301

Land warrants, 105

Lansdowne, Lord. See Shelburne, Lord

Laussat, 207, 209, 361

Lee, Arthur, 118–119

Lee, Richard Henry, 174, 183

Lewis, Andrew, 32

Lewis and Clark expedition, 234–235

Liston, Robert, 197

Livestock, 324–325, 327–328, 339, 357–358

Livingston, Robert, 76, 226; and La. Purchase, 206, 209, 213, 215, 217

Lochaber, Treaty of, 32, 40

Louisiana, 164, 166, 169–171; European policy toward, 201–203; Spanish cession to France, 203–205, 207–209; U.S. interest in, 206, 208; New Orleans deposit right, 206, 209; and trade, 208, 221–222, 335; U.S. procures, 210–211; value to U.S., 217–218; as Indian reserve, 211, 284; boundary negotiation, 225–226, 228; and W. Fla., 225, 231; Act of 1804, 284; land titles, 290–291; settlement, 316–317, 325–326

Louisiana, State of, 232, 234

Louisiana Purchase, 210–211, 317; boundary ambiguity, 212–215; and nationalism, 234; and constitutional question, 235

Loyal Company, 32, 40

Loyalists, 7, 57, 61–62, 91, 109, 134–135, 141, 151, 166, 197, 231, 355, 360, 362; and peace negotiations, 71–75, 77–78; in Canada, 256, 274, 279–280

Luzerne, 65–68, 71

Macadamized roads, 307, 333

Madison, James, 190, 212, 222, 228, 268n, 285; and Miss. R. navigation, 174; and La. Purchase, 215, 217–218; and Fla., 229–231; and War of 1812, 264–265

Madrid, Treaty of, 205

Manufacturing, 330–331

Marshall, John, 23, 114; and Burr trial, 243–246, 249

Maryland, land system, 105; land claims, 112; and cession, 114–116; and west settlement, 305, 312

Mason, Steven T., 349n

Massachusetts, land system, 108; land claims, 111; and cession, 120; rebellion in, 145; and public land, 293; and west settlement, 319, 327

McGillivray, Alex, 164, 167–168, 360n

McKee, Alexander, 144, 150, 157, 285

Mercantilism, British, 51–52, 201, 255–257, 281; repudiated, 274

Merry, Anthony, and Burr, 239, 240n

Mexican Association, 237–238, 242, 248

Mexico, 164; and Burr, 229, 236, 239–241, 248–249

Miami, 22

Michigan, 129–130; and War of 1812, 276–277; Indians, 285–286; settlement, 283, 309, 315–316, 319, 327, 338; timber, 329; self-government, 365

Michigan Territory, 266, 349n, 369

Migration, to west, causes, 310, 319–321, 344–349, 355, 359, 364, 367; trips, 311–314; population, 315–319; and salt licks, 326; habits, 354–356, 365, 373; as Constitutional right, 363

Minnesota, settlement, 317

Miranda, Francisco de, 204, 249

Miró, Governor Estevan, 166, 177–181

Mississippi, 123, 303, 316, 321; settlement, 91; crops, 325–326

Mississippi Company, 15

Mississippi River, as boundary, 62, 67–68, 166, 173, 189–191, 271–272, 278; control of, 65, 152, 160–161; right of navigation, 62, 67–68, 145, 147, 163–164, 171–173, 175, 177–178, 185, 190–192, 199, 261, 271n, 273, 278–279, 360n, 363; natural law, 164; American interests, 165, 169–170, 172–174; closed by Spain, 170; international law re, 171–172; and U.S.-Spanish negotiations, 172–174, 190–191; use for trade, 174–175, 179, 183, 257, 330, 335–337; opened to westerners, 179–181; and immigration policy, 179–180; and Jay's treaty, 194–195; and La. cession, 206–208, 210; and Canadian traders, 260–261

Mississippi Territory, 227, 242–243, 270, 357; settlement in, 216, 219, 222; trade with, 223–224; anarchy, 231; rivalry with Territory of Orleans, 232

Missouri, 185, 188, 234–236, 288; as state, 283; and Indians, 287–289; land titles, 290; population, 317; trade, 325, 336; iron, 330

Missouri River, as boundary, 186; settlement, 260, 317, 337; as travel route, 316

Mohawks, 2, 56, 141, 151

Monroe, James, 128–130, 278, 323; and La. Purchase, 195, 208–209, 213, 215, 218; to Madrid, 225–227; and Indians, 285, 288

Montmorin, Comte de, and U.S., 163, 165

Morales, Juan Ventura, 206, 209, 219, 227; and closing of deposit right, 222; and trade, 223–224

Morgan, George, 180

Morris, Gouverneur, 151, 174

Morris, Robert, 43n

Moûstier, Comte de, 163, 165, 190

Murray, John, 34, 43

Napoleon, 229, 274; and La., 205, 207, 209–210, 217, 226, 228

National Highway, 305–307, 312n

Nationalism, 321, 355, 362–363; and La. Purchase, 234; and War of 1812, 273

Nationality, international law, 178

Natural right, and Miss. R., 191, 194

Navarro, Martín, 164, 169–170, 177–178

Navigation system, British, 255, 258

Netherlands, and U.S. trade, 254

Neutral rights, 134, 280; and Jay's treaty, 195, 202; and War of 1812, 262, 264, 271, 274

Neutral trade, 202, 204, 227, 222–223; and War of 1812, 264–265

Neutrality, of Indians, 41; of U.S., 172, 188–189, 196

New Hampshire, and Vt. claim, 145–146

New Jersey, land system, 107

New Orleans, cession of, 191; right of deposit, 206–207, 209; and La. Purchase, 213; discontent, 234

New Spain, 210, 217, 251

New York, lands, 105, 107–109, 111, 114–116, 120, 293; boundary, 146, 154; and west settlement, 304, 310, 315–316; and roads, 307–308, 337–338

Nootka Sound incident, 146, 165, 184, 190

North, Lord, 137, 143, 366; and U.S. trade, 255

North Carolina, 346; and cessions, 85–86, 115, 122, 127; land system, 105, 108; and Watauga, 126; and Indians, 168; and separatism, 184; lands, 299; settlement, 82, 304, 315

Northwest, reorganization, 38, 44; and settlement under Ordinance of 1787, 180; and Indians, 284, 286; land titles, 290; settlement, 261, 303, 308, 321; roads to, 307–308, 316

Northwest Fur Company, 275

Northwest Territory, 124, 142, 323, 357–358, 365, 369

O'Fallon, James, 168, 184–185, 187, 360

Ohio, settlement of, 81, 185, 303, 308–310, 312, 315–316, 327, 365; population, 261; as state, 283; public land system, 294; and roads, 307, 316, 331–333; and products, 325–326, 328–330; and canals, 334–335; and trade, 336, 338; banking, 340–342

Ohio Company, 36, 94–95, 124–125, 155, 294–295; and settlement, 308

Ohio Company of Connecticut, 124

Ohio Company of Virginia, 113n

Ohio country, 73–75, 110–111, 137, 293

Ohio Indians, 285–286
Ohio River, as route west, 304–306, 308, 311, 313–315; use in trade, 331, 333–334, 336–337
Oklahoma, 317
Old Northwest, Indians, 22–25, 289; and settlement, 261–262
Old Southwest, 133, 184, 287, 359
Oneida, 56n
Ordinance of 1783, 140
Ordinance of 1784 ("Jefferson's Ordinance"), 121, 125–130, 132
Ordinance of 1785, 106, 292n
Ordinance of 1787, xii, 90, 127, 130–132, 180, 293, 317, 322, 354n, 365, 368–369
Osage, 289
Oswald, Richard, 70–74, 77–78
Owen, David Dale and Robert, 346

Paine, Thomas, 187
Panic of 1819, 296, 309, 342–343
Panton firm, 167
Paris, Treaty of, 1763, 1, 23, 50, 171, 201–202, 221; and Miss. R. navigation, 191; and La. Purchase, 213
Paris, Treaty of, 1783, 23, 134–138, 141, 148, 151–152, 155, 156, 160, 221; secret U.S.-British article, 170–171, 191; and Miss. R., 171, 191; boundaries, 219; and Great Lakes, 277–278; and land titles, 290
Pennsylvania, 107, 346; dispute with Va., 40, 59, 82; and west settlement, 81–82, 304–306, 309; and transportation, 307–308, 330, 332, 337–338; products, 326, 329–330
Peoria, 285n
Perry, Commodore Oliver, 268
Pichon, Stéphen, 208–209
Pickering, Timothy, 195–215
Pike's expedition, 235
Pinckney, Charles, 174, 183, 218, 225
Pinckney, Gen. Thomas, 193–194
Pinckney's treaty, 202, 206, 208; nonexecution, 195, 200; signed, 196
Pitt, William, 151, 254–255
Plan of 1764, 9–11, 14, 27, 55
Plantation, system, 316; economy, 325–326
Pollock, Oliver, 60, 62
Pontiac's War, xvi, 6, 26–28, 81, 140

Population, emigration, 315–320
Posts, in northwest, 18–21, 47, 49–51, 55, 151–152, 154–157, 159–162, 190, 258, 259, 292; U.S.-British relations, 134–137, 143–148; British abandonment, 202
Potawatomi, 22
Pownall, John, 25, 49
Pownall, Governor Thomas, 14
Pre-emption, 109, 112; rights, 293, 297–301; Act of 1830, 298n; laws, 354, 368
Primogeniture, 91, 109
Proclamation of 1763, 39, 43, 48, 51, 80, 91, 150; provisions and effect, 4–9, 12–13; land title and boundaries, 24–26, 112, 114, 119–120
Proclamation Line of 1763, xii, 14, 21, 27–31, 37, 55
Prophet, The, 143, 263
Proprietary lands, 107
Public lands, 290–298, 300–302, 331, 333–334, 347; sales, 326

Quapaw, 288
Quebec Act, 41, 43–44, 72–73, 256; passed, 38; intent of, 39

Railroads, and trade, 337
Randolph, Edmund, 159n, 221n
Rayneval, M., 75–76
Relief laws, 342–343
Religion, 39n, 256, 319, 349, 369
Removal Act of 1830, 289
Revolution, 62; and Quebec Act, 39; and West, 53–54, 84; and Indians, 55–56, 58–59
Roads, financing, 305, 307; for travel west, 306–309; 315–316; construction, 331–335, 338; state, 305, 307
Robertson, James, 83–84, 179, 359
Rockingham, Lord, 71, 73
Rodney, Adm. George, 72–73, 79
Routes, to West, 303–306, 309, 315–316
Rush, Richard, 298n
Russia, 270–271, 329

"Safety-valve" theory, 319n
St. Clair, Gen. Arthur, 142, 148–149, 157, 186, 189, 308–309, 323, 346, 365

St. Lawrence River, 172n, 257–258, 307

Salt licks, 326

San Ildefonso, Treaty of, 204–205

Sargent, Winthrop, 124

Sayre, Stephen, 187

Scioto Company, 124–125, 294

Sebastian, Benjamin, 176

Sectionalism, 165, 173, 301

Self-government, 351–353, 355, 364–365, 367, 370–371

Seneca, 26, 34

Separatism, 84, 87, 99–101, 175–180, 198–199, 359, 363–364

Sevier, John, 179, 359; and treason, 182n

Shawnee, 22, 25–28, 30, 34–35, 41, 44, 56, 142; and removal, 285

Shays, Daniel, rebellion, 145

Shelburne, Lord (Lord Lansdowne), 48–49, 54–55, 70, 78, 111, 137–138, 172, 201, 274, 278; Proclamation of 1763, 3–7; Plan of 1764, 12; policy in west, 16–17, 19–20, 25, 30; U.S. trade, 254–255; Franklin negotiations, 257; Canada trade, 259

Short, William, 191

Simcoe, Lt. Gov. John Graves, 144, 150, 155–156, 158, 196, 259, 262

Six Nations, 25–27, 29, 34–35, 41, 138, 142, 304; Ft. Stanwix treaty, 30; peace with Am., 55–56

Slavery, 125, 127–128, 131–132, 312, 317, 369

Smith, Sen. John, 219–220; and Burr, 236, 238–240, 242

Smuggling, 258–259, 263–264, 273, 277

Social structure, 107; and migration, 345–350; in west, 351–369

South Carolina, 166, 168; settlement, 83, 91, 304, 316; lands, 107–108, 122, 293

South Carolina Company, 184–185

South Carolina Yazoo Company, 187

Southwest, and British plan, 197; and smuggling, 263; and Indians, 287; settlement, 303, 316–317, 321; roads, 308, 316

Spain, and Revolution, 62–68, 75, 78; U.S. relations, 134, 146–147, 173, 192, 194–195; and Gt. Br., 146–148, 165, 191, 239; and west, 163–173, 175, 181, 192, 184–185, 189–190; negotiations with U.S., 172–173, 193, 198–199, 225; Spanish posts, 196–197; and La., 201–208, 216–218; and Fla., 217–218, 290

"Spanish Conspiracies," 175–184, 359–360, 363

Speculation, land, gov't measures to control, 55; Confederation, 82, 84–87, 104–108, 122–125; western settlement, 91–97, 100. *See also individuals and companies*

Squatters, 106–107; and law, 297–300

Squatter sovereignty, 87, 101–102

Steamboats, 314–315, 317, 329, 336–338

Stuart, John, 2, 9–10, 12, 29, 32, 50, 56–57, 105

Suffering Traders of 1763, 28, 35, 42, 95n, 117

Suffrage, 100–101, 126, 130, 320, 350–352, 355n, 367

Symmes Assoc., 125, 155, 294–295, 299

Talleyrand, 203–204, 209, 218, 228, 363

Taxation, and Revolution, 53–54; during Confederation, 86–87, 93–94, 98, 100–101; role in migration, 319

Tecumseh, 143, 263, 268–269

Tennessee, settlement, 31, 84, 91, 97, 109, 185, 315, 317; cession, 122; loyalty to Confederation, 145; Indians, 288; land, 293; roads, 308, 316; crops, 325–326

Territory of Orleans, 211, 231–232, 234, 284

Texas, 225–227, 229

Toulmin, Harry, 232, 305, 309, 312, 326–327, 346

Trade, U.S.-Spanish, 173; U.S.-Canada, 253, 256–258, 260–261, 273; U.S.-France, 254, 256, 263; U.S.-Gt. Br., 254–255, 257, 273–274; smuggling, 258–259, 263–264; west, 330, 334–339, 341–342, 373; barter, 339–340

Trade plan of 1764, 48

Transportation, 306, 313–315, 330–339, 342

Transylvania, 45–46, 90, 98, 102, 168, 359

Transylvania Co., 46, 84, 89–90, 95–96, 112–113

Treason, in U.S., 177, 182–184, 237, 243–246; in Canada, 280

Treaties. *See under treaty name*

Treaty of 1744, 25–26

Treaty of 1748, 23

Treaty of 1751, 25–26

Treaty of 1752, 25–26

Treaty of 1758, 3

Treaty of 1784, 156

Treaty of 1789, 156

Treaty of 1828, 289

Trent, William, 42

Tucker, Josiah, 254, 281n

Turner, Frederick Jackson, xi–xii, 50, 109, 189, 312, 350, 366–371, 374; on settlement, 98–99; on Wilkinson, 252n; and War of 1812, 264–265; thesis, 379 ff

Turnpikes, 307–308, 315, 331, 333, 337

Tuscarora, 56n

Vagabondage, 256, 363

Vandalia, 40–41, 44, 47, 80, 81n, 82, 117

Vaudreuil map, 65n

Vergennes, Comte de, 63–68, 71, 73, 75–79, 163, 213

Vermont, 87, 126, 145–146, 258–259, 279n

Victor, General, 207, 209

Virginia, Penna. dispute, 40, 59, 82; cessions, 60, 115–117, 120, 122, 125, 129, 132–133, 166, 168, 175, 298; lands, 105–120, 299; Miss. R. navigation, 174–182; land act, 1779, 293; settlement, 304–319, 332

Wabash Company, 42–43, 112

Walker, Dr. Thomas, 32, 43n

Walpole Company, 35, 37, 40, 96n, 97; claims, 112, 115, 117

War of 1812, 258, 262–269, 296, 325, 332–333, 337, 349; peace, 270–278; and settlement, 309, 316, 321

Washington, George, and speculation, 40, 45, 85, 94; on Miss. R. navigation, 174

Watauga, 45, 83–84, 86, 89, 98, 100, 109, 126, 304, 363

Wayne, Gen. Anthony, 189, 198, 268, 309; and Indian war, 156–159

Webster-Hayne debate, 298n

West, Far, 368

West Florida. *See* Florida

West Indies, 73, 174, 185, 256–257, 274, 329, 335

West Virginia, 31, 80–81, 326

Western Reserve, 96n, 120, 294–295, 324, 328

Westerners, character of, 345–363, 366–373

Westsylvania, 41, 81n, 82, 102–103, 359, 366

Wharton, Samuel, 35, 36n, 95n, 117

Whisky Insurrection, 198, 363

Wilderness Road, 305–306, 308, 316, 324

Wilkinson, James, xii, 186, 197–200, 218, 230–231, 234–236, 261, 288, 317, 359, 360n; and Spanish conspiracy, 175–184; and Burr, 229–252

Willing's raid, 360n

Winchester, James, 268

Wisconsin, 129–130; Indians, 285–286; settlement, 317, 365

Wraxell, Peter, 92

Wyandot, 22, 142, 159

Yazoo frauds, 97, 107, 123, 184, 187–188, 192–193, 197

Yrujo, Marquis de, 239

Zane's Road, 313

Zane's Trace, 316

72 73 74 75 10 9 8 7 6 5 4 3